CONTEMPORARY PUBLIC ADMINISTRATION

CONTEMPORARY PUBLIC ADMINISTRATION

DAVID H. ROSENBLOOM

American University

DEBORAH D. GOLDMAN, Esq.

PATRICIA W. INGRAHAM

Syracuse University

McGraw-Hill, Inc.

New York   St. Louis   San Francisco   Auckland   Bogotá   Caracas
Lisbon   London   Madrid   Mexico City   Milan   Montreal   New Delhi
San Juan   Singapore   Sydney   Tokyo   Toronto

CONTEMPORARY PUBLIC ADMINISTRATION

 This book is printed on recycled, acid-free paper containing 10% postconsumer waste.

2 3 4 5 6 7 8 9 0 DOC DOC 9 0 9 8 7 6 5 4

ISBN 0-07-053939-1

This book was set in Melior by The Clarinda Company.
The editors were Peter Labella and Fred H. Burns;
the production supervisor was Denise L. Puryear.
The cover was designed by Rafael Hernandez.
R. R. Donnelley & Sons Company was printer and binder.

Library of Congress Cataloging-in-Publication Data

Contemporary public administration / David H. Rosenbloom, Deborah D.
Goldman, Patricia W. Ingraham [editors].
    p.   cm.
  Includes bibliographical references.
  ISBN 0-07-053939-1
  1. Public administration   I. Rosenbloom, David H.   II. Goldman,
Deborah D.   III. Ingraham, Patricia W.
JF1351.C64   1994
350—dc20   93-47904

About the Editors

David H. Rosenbloom is Distinguished Professor of Public Administration in the School of Public Affairs at the American University. He received his Ph.D. in political science from the University of Chicago (1969). His published work focuses on the politics, personnel, and law of public bureaucracy as well as on public administrative history. He became Editor-in-Chief of *Public Administration Review* in 1991. A member of the National Academy of Public Administration, Rosenbloom was appointed to the Clinton-Gore Presidential Transition of 1992–1993 to work on the transition at the U.S. Office of Personnel Management. He has testified before the U.S. Senate Governmental Affairs Committee and his work has been relied on as authoritative by the U.S. Supreme Court. Rosenbloom received the 1992 Distinguished Research Award and the 1993 Charles H. Levine Memorial Award for Excellence in Public Administration from the American Society for Public Administration and the National Association of Schools of Public Affairs and Administration. Among his recent publications is *Public Administration: Understanding Management, Politics, and Law in the Public Sector,* third edition (McGraw-Hill, 1993, with Deborah D. Goldman).

Deborah D. Goldman, Esq., is a professional legal writer. She received her B.A. from Cornell University, cum laude in history and the J. D. and M.P.A. degrees in 1982 from Syracuse University's E. I. White College of Law and Maxwell School of Citizenship and Public Affairs. She was admitted to the New York State Bar in 1983. She worked in the area of consumer fraud in the New York State Attorney General's Office. She also practiced appellate law in central New York. She is the author of numerous legal references on New York State estate law and Surrogate's Court procedure, published by Matthew Bender and Co., Inc. She is a contributing author of *Public Administration: Understanding Management, Politics, and Law in the Public Sector,* currently in its third edition (McGraw-Hill, 1993).

Patricia W. Ingraham is a Professor of Public Administration at the Maxwell School of Citizenship and Public Affairs, Syracuse University. She received her Bachelor's Degree from Macalester College, her M.A. from Michigan State University, and her Ph.D. from SUNY/Binghamton.

She served as an Associate Professor of Political Science and Director of the Masters Program in Policy and Administration at the State University of New York at Binghamton. She worked as Project Director of the Task Force on Recruitment and Retention for the National Commission on the

Public Service (the Volcker Commission). She has testified before both the U.S. House of Representatives and the U.S. Senate on issues related to recruiting and managing a quality federal workforce. She has lectured widely in the United States and in Europe on that issue and on the American policial management system. She was elected a Fellow of the National Academy of Public Administration in 1990.

Professor Ingraham is the co-editor of three books: *Legislating Bureaucratic Change: The Civil Service Reform Act of 1978,* with Carolyn Ban; *The Promise and Paradox of Bureaucratic Reform,* with David Rosenbloom; and the *Federal Service: An Agenda for Excellence,* with Donald Kettl. She is the author of a number of articles dealing with civil service reform, public management, and the relationship between the president and the career civil service.

To students of public administration everywhere who would improve government and advance civilization.

Contents

Preface

Public administration is often characterized as a fragmented field—one that is pulled in competing directions by different intellectual and disciplinary perspectives, as well as by the concerns of practice and theory. Nevertheless, it does have a common core of knowledge and a coherent intellectual history. The purpose of *Contemporary Public Administration* is to provide an essential resource for teaching this core and central set of ideas to graduate and undergraduate students. The book presents concepts, ideas, historical perspectives, discussions of administrative values, and intellectual frameworks that are fundamental to understanding contemporary public administration. It does so parsimoniously and efficiently. It includes only concise and easily accessible writings that clearly frame the central issues and/or present up-to-date analyses of all the major topics that comprise today's public administration. Many of the selections were written during the past few years; others, though older, continue to inform cutting-edge thinking in the field. Whether an original contribution, a synthesis, or a review, each selection provides ingredients that are essential to understanding public administration as a practice and as an area of study.

Contemporary Public Administration differs fundamentally from other anthologies in the field. The book is a guide to the issues, perspectives, vocabulary, and knowledge that comprise contemporary public administration. It presents selections that are basic to fluency in the language, concepts, analysis, and practice of public administration. It is not a handbook, intended to provide comprehensive detailed coverage of all aspects of the field. It is not confined to "classics," though it does include some. It addresses current issues, but is not limited to them. It treats the enduring concerns along with newer themes.

The book recognizes that public administration is in greater flux today than it has been for some time. "Market-based" initiatives, such as privatization, public entrepreneurship, public choice, deregulation, and the total quality management (TQM) movement have become increasingly significant. Although they have not transformed the field, they have been integrated into administrative thought and practice. But it is difficult to know whether they will make further substantial inroads. Public administration has had a history of faddish adoptions of new techniques and processes. *Contemporary Public Administration* deals with this uncertainty by including several selections on market-based public administration that address the fundamental questions it presents. Among these are Vincent Ostrom and Elinor Ostrom's "Public Choice: A Different Approach to the Study of Public Administration" (number 3); James Swiss's "Adapting Total Quality Management (TQM) to Government" (number 13); and Carl Bellone and George Goerl's "Reconciling Public Entrepreneurship and Democracy" (number 32). The book also includes an excellent discussion of economically based "formal models," Jonathan Bendor's "Formal Models of Bureaucracy: A Review" (number 14). These foundational pieces will serve students well regardless of the directions public administrative theory and practice take in the next serveral years.

Contemporary Public Administration is organized into ten sections. Each corresponds to chapters usually included in public administration texts. Sections 1 and 2 on "The Practice and Discipline of Public Administration" and "The American Administrative State" logically should be read before the remaining sections. However, the book is organized so that sections 3 through 10 are sufficiently self-contained to allow their use in any order. These sections are: "Federalism and Intergovernmental Relations"; "Administrative Organization"; "Public Personnel Systems"; "Budgeting"; "Decision Making"; "Public Policy"; "Public Administration and the Public"; and "Accountability and Ethics."

Deciding what to include in *Contemporary Public Administration* was a formidable task. The public administration literature is diffuse and vast; selecting the materials that would most efficiently capture the knowledge and information essential to understanding today's public administration was a difficult challenge. The book's final contents are informed by countless discussions with colleagues and students too numerous to thank individually. But we want to acknowledge our gratitude to them for their interest, enthusiasm, and advice. We are also grateful to American University's School of Public Affairs and Syracuse University's Maxwell School of Citizenship and Public Affairs for providing highly supportive environments in which to develop and complete the book.

We would like to specifically mention five reviewers and to thank them for their comments and suggestions: Patricia Bodelson, St. Cloud State University; Robert D. Hamm, University of Wyoming; Rebecca Hendrick, University of Wisconsin at Milwaukee; Stephen S. Jenks, University of North Carolina at Chapel Hill; and B. Dan Wood, Texas A & M University.

David H. Rosenbloom
Deborah D. Goldman
Patricia W. Ingraham

CONTEMPORARY
PUBLIC
ADMINISTRATION

The Practice and Discipline of Public Administration: Competing Concerns

Public administration is a central activity of government. It is often large in scale and almost always complicated. In highly developed nations, it touches upon virtually all aspects of life. But, as Dwight Waldo observes in "What Is Public Administration?" there is no good definition of it! He dismisses all one-sentence or one-paragraph definitions as productive only of "mental paralysis." Taken together, the selections in this section may raise as many or more questions than they answer. That is the nature of contemporary public administration. But they will also make the reader fully conversant with the major intellectual currents in the field today.

Waldo, who has been among the most important American public administrative thinkers during the past half-century, views public administration as a technology for human cooperation. It emphasizes rationality, organization, and management in the pursuit of cooperation. It is embedded in human cultures and is a means by which "societies try to control their culture, by which they seek simultaneously to achieve . . . the goals of stability and the goals of change."

Any definition or discussion of public administration is certain to involve bureaucracy. The classic analysis of this form of organization, which is so frequently relied upon in public administration, was developed by Max Weber. Writing during the decades preceding and following the turn of the nineteenth century, Weber mentally constructed an "ideal type" of bureaucracy as a way of uncovering its essential, core aspects. The ideal type is best thought of as what bureaucracy would be if it were allowed to develop to its fullest extent, without facing any militating forces or counter pressures. Consequently, the analysis pays scant attention to how bureaucracy might function differently in accordance with changes in resources, technologies, governmental structures, legal systems, or cultural settings. When reading the selection from Weber on "The Essentials of Bureaucratic Organization: An Ideal-Type Construction," it is important to bear in mind that the "ideal type" is not the "best" bureaucracy in a normative sense; rather it is the most fully developed. Indeed, toward the end of his life, Weber lamented the spread of bureaucracy.

For Weber, bureaucracy is first and foremost a form of organization for exercising a type of authority, namely "rational legal" authority. The selection in this section lists the characteristics of such authority and proceeds to propose that "the purest type of exercise of legal authority is that which employs a bureaucratic administrative staff." Weber describes the leading features of bureaucracy, noting that such organization is not socially neutral, but rather tends to break down systems of social privilege, while also promoting advantages for those who can afford prolonged technical education. He also claims that as bureaucracy pervades a society, norms of impersonality become stronger.

Both Waldo and Weber view public administration and its frequently bureaucratic organization as a means, whether to promote cooperation or exercise authority. In the third selection, "Public Choice: A Different Approach to the Study of Public Administration," Vincent and Elinor Ostrom outline a fundamentally new way of thinking about cooperation, administrative organization, and the purposes of public administration. Relying on the field of "public choice" economics, which Ostrom and Ostrom admirably describe, they argue that theories of public administration would benefit by focusing on individual behavior, especially that of public administrators and citizens in the production and consumption of public goods and services. They also call for further analysis of the advantages and disadvantages of public administration and bureaucratic organization relative to other means (such as markets) and organizational forms for achieving public policy objectives. Their article, first published in 1971, is probably more relevant to public administration today than ever before in its discussion of developing "market arrangements" such as voucher systems and user fees among the "consumers" of public services.

This section is rounded out by Donald Kettl's "The Perils—and Prospects—of Public Administration." Kettl is concerned with public administration as a field of study. He reviews several contemporary intellectual challenges to which public administration must respond if it is to advance. These are (1) implementation studies, (2) public management studies focusing on the roles and functions of high level administrative officials, and (3) models of administrative behavior based on formal theories assuming that public administrators rationally seek to maximize their satisfaction. Kettl succinctly notes the strengths and limitations of these approaches. He concludes by suggesting that public administration should refocus analysis on agencies as governmental actors, an approach sometimes called "new institutionalism," and that the field should seek to "map" the variety of agency behavior.

1.   **What Is Public Administration?**

Dwight Waldo

When announcement of the first atomic explosions was made there was a deep sense of awe at the power unleashed. Imagination and reason strained to comprehend what had happened and how it had been brought to pass. The sense of awe was extended to the physical science and engineering which had made this stupendous phenomenon possible.

Along with an account of the general principles of physics involved and how they had been conceived and brought to successful test by the various physicists, the government of the United States gave also an account of the human science and engineering that lay behind the achievement. In brief, a special administrative system named the Manhattan Engineer District had been set up as a subdivision of the government of the United States. The Manhattan Engineer District spent two billion dollars, under conditions of such great secrecy that comparatively few Americans knew it existed and many of its own employees did not know its purpose. It brought together thousands of variously and highly trained men, and many and rare materials and objects, from all over the earth. It built extensive facilities and created specialized subadministrative systems across the continent, tying them together in intricate ways with the administrative systems we know as business enterprises and universities. The success of the Manhattan Engineer District lies before all: its purpose was the achievement of militarily usable explosions based on nuclear fission.

Now it is a reasonable conclusion,

based upon evidence, that most people regarded the atomic bomb as an achievement of physical science alone, and that the account of the Manhattan Engineer District did not make much of an impression—and has been generally forgotten. *But might we not seriously entertain another point of view: that the atomic bomb was as much an achievement on the human side as on the side of physical science?*

Not that the atomic bomb was a triumph of human morality. Perhaps the reverse was true, though judgment upon the atomic bomb cannot be dissociated from judgment upon war itself and all its modern machinery. What should be noticed is that in the perspective of history the human technology in achieving the bomb was a remarkable thing—perhaps as far removed from the social experience and imagination of any primitive people as the bomb itself from their physical experience and imagination.

To be sure, the all-but-universal judgment of the day is that our physical science is progressive or mature, while our social science is backward, infantile, or adolescent. This may be true. Certainly it is true by definition if the criteria commonly used in making this judgment are accepted as the proper ones: these criteria (for example, mathematical sophistication) are the distinguishing marks of the physical sciences! But though it may be true, this judgment tends to obscure and to depreciate what we have achieved in the area of human "technology," to use a word not as hard and argumentative as science.

Because we have lived from birth in a society with an advanced technology of cooperation and have learned so much of this technology without awareness, we accept the miracles of human coop-

SOURCE: From *The Study of Public Administration,* by Dwight Waldo. Copyright © 1955 by Random House, Inc. Reprinted by permission of the publisher.

eration all about us as though they were natural or indeed inevitable. But they are not. Far from it. This technology was achieved through incalculable human industry, much systematic thought, and the flashes of inspiration of occasional geniuses. The technology of human co-operation must be learned afresh with each generation. Still fuller achievement of human purposes depends upon its extension by study and invention.

This essay is intended as an intro-duction to the study of one phase or as-pect of human cooperation, namely, public administration. Public adminis-tration is much less than the whole process or concept of human coopera-tion. Those who study law, or anthro-pology, or economics, for example, are also studying human cooperation. There are specialized technologies within the technology of human cooperation; and there are also varying conceptual appa-ratuses by which study *in* or the study *of* these technologies may be ap-proached. Public administration in our society is one of the technologies within the technology, and has its own special conceptual apparatuses in its practice and in its study.

THE PROBLEM OF DEFINITION

Logic and convention both require that we now deal more carefully with the problem of definition: What is public administration? But in truth there is no good definition of public administra-tion. Or perhaps there are good short de-finitions, but no good short explanation. The immediate effect of all one-sentence or one-paragraph definitions of public administration is mental paralysis rather than enlightenment and stimulation. This is because a serious definition of the term—as against an epigrammatical definition, however witty—inevitably contains several abstract words or phrases. In short compass these abstract words and phrases can be explained

only by other abstract words and phras-es, and in the process the reality and im-portance of "it" become fogged and lost. With this warning let us consider two typical definitions:

1. Public administration is the organiza-tion and management of men and materials to achieve the purposes of government.
2. Public administration is the art and science of management as applied to affairs of state.

These are the ways public administra-tion is usually defined. There is nothing wrong with such definitions—except that in themselves they do not help much in advancing understanding. Per-haps these definitions do evoke sharp concepts and vivid images in the read-er's mind. But if they do not, it is better to proceed, rather than puzzle over each word, in the hope that the following ex-planations, descriptions, and comments will bring understanding in their train.

Administration: Art or Science?

Let us give a moment's attention to a tra-ditional dispute in the definition of pub-lic administration, and a related source of frequent confusion in the use of the term. The conflict has concerned whether public administration is an art or science. Some students and adminis-trators, impressed with the achieve-ments of the natural and physical sci-ences, have been insistent that public administration can and should become a science in the same sense. Other stu-dents and administrators, impressed with a fluid, creative quality in actual administration, with such intangibles as judgment and leadership, have been equally insistent that public administra-tion cannot become a science, that it is an art.

Much nonsense has resulted from the debates of the science-art controversy, but also considerable clarification of concepts and agreement on usage. It is fashionable nowadays to refer to the "art *and* science" of public administration, in the manner of the second definition above. This usage reflects a general conclusion that public administration has important aspects of *both* science and art. It reflects also, however, a desire to bypass the definitional problems, to compromise the issues by yielding to both sides, to get on with the study and practice of public administration, whatever it is. This disposition to get on is no doubt healthy, and diminishes a picayune and wasteful squabbling over words alone. But it must not be forgotten that definitions are important to fruitful study and effective action. The problem of how people are to be educated or trained for participating in public administration, for example, is one that can be solved only after a decision as to what, after all, is meant by public administration.[1]

Dual Usage of the Words Public Administration

A fertile source of confusion and error, closely related to the science-art controversy, is the fact that the words "public administration" have two usages. They are used to designate and delineate both (1) an area of intellectual inquiry, a discipline or study, and (2) a process or activity—that of administering public affairs. While the two meanings are of course closely related, they are nevertheless different; it is a difference similar to that between biology as the study of organisms and the organisms themselves.

Now if this distinction seems so obvious as not to warrant the making, the excuse must be that it is nevertheless a distinction often missed. It is obvious, in retrospect, that a great deal (but not all) of the controversy over whether public administration is a science or an art stemmed from failure to agree on which public administration was being discussed, the discipline or the activity. It is quickly apparent that it is easier to make the case for science on the *systematic study,* and the case for art on the *practice,* of public administration.

A student of public administration must cultivate a sharp eye for the two usages of the term. Sometimes the meaning will be clear from definition or context, but often there is simply ambiguity and confusion. Sometimes this is true because a writer begins with a definition of public administration as a process or activity, and then proceeds, abruptly or gradually, to use the term also to refer to the systematic study of public administration. Sometimes too the attempt is made to embrace both meanings within the same definition, which opens great opportunity for confusion. (Turn back now and scrutinize the two definitions given on an earlier page. In terms of the distinction made, is their intent clear?)

Let us confess that in attempting to clarify a distinction which is important we have made it sharper than it is in fact. To explain, recall the analogy drawn above between biology as the study of organisms and the organisms themselves. In this case the distinction is sharp, because while biology includes the study of man as an organism, this is but a small part of the whole; and on the other hand, no organism except man makes much of a study of other organisms. In the case of public administration, however, the central concern of the study is man himself, in certain aspects and sets of relationships; and on the other hand, much studying of public administration is carried on by men while engaged in the activities and process of public administration. The file clerk meditating on a better filing system for his needs, the supervisor deciding upon a new distribution of work among his staff, the group of publicly employed social scientists making an elaborate study of how employee morale can be maintained, are all studying public administration in some sense or aspect.

THE CONCEPT OF RATIONAL ACTION

The point will be made clearer by the introduction of the concept of *rational action,* defined here as action correctly[2] calculated to realize given desired goals with minimum loss to the realization of other desired goals. We will use the concept somewhat crudely, and not pause here to consider such interesting and important questions as whether man does wish or should wish that all his actions be rational. We will be content for the moment with the general observation or belief that man can and does maximize his goal achievement by taking thought, by correctly relating means to ends.

Now public administration in *both* senses is rational action as just defined. It is action designed to maximize the realization of goals that are public by definition. In public administration *as an activity* there is continuous calculation of the means to maximize public goals, although there is great variation in the goal awareness, knowledge, and level of abstraction of those engaged in the activity. A top leader may be highly trained and spend his time and energy in a conscious and careful calculation of means to realize given public goals. A machine-operator, on the other hand, may not know or care about the "public" goals of the agency for which he works. Still, the work of the machine-operator will be rational, in the sense that it is a joining of means to ends— say, the operation of a calculating machine for the solving of arithmetical problems. Rationality may be built into a mechanical operation or even a profession. The task of a leader or administrator is then to relate such built-in ra-

tionality to goals which *he* seeks in such a way that these goals are maximized.

In public administration *as a study* there is also continuous calculation of the means by which public goals may be maximized. In fact this is not only a central concern of the discipline but, many would say, its sole legitimate concern. In this case too, however, there is great variation—in types of approach, in level of abstraction, in size of problem, in the generality or particularity of goals to be maximized, and so forth. Time-and-motion studies of mechanical operations, leadership decision-making, community value-structures affecting administration, auditing procedures, trade-union characteristics in public administration—these are random examples suggesting the range and variation of studies.

To visualize how study and action can blend together in the concept of rational action, let us imagine a case. Suppose that a firm of management consultants is hired on contract by a state department of public works, with the specific task of determining whether use of mechanical equipment might be made more rational. The persons assigned to the study would observe and gather data and enlist the interest and support of those employees in the department who are concerned with mechanical equipment. Eventually they would present recommendations, and these recommendations might be accepted and put into effect immediately, by the consultants working together with those in the department. In such a case, study and action are so blended that the distinction does not make much sense; and of course study is also a form of action, in the final analysis. Still, at the extreme instead of at the mean, the distinction is a very useful one. A helpful analogy is the familiar range of the spectrum: between the extreme bands are many variations and gradations.

THE MEANING OF ADMINISTRATION: COOPERATIVE RATIONAL ACTION

Up to this point we have invariably dealt with the expression *public administration* and at no time with the noun *administration* alone. An appropriate next step is to examine into the meaning of the noun alone, and then into that of the adjective.

We may proceed by analogy: Public administration is a species belonging to the genus administration, which genus in turn belongs to a family which we may call *cooperative human action.* The word *cooperative* is here defined in terms of results: human activity is cooperative if it has effects that would be absent if the cooperation did not take place. Thus—to take a frequently used illustration—when two men roll a stone which neither could roll alone, they have cooperated. The result, the rolled stone, is the test. But what if one of the two men has lent his effort unwillingly, perhaps under threat of bodily harm from the other: Is this cooperation? It is, in the meaning here assigned. Cooperation as ordinarily used suggests willingness, even perhaps enthusiasm; so we are straining the customary meaning. But the English language seems to have no word better adapted to the meaning here desired. The expression *antagonistic cooperation,* incidentally, is sometimes used in the social sciences to distinguish unwilling from willing cooperation.

We are now in a position to describe administration. Administration is a type of cooperative human effort that has a high degree of rationality. This description in turn needs some qualification.

First, administration is not necessarily the only type of human cooperation that is rational. For example, the American economic system utilizes competition between companies—antagonistic cooperation—as well as administration within them to achieve rational action in the production and distribution of economic goods.[3]

Second, there is an important question implicit in the phrase "high degree of rationality." It is well to note this question, though it cannot be discussed fully here. Whose goals or ends shall be used in assessing rationality? A little reflection will suggest that the *personal* goals of many if not all of the people in a particular administrative system are different from the formally stated goals of that system; sometimes, indeed, a product (for example, a military item) may be secret, its use unknown to many of those engaged in its manufacture. The idea of purpose or goal is essential to the definition of administration. But like quicksilver it is hard to grasp; it eludes and scatters. What shall we say is the purpose or goal of the Chevrolet Division of General Motors? In one sense certainly to make automobiles; and in another sense certainly to make profits for the stockholders. But the personal goals of all officers and employees are certainly in some senses neither of these, or at least not wholly these.[4]

Administration was described as a type of cooperative human endeavor with a high degree of rationality. What distinguishes it as a *type?* The answer depends in part upon the perspective. In one perspective the sociologist views the distinguishing characteristics as those he subsumes under the concept of *bureaucracy* (this is discussed in Chapter Five). In the conventional perspective of the student of administration these characteristics are best subsumed under the two terms *organization* and *management.*

The Nature of Organization

The terms *organization* and *management* require explanation in turn. We may begin with another analogy: organization is the anatomy, management the physiology, of administration. Organization is structure; management is functioning. But each is dependent upon and inconceivable without the other in any existing administrative system, just as anatomy and physiology are intertwined and mutually dependent in any living organism.[5] We are close to the truth, in fact, when we assert that organization and management are merely convenient categories of analysis, two different ways of viewing the same phenomena. One is static and seeks for pattern; the other is dynamic and follows movement.

More precisely, organization may be defined as *the structure of authoritative and habitual personal interrelations in an administrative system.* In any administrative system some persons give orders to others, for certain activities if not for all, and these orders or instructions are habitually followed by other persons; that is to say, some have more power than others, as evidenced by habitual command-obedience or instruction-response relationships. Usually there is an official theory or statement of what the authoritative interrelationships should be in a given administrative system. In an army unit, for example, authority is officially exercised according to the ranks (lieutenant, major, etc.) in the chain of command.

There may be considerable discrepancy, however, between the official theory or statement of authoritative interrelations and the actual, habitual exercise of authority, as evidenced by the actual giving and following of orders or directions. In truth, in any actual administrative system there is usually some discrepancy between the official theory or statement and the facts of authority as evidenced by customary action; and in some cases the official theory or statement may even be no more than a polite fiction, so far do the facts depart from it. Moreover, all or nearly all so-called subordinates, those we think of as docilely taking orders, have means or techniques for changing the behavior of their superiors—for example, the workers' slowdown, or the secretary's smile or frown. A pure one-way power relationship in human affairs is very rare, if indeed it exists. In short, the word *authoritative* in the above definition is ambiguous, since the test of authority may be either the official theory or habitual response. The definition was framed in the knowledge of this ambiguity, which is important but cannot be explored further here. In any case—this is our present point—there are more or less firm structures of personal interrelationships in an administrative system, and these we designate *organization.*

The Nature of Management

Turning to *management,* we may define it as *action intended to achieve rational cooperation in an administrative system.* An administrative system is what we are seeking to explain, and rational cooperation has already been defined. Our attention focuses, then, upon the phrase *action intended to achieve.*

Action is to be construed very broadly: *any change intended to achieve rational cooperation.* It includes self-change or activity, all effects of man upon man, and all effects of man upon nonhuman things. In the postal system, for example, action includes the deliberations of the Postmaster General on such a matter as the desirability of a system of regional postal centers, the instructions of a city postmaster in supervising his staff, and the activities of a deliverer in sorting his daily batch of mail. There is an authoritative quality involved in many of these actions: some men habitually give more instructions (which are followed) than others. Hence some writers define management in terms of direction or control. But this definition is likely to lead to an undesirable narrowing of attention.

The word *intended* in the definition has this significance: there may be a distinction between actions intended to achieve rational cooperation and actions which in fact do so. The reason for this is that in terms of given goals, actions intended to be rational may fail because not all the relevant facts and conditions are known or properly included in judgments and decisions—something which occurs in private life as well as in group activity. On the other hand, actions which are not part of any conscious rational calculation may nevertheless contribute to rational cooperation. Such actions may be sheerly accidental, or they may be actions we associate with emotions, personality, and so forth—areas beyond full scientific statement and calculation, for the present at least. *Management* is customarily used of actions *intended* to achieve rationality (and carries the presumption that the intention is usually realized), but of course an astute practitioner or student will be aware of the difference between intention and actuality and will never forget the large area still unmanageable. Incidentally, a great deal of political theory, especially in modern centuries, has concerned itself with the question of the general scope and the particular areas of human manageability. Students of administration can profit from the literature of this debate. And their findings and experience are in turn an important contribution to it.

THE MEANING OF PUBLIC

After this attempt at a formal definition of administration we return to the question, What is *public* administration? What qualities are signified by the adjective? How is public administration distinguished from administration in general, the species differentiated from the genus?

This is a difficult question. We might begin by defining *public* in terms of such words as *government* and *state,* as is often done. An attempt to understand these words in turn leads to an inquiry into such legal and philosophical concepts as sovereignty, legitimacy, and general welfare. These are important matters, and a student or practitioner of public administration ought to have made serious inquiry into general political theory. Such inquiry helps in understanding various phenomena, such as the coercions sometimes exercised in public administration.

Or we might take a quite different, empirical tack and attempt to define *public* simply by the test of opinion: In a particular society what functions or activities are believed to be public? This proposal has a certain crude truth or usefulness. In the United States, for example, there is certainly a general opinion that, say, the administration of military affairs is public, whereas the administration of automobile sales is private. But complications arise quickly in following this approach. People's opinions differ and are extremely hard to determine and assess (and to suggest another type of complication, the administration of automobile sales is subject to much public control, even in peacetime).

Or we might take the common-sense approach and ask simply, Does the government carry on the function or activity? For many common-sense purposes this approach is quite adequate. It will satisfy most of the purposes of the citizen, and many of those of the student and practitioner of administration. But for many purposes of study, analysis, and informed action it is quite inadequate. Even at the level of common sense it is not completely adequate. For example, there are unstable political situations in which it is difficult to identify "the government" and what is "legal." And there are borderline activities of which one is hard put to it to say whether the government carries them on or not, such are the subtleties of law and circumstances. For example, the development of atomic energy is public in the sense that the government of the United States is in charge. Indeed, there is much secrecy, and tight controls; the situation is sometimes referred to as a monopoly. Yet this program involves an intricate network of contractual relationships, not only with state and local authorities, but with private corporations and individuals. Shall we call developmental programs carried on under contract by Union Carbide and Carbon Corporation public administration?

The most fruitful approach to the meaning and significance of *public* for the student of administration is through use of certain concepts which have been developed most fully in such disciplines as sociology and anthropology. The ones suggested as being particularly useful are associated with the expressions *structural-functional analysis* and *culture.* The concepts involved in these terms are by no means completely clear and precise. About them highly technical and intense professional debates are carried on. Nevertheless they are very useful to the student of administration even if used crudely. They provide needed insight, if not firm scientific generalizations.

Clarification through Structural-Functional Analysis

Structural-functional analysis seeks the basic or enduring patterns of human needs, wants, dispositions, and expressions in *any* society. Recognizing the great diversity in human societies, it yet seeks for common denominators, for the universal grammar and syntax of collective living.

Such studies provide the basis for a meaning of *public* which one could designate universal or inherent. What is indicated—if not precisely concluded—is that institutions and activities that are associated with the identity of a group, with group life as a whole, have special coercive, symbolic, and ceremonial aspects. There is inevitably a sacred aura surrounding some aspects of government. In some societies, of course, Church and State are one, or closely joined. But even where they are officially separated, and even indeed when religion, as such, is officially proscribed by the government, the government—if it is "legitimate"—has this sacred quality. (Nationalism is, of course, often described as a secular religion.)

This approach helps us to understand the special public quality of certain functions of government, for example, the apprehension and trial at law of persons accused of crimes, and the punishment or incarceration of the convicted; the manufacture and control of money; the conduct of foreign relations; or the recruitment, training, and control of armed forces. There is about such activities a monopoly aspect, and they are heavily vested with special coercions, symbolisms, and ceremonies. It is especially in such areas of activity that when a private citizen becomes a public official we expect him to play a new role, one which gives him special powers and prestige, but also requires of him observance of certain proprieties and ceremonies.

Incidentally, though the concept of rational action seems the most useful one in defining administration, we could also use the ideas and findings of structural-functional analysis for this purpose. We could, that is to say, construct a model of what an administrative system is like as a general type, using the concepts and idiom of structural-functional analysis.

Clarification through the Concept of Culture

The concept of culture is used in the social sciences—especially anthropology and sociology—to denote the entire complex of beliefs and ways of doing things of a society. We may analyze it as follows for our purposes: By *beliefs* is meant the systems of ideas held with respect to such matters as religion, government, economics, philosophy, art, and personal interrelations. By *ways of doing things* is meant patterns of activity with respect to food, clothing, shelter, courtship and marriage, child-rearing, entertainment, aesthetic expression, and so forth. The concept implies or asserts that there is a close connection between beliefs and ways of doing things—for example, between ideas concerning art, and modes of aesthetic expression. It further implies or asserts that the various beliefs and ways of doing things in a particular culture are a system in the sense that they are dependent one upon the other, in such a way that a change in one sets off a complicated (and given the present state of our knowledge, at least, often unanticipated and uncontrollable) train of results in others. For example, the introduction of firearms or of the horse into the culture of a primitive people is likely ultimately to affect such matters as artistic expression and marriage customs.

Now the concept of culture tends somewhat to turn attention in the opposite direction from structural-functional analysis. It emphasizes the variety of human experience in society rather than the recurrent patterns. Indeed, the concept has been used in arguing the almost complete plasticity of human beings and of society—and this is the source of one of the professional controversies referred to above. The professional controversies as to the *limits* of the truth or usefulness of concepts should not mislead us, however. The two concepts or sets of concepts we are dealing with here are not necessarily antithetical, but rather are customarily supplementary over a large area of social analysis.

As structural-functional analysis provides tools for dealing with recurrent phenomena, the concept of culture provides tools for dealing with *variety*. The feeling or intuition that administration is administration wherever it is comes very quickly to the student of administration; and this theme is heavily emphasized in the American literature dealing with administration. Yet the student will also become aware, as he advances, that there are important *differences* between administrative systems, depending upon the location, the tasks, the environment, and the inhabitants of the system. And he needs handles by which he can grasp and deal with the differences.

Our present concern is with the differences between private and public administration. The thesis here is that unless we take the broad view provided by intercultural comparison, we are likely to fall into error, designating a distinction as universal when it is a true or important distinction only in our own country or cultural tradition. There come to mind here the common generalizations of writers in the United States which are true of a significant part or aspect of public administration in liberal democratic societies, but are by no means true of public administration by definition, as is implied or suggested. Precisely, consider the generalization that public administration is distinguished by special care for equality of treatment, legal authorization of and responsibility for action, public justification or justifiability of decisions, financial probity and meticulousness, and so forth. It does not take much knowledge of comparative administration to appreciate the very limited applicability of these characteristics to some "public" administration.

The concept of culture—plus knowledge about the actual culture—enables us to see administration in any particular society in relation to all factors which surround and condition it: political theories, educational system, class and caste distinctions, economic technology, and so forth. And enabling us to see administration in terms of its environment, it enables us to understand differences in administration between different societies which would be inexplicable if we were limited to viewing administration analytically in terms of the universals of administration itself. *For as the constituent parts of culture vary within a society, or between societies, so does administration vary as a system of rational cooperative action in that society, or between societies.* Administration is a part of the cultural complex; and it not only is acted upon, it acts. Indeed, by definition a system of rational cooperative action, it inaugurates and controls much change. Administration may be thought of as the major invention and device by which civilized men in complex societies try to control their culture, by which they seek simultaneously to achieve—within the limitations of their wit and knowledge—the goals of stability and the goals of change.

WHAT IS PUBLIC ADMINISTRATION? A SUMMARY EXPLANATION

Let us return again to the question: What is *public* administration? The ideas associated with structural-functional analysis and culture will not enable us to *define* public with precision, but they help us in understanding the significance and implications of the term. They help us to understand why public administration has some general or generic aspects but also why the line between public and private is drawn in different places and with differing results—why "public" doesn't have precisely the same meaning in any two different cultural contexts. They help make some sense of the undoubted facts of similarity in diversity and diversity in similarity that characterize the Universe of Administration.

Whether public administration is an art or a science depends upon the meaning and emphasis one assigns these terms. The answer is affected too by the kind of public administration referred to—the study or discipline on the one hand, the activity or process on the other.

The central idea of public administration is rational action, defined as action correctly calculated to realize given desired goals. Public administration both as a *study* and as an *activity* is intended to maximize the realization of goals; and often the two blend into each other, since in the last analysis study is also a form of action.

Administration is cooperative human action with a high degree of rationality. Human action is *cooperative* if it has effects that would be absent if the cooperation did not take place. The significance of *high degree* of rationality lies in the fact that human cooperation varies in effectiveness of goal attainment, whether we think in terms of formal goals, the goals of leaders, or the goals of all who cooperate.

The distinguishing characteristics of an administrative system, seen in the customary perspective of administrative students, are best subsumed under two concepts, organization and management, thought of as analogous to anatomy and physiology in a biological system. *Organization* is the structure of authoritative *and* habitual personal interrelations in an administrative system. *Management* is action intended to achieve rational cooperation in an administrative system.

The significance of *public* can be sought in varying ways, each having some utility. For some purposes, for example, a simple determination of the legal status of an administrative system will suffice. For some important purposes, however, it is desirable to go beyond the boundaries of public administration as it has conventionally been studied and to adopt some of the concepts and tools of sociology and anthropology. *Structural-functional analysis* helps to identify the generic meaning or enduring significance of *public* in all societies. The concept of culture, on the other hand, helps in identifying and dealing with the varying aspects of *public* between societies, as well as with various relations of administration within in a society.

THE IMPORTANCE OF NONRATIONAL ACTION

In this attempt to define and explain public administration in brief compass we have constructed a simple model. Of necessity many concepts of importance in the study of public administration have been omitted, and some of the concepts included have been dealt with rather summarily. Some of the omitted concepts are introduced, and perhaps some of the inadequacies repaired, in the following chapters. This is the appropriate place, however, to deal with what is perhaps a bias or distortion in our model, since the basis or source of the distortion largely lies outside of the later discussions.

The point is this: perhaps the model, by stressing rational action, creates a false impression of the amount of rationality (as defined) existing or possible in human affairs.

Now we may properly hold that the concept of rational action is placed at the center of administrative study and action. This is what it is about, so to speak. But the emphasis needs to be qualified—mellowed—by knowledge and appreciation of the nonrational. It is now generally agreed that earlier students of administration had a rationalist bias that led them to overestimate the potentialities of man (at least in the foreseeable future) for rational action.

Most of the streams of modern psychology emphasize—indeed perhaps overemphasize—the irrational component in human psychology: the role of the conditioned response, the emotive, the subconscious. Much of anthropology and sociology stresses complementary themes: the large amount of adaptive social behavior that is below the level of individual—and even group—conscious choice of goals and means to realize the goals. (The fact that goals are not chosen consciously does not mean that there are no goals in this behavior, nor that the goals are necessarily unimportant, nor even that they are any less true or meaningful than those consciously chosen. A baby responding to food stimuli, for example, is not choosing the goal of survival—but survival is usually thought a highly important goal. Actually, though such words as *conscious* and *unconscious* or *deliberate* and *adaptive* suggest two different realms of behavior, there is probably no sharp break, but rather varying levels of awareness of ends and means.)

The general picture that the nonrationalist conclusion of the psychologists, anthropologists, and sociologists (and others—the sources and manifestations of this mode of thought are many) present for the student of administration is this: An administrative organization has an internal environment and an external environment that are largely nonrational, at least so far as the formal goals of the administrative organization are concerned. People do not come into administrative organizations as pieces of putty, as units of abstract energy, nor as mere tools sharpened to some technical or professional purpose. They bring with them their whole cultural conditioning and their personal idiosyncrasies. Each is genetically unique, and all are members of institutions—families, churches, clubs, unions, and so forth—outside the administrative organization; and within the administrative organization they form into natural or adaptive groups of various kinds—friendships, cliques, car pools, and so forth—that flow across the lines of formal administrative organization, sometimes darkening, sometimes lightening, and sometimes erasing these lines.

Students of administration have become increasingly aware of the nonrational factors that surround and condition administration. They have broadened the base of their study to include much information that was formerly either unavailable or ignored. The goal of rationality has not been abandoned. Rather, it has been put in a new perspective: to achieve rationality demands a respect for the large area of the nonrational and much knowledge of it. Partly this new perspective is but a more serious heeding of Bacon's maxim: "Nature to be commanded must be obeyed." (These nonrational factors are not to be understood as, by definition, working against formal organization goals, but rather, paradoxically, as phenomena which, properly understood, can often be directed toward the realization of organization goals. They are resources as well as liabilities. Thus personal rivalries can be channeled—as by an official contest—to help rather than hinder goal achievement.) Partly the new perspective is a philosophical or psychological reorientation, as implied in the word *respect*. Students of administration now know that they are not going to take heaven by storm, that is to say, quickly reduce human affairs to rule and chart. Some of them, even, without ceasing to desire and strive for more rationality than we have now achieved, are heard to say that complete rationality in human affairs is not the proper goal; that a world in which *all* is orderly and predictable, with no room for spontaneity, surprise, and emotional play, is an undesirable world.

NOTES

1. Another distinction, related and similar to the distinction between science and art, is that between pure and applied, or theoretical and practical, science. This distinction, which has important uses, is discussed below in connection with logical positivism. For a statement of it see Herbert A. Simon: *Administrative Behavior: A Study of Decision-Making Processes in Administrative Organization* (New York, Macmillan, 1947), Appendix.

2. This is an important—and difficult—word. One source of difficulty lies in the fact that given actions may produce desired results for the wrong reasons. Thus actions enjoined by superstition are found sometimes to be correct (i.e., goal-maximizing) by science, but the explanations in the two systems of interpretation are quite different. Another source of difficulty or ambiguity is discussed under The Meaning of Management.

3. See *Politics, Economics and Welfare* (New York, Harper & Row, 1953) by Robert A. Dahl and Charles E. Lindblom for a discussion of different forms of rational cooperation.

4. Sometimes a distinction is made between *purpose* and *function* in an attempt to deal with this problem. Dahl and Lindblom (p. 38) apply the idea of *net* goal achievement to the problem of multiple goals. "What do we mean by 'rationality'? And how can one test whether one action is more rational than another? The first question is easier to answer than the second. An action is rational to the extent that it is 'correctly' designed to maximize goal achievement, given the goal in question and the real world as it exists. Given more than one goal (the usual human situation), an action is rational to the extent that it is correctly designed to maximize *net* goal achievement."

5. This analogy is for introductory and explanatory purposes, and is to be viewed in this light. The definitions of organization and management that

follow in the text admittedly comprehend less than the whole of societal
anatomy and physiology respectively.
And we are not here concerned with
the familiar sociological distinction
between patterns and consequences,
or with distinguishing between static
and dynamic models.

2. The Essentials of Bureaucratic Organization: An Ideal-Type Construction

Max Weber

The effectiveness of legal authority
rests on the acceptance of the validity
of the following mutually inter-depen-
dent ideas.

1. That any given legal norm may be
established by agreement or by imposition, on grounds of expediency or rational values or both, with a claim to obedience at least on the part of the members
of the corporate group. This is, however,
usually extended to include all persons
within the sphere of authority or of
power in question—which in the case of
territorial bodies is the territorial area—
who stand in certain social relationships
or carry out forms of social action which
in the order governing the corporate
group have been declared to be relevant.

2. That every body of law consists essentially in a consistent system of abstract rules which have normally been
intentionally established. Furthermore,
administration of law is held to consist
in the application of these rules to particular cases; the administrative process
is the rational pursuit of the interests
which are specified in the order governing the corporate group within the limits laid down by legal precepts and following principles which are capable of

generalized formulation and are approved in the order governing the group,
or at least not disapproved in it.

3. That thus the typical person in authority occupies an "office." In the action associated with his status, including the commands he issues to others,
he is subject to an impersonal order to
which his actions are oriented. This is
true not only for persons exercising
legal authority who are in the usual
sense "officials," but, for instance, for
the elected president of a state.

4. That the person who obeys authority does so, as it is usually stated, only in
his capacity as a "member" of the corporate group and what he obeys is only
"the law." He may in this connexion be
the member of an association, of a territorial commune, of a church, or a citizen
of a state.

5. In conformity with point 3, it is
held that the members of the corporate
group, in so far as they obey a person in
authority, do not owe this obedience to
him as an individual, but to the impersonal order. Hence, it follows that there
is an obligation to obedience only within the sphere of the rationally delimited
authority which, in terms of the order,
has been conferred upon him.

The following may thus be said to be
the fundamental categories of rational
legal authority:—

(1) A continuous organization of official functions bound by rules.

(2) A specified sphere of competence.

SOURCE: Reprinted with the permission of
The Free Press, a Division of Macmillan, Inc.,
from *The Theory of Social and Economic Organization* by Max Weber, translated by A. M.
Henderson and Talcott Parsons, edited by Talcott Parsons. Copyright © 1947, renewed
1975 by Talcott Parsons.

This involves (a) a sphere of obligations to perform functions which has been marked off as part of a systematic division of labour. (b) The provision of the incumbent with the necessary authority to carry out these functions. (c) That the necessary means of compulsion are clearly defined and their use is subject to definite conditions. A unit exercising authority which is organized in this way will be called an "administrative organ."

There are administrative organs in this sense in large-scale private organizations, in parties and armies, as well as in the state and the church. An elected president, a cabinet of ministers, or a body of elected representatives also in this sense constitute administrative organs. This is not, however, the place to discuss these concepts. Not every administrative organ is provided with compulsory powers. But this distinction is not important for present purposes.

(3) The organization of offices follows the principle of hierarchy; that is, each lower office is under the control and supervision of a higher one. There is a right of appeal and of statement of grievances from the lower to the higher. Hierarchies differ in respect to whether and in what cases complaints can lead to a ruling from an authority at various points higher in the scale, and as to whether changes are imposed from higher up or the responsibility for such changes is left to the lower office, the conduct of which was the subject of complaint.

(4) The rules which regulate the conduct of an office may be technical rules or norms.[1] In both cases, if their application

---

[1]Weber does not explain this distinction. By a "technical rule" he probably means a prescribed course of action which is dictated primarily on grounds touching efficiency of the performance of the immediate functions, while by "norms" he probably means rules which limit conduct on grounds other than those of efficiency. Of course, in one sense all rules are norms in that they are prescriptions for conduct, conformity with which is problematical.—Ed. [Parsons.]

is to be fully rational, specialized training is necessary. It is thus normally true that only a person who has demonstrated an adequate technical training is qualified to be a member of the administrative staff of such an organized group, and hence only such persons are eligible for appointment to official positions. The administrative staff of a rational corporate group thus typically consists of "officials," whether the organization be devoted to political, religious, economic—in particular, capitalistic—or other ends.

(5) In the rational type it is a matter of principle that the members of the administrative staff should be completely separated from ownership of the means of production or administration. Officials, employees, and workers attached to the administrative staff do not themselves own the nonhuman means of production and administration. These are rather provided for their use in kind or in money, and the official is obligated to render an accounting of their use. There exists, furthermore, in principle complete separation of the property belonging to the organization, which is controlled within the sphere of office, and the personal property of the official, which is available for his own private uses. There is a corresponding separation of the place in which official functions are carried out, the "office" in the sense of premises, from living quarters.

(6) In the rational type case, there is also a complete absence of appropriation of his official position by the incumbent. Where "rights" to an office exist, as in the case of judges, and recently of an increasing proportion of officials and even of workers, they do not normally serve the purpose of appropriation by the official, but of securing the purely objective and independent character of the conduct of the office so that it is oriented only to the relevant norms.

(7) Administrative acts, decisions, and rules are formulated and recorded in writing, even in cases where oral discus-

sion is the rule or is even mandatory. This applies at least to preliminary discussions and proposals, to final decisions, and to all sorts of orders and rules. The combination of written documents and a continuous organization of official functions constitutes the "office"[2] which is the central focus of all types of modern corporate action.

(8) Legal authority can be exercised in a wide variety of different forms which will be distinguished and discussed later. The following analysis will be deliberately confined for the most part to the aspect of imperative coordination in the structure of the administrative staff. It will consist in an analysis in terms of ideal types of officialdom or "bureaucracy."

In the above outline no mention has been made of the kind of supreme head appropriate to a system of legal authority. This is a consequence of certain considerations which can only be made entirely understandable at a later stage in the analysis. There are very important types of rational imperative co-ordination which, with respect to the ultimate source of authority, belong to other categories. This is true of the hereditary charismatic type, as illustrated by hereditary monarchy and of the pure charismatic type of a president chosen

by plebiscite. Other cases involve rational elements at important points, but are made up of a combination of bureaucratic and charismatic components, as is true of the cabinet form of government. Still others are subject to the authority of the chief of other corporate groups, whether their character be charismatic or bureaucratic; thus the formal head of a government department under a parliamentary regime may be a minister who occupies his position because of his authority in a party. The type of rational, legal administrative staff is capable of application in all kinds of situations and contexts. It is the most important mechanism for the administration of everyday profane affairs. For in that sphere, the exercise of authority and, more broadly, imperative co-ordination, consists precisely in administration.

The purest type of exercise of legal authority is that which employs a bureaucratic administrative staff. Only the supreme chief of the organization occupies his position of authority by virtue of appropriation, of election, or of having been designated for the succession. But even *his* authority consists in a sphere of legal "competence." The whole administrative staff under the supreme authority then consists, in the purest type, of individual officials who are appointed and function according to the following criteria:[3]

(1) They are personally free and subject to authority only with respect to their impersonal official obligations.

(2) They are organized in a clearly defined hierarchy of offices.

(3) Each office has a clearly defined sphere of competence in the legal sense.

(4) The office is filled by a free contractual relationship. Thus, in principle, there is free selection.

[2]*Bureau.* It has seemed necessary to use the English word "office" in three different meanings, which are distinguished in Weber's discussion by at least two terms. The first is *Amt*, which means "office" in the sense of the institutionally defined status of a person. The second is the "work premises" as in the expression "he spent the afternoon in his office." For this Weber uses *Bureau* as also for the third meaning which he has just defined, the "organized work process of a group." In this last sense an office is a particular type of "organization," or *Betrieb* in Weber's sense. This use is established in English in such expressions as "the District Attorney's Office has such and such functions." Which of the three meanings is involved in a given case will generally be clear from the context.—Ed. [Parsons.]

[3]This characterization applies to the "monocratic" as opposed to the "collegial" type, which will be discussed below.

(5) Candidates are selected on the basis of technical qualifications. In the most rational case, this is tested by examination or guaranteed by diplomas certifying technical training, or both. They are *appointed,* not elected.

(6) They are remunerated by fixed salaries in money, for the most part with a right to pensions. Only under certain circumstances does the employing authority, especially in private organizations, have a right to terminate the appointment, but the official is always free to resign. The salary scale is primarily graded according to rank in the hierarchy; but in addition to this criterion, the responsibility of the position and the requirements of the incumbent's social status may be taken into account.

(7) The office is treated as the sole, or at least the primary, occupation of the incumbent.

(8) It constitutes a career. There is a system of "promotion" according to seniority or to achievement, or both. Promotion is dependent on the judgment of superiors.

(9) The official works entirely separated from ownership of the means of administration and without appropriation of his position.

(10) He is subject to strict and systematic discipline and control in the conduct of the office.

This type of organization is in principle applicable with equal facility to a wide variety of different fields. It may be applied in profit-making business or in charitable organizations, or in any number of other types of private enterprises serving ideal or material ends. It is equally applicable to political and to religious organizations. With varying degrees of approximation to a pure type, its historical existence can be demonstrated in all these fields.

1. For example, this type of bureaucracy is found in private clinics, as well as in endowed hospitals or the hospitals maintained by religious orders. Bureaucratic organization has played a major role in the Catholic Church. It is well illustrated by the administrative role of the priesthood in the modern church, which has expropriated almost all of the old church benefices, which were in former days to a large extent subject to private appropriation. It is also illustrated by the conception of the universal Episcopate, which is thought of as formally constituting a universal legal competence in religious matters. Similarly, the doctrine of Papal infallibility is thought of as in fact involving a universal competence, but only one which functions "ex cathedra" in the sphere of the office, thus implying the typical distinction between the sphere of office and that of the private affairs of the incumbent. The same phenomena are found in the large-scale capitalistic enterprise; and the larger it is, the greater their role. And this is not less true of political parties, which will be discussed separately. Finally, the modern army is essentially a bureaucratic organization administered by that peculiar type of military functionary, the "officer."

2. Bureaucratic authority is carried out in its purest form where it is most clearly dominated by the principle of appointment. There is no such thing as a hierarchy of elected officials in the same sense as there is a hierarchical organization of appointed officials. In the first place, election makes it impossible to attain a stringency of discipline even approaching that in the appointed type. For it is open to a subordinate official to compete for elective honours on the same terms as his superiors, and his prospects are not dependent on the superior's judgment.

3. Appointment by free contract, which makes free selection possible, is essential to modern bureaucracy. Where there is a hierarchical organization with impersonal spheres of competence, but

occupied by unfree officials—like slaves or dependents, who, however, function in a formally bureaucratic manner—the term "patrimonial bureaucracy" will be used.

4. The role of technical qualifications in bureaucratic organizations is continually increasing. Even an official in a party or a trade-union organization is in need of specialized knowledge, though it is usually of an empirical character, developed by experience, rather than by formal training. In the modern state, the only "offices" for which no technical qualifications are required are those of ministers and presidents. This only goes to prove that they are "officials" only in a formal sense, and not substantively, as is true of the managing director or president of a large business corporation. There is no question but that the "position" of the capitalistic entrepreneur is as definitely appropriated as is that of a monarch. Thus at the top of a bureaucratic organization, there is necessarily an element which is at least not purely bureaucratic. The category of bureaucracy is one applying only to the exercise of control by means of a particular kind of administrative staff.

5. The bureaucratic official normally receives a fixed salary. By contrast, sources of income which are privately appropriated will be called "benefices." Bureaucratic salaries are also normally paid in money. Though this is not essential to the concept of bureaucracy, it is the arrangement which best fits the pure type. Payments in kind are apt to have the character of benefices, and the receipt of a benefice normally implies the appropriation of opportunities for earnings and of positions. There are, however, gradual transitions in this field with many intermediate types. Appropriation by virtue of leasing or sale of offices or the pledge of income from office are phenomena foreign to the pure type of bureaucracy.

6. "Offices" which do not constitute the incumbent's principal occupation, in particular "honorary" offices, belong in other categories. . . . The typical "bureaucratic" official occupies the office as his principal occupation.

7. With respect to the separation of the official from ownership of the means of administration, the situation is essentially the same in the field of public administration and in private bureaucratic organizations, such as the large-scale capitalistic enterprise.

8. . . . At the present time [collegial bodies] are rapidly decreasing in importance in favour of types of organization which are in fact, and for the most part formally as well, subject to the authority of a single head. For instance, the collegial "governments" in Prussia have long since given way to the monocratic "district president." The decisive factor in this development has been the need for rapid, clear decisions, free of the necessity of compromise between different opinions and also free of shifting majorities.

9. The modern army officer is a type of appointed official who is clearly marked off by certain class distinctions . . . In this respect such officers differ radically from elected military leaders, from charismatic "condottieri," from the type of officers who recruit and lead mercenary armies as a capitalistic enterprise, and, finally, from the incumbents of commissions which have been purchased. There may be gradual transitions between these types. The patrimonial "retainer," who is separated from the means of carrying out his function, and the proprietor of a mercenary army for capitalistic purposes have, along with the private capitalistic entrepreneur, been pioneers in the organization of the modern type of bureaucracy. . . .

The Monocratic Type of Bureaucratic Administration. Experience tends universally to show that the purely bureaucratic type of administrative organization—that is, the monocratic variety of bureaucracy—is, from a purely technical point of view, capable of attaining the highest degree of efficiency and is in this sense formally the most rational known means of carrying out imperative control over human beings. It is superior to any other form in precision, in stability, in the stringency of its discipline, and in its reliability. It thus makes possible a particularly high degree of calculability of results for the heads of the organization and for those acting in relation to it. It is finally superior both in intensive efficiency and in the scope of its operations, and is formally capable of application to all kinds of administrative tasks.

The development of the modern form of the organization of corporate groups in all fields is nothing less than identical with the development and continual spread of bureaucratic administration. This is true of church and state, of armies, political parties, economic enterprises, organizations to promote all kinds of causes, private associations, clubs, and many others. Its development is, to take the most striking case, the most crucial phenomenon of the modern Western state. However many forms there may be which do not appear to fit this pattern, such as collegial representative bodies, parliamentary committees, soviets, honorary officers, lay judges, and what not, and however much people may complain about the "evils of bureaucracy," it would be sheer illusion to think for a moment that continuous administrative work can be carried out in any field except by means of officials working in offices. The whole pattern of everyday life is cut to fit this framework. For bureaucratic administration is, other things being equal, always, from a formal, technical point of view, the most rational type. For the needs of mass administration to-day, it is completely indispensable. The choice is only that between bureaucracy and dilettantism in the field of administration.

The primary source of the superiority of bureaucratic administration lies in the role of technical knowledge which, through the development of modern technology and business methods in the production of goods, has become completely indispensable. In this respect, it makes no difference whether the economic system is organized on a capitalistic or a socialistic basis. Indeed, if in the latter case a comparable level of technical efficiency were to be achieved, it would mean a tremendous increase in the importance of specialized bureaucracy.

When those subject to bureaucratic control seek to escape the influence of the existing bureaucratic apparatus, this is normally possible only by creating an organization of their own which is equally subject to the process of bureaucratization. Similarly the existing bureaucratic apparatus is driven to continue functioning by the most powerful interests which are material and objective, but also ideal in character. Without it, a society like our own—with a separation of officials, employees, and workers from ownership of the means of administration, dependent on discipline and on technical training—could no longer function. The only exception would be those groups, such as the peasantry, who are still in possession of their own means of subsistence. Even in case of revolution by force or of occupation by an enemy, the bureaucratic machinery will normally continue to function just as it has for the previous legal government.

The question is always who controls the existing bureaucratic machinery. And such control is possible only in a very limited degree to persons who are not technical specialists. Generally speaking, the trained permanent official is more likely to get his way in the long run than his nominal superior, the Cabinet minister, who is not a specialist.

Though by no means alone, the capitalistic system has undeniably played a major role in the development of bureaucracy. Indeed, without it capitalistic production could not continue and any rational type of socialism would have simply to take it over and increase its importance. Its development, largely under capitalistic auspices, has created an urgent need for stable, strict, intensive, and calculable administration. It is this need which gives bureaucracy a crucial role in our society as the central element in any kind of large-scale administration. Only by reversion in every field—political, religious, economic, etc.—to small-scale organization would it be possible to any considerable extent to escape its influence. On the one hand, capitalism in its modern stages of development strongly tends to foster the development of bureaucracy, though both capitalism and bureaucracy have arisen from many different historical sources. Conversely, capitalism is the most rational economic basis for bureaucratic administration and enables it to develop in the most rational form, especially because, from a fiscal point of view, it supplies the necessary money resources.

Along with these fiscal conditions of efficient bureaucratic administration, there are certain extremely important conditions in the fields of communication and transportation. The precision of its functioning requires the services of the railway, the telegraph, and the telephone, and becomes increasingly dependent on them. A socialistic form of organization would not alter this fact. It would be a question whether in a socialistic system it would be possible to provide conditions for carrying out as stringent bureaucratic organization as has been possible in a capitalistic order. For socialism would, in fact, require a still higher degree of formal bureaucratization than capitalism. If this should prove not to be possible, it would demonstrate the existence of another of those fundamental elements of irra-

tionality in social systems—a conflict between formal and substantive rationality of the sort which sociology so often encounters.

Bureaucratic administration means fundamentally the exercise of control on the basis of knowledge. This is the feature of it which makes it specifically rational. This consists on the one hand in technical knowledge which, by itself, is sufficient to ensure it a position of extraordinary power. But in addition to this, bureaucratic organizations, or the holders of power who make use of them, have the tendency to increase their power still further by the knowledge growing out of experience in the service. For they acquire through the conduct of office a special knowledge of facts and have available a store of documentary material peculiar to themselves. While not peculiar to bureaucratic organizations, the concept of "official secrets" is certainly typical of them. It stands in relation to technical knowledge in somewhat the same position as commercial secrets do to technological training. It is a product of the striving for power.

Bureaucracy is superior in knowledge, including both technical knowledge and knowledge of the concrete fact within its own sphere of interest, which is usually confined to the interests of a private business—a capitalistic enterprise. The capitalistic entrepreneur is, in our society, the only type who has been able to maintain at least relative immunity from subjection to the control of rational bureaucratic knowledge. All the rest of the population have tended to be organized in large-scale corporate groups which are inevitably subject to bureaucratic control. This is as inevitable as the dominance of precision machinery in the mass production of goods.

The following are the principal more general social consequences of bureaucratic control:—

(1) The tendency to "levelling" in the interest of the broadest possible basis of

recruitment in terms of technical competence.

(2) The tendency to plutocracy growing out of the interest in the greatest possible length of technical training. Today this often lasts up to the age of thirty.

(3) The dominance of a spirit of formalistic impersonality, *"Sine ira et studio,"* without hatred or passion, and

hence without affection or enthusiasm. The dominant norms are concepts of straightforward duty without regard to personal considerations. Everyone is subject to formal equality of treatment; that is, everyone in the same empirical situation. This is the spirit in which the ideal official conducts his office.

3. Public Choice: A Different Approach to the Study Of Public Administration

Vincent Ostrom and Elinor Ostrom

In November 1963, a number of economists and a sprinkling of other social scientists were invited by James Buchanan and Gordon Tullock to explore a community of interest in the study of nonmarket decision making. That conference was reported in PAR as "Developments in the 'No-Name' Fields of Public Administration."* A shared interest prevailed regarding the application of economic reasoning to "collective," "political" or "social" decision making, but no consensus developed on the choice of a name to characterize those interests. In December 1967 the decision was taken to form a Public Choice Society and to publish a journal, *Public Choice.*** The term "public choice" will be used here to refer to the

SOURCE: "Public Choice: A Different Approach to the Study of Public Administration," by Vincent and Elinor Ostrom, *Public Administration Review:* 31 (March/April 1971). Reprinted by permission of the American Society for Public Administration.
Public Administration Review, Vol. XXIV (March 1964), pp. 62-63.
**Originally issued as *Papers on Non-Market Decision Making*, *Public Choice* first appeared in Spring 1968. Professor Gordon Tullock, Center for the Study of Public Choice, Virginia Polytechnic Institute, Blacksburg, Virginia, is editor of *Public Choice.*

work of this community of scholars. The bibliography following this article refers to only a small fraction of the relevant literature, but will serve to introduce the reader to public choice literature.

The public choice approach needs to be related to basic theoretical traditions in public administration. As background, we shall first examine the theoretical tradition as formulated by Wilson and those who followed. We shall next examine Herbert Simon's challenge to that tradition which has left the discipline in what Dwight Waldo has characterized as a "crisis of identity." (118) The relevance of the public choice approach for dealing with the issues raised by Simon's challenge will then be considered.

THE TRADITIONAL THEORY OF PUBLIC ADMINISTRATION

Woodrow Wilson's essay, "The Study of Administration," called for a new science of administration based upon a radical distinction between politics and administration. (130, p. 210) According to Wilson, governments may differ in the political principles reflected in their constitutions, but the principles of good administration are much the same in any system of government. There is ". . . but one rule of good administration for all governments alike," was Wilson's major thesis. (130, p. 218) "So far as administrative functions are concerned, all governments have a strong structural likeness; more than that, if they are to be uniformly useful and efficient, they must have a strong structural likeness." (130, p. 218)

Good administration, according to Wilson, will be hierarchically ordered in a system of graded ranks subject to political direction by heads of departments at the center of government. The ranks of administration would be filled by a corps of technically trained civil servants ". . . prepared by a special schooling and drilled, after appointment, into a perfected organization, with an appropriate hierarchy and characteristic discipline. . . ." (130, p. 216) Perfection in administrative organization is attained in a hierarchically ordered and professionally trained public service. Efficiency is attained by perfection in the hierarchical ordering of a professionally trained public service. Wilson also conceptualizes efficiency in economic terms: ". . . the utmost possible efficiency and at the least possible cost of either money or of energy." (130, p. 197)

For the next half-century, the discipline of public administration developed within the framework set by Wilson. The ends of public administration were seen as the "management of men and material in the accomplishment of the purposes of the state." (125, p. 6) Hierarchical structure was regarded as the ideal pattern of organization. According to L. D. White, "All large-scale organizations follow the same pattern, which in essence consists in the universal application of the superior-subordinate relationship through a number of levels of responsibility reaching from the *top to the bottom* of the structure." (Emphasis added, 125, p. 33)

SIMON'S CHALLENGE

Herbert Simon, drawing in part upon previous work by Luther Gulick, (53) sustained a devastating critique of the theory implicit in the traditional study of public administration. In his *Administrative Behavior,* Simon elucidated some of the accepted administrative principles and demonstrated the lack of logical coherence among them. (104) Simon characterized those principles as "proverbs." Like proverbs, incompatible principles allowed the administrative analyst to justify his position in relation to one or another principle. "No single one of these items is of sufficient importance," Simon concluded, "to suffice as a guiding principle for the administrative analyst." (104, p. 36)

After his indictment of traditional administrative theory, Simon began an effort to reconstruct administrative theory. The first stage was "the construction of an adequate vocabulary and analytic scheme." Simon's reconstruction began with a distinction between facts and values. Individuals engage in a consideration of facts and of values in choosing among alternative possibilities bounded by the ordered rationality of an organization. Simon envisioned the subsequent stage of reconstruction to involve the establishment of a bridge between theory and empirical study "so that theory could provide a guide to the design of 'critical' experiments and studies, while experimental study could provide a sharp test and corrective of theory." (104, p. 44)

One of Simon's central concerns was to establish the criterion of efficiency as a norm for evaluating alternative administrative actions. Simon argued that the "criterion of efficiency dictates that choice of alternatives which produce the largest result for the given application of resources." (104, p. 179) In order to utilize the criterion of efficiency, the results of administrative actions must be defined and measured. Clear conceptual definitions of output are necessary before measures can be developed.

No necessary reason existed, Simon argued, for assuming that perfection in hierarchical ordering would always be the most efficient organizational arrangement. [But see also (106) and (107).] Alternative organizational forms needed to be empirically evaluated to determine their relative efficiency. Simon's own work with Ridley on the measurement of municipal activities represented a beginning effort to identify the output of government agencies and to develop indices to measure those outputs. (92)

THE WORK OF THE POLITICAL ECONOMISTS

During the period following Simon's challenge, another community of scholars has grappled with many of these same intellectual issues. This community of scholars has been composed predominantly of political economists who have been concerned with public investment and public expenditure decisions. One facet of this work has been manifest in benefit-cost analysis and the development of the PPB system. (116) PPB analysis rests upon much the same theoretical grounds as the traditional theory of public administration. The PPB analyst is essentially taking the methodological perspective of an "omniscient observer" or a "benevolent despot." Assuming that he knows the "will of the state," the PPB analyst selects a program for the efficient utilization of resources (i.e., men and material) in the accomplishment of those purposes. As Senator McClelland has correctly perceived, the assumption of omniscience may not hold; and, as a consequence, PPB analysis may involve radical errors and generate gross inefficiencies. [See (126).]

Public choice represents another facet

of work in political economy with more radical implications for the theory of public administration. Most political economists in the public choice tradition begin with the individual as the basic unit of analysis. Traditional "economic man" is replaced by "man: the decision maker."

The second concern in the public choice tradition is with the conceptualization of public goods as the type of event associated with the output of public agencies. These efforts are closely related to Simon's concern for the definition and measurement of the results of administrative action. In addition, public choice theory is concerned with the effect that different decision rules or decision-making arrangements will have upon the production of those events conceptualized as public goods and services. Thus, a model of man, the type of event characterized as public goods and services, and decision structures comprise the analytical variables in public choice theory. Our "man: the decision maker" will confront certain opportunities and possibilities in the world of events and will pursue his relative advantage within the strategic opportunities afforded by different types of decision rules or decision-making arrangements. The consequences are evaluated by whether or not the outcome is consistent with the efficiency criterion.

Work in public choice begins with methodological individualism where the perspective of a representative individual is used for analytical purposes. (20) Since the individual is the basic unit of analysis, the assumptions made about individual behavior become critical in building a coherent theory. (32) (33) Four basic assumptions about individual behavior are normally made.

First, individuals are assumed to be self-interested. The word "self-interest" is not equivalent to "selfish." The assumption of self-interest implies primarily that individuals each have their own preferences which affect the decisions they make, and that those preferences may differ from individual to individual. (25)

Secondly, individuals are assumed to be rational. Rationality is defined as the ability to rank all known alternatives available to the individual in a transitive manner. Ranking implies that a rational individual either values alternative "A" more than alternative "B," or that he prefers alternative "B" to alternative "A," or that he is indifferent as between them. Transitivity means that if he prefers alternative "A" to alternative "B," and "B" is preferred to "C," then "A" is necessarily preferred to "C." [See also (13) and (48).]

Third, individuals are assumed to adopt maximizing strategies. Maximization as a strategy implies the consistent choice of those alternatives which an individual thinks will provide the highest net benefit as weighed by his own preferences. (117) At times the assumption of maximization is related to that of satisfying, depending upon assumptions about the information available to an individual in a decision-making situation. (105)

Fourth, an explicit assumption needs to be stated concerning the level of information possessed by a representative individual. Three levels have been analytically defined as involving certainty, risk, and uncertainty. (68) (72) The condition of certainty is defined to exist when: (1) an individual knows all available strategies, (2) each strategy is known to lead invariably to only one specific outcome, and (3) the individual knows his own preferences for each outcome. Given this level of information, the decision of a maximizing individual is completely determined. He simply chooses that strategy which leads to the outcome for which he has the highest preference. (50)

Under conditions of risk, the individual is still assumed to know all available strategies. Any particular strategy may lead to a number of potential outcomes, and the individual is assumed to know the probability of each outcome. (1) Thus, decision making becomes a weighting process whereby his preferences for different outcomes are combined with the probability of their occurrence prior to a selection of a strategy. Under risk, an individual may adopt mixed strategies in an effort to obtain the highest level of outcomes over a series of decisions in the long run.

Decision making under uncertainty is assumed to occur either where (1) an individual has a knowledge of all strategies and outcomes, but lacks knowledge about the probabilities with which a strategy may lead to an outcome, or (2) an individual may not know all strategies or all outcomes which actually exist. (57) (91) Uncertainty is more characteristic of problematical situations than either certainty or risk. Under either certainty or risk, an analyst can project a relatively determinant solution to a particular problem. Under conditions of uncertainty, the determinateness of solutions is replaced by conclusions about the range of possible "solutions." (102)

Once uncertainty is postulated, a further assumption may be made that an individual learns about states of affairs as he develops and tests strategies. (108) (110) Estimations are made about the consequences of strategies. If the predicted results follow, then a more reliable image of the world is established. If predicted results fail to occur, the individual is forced to change his image of the world and modify his strategies. (83) Individuals who learn may adopt a series of diverse strategies as they attempt to reduce the level of uncertainty in which they are operating. (35) (109)

THE NATURE OF PUBLIC GOODS AND SERVICES

Individuals who are self-interested, rational, and who pursue maximizing strategies find themselves in a variety of situations. Such situations involve the production and consumption of a variety of goods. Political economists in the public choice tradition distinguish situations involving purely private goods as a logical category from purely public goods. (39) (97) (98) Purely private goods are defined as those goods and services which are highly divisible and can be (1) packaged, contained, or measured in discrete units, and (2) provided under competitive market conditions where potential consumers can be excluded from enjoying the benefit unless they are willing to pay the price. Purely public goods, by contrast, are highly indivisible goods and services where potential consumers cannot be easily excluded from enjoying the benefits. (17) Once public goods are provided for some, they will be available for others to enjoy without reference to who pays the costs. National defense is a classic example of a public good. Once it is provided for some individuals living within a particular country, it is automatically provided for all individuals who are citizens of that country, whether they pay for it or not.

In addition to the two logical categories of purely private and purely public goods, most political economists would postulate the existence of an intermediate continuum. Within this continuum, the production or consumption of goods or services may involve spill-over effects or externalities which are not isolated and contained within market transactions. (5) (23) (38) (75) Goods with appreciable spill overs are similar to private goods to the extent that some effects can be subject to the exclusion principle; but other effects are like public goods and spill over

onto others not directly involved. (31) The air pollution which results from the production of private industry is an example of a negative externality. Efforts to reduce the cost of a negative externality is the equivalent of providing a public good. The benefits produced for a neighborhood by the location of a golf course or park is a positive externality.

The existence of public goods or significant eternalities creates a number of critical problems for individuals affected by those circumstances. (26) (58) (89) Each individual will maximize his net welfare if he takes advantage of a public good at minimum cost to himself. (42) He will have little or no incentive to take individual action where the effect of individual action would be to conserve or maintain the quality of the good that each shares in common. Each individual is likely to adopt a "dog-in-the-manger" strategy by pursuing his own advantage and disregarding the consequences of his action upon others. Furthermore, individuals may not even be motivated to articulate their own honest preferences for a common good. (43) (78) (111) If someone proposes an improvement in the quality of a public good, some individuals may have an incentive to withhold information about their preferences for such an improvement. (101) If others were to make the improvement, the individual who had concealed his preference could then indicate that he was not a beneficiary and might avoid paying his share of the costs. If voluntary action is proposed, some individuals will have an incentive to "hold-out," act as "free-riders," and take advantage of the benefits provided by others. (34) (63) Garret Hardin had indicated that these strategies typically give rise to "the tragedy of the commons" where increased individual effort leaves everyone worse off. (56)

THE EFFECT OF DECISION STRUCTURES UPON COLLECTIVE ACTION

The Problem of Collective Inaction

The problem arising from the indivisibility of a public good and the structure of individual incentives created by the failure of an exclusion principle is the basis for Mancur Olson's *The Logic of Collective Action.* (81) Olson concludes that individuals cannot be expected to form large voluntary associations to pursue matters of public interest unless special conditions exist. (77) Individuals will form voluntary associations in pursuit of public interests only when members will derive separable benefits of a sufficient magnitude to justify the cost of membership or where they can be coerced into bearing their share of the costs. (27) (51) (69) Thus, we cannot expect persons to organize themselves in a strictly voluntary association to realize their common interest in the provision of public goods and services. An individual's actions will be calculated by the probability that his efforts alone will make a difference. If that probability is nil, and if he is a rational person, we would expect his effort to be nil.

Constitutional Choice and Collective Action

The analysis of Mancur Olson would lead us to conclude that undertaking collective actions to provide public goods and services such as national defense, public parks, and education is not easily accomplished. If unanimity were the only decision rule that individuals utilized to undertake collective action, most public goods would not be provided. (8) Yet, individuals do surmount the problems of collective inaction to constitute enterprises which do not rely strictly upon the voluntary consent of all who are affected. Buchanan and Tul-

lock begin to develop a logic that a representative individual might use in attempting to establish some method for gaining the benefits of collective action. (25) While many students of public administration would not immediately see the relevance of a logic of constitutional decision making for the study of public administration, we feel that it provides an essential foundation for a different approach to the field. Using this logic, public agencies are not viewed simply as bureaucratic units which perform those services which someone at the top instructs them to perform. Rather, public agencies are viewed as means for allocating decision-making capabilities in order to provide public goods and services responsive to the preferences of individuals in different social contexts.

A constitutional choice is simply a choice of decision rules for making future collective decisions. Constitutional choice, as such, does not include the appropriation of funds or actions to alter events in the world except to provide the organizational structure for ordering the choices of future decision makers. A representative individual wanting to create an organization to provide a public good would, according to Buchanan and Tullock, need to take two types of costs into account: (1) external costs—those costs which an individual expects to bear as the result of decisions which deviate from his preferences and impose costs upon him—and (2) decision-making costs—the expenditure of resources, time, effort, and opportunities foregone in decision making. (22) Both types of costs are affected by the selection of decision rules which specify the proportion of individuals required to agree prior to future collective action. (87)

Expected external costs will be at their highest point where any one person can take action on behalf of the entire collectivity. Such costs would decline as the proportion of members participating in collective decision making increases. Expected external costs would reach zero where all were required to agree prior to collective action under a rule of unanimity. However, expected decision-making costs would have the opposite trend. Expenditures on decision making would be minimal if any one person could make future collective decisions for the whole group of affected individuals. Such costs would increase to their highest point with a rule of unanimity.

If our representative individual were a cost minimizer, and the two types of costs described above were an accurate representation of the costs he perceives, we would expect him to prefer the constitutional choice of a decision rule where the two cost curves intersect. When the two cost curves are roughly symmetrical, some form of simple majority vote would be a rational choice of a voting rule. If expected external costs were far greater than expected decision-making costs, an extraordinary majority would be a rational choice of a voting rule. On the other hand, if the opportunity costs inherent in decision making were expected to be very large in comparison to external costs, then reliance might be placed on a rule authorizing collective action by the decision of one person in the extreme case requiring rapid response. An optimal set of decision rules will vary with different situations, and we would not expect to find one good rule that would apply to the provision of all types of public goods and services.

Majority Vote and the Expression of Social Preferences

Scholars in the public choice tradition have also been concerned with the effect of decision rules upon the expression of individual preferences regarding the social welfare of a community of individuals. (2) (15) (16) (46) Particular attention has been paid to majority vote as a means of expressing such preferences. (44) (49) (59) (90) (94) (95) (96) Duncan Black in *The Theory of Committees and Elections* has demonstrated that if a community is assumed to have a single-peaked preference ordering, then a choice reflecting the median preference position will dominate all others under majority vote, providing the numbers are odd. (11) (12) Edwin Haefele and others have pointed out that this solution has interesting implications for the strategy of those who must win the approval of an electorate. (37) (40) (55) If representatives are aware of their constituents' preferences, the task of developing a winning coalition depends upon the formulation of a program that will occupy the median position of voter preferences, providing that voters are making a choice between two alternatives. Under these circumstances, persons in political or administrative leadership would have an incentive to formulate a program oriented to the median preference position of their constituents. Voters would then choose the alternative, if presented with a choice, which most closely approximates the median position. (45) (66) Single peakedness implies a substantial homogeneity in social preference with the bulk of preferences clustering around a single central tendency. Such conditions might reasonably apply to a public good for which there is a relatively uniform demand in relation to any particular community of interest. Substantial variations in demand for different mixes of public goods, as might be reflected in the differences between wealthy neighborhoods and ghetto neighborhoods in a big city, would most likely not meet the condition of single peakedness when applied to the provision of educational services, police services, or welfare services. Majority voting under such conditions would fail to reflect the social preference of such divers neighborhoods if they were subsumed in the same constituency.

Bureaucratic Organization

If the essential characteristic of a bureaucracy is an ordered structure of authority where command is unified in one position and all other positions are ranked in a series of one-many relationships, then we would assume from the Buchanan and Tullock cost calculus that a constitutional system based exclusively upon a bureaucratic ordering would be an extremely costly affair. Presumably, an ordered system of one-man rule might sustain considerable speed and dispatch in some decision making. However, the level of potential deprivations or external social costs would be very high. If external costs can be reduced to a low order of magnitude, then reliance upon a bureaucratic ordering would have considerable advantage.

The possibility of reducing expected external costs to a low order of magnitude so that advantage might be taken of the low decision costs potentially inherent in a bureaucratic ordering can be realized only if (1) appropriate decision-making arrangements are available to assure the integrity of substantial unanimity at the level of constitutional choice, and (2) methods of collective choice are continuously available to reflect the social preferences of members of the community for different public goods and services. The rationale for bureaucratic organization in a democratic society can be sustained only if both of these conditions are met.

In the political economy tradition, two different approaches have been taken in the analysis of bureaucratic organizations. R. H. Coase in an article on "The Nature of a Firm" has developed an explanation for bureaucratic organization in business firms. (30) According to Coase, rational individuals might be expected to organize a firm where management responsibilities would be assumed by an entrepreneur, and others would be willing to become employees if the firm could conduct business under direction of the entrepreneur at a lesser cost than if each and every transaction were to be organized as market transactions. The firm would be organized on the basis of long-term employment contracts, rather than short-term market transactions. Each employee would agree, for certain remuneration, to work in accordance with the directions of an entrepreneur within certain limits. The employment contract is analogous to a constitution in defining decision-making arrangements between employer and employee.

Coase anticipates limits to the size of firms where the costs of using a factor of production purchased in the market would be less than adding a new component to the firm to produce that added factor of production. As more employees are added, management costs would be expected to increase. A point would be reached where the saving on the marginal employee would not exceed the added costs of managing that employee. No net savings would accrue to the entrepreneur. If a firm became too large, an entrepreneur might also fail to see some of his opportunities and not take best advantage of potential opportunities in the reallocation of his work force. Another entrepreneur with a smaller, more efficient firm would thus have a competitive advantage over the larger firm which had exceeded the limit of scale economy in firm size.

Gordon Tullock in *The Politics of Bureaucracy* develops another analysis using a model of "economic man" to discern the consequences which can be expected to follow from rational behavior in large public bureaucracies. (114) Tullock's "economic man" is an ambitious public employee who seeks to advance his career opportunities for promotions within the bureaucracy. Since career advancement depends upon favorable recommendations by his superiors, a career-oriented public servant will act so to please his superiors. Favorable information will be forwarded; unfavorable information will be repressed. Distortion of information will diminish control and generate expectations which diverge from events sustained by actions. (80) Large-scale bureaucracies will, thus, become error prone and cumbersome in adapting to rapidly changing conditions. Efforts to correct the malfunctioning of bureaucracies by tightening control will simply magnify errors.

Coase's analysis would indicate that elements of bureaucratic organization can enhance efficiency if the rule-making authority of an entrepreneur is constrained by mutually agreeable limits and he is free to take best advantage of opportunities in reallocating work assignments within those constraints. Both Coase and Tullock recognize limits to economies of scale in bureaucratic organization. (128) No such limits were recognized in the traditional theory of public administration. Bureaucratic organization is as subject to institutional weaknesses and institutional failures as any other form of organizational arrangement.

Producer Performance and Consumer Interests in the Provision of Public Goods and Services

The problem of collective inaction can be overcome under somewhat optimal conditions provided that (1) substantial unanimity can be sustained at the level of constitutional choice, (2) political and administrative leadership is led to search out median solutions within a community of people which has a single-peaked order of preferences, and (3) a public service can be produced by an enterprise subject to those constraints. Some difficult problems will always remain to plague those concerned with the provision of public goods and services.

Once a public good is provided, the absence of an exclusion principle means that each individual will have little or no choice but to take advantage of whatever is provided unless he is able to move or is wealthy enough to provide for himself. (112) Under these conditions, the producer of a public good may be relatively free to induce savings in production costs by increasing the burden or cost to the user or consumer of public goods and services. Shifts of producer costs to consumers may result in an aggregate loss of efficiency, where the savings on the production side are exceeded by added costs on the consumption side. Public agencies rarely, if ever, calculate the value of users' time and inconvenience when they engage in studies of how to make better use of their employees' time. What is the value of the time of citizens who stand in line waiting for service as against the value of a clerk's time who is servicing them? (67) (119) (122) If the citizen has no place else to go and if he is one in a million other citizens, the probability of his interest being taken into account is negligible. The most impoverished members of a community are the most exposed to deprivations under these circumstances. A preoccupation with producer efficiency in public administration may have contributed to the impoverishment of ghettos.

This problem is further complicated by conditions of changing preferences among any community of people and the problem of changing levels of demand in relation to the available supply of a public good or service. No one can know the preferences or values of other persons apart from giving those persons an opportunity to express their preferences or values. If constituencies and collectivities are organized in a way that does not reflect the diversity of interests among different groups of people, then producers of public goods and services will be taking action without information as to the changing preferences of the persons they serve. Expenditures may be made with little reference to consumer utility. Producer efficiency in the absence of consumer utility is without meaning. Large per capita expenditures for educational services which are not conceived by the recipients to enhance their life prospects may be grossly unproductive. Education can be a sound investment in human development only when individuals perceive the effort as enhancing their life prospects.

Similar difficulties may be engendered when conditions of demand for a public good or service increase in relation to the available supply. When demands begin to exceed supply, the dynamics inherent in "the tragedy of the commons" may arise all over again. (76) (79) (96) (100) (129) A congested highway carries less and less traffic as the demand grows. What was once a public good for local residents may now become a public "bad" as congested and noisy traffic precludes a growing number of opportunities for the use of streets by local residents. (24) In short, the value of public goods may be subject to serious erosion under conditions of changing demand.

Finally, producer performance and consumer interests are closely tied together when we recognize that the capacity to levy taxes, to make appropriate expenditure decisions, and to provide the necessary public facilities are insufficient for optimality in the use of public facilities. One pattern of use may impair the value of a public facility for other patterns of use. The construction of a public street or highway, for example, would be insufficient to enhance the welfare potential for members of a community without attention to an extensive body of regulations controlling the use of such facilities by pedestrian and vehicular traffic. As demand for automobile traffic turns streets into a flood of vehicles, who is to articulate the interests of pedestrians and other potential

users, and allocate the good among all potential users?

The interests of the users of public goods and services will be taken into account only to the extent that producers of public goods and services stand exposed to the potential demands of those users. If producers fail to adapt to changing demands or fail to modify conditions of supply to meet changing demands, then the availability of alternative administrative, political, judicial, and constitutional remedies may be necessary for the maintenance of an efficient and responsive system of public administration. Efficiency in public administrations will depend upon the sense of constitutional decision making that public administrators bring to the task of constituting the conditions of public life in a community.

Most political economists in the public choice tradition would anticipate that no single form of organization is good for all social circumstances. [See also (3) and (4).] Different forms of organization will give rise to some capabilities and will be subject to other limitations. Market organization will be subject to limitations which will give rise to institutional weaknesses or institutional failure. Bureaucratic organization will provide opportunities to develop some capabilities and will be subject to other limitations. Those limitations will in turn generate institutional weakness or institutional failure if they are exceeded. A knowledge of the capabilities and limitations of diverse forms of organizational arrangements will be necessary for both the future study and practice of public administration.

TOWARD NEW PERSPECTIVES IN THE STUDY OF PUBLIC ADMINISTRATION

Our prior analysis has been largely, though not exclusively, oriented toward a circumstance involving calculations relative to the provision of a single public good. If we proceed with an assumption that we live in a world involving a large variety of potential public goods which come in different shapes and forms, we may want to consider what our representative individual as a self-interested calculator pursuing maximizing strategies would search out as an appropriate way for organizing an administrative system to provide an optimal mix of different public goods and services. Would a representative individual expect to get the best results by having all public goods and services provided by a single integrated bureaucratic structure subject to the control and direction of a single chief executive? Or would he expect to get better results by having access to a number of different collectivities capable of providing public services in response to a diversity of communities of interest? (9) (47) (54) (64) (73) (88)

If the answer to the first question is "no" then the presumptions inherent in Wilson's theory of administration and in the traditional principles of public administration will not stand as a satisfactory basis for a theory of administration in a democratic society. If the answer to the second question is "yes" then we are confronted with the task of developing an alternative theory of public administration that is appropriate for citizens living in a democratic society. (71)

If a domain that is relevant to the provision of a public good or service can be specified so that those who are potentially affected can be contained within the boundaries of an appropriate jurisdiction and externalities do not spill over onto others, then a public enterprise can be operated with substantial autonomy, provided that an appropriate structure of legal and political remedies are available to assure that some are not able to use the coercive powers of a collectivity to deprive others of unlawful rights or claims. (61) (62) Even where

such conditions could not be met, solutions can be devised by reference to overlapping jurisdictions so that the larger jurisdictions are able to control for externalities while allowing substantial autonomy for the same people organized as small collectivities to make provision for their own public welfare.

In the traditional theory of public administration, the existence of overlapping jurisdictions has often been taken as *prima facie* evidence of duplication of effort, inefficiency, and waste. If we contemplate the possibility that different scales of organization may be appropriate to different levels of operation in providing a particular type of public service, substantial advantage may derive from the provision of services by overlapping jurisdictions. (41) (60) (127) For example, local police may not be very proficient in dealing with organized crime operating on a state, interstate, national, or international basis. Large-scale national police agencies may be a necessary but not sufficient condition for dealing with such problems. Control over the movement of traffic in and out of urban centers may pose problems of an intermediate scale in policing operations. Crimes in the street, however, may reflect the absence of police services responsive to local neighborhood interests.

Once we contemplate the possibility that public administration can be organized in relation to diverse collectivities organized as concurrent political regimes, we might further contemplate the possibility that there will not be one rule of good administration for all governments alike. Instead of a single integrated hierarchy of authority coordinating all public services, we might anticipate the existence of multiorganizational arrangements in the public sector that tends to take on the characteristics of public-service industries composed of many public agencies operating with substantial independence of one another. (84) Should we not begin to look at the police industry, (82) (103) the education industry, (7) (65) (74) the water industry, (6) (99) (123) and other public service industries on the assumption that these industries have a structure that allows for coordination without primary reliance upon hierarchical structures? (120) Once we begin to look for order among multiorganizational arrangements in the public sector, important new vistas will become relevant to the study of public administration. (10) So-called grants-in-aid may take on the attributes of a transfer of funds related to the purchase of a mix of public services to take appropriate account of externalities which spill over from one jurisdiction to another. (18) (121)

A combination of user taxes, service charges, intergovernmental transfers of funds, and voucher systems may evoke some of the characteristics of market arrangements among public service agencies. (19) (21) (36) (85) (86) Instead of a bureaucratic hierarchy serving as the primary means for sustaining legal rationality in a political order as Max Weber has suggested, we should not be surprised to find that legal rationality can be sustained by recourse to judicial determination of issues arising from conflicts over jurisdiction among administrative agencies. Given the high potential cost of political stalemate for the continuity and survival of any administrative enterprise, we should not be surprised to find rational, self-interested public administrators consciously bargaining among themselves and mobilizing political support from their clientele in order to avoid political stalemate and sustain the political feasibility of their agencies. (70) Perhaps a system of public administration composed of a variety of multiorganizational arrangements and highly dependent upon mobilizing clientele support will come reasonably close to sustaining a high level of performance in advancing the public welfare.

REFERENCES*

*Abbreviations for journal references most frequently cited:

AER	American Economic Review
AJS	American Journal of Sociology
APSR	American Political Science Review
CJE&PS	Canadian Journal of Economics and Political Science
JLE	Journal of Law and Economics
JPE	Journal of Political Economy
MJ of PS	Midwest Journal of Political Science
Papers	Papers on Non-Market Decision Making
PAR	Public Administration Review
PC	Public Choice
PF	Public Finance
QJE	Quarterly Journal of Economics

1. Kenneth F. Arrow, "Alternative Approaches to the Theory of Choice in Risk-Taking Situations," *Econometrica,* 19 (October 1951), pp. 404–437.
2. ———, *Social Choice and Individual Values,* second edition (New York: John Wiley & Sons, 1963).
3. W. Ross Ashby, "Principles of the Self-Organizing System," in *Principles of Self-Organization,* H. Von Foerster and G. W. Zopf (eds.). (New York: The Macmillan Co., 1962), pp. 255–278.
4. ———, *Design for a Brain,* second edition (New York: John Wiley & Sons, 1960).
5. Robert U. Ayres and Allen V. Kneese, "Production, Consumption and Externalities," *AER,* 59 (June 1969), pp. 282–297.
6. Joe S. Bain, Richard E. Caves, and

Julius Margolis, *Northern California's Water Industry: The Comparative Efficiency of Public Enterprise in Developing a Scarce Natural Resource* (Baltimore: The Johns Hopkins Press, 1966).

7. Robin Barlow, "Efficiency Aspects of Local School Finance," *JPE,* 78 (October 1970), pp. 1028–1040.

8. Francis Bator, "The Anatomy of Market Failure," *QJE,* LXXII (August 1958), pp. 351–379.

9. Robert L. Bish, "A Comment on V. P. Duggal's 'Is There an Unseen Hand in Government?'" *Annals of Public and Cooperative Economy,* XXXIX (January/March 1968), pp. 89–94.

10. ———, *The Public Economy of Metropolitan Areas* (Chicago: Markham Publishing Company, 1971).

11. Duncan Black, *The Theory of Committees and Elections* (Cambridge, England: Cambridge University Press, 1958).

12. ——— and R. A. Newing, *Committee Decisions with Complementary Valuation* (London: William Hodge, 1951).

13. Kenneth E. Boulding, "The Ethics of Rational Decision," *Management Science,* 12 (February 1966), pp. 161–169.

14. ———, "Towards a Pure Theory of Threat Systems" *AER,* 53 (May 1963), pp. 424–434.

15. Howard R. Bowen, "The Interpretation of Voting in the Allocation of Economic Resources," *QJE,* LVIII (November 1943), pp. 27–48.

16. D. V. Bradford, "Constraints on Public Action and Rules for Social Decision," *AER,* 60 (September 1970), pp. 642–654.

17. Albert Breton, "A Theory of the Demand for Public Goods," *CJE&PS,* XXXII (November 1966), pp. 455–467.

18. ———, "A Theory of Government Grants," *CJE&PS,* XXXI (May 1965), pp. 175–187.

19. ———, *Discriminatory Government Policies in Federal Countries* (Montreal: The Canadian Trade Committee, Private Planning Association of Canada, 1967).

20. May Brodbeck, "Methodological Individualism: Definition and Reduction," *Philosophy of Science,* 25 (January 1958), pp. 1–22.

21. James M. Buchanan, "A Public Choice Approach to Public Utility Pricing," *PC,* 5 (Fall 1968), pp. 1–17.

22. ———, *Cost and Choice: An Inquiry in Economic Theory* (Chicago: Markham Publishing Company, 1969).

23. ——— and W. Craig Stubblebine, "Externality," *Economica,* XXIX (November 1962), pp. 371–384.

24. ———, "Public Goods and Public Bads," in *Financing the Metropolis,* John P. Crecine (ed.) (Beverly Hills: Sage Publications, 1970).

25. ——— and Gordon Tullock, *The Calculus of Consent: Logical Foundations of Constitutional Democracy* (Ann Arbor, Mich.: University of Michigan Press, 1965).

26. ———, *The Demand and Supply of Public Goods* (Chicago: Rand McNally, 1968).

27. Philip M. Burgess and James A. Robinson, "Alliances and the Theory of Collective Action: A Simulation of Coalition Processes," *MJ of PS,* XII (May 1969), pp. 194–219.

28. Colin D. Campbell and Gordon Tullock, "A Measure of the Importance of Cyclical Majorities," *Economic Journal,* 75 (1965), pp. 853–857.

29. ——— and Gordon Tullock, "The Paradox of Voting: A Possible Method of Calculation," *APSR,* LX (September 1966), pp. 684–685.

30. R. H. Coase, "The Nature of the Firm," *Economica*, 4 (1937), pp. 386–485.

31. ———, "The Problem of Social Cost," *JLE*, III (October 1960), pp. 1–44.

32. James S. Coleman, "Foundations for a Theory of Collective Decisions," *AJS*, 71 (May 1966), pp. 615–627.

33. ———, "Individual Interests and Collective Action," *Papers*, 1 (1966), pp. 49–63.

34. R. L. Cunningham, "Ethics and Game Theory: The Prisoners Dilemma," *Papers*, 2 (1967), pp. 11–26.

35. Richard M. Cyert, and James G. March, *A Behavioral Theory of the Firm* (Englewood Cliffs, N.J.: Prentice Hall, 1963).

36. J. H. Dales, *Pollution, Property and Prices: An Essay in Policy–Making and Economics* (Toronto: University of Toronto Press, 1968).

37. Otto A. Davis, and Melvin Hinich, "A Mathematical Model of Policy Formation in a Democratic Society," *Mathematical Applications in Political Science*, II (1966), pp. 175–208.

38. ——— and Andrew Winston, "Externalities, Welfare and the Theory of Games," *JPE*, 60 (June 1962), pp. 241–262.

39. ——— and ———, "On the Distinction Between Public and Private Goods," *AER*, 57 (May 1967), pp. 360–373.

40. ——— and Melvin Hinich, "Some Results Related to a Mathematical Model of Policy Formation in a Democratic Society," *Mathematical Applications and Political Science*, III (1967), pp. 14–38.

41. D. A. Dawson, *Economies of Scale in the Public Secondary School Education Sector in Ontario* (Hamilton, Ontario: McMaster University, Department of Economics, Working Paper No. 70-04, 1970).

42. Harold Demsetz, "Private Property, Information and Efficiency," *AER*, LVII (May 1967), pp. 347–360.

43. ———, "The Private Production of Public Goods" *JLE*, XII (October 1970), pp. 293–306.

44. Anthony Downs, *An Economic Theory of Democracy* (New York: Harper & Row, 1957).

45. ———, "In Defense of Majority Voting," *JPE*, LXIX (April 1961), pp. 192–199.

46. ———, "Why the Government Budget is Too Small in a Democracy," *World Politics*, XII (July 1960), pp. 541–564.

47. V. P. Duggal, "Is There an Unseen Hand in Government?" *Annals of Public and Comparative Economy*, 37 (April-June 1966), pp. 145–150.

48. Heinz Eulau, "Logic of Rationality in Unanimous Decision Making," in *Nomos VII: Rational Decision*, Carl J. Friedrich (ed.) (New York: Atherton Press, 1964), pp. 26–54.

49. Robin Farquharson, *Theory of Voting* (New Haven: Yale University Press, 1969).

50. Peter C. Fishburn, *Decision and Value Theory* (New York: John Wiley & Sons, Inc., 1964).

51. Gerald Garvey, "The Political Economy of Patronal Groups," *PC*, VII (Fall 1969), pp. 33–45.

52. ———, "The Theory of Party Equilibrium," *APSR*, LX (March 1966), pp. 29–38.

53. Luther Gulick and L. Urwick (eds.), *Papers on the Science of Administration* (New York: Columbia University, Institute of Public Administration, 1937).

54. Edwin T. Haefele, "Coalitions, Minority Representation, and Vote-Trading Probabilities," *PC*, VII (Spring 1970), pp. 75–90).

55. ———, "Environmental Quality as a Problem of Social Choice," in *Environmental Quality Analysis: Studies in the Social Sciences*, RFF (forthcoming).

56. Garrett Hardin, "The Tragedy of the Commons," *Science*, 162 (December 13, 1968), pp. 1243–1248.

57. Albert G. Hart, *Anticipations, Uncertainty and Dynamic Planning* (New York: Augustus M. Kelley, 1965).

58. J. G. Head, "Public Goods and Public Policy," *Public Finance*, 17 (1962), pp. 197–219.

59. Melvin J. Hinich and Peter Ordeshook, "Plurality Maximization vs. Vote Maximization: A Spatial Analysis with Variable Participation," *APSR*, 64 (September 1970), pp. 772–791.

60. Werner Z. Hirsch, "Local Versus Areawide Urban Government Services," *National Tax Journal*, 17 (December 1964), pp. 331–339.

61. ———, "The Supply of Urban Public Services," in *Issues in Urban Economics*, Harvey S. Perloff and Lowden Wingo (eds.) (Baltimore: Johns Hopkins Press, 1968), pp. 477–526.

62. ———, "Urban Government Services and Their Financing," in *Urban Life and Form*, Werner Z. Hirsch (ed.) (New York: Holt, Rinehart and Winston, 1963), pp. 129–166.

63. Jack Hirshleifer, James C. DeHaven, and Jerome W. Milliman, *Water Supply Economics, Technology, and Policy* (Chicago: The University of Chicago Press, 1960).

64. A. O. Hirschman, "The Principles of the Hiding Hand," *The Public Interest*, 6 (Winter 1967).

65. A. G. Holtmann, "A Note on Public Education and Spillovers through Migration," *JPE* 74 (October 1966), pp. 524–525.

66. Harold Hotelling, "Stability in Competition," *Economic Journal*, 39 (1929), pp. 41–57.

67. Madelyn L. Kafoglis, "Participatory Democracy in the Community Action Program," *PC*, V (Fall 1968), pp. 73–85.

68. Frank H. Knight, *Risk, Uncertainty and Profit* (New York: Harper and Row, reissued 1965).

69. Bruno Leoni, "The Meaning of 'Political' in Political Decisions," *Political Studies*, V (October 1957), pp. 225–239.

70. Charles E. Lindblom, *Bargaining: The Hidden Hand in Government* (Santa Monica: The RAND Corporation, 1955).

71. ———, *The Intelligence of Democracy: Decision Making through Mutual Adjustment* (New York: The Free Press, 1965).

72. R. Duncan Luce and Howard Raiffa, *Games and Decisions: Introduction and Critical Survey* (New York: John Wiley & Sons, 1957).

73. Roland L. McKean, "The Unseen Hand in Government," *AER*, 55 (June 1965), pp. 496–506.

74. Fritz Machlup, *The Production and Distribution of Knowledge in the U.S.* (Princeton, N.J.: Princeton University Press, 1962).

75. Ezra J. Mishan, *The Costs of Economic Growth* (New York: Frederick A. Praeger, 1967).

76. H. Mohring, "The Peak Load Problem with Increasing Returns and Pricing Constraints," *AER*, 60 (September 1970), pp. 693–705.

77. Richard Musgrave, "The Voluntary Exchange Theory of Public Economy," *QJE*, LIII (February 1939), pp. 213–237.

78. ———, *The Theory of Public Finance* (New York: McGraw-Hill, 1959).

79. James C. Nelson, "The Pricing of Highway, Waterway, and Airway

Facilities," *AER,* 52 (May 1962), pp. 426–435.

80. William A. Nishanen, *Bureaucracy and Representative Government,* review draft (Arlington, Va.: Institute for Defense Analysis, 1970).

81. Mancur Olson, *The Logic of Collective Action* (Cambridge, Mass.: Harvard University Press, 1965).

82. Elinor Ostrom, "Institutional Arrangements and the Measurement of Policy Consequences in Urban Affairs," *Urban Affairs Quarterly* (June 1971).

83. ———, "Some Postulated Effects of Learning on Constitutional Behavior," *PC,* V (Fall 1968), pp. 87–104.

84. Vincent Ostrom, and Elinor Ostrom, "A Behavioral Approach to the Study of Intergovernmental Relations," *Annals of the American Academy of Political and Social Science,* 359 (May 1965), pp. 137–146.

85. Vincent Ostrom, "Operational Federalism: Organization for the Provision of Public Services in the American Federal System," *PC,* VI (Spring 1969), pp. 1–17.

86. ———, Charles M. Tiebout, and Robert Warren, "The Organization of Government in Metropolitan Areas: A Theoretical Inquiry," *APSR,* 55 (December 1961), pp. 831–842.

87. ———, "Water Resource Development: Some Problems in Economic and Political Analysis of Public Policy," in *Political Science and Public Policy,* Austin Ranney (ed.) (Chicago: Markham Publishing Company, 1968).

88. Mark V. Pauly, "Optimality, 'Public' Goods and Local Governments: A General Theoretical Analysis," *JPE,* 78 (May/June 1970), pp. 572–585.

89. Edmund Phelps, *Private Wants and Public Needs* (New York: W. W. Norton, 1965).

90. Charles R. Plott, "A Notion of Equi-

librium and its Possibility Under Majority Rule," *AER,* 57 (September 1967), pp. 787–806.

91. Roy Radner, "Problems in the Theory of Markets under Uncertainty," *AER,* LX (May 1970), pp. 454–460.

92. Clarence E. Ridley, and Herbert A. Simon, *Measuring Municipal Activities* (Chicago: The International City Manager's Association, 1938).

93. William H. Riker, "Arrow's Thereom and Some Examples of the Paradox of Voting," *Mathematical Applications in Political Science,* I (1965).

94. ———, "The Paradox of Voting and Congressional Rules for Voting on Amendments," *APSR,* 52 (1958), pp. 349–366.

95. ———, *The Theory of Political Coalitions* (New Haven: Yale University Press, 1962).

96. Jerome Rothenberg, "The Economics of Congestion and Pollutions: An Integrated View," *AER,* LX (May 1970), pp. 114–121.

97. Paul A. Samuelson, "Diagrammatic Exposition of a Theory of Public Expenditure," *Review of Economics and Statistics,* XXXVII (November 1955), pp. 350–356.

98. ———, "The Pure Theory of Public Expenditure," *Review of Economics and Statistics,* XXXVI (November 1954), pp. 387–389.

99. A. Allan Schmid, "Nonmarket Values and Efficiency of Public Investments in Water Resources," *AER,* LVII (May 1967), pp. 158–168.

100. Joseph J. Seneca, "The Welfare Effects of Zero Pricing of Public Goods," *PC,* VII (Spring 1970), pp. 101–110.

101. Thomas C. Schelling, *The Strategy of Conflict* (Cambridge, Mass.: Harvard University Press, 1963).

102. G. L. S. Shackle, *Decision, Order and Time in Human Affairs* (Cambridge, England: Cambridge University Press, 1961).

103. Carl S. Shoup, "Standard for Distributing of Free Government Service: Crime Prevention," *PF,* 19 (1964), pp. 383–392.

104. Herbert A. Simon, *Administrative Behavior: A Study of Decision–Making Processes in Administrative Organizations* (New York: Macmillan, 1964).

105. ———, *Models of Men, Social and Rational* (New York: Wiley and Sons, 1957).

106. ———, "The Architecture of Complexity," *Proceedings of the American Philosophical Society,* 106 (December 1962), pp. 467–482.

107. ———, *The Sciences of the Artificial* (Cambridge, Mass.: The M.I.T. Press, 1969).

108. ———, "Theories of Decision-Making in Economics and Behavioral Science," *AER,* XLIX (June 1959), pp. 253–283.

109. George J. Stigler, "The Economics of Information," *JPE,* LXIX (June 1961), pp. 213–225.

110. E. A. Thompson, "A Pareto-Optimal Group Decision Process," *Papers,* I (1966), pp. 133–140.

111. Wilbur Thompson, "The City as a Distorted Price System," *Psychology Today* (August 1968), pp. 28–33.

112. Charles M. Tiebout, "A Pure Theory of Local Expenditures," *JPE,* 64 (October 1956), pp. 416–424.

113. Gordon Tullock, "A Simple Algebraic Logrolling Model," *AER,* LX (June 1970), pp. 419–426.

114. ———, *Politics of Bureaucracy* (Washington, D.C.: The Public Affairs Press, 1965).

115. ———, "The General Irrelevance of the General Impossibility Theorem," *QJE,* 81 (May 1967), pp. 256–270.

116. U.S. Congress, Joint Economic Committee, Subcommittee on Economy in Government, *A Compendium of Papers on the Analysis and Evaluation of Public Expenditures: The PPB System,* three volumes (Washington, D.C.: U.S. Government Printing Office, 1969).

117. L. L. Wade, and R. L. Curry, Jr., *A Logic of Public Policy: Aspects of Political Economy* (Belmont, Calif.: Wadsworth Publishing Company, 1970).

118. Dwight Waldo, "Scope of the Theory of Public Administration" in *Theory and Practice of Public Administration: Scope, Objectives, and Methods,* James C. Charlesworth (ed.) (Philadelphia: The American Academy of Political and Social Science, 1968).

119. Robert Warren, "Federal-Local Development Planning: Scale Effects in Representation and Policy Making," *PAR,* XXX (November/December 1970), pp. 584–595.

120. ———, *Government in Metropolitan Regions: A Reappraisal of Fractionated Political Organization,* (Davis, Calif.: University of California, Davis, Institute of Governmental Affairs, 1966).

121. J. C. Weldon, "Public Goods and Federalism," *CJE&PS,* 32 (1966), pp. 230–238.

122. Louis F. Weschler, Paul D. Marr, and Bruce M. Hackett, *California Service Center Program* (Davis, Calif.: University of California, Davis, Institute of Governmental Affairs, 1968).

123. ———, *Water Resources Management: The Orange County Experience* (Davis, Calif.: University of California, Davis, Institute of Governmental Affairs, 1968).

124. H. J. Wheeler, "Alternative Voting Rules and Local Expenditures: The Town Meeting vs. City," *Papers,* 2 (1967), pp. 61–70.

125. Leonard D. White, *Introduction to the Study of Public Administration* (New York: The Macmillan Company, 1926).

126. Aaron Wildavsky, "The Political

Economy of Efficiency," *PAR,* XXVI (December 1966), pp. 292–310.

127. Alan Williams, "The Optimal Provision of Public Goods in a System of Local Government," *JPE,* 74 (February 1966), pp. 18–33.

128. Oliver E. Williamson, "Hierarchical Control and Optimum Firm Size," *JPE,* 75 (April 1967), pp. 123–138.

129. ———, "Peak Load Pricing and Optimal Capacity Under Indivisibility Constraints," *AER,* LVI (September 1966), pp. 810–827.

130. Woodrow Wilson, "The Study of Administration," *Political Science Quarterly,* II (June 1887), pp. 197–222.

4.   The Perils—and Prospects—of Public Administration

Donald F. Kettl

Every discipline periodically goes through a period of sometimes wrenching reassessment. For public administration, this reassessment has been nearly constant. Americans have always been distrustful of governmental power and, especially, administrative power. They have long believed that public administration is more inefficient and corrupt than private administration. Woodrow Wilson's memorable call to study the importance of running a constitution shows how, even in its earliest days, the modern study of American public administration has struggled for acceptance.

Public administration marked its high point of public and political acceptance with the New Deal. The Brownlow Committee's recommendations in 1938 that "the president needs help" from assistants with a "passion for anonymity" shaped the modern presidency and ushered public administration scholars onto center stage in national politics.[1] Then, during World War II, an entire genera-

tion of the field's key figures staged their own invasion of Washington and, from one end of town to the other, they managed key positions in the war effort. At the same time, institutes of government and bureaus of municipal research provided important service to state and local governments. Government searched for a strong and positive role, pursued with economy and efficiency. Public administration stood eager to help, and its assistance was eagerly received.[2]

Almost immediately after World War Two, however, public administration's prominence slipped precipitously. The growth of the modern social sciences, especially a more behaviorally oriented political science and a more statistically oriented economics, weakened public administration's hold on the study and practice of government. Leading scholars argued that public administration's prewar proverbs had borne little fruit and that public administration was unlikely to become a science.[3] Political science and much—but certainly not all—of the public administration community began a prolonged but never completely consummated divorce. Meanwhile, the emerging policy sciences challenged public administration's

SOURCE: "The Perils—and Prospects—of Public Administration" by Donald F. Kettl, *Public Administration Review:* 50 (July/August 1990). Reprinted by permission of the American Society for Public Administration.

claim to prescriptions for effective management.

Social and political changes coupled with old problems to undermine the discipline further. The perception of governmental failure that plagued the late 1960s and early 1970s undermined the nation's belief that government could play a positive role. These perceptions, coupled with bureaucrat bashing by top politicians during the 1970s and 1980s, caused the public image of public administration to sink to a new low.[4] More subtle intellectual currents also weakened public administration's intellectual claims. New professions, from engineering and accounting to medicine and law, developed a cult of specialization, while the social sciences pressed toward "scientific" explanations of phenomena. Public administration's traditional focus on generalism stirred little enthusiasm and much outright hostility.[5] Public administration was certainly no longer queen of the social sciences. Indeed, it had trouble winning a place at court.

Throughout the 1960s and 1970s, public administration found itself under attack by other approaches to understanding governmental performance. These perils—especially challenges from the implementation, public-management, and rationalist perspectives— wounded the field's self-confidence and its self-awareness. Each of the attacks contributed important insights into administrative practice. After two decades of criticisms, though, public administration as a field retains important insights and good prospects. To realize those prospects, however, public administration must take two steps. First, it must rediscover the central questions of the discipline. Second, it must develop new answers to those questions that fit the changing realities of public programs. Let me first explore the perils that public administration has suffered and then examine the prospects the field offers.

THE PERILS OF PUBLIC ADMINISTRATION

In the decades after World War Two, public administration faced three especially important intellectual challenges: the implementation challenge, from those trying to explain why agencies so often seemed to perform so badly; the public-management challenge, from those seeking to develop practical guides for top-level government officials; and the rationalist challenge, from those venturing a positivist/minimalist theory of bureaucratic behavior.

The Implementation Challenge

Many political scientists in the 1960s were struck by the failure of the Great Society to win the war (or even major skirmishes) on poverty. They developed a new field—implementation—to provide the "missing link" in public policy analysis between decision making and program evaluation.[6] Most of the implementation literature, however, quickly moved to the analysis of failure. In one early book, Pressman and Wildavsky describe their investigation into one Oakland, California, federal grant program with a famous subtitle: "How Great Expectations in Washington Are Dashed in Oakland; Or, Why It's Amazing That Federal Programs Work At All."[7] Students of implementation concentrated on why so often government programs failed to achieve the goals that Congress set for them.[8]

They rejected, at least implicitly, the nearly 100-year tradition of public administration as useless. "There is (or there must be) a large literature about implementation in the social sciences," Pressman and Wildavsky wrote in 1974. "It must be there; it should be there; but in fact it is not."[9] Pressman and Wildavsky began from the proposition that public administration had little to offer anyone studying program performance.

That statement struck many public administration scholars by surprise because, even though they did not work under that label, most of them believed that the entire field was devoted to precisely that question. Implementation was different, however. Unlike public administration, which focuses on the behavior of agencies and of their employees, implementation focuses on the outcomes of public programs. Goals and resources are put into the system, peopled principally by bureaucrats, and results—often at variance with intentions—result. Thus, instead of being the central focus of the school, the agency and its employees are instruments.

For students of implementation, failure was centrally defined as the inability of a program to achieve its legislative goals. (Later research examined problems in decision making and the design of public policy as well,[10] but the failure to achieve goals was the central and initial focus of implementation.) The causes of failure were legion, rooted especially in fundamental pathologies of public bureaucracy.[11] The problem most often was one of control: the inability of policy makers at the top to regulate the behavior of others in the policy process. They saw the environment of public policy implementation as very complex, however, and the many participants played endless games that distorted and delayed implementation.[12] The odds thus were stacked heavily against successful implementation. Nearly everything along the line from top policy makers to lower-level managers had to work perfectly if a program was not to become bogged down. In a process requiring 70 separate agreements, even if the chances of a successful agreement at each step were 99 percent, the odds of program success were less than 50-50.[13]

In the implementation school, public agencies are instruments toward the goals set by policy makers like members of Congress and the president. Members of these agencies have many personal goals and political cross pressures that frequently distort their behavior away from legislative goals and consequently produce failures. Problems persist because bureaucrats delay, obstruct, create red tape, vacillate, and hesitate. Agencies ideally should be self-evaluating and skilled at adapting new behavior to prevent old mistakes. The need of organizations for political support, however, makes them more cautious and conservative.[14] They get caught up in their own routines and ruling orthodoxies and become blinded to new signs and signals. Bureaucracy demonstrates "a preference for procedure over purpose."[15]

Of all the impediments to success, students of implementation rate bureaucracy the worst. "No one is clearly in charge of implementation," Ripley and Franklin conclude. Therefore, "Domestic programs virtually never achieve all that is expected of them."[16] The result is a depressing forecast of the prospects for learning and achievement. The implementation school thus provides a well-accepted explanation for learning failures and the frequent problems of performance that plague government agencies.

Two important weaknesses characterize the implementation approach, however. First, implementation looks especially bleak because of the negative cases its students have chosen to study. The implementation literature is based in failure; its scholars have rarely studied program successes, which are legion. Failures, of course, are often more intriguing, but they are not always more important. Stories such as "Mail Delivered Yet Again Today," "Social Security Checks Arrive on Time," or "Air-Traffic Control System Safely Guides Thousands of Planes" never make the papers and rarely attract scholars' attention. Because success stories have only rarely been studied, implementation scholars have not systematically compared successes and failures. Nor have they carefully differentiated the forces that produce failures instead of successes (or vice versa). It is, therefore, almost impossible to understand fully why failures occur, how frequently they happen, or what could have been done to prevent them.

Second, "success" and "failure" are far more elusive terms than the implementation literature suggests. The ultimate benchmark for most studies is the law as enacted by Congress and Congress's intent. The fuzziness of congressional goals, however, is legendary. Defining and redefining those goals as programs evolve is inevitable. So, too, is adapting broad national goals to the vast variety of local conditions. In many intergovernmental programs, in fact, adapting national goals to local needs was the central focus. The programs delegated substantial policy-making authority to state and local officials. Observations of "success" and "failure" therefore often varied greatly depending on who was conducting the observations. One would scarcely expect that every observer would draw the same conclusions about a program's results, especially when the very process of developing its goals was a complex affair. A "success" to a local official might seem a "failure" to a federal official. Moreover, judgments can change radically over time as well. Programs delayed sometimes become eventual successes, and some early successes turn sour. Even a program brought to a standstill, such as construction of a new highway, may well be a "success" for an interest which did not want it finished.

Judgments of success and failure thus are most elusive. The implementation literature has produced a lively set of case studies and some intriguing explanations of governmental behavior. It has not, however, developed a systematic explanation of why some programs succeed while others fail, how implementation might vary among different program strategies (such as regulation on contracting or transfer programs), or even an acceptable definition of what constitutes "success" and "failure."

The Public Management Challenge

On the heels of the implementation movement came a new public-management school. Public administration focuses on agencies and their employees, and implementation concentrates on programs and their outcomes. The more-recent public management movement, by contrast, is based on the role of top administrative leaders, typically political appointees such as cabinet secretaries and agency administrators, and the strategies they set. In fact, the movement has its foundation on writing *about* such top officials *by* former officials.[17] (Public management, to some degree, has become a popular catchword for many different approaches to administration. Among many others, the public management net snares the bureaucratic politics and more-generic administrative science approaches. The discussion here focuses on the approach, circulated through case studies, that has seized the high ground at many policy schools.)

According to these studies, the strategies of public managers have three objects. First, they must develop strategies for efficiently and effectively overseeing their agency's programs. Second, since there usually are competing strategies that could be adopted, they must build political support, both inside and outside the agency, for their own views of their agencies' directions. Finally, they must maintain their agencies' health—its organizational capacity and credibility—and obtain needed resources—especially funding, personnel, legislation, and favorable constituencies.[18]

Management problems, according to this school, are especially likely to come from an organization's environment, and the public manager must devote considerable time to learning about, coping with, adapting to, and sometimes trying to shape that environment. Such adaptation, however, is limited by the constraints that public managers face: from the political environment, which sometimes can be hostile; from their own organizations, which sometimes resist managerial strategies; and from their own personalities and cognitive styles, which may limit the managers' vision and ability to persuade. The public-management movement thus has developed along three fronts. In looking to the outside world, the movement has examined relations between top executives and other political forces, especially the president, Congress, and interest groups.[19] In looking within the agency, the movement has adopted the pathological approach of implementation to chart the games that bureaucrats play in frustrating the strategies of top officials.[20] Finally, in looking at public managers' own styles, the movement has developed personality studies on the behavior of individual public managers.[21]

The public-management school is largely case-based. It is dominated by the personal reflections of individuals who have served in top administrative positions and by case studies of individual public managers.[22] Indeed, Lynn contends that "there is no intellectual alternative to regarding the experience of each public executive as a unique case." Every manager finds himself or herself in a different situation, and broad generalizations are impossible.[23] The public-management school's approach to the problems of administering public programs is to present broad propositions about the need to adapt (and about the problems that can hinder adaptation); to add rich case studies about public managers who have been perceived as successful and unsuccessful; and to ground it all in Neustadt's dictum that executive power is the power to persuade.[24]

The public-management school has made useful contributions to the study of public policy and administration. Far more than implementation, it celebrates the art of the possible. Far more than traditional public administration, it focuses on the unique role played by top-level administrators and on the special problems they face.[25] However, the problems of public management include much more than the behavior of people at the top of government agencies. Decision making is the very essence of administrative behavior, and it permeates bureaucracy from top to bottom. In fact, it is the central administrative act.[26] By giving short shrift to management at any but the agency's top levels, the public-management school blinds itself to important questions.

Top NASA managers, for example, never had the chance to decide whether the cold made launching the *Challenger* too risky on that fateful January 1986 morning because mid-level NASA administrators did not pass crucial information on to them. Top NASA managers did receive signals months before the explosion that the O-rings performed badly in cold weather, but the signals did not come in a form that demanded attention and strategy setting. The heavy concern in the public-management literature with building political support does not address why such problems come about or what public managers should do about them. The public-management school gives few clues about how to deal with other levels of the bureaucracy, or how those levels behave (except, perhaps, as an impediment to executive action). The public-management school thus gives few clues about how administration works—and why sometimes it does not.

The Rationalist Challenge

Economists, and political scientists following basic economic constructs, have developed a different approach. They have sought to develop a formal theory of bureaucratic behavior from the foundation of only a few assumptions, principally that bureaucrats (like all individuals) seek to maximize their utility, or satisfaction. The approach then asks how utility-maximizing individuals, when placed within an agency, are likely to respond.[27] It builds a framework on the assumption of rationally self-interested behavior that leads to a deductive theory of bureaucratic behavior.[28]

In one of the leading elements of the rationalist school, an agency can be considered a market in which employers seek to purchase the skills of employees. The employer can be considered the principal actor, who hires the employee as an agent to perform the organization's tasks. (More broadly, an organization, such as a government agency, can hire other organizations, such as contractors, for similar purposes. The agency then becomes the principal, the contractor the agent.) This structure allows the application of economic theories to bureaucratic behavior.

This principal-agent theory, as it is known, argues that principals must solve two basic tasks in choosing their agents. Principals must select the best agents, whether employees or contractors (or, for that matter, other third parties who serve as agents), and create inducements for them to behave as desired. Principals must also monitor the behaviors of their agents to ensure that they are performing their tasks well. Economists' elaboration of principal-agent theory is extremely mathematical, with individual behaviors modeled in complex algorithms. The theory can, however, be reduced to two basic problems.

First, the principal can never know everything about an agent. A supervisor can examine a potential employee's education, skills, personality, and background, but he or she can never be sure of selecting the best person for the job. Potential employees will know more about their own qualifications than potential employers can ever learn. Thus, the theory contends, employers tend to hire lower-quality applicants than desired. Principal-agent theorists have christened this the "adverse-selection" problem. Second, the principal can never be sure of knowing the full details of the agent's performance. There are always signals about an employee's performance, such as reports, complaints, direct observation, and work habits, but the employer can never know the full story. Principals are thus typically at an information disadvantage with respect to their agents, and agents therefore have an incentive to work to less than their capacity, since they know that performance inadequacies may not be detected. Principal-agent theorists call this the "moral hazard" problem.[29] Put together, the problems explain why control by managers of organizations is difficult.[30]

Principal-agent theory offers insight into problems, such as why the Department of Energy has had such difficulty in managing the contractors that manufacture the nation's nuclear weapons. It is difficult to choose good contractors (adverse selection). It is also hard to know what the contractor is doing, and whether its performance matches the department's goals (moral hazard). Furthermore, principal-agent theory identifies the flow of information as the critical problem. Principals can improve their selection of agents if they can learn more about them before hiring them. Principals can reduce moral hazard by altering their agents' incentives and by improving the monitoring of their agents' behaviors.

As with implementation and public-management theories, however, principal-agent theory does not explain several important administrative issues. While the market approach produces interesting insights, market metaphors in the public sector often produce distortions because the "markets" themselves have imperfections. On the supply side, government often has relatively few choices in purchasing services. From mass-transit buses and subway cars to submarines and airliners, government rarely can call on more than a few suppliers. These suppliers enjoy a near-monopoly in the market, and as purchaser the government must solve all of the problems that exist in monopoly markets. Even in such mundane services as garbage collection, the number of potential contractors is often deceptively small.

The market is further distorted on the demand side because, for some items, government is often the only purchaser. The Department of Energy's contractors are not allowed to sell plutonium triggers for nuclear weapons to anyone but the government. The Newport News shipyard does not build aircraft carriers for anyone but the U.S. Navy, and many urban planning firms have few clients other than local governments and their redevelopment agencies. Economists call a high concentration of buyers a "monopsony," and in such conditions the flexibility of the government as buyer is often limited. Does the Navy dare, for both strategic and economic reasons, to allow one of the two manufacturers of nuclear submarines to go out of business?

Principal-agent theory, moreover, does not recognize well the role that power plays in organizational (or, more broadly, in political) life.[31] Because it is based on market behavior, it assumes relationships among equals, with principals and agents each seeking to develop an acceptable exchange. It thus neglects what Parsons calls "the central phenomenon of organizations."[32] It also neglects the considerable complexity in the environment of agencies and the many cross-cutting political pressures on administrators. The mathematical models could theoretically capture these additional complexities, but it is unrealistic to think that the full range of power relationships facing public administrators could be modeled in equations.

Furthermore, organizational goals are far more dynamic and evolutionary than the relatively static principal-agent models tend to capture.[33] Members of Congress frequently change their minds about which goals administrators should emphasize, and administrators themselves must set priorities among the many competing demands on their time and expertise. Goals, moreover, often evolve in collaboration between principals and agents. Defense contracts, for example, frequently are modified as Pentagon officials and contractors learn more about what works and what does not in a new weapons system. In intergovernmental grant programs, moreover, it is often difficult to recognize who is the principal and who is the agent. Different levels of government take different responsibilities for different pieces of the same program. The relationship here is less one of exchange than of constitutional collaboration. While dynamic goals theoretically are possible to model, they move far beyond the static models of principal-agent theory and enter into a realm of enormous complexity.

Market models offer important insights into the problems that government must solve. They focus attention on information flows in the relationship between principal and agent. Looking at public services in terms of the nature of the principal-agent relationship can also produce valuable insights about constraints on government's control of its agents. Market-based models, however, tend to be far better at asking questions than in answering them.

THE PROSPECTS OF PUBLIC ADMINISTRATION

Since World War Two, the field of public administration has taken its lumps from many different directions. None of the competing theories, however, has succeeded in supplanting the more-traditional study of public administration. While each one has its important attractions, each one leaves critical questions unanswered. And these unanswered questions lead back to public administration's doorstep.

The prospects of public administration lie in rediscovering the fundamental issues on which the discipline is based. This in turn requires two steps. First, it requires recognizing and redefining the importance of agencies as actors within the political process.[34] Second, it requires understanding how the behaviors of agencies as actors vary and how to map that variance.

Agencies as Actors

Agencies need to be understood as more than instruments that produce (or distort) policy outcomes, as stressed in the implementation school; as shaped by more than the decisions of political appointees, as discussed by the public-management school; and as more than the accumulation of individual transactions between employers and employees, as analyzed by the principal-agent school. Agencies, as agencies, need to be considered as important participants in their own right. One of the most important arguments of the early public-administration school was, quite simply, that organization matters, and that different organizational structures are likely to produce different outcomes.[35]

Between these early works and the perils of public administration came the important observation of open-systems theorists: the agencies must adapt to changes in their environment to be effective.[36] The political forces and technical problems with which bureaucracies must deal constantly change. Agencies shape and are shaped by the environment.

This leads to two important implications. First, agencies frequently are creatures of their past. Rules, standard operating procedures, and norms all are products of accumulated experience. They, in fact, often acquire lives independent of the forces that produced them. Members of bureaucracies may have long ago forgotten why rules were adopted or why they follow the norms that they do. Regulations, procedures, and standards, often are products of the bureaucracy's adaptation to previous situations, and they take on lives independent of the forces that created them.[37] Agencies often therefore tend to be backward looking.

Second, the major challenge facing agencies as actors is to adapt to future problems from their backward-looking views. Behavior conditioned by the past provides a useful administrative shortcut, since every new problem does not require a new solution. Such behavior does not always produce the best answers to new problems, however. Organizations must therefore develop approaches to learning from mistakes and adapting to the future.[38]

This "new institutionalist" approach borrows heavily from the other schools. Like implementation, it self-consciously focuses attention on the relationship between the bureaucracy's behavior and its results, past and future. Like public management, it pays heed to both internal problems, such as communication, and external problems, such as political support. Like principal-agent theory, it recognizes the critical importance of information asymmetries. But unlike any of these other approaches, it focuses centrally on the importance of the agencies as independent actors. The burden of the argument is that agencies develop behaviors separate from the behaviors of those who happen to populate them at any one moment. The first step to understanding the prospects of public administration therefore is to develop better knowledge about how such behaviors are shaped, how behaviors shape bureaucratic outcomes, and what bureau leaders can do to improve those outcomes.[39]

Varying Behavior

Not all bureaucratic behavior is the same, of course. One of the principal arguments of public administration's post-World War Two critics was that the generalized principles of administrative theory did not answer questions then asked by theorists. To an important extent, the first century of American public administration was devoted to understanding basic forces and processes at work within agencies of all kinds and at all levels of government. When the search for generalizable common features ran dry, competing schools sprang up. Bureaucratic institutions have self-evidently evolved into large numbers and remarkable variety. American public administration must now be devoted to understanding better how administrative practice varies.

Can the variety be systematically mapped? The answer is "yes," but the answer depends on understanding the problems that government agencies must solve in adapting to their environments. Consider two federal bureaus, for example. In the Federal Aviation Administration (FAA), some employees provide a direct service for the flying public. They guide, with great skill and rare failure, thousands of airplanes to their destination every day. Other FAA employees, however, regulate and inspect the airline industry to ensure the safe maintenance and operation of their fleets. These jobs are distinctively different. The FAA's controllers work with willing clients who want nothing more than to be separated safely from nearby traffic. The controllers' radar, meanwhile, enables them to observe precisely what is happening in the skies they are supervising. That role is very different from that of the FAA's safety inspectors who often deal with airlines seeking to minimize expense and down time and who can only indirectly, at best, observe the effects of their activities. The administration of these programs, even though they exist within the same agency, is very different.

In the U.S. Department of Health and Human Services, officials know how much money is being spent on different medical services through the Medicare program because they know to whom they are writing checks and in which categories. Beyond the mailing of checks by HHS and cashing those checks by recipients, there needs to be little coordination. That is not the case with the administrative services that the many contractors working for HHS on the Medicare program provide. The very process of negotiating the contract ensures high agreement on goals; if agreement on aims is not reached, there is no contract. On the other hand, because contractors work at arm's length from HHS, simply determining what the contractors are actually doing is problematic.[40]

Can systematic differences be discerned among these programs and among the many other governmental programs that challenge administrators? Two concepts are useful for that purpose.

First, the agencies' behavior depends importantly on information. Information flow is most "sticky"—most threatened by distortions, losses, filtering, and condensation—at bureaucratic boundaries.[41] For air-traffic control and the distribution of Medicare checks, information flow is relatively clear. Air-traffic controllers look down at the radar screens in front of them, while HHS employees who process Medicare checks work from claim forms showing the services performed. In Medicare contracting and air-safety regulation, however, information about performance is only indirect and typically costly to obtain. That clearly makes a difference in the way agencies behave.[42]

Second, the agencies' behaviors depend also on the congruence between their goals and the goals of those with whom they deal outside the agency. While no airline wants to fly an unsafe plane, there is constant disagreement on just how much maintenance, to which standards, is enough. Disagreement on just how much medical care is enough and about how much the government should pay is common in Medicare benefits as well. In contrast, goal congruence in the air-traffic control system is absolute—everyone wants safe procedures. The contracting process between Medicare and its contractors at least assures basic agreement on goals. These differences also make a difference in how agencies behave.

In short, public administration is likely to be different in different kinds of governmental programs. In particular, public administration is likely to differ when the relative costs of obtaining information about an agency's outputs are relatively high or low. It is also likely to differ when the congruence between an agency's goals and the goals of those outside the agency's boundaries are relatively high or low. As Figure 4.1 shows, four major governmental policy strategies can be sorted among these categories. Programs administered through grants and contracts (such as supplementary Medicare services) are likely to have relatively high information costs but relatively high goal congruence. Regulatory programs (such as the FAA's air-safety regulations) are likely to have relatively high information costs but relatively low goal congruence. Directly administered programs (such as the FAA's air-traffic control) are likely to have relatively low information costs and relatively high goal congruence. Finally, transfer

Information Costs

Figure 4.1
Variance of Programs by Information and Goals

	High	Low
High	INDIRECT Department of Energy: nuclear weapons contracting	DIRECT FAA: air-traffic control
Low	REGULATORY IRS: tax administration	TRANSFER HHS: disability insurance

Goal Congruence

programs (such as Medicare's benefits program) are likely to have relatively low goal congruence and relatively low information costs.

Public administration is likely to vary accordingly. This scheme suggests that directly administered programs, in general, will be the least problematic because goal congruence is relatively high and information costs are relatively low.[43]

Indirectly administered programs, such as grants and contracts, must seek a negotiated agreement on goals and struggle to acquire good feedback on performance. Administrators of transfer programs, such as Medicare and welfare, must worry about getting the checks into the hands of recipients and then about whether the recipients spend the money according to the government's goals. Regulatory administrators face the difficult challenge of trying to enforce changes in behaviors (and thus in goals) while having relatively poor information on whether they are successful.

RESCUING PUBLIC ADMINISTRATION

While its critics would not unanimously agree that public administration needs or deserves rescuing, several decades of alternative approaches to the field's basic problems have not supplanted it. The alternatives have been interesting, in part because of the weaknesses in more-traditional public administration to which they have pointed and in part because of the different questions they have asked. These weaknesses and questions, however, lead public administration back to basic questions: the importance of understanding agencies as actors, in their own right, in the political process; and the relationship between those agencies and the political environments in which they act.

Rescuing public administration, how-

ever, will require more than simply reestablishing the importance of agencies as actors in the political process. Its critics rejected public administration after World War Two because it attempted to offer universal principles when a sophisticated, differentiated vision was needed. That requires recognizing not only what ties public administration together—such as a sense of the agency and its officials as political actors—but also how it varies. Different forms of the administrative process present different kinds of political and managerial problems. Rescuing public administration means recognizing and understanding these differences as well as the similarities. Perhaps the most important differences revolve around the costs of obtaining information and the difficulties in obtaining congruence on goals.

Finally, rescuing public administration means being alert to its changing forms and emerging issues. If understanding the variation in public administration replaces the search for principles, it will be easier to spot the shifting forms of administrative action. The administrative issues surrounding the emergence of contracting for high-technology projects, the spread of transfer and regulatory programs, and the invention of new governmental forms such as government-sponsored enterprises and government corporations (in all their hybrid patterns) will be more apparent to students alert to both similarities and differences. Comprehending such forms of administrative life, and the different problems they bring to the public service, is key to bringing public administration home and restoring its life and vision.

NOTES

I am indebted to incisive comments by Erwin C. Hargrove and by an anonymous *PAR* reviewer which improved this article. The Earhart Foundation generously provided support for a portion of the research on which the article is based, and the foundation has my deep thanks.

1. President's Committee on Administrative Management, *Report of the President's Committee, Administrative Management in the Government of the United States* (Washington: U.S. Government Printing Office, 1937).

2. An excellent self-examination of public administration's role is Frederick C. Mosher, ed., *American Public Administration: Past, Present, Future* (University: University of Alabama Press, 1975).

3. Herbert Simon, "The Proverbs of Administration," *Public Administration Review*, vol. 6 (Winter 1946), pp. 53-67; and Robert A. Dahl, "The Science of Public Administration: Three Problems," *Public Administration Review*, vol. 7 (Winter 1947), pp. 1–11.

4. National Commission on the Public Service (Volcker Commission), *Leadership for America: Rebuilding the Public Service* (Lexington, MA.: Lexington Books, 1989), esp. pp. 53–11.

5. See Frederick C. Mosher, "Introduction: The American Setting," in Mosher, ed., *American Public Administration*, pp. 6–7.

6. Erwin C. Hargrove, *The Missing Link: The Study of the Implementation of Social Policy* (Washington: The Urban Institute, 1975).

7. Jeffrey L. Pressman and Aaron B. Wildavsky, *Implementation* (Berkeley: University of California Press, 1973).

8. See, for example, Martha Derthick, *New Towns In-Town* (Washington: Urban Institute, 1972); Eugene Bardach, *The Implementation Game: What Happens After a Bill Becomes a Law* (Berkeley: University of California Press, 1977); Paul Berman, "The Study of Macro- and Micro-Implementation," *Public Policy*, vol. 26 (Spring 1978), pp. 157-84; Richard F. Elmore, "Organizational Models of Social Program Implementation," *Public Policy*, vol. 26 (Spring 1978), pp. 185-228; Carl E. Van Horn, *Policy Implementation in the Federal System: National Goals and Local Implementors* (Lexington, MA: Heath, 1979); D. A. Mazmanian and P. A. Sabatier, *Implementation and Public Policy* (Glenview, IL: Scott, Foresman, 1983); and Randall B. Ripley and Grace A. Franklin, *Policy Implementation and Bureaucracy*, 2d ed. (Chicago: Dorsey Press, 1986).

9. Pressman and Wildavsky, *Implementation, supra*, p. 166. In fact, a handful of studies on implementation had already been published, including Stephen K. Bailey and Edith K. Mosher, *ESEA: The Office of Education Administers A Law* (Syracuse, NY: Syracuse University Press, 1968); and Jerome T. Murphy, "Title I of ESEA: The Politics of Implementing Federal Educational Reform," *Harvard Educational Review*, vol. 41 (February 1971), pp. 35–63.

10. For a survey of these approaches, see Charles O. Jones, *An Introduction to the Study of Public Policy*, 3d ed. (Monterey, CA: Brooks/Cole, 1984).

11. Brian W. Hogwood and B. Guy Peters, *The Pathology of Public Policy* (Oxford: Oxford University Press, 1985).

12. See Bardach, *The Implementation Game, supra.*

13. A notably more positive view is Malcolm L. Goggin, Ann O'M. Bowman, James P. Lester, and Laurence J. O'Toole, Jr., *Implementation Theory and Practice: Toward A Third Generation* (Glenview, IL: Scott, Foresman, 1990).

14. Aaron Wildavsky, "The Self-Evaluating Organization," *Public Admin-*

istration Review, vol. 32 (Sept-ember/October 1972), pp. 509–520.

15. Pressman and Wildavsky, *supra,* p. 133.

16. Ripley and Franklin, *Policy Implementation and Bureaucracy, supra,* p. 12.

17. Richard R. Elmore, "Graduate Education in Public Management: Working the Seams of Government," *Journal of Policy Analysis and Management,* vol. 6 (Fall 1986), pp. 69–83. Excluded from this discussion are more-traditional approaches to public administration that have been rechristened "public management."

18. Laurence E. Lynn, Jr., *Managing the Public's Business: The Job of the Government Executive* (New York: Basic Books, 1981) and *Managing Public Policy* (Boston: Little, Brown, 1987). See also Elmore, "Graduate Education in Public Management"; and Philip B. Heymann, *The Politics of Public Management* (New Haven: Yale University Press, 1987). An excellent summary of public management literature is Hal G. Rainey, "Public Management: Recent Developments and Current Prospects," in *Public Administration: The State of the Discipline,* Naomi B. Lynn, Aaron Wildavsky (Chattham, NJ: Chatham House Publishers, 1990), pp. 157–184.

    The public-management movement builds self-consciously on the foundation of bureaucratic politics established by Graham T. Allison in "Conceptual Models and the Cuban Missile Crisis," *American Political Science Review,* vol. 63 (September 1969), pp. 689–718; and *Essence of Decision: Explaining the Cuban Missile Crisis* (Boston: Little, Brown, 1971). See also Morton H. Halperin with Priscilla Clapp and Arnold Kanter, *Bureaucratic Politics and Foreign Policy* (Washington: Brookings Institution, 1974).

19. See Heyman, *The Politics of Public Management, supra.;* and Hugh Heclo, *A Government of Strangers: Executive Politics in Washington* (Washington: Brookings Institution, 1977).

20. See Lynn, *Managing Public Policy, supra.*

21. See Jameson W. Doig and Erwin C. Hargrove, eds., *Leadership and Innovation: A Biographical Perspective on Entrepreneurs in Government* (Baltimore: Johns Hopkins University Press, 1987).

22. Case studies prepared at Harvard's Kennedy School of Government are a special example of this approach. See, for example, Robert Reich, *Public Management in a Democratic Society* (Englewood Cliffs, NJ: Prentice-Hall, 1990).

23. Lynn, *Managing Public Policy, supra.,* p. 5.

24. Richard E. Neustadt, *Presidential Power: The Politics of Leadership* (New York: John Wiley and Sons, 1960).

25. This problem, however, has scarcely been ignored in the public-administration literature. See, for example, James W. Fesler, "Politics, Policy, and Bureaucracy at the Top," *Annals of the Academy of Political and Social Science,* vol. 466 (March 1983), pp. 23–41.

26. Herbert A. Simon, *Administrative Behavior: A Study of Decision-Making Processes in Administrative Organization,* 3d ed. (New York: Free Press, 1976).

27. See, for example, William A. Niskanen, Jr., *Bureaucracy and Representative Government* (Chicago: Aldine, Atherton, 1971).

28. For a summary of principal-agent theory, see Kenneth J. Arrow, "The Economics of Agency," in John W. Pratt and Richard J. Zeckhauser, eds., *Principals and Agents: The Structure of Business* (Boston: Harvard Busi-

ness School Press, 1985), pp. 37-51. Terry M. Moe examines the potential of principal-agent theory for public agencies in "The New Economics of Organization," *American Journal of Political Science,* vol. 20 (November 1984), pp. 739–777.

29. The term comes from the insurance literature. Those who buy insurance know they are covered in case of harm and therefore do not have as strong an incentive to protect themselves from potential losses. They also know that the risks of a serious problem are relatively small, so their incentives for self-protection may further decrease. The insurance company, which must pay for any losses, cannot know how policy holders are behaving and finds it difficult to evaluate the safety habits of individual policy holders. This mismatch exposes the insurance company to greater risks and points to fundamental uncertainties in its operations.

30. See, for example, Harrison C. White, "Agency as Control," in *Principals and Agents: The Structure of Business,* John W. Pratt and Richard J. Zeckhauser, eds. (Boston: Harvard Business School Press, 1985), p. 188.

31. Charles Perrow, *Complex Organizations: A Critical Essay,* 3d ed. (New York: Random House, 1986), pp. 230–231.

32. Talcott Parsons, *Structure and Process in Modern Societies* (New York: The Free Press, 1960), p. 41.

33. James G. March and Johan P. Olsen, *Rediscovering Institutions: The Organizational Basis of Politics* (New York: Free Press, 1989), p. 66.

34. This, in turn, means placing public administration within the new institutionalist school. See March and Olsen, *Rediscovering Institutions;* Stephen Skowronek, *Building a New Administrative State: The Expansion of National Administrative Capaci-*

ties, 1877-1920 (Cambridge: Cambridge University Press, 1982); James G. March and Johan P. Olsen, "The New Institutionalism: Organizational Factors in Political Life," *American Political Science Review,* vol. 78 (September 1984), pp. 734–749.

35. See, in addition to the Brownlow Committee report, Luther Gulick and Lyndall Urwick, eds., *Papers on the Science of Administration* (New York: Institute of Public Administration, 1937), especially Gulick's paper, "Notes on the Theory of Organization," pp. 1–45.

36. See Daniel Katz and Robert L. Kahn, *The Social Psychology of Organizations* (New York: John Wiley and Sons, 1966); and James D. Thompson, *Organizations in Action* (New York: McGraw Hill, 1967).

37. March and Olsen, *Rediscovering Institutions, supra,* p. 38.

38. See, for example, Chris Argyris and Donald A. Schon, *Organizational Learning: A Theory of Action Perspective* (Reading, MA: Addison-Wesley, 1978); Richard L. Daft and George P. Huber, "How Organizations Learn: A Communication Framework," *Research in the Sociology of Organizations,* vol. 5 (1987), pp. 1–36.

39. Several public-administration scholars have made important contributions to these issues. See, for example, Frederick C. Mosher, *Democracy and the Public Service,* 2d ed. (New York: Oxford University Press, 1978), on personnel policy; Irene S. Rubin, *The Politics of Public Budgeting* (Chatham, NJ: Chatham House Publishers, 1990), on budgeting; and Barbara S. Romzek and Melvin J. Dubnick, "Accountability in the Public Sector: Lessons from the Challenger Tragedy," *Public Administration Review,* vol. 47 (May/June 1987), pp. 227-38, on organization theory.

40. See U.S. Comptroller General, *Medicare: Contractor Services to Beneficiaries and Providers* (Washington: U.S. Government Printing Office, 1988).

41. Parsons, *Structure and Process in Modern Societies, supra,* p. 18; Michael L. Tushman, "Special Boundary Roles in the Innovation Process," *Administrative Science Quarterly,* vol. 22 (December 1977), pp. 587-605; and Michael L. Tushman and Ralph Katz, "External Communication and Project Performance: An Investigation into the Role of Gatekeepers," *Management Science,* vol. 26 (November 1980), pp. 1071–1085.

42. Information flow at the "seams of government" is an important part of some public-management approaches as well. See Elmore, "Graduate Education in Public Management," *supra,* p. 77.

43. Critics from the privatization movement, of course, have suggested that such high goal congruence also produces inefficient administration that other strategies, such as contracting out, can solve.

SECTION 2

The American Administrative State

All modern countries can be characterized as "administrative states." They all have large and powerful administrative components that are central to the formulation and implementation of public policy. But there is also great variation among administrative systems. For instance, career public administrators and agencies may be more or less subordinate to legislatures, presidents, prime ministers, and other political authorities. The American administrative state is set apart by the combination of two of its constitutional provisions: (1) the separation of powers and (2) federalism.

In the United States, public bureaucracies are not simply arms of the president or of the state governors. They must be responsive to these chief executives, of course, but also to legislatures and courts. Because each of these constitutional branches has different governmental responsibilities, concerns, and (consequently) values, public administrators can find themselves pushed and pulled in opposing directions. The impact of the separation of powers pervades every significant aspect of American public administration: administrative law, bureaucratic politics, organization, personnel, budgeting, policy formulation, implementation, and evaluation, as well as the theories and values that inform administrative practice in general.

Power over administration is fragmented further by American federalism. Federalism became a complicating factor for effective public administration as the federal government began taking on greater responsibility for the economy and society in the 1880s. By the mid-1900s, federal and state administrative activities overlapped so much that it was no longer possible to think constructively in terms of a "dual federalism," in which powers were clearly divided between the states and the national governments. Instead, the emphasis was on developing effective cooperation and coordination whereby the state and local administrators would implement federal policies and mandates. Like the separation of powers, federalism and the complexities it presents are rooted in the Constitution's peculiar mixing of distinct and shared powers.

Collectively, the essays in this section provide a comprehensive overview of how public administration fits and misfits the constitutional design. They also outline the main dimensions of public administration's relationships with legislatures, political executives, and the courts.

What did the Framers of the Constitution have in mind for public administration in the United States? The document itself contains only rudimentary provisions for the establishment and maintenance of civilian administrative agencies. It is certainly not a blueprint for integrating today's large federal bureaucracy into the constitutional scheme. Nor, of course, could the Framers have anticipated that there would be almost as many federal civilian employees two centuries later as there were people in the nation when they drafted the Constitution in 1787. Time, scope, and vagueness would seem to have rendered their thoughts largely irrelevant to today's public administration were it not for the brilliant analysis of administration put forth in *The Federalist Papers.* Written in 1787–1788 by Alexander Hamilton, James Madison, and John Jay under the pen name of "Publius," the *Federalist* sought to convince the citizens of New York that the Constitution would yield effective, but restrained, public administration. In the first paper, Hamilton, who was a very strong proponent of a powerful executive branch at the constitutional convention, argues that "the vigor of government is essential to the security of liberty." Therefore, strong public administration is a prerequisite to freedom rather than merely a danger to it. In No. 51, James Madison, who influenced the constitutional design perhaps more than anyone else, addresses the importance of fragmenting political power and influence in the political system in order to prevent the accumulation of overbearing power in one branch. His argument is compelling, though nowadays fragmentation presents public administrators with myriad obstacles to coordination. In Nos. 68 and 70, Hamilton elaborates on his earlier claim that vigorous government is essential. He writes that "the true test of a good government is its aptitude and tendency to produce a good administration" and goes on to argue that the constitutional government would meet this test because it provides for energy in the executive branch. He reminds us of the fundamental importance of public administration: "a government ill executed, whatever it may be in theory, must be in practice a bad government."

The themes regarding public administration outlined in the *Federalist* are explored in the context of the modern American administrative state in the selection on "Bureaucracy and Constitutionalism" by Norton Long. Long was among the first scholars to recognize that, by the 1940s, the federal bureaucracy could no longer be simply subordinate to the president and Congress. Rather it had to be integrated into the constitutional scheme: "we have worked out a complex system in which the bureaucracy and legislature perform complementary and interlocking functions. Both are necessary, and the supremacy of either would be a constitutional misfortune." Long correctly predicted that

> the role of the legislature and of the political executive may come to consist largely of encouraging, discouraging and passing on policy which wells up from the agencies of administration. All of this is because the bureaucracy is

not just an instrument to carry out a will formed by the elected Congress and President. It is itself a medium for registering the diverse wills that make up the people's will and for transmuting them into responsible proposals for public policy.

In sum, the bureaucracy has become a central actor in American politics.

In essence, Long identified a new field of study, that of "bureaucratic politics." The section is rounded out by discussions of several aspects of such politics: the relationships between the bureaucracy and Congress, the political executive, and the federal judiciary. In "Congress and the Administrative State," Lawrence Dodd and Richard Schott note that to a very large extent the administrative state is a creation of Congress. In order to control it, however, Congress has tended to strengthen the presidency and in some ways weaken itself. Nevertheless, the bureaucracy is hardly irrelevant to Congress and vice versa: their relationship to one another affects their organization and functions. Looking at the relationship between the president and public administration, Joel Aberbach and Bert Rockman are skeptical about the viability of models that would strictly subordinate the bureaucracy to the chief executive. In their view, the separation of powers gives the legislature and the judiciary sufficient motives and powers to resist transformation of the civil service into an adjunct of the presidency. Conversely, they are apprehensive that if Congress and the courts do not react "when presidents arrogate for their exclusive use constitutionally shared authority," then "presidents will take as theirs what Congress by its inaction bestows." The relationship between the courts and public administration is analyzed by Rosemary O'Leary and Charles Wise in "Public Managers, Judges, and Legislators: Redefining the 'New Partnership.'" Their study uses the case of *Missouri* v. *Jenkins* (1990) as an illustration of how deeply the separation of powers and federalism, taken together, may affect public administration. In that case the federal courts essentially took control of an important aspect of local administration, public education, and also required that local taxes be raised.

5.   The Federalist No. 1

Alexander Hamilton

INTRODUCTION

To the People of the State of New York:
After an unequivocal experience of the inefficiency of the subsisting federal government, you are called upon to de-

SOURCE: From *The Federalist Papers,* Nos. 1, 51, 68, and 70.

liberate on a new Constitution for the United States of America. The subject speaks its own importance; comprehending in its consequences nothing less than the existence of the UNION, the safety and welfare of the parts of which it is composed, the fate of an empire in many respects the most interesting in the world. It has been frequently remarked that it seems to have been reserved to the people of this country, by their conduct and example, to decide the important question, whether societies of men are really capable or not of establishing good government from reflection and choice, or whether they are forever destined to depend for their political constitutions on accident and force. If there be any truth in the remark, the crisis at which we are arrived may with propriety be regarded as the era in which that decision is to be made; and a wrong election of the part we shall act may, in this view, deserve to be considered as the general misfortune of mankind.

This idea will add the inducements of philanthropy to those of patriotism, to heighten the solicitude which all considerate and good men must feel for the event. Happy will it be if our choice should be directed by a judicious estimate of our true interests, unperplexed and unbiased by considerations not connected with the public good. But this is a thing more ardently to be wished than seriously to be expected. The plan offered to our deliberations affects too many particular interests, innovates upon too many local institutions, not to involve in its discussion a variety of objects foreign to its merits, and of views, passions and prejudices little favorable to the discovery of truth.

Among the most formidable of the obstacles which the new Constitution will have to encounter may readily be distinguished the obvious interest of a certain class of men in every State to resist all changes which may hazard a diminution of the power, emolument, and consequence of the offices they hold under the State establishments; and the perverted ambition of another class of men, who will either hope to aggrandize themselves by the confusions of their country, or will flatter themselves with fairer prospects of elevation from the subdivision of the empire into several partial confederacies than from its union under one government.

It is not, however, my design to dwell upon observations of this nature. I am well aware that it would be disingenuous to resolve indiscriminately the opposition of any set of men (merely because their situations might subject them to suspicion) into interested or ambitious views. Candor will oblige us to admit that even such men may be actuated by upright intentions; and it cannot be doubted that much of the opposition which has made its appearance, or may hereafter make its appearance, will spring from sources, blameless at least, if not respectable—the honest errors of minds led astray by preconceived jealousies and fears. So numerous indeed and so powerful are the causes which serve to give a false bias to the judgment, that we, upon many occasions, see wise and good men on the wrong as well as on the right side of questions of the first magnitude to society. This circumstance, if duly attended to, would furnish a lesson of moderation to those who are ever so much persuaded of their being in the right in any controversy. And a further reason for caution, in this respect, might be drawn from the reflection that we are not always sure that those who advocate the truth are influenced by purer principles than their antagonists. Ambition, avarice, personal animosity, party opposition, and many other motives not more laudable than these, are apt to operate as well upon those who support as those who oppose the right side of a question. Were there not even inducements to moderation, nothing could be more ill-judged than that intolerant spirit which has, at all times, characterized political parties. For in politics, as in religion, it is equally absurd to aim at making proselytes by fire and sword. Heresies in either can rarely be cured by persecution.

And yet, however just these sentiments will be allowed to be, we have already sufficient indications that it will happen in this as in all former cases of great national discussion. A torrent of angry and malignant passions will be let loose. To judge from the conduct of the opposite parties, we shall be led to conclude that they will mutually hope to evince the justness of their opinions, and to increase the number of their converts by the loudness of their declamations and the bitterness of their invectives. An enlightened zeal for the energy and efficiency of government will be stigmatized as the offspring of a temper fond of despotic power and hostile to the principles of liberty. An overscrupulous jealousy of danger to the rights of the people, which is more commonly the fault of the head than of the heart, will be represented as mere pretence and artifice, the stale bait for popularity at the expense of the public good. It will be forgotten, on the one hand, that jealousy is the usual concomitant of love, and that the noble enthusiasm of liberty is apt to be infected with a spirit of narrow and illiberal distrust. On the other hand, it will be equally forgotten that the vigor of government is essential to the security of liberty; that, in the contemplation of a sound and well-informed judgment, their interest can never be separated; and that a dangerous ambition more often lurks behind the specious mask of zeal for the rights of the people than under the forbidding appearance of zeal for the firmness and efficiency of government. History will teach us that the former has been found a much more certain road to the introduction of despotism than the latter, and that of those men who have overturned the liberties of republics, the greatest number have begun their career by paying an obsequious court to the people; commencing demagogues, and ending tyrants.

In the course of the preceding observations, I have had an eye, my fellow-citizens, to putting you upon your guard against all attempts, from whatever quarter, to influence your decision in a matter of the utmost moment to your welfare, by any impressions other than those which may result from the evidence of truth. You will, no doubt, at the same time, have collected from the general scope of them, that they proceed from a source not unfriendly to the new Constitution. Yes, my countrymen, I own to you that, after having given it an attentive consideration, I am clearly of opinion it is your interest to adopt it. I am convinced that this is the safest course for your liberty, your dignity, and your happiness. I affect not reserves which I do not feel. I will not amuse you with an appearance of deliberation when I have decided. I frankly acknowledge to you my convictions, and I will freely lay before you the reasons on which they are founded. The consciousness of good intentions disdains ambiguity. I shall not, however, multiply professions on this head. My motives must remain in the depository of my own breast. My arguments will be open to all, and may be judged of by all. They shall at least be offered in a spirit which will not disgrace the cause of truth.

I propose, in a series of papers, to discuss the following interesting particulars: —The utility of the UNION to your political prosperity—The insufficiency of the present Confederation to preserve that Union—The necessity of a government at least equally energetic with the one proposed, to the attainment of this object— The conformity of the proposed Constitution to the true principles of republican government—Its analogy to your own State constitution— and lastly, The additional security which its adoption will afford to the preservation of that species of government, to liberty, and to property.

In the progress of this discussion I shall endeavor to give a satisfactory answer to all the objections which shall have made their appearance, that may seem to have any claim to your attention.

It may perhaps be thought superfluous to offer arguments to prove the utility of the UNION, a point, no doubt, deeply engraved on the hearts of the great body of the people in every State, and one, which it may be imagined, has no adversaries. But the fact is, that we already hear it whispered in the private circles of those who oppose the new Constitution, that the thirteen States are of too great extent for any general system, and that we must of necessity resort to separate confederacies of distinct portions of the whole.* This doctrine will, in all

*The same idea, tracing the arguments to their consequences is held out in several of the late publications against the new Constitution.—PUBLIUS

probability, be gradually propagated, till it has votaries enough to countenance an open avowal of it. For nothing can be more evident, to those who are able to take an enlarged view of the subject, than the alternative of an adoption of the new Constitution or a dismemberment of the Union. It will therefore be of use to begin by examining the advantages of that Union, the certain evils, and the probable dangers, to which every State will be exposed from its dissolution. This shall accordingly constitute the subject of my next address.

PUBLIUS

The Federalist No. 51

James Madison

February 6, 1788

To the People of the State of New York:

To what expedient then shall we finally resort for maintaining in practice the necessary partition of power among the several departments, as laid down in the constitution? The only answer that can be given is, that as all these exterior provisions are found to be inadequate, the defect must be supplied, by so contriving the interior structure of the government, as that its several constituent parts may, by their mutual relations, be the means of keeping each other in their proper places. Without presuming to

SOURCE: From *The Independent Journal,* February 6, 1788. This essay appeared on February 8 in *The New-York Packet* and on February 11 in *The Daily Advertiser.* It was numbered 51 in the McLean edition and 50 in the newspapers.

undertake a full development of this important idea, I will hazard a few general observations, which may perhaps place it in a clearer light, and enable us to form a more correct judgment of the principles and structure of the government planned by the convention.

In order to lay a due foundation for that separate and distinct exercise of the different powers of government, which to a certain extent, is admitted on all hands to be essential to the preservation of liberty, it is evident that each department should have a will of its own; and consequently should be so constituted, that the members of each should have as little agency as possible in the appointment of the members of the others. Were this principle rigorously adhered to, it would require that all the appointments for the supreme executive, legislative, and judiciary magistracies, should be drawn from the same fountain of authority, the people, through channels, having no communication whatever with one another. Perhaps such a plan of constructing the several departments would be less difficult in practice than it may in contemplation appear. Some difficulties however, and some additional expence, would attend the execution of it. Some deviations therefore from the principle must be admitted. In the constitution of the judiciary department in particular, it might be inexpedient to insist rigorously on the principle; first, because peculiar qualifications being essential in the members, the primary consideration ought to be to select that mode of choice, which best secures these qualifications; secondly, because the permanent tenure by which the appointments are held in that department, must soon destroy all sense of dependence on the authority conferring them.

It is equally evident that the members of each department should be as little dependent as possible on those of the others, for the emoluments annexed to their offices. Were the executive magistrate, or the judges, not independent of the legislature in this particular, their independence in every other would be merely nominal.

But the great security against a gradual concentration of the several powers in the same department, consists in giving to those who administer each department, the necessary constitutional means, and personal motives, to resist encroachments of the others. The provision for defence must in this, as in all other cases, be made commensurate to the danger of attack. Ambition must be made to counteract ambition. The interest of the man must be connected with the constitutional rights of the place. It may be a reflection on human nature, that such devices should be necessary to controul the abuses of government. But what is government itself but the greatest of all reflections on human nature? If men were angels, no government would be necessary. If angels were to govern men, neither external nor internal controuls on government would be necessary. In framing a government which is to be administered by men over men, the great difficulty lies in this: You must first enable the government to controul the governed; and in the next place, oblige it to controul itself. A dependence on the people is no doubt the primary controul on the government; but experience has taught mankind the necessity of auxiliary precautions.

This policy of supplying by opposite and rival interests, the defect of better motives, might be traced through the whole system of human affairs, private as well as public. We see it particularly displayed in all the subordinate distributions of power; where the constant aim is to divide and arrange the several offices in such a manner as that each may be a check on the other; that the private interest of every individual, may be a centinel over the public rights. These inventions of prudence cannot be less requisite in the distribution of the supreme powers of the state.

But it is not possible to give to each department an equal power of self defence. In republican government the legislative authority, necessarily, predominates. The remedy for this inconveniency is, to divide the legislature into different branches; and to render them by different modes of election, and different principles of action, as little connected with each other, as the nature of their common functions, and their common dependence on the society, will admit. It may even be necessary to guard against dangerous encroachments by still further precautions. As the weight of the legislative authority requires that it should be thus divided, the weakness of the executive may require, on the other hand, that it should be fortified. An absolute negative, on the legislature, appears at first view to be the natural defence with which the executive magistrate should be armed. But perhaps it would be neither altogether safe, nor alone sufficient. On ordinary occasions, it might not be exerted with the requisite firmness; and on extraordinary occasions, it might be perfidiously abused. May not this defect of an absolute negative be supplied, by some qualified connection between this weaker department, and the weaker branch of the stronger department, by which the latter may be led to support the constitutional rights of the former, without being too much detached from the rights of its own department?

If the principles on which these observations are founded be just, as I persuade myself they are, and they be applied as a criterion, to the several state constitutions, and to the federal constitution, it will be found, that if the latter does not perfectly correspond with them, the former are infinitely less able to bear such a test.

There are moreover two considerations particularly applicable to the federal system of America, which place that system in a very interesting point of view.

First. In a single republic, all the power surrendered by the people, is submitted to the administration of a single government; and usurpations are guarded against by a division of the government into distinct and separate departments. In the compound republic of America, the power surrendered by the people, is first divided between two distinct governments, and then the portion allotted to each, subdivided among distinct and separate departments. Hence a double security arises to the rights of the people. The different governments will controul each other; at the same time that each will be controuled by itself.

Second. It is of great importance in a republic, not only to guard the society against the oppression of its rulers; but to guard one part of the society against the injustice of the other part. Different interests necessarily exist in different classes of citizens. If a majority be united by a common interest, the rights of the minority will be insecure. There are but two methods of providing against this evil: The one by creating a will in the community independent of the majority, that is, of the society itself; the other by comprehending in the society so many separate descriptions of citizens, as will render an unjust combination of a majority of the whole, very improbable, if not impracticable. The first method prevails in all governments possessing an hereditary or self appointed authority. This at best is but a precarious security; because a power independent of the society may as well espouse the unjust views of the major, as the rightful interests, of the minor party, and may possibly be turned against both parties. The second method will be exemplified in the federal republic of the United States. Whilst all authority in it will be derived from and dependent on the society, the society itself will be broken into so many parts, interests and classes of citizens, that the rights of individuals or of the minority, will be in little danger from interested combinations of the majority. In a free government, the security for civil rights must be the same as for religious rights. It consists in the one case in the multiplicity of interests, and in the other, in the multiplicity of sects. The degree of security in both cases will depend on the number of interests and sects; and this may be presumed to depend on the extent of country and number of people comprehended under the same government. This view of the subject must particularly recommend a proper federal system to all the sincere and considerate friends of republican government: Since it shews that in exact proportion as the territory of the union may be formed into more circumscribed confederacies or states, oppressive combinations of a majority will be facilitated, the best security under the republican form, for the rights of every class of citizens, will be diminished; and consequently, the stability and independence of some member of the government, the only other security, must be proportionally increased. Justice is the end of government. It is the end of civil society. It ever has been, and ever will be pursued, until it be obtained, or until liberty be lost in the pursuit. In a society under the forms of which the stronger faction can readily unite and oppress the weaker, anarchy may as truly be said to reign, as in a state of nature where the weaker individual is not secured against the violence of the stronger: And as in the latter state even the stronger individuals are prompted by the uncertainty of their condition, to submit to a government which may protect the weak as well as themselves: So in the former state, will the more powerful factions or parties be gradually induced by a like motive, to wish for a government which will protect all parties, the weaker as well as the more powerful. It can be little doubted, that if the state of Rhode Island was separated from the confederacy, and left to itself, the insecurity of rights under the popular form of government within such narrow limits, would be displayed by such reiterated oppressions of factious majorities, that some power altogether independent of the people would soon be called for by the voice of the very factions whose misrule had proved the necessity of it. In the extended republic of the United States, and among the great variety of interests, parties and sects which it embraces, a coalition of a majority of the whole society could seldom take place on any other principles than those of justice and the general good; and there being thus less danger to a minor from the will of the major party, there must be less pretext also, to provide for the security of the former, by introducing into the government a will not dependent on the latter; or in other words, a will independent of the society itself. It is no less certain than it is important, notwithstanding the contrary opinions which have been entertained, that the larger the society, provided it lie within a practicable sphere, the more duly capable it will be of self government. And happily for the *republican cause,* the practicable sphere may be carried to a very great extent, by a judicious modification and mixture of the *federal principle.*

PUBLIUS

The Federalist No. 68

Alexander Hamilton

THE METHOD OF ELECTING THE PRESIDENT

To the People of the State of New York:
The mode of appointment of the Chief Magistrate of the United States is almost the only part of the system, of any consequence, which has escaped without severe censure, or which has received the slightest mark of approbation from its opponents. The most plausible of these, who has appeared in print, has even deigned to admit that the election of the President is pretty well guarded.* I venture somewhat further, and hesitate not to affirm that if the manner of it be

* *Vide* FEDERAL FARMER.—Publius

not perfect, it is at least excellent. It unites in an eminent degree all the advantages the union of which was to be wished for.

It was desirable that the sense of the people should operate in the choice of the person to whom so important a trust was to be confided. This end will be answered by committing the right of making it, not to any preëstablished body, but to men chosen by the people for the special purpose, and at the particular conjuncture.

It was equally desirable, that the immediate election should be made by men most capable of analyzing the qualities adapted to the station, and acting under circumstances favorable to deliberation, and to a judicious combination of all the reasons and inducements which were proper to govern their choice. A small number of persons, selected by their fellow-citizens from the general mass, will be most likely to possess the information and discernment requisite to such complicated investigations.

It was also peculiarly desirable to afford as little opportunity as possible to tumult and disorder. This evil was not least to be dreaded in the election of a magistrate, who was to have so important an agency in the administration of the government as the President of the United States. But the precautions which have been so happily concerted in the system under consideration, promise an effectual security against this mischief. The choice of *several,* to form an intermediate body of electors, will be much less apt to convulse the community with any extraordinary or violent movements, than the choice of *one* who was himself to be the final object of the public wishes. And as the electors, chosen in each State, are to assemble and vote in the State in which they are chosen, this detached and divided situation will expose them much less to heats and ferments, which might be communicated from them to the people, than if they were all to be convened at one time, in one place.

Nothing was more to be desired than that every practicable obstacle should be opposed to cabal, intrigue, and corruption. These most deadly adversaries of republican government might naturally have been expected to make their approaches from more than one quarter, but chiefly from the desire in foreign powers to gain an improper ascendant in our councils. How could they better gratify this, than by raising a creature of their own to the chief magistracy of the Union? But the convention have guarded against all danger of this sort, with the most provident and judicious attention. They have not made the appointment of the President to depend on any preëxisting bodies of men, who might be tampered with beforehand to prostitute their votes; but they have referred it in the first instance to an immediate act of the people of America, to be exerted in the choice of persons for the temporary and sole purpose of making the appointment. And they have excluded from eligibility to this trust, all those who from situation might be suspected of too great devotion to the President in office. No senator, representative, or other person holding a place of trust or profit under the United States, can be of the numbers of the electors. Thus without corrupting the body of the people, the immediate agents in the election will at least enter upon the task free from any sinister bias. Their transient existence, and their detached situation, already taken notice of, afford a satisfactory prospect of their continuing so, to the conclusion of it. The business of corruption, when it is to embrace so considerable a number of men, requires time as well as means. Nor would it be found easy suddenly to embark them, dispersed as they would be over thirteen States, in any combinations founded upon motives, which though they could not properly be denominated corrupt, might yet be of a nature to mislead them from their duty.

Another and no less important desideratum was, that the Executive should be independent for his continuance in the office on all but the people themselves. He might otherwise be tempted to sacrifice his duty to his complaisance for those whose favor was necessary to the duration of his official consequence. This advantage will also be secured, by making his reëlection to depend on a special body of representatives, deputed by the society for the single purpose of making the important choice.

All these advantages will happily combine in the plan devised by the convention; which is, that the people of each State shall choose a number of persons as electors, equal to the number of senators and representatives of such State in the national government, who shall assemble within the State, and vote for some fit person as President. Their votes, thus given, are to be transmitted to the seat of the national government, and the person who may happen to have a majority of the whole number of votes will be the President. But as a majority of the votes might not always happen to centre in one man, and as it might be unsafe to permit less than a majority to be conclusive, it is provided that, in such a contingency, the House of Representatives shall select out of the candidates who shall have the five highest number of votes, the man who in their opinion may be best qualified for the office.

The process of election affords a moral certainty, that the office of President will never fall to the lot of any man who is not in an eminent degree endowed with the requisite qualifications. Talents for low intrigue, and the little arts of popularity, may alone suffice to elevate a man to the first honors in a single State; but it will require other talents, and a different kind of merit, to establish him in the esteem and confidence of the whole Union, or of so considerable a portion of it as would be necessary to make him a successful candidate for the distinguished office of President of the United States. It will not be too strong to say, that there will be a constant probability of seeing the station filled by characters preëminent for ability and virtue. And this will be thought no inconsiderable recommendation of the Constitution, by those who are able to estimate the share which the executive in every government must necessarily have in its good or ill administration. Though we cannot acquiesce in the political heresy of the poet who says:

> "For forms of government let fools contest—
> That which is best administered is best,"—

yet we may safely pronounce, that the true test of a good government is its aptitude and tendency to produce a good administration.

The Vice-President is to be chosen in the same manner with the President; with this difference, that the Senate is to do, in respect to the former, what is to be done by the House of Representatives, in respect to the latter.

The appointment of an extraordinary person, as Vice-President, has been objected to as superfluous, if not mischievous. It has been alleged, that it would have been preferable to have authorized the Senate to elect out of their own body an officer answering that description. But two considerations seem to justify the ideas of the convention in this respect. One is, that to secure at all times the possibility of a definite resolution of the body, it is necessary that the President should have only a casting vote. And to take the senator of any State from his seat as senator, to place him in that of President of the Senate, would be to exchange, in regard to the State from which he came, a constant for a contingent vote. The other consideration is, that as the Vice-President may occasionally become a substitute for the President, in the supreme executive magistracy, all the reasons which recommend the mode of election prescribed for the one, apply with great if not with equal force to the manner of appointing the other. It is remarkable that in this, as in most other instances, the objection which is made would lie against the constitution of this State. We have a Lieutenant-Governor, chosen by the people at large, who presides in the Senate, and is the constitutional substitute for the Governor, in casualties similar to those which would authorize the Vice-President to exercise the authorities and discharge the duties of the President.

PUBLIUS

The Federalist No. 70

Alexander Hamilton

March 15, 1788

To the People of the State of New York:
There is an idea, which is not without its advocates, that a vigorous executive is inconsistent with the genius of republican government. The enlightened well wishers to this species of government must at least hope that the supposition is destitute of foundation; since they can never admit its truth, without at the same time admitting the condemnation of their own principles. Energy in the executive is a leading character in the definition of good government. It is essential to the protection of the community against foreign attacks: It is not less essential to the steady administration of the laws, to the protection of property against those irregular and high handed-combinations, which sometimes interrupt the ordinary course of justice, to the security of liberty against the enterprises and assaults of ambition, of faction and of anarchy. Every man the least conversant in Roman story knows how often that republic was obliged to take refuge in the absolute power of a single man, under the formidable title of dictator, as well against the intrigues of ambitious individuals, who aspired to the tyranny, and the seditions of whole classes of the community, whose conduct threatened the existence of all government, as against the invasions of external enemies, who menaced the conquest and destruction of Rome.

There can be no need however to multiply arguments or examples on this head. A feeble executive implies a feeble execution of the government. A feeble execution is but another phrase for a bad execution: And a government ill executed, whatever it may be in theory, must be in practice a bad government.

Taking it for granted, therefore, that all men of sense will agree in the necessity of an energetic executive; it will only remain to inquire, what are the ingredients which constitute this energy—how far can they be combined with those other ingredients which constitute safety in the republican sense? And how far does this combination characterise the plan, which has been reported by the convention?

The ingredients, which constitute energy in the executive, are first unity, secondly duration, thirdly an adequate provision for its support, fourthly competent powers.

SOURCE: From *The Independent Journal,* March 15, 1788. This essay appeared on March 18 in *The New-York Packet.* It was numbered 70 in the McLean edition and 69 in the newspapers.

The circumstances which constitute safety in the republican sense are, Ist. a due dependence on the people, secondly a due responsibility.

Those politicians and statesmen, who have been the most celebrated for the soundness of their principles, and for the justness of their views, have declared in favor of a single executive and a numerous legislature. They have with great propriety considered energy as the most necessary qualification of the former, and have regarded this as most applicable to power in a single hand; while they have with equal propriety considered the latter as best adapted to deliberation and wisdom, and best calculated to conciliate the confidence of the people and to secure their privileges and interests.

That unity is conducive to energy will not be disputed. Decision, activity, secrecy, and dispatch will generally characterise the proceedings of one man, in a much more eminent degree, than the proceedings of any greater number; and in proportion as the number is increased, these qualities will be diminished.

This unity may be destroyed in two ways; either by vesting the power in two or more magistrates of equal dignity and authority; or by vesting it ostensibly in one man, subject in whole or in part to the controul and co-operation of others, in the capacity of counsellors to him. Of the first the two consuls of Rome may serve as an example; of the last we shall find examples in the constitutions of several of the states. New-York and New-Jersey, if I recollect right, are the only states, which have entrusted the executive authority wholly to single men.* Both these methods of destroying

*New-York has no council except for the single purpose of appointing to offices; New-Jersey has a council, whom the governor may consult. But I think from the terms of the constitution their resolutions do not bind him. (Publius)

the unity of the executive have their partisans; but the votaries of an executive council are the most numerous. They are both liable, if not to equal, to similar objections; and may in most lights be examined in conjunction.

The experience of other nations will afford little instruction on this head. As far however as it teaches any thing, it teaches us not to be inamoured of plurality in the executive. We have seen that the Achæans on an experiment of two Prætors, were induced to abolish one. The Roman history records many instances of mischiefs to the republic from the dissentions between the consuls, and between the military tribunes, who were at times substituted to the consuls. But it gives us no specimens of any peculiar advantages derived to the state, from the circumstance of the plurality of those magistrates. That the dissentions between them were not more frequent, or more fatal, is matter of astonishment; until we advert to the singular position in which the republic was almost continually placed and to the prudent policy pointed out by the circumstances of the state, and pursued by the consuls, of making a division of the government between them. The Patricians engaged in a perpetual struggle with the Plebians for the preservation of their antient authorities and dignities; the consuls, who were generally chosen out of the former body, were commonly united by the personal interest they had in the defence of the privileges of their order. In addition to this motive of union, after the arms of the republic had considerably expanded the bounds of its empire, it became an established custom with the consuls to divide the administration between themselves by lot; one of them remaining at Rome to govern the city and its environs; the other taking the command in the more distant provinces. This expedient must no doubt have had great influence in preventing those collisions and rivalships, which might otherwise have embroiled the peace of the republic.

But quitting the dim light of historical research, and attaching ourselves purely to the dictates of reason and good sense, we shall discover much greater cause to reject than to approve the idea of plurality in the executive, under any modification whatever.

Wherever two or more persons are engaged in any common enterprize or pursuit, there is always danger of difference of opinion. If it be a public trust or office in which they are cloathed with equal dignity and authority, there is peculiar danger of personal emulation and even animosity. From either and especially from all these causes, the most bitter dissentions are apt to spring. Whenever these happen, they lessen the respectability, weaken the authority, and distract the plans and operations of those whom they divide. If they should unfortunately assail the supreme executive magistracy of a country, consisting of a plurality of persons, they might impede or frustrate the most important measures of the government, in the most critical emergencies of the state. And what is still worse, they might split the community into the most violent and irreconcilable factions, adhering differently to the different individuals who composed the magistracy.

Men often oppose a thing merely because they have had no agency in planning it, or because it may have been planned by those whom they dislike. But if they have been consulted and have happened to disapprove, opposition then becomes in their estimation an indispensable duty of self love. They seem to think themselves bound in honor, and by all the motives of personal infallibility to defeat the success of what has been resolved upon, contrary to their sentiments. Men of upright, benevolent tempers have too many opportunities of remarking with horror, to what desperate lengths this disposition

is sometimes carried, and how often the great interests of society are sacrificed to the vanity, to the conceit and to the obstinacy of individuals, who have credit enough to make their passions and their caprices interesting to mankind. Perhaps the question now before the public may in its consequences afford melancholy proofs of the effects of this despicable frailty, or rather detestable vice in the human character.

Upon the principles of a free government, inconveniencies from the source just mentioned must necessarily be submitted to in the formation of the legislature; but it is unnecessary and therefore unwise to introduce them into the constitution of the executive. It is here too that they may be most pernicious. In the legislature, promptitude of decision is oftener an evil than a benefit. The differences of opinion, and the jarrings of parties in that department of the government, though they may sometimes obstruct salutary plans, yet often promote deliberation and circumspection; and serve to check excesses in the majority. When a resolution too is once taken, the opposition must be at an end. That resolution is a law, and resistance to it punishable. But no favourable circumstances palliate or atone for the disadvantages of dissention in the executive department. Here they are pure and unmixed. There is no point at which they cease to operate. They serve to embarrass and weaken the execution of the plan or measure, to which they relate, from the first step to the final conclusion of it. They constantly counteract those qualities in the executive, which are the most necessary ingredients in its composition, vigour and expedition, and this without any counterballancing good. In the conduct of war, in which the energy of the executive is the bulwark of the national security, every thing would be to be apprehended from its plurality.

It must be confessed that these observations apply with principal weight to the first case supposed, that is to a plurality of magistrates of equal dignity and authority; a scheme the advocates for which are not likely to form a numerous sect: But they apply, though not with equal, yet with considerable weight, to the project of a council, whose concurrence is made constitutionally necessary to the operations of the ostensible executive. An artful cabal in that council would be able to distract and to enervate the whole system of administration. If no such cabal should exist, the mere diversity of views and opinions would alone be sufficient to tincture the exercise of the executive authority with a spirit of habitual feebleness and dilatoriness.

But one of the weightiest objections to a plurality in the executive, and which lies as much against the last as the first plan, is that it tends to conceal faults, and destroy responsibility. Responsibility is of two kinds, to censure and to punishment. The first is the most important of the two; especially in an elective office. Man, in public trust, will much oftener act in such a manner as to render him unworthy of being any longer trusted, than in such a manner as to make him obnoxious to legal punishment. But the multiplication of the executive adds to the difficulty of detection in either case. It often becomes impossible, amidst mutual accusations, to determine on whom the blame or the punishment of a pernicious measure, or series of pernicious measures ought really to fall. It is shifted from one to another with so much dexterity, and under such plausible appearances, that the public opinion is left in suspense about the real author. The circumstances which may have led to any national miscarriage or misfortune are sometimes so complicated, that where there are a number of actors who may have had different degrees and kinds of agency, though we may clearly see upon the whole that there

has been mismanagement, yet it may be impracticable to pronounce to whose account the evil which may have been incurred is truly chargeable.

"I was overruled by my council. The council were so divided in their opinions, that it was impossible to obtain any better resolution on the point." These and similar pretexts are constantly at hand, whether true or false. And who is there that will either take the trouble or incur the odium of a strict scrutiny into the secret springs of the transaction? Should there be found a citizen zealous enough to undertake the unpromising task, if there happen to be a collusion between the parties concerned, how easy is it to cloath the circumstances with so much ambiguity, as to render it uncertain what was the precise conduct of any of those parties?

In the single instance in which the governor of this state is coupled with a council, that is in the appointment to offices, we have seen the mischiefs of it in the view now under consideration. Scandalous appointments to important offices have been made. Some cases indeed have been so flagrant, that ALL PARTIES have agreed in the impropriety of the thing. When enquiry has been made, the blame has been laid by the governor on the members of the council; who on their part have charged it upon his nomination: While the people remain altogether at a loss to determine by whose influence their interests have been committed to hands so unqualified, and so manifestly improper. In tenderness to individuals, I forbear to descend to particulars.

It is evident from these considerations, that the plurality of the executive tends to deprive the people of the two greatest securities they can have for the faithful exercise of any delegated power; first, the restraints of public opinion, which lose their efficacy as well on account of the division of the censure attendant on bad measures among a number, as on account of the uncertainty on whom it ought to fall; and secondly, the opportunity of discovering with facility and clearness the misconduct of the persons they trust, in order either to their removal from office, or to their actual punishment, in cases which admit of it.

In England the king is a perpetual magistrate; and it is a maxim, which has obtained for the sake of the public peace, that he is unaccountable for his administration, and his person sacred. Nothing therefore can be wiser in that kingdom than to annex to the king a constitutional council, who may be responsible to the nation for the advice they give. Without this there would be no responsibility whatever in the executive department; an idea inadmissible in a free government. But even there the king is not bound by the resolutions of his council, though they are answerable for the advice they give. He is the absolute master of his own conduct, in the exercise of his office; and may observe or disregard the council given to him at his sole discretion.

But in a republic, where every magistrate ought to be personally responsible for his behaviour in office, the reason which in the British constitution dictates the propriety of a council not only ceases to apply, but turns against the institution. In the monarchy of Great-Britain, it furnishes a substitute for the prohibited responsibility of the chief magistrate; which serves in some degree as a hostage to the national justice for his good behaviour. In the American republic it would serve to destroy, or would greatly diminish the intended and necessary responsibility of the chief magistrate himself.

The idea of a council to the executive, which has so generally obtained in the state constitutions, has been derived from that maxim of republican jealousy, which considers power as safer in the hands of a number of men than of a single man. If the maxim should be admit-

ted to be applicable to the case, I should contend that the advantage on that side would not counterballance the numerous disadvantages on the opposite side. But I do not think the rule at all applicable to the executive power. I clearly concur in opinion in this particular with a writer whom the celebrated Junius pronounces to be "deep, solid and ingenious," that, "the executive power is more easily confined when it is one": That it is far more safe there should be a single object for the jealousy and watchfulness of the people; and in a word that all multiplication of the executive is rather dangerous than friendly to liberty.

A little consideration will satisfy us, that the species of security sought for in the multiplication of the executive is unattainable. Numbers must be so great as to render combination difficult; or they are rather a source of danger than of security. The united credit and influence of several individuals must be more formidable to liberty than the credit and influence of either of them separately. When power therefore is placed in the hands of so small a number of men, as to admit of their interests and views being easily combined in a common enterprise, by an artful leader, it becomes more liable to abuse and more dangerous when abused, than if it be lodged in the hands of one man; who from the very circumstance of his being alone will be more narrowly watched and more readily suspected, and who cannot unite so great a mass of influence as when he is associated with others. The Decemvirs of Rome, whose name denotes their number, were more to be dreaded in their usurpation than any ONE of them would have been. No person would think of proposing an executive much more numerous than that body, from six to a dozen have been suggested for the number of the council. The extreme of these numbers is not too great for an easy combination; and from such a combination America would have more to fear, than from the ambition of any single individual. A council to a magistrate, who is himself responsible for what he does, are generally nothing better than a clog upon his good intentions; are often the instruments and accomplices of his bad, and are almost always a cloak to his faults.

I forbear to dwell upon the subject of expence; though it be evident that if the council should be numerous enough to answer the principal end, aimed at by the institution, the salaries of the members, who must be drawn from their homes to reside at the seat of government, would form an item in the catalogue of public expenditures, too serious to be incurred for an object of equivocal utility.

I will only add, that prior to the appearance of the constitution, I rarely met with an intelligent man from any of the states, who did not admit as the result of experience, that the UNITY of the Executive of this state was one of the best of the distinguishing features of our constitution.

PUBLIUS

6.   Bureaucracy and Constitutionalism

Norton E. Long

There is an old aphorism that fire is a good servant but a bad master. Something like this aphorism is frequently applied to the appropriate role of the bureaucracy in government. Because bureaucracy is often viewed as tainted with an ineradicable lust for power, it is alleged that, like fire, it needs constant control to prevent its erupting from beneficent servitude into dangerous and tyrannical mastery.

The folklore of constitutional theory relegates the bureaucracy to somewhat the same low but necessary estate as Plato does the appetitive element of the soul. In the conventional dichotomy between policy and administration, administration is the Aristotelian slave, properly an instrument of action for the will of another, capable of receiving the commands of reason but incapable of reasoning. The amoral concept of administrative neutrality is the natural complement of the concept of bureaucracy as instru-

ment; for according to this view the seat of reason and conscience resides in the legislature, whatever grudging concession may be made to the claims of the political executive, and a major, if not the major, task of constitutionalism is the maintenance of the supremacy of the legislature over the bureaucracy. The latter's sole constitutional role is one of neutral docility to the wishes of the day's legislative majority.

The source of this doctrine is found in part in a reading of English constitutional history and in part in the political metaphysics of John Locke. The drama of English constitutional development may be seen as first the concentration of power in the Norman kings, with the suppression of feudal anarchy, and then the gradual attainment of parliamentary supremacy. Because the bureaucracy was created by the kings as an instrument of national unification, it became identified with them and was envisaged as a monarchical rather than a popular element, and one which required control. At a later date the class monopoly of the upper hierarchy of the civil ser-

SOURCE: "Bureaucracy and Constitutionalism" by Norton Long, *American Political Science Review,* Vol. 46, September 1952.

vice reinforced liberal suspicions of the bureaucracy, and it seemed especially clear that the most bureaucratic part of the bureaucracy, the military, had to be placed firmly under civilian, i.e., legislative, control.

John Locke, writing the apologia for the Glorious Revolution and its accompanying shift in political power, held that "there can be but one supreme power, which is the legislative, to which all the rest are and must be subordinate. . . ."[1] To be sure, Locke conceived of the legislature only as the fiduciary of the people, from whom all legitimate power ultimately stemmed. But since the legislature was considered the authentic voice of the people changeable only by revolution, this limitation could be forgotten in practice. Despite Locke's qualifications, the latter-day exponents of his views have given currency to what Jackson called the "absurd doctrine that the legislature is the people." Professor Charles Hyneman, accepting the majority will metaphysics of Willmoore Kendall, has ably expounded the consequence of that point of view in his recent *Bureaucracy in a Democracy*. It is his position that in a democracy the people should get what they want, and that what the legislature wants is the best approximation of what the people want; ergo, we should fashion our institutions for legislative supremacy, at least with respect to the bureaucracy.[2] Hyneman's position is extreme but not substantially different from others who argue that Congress is our board of directors. Even Paul Apple-

by reflects at times the conventional bureaucratic homage to Congress, though his central position rejects the claim of any single organ to monopolize the democratic process.[3] Acceptance of the principle of legislative supremacy by practicing administrators is, of course, more a counsel of expediency than an article of faith. It pays for the administrator to call Congress our board of directors, whatever his private conviction may be.

Unfortunately for the simplicity of the theory that democracy means giving the people what they want and that this means giving the legislature what it wants, the legislature is divided into two branches and the President is an independently elected official. In case of conflict between any or all of these, who should be supreme as the authentic representative of what the people want? Professor Hyneman has his uneasy moments between President and legislature. Realism compels some doubts as to the validity of the voice of congressional committees, and closer examination bogs the theory down in exceptions and qualifications.

The will of the people, like sovereignty, is regarded as a metaphysical first principle, supplying an absolute from which certain consequences can be deduced. Yet to possess meaning in political analysis, the concept must be defined in operational terms. How do you discover what the people want? The mode of consultation can make a world of difference. At various times President, Senate, House, Supreme Court, Dr. Gallup, and a host of other agents and agencies have claimed a special ability to express the people's will. The Achilles heel of Rousseau's *volonté gen-*

[1]John Locke, *The Second Treatise of Civil Government and A Letter concerning Toleration* (Oxford, 1947), Ch. 8, p. 87.

[2]See Part 1 of *Bureaucracy in a Democracy* (New York 1950). For a penetrating but sympathetic criticism of Hyneman's views, see Chester I. Barnard's review of the book in AMERICAN POLITICAL SCIENCE REVIEW, Vol. 44, pp. 990–1004 (Dec., 1950).

[3]For Appleby's central position, see Ch. 16 of his *Big Democracy* (New York, 1945) and p. 164 of his *Policy and Administration* (University, Alabama, 1949).

erale was that it had to find a voice, and his solutions ranged from enlightened dictatorship to counting the votes. The will of the people in Professor Elliott's sense is the democratic myth, and in Mosca's the political formula. It serves as a symbol to legitimatize the acts of any group that can successfully identify itself with it in the public mind. Properly understood, it probably should be treated as a value symbol of our political culture, an object for investigation involving a political process—and not a principle from which we can logically excogitate the appropriate role of bureaucracy.

Dissatisfaction with the view of bureaucracy as instrument and Caliban has grown among students of government as first-hand experience in government and historical research have undermined accepted dogma. Professor C. J. Friedrich has pointed to the beneficent role of bureaucracy as the core of modern government.[4] Dr. Fritz Morstein Marx has described the vital role of the Prussian bureaucracy in developing the *Rechtsstaat*.[5] The studies of Pendleton Herring, John M. Gaus and Leon O. Wolcott, Arthur W. MacMahon and John D. Millett have illustrated the genuinely representative part played by the bureaucracy in American government.[6] And in a widely used text Professor J. A. Corry has not hesitated to refer to administration as the mainspring of government and to the administrative, as distinguished from the political, executive as a fourth branch of government. An assessment of the vital role of bureaucracy in the working American constitution seems to be overdue.

The most ardent advocate of legislative supremacy can no longer blink the fact of administrative discretion and even administrative legislation. Nor does any one seriously suppose that the clock can be turned back. Improvement there may be in the capacity and willingness of the legislature to exercise general policy superintendence, but anything approaching the conditions necessary to achieve a separation of policy from administration is highly doubtful. The bureaucracy is in policy, and major policy, to stay; in fact, barring the unlikely development of strong majority party legislative leadership, the bureaucracy is likely, day in and day out, to be our main source of policy initiative.[7] The role of the legislature and of the political executive may come to consist largely of encouraging, discouraging and passing on policy which wells up from the agencies of administration. All of this is because the bureaucracy is not just an instrument to carry out a will formed by the elected Congress and President. It is itself a medium for registering the diverse wills that make up the people's will and for transmuting them into responsible proposals for public policy.

Growth in the power of the bureaucracy is looked upon as a menace to constitutionalism. By some it is seen as a dangerous enhancement of the power of the President, by others as an alarming accretion of power to a non-elective part of the government. The logic of *either-or* sees a cumulative process in which the supremacy of the elected legislative is re-

[4]*Constitutional Government and Democracy*, rev. ed. (Boston, 1950), Ch.2.

[5]"Civil Service in Germany," in *Civil Service Abroad* (New York, 1935).

[6]Pendleton Herring, *Public Administration and the Public Interest* (New York, 1936); J. M. Gaus and L. O. Wolcott, *Public Administration and the United States Department of Agriculture* (Chicago, 1940); A. W. MacMahon and J. D. Millett, *Federal Administrators; A Boigraphical Approach to the Problem of Departmental Management* (New York, 1939).

[7]Cf. George B. Galloway, *Congress at the Cross Roads* (New York, 1946), pp. 150–151; Roland A. Young, *This Is Congress* (New York, 1943), Ch. 2.

placed by the supremacy of an appointed bureaucracy. Given the alternative, the choice of the supremacy of an elected legislature would be clear, but that choice is an unreal bogy. To meet our needs, we have worked out a complex system in which the bureaucracy and legislature perform complementary and interlocking functions.[8] Both are necessary, and the supremacy of either would be a constitutional misfortune. We sometimes forget that the authors of the *Federalist* and Jefferson alike were aware of the danger of legislative tyranny.

Professor Friedrich and others have argued that the essence of constitutionalism is the division of power in such a way as to provide a system of effective regularized restraints upon governmental action.[9] The purpose of this division of power is not to create some mechanical equipoise among the organs of government but so to represent the diversity of the community that its own pluralism is reflected in a pluralism within the government. As Mosca has well said, "the only demand that is important, and possible, to make of a political system is that all social values shall have a part in it, and that it shall find a place for all who possess any of the qualities which determine what prestige and what influence an individual, or a class, is to have."[10] Now it is extremely clear that our Congress fails to do this and that the bureaucracy in considerable measure compensates for its deficiency. Important and vital interests in the United States are unrepresented, underrepresented, or malrepresented in Congress. These interests receive more effective and more responsible representation through administrative channels than through the legislature.

In considerable part this is due to the nature of the presidency and its constituency. Responsible behavior in the sense of sensitivity to long-range and broad considerations, the totality of interests affected, and the utilization of expert knowledge by procedures that ensure a systematic collection and analysis of relevant facts, is more characteristic of the executive than of Congress. Despite the exceptions, and there are many, this kind of responsible behavior is more expected, more politically feasible, and more frequently practiced in the administrative branch. The bureaucracy headed by the presidency is both compelled and encouraged to respond to, and even to assist in the development of broad publics (e.g., the public for Ewing's Health Insurance Program); but broad publics seldom emanate from the organization and the geographic concentration necessary for effectiveness in the congressional committee process. The public's conception of the President as national leader creates an expectation as to his role that differs markedly from any stereotype of Congress or Congressman. This general conception of the presidency not only imposes itself on the incumbent of the office, enforcing a degree of responsibility for playing a national part, but also provides the political means for its performance by organizing a nationwide public. As one President has remarked, the presidency is the best pulpit in the land. It has a nation for its congregation. But what is important here is the expectation that the President should offer a national and party program which provides a degree of synthesis for the agencies of administration. Imperfectly effective as are the organs of coordination—Cabinet, Bureau of the Budget, National Security Council, inter-Departmental committees, and the rest—they are far more effective at ensuring integration than is even the well-disciplined House Appropriations Committee, with its stubbornly fragmented procedures.

[8]Appleby, *Policy and Administration,* Ch. 2.
[9]Friedrich, Ch. 1.
[10]Gaetano Mosca, *The Ruling Class,* trans. Hannah D. Kahn, ed. Arthur Livingston (New York, 1939), p. 258.

In addition to the broader constituency represented by the presidency and the national concern imposed by this office on the subordinate agencies of administration, there is another factor to account for the vital role of these agencies in supplementing congressional representation. It is simply that the shield of presidential power permits the development of the agencies of administration into institutions to mediate between the narrow and the broad interests at work in the subject matter of their concern. The presidency provides a balancing power that permits and sustains a perspective which the overwhelming concentration of narrow interests in the congressional subject matter committee makes difficult in the legislative process. Representation of consumer interests in the Bureau of Agricultural Economics, for example, depends upon presidential protection. Under this same shelter, agencies may develop organizational codes, stereotyped in public expectations, that permit the continuance of broader representation and encourage responsibility in the range and manner in which problems are considered and solutions sought.

To the modern student of government, Aristotle's characterization of an election as an oligarchical device always comes somewhat as a shock. Nonetheless, its implications for representative democracy are significant. If one were to set forth in law the facts of life of the American Congress, it would appear that, to be eligible, overwhelmingly a candidate had first to be in the upper upper-income bracket or second, either personally or through his associates, to be able to command substantial sums of money.[11] Expressed as custom, such conditions are passed over save for the carping criticism of Marxists; yet if they were expressed in law, they would clearly characterize our constitution as oligarchic.

While the Jacksonian conception of the civil service as a domain for the common man was not expressly designed as a balance to the inevitably oligarchical aspects of an elected legislature, it has been influential in that direction. Accustomed as we are to the identification of election with both representation and democracy, it seems strange at first to consider that the non-elected civil service may be both more representative of the country and more democratic in its composition than the Congress.

As it operates in the civil service, the recruitment process brings into federal employment and positions of national power, persons whose previous affiliations, training, and background cause them to conceive of themselves as representing constituencies that are relatively uninfluential in Congress. These constituencies, like that of the presidency, are in the aggregate numerically very large; and in speaking for them as self-appointed, or frequently actually appointed, representatives, the bureaucrats fill in the deficiencies of the process of representation in the legislature. The importance of this representation lies not only in offsetting such defects as rural overrepresentation, the self-contained district, and other vagaries of our system of nominations that leave many without a voice, but in the qualitative representation of science, the professions, the institutions of learning, and the conscience of society as it is expressed in churches, civil liberties groups, and a host of others.

The democratic character of the civil service stems from its origin, income level, and associations. The process of selection of the civil service, its contacts, milieu, and income level after induction make the civil service as a body a better sample of the mass of the people

---

[11]Galloway, pp. 28 ff.; Young, pp. 173 ff.; F. A. Ogg and P. O. Ray, *Introduction to American Government*, 9th ed. (New York, 1948), pp. 304–305; and M. M. McKinney, "The Personnel of the Seventy-seventh Congress," AMERICAN POLITICAL SCIENCE REVIEW, Vol. 36, pp. 67–75 (Feb., 1942).

than Congress. Lacking a caste system to wall them off from their fellows, the members of this sample are likely to be more responsive to the desires and needs of the broad public than a highly selected slice whose responsiveness is enforced by a mechanism of elections that frequently places more power in the hands of campaign-backers than voters. Furthermore, it is unlikely that any overhauling of our system of representation in Congress will remove the need for supplementary representation through the bureaucracy. The working interaction of President, Congress, courts, and the administrative branch makes the constitutional system a going concern—not the legal supremacy of anyone of them.

Given the seemingly inevitable growth in the power of the bureaucracy through administrative discretion and administrative law, it is of critical importance that the bureaucracy be both representative and democratic in composition and ethos. Its internal structuring may be as important for constitutional functioning as any theoretical or practicable legislative supremacy. That wonder of modern times, the standing army possessed of a near-monopoly of force yet tamely obedient to the civil power, is a prime example of the efficacy of a balance of social forces as a means to neutralization as a political force. A similar representation of the pluralism of our society in the vitals of the bureaucracy insures its constitutional behavior and political equilibrium.

It is not by any means sure that the people think that what they want is the same as what Congress wants. In fact, there is considerable evidence that the ordinary man views Congressmen, if not Congress as an institution, with considerable skepticism. The retort that the people elected the Congress falls somewhat wide of the mark. Given the system of parties and primaries, rural over-representation, seniority rule, interest-dominated committees, and all the devices that give potent minorities a

disproportionate say, if should occasion no surprise if Congress' claim exclusively to voice what the people want be taken with reservations.[12] Skepticism of the exclusiveness of the claim, however, is no warrant for denying the vital contribution of the representative legislature to the maintenance of constitutionalism. Without it bureaucratic absolutism would be well-nigh unavoidable.

If one rejects the view that election is the *sine qua non* of representation, the bureaucracy now has a very real claim to be considered much more representative of the American people in its composition than the Congress. This is not merely the case with respect to the class structure of the country but, equally significantly, with respect to the learned groups, skills, economic interests, races, nationalities, and religions. The rich diversity that makes up the United States is better represented in its civil service than anywhere else.

While it has distressed those who see in the bureaucracy merely an efficient instrument for executing policy framed elsewhere, its persistent refusal to block the path of the common man by educational qualifications beyond the reach of the poor has made the civil service a democratic *carrière ouverte aux talentes.*

---

[12] Cf. Barnard, *op cit.* (above, n. 2), p. 1004, and James MacGregor Burns, *Congress on Trial* (New York, 1949). Hyneman is aware of these misgivings; "If there is widespread and serious doubt that Congress can make the major decisions—including the decision as to what authority the President shall have—in a way that the American people as a whole will find acceptable, then we had better get busy with the improvement of our political organization, our electoral system, and the organization of Congress so that the grounds for such doubt will be removed" (*op. cit.,* p. 217). Burns and others have pointed out the road blocks in the way of such reform. Compensation for congressional deficiencies through the presidency and bureaucracy seems the normal course of our development. Had Professor Hyneman considered the possibilities of moral restraints, as Barnard suggests, this road might not have seemed so perilous.

Like Napoleon's soldiers, the humble clerk carries a marshals' baton in his knapsack. And the open avenue of opportunity in the government has meant much in providing substance to the forms of democracy. At a time when administration has become a towering fact, the significance of our recruitment process for a democratic and representative bureaucracy over-shadows an academic preoccupation with the objective of a merely technical proficiency. One has only to consider seriously the role of bureaucracy as formulator of the bulk of the policy alternatives for legislature and political executive alike—as rule-maker-in-chief—to recognize that representativeness must be a prime consideration in the recruitment process.

It can hardly be denied that, despite the attempt to achieve it by the recruitment process, representativeness in the agencies of government is seriously inadequate.[13] The capture of commissions such as the I.C.C. by the regulated interests has often been charged, not without persuasive evidence. In his pioneering work, *Public Administration and the Public Interest,* Pendleton Herring has documented the problem. Yet however crassly one-sided an agency of government may become, few indeed will be found so completely under the dominance of a single interest as the subject matter committees of Congress. And those that are so dominated have a bad conscience not shared by their brethren on the Hill.

The Department of Agriculture is probably as clearly a clientele department as any in the United States government. Nevertheless, it compares most favorably with the Senate and House Agricultural Committee in the breadth

of its conception of the public interest. (In point of fact, the luckless Bureau of Agriculture Economics incurred congressional wrath for daring to act on the assumption that it had a responsibility to the consumer.) As mediator, moderator, and synthesizer of the raw demands of the agricultural pressure groups, the Department works to attain a feasible national farm policy in a context of political and group demands. The structure of the Department in itself insures some consideration of the many aspects of the nation's agriculture in the formation and formulation of policy alternatives. Agronomists, soil chemists, nutritionists, economists, market analysts, and a host of others organized in bureaus and divisions bring together and into focus the elements necessary for responsible decisions. The point of view of personnel trained to think of a national economy and to utilize a scientific outlook is a needed counterpoise to the immediacy of political demands and the narrowness of pressure group perspective. In addition, the very permanence of the Department and the comparative permanence of many of its personnel provide a range of vision that at least partially transcends the headlines of the moment. Of course, it is true that sometimes, as in the Forest Service, the interest of the Department seems to be a bureaucratic contemplation of its own navel. Still the Department institutionalizes, however inadequately in its bad moments, the long view and the broad look on the nation's agricultural problems. While occasional Congressmen and occasional pressure groups also may take the long view, in the main such behavior is exceptional and little reliance can be placed on it.

Responsibility is a product of responsible institutions; and with all their deficiencies—which are many indeed—the departments of administration come closer than any other organs of government to achieving responsible behavior

---

[13] A thoughtful interpretation of the whole problem of interests and the bureaucracy is contained in David B. Truman, *The Government Process* (New York, 1951), esp. Chs. 8 and 9.

by virtue of the breadth and depth of their consideration of the relevant facts and because of the representative character of their personnel.[14] As continuing organizations, they can learn from their mistakes. They can even make their mistakes meaningful. That is, they can make explicit to themselves the hypotheses on which they act and so make failure itself a source of knowledge. In however limited a form, these agencies are organized to make self-corrective behavior possible.

The difficulties of arriving at self-corrective behavior in the disorganized and heatedly partisan atmosphere of Congress are all too apparent. Legislatures such as the British Parliament have at times developed wisdom and perpetuated it in a sound tradition workably related to the problems confronting the nation. But in the absence of a disciplined party system with reasonable continuity of leadership, conditions are too anarchical in our Congress to permit that body to try to organize its experience for the production of knowledge. The conditions of political success do not encourage the cooperative corporate endeavor that characterizes our successful disciplines dedicated to the discovery of fact and the testing of hypotheses. One must hasten to admit that few agency heads willingly admit failure and search for its causes. The extraordinary but explicable overestimate of the magnitude of reconversion unemployment by the O.W.M.R. after World War II was regarded less as an opportunity and a first-rate challenge to reëxamine some fundamental economic thinking than as a botch to be dealt with by the palliative arts of propaganda. Even the eminently sane strategic bombing survey was frequently imperiled by an expediential urge to color the facts. Nonetheless, for the Air Force to undertake a strategic bombing survey at all is an encouraging instance of the recognition of the need of self-corrective behavior. Similarly, the State Department may undertake a review of China policy not simply to provide a brief for the defense but to examine the causes of past failure and to extract the lessons that may lead to future success. Given the current situation, such a review is beyond the capacity of Congress to undertake. In addition to the anarchic conditions already noted, a major reason for this lies in a phenomenon pointed out by Roland Young: the members of Congress, majority as well as minority, do not identify themselves with administration.[15] Law in action is administration—and it is the work of the bureaucrats from whom and from whose works Congressmen instinctively dissociate themselves. Policy in practice thus is never the responsibility of Congress. The "foul up" is always the fault of the Administration, and Congress is well-nigh in the position of the British King who can do no wrong. Yet the penalty for the failure to accept responsibility for the test of legislation in administration is blindness to the possible lessons of experience. It may be that if government is ever to learn from its experience, the learning process will in large measure depend on the functioning of the bureaucracy.

Through the breadth of the interests represented in its composition, the bureaucracy provides a significant constitutionalizing element of pluralism in our government. Through its structure, permanence, and processes, it provides a medium in which the conditions requisite for the national interpretation of experience can develop. Thus it has a substantial part to play in the working constitution as representative organ and as source of rationality.

[14]Cf. George A. Graham, "Essentials of Responsibility," in F. M. Marx (ed.), *Elements of Public Administration* (New York, 1946).

[15]Young, Ch. 1.

Returning now to Aristotle's suggestive analysis of the real components of a constitution, it is interesting to consider the ethical constitution of the bureaucracy. What is the prevailing ethos of the leading elements in the bureaucracy and how does it compare with those of the other branches of government, notably that of Congress? A detailed analysis of working attitudes towards the rule of law, civil liberties, and due process would be illuminating. A powerful case might well be made that in practice the bureaucracy shows far more concern and respect for each of these constitutional fundamentals than does the Congress. Certainly no agency shows such blatant disregard for due process as is customary with congressional committees, while the entire body's acquiescence in the abuse of congressional immunity bespeaks a disregard for constitutional safeguards that goes beyond committee excesses.

It was the bureaucracy, acting through the Department of Justice, that drafted Truman's unsuccessful veto of the McCarran Act, despite the potentially great power which the administration of this act could place in the hands of reputedly power-hungry bureaucrats. And if the executive branch has a sorry record on a loyalty program whose procedures give less opportunity to the accused than to a common felon, the explanation lies in a pusillanimous attitude to Congress rather than in a lack of scruples. One may search the records of Congress for a wigging administered to the F. B. I. similar to that frequently administered to the Home Office by the British Parliament. It is the nation's good fortune in having a man of the character of J. Edgar Hoover heading the F. B. I. rather than careful congressional scrutiny that has thus far secured us from the danger inherent in a national police.

Clearly the difference in ethos in the congressional and administrative branches of the government is not due to any mysterious vice in the one or virtue in the other. The difference must relate to the backgrounds and education of the personnel recruited for each and the seemingly wide difference in what constitutes successful practice in each as well as to the forces that bear upon them. Both branches are products of the effective political sentiments bearing upon them; they are rivals in political competence, varying according to their respective patterns of representativeness and responsibility. (For example, criticism of law schools and law reviews wrings the withers of no Congressman; it does have effect upon the bureaucracy and the courts.) Altogether, the climate of influential opionion is different, and the working of the group structure through the relevant institutions of selection and election produces a different result.

Given the views and composition of Congress, it is a fortunate fact of our working constitution that it is complemented by a bureaucracy indoctrinated with the fundamental ideals of constitutionalism. This varied group, rooted in the diversity of the country, can be counted on to provide important representation for its pluralism. In a real and important sense, it provides a constitutional check on both legislature and executive.

It is no neutral instrument like the German bureaucracy, available to Nazi and democrat alike, pleading its orders from *"die höhe Tiere"* as an excuse for criminal acts. Be it noted that this plea of duty to carry out orders neutrally met short shrift at Nuremberg. Facing the facts should lead to some interesting changes in the theory of the desirability of administrative neutrality. It is the balance of social forces in the bureaucracy that enables it both to perform an important part in the process of representation and to serve as a needed addition to a functioning division of power in government. Were the administrative branch ever to become a neutral instrument, it would, as a compact and homogeneous power group, either set up shop on its own account or provide the weapon for some other group bent on subverting the constitution.

A candid review of the causes leading to the overthrow of constitutional governments in recent years will show few, if any, examples where prime responsibility can be placed on the bureaucracy. With the exception of the military in Spain and South America, one must look elsewhere. Indeed, the very weakness of bureaucracies incapable of maintaining order has been a major chink in the constitutional armor; but anarchical legislatures incompetent to govern, accompanied by the rise of totalitarian political parties, have been the political causes of the debacle of constitutionalism. It is high time that the administrative branch is recognized as an actual and potentially great addition to the forces of constitutionalism. The advice of the devotees of Locke would make it a neutral instrument, a gun for hire by any party. Fortunately, such advice cannot be taken. Far better would be to recognize that, by appropriate recruitment, structure, and processes, the bureaucracy can be made a vital part of a functioning constitutional democracy, filling out the deficiencies of the Congress and the political executive. The theory of our constitution needs to recognize and understand the working and the potential of our great fourth branch of government, taking a righful place beside President, Congress, and Courts.

7. Congress and the Administrative State

Lawrence C. Dodd and Richard L. Schott

A distinguishing feature of political life in twentieth century America has been the spectacular growth of the functions and services provided by our national government. Along with this growth has come the creation of a federal bureaucracy of great size, scope, and power— an "administrative state" composed of a multitude of federal departments, agencies, boards, and commissions. Few areas of our daily lives go untouched by a national bureaucracy that delivers our mail, regulates our drugs, our industry, and commerce; provides food stamps to the hungry and relief payments to the

SOURCE: "Congress and the Administrative State" by Lawrence Dodd and Richard Schott, *Congress and the Administrative State,* Introduction (New York: Wiley, 1979). Reprinted by permission of the authors.

poor; subsidizes our education; helps ensure our national security; and also collects a part of our personal incomes to finance its activities. Due in part to the vast reservoir of information at its disposal and to its political muscle, this federal bureaucracy has emerged as a fourth branch of American national government. As such, it is engaged in struggle for control of public policy with the three branches created by the Constitution: the Congress, the executive, and the courts.

The ascendancy of this powerful and pervasive administrative state has not come by accident, nor by some deep and sinister bureaucratic conspiracy, but by the conscious choice (or series of choices) of the American people acting through their elected representatives. For it is the Congress that, in response to the needs and demands of the population, has given birth to our national administrative system. No federal department, agency, administration, or major federal program has ever been created without the express or implicit consent of Congress, nor may one be abolished without its approval.

The administrative state is, however, in many respects a prodigal child. Although born of congressional intent, it has taken on a life of its own and has matured to a point where its muscle and brawn can be turned against its creator. Over the past several decades, the federal bureaucracy has come to rival the president and the Congress, challenging both for hegemony in the national political system. Protected by civil service tenure, armed with the power to issue orders and rules that have the force of law, supported by strong clientele and interest groups, and possessing a wealth of information, knowledge, and technical expertise, it goes forth to battle its institutional rivals on equal, and sometimes superior, terms. And, though occasionally defeated, it rarely returns home repentant.

The modern federal bureaucracy is a formidable force not only in the execution of policy (its original task) but increasingly also in its formulation. Its agencies are staffed by specialists, career civil servants who have spent a lifetime immersed in the details of a particular program. Strong among their ranks are professionals and scientists whose special training has given them fresh insights into how a proposal might be improved or a new policy initiated. The expertise of these career bureaucrats, combined with the technical facilities for data collection and analysis that are at their disposal, allows them to bring to policy struggles an authority and knowledge that is difficult for members of Congress, presidents, or political appointees to match. These specialists, working through the political ap-

pointees that head their departments, or working directly with members of Congress and their staffs, can mold and constrain the legislative options open to both Congress and the president. In more cases than generally recognized, the germs of policy ideas emanating from the White House originate with these career officials.

The implementation of these policies is, among other things, a constant refinement of congressional intent as expressed in legislation. This refinement involves the formulation of rules and regulations, their application to specific programs and cases, and numerous administrative decisions interpreting their application—a translation into tangible programs of broad public policy guidelines laid down by the Congress. This process whereby law is distilled into administrative action, known as "sub-legislation," gives the bureaucracy a great deal of discretionary latitude. To the degree that an agency opposes congressional policy, this latitude can be exploited to undercut, even destroy, legislative intent. And to the degree an agency supports a policy, this latitude provides an aggressive agency the opportunity to aggrandize power by interpreting broadly its legislative mandate.

PRESIDENTS, CONGRESS, AND THE ADMINISTRATIVE STATE

The coming of age of the administrative state has not gone unnoticed by those whom it has challenged. With the growth of the bureaucracy, presidents have sought from Congress (and have been given) substantial power to coordinate and control the agencies of the executive branch. These include: (1) authorization of large-scale assistance to the president; (2) presidential power to control the bureaucracy and change executive branch structure; and (3) a relatively free hand in high level appointments. Among the mechanisms that

Congress has provided presidents is the Executive Office of the President. This powerful organization consists of a group of personal advisors, staff offices, and advisory councils (among them the Office of Management and Budget, the National Security Council, the Council of Economic Advisors) designed to supply presidents not only with intelligence about what is happening in the depths of the administration, but also with public policy options and the organizational tools to coordinate both the formulation and execution of public policy. In addition to the Executive Office, Congress has given Presidents substantial budgetary powers, including the authority to formulate a unified national budget and to oversee its administration.

To help control the bureaucracy, Congress has given occupants of the Oval Office the right—subject to congressional approval—to reorganize executive branch structure. Rolling back the high-water mark of civil service domination of federal agencies reached in the 1950s, Congress has provided presidents with a second tier of political appointees serving in responsible policymaking positions below the secretary level. And Congress has traditionally accorded presidents wide latitude in the confirmation of those individuals who a president nominates to head the various federal departments, commissions, and agencies. In granting presidents this wide range of checks and controls over the federal bureaucracy, Congress has chosen to institutionalize the presidency as a counterweight to the administrative state. The Executive Office, a key feature of the "institutionalized presidency," is, like the federal bureaucracy, a creation of Congress.

Inevitably, many of the very devices that Congress has given presidents in an effort to strengthen their hand over the bureaucracy have led as well to the strengthening of the presidency vis-à-vis

Congress, thus returning to haunt the Congress as ghosts of decisions past. For example, the authority to prepare a nation's budget carries with it the opportunity to manage the nation's pursestrings and thereby to determine programmatic priorities. The power of the purse, Madison writes in Federalist #58, provides the legislature "the most complete and effectual weapon with which any constitution can arm the immediate representatives of the people, for obtaining a redress of every grievance, and for carrying into effect every just and salutory measure." A Revolutionary War slogan captured the point a bit more succinctly: "No taxation without representation!" The power Congress has given presidents to prepare an executive budget from agency recommendations and to present it to Congress as basic policy exalts the presidency as the central budget office of our government. The president's role as chief budgetary officer undermines congressional control of the national pursestrings and limits thereby the ability of Congress to have an independent influence on public policy.

The power vis-à-vis Congress inherent in presidential formulation of the national budget is augmented by a second, presidential access to information. Information, the saying goes, is power. It provides the raw material from which to formulate, justify, and implement public policy. Through the institutional capability to collect, organize, and present information provided by the Executive Office, the president has attempted to centralize control of this resource. Moreover, presidents have moved in recent years to gain control of this information by expanded use of the claim of executive privilege and by restrictive classification of executive branch documents. This near-monopoly of information and the system of secrecy associated with it, Arthur Schlesinger, Jr., has argued, are key elements of the "imperial presidency." Restoring "constitutional comity" between Congress and the presidency and the "hope of democratic control" over policymaking, he suggests, rest at least in part on the "loosening of the executive monopoly of information."[1]

The emergence of the administrative state and numerous congressional grants of authority over it to the president have contributed to a dramatic shift in the constitutional balance of power in America. The intent of the founding fathers, as represented in the *Federalist Papers,* was to construct a representative government of limited powers, which would serve primarily to conduct foreign policy, provide for domestic tranquility and national security, and ensure the ease of commerce among separate states. Authority to act in the areas of foreign policy, national security, and interstate commerce, along with a limited number of other jurisdictional areas, was explicitly delegated to the national government, with all other powers reserved to the states or the people.

The goal of the founders was to construct a government with the ability to preserve the nation (and its existing structure of social and economic power) and to create an aura of civil liberties and democratic processes. But they also intended to limit the possibility that the national government might be used aggressively by a new majority to redirect or redistribute economic and social power. While delegating specific powers to the national government, therefore, the founders chose to separate governmental functions among three branches, the Congress, the presidency, and the courts, giving each specific checks against the others. Because the founders did not plan for (or desire) an extensive national government, they did not foresee the emergence of a large bureaucracy and thus made no provisions concern-

ing the constitutional role it would play. As an unanticipated national bureaucracy has grown, it has been drawn into the president's orbit and thereby "tilted" the balance of American politics toward the executive branch—a tilt sanctioned in congressional grants of authority.

It would be misleading, of course, to assert that the courts or Congress have been eclipsed. First, considerable tension remains between the president and the bureaucracy. This tension often enables Congress to find allies among bureaucratic agencies on certain issues. Second, Congress has developed and employed a variety of devices to help it stand guard over the conduct and behavior of administrative agencies, devices discussed extensively later. Third, the judiciary may provide a court of last resort. The Supreme Court, for example, may rule on the constitutionality of specific acts of the executive. By appeal to the courts, Congress was able to overturn the majority of attempts by the Nixon administration to impound funds appropriated by the legislature. The avenue of judicial appeal, however, is cumbersome and time-consuming. It forces the Congress into direct confrontation with the executive and heightens a struggle between institutions rather than promotes a mutual quest for consensus over national public policy.

The struggle for institutional power, and the ensuing decrease in constitutional comity, have produced a serious challenge to representative government in America. Representative government rests on the assumption that fundamental policy decisions will be made by elected representatives of the people. Within the entire executive apparatus of our national government, from the White House to the Washington agencies to the local post office, only the president and vice president are elected; all others are appointed by the president or his appointees or selected by merit system procedures. Presidents are limit-

[1]Arthur Schlesinger, Jr., *The Imperial Presidency* (Boston: Houghton Mifflin, 1973), p. 317.

ed by the 22nd Amendment to two elective terms, so that two-term presidents serve half of their tenure without the spectre of electoral accountability. In addition, the 25th Amendment provides the possibility that both a president and vice president can be installed by nonelective means: the elevations of Gerald Ford and Nelson Rockefeller are examples. There is, therefore, no set of individuals within the executive branch who necessarily derive their positions from election and who are continually subject to electoral accountability.

In our national government, Congress is the only truly elective branch. Only in the halls of Congress can citizens seeking political redress of their grievances be assured of finding government officials whose fate depends directly on the vote of the people. The historic shift in power toward the executive and away from Congress makes more serious the fact that critical policy decisions are made by administrative officials who may have never served in elective office, who are largely hidden from public view, and who gain their jobs through political appointment or technical expertise instead of direct popular mandate. As Sam Rayburn commented to Lyndon Johnson concerning President John Kennedy's cabinet appointees: "They may be every bit as intelligent as you say, but I'd feel a whole lot better about them if just one of them had run for sheriff once."[2]

STUDYING EXECUTIVE– LEGISLATIVE RELATIONS

The growth of executive power at the expense of Congress and the threat to representative government that this growth implies have received considerable scholarly attention. Most analyses,

[2]Quoted in David Halberstram, *The Best and the Brightest* (New York: Random House, 1969), p. 41.

however, tend to personalize the presidency and to treat the relationship of the executive to the legislative as if it were primarily or exclusively a relationship between president and Congress. Studies in the latter vein offer material that is often dramatic, in which the issues are clear-cut and the action exciting—as, for example, in a successful attempt by Congress to override a presidential veto—and the clash of institutions more visible. Such a perspective, however, tends to ignore the fact that the "executive" is much more than the presidency; the executive is essentially two related but often conflicting institutions: the presidency and the bureaucracy. The increased power of the executive, in short, results from not only the emergence of an imperial presidency but also the emergence of the modern administrative state.

To comprehend fully the challenge to representative government, to assess the problems and potentials facing Congress as it attempts to reassert its independent role, to understand Congress in relation to the executive and vice versa, it is necessary to investigate the relationship between Congress and the administrative state. By this we mean, however, not necessarily the relationship between an agency and a congressional committee but instead the dynamic, changing impact that each institution has on the other. It is our basic thesis that both Congress and the administrative state have a significant influence on the other's organization and function. Just as Congress created the administrative state, the rise of the administrative state influenced the emergence of the modern Congress at the turn of the century. This modern Congress has encountered significant problems in performing its constitutional role, problems that have led to recurrent and wide-ranging reforms of Congress, particularly during the 1970s. These reforms have been designed in part to give Congress better leverage over the administrative state—they are reforms that have influenced how the administrative state is organized and how it functions. . . .

POLICY FORMULATION AND SUBSYSTEM POLITICS

In approaching the study of congressional-bureaucratic relations, a first connection to examine is their *legislative* interaction in the formulation of policy. Although Congress is constitutionally the wellspring of law and legislation, it has long been recognized that in this complex modern age, it is no longer the sole source of those proposals that provide grist for the legislative mill. Indeed, the present century has witnessed the growing dependence of Congress on the stimulus and initiatives for legislation developed in the executive branch. These initiatives may come from the president as a part of his legislative program, and are transmitted to Congress with the State-of-the-Union message, the budget message, and occasional special messages concerning specific policy or program areas. The president thus helps set the legislative machine in motion, and a significant part of its yearly output of bills is a modification of such initiatives.

Yet it would be a mistake to suggest that we have moved from an era in which Congress proposed and the president disposed to one in which the reverse is true. In reality, the bureaucratic agencies, as well as the president, members of Congress, and major interest groups play significant roles in formulating and lobbying for legislation. Neither the bureaucracy, the president, nor the Congress is the sole arbiter of public policy. Nor is any one of them a monolithic entity. Power, influence, and authority in the federal government are diffused among and within the major institutions, and policy formulation reflects this pluralism. Much of the ongoing process of national policy determination actually takes place outside the glare of television klieg lights, outside the public view in small "whirlpools" or "subsystems" of government. The major actors in these isolated dramas are generally congressional subcommittees, an executive agency or bureau, and an interest group or groups that are affected by or benefit from a given policy.[3] Debates over the regulation of the fares and frills offered by the nation's airlines, for example, involve a triangle composed of the Civil Aeronautics Board (the federal regulatory agency), the House and Senate transportation (aviation) subcommittees of the respective Commerce committees, and the interest or pressure groups associated with the airline industry, chief among them the Air Transport Association.[4] It is in a subsystem such as this that much legislation in a particular policy area will be proposed, debated, drafted, and ratified.

Nearly every major program or policy of national government is at least partly formulated in one or more legislative subsystems. These subsystems, little groups of policy neighbors, are often in substantial agreement on the basic policy issues confronting them—an agreement that may not coincide with the majority views of the larger institutions of which they are a part. These subsystems tend to develop a momentum of their own, proceeding along policy lines that are mutually advantageous to the members of the subsystem until some

[3]Among the first to identify and discuss the notion of the subsystem and its implications were Arthur Maass, *Muddy Waters—The Army Engineers and the Nation's Rivers* (Cambridge: Harvard University Press, 1951) and J. Lieper Freeman, *The Political Process* (New York: Random House, 1955).

[4]A discussion of the civil aviation subsystem may be found in Emmette S. Redford, "A Case Analysis of Congressional Activity: Civil Aviation, 1957–58," *Journal of Politics* (May, 1960), pp. 228–258.

outside crisis or force challenges their existing consensus (or threatens the balance of power among them). When this happens, the traditional triangle is broken, and the arena in which policy decisions are made shifts to other competing subsystems or into the larger institutions of which the subsystem members are a part—the Congress, the presidency, the bureaucratic departments, and the public.

Much (perhaps too much) of the daily policymaking of national government takes place in or through these subsystems, an arena in which the agencies of the administrative state play a crucial role. The power of Congress or the majority of its members to control public policy and determine policy priorities depends very much on the ability of Congress to play a forceful role in subsystem politics, to control the behavior of its own members at the subsystem level, and to coordinate the decisions made in the different policy subsystems.

POLICY SURVEILLANCE AND SUBSYSTEM POLITICS

The second major relationship between Congress and the bureaucracy involves the surveillance and supervision by Congress of the execution of public policy and administration. Without the power to know how the executive branch is translating its policy directives into action, Congress cannot gauge the adequacy of policy or ascertain whether agency behavior is consistent with Congressional intent. Without the power to ensure that policies are actually implemented, the legislative power of Congress is meaningless. As Woodrow Wilson wrote in *Congressional Government*, "quite as important as legislation is vigilant oversight of administration":

It is the proper duty of a representative body to look diligently into every affair of government and to talk much about what it sees. It is meant to be the eyes and the voice, and to embody the wisdom and the will of its constituents. Unless Congress have and use every means of acquainting itself with the acts and disposition of the administrative agents of the government, the country must be helpless to learn how it is being served.[5]

In his classic book, Wilson concludes that the "argument is not only that discussed and interrogated administration is the only pure and efficient administration, but, more than that, that the only really self-governing people is that people which discusses and interrogates its administration."[6]

As with legislative interaction, much of congressional surveillance and supervision of bureaucratic action occurs largely at the subsystem level. Although Congress has attempted, through the use of Government Operations committees in both houses, to establish some kind of central mechanism for investigating bureaucratic agencies to ascertain whether they are performing their given tasks, this attempt has been less than successful. One reason—related to the distribution of power among committees—appears to be a reluctance on the part of the Government Operations committees to intrude on the domain of the other standing committees. As a result, oversight responsibilities have fallen largely to the same committees and subcommittees involved originally in drafting legislation. To a large extent, therefore, the subsystems in which policy is initially formulated and funded are also the subsystems in which the implementation of policy is debated, investigated, and assessed.

The power of Congress to ensure that

[5]Woodrow Wilson, *Congressional Government* (Gloucester, Mass: Peter Smith, 1885, 1965), p. 195.
[6]*Ibid,* p. 198.

legislative intent is carried out by the bureaucracy depends on the quality of the resources and information that the subcommittees possess and on coordination among relevant subcommittees to ensure that the president, key agencies, or interested lobbies cannot play one subcommittee off against another. It depends further on the ability of Congress as a whole to break the subsystem triangle through other mechanisms when subcommittees cannot or will not perform the desired roles of policy surveillance and supervision. The critical nature of subsystem politics means that the ability of Congress to assert its policy roles and keep executive action in bounds depends on the success of Congress in organizing and disciplining itself.

THE CENTRAL QUESTIONS

Congress must be able to surmount the barriers to representative government that the federal agencies may devise without destroying the effectiveness of the bureaucracy as an instrument of governmental administration. Congress must be able to ensure that a national majority can act to formulate policy and to ensure that it is carried out—yet it must be able to guide and constrain both the president and the bureaucracy without hamstringing either.

This challenge raises a set of fundamental questions. Can Congress oversee the executive without reducing it, and government in general, to impotence? Is the problem ultimately one of finding the appropriate mechanisms of Congressional supervision and control, or does it lie elsewhere, for example, in congressional structure or constitutional system? Can representative government, within the current system of checks and balances, allow for legislative decision-making, supervision, and control while also ensuring that legislation will in fact be implemented? How can representative democracy, within the context of our constitution, be reconciled with the existence of the administrative state? Can the people rule through the representative institutions provided in the American constitutional system without destroying the ability of the government to govern? . . .

8.   Mandates or Mandarins? Control and Discretion in the Modern Administrative State

Joel D. Aberbach and Bert A. Rockman

The development of the administrative state and the growth of political democracy constitute two of the most distinctive tendencies of modern government. The development of an advanced ad-

SOURCE: "Mandates or Mandarins? Control and Discretion in the Modern Administrative State" by Joel Aberbach and Bert Rockman, *Public Administration Review: 48* (March/April 1988). Reprinted by permission of the American Society for Public Administration.

ministrative apparatus carries with it claims to the values of continuity, professionalism, expertise, and effectiveness. The other development, that of political democracy, encompasses claims to the values of responsiveness, direction, and revitalization. Notwithstanding the desirability of each set of values, the means for meshing them in an optimal mix are hardly obvious. Even though it is widely accepted in democratic settings that the permanent administration must be accountable to constitutionally elected or delegated political overseers, the precise terms of this agreement are much more controversial.

Almost certainly, few of us come to see the struggle between political control and administrative discretion in entirely neutral terms. Typically, depending on our particular inclination, we tend to adopt perspectives that place more weight either on "political" or on "administrative" values, regardless of the importance we attach to the need for an optimal mix.

Partisans of political leadership (and these almost always include the incumbent set of leaders) are doers, not doubters. They want tools, not obstacles. To the extent that doubt exists about the willingness of career administrators to carry out faithfully the policy directions of the political leadership, career administrators are viewed by political actors as impediments rather than implements. Partisans of politics, consequently, typically look to enhance procedures for control and supervision of the permanent administrative apparatus and, when deemed necessary, to politicize it.

Partisans of the career administration, on the other hand, view it as the ballast that maintains the ship of state in unsteady seas. Its resistor-like qualities to the super-charged enthusiasms of new political leaders are seen as a virtue, not a vice—a deterrent, in fact, to longer-run damage inflicted by political leaders on themselves as well as on the organizational fabric of government. Partisans of public administration thus decry efforts to reduce the independence of career officialdom or to restrict severely administrative discretion.

The political leadership view in the modern democratic polity is one that we characterize as the "mandate" perspective. Underlying it is the logic that the elected political authorities have either a right, an obligation, or a legitimate need to pursue their goals and policy proposals and that it is essential for the operative instruments of government to be in strict compliance with these. The next step in this logic goes farther— indeed, a critical distance. The next step is that discretionary authority within the administrative apparatus can be meted out only to those who meet requisite tests of ardor for the goals and methods of the elected authorities.

The administrative view we shall characterize as the "mandarin" perspective—a term that resonates, for historical reasons, better in Europe than in the United States. The essence of this view is surely applicable to the American setting as well. It is that a professionalized bureaucracy (which came late to the United States, we should note) elevates the effectiveness of government. The "good government" inclinations of the Progressives, for example, predisposed them to what might be called a democratic mandarinate—the synergistic fusion of executive leadership from a democratically-inspired elected executive and an efficiency-inspired professional civil service. Historically in the United States, much of the modern administrative apparatus was created largely to advance the goals of proficiency and universalistic standards sought by the Progressives, and later it was used to advance the goals of social and economic reform and the development of the welfare state through the New Deal, later fortified by the Great Society. A high degree of congruence in purpose between the presidency and the career executive was once thought to exist—a truly democratic (but probably also Democratic) mandarinate was seen to be in the service of the national interest (as that largely was defined by the president).

Although no president is ever prepared to leave what he regards as truly central activities to the career executive, the broad premises of what presidents and their administrative apparatus were about appeared to be in general concordance. Well-articulated and clear-cut strategies for controlling the administrative apparatus or cutting it out of the action would await the machinations of the Nixon White House and its successors, most notably, the Reagan Administration. What the Nixon White House made clear in its operative premise about the bureaucracy was that it assumed noncompliance rather than concordance. Moreover, it conceived of the Washington bureaucracy as tending toward uncontrollable fission rather than synergistic fusion. Whatever the realities of the situation, the underlying attitudes and perceptions of the relevant actors have determined the atmosphere in which these relationships recently have developed. The self-perceived possessors of the democratic mandate worked to tighten the leash, to diminish the possibilities of noncompliant bureaucratic tactics, and wherever possible, to ensure that implementation be carried out only by trusted agents. The imperative to command has grown increasingly compelling from the perspective of the White House.

THE INTELLECTUAL JUSTIFICATION OF POLITICAL COMMAND

In the American case, however, the constitutional basis of hierarchical command is absent or, more properly, it is plural and thus potentially contradictory. In Richard Nathan's words, "it is the wonderfully animated, competitive, and open character of the American political system that distinguishes it among the democracies of the Western world."[1]

It is exactly this competitiveness—a political market system as we shall think of it—that makes the administrative apparatus a resource worth competing for in an effort to influence programmatic control over federal policy. A system of segmented power such as that exhibited in the syndrome of subgovernmental domination over programs (the triad of congressional committee or subcommittee, clientele group, and bureau) produces what economists and, in their own way, presidents see as inefficient equilibria.[2] While economic theorists might define these inefficient equilibria in the form of misallocated resources, presidents tend to define them in the form of subsystemic resistances to policy change.

In recent years, the president's side of this problem—his ability to manage the executive branch and his need to procure resources in the competitive struggle to govern—has been voiced in sophisticated ways. Richard Nathan articulates well the view that presidents not only need to, but properly ought to, "influence administrative processes in a way that enables (them) to move forward on important policy objectives."[3] Clearly, it is within the power of a presidential administration and within, broadly speaking, the norms of American politics and government to make ideological harmony an important criterion for noncareer administrative appointments. The key obviously is how the "reds" interact with the "experts," and whether the "change agents" recognize any legitimate bounds to their strategies for effecting change. Above all, the central issue is how the presidential administration in its efforts to influence administrative processes interacts with other legitimate authorities, especially Congress and the judiciary.

Nathan concludes, however, that because the American political system is dynamic and competitive, "leadership is hard to exercise. . . . Policy changes are not easy to achieve, yet are often needed. . . . [Consequently, because] American national government at high levels is not a subtle business . . . the administrative strategy of the presidency is a valid and valuable instrument of presidential leadership."[4] In other words, it is legitimate for presidents to seek to politicize the bureaucracy on behalf of their goals because presidential leadership is essential to the system. When the wheel turns, other presidents with different goals may also legitimately seek to politicize the bureaucracy to their own ends. The model is, as a former president used to say, perfectly clear. It is collectively rational for the system that presidents should command, and it is individually rational for presidents to seek to command.

In an especially sophisticated analysis, Terry Moe argues correspondingly that a system such as that described by Nathan gives a rational president few options.[5] Whether individual rationality leads to collectively rational solutions is a matter that Moe leaves open to debate. Even though Moe seems strongly to imply that presidential politicization of the bureaucracy, including the institutional presidency, is a good, his argument is couched very much in the language of individual rationality. What is a rational president to do given the logic prevailing between incentives and institutions? The answer seems to be to strive for control over everything that is not nailed down.

Whether presidential command is a good or a bad is not Moe's fundamental point. Presidents seek to assert control over what they can, he asserts, mostly because they must. The maximization of control is viewed as a systemically necessary strategy.

In the final analysis, writers as different as Lowi, Rose, Nathan, and Moe all have bought into the mandate theory. Putting other analytic problems with such a theory to one side, however, only the system of government that Rose discusses (British party government and parliamentary supremacy) has institutions that are consistent with the premises of the mandate theory.[6] In the more structurally complex American

system, Lowi has chosen the statutory instrument as the anchor.[7] This implies a kind of congressional supremacy even while it promotes both administrative and political inflexibility. Nathan and Moe, on the other hand, appear to gravitate to the opposite pole, namely that executive command is an appropriate (either desirable or simply necessary) form of politicization. Yet, the theory of organizational command and the theory that constitutionally organizes the American system of government are at odds.[8] The point is that in the United States it is not enough to talk about what politicians have a right to; one must specify *which* politicians. That being said, an even more fundamental point about the American system that follows from it is that in a system of divided authority, to say that politicians have the right to control is not the equivalent of saying that the president has the right to control. Such rights, as Neustadt once noted, are joint property rights.[9] And, as Neustadt, in essence, also saw, for such rights to be exercised, they would have to be jointly authorized.[10] It is possible, perhaps even probable, to suggest that this may be asking too much of a system of divided authority and of a system that frequently also divides this authority along partisan lines. But it also is likely that such a system requires either unusual consensus-building skills and/or exceedingly clear political signals from the electorate to alter existing equilibria. Otherwise, presidents belatedly may come to discover many adverse political effects from their efforts to monopolize a shared resource.

THE PRESIDENTIAL ROLE IN THE ADMINISTRATIVE PROCESS

More and more, however, what the White House wants of civil servants, as ex-White House aide (and not just coincidentally also ex-convict) John Ehrlichman so picturesquely put it, is the following: "When we say jump, the answer should be 'how high?'"

In recent decades, though, presidents and their entourages have come to conclude that when asked "to jump," bureaucrats are not immediately inclined to ask "how high?" but rather "to where?" For administrations bent on redefining the role of the state or just simply jamming through their definition of priorities, questions and conditionals are mere impediments. Accordingly, they conclude that it is best to cut the operating agencies out of the action as much as possible (centralization) and, when that is not possible, to cut the careerists out of the sphere of potential influence while relying on increased layers of politically faithful appointees (politicization).

The logic, as presidents are inclined to see it, is that popular sovereignty empowers them to command the apparatus of government. Even if one were to conclude that the only concrete expression that could be given to the public interest lies in the momentary will of the authorized political leadership, the fundamental flaw in this conception is that this will is not derivable from a single source. Members of Congress also lay claim to a piece of the mandate. When the political will of Congress and the president are coincident, ironically, the need for exclusivity of control over the administrative apparatus diminishes. When they are in conflict, it is likely that exclusivity of claims for control will be countered. It is certainly likely that when institutional interests clash and presumptive behavior increases, nothing in Washington will stay uncontested for long. That includes control of the administrative process.

Increasingly, it seems, presidents and political theorists find the idea of "neutral competence" impossible to describe. No one plausibly can lack interests; thus, all advice or discretionary possi-

bilities are skewed. The sentiment on behalf of politicization necessarily assumes this. Consequently, it follows that if all "parties" have interests, the concept of "neutral competence" lacks operational meaning. If that is so, then it is clear that the career executives themselves have to meet political criteria or, as a group, be buried sufficiently far from the centers of power to prevent them from exercising meaningful discretion or from being able to influence decision makers. The decline of the neutral competence ideal corresponds to the rise in Washington of the adversarial ideal—the belief that everyone has an interest that they are seeking to optimize and that all expressions of collective or public interest are only facades (even if these are internalized) for the operation of individual interest or preference. Accordingly, without presidential control of the executive, it is believed by many advocates of presidential control that the expression of those interests and preferences will be chaotic overall and unaccountable.

The case for presidential politicization of the executive boils down to these suppositions. The president is the supreme legitimate governor in the American system. And since no one possibly can be neutral, it is necessary to assure that the apparatus works unequivocally on behalf of presidential goals and needs.

COLLECTIVE RATIONALITY: CONTROL OR SYNTHESIS?

Politics provides energy and revitalization while bureaucracy brings continuity, knowledge, and stability.[11] One can exist without the other but only to the detriment of effective government. The problem for government and, in our view, the public interest is not to have one of these values completely dominate the other, but to provide a creative dialogue or synthesis between the two.

In recent times the dialogue has turned into monologue as deinstitutionalization and centristic command have grown apace.

Each president in recent times has begun office with the supposition that the government has no organic past. At each turn, the wheel is to be reinvented anew. At their core, arguments for furthering the process of politicization and centristic command also conclude that leadership is equivalent to the introduction of novelty and that institutionalization is an obstacle to both.

Since politicians are constitutionally empowered to direct government, there can be no argument that the administrative apparatus, other things being equal, must be responsive to the political leadership. The question is what that responsiveness may mean and what, therefore, is the responsibility of the senior civil servant. We quote here from our earlier studies the reaction of a German civil servant to this problem:

> We are not here to receive orders, mentally to click our heels, and to say "Jawohl!"—that's not why we are here. On the contrary, if (senior civil servants) have a different conception (of the problem)—and they should always have a political conception—they must under certain circumstances use their conception in conjunction with their expertise and simply say, "But I would propose thus and such for this reason." And if the minister says, "No, politically we can't do that on account of these reasons," then all right, it already will be done as proposed (by the minister). It must be this way, because the minister is the responsible official, who must have the last word. That can't be avoided.[12]

Even though senior career executives in the United States are more likely to be talking to assistant secretaries instead of the ministerial equivalents of their departments, it is not difficult to imagine discussions of the sort exemplified in the quote taking place much of the time.

Although a good many claims have been made about the recalcitrance of career civil servants to follow the policy and program course that a presidential administration is embarking on, little evidence supports these assertions when effective administrative leadership is brought to bear. Good management, as reflected in open channels of communication, willingness to listen to advice, clear articulation of goals, and mutual respect, in fact, may also constitute good politics for department secretaries or their assistant secretaries. No evidence shows that good management is incompatible with effective politics unless the imposition of stringent command procedures is regarded as an integral part of a presidential administration's political style. The antibureaucratic styles of recent administrations suggest that this symbolic component has become at least as important as achieving results.

Responsive competence from the executive apparatus is a legitimate request of presidents up to the limits we have described. No one seriously would argue that the administrative mandarinate should be unaccountable. So, the issue is what can, and should, presidents try to control. That, it turns out, is a matter that presidential administrations often must settle internally amongst their own appointees. Even more, it is a matter that presidential administrations must define in the context of other institutions that the American system constitutes as authoritative principals. Thus, it turns out that the real issue often is not politics versus neutral competence but clarifying the principals (and their underlying principles) in the principal-agent relationship. Politicization and centralization are appropriate presidential responses in efforts to define the terms of the relationship—to a degree. Beyond that unspecifiable point, however, strategies for achieving presidential responsiveness turn into tactics for exclusive presidential rule. Efforts to achieve that level of aggrandizement are ruinous for governance in the American system; that is, they are collectively irrational. They also are ultimately ruinous for presidents whose political well-being probably is essential for effective governance and are thus likely to be individually irrational as well.

The key issue, therefore, is not whether some degree of politicization is necessary to promote responsiveness, but rather how much. The issue is not whether responsiveness should be promoted, but rather how reflexively and to whom. The model proposed for more presidential aggrandizement, ironically, is a prescription to rob government of its capability for reality testing, and it is without doubt a model for demoralization of the career service.

INDIVIDUAL RATIONALITY: WHAT IS IN A PRESIDENT'S INTERESTS?

The argument that presidential command of the bureaucracy needs to be furthered is rooted in the value ascribed to presidential leadership and in the view that presidential goals and directions are overriding. In this view, the bureaucracy needs to be mobilized in accordance with these goals and directions. At the basis of the contention that furthering politicization of the bureaucracy is in the collective interest is the belief that presidential leadership is essential and whatever enhances it is a good.

While we believe that Terry Moe's analysis also is sympathetic to this general view, his more fundamental argument is that presidents ineluctably are driven to politicization and centralization because of the relationship between structures and incentives in the American governmental system.

As Moe asserts:

In an ideal world, presidents might pursue a variety of institutional reforms in righting the imbalance between expectations and capacity. In the real world, they readily embrace politicization and centralization because they have no attractive alternatives. The causes are systemic—they are rooted in the way the larger institutionalized system is put together.[13]

Two points are necessary to address because they represent important ambiguities in any analysis of the subject of presidential prerogatives and the use of the executive. The first is what it is that constitutes politicization and centralization. The second is the need to distinguish between the apparent incentives a president has (or more properly is inclined to see) and his interests.

The first point is especially difficult. It is impossible, we agree, to deny the need for politics or for political leadership of the administrative apparatus. However, the reverse argument, that which implicitly denies the need for deliberation, skepticism, and continuity, has become more frequent. What makes this issue so complex is not the readily agreed upon notion that the bureaucracy requires political leadership and supervision, but the problem of defining the legitimate thresholds of this. At what point, for example, should an issue be politicized in decision making?

Rather than the broad argument as to whether politicization and centralization are goods or bads, we need to specify the mechanisms and also the political conditions under which these operate. Some mechanisms are legitimate; others are not. Some may be wise; others are not.

With regard to the second point—that of presidential incentives and inter-

ests—we distinguish different conceptions of "interest." The discipline of
economics tends to define a person's interests by what one is willing to pay for.
Interest has an operative meaning.
Therefore, by this logic, how presidents
behave in a situation expresses their interest. When they behave so as to aggrandize power, that expresses their interest and reflects the structure of
incentives around them. But presidents,
like consumers, make choices with uncertain information. Put in front of a
candy counter, a child is likely to make
dietary decisions inconsistent with his
interests. When presidents come to office without having been exposed to career officials, but often only to horror
stories told about them, they too may
make decisions inconsistent with their
interests.

The fact is that presidents can get into
very deep trouble when they do end-
runs around the bureaucracy, when
command replaces deliberation, and
when White House centrism brings forth
the illusion of central control. Nixon's
fall from power was paved by the Watergate break-in, but it had as much to do
with abuses of the executive as anything
else. Even had Watergate not occurred,
but with Congress remaining in the
hands of the Democratic opposition, it is
hard to imagine that the congressional
hand would have been stayed for long.
The revelations of 1986–87 involving
the White House–NSC operation of arms
shipments to Iran and laundered funds
to the Nicaraguan contras also threatens
to erode fatally the political standing
and the policy credibility of the Reagan
presidency. Operating through the back
door and around the institutionalized
apparatus of government can lead to decisions and illegalities that are truly
presidency-threatening. It is hard to
imagine that this is in a president's interests.

One of the major functions, in short,
of the permanent apparatus is to serve

presidents by helping them avoid stupid
mistakes that threaten their political viability. The urge to command and to centralize often fails to recognize that political impulses should be subjected to
tests of sobriety. Though there are a
good many reasons to argue on behalf of
the basic idea of "neutral competence"
and against the politicization of all executive organizations, the most fundamental one that a president ought to consider is the avoidance of error and illegality
that have wracked recent presidencies.

CONCLUSION: MONOPOLY AND COMPETITION IN AMERICAN GOVERNMENT

As we read the insightful and provocative analyses of Richard Nathan and
Terry Moe about the need for more presidentialism (or, in Moe's case especially,
the needs of presidents themselves), we
are struck by how similar their and our
descriptions of the American system
are. We see, as they do, a system of intense competition for resources in the
struggles to define public policy and to
jockey for political advantage. In broad
contours, the system looks to us (two
centuries removed) as Madison hoped it
would. The competitive struggle leaves
no single institutional actor with sufficient resources to fully dominate the
system in the absence of extensive and
deep consensus.

The analyses of Nathan and Moe,
while imbued with some novel twists,
fit broadly into a long line of presiden-
tialist literature that urges reform to
make the system more compliant with
presidential objectives. The difference,
as Moe indicates, is that most of that literature is organized around nonexecu-
tive reforms whose prospects are implausible. The only significant tools
available, according to this logic, are executive ones—politicizing the bureaucracy and centralizing executive command. In essence, presidents do what

they have to do with what they have available. But the spirit of presidentialism is the motivating ideal. In the end, it is the president on whom falls the responsibility of governing.

That being the case, presidents need, in this line of analysis, to maximize their advantages in a system that endows them with too few. Maximizing advantage through the executive, in Moe's view, is a norm that has evolved because presidents increasingly have found it essential as a means of accomplishing their goals. The trouble with this norm, among other things, is that it tends to induce retaliatory behavior. When U.S. Office of Management and Budget (OMB) or presidential emissaries decide to rewrite regulations to fit their, rather than statutory, definitions of policy, Congress will retaliate when it has the political will. Because presidents have the advantage of initiative in these situations, however, they may see little to lose in pressing that advantage. But retaliatory behavior—and with it, a loss of credibility—has a good chance of being provoked.

In the short run, the system, as Moe argues, provides incentives for maximizing advantage, and since the players, especially the presidential ones, are short-term actors, it is understandable that these incentives seem compelling. Norms have evolved in the White House, particularly among Republican presidents, to politicize and centralize the executive apparatus in especially exuberant fashion. But other norms can evolve as well if, *in the long run,* ceaseless politicization and centrism are seen as having disadvantages.

Through his experiments, Robert Axelrod draws some interesting lessons about how norms of cooperation evolve. In Axelrod's model, which he calls TIT for TAT, time and the continuity of relationship are important elements.[14] Negative sanctions must be timely so that they can be linked clearly to a player's

move to defect. Thus, we can infer that using the executive in illegal ways should be met more swiftly than not with congressional or judicial retribution. A larger time horizon is necessary, however, to ensure that a benefit to improving a continuous relationship is perceived. When the marginal cost to defect is low, stemming from a failure to retaliate in a timely way, and, above all, from a belief that a relationship is noncontinuous, it is difficult for norms of reciprocity and cooperation to develop.

Of course, the extent to which Congress or the judiciary will react will depend largely on the prevailing political climate, and to the extent that there is reaction, it likely means that senior career officials will be squeezed from all sides. That is not likely to be a condition that enhances either the status or the role of career officials or the quality of governance. And the slowness of reaction under most circumstances means that presidents often learn the necessary lessons late, perhaps too late.

The incentives toward reciprocity need to be strengthened. If presidents are quickly and forcefully reminded about what they cannot as well as about what they can achieve by efforts to monopolize institutional power through command, perhaps, then, they will be more inclined to seek other means for influencing a government that they only partially head and which has an executive apparatus that is not under their exclusive control. Respect for that principle may turn out to afford presidents the best opportunity to achieve their goals without recurrent backlash. In a system such as ours, it is vital to develop norms of cooperative behavior. That, of course, is a different model of how a system structured around competition might work.

It is hard, however, to be optimistic about this. Precisely because the president and presidential appointees in the executive have such short time horizons, the norms of cooperation are difficult to develop, especially once noncooperative norms of behavior have taken hold.

This is the crux of a crucial current dilemma facing the American presidency as an institution. If presidents follow their short-term interests, they are likely to stimulate more and more restrictive congressional bonds on their behavior, thereby giving presidents incentives to engage in the types of behavior exemplified by the Iran-Contra Affair. Yet each individual president is likely to put his short term interests above the institution's interests. As in many other aspects of American politics, Congress is key here. It will ultimately determine the kind of presidency we get. It must act expeditiously when presidents arrogate for their exclusive use constitutionally shared authority. Otherwise, presidents will take as theirs what Congress by its inaction bestows.

NOTES

The authors are grateful to Paul Quirk, Terry Moe, Mark Petracca, and Michael Reagan for comments on an earlier, more extended version of this paper.

1. Richard P. Nathan, "Institutional Change Under Reagan," in John L. Palmer, ed., *Perspectives On The Reagan Years* (Washington: The Urban Institute Press, 1986), p. 121.
2. Richard Rose, "Government Against Sub-Governments: A European Perspective on Washington," in Richard Rose and Ezra N. Suleiman, eds., *Presidents and Prime Ministers* (Washington: American Enterprise Institute, 1980), pp. 284–347.
3. Nathan, "Institutional Change," p. 128.
4. Nathan, "Institutional Change," pp. 133, 132.
5. Terry Moe, "The Politicized Presidency," in John E. Chubb and Paul E. Peterson, eds., *The New Direction in American Politics* (Washington: The Brookings Institution, 1985), pp. 235–272.
6. Richard Rose, *The Problem of Party Government* (New York: The Free Press, 1974).
7. Theodore J. Lowi, *The End of Liberalism: The Second Republic of the United States,* 2d ed. (New York: W. W. Norton, 1979).
8. Bert A. Rockman, "The Modern Presidency and Theories of Accountability: Old Wine *and* Old Bottles," *Congress and the Presidency,* vol. 13 (Autumn 1986), p. 138.
9. Richard E. Neustadt, "Politicians and Bureaucrats," in David B. Truman, ed., *The Congress and America's Future* (Englewood Cliffs, NJ: Prentice-Hall, 1965), pp. 102–120.
10. Speaking of both the White House and Capitol Hill, in regard to direction of the bureaucracy, Neustadt comments (from present perspectives, ironically) that "at both ends of the Avenue, to urge awareness of joint stakes and common risks is not perhaps to ask too much of our established system." Neustadt, p. 120.
11. Joel D. Aberbach, Robert D. Putnam, and Bert A. Rockman, *Bureaucrats and Politicians in Western Democracies* (Cambridge: Harvard University Press, 1981), especially Chapter 8.
12. Aberbach *et al.,* p. 249.
13. Moe, p. 246.
14. Robert Axelrod, *The Evolution of Cooperation* (New York: Basic Books, 1984).

9.   Public Managers, Judges, and Legislators: Redefining the "New Partnership"

Rosemary O'Leary and Charles R. Wise

On September 15, 1987, United States District Court Judge Russell Clark ordered a doubling of property taxes in Kansas City, Missouri, in order to aid in the desegregation of the school system. Nine thousand Kansas Citians voiced their disapproval by paying their property taxes under protest, while others responded by staging a series of "tea parties" to complain about "taxation without representation." Two and one-half years later in the landmark decision of *Missouri* v. *Jenkins,* a majority of the U.S. Supreme Court surprised many by supporting Judge Clark's actions in part. It upheld the authority of a federal judge to order a local government to levy a tax increase in order to remedy constitutional violations, even though state laws prohibited such a tax increase.

Although the case has immense fiscal implications, the significance of *Missouri* v. *Jenkins* for public administration extends beyond its consequences for fiscal policy. It has broad implications for the increasingly important aspect of American governance embodied in the relationships between judges and public administrators—the so-called "new partnership." The thrust of this article is that *Missouri* v. *Jenkins* demonstrates that the relationship between judges and public administrators has evolved to a new level with profound effects.

THE NEW PARTNERSHIP

Judge Bazelon (1976), who coined the term "new partnership," called for

SOURCE: "Public Managers, Judges, and Legislators: Redefining the 'New Partnership'" by Rosemary O'Leary and Charles Wise, *Public Administration Review: 51* (July/August 1991). Reprinted by permission of the American Society for Public Administration.

judges and administrators to work collaboratively to assure fair implementation of public policies. The view of harmonious collaboration has not gone unchallenged. Melnick (1985), among others, held a little over a decade later that the new partnership had evolved into a cover for judicial usurpation of administrative power. The evolution of the new partnership has proceeded apace in many areas of public administration including schools, prisons and jails, and mental health facilities. An examination of *Missouri* v. *Jenkins,* however, yields the conclusion that the new partnership involves a more complex set of relationships than connoted by either simple collaboration or usurpation; rather, the case signifies a transformation of the positions of judges, administrators, and also legislators brought about by the evolution of the new partnership.

This article examines what this case implies about the evolution of judicial-administrative relations and their impact on American governance. It focuses on the consequences for the constitutional principles of separation of powers and federalism, as well as the concept of representative democracy. The consequences for management effectiveness and implications for other public organizations beyond the school setting are also examined.

Missouri v. *Jenkins* is a particularly germane case to scrutinize in order to delineate the condition of the new partnership. It not only deals with a basic issue of government, taxation and representation, but also exemplifies the types of alternative choices before both public administrators and judges as they carry out their partnership roles.

THE POSSIBLE IMPACTS
OF THE JUDICIARY

The literature is replete with works by scholars arguing about the appropriateness of judges intervening in policy and administrative disputes. With few exceptions (Monti, 1980; Wasby, 1981; Wood, 1990), the literature suggests that judges are becoming increasingly active in their oversight of administrative agencies (Frug, 1978; Melnick, 1983; Rosenbloom, 1983). Judges in many instances are no longer passive reviewers of agency actions, but are full participants, shaping litigation and its outcomes (Chayes, 1986). Although researchers have examined what happens when judges do intervene in a specific instance or two (Harris and Spiller, 1976; Wood, 1982; O'Leary, 1989), they have generally been less attentive to the impact of such intervention on the responsibilities of public managers.

Judicial involvement in the management of public institutions increasingly comes about as a result of suits filed in federal courts on the basis of alleged constitutional violations by state and local officials. These are often broad based attacks alleging systemic violations requiring comprehensive programmatic changes. Once the federal district court judge makes a finding that the condition of the service constitutes a violation of the U.S. Constitution, the judge (with the involvement of the various parties) fashions a series of mandatory program steps to remedy the effects of the violation.

As Cooper's analysis (1988) of cases involving various public services shows, the determination of who is liable for what type of constitutional violation as well as the specifications as to how the service is to be altered are much more complex than a judge contemplating and then deciding what would be fair and then imposing that solution on the parties. The remedy phase of the case can involve multiple parties including various interest groups, local administrators and elected officials, state officials, state legislators, the U.S. Justice Department, federal district court judges, and federal appellate judges. The final remedial program to be implemented is a product of a multilevel process of interaction among the participants that typically takes place over a period of years. Such "partnerships" are not short term affairs, but typically go on for years or decades.[1] The results of the remedy phase are significantly affected by the perspectives of the participants regarding their appropriate roles and responsibilities.

THE ROLES OF STATE AND
LOCAL OFFICIALS

State and local public administrators and elected officials in the process are seldom passive recipients of the program remedy that a federal judge imposes on them. Instead, they have significant choices of roles and responsibilities which, along with the decisions of the other parties, have serious implications for the public service outcomes, American governance, and public administration. Public administrators and elected officials do not necessarily play the role of the defendant in the traditional sense, resisting the challenged state of affairs. Nor does either automatically resist the changes that come with the court-imposed remedy. Either can choose to see their responsibilities as defender and/or resister if they feel important values are involved. Administrators may resist if they feel the prospective judicial intervention constitutes an inappropriate interference with their administrative responsibilities. Officials of the executive branch of government have constitutional responsibilities to "take care that the laws are faithfully executed" and to defend executive branch prerogatives against encroachment of the other branches. They also have responsibilities to represent the interests and views of their constituents. These responsibilities, of course, must be balanced with the responsibility to uphold the rights found in the U.S. and state constitutions. How executive branch officials see their role inevitably involves a judgment balancing these factors. Administrators may also resist if they believe judicial involvement will exacerbate their relationships with other important governmental actors.

Alternatively, administrators can choose the role of collaborator, either believing they can advance important constitutional values and/or obtain desirable program choices through the federal courts that they can not achieve through other administrative and political processes. Prominent among these latter are additional budgetary resources. As Diver points out:

> The interests of officials with direct operating responsibility—for example, institutional superintendents and their deputies—often overlap substantially with those of the plaintiffs. They are most likely to support demands that can be satisfied by expending more funds or hiring more personnel. Translating a grievance into a demand for resources, even when alternative remedial approaches exist, not only deflects responsibility for the institution's defects away from the operating manager but also gives him [or her] a powerful ally in his [or her] unending quest for additional funds (Diver: 1979, pp. 70–71).

Administrators and officials, however, need to focus on more than the likelihood of obtaining additional resources. As Allerton (1976), Frug (1978), Hale (1979), Horowitz (1983), and Straussman (1986) contend, litigation imports considerable loss of predictability into budgetary decisionmaking. Involvement of the courts makes calculation of the outcomes of strategies more difficult. In addition, officials should consider what

the public wants in a possibly altered public service situation. Courts may order remedies, but public reaction and support, or lack of it, will ultimately influence the effectiveness of such remedies.

Additionally, administrators need to give consideration to the effects of the remedy on relationships within the governmental system and constitutional values. For example, state and local administrators often complain about a lack of respect for federalism in national decision making, but actions they take in liability suits can have significant consequences for either supporting or undermining such values. The issue is complicated by the fact that state and local officials are not monolithic. They often represent different constituencies and have different interests. These intrastate intergovernmental differences have important impacts on the strategies taken in the course of litigation, and conflicts in positions among state and local litigants can invite the federal courts to settle the issues with the resulting effect of rearranging intergovernmental relationships. Thus, administrators and elected officials must weigh constitutional, political, and management considerations in choosing a strategy for their participation in both liability phases and remedy-crafting phases of such suits.

THE ROLE OF JUDGES

The judicial side of the equation is not monolithic either, with judges at both the trial and appellate levels in the federal court system adopting certain roles and responsibilities. It should be understood that the "sides" of the partnership are not equal. Judge Bazelon observed that the advent of the new partnership places the judiciary in the role of "senior partner," and Rosenbloom (1983) observed that this not only enables the judiciary to assert some control over public administration, but to strengthen its own power in the administrative state. As Diver put it, "among the many players in the game of reform litigation . . . there is one whose capacity to manipulate its political impact exceeds all others: the trial judge."

The trial judge's responsibilities are given effect not only in how narrowly or broadly he or she finds the liability and how widely he or she casts the net of those responsible, but also in the extensiveness of the remedy that is crafted. The doctrines of legal equity are broad, and the Supreme Court has emphasized to district court judges the use of the broad discretion afforded. "The scope of the district court's equitable powers to remedy past wrongs is broad, for breadth and flexibility are inherent in equitable remedies" (*Swann* v. *Charlotte-Mecklenburg Board of Education,* 1976, p. 15; *Milliken* v. *Bradley,* 1977, p. 281). As Cooper pointed out, the trial judge's remedy-crafting decisions are a function of the doctrinal limits constructed by the appellate courts and how the judge chooses to see and use the resulting judicial policy range.

Although the Supreme Court has stated that the doctrinal limits of equitable remedies are quite broad, in the past it has also said this does not mean they are limitless. In *Milliken* v. *Bradley* (1974), a leading desegregation case prior to the case under review here, the Supreme Court, in its first of two decisions, overturned a district court decision that would have consolidated Detroit's school system with those of its suburbs, in part because of a fear that the lower court's actions would "deprive the people of control of the schools through their elected representatives" (*Milliken* v. *Bradley* 1974, p. 717). In its second *Milliken* decision (1977), the Supreme Court upheld a modified remedy in part because the district court had not attempted "to mandate a particular method or structure of state or local financing" (*Milliken*

v. *Bradley:* 1977, p. 267). The majority said the application of "equitable principles" required the trial courts to focus upon three factors:

> [First,] the nature and scope of the constitutional violation . . . [must] be related to the *condition* alleged to offend the Constitution. . . . Second, the decree must indeed be remedial in nature, that is it must be designed as nearly as possible to restore the victims of discriminatory conduct to the position they would have occupied in the absence of such conduct. . . . Third, the federal courts in devising the remedy must take into account the interests of state and local government authorities in managing their own affairs, consistent with the Constitution (*Milliken* v. *Bradley,* 1977, pp. 281–282).

These factors do not necessarily limit the district courts very much. As one analyst (Nagel: 1978, p. 713) articulated, "the judgment of what is necessary to rectify the condition that offends the Constitution requires an essentially imaginary determination of the state of affairs that would have existed but for the violation. The consequences of the violation are speculative and potentially unlimited."

All three factors still preserve considerable policy range that trial judges control. Just how considerable is vividly demonstrated in *Missouri* v. *Jenkins.* The third factor places a responsibility on state and local officials to assert their interests, as well as those of their constituents. The problem is that all of their interests will not necessarily coincide, and the federal district court judge is in the preeminent position to determine which interests will be recognized. As Diver delineates, "through selective intervention he [or she] can identify and strengthen the position of allies on whom he [or she] can depend to champion the favored remedial objectives in subsequent political games. Litigation presents the politically sensitive judge with almost limitless opportunities for political impact" (Diver: 1979, p. 79). Litigation in federal courts transforms the normal processes and limits of the U.S. federal governmental system and opens up the fundamental decision of who will have what powers among appointed and elected officials and among local, state, and federal officials. The roles of trial judges in terms of more active or more neutral determination of which parties and issues will be assigned priority will not only have effects on the policy dispute at issue, but on the wider political system in the future. If their actions seek to enlarge the judicial policy range, then the appellate courts occupy the crucial position in further definition of doctrinal limits which determines if the expansion will stand, and thus, further defines the new partnership.

THE TRIAL COURT— EXERCISING AND EXPANDING POLICY RANGE

It is important to understand the levels as well as the direction of the conflict at the initial stages of the litigation. All public officials do not necessarily see their roles or interests in the same way. In this case, the superintendent and the school board actually initiated the litigation. The case began in 1977, when the Kansas City Missouri School District (KCMSD)—a creation of the state of Missouri—sued itself. More specifically, in 1977, the KCMSD's board and superintendent, along with several students, filed suit in federal district court against several parties, including the state of Missouri, the state board of education, nineteen suburban school districts, and three federal agencies. The plaintiffs alleged that the state had failed to carry out its duty to eliminate racial segregation after the U.S. Supreme Court decision *Brown* v. *Board of Education* (1954), and initially sought a judicially mandated desegregation plan.

The judge to whom the case was assigned, Russell Clark, realigned the KCMSD as a defendant in the lawsuit and dismissed several other defendants. (This action raises the question of whether there was actually a "case or controversy" under Article III of the Constitution.) KCMSD immediately filed a cross-claim against the state of Missouri. Kalima Jenkins and other KCMSD students stepped into the picture as plaintiffs and reasserted the original complaint. Thus, the school superintendent and the school board collaborated with the plaintiff at the initiation of the lawsuit, through the phase in which liability was found, and into court-imposed efforts to remedy the violation. Throughout the lengthy trial, the defendant KCMSD worked closely with the plaintiffs in developing arguments, writing complaints, and in styling the relief requested. On June 6, 1984, to the delight of the KCMSD, Judge Clark found that the state of Missouri and the KCMSD had violated the Equal Protection Clause of the U.S. Constitution by operating a racially segregated school system. The court also held in favor of the KCMSD on its cross-claim against the state (*Jenkins* v. *Missouri,* 1984).

The district court then issued an order detailing the remedies necessary to desegregate the school district, including the finances required to implement those remedies (*Jenkins* v. *Missouri,* 1985). In the original remedial order, the judge estimated the costs to be almost $88,000,000 over three years of which he expected the state to pay $67,592,072 and KCMSD to pay $20,140,472. The judge also ordered KCMSD to do something that would prove to have a momentous impact on the case. He directed the KCMSD to prepare a study addressing the usefulness of "magnet schools" to promote desegregation (*Jenkins* v. *Missouri*, 1985). (A magnet school is one with reputedly superior teaching, as well as better and more elaborate programs and facilities in a specific area designed to "attract" students with interests in that area.)[2]

The state of Missouri appealed the judge's state allocation decision to the Eighth Circuit Court of Appeals alleging that the judge had failed to explain adequately why he had imposed most of the cost on the state. The Eighth Circuit ultimately agreed with the state on that point. During the appeal period, however, the district court's proceedings continued. In May 1986, KCMSD proposed to the court that it be ordered to operate new magnet schools. On June 16, 1986, the judge approved KCMSD's proposal to operate six magnet schools during 1986–87, and authorized $12,972,727 for magnet school operations and $12,877,330 for further capital improvements (*Jenkins* v. *Missouri,* 1986). However, perhaps as a harbinger of things to come, Judge Clark stated in his opinion his long term goal "to make available to all KCMSD students educational opportunities equal to *or greater than* those presently available in the average Kansas City Missouri Metropolitan school district" (*Jenkins* v. *Missouri:* 1986, p. 54; emphasis added). Presumably restoring those affected by the segregated school system meant that Kansas City Schools would have been superior to surrounding schools, and the court could order the district to go further than other school districts had gone.

In August 1986, KCMSD submitted its long-range magnet school plan and proposed an expansion of the magnet schools program to essentially make the whole school district a magnet schools system. In November 1986, Judge Clark adopted the KCMSD plan and ordered that every high school, every middle school, and half of the elementary schools become magnet schools by the 1991–1992 school year. Exceeding original budgetary projections, the judge authorized $142,736,025 for operations and $52,858,301 for additional capital improvements. The judge also found that the state was 75 percent at fault and KCMSD was 25 percent at fault, and ordered them to share the costs of the remedy in that proportion. He also found the state and KCMSD "jointly and severally" liable for the costs of the plan. Under the principles of joint and several liability, each of the two responsible parties pays a prescribed allocation, but each party also is obligated to pay more than its allocation or even all of the costs if the other cannot pay. On September 15, 1987, the judge boosted the amount necessary for capital improvements to $187,450,334 (*Jenkins* v. *Missouri,* 1987).

At this point, it became clear to Judge Clark that the KCMSD would lack the resources to pay for its 25 percent share of the now more expensive plan. The court confronted the fact that the Missouri Constitution (Art. X, Sec. 11[b][c]) limits local property taxes to $1.25 per $100 of assessed valuation unless a majority of the voters in the district approve a higher levy, up to $3.26 per $100. The levy may be raised above $3.26 only if two-thirds of the voters agree. Complicating the situation was another provision of the Missouri Constitution (Art. X, Sec. 22[a]) which states that no revenue increase may be obtained through increases in the assessed valuation of real property. Further exacerbating the case was Missouri's "Proposition C" (Missouri Rev. Stat. Sec. 137.073.2 [1986]) which allocates one cent of every dollar raised by the state sales tax to schools, but had the effect of diverting nearly one-half of the sales tax collected in the KCMSD to other parts of the state.

In a series of actions aimed at raising

the needed funds to carry out the school desegregation (which included the building of new state-of-the-art schools), the court ordered the KCMSD to submit to the voters a proposal for an increase in taxes (*Jenkins* v. *Missouri,* 1985, p. 45). The voters responded by defeating the proposal as they had done five times previously in 1971, 1974, 1983, 1986, and 1987. Further efforts to obtain funds from the city council and the state legislature failed.

Voters interviewed by the local paper indicated that they did not support the proposal because the KCMSD already was spending more per pupil than all but one other district on the Missouri side of the metropolitan area. Yet the KCMSD was the only one in the metropolitan area without the state's highest rating, AAA, and ranked last in scores on the state's minimum competency test (*Kansas City Star,* June 2, 1986). The Kansas City newspaper portrayed the KCMSD as "wasteful, top-heavy, and insensitive to the needs of children."

Convinced that the KCMSD had exhausted all avenues of raising revenue and chastised by an appeals court that a lack of money could not be allowed to impede the desegregation plan, Judge Clark took the unusual action of ordering the KCMSD property tax levy raised from $2.05 to $4.00 per $100 of assessed valuation. Outraged residents and the state of Missouri appealed the decision to the Eighth Circuit Court of Appeals.

The state argued to the appeals court that the facility improvements were more than was necessary to carry out the educational components of the desegregation plan and that the capital improvements plan was extravagant. The Eighth Circuit dismissed these arguments summarily noting only that "the district court found that the overall condition of the school buildings adversely affects the learning environment and continues to discourage parents who might otherwise enroll their children in

the KCMSD" (*Jenkins* v. *Missouri,* 1988, p. 1306). The appeals court was quite ready to allow the lower court judge vast policy range, dismissing for example, the state's objection that a twenty-five acre farm and a twenty-five acre wildlife area were excessive by noting that one suburban school district had a twenty-three acre museum and laboratory (*Jenkins* v. *Missouri,* 1988, p. 1306). What expenditures were necessary to remedy the constitutional violation were to be determined very much by the trial judge, the court said.

The appeals court also upheld the tax increase, but strongly cautioned Judge Clark in the future not to set the property tax rate himself. The two-judge majority cautioned that the "least intrusive" strategy would entail authorizing the KCMSD to set a "reasonable" levy increase and then to enjoin the operation of state laws preventing such a remedy. Acknowledging that the levy would have to be subject to some limitation, the majority concluded ". . . it is best to leave the appropriate limitation to the district court's discretion" (*Jenkins* v. *Missouri,* 1988, p. 1314). Thus, the district court would, in effect, act as a continuing appropriations and revenue committee, as well as a legislature for the school district.

Judge Lay, in dissent against allowing the district court to order the district to levy a tax increase, stated that the court had another alternative. Noting that the trial court had found the school district and the state jointly and severally liable, he observed that the court could have held the state liable for that portion of the costs that the district could not pay under state laws (*Jenkins* v. *Missouri,* 1988, pp. 1318–1319). This would then have left it up to the state legislature to decide whether it wanted to change the laws to allow higher school district taxes, raise state taxes, or to shift resources from other programs. The two-judge majority rejected that alternative on the grounds it "would simply prolong the controversy." Notions of separation of powers and federalism would have to give way to issues of rapidity.

The Eighth Circuit's decision was further appealed by the state of Missouri to the Supreme Court. The Court denied the state's petition for review of the scope of the remedy (the budget) and agreed to only a limited review of that part of the case dealing with the tax increase, even though the Eighth Circuit concluded that the remedies ordered by the district court went far beyond anything previously ordered by a court.[3] On April 18, 1990, the Supreme Court issued its opinion. The Court first held unanimously that the district court itself could not impose the tax directly. The opinion then went on to uphold, in a five to four vote, the authority of a federal judge to direct a local government body to levy taxes, despite state law limitations, in order to remedy a constitutional violation. Three months later, Judge Clark ordered the Kansas City school board to bypass taxpayers and raise taxes another 24 percent to $4.96 per $100 of assessed value.

IMPLICATIONS FOR CONSTITUTIONAL PRINCIPLES

Many cases involving remedies based on the Constitution involve competing constitutional principles, and *Missouri v. Jenkins* is no exception. An argument persuasively has been made by Rosenbloom and Carroll (1990) that competent public officials need to be aware of constitutional imperatives and conduct their affairs accordingly. However, the officials in the executive, legislative, and judicial branches also have to decide which of the competing constitutional principles shall have priority and how far the dominant constitutional principle should extend over the others. How the courts see the relative importance of the principles and the latitude

such principles create for district court judges profoundly affects public service outcomes and our system of governance.

Missouri v. *Jenkins* involves four competing constitutional principles: (1) equal protection (guaranteed by the Fourteenth Amendment); (2) separation of powers (implicated by Article III covering the powers of the judiciary); (3) federalism (provided for by the Tenth Amendment) and principles of state and local comity; and (4) the guarantee of a republican form of government. The primary basis for justifying the remedy is equal protection guaranteed by the Fourteenth Amendment. At this point, there can be little dispute that the children of Kansas City are guaranteed equal protection of laws in education. The guarantee of equal protection for our nation's children is no less important today than it was when *Brown* v. *Board of Education* was decided in 1954. Further, the judges themselves did not file suit in this case, nor did they create the discriminatory conditions in the KCMSD. (Indeed, the government could have avoided the entire case by not violating the Fourteenth Amendment.)

Yet, there are different ways to respond to such discriminatory practices. The decision as to how to meet the command of the Fourteenth Amendment leaves enormous discretion to district court judges. Their decisions regarding what constitutes "equal" and how to achieve such equality are subject to debate. For example, how broad in scope in terms of programmatic, budgetary, and revenue decisions is it necessary to make the remedy? How much realignment of governmental authority at state and local levels is necessary to assure the remedy? The Supreme Court majority did not delve deeply into these issues except to say that the Fourteenth Amendment was sufficient justification. Instead the Court seemed intent on erring on the side of preserving great policy range for district court judges in making all kinds of decisions pursuant to the broad mandate of the Fourteenth Amendment. As the dissent in *Missouri v. Jenkins* stated, the act of the Court's majority "seems motivated by the fear that failure to endorse judicial taxation power might in some extreme circumstance leave a court unable to remedy a constitutional violation" (*Missouri v. Jenkins,* 1990, p. 1675).

This fear seems baseless, however, given the fact that there was never a finding by any court that without the imposition of the tax, the constitutional violations would not be remedied. Nor was there a finding that the district court's plan was the only possible means for correcting the constitutional violation. If the judge or the appeals court had assigned costs that the school district could not pay under existing Missouri law to the state itself, then the issue of extending the judicial power over taxation might never have arisen. In addition, as the Supreme Court dissent pointed out, "there is no showing in the record that, faced with the revenue shortfall, the district court gave due consideration to the possibility that another remedy among the 'wide range of possibilities' would have addressed the constitutional violations without giving rise to the funding crisis" (*Missouri v. Jenkins,* 1990, pp. 1677–1678).

The unprecedented court-mandated budget increases were not even reviewed by the Supreme Court. The dissenters took the majority to task for not considering the scope of the budgetary remedy (which the district court judge said gave him no choice but to impose a tax), and stated ". . . attention to the extraordinary remedy here is the Court's duty" (*Missouri v. Jenkins:* 1990, p. 1678). There is substantial room for debate concerning whether the Fourteenth Amendment requires magnet school facilities having classrooms with:

air conditioning, an alarm system and 15 microcomputers; a 2,000-square-foot planetarium; greenhouses and vivariums, a 25-acre farm with an air-conditioned meeting room for 104 people; a model United Nations wired for language translation; broadcast capable radio and television studios with an edition and animation lab; a temperature controlled art gallery; movie editing and screening rooms; a 3,500-square-foot dust-free diesel mechanics room; 1,875-square-foot elementary school; animal rooms for use in a Zoo Project; swimming pools; and numerous other facilities (*Missouri v. Jenkins,* 1990, p. 1677).

The Supreme Court majority extended the judicial power over taxes without examining the issue of what type of programmatic and budgetary remedy would justify that step, and whether the one fashioned for Kansas City met or vastly exceeded the requirements of the Fourteenth Amendment. As the dissent put it, "if the Court takes upon itself the power to tax, respect for its own integrity demands that the power be exercised in support of true constitutional principles, not 'suburban comparability' and 'visual attractiveness'" (*Missouri v. Jenkins:* 1990, p. 1678).

There is no other power more central to the legislative function than the power to impose taxes. Nowhere in the constitutional description of judicial power in Article III is the word tax included. In addition, Alexander Hamilton (Federalist No. 78) seeking to assure that legislators had nothing to fear from the proposed Supreme Court in terms of threatening their basic prerogatives, wrote: "The judiciary . . . has no influence over either the sword or the purse, no direction either of the strength or of the wealth of the society, and can take no active resolution whatever."[4]

The Supreme Court has said many times in other cases that federal courts may not assess or levy taxes (*Moses* v. *Grant County*, 1961; *Davis* v. *Michigan*, 1989). Although a federal court, under certain circumstances, can order a public entity to levy a tax which the law authorizes (*Griffin* v. *Prince Edward County*, 1964), the Supreme Court has never before permitted the ordering of a tax which the state law explicitly does not authorize (if the state law was not found to be unconstitutional). Nowhere in *Missouri* v. *Jenkins* was the state law held to be unconstitutional. The majority did not significantly examine the separation of powers question, but simply stated ". . . a court order directing a local government body to levy its own taxes is plainly a judicial act within the power of a federal court" (*Missouri* v. *Jenkins*, 1990, p. 1665). As long as the district court judge had "reason based in the Constitution," the majority saw no separation of powers problem in his ordering a tax increase (*Missouri* v. *Jenkins*, 1990, p. 1666). With this decision, a majority of the Supreme Court left no doubt that it considers that the separation of powers principle does not apply to the federal courts' relationship to the states, and provided no limitation at all to the "new partnership."[5]

The related principle of representative democracy is likewise affected by the majority's decision. The act of the Court binds individuals, the taxpayers of Kansas City, who were not directly represented in the suit. There was no notice and therefore no opportunity to be heard, as is the case in more traditional local government taxation efforts. There was no forum for the public to discuss the balancing of demands for resources with the availability of resources. From this perspective, there was no due process.[6]

With respect to federalism, the majority quickly dismissed the state's contention that the Tenth Amendment applied, proclaiming only that the Fourteenth Amendment underlying the judge's decision overcame it (*Missouri* v. *Jenkins*, 1990, p. 1665). The majority did recognize the principle of federal/state comity, but in an ironic way. The majority claimed that the appeals court's act of striking down the district court's direct imposition of the tax and substituting an order that the local government levy the tax itself preserved federal/state comity.[7] In other words, if the district court judge does not pull the local tax lever with his or her own hand, but grasps the wrist of the local official and makes him or her pull it, federal/state comity is preserved.

In sum, the Supreme Court majority in *Missouri* v. *Jenkins* appeared to see its role as preserving as much policy range as possible for the trial courts in fashioning a remedy, and not in placing any significant limits based on other constitutional principles. As a result, the reach of district court judges under the broad prescriptions of the Fourteenth Amendment has been extended even further into other core constitutional principles.

IMPLICATIONS FOR MANAGEMENT EFFECTIVENESS

Administrators and elected officials can discern several lessons from the outcome of this litigation to date. Both programmatic gains and unanticipated consequences[8] result from managing under federal court supervision. As noted previously, a district court judge can determine what interests will be recognized and which officials will be affected. In this case, local school officials have been empowered, some charge, at the expense of the state and local taxpayers. The district itself, even though a defendant in the case, has been active behind the scenes from the very beginning, shaping the litigation and its outcomes. Superintendent Garcia, for example, has been described by the plaintiff's attorney as the "lead witness" to convince the court of the appropriateness of plans. Hence, the court decision has given power and legitimacy to the ideas of the superintendent, as well as others, that might never have been implemented. School district officials have been enabled to create new and innovative programs which many consider "cutting edge reforms." The largest enterprise has been the creation of magnet schools that specialize in areas such as computer science, the performing arts, and languages. Another program created prepares 3- and 4-year-old "at risk" children for school. Other examples include a "Parents as Teachers" program and an extended day-care program for the children of working parents.

As discussed, those officials choosing the collaborator role may be motivated by the prospect of additional resources. Additional resources are a most visible result in Kansas City. The court decision has dramatically increased the budget of the school district. The budget grew from $115 million in 1986 to $300 million in 1988—nearly a threefold increase. Moreover, the bill just for new school buildings and renovations of older buildings is expected to reach $350 million or more. Finally, the total monetary cost of implementing the desegregation plan is estimated to be $1 billion, a significant infusion of funds into the KCMSD. The resources have allowed the rebuilding of the aging, asbestos-laden, mice and roach-infested infrastructure of thirty-nine schools. They have also yielded a $68 million salary increase for district teachers and support staff. This averages to at least a 20 percent raise for every district employee. Moreover, smaller classes have been possible through the hiring of additional teachers. This has yielded a reduction in the pupil to teacher ratio.

Unanticipated consequences resulting from the court order include impacts on priorities, implementation, interorganizational relations, and accountability mechanisms. First there has been a loss of control over priority-setting by school officials. From a "macro" or school district-wide perspective, compliance with the courts' orders has become the KCMSD's top priority, at times overshadowing its educational mandate. The courts have dictated which issues get attention in the school district. The court orders are the sole components of the district's strategic plan.

Second, the court decision has been an implementation nightmare, yielding "overwhelming" budgeting, planning, and staffing problems. Simply put, the changes have been too much too soon. Deadlines have been devised and missed as the district has struggled with issues such as land acquisition, school design, and lack of staff. New deadlines have been formulated and ignored.

Moreover, while the budget grew, the staffing of the business office initially did not. Hundreds of financial transactions flooded the antiquated business office, overwhelming the staff. For example, millions of dollars of purchases budgeted for the newly renovated schools in the 1989 fiscal year were not processed before the end of the year. The court held that KCMSD could not obtain reimbursement for these purchases even though similar purchases in the future might be acceptable (Court Order, January 25, 1990). Under court guidelines, money budgeted but not spent in a fiscal year may not be recovered. Teachers have complained that the purchasing department has lost their records, and schools have opened without needed supplies.

Further, the human resources division, unequipped for its new responsibilities, has fumbled the recruiting of many new teachers. Reports of applications withdrawn because of lengthy waits, misplaced files, and letters of appointment sent two weeks after the opening of schools, were rampant. In some instances, the teachers needed to fill specialty slots have not been located. Exacerbating the situation, the human resources division has been without a permanent director for one and one-half years.

The court decisions also put pressure on and magnified deficiencies in district planning processes. For example, the scheduled opening of the Metropolitan Advanced Technical High School was delayed because officials had not anticipated vacating the school for renovations and installation of specialized equipment. While granting the delay, the court called the move a "tragic result" of "KCMSD's poor planning process." Further, the court warned that "if the proper planning does not occur, desegregation funds will not be approved" for the school (Court Order, July 5, 1989, p. 16). In another project, the officials did not plan for asbestos removal, and unanticipated costs exceeded $910,000.

Additionally, the opening of a magnet program at the King middle school was delayed by a year because KCMSD expected less than one-third of the 125 student slots to be filled. The court again criticized the district's poor planning and threatened to withhold funds, but also threatened to hold key district administrators in contempt of court "if the planning process for King . . . [was] not improved" (Court Order, July 5, 1989, p. 21). Decisionmaking under court order has often been delayed, because all major actions have had to be approved by the judge. A May 3, 1990, memo from the KCMSD superintendent to the school board, for example, indicates that the standard operating procedure has been to seek "*prior* approval . . . from the court." This has often been a slow process because of the court's busy docket.

Administrators have also lost control over numerous details of administration. When the plaintiffs and defendants filed a joint motion to request an independent study to determine the extent to which KCMSD was able to meet certain financial obligations under the de-

segregation plan, Judge Clark ordered that the study must include a complete analysis of organizational structure and an assessment of the "leadership performance of key personnel involved in organization development within the KCMSD" (Court Order, April 13, 1990, pp. 2–3). Judge Clark has also reduced architect's fees from 8 percent to 6 percent, and denied a district request for furniture because he was not supplied with information he wanted concerning its quantity and quality.

All of these implementation problems have created an immense amount of stress in the workplace, and have not led to confidence in the management capacity of the district administration or the school board. A governor's task force survey (1990) found that in terms of how it functions in eleven areas, the KCMSD board was rated below average by the administration in nine areas, very low by the faculty in nine areas, very low by the parents/residents in eight areas, and low or very low by members of the board itself in nine categories. The superintendent was seen functioning as average by the board as well as by the administration, and very low by parent/resident respondents. Several assistant superintendents, the deputy superintendent, and finally the superintendent himself, have resigned.

Third, the court decision has complicated the management of interorganizational relations leading to increased conflict. The largest source of interorganizational conflict for the KCMSD superintendent has come from the thirteen person desegregation monitoring committee (DMC), appointed by the judge to oversee all desegregation efforts and to report to the judge. The existence of this committee, which has no statutory limits, has yielded a loss of administrative power for the district's chief administrator, with the committee dissecting or "micromanaging" virtually everything the district does. For example, in the summer of 1990, the DMC had a one-hour discussion on the width of a creek on a proposed elementary school campus. The DMC has also intervened in appointments for key personnel responsible for desegregation plan implementation. A May 1990, memo from the superintendent to the school board called this particularly "problematic because . . . [the DMC members] question district actions in an area in which the administration traditionally has had wide discretion. It is unclear how the tension over personnel appointments will be resolved." The committee has also involved itself in choosing sites for the new schools, recruiting students for the magnet schools, and advertising for new teachers. The DMC repeatedly has questioned the superintendent's leadership skills, scolding him in public for not being "charismatic enough." A report issued in the fall of 1990 by the DMC concluded that the superintendent did not have the "administrative expertise to implement so ambitious a desegregation plan." When the DMC threatened to take over the administration of the school district or have the court take it over, the superintendent replied, "if they think they can do a better job, they should go ahead and do it" (*Kansas City Star,* July 10, 1990).

Fourth, the administration has been beset by numerous demands to install new accountability mechanisms. One source of challenge has been the result of the rapid influx of money which has yielded a public demanding enhanced scrutiny and accountability. Such demands have been intensified by allegations of corruption. One cab company, for example, recently admitted overcharging the district by $137,000 for transporting students, while another cab company admitted overcharging by $84,800. In October 1988, more than 6,100 Kansas City voters signed a petition calling on the state auditor to examine district records for wasteful spending or misuse of funds. The audit, which found inadequate recordkeeping, lax control systems, the existence of employee fraud, accounting irregularities, poor management practices, and no competitive bidding in certain instances, was released two years late, after most of the problems had been detected and addressed. The DMC has also demanded accountability to it and told the superintendent that its support was contingent upon his solving the accounting and financial reporting problems in ways dictated by the DMC. The state also has demanded strict separation of desegregation costs.[9] New data systems have had to be established to aid in the internal control of spending, student record keeping, purchasing, insurance tracking, and security.

THE IMPACT ON PUBLIC ADMINISTRATION

While *Missouri* v. *Jenkins* has had a great impact on the ability of the KCMSD superintendent to manage and lead the school district, it potentially could have an even more significant impact on public administration as a whole. The principles discussed in the case are not limited to its discreet factual situation, or to school desegregation cases. The majority cited 42 U.S.C. Sec. 1983 (a broad-based civil rights liability statute applicable to all state and local officials and local governments—see Wise [1989]) as providing the authority for the plaintiff's claim and the district court's exercise of its equitable powers. Justice Kennedy wrote:

There is no obvious limit to today's discussion that would prevent judicial taxation in cases involving prisons, hospitals, or other public institutions, or indeed to pay a large damages award levied against a municipality under 42 U.S.C. Sec. 1983. This assertion of judicial power in one of the most sensitive policy areas, that involving taxation, begins a process that over time could threaten fundamental alteration of the form of government our Constitution embodies (*Missouri* v. *Jenkins,* 1990, pp. 1678–79).

Any of our nation's local government entities with taxing authority may be ordered to levy taxes in excess of the limit set by state statute where there is reason based in the Constitution for not observing the statutory limitation. In 1987, there were 3,042 county, 19,200 municipal, 16,691 township, and 14,721 school district governments legally authorized to levy property taxes. In addition, 41 percent of special district governments, or 12,108 more public entities were legally authorized to levy property taxes (U.S. Dept. of Commerce, 1988). Not all of these 65,762 local governments were subject to state imposed limits, however. Nine states and the District of Columbia have no limits,[10] while the other forty-one states vary considerably in the type of local government entity limited by statute as well as the type of tax power limited (Advisory Commission on Intergovernmental Relations, 1986). Examples of potentially vulnerable functions include hospitals, airports, sewerage, water supply, fire protection, housing, and highways.

As the budgetary effects of a national policy which has shifted responsibility for programs mandated by the federal government to state and local governments becomes clearer, judicial taxation could come into play in many different instances. Groups unsuccessful in the legislature may increasingly turn to the judiciary for help. In the earlier years of public service litigation when federal grants were more plentiful, courts reduced the impact on state treasuries by directing institutional defendants into the frequently open embrace of federal grant administrators (Cavanagh and Sarat, 1980). This softened the blow to the public and diffused federalism concerns in that the federal government would help pay for what the federal courts ordered.

Given the federal fiscal situation, however, such grants are largely extinct. This brings those seeking institutional change face to face with legislatures. Public institutions could join forces with interest groups to enlist the backing of a federal court in financing policy initiatives that do not have public support. Such litigation may have less to do with constitutional rights than with intergovernmental warfare over resources. As Justice Powell stated in his concurring opinion in *Milliken* v. *Bradley,* the plaintiffs and the defendant "have now joined forces apparently for the purpose of extracting funds from the state treasury." Credence for this motivation in Kansas City is provided by the school superintendent who stated in an interview

> I think one thing that's been missed by a lot of Kansas City residents is yes the property tax has been doubled, but there is no other district—well a couple of districts in the country—where the state, all the taxpayers in the whole state, are rebuilding our capital facilities in Kansas City. It is unique. So the city is getting new school facilities and paying only about 30 percent of the cost (Rodgers, 1990).[11]

Local governments may be facing a dramatic change in the way that priorities are determined and funded. Local control and long established service priorities may be jeopardized as judges who deal with only one of hundreds of competing issues facing local governments order taxes to support a single purpose. In such situations, no one person or entity will be responsible for a total budget, yet the public will continue to demand accountability.

CONCLUSION: REASSESSING THE "NEW PARTNERSHIP"

If, as the foregoing discussion suggests, *Missouri* v. *Jenkins* yields a redefinition of the role of public managers in our local governments, then it also must bring with it a redefinition of the term "new partnership." Judges are not making changes in public services on their own. The on-going interaction among multiple parties under federal court supervision of a public service requires public managers to consider their roles and responsibilities within the litigation context. The decisions they make not only will affect the priorities for public programs, but also can bring new players into the management of public organizations, accompanied by numerous unanticipated consequences for management effectiveness. It is difficult for public managers to control or adjust these consequences because so much decisionmaking becomes susceptible to forces within the judicial decisionmaking arena.

In addition, the decisions by public managers in litigation can have profound consequences for the arrangement of governmental power, priorities among constitutional principles, and relationships with other officials and the public. The school administrators' quest for resources, quality schooling, and equal protection in Kansas City has significant implications for federalism, the separation of powers, and representative democracy. Public managers are by no means the primary agents in determining the outcomes noted above. The senior judicial partner is in the position to arrange decisionmaking power over the public service among the various parties. Local officials are very much in a junior

partner position, along with state executive officials, and other administrators of other related jurisdictions. The choice to play the collaborative role, however, may bring a rearrangement of power and priorities within state and local governments favorable to the local jurisdiction if it fits within the goals of the judicial partner. Nonetheless, local public managers need to consider the implications of how their choices can reverberate throughout the judicial system not only to affect their future management effectiveness, but the governing and management effectiveness of other state and local jurisdictions as well. For example, it is inconsistent to call for respect for the principles of federalism from the federal government for regulations considered oppressive, and then to ask the federal courts to set aside state laws and the wishes of local voters to attain programmatic goals considered desirable.

Missouri v. *Jenkins* also demonstrates the capacity of federal judges to choose their responsibilities and play their roles to determine who will have administrative, and even legislative power, at the state and local level. Once litigation begins federal district court judges are clearly in the preeminent powerbroker position. If the judge chooses to play the role expansively, there are no hard and fast limits. Rather, the regulators of judicial policy range have demonstrated that if they are likely to err in setting limits, they are disposed to err on the side of preserving an extensive range for judicial choice.

The judicial policy range for the federal courts may not be without limits, but *Missouri* v. *Jenkins* demonstrates that those limits are certainly flexible enough to permit further expansion by the district courts. Tied in with this, state legislatures have been welcomed to the new partnership with notice being served that even the core legislative power of taxation is not outside the purview of judicial decision. With the Supreme Court's decision in *Missouri* v. *Jenkins,* a redefinition of the term new partnership to include the judicial surpation of legislative functions is needed. Perhaps the term "new triumvirate" is appropriate. But it must be acknowledged that in this ruling body of three, all players are not created equal, and the formerly "least dangerous" player is now holding most of the cards. Clearly the "new triumvirate" will affect the administration of our governments for years to come.

NOTES

The authors thank Robin Lamott, Dan McNamara, and John Lindeman for their research assistance. The authors also thank three anonymous reviewers for their helpful comments on an earlier draft.

1. The U.S. Department of Justice has a list of 235 school cases which resulted in court orders involving 506 school districts. Most of these cases were decided in the late 1960s or early 1970s. Of the 506, 335 were still under court order in 1990 (House Select Committee on Kansas City Schools: 1990, p. 4).

2. A recent study (Rossell, 1990) concluded that "voluntary" magnet plans such as the Kansas City plan, characterized in part by voluntary white transfers to magnet schools placed in minority neighborhoods as well as voluntary minority transfers to white schools, produce more desegregation than mandatory magnet plans in which students are assigned to other-race schools.

3. The Eighth Circuit stated that the remedies had gone "far beyond anything previously seen in desegregation cases. The sheer immensity of the programs encompassed by the district court's order—the large number of magnet schools and the quantity of capital renovations and new construction—are concededly without parallel in any other school district in the country" (*Missouri* v. *Jenkins,* 1988, p. 1319).

4. James Madison (Federalist No. 48) wrote at the same time: "[In our system] the legislative department alone has access to the pockets of the people."

5. For the evolution of this doctrine, see Robert F. Nagel, 1978, "Separation of Powers and the Scope of Federal Equitable Remedies." *Stanford Law Review,* vol. 30, pp. 661–724.

6. As the dissent stated with respect to the nature of the court order: "It has the purpose and direct effect of extracting money from persons who have had no presence or representation in the suit. For this reason, the district court's order imposing a tax was more than an abuse of discretion, for any attempt to collect the taxes from the citizens would have been a blatant denial of due process" (*Missouri* v. *Jenkins,* 1990, p. 1671).

7. The majority stated that the difference between having the court impose the tax and ordering the local authority to do it ". . . is far more than a matter of form. Authorizing and directing local government institutions to devise and implement remedies not only protects the function of those institutions, but, to the extent possible, also places the responsibility for the solutions to the problem of segregation upon those who have themselves created the problem" (*Missouri* v. *Jenkins,* 1990, p. 1663).

8. The data upon which the conclusions of this section are based were derived from interviews with KCMSD employees and residents conducted in summer, 1990, as well

as an analysis of archival materials, KCMSD internal memos, court documents, government reports, and newspaper articles.

9. A memo (May 3, 1990) from the superintendent to the school board states, "The District thus does not have unrestricted funds from its operating budget, but should assume that operating expenditures will be scrutinized closely to determine whether they would more properly be used to repay the State or for other desegregation needs."

10. States which do not impose limits on local government tax rates or tax levies include: Connecticut, Hawaii, Maine, Maryland, New Hampshire, South Carolina, Tennessee, Vermont, and Virginia.

11. Justice Kennedy observed, "The State's complaint that this suit represents the attempt of a school district that could not obtain public support for increased spending to enlist the District Court to finance its educational policy cannot be dismissed out of hand" (*Missouri* v. *Jenkins,* 1990, p. 1676).

REFERENCES

Advisory Commission on Intergovernmental Relations, 1986. *Significant Features of Fiscal Federalism, 1985–86 Edition.* Washington, D.C.: U.S. Advisory Commission on Intergovernmental Relations.

ALLERTON, W. S., 1976. "An Administrator Responds," in V. Bradley and G. Clark, eds., *Paper Victories and Hard Realities.* Washington D.C.: Georgetown University Health Policy Center.

BAZELON, DAVID L., 1976. "The Impact of the Courts on Public Administration." *Indiana Law Journal,* vol. 52, pp. 101–110.

CAVANAGH, RALPH AND AUSTIN SARAT, 1980. "Thinking About Courts: Toward and Beyond a Jurisprudence of Judicial Competence." *Law and Society Review,* vol. 14, pp. 371–415.

CHAYES, ABRAM, 1976. "The Role of the Judge In Public Law Litigation." *Harvard Law Review,* vol. 89, p. 1281.

COOPER, PHILLIP J., 1988. *Hard Judicial Choices.* New York: Oxford University Press.

DIVER, COLIN, 1979. "The Judge as Political Powerbroker: Superintending Structural Change in Public Institutions." *Virginia Law Review,* vol. 65, pp. 43–106.

FRUG, GERALD E., 1978. "The Judicial Power of the Purse." *University of Pennsylvania Law Review,* vol. 126, pp. 715–794.

HALE, GEORGE E., 1979. "Federal Courts and the State Budgetary Process." *Administration and Society,* vol. 11, no. 3, pp. 357–368.

HARRIS, M. KAY and DUDLEY SPILLER, JR., 1976. *After Decision: Implementation of Judicial Decrees in Correctional Settings.* Washington D.C.: U.S. Government Printing Office.

HOROWITZ, DONALD L., 1983. "Decreeing Organizational Change: Judicial Supervision of Public Institutions." *Duke Law Journal,* vol. 1983, p. 1265.

House Select Committee on Kansas City Schools, January, 1990. *Report to the Speaker.* Jefferson City, Missouri: Missouri House of Representatives.

Kansas City Star, June 2, 1986.

Kansas City Star, July 10, 1990.

MELNICK, R. SHEP, 1983. *Regulation and the Courts: The Case of the Clean Air Act.* Washington, D.C.: The Brookings Institution.

MELNICK, R. SHEP, 1985. "The Politics of Partnership." *Public Administration Review,* vol. 45 (Special Issue), pp. 653–660.

Missouri Constitution, Article X, Section 11(b)(c).

Missouri Constitution, Article X, Section 22 (a).

Missouri Revenue Statute Section 137.073.2 (1986).

MONTI, DANIEL J., 1980. "Administrative Foxes in Educational Chicken Coops: An Examination of the Critique of Judicial Activism in School Desegregation Cases." *Law and Policy Quarterly,* vol. 2, no. 2, pp. 233–256.

NAGEL, ROBERT F., 1978. "Separation of Powers and the Scope of Federal Equitable Remedies." *Stanford Law Review,* vol. 30, pp. 661–724.

O'LEARY, ROSEMARY, 1989. "The Impact of Federal Court Decisions on the Policies and Administration of the U.S. Environmental Protection Agency." *Administrative Law Review.* vol. 41, no. 4, pp. 549–574.

RODGERS, BRUCE, 1990. "A Good Guy Leaving a Tough Job." *The View* (November 2) p. 9.

ROSENBLOOM, DAVID H., 1983. *Public Administration and Law.* New York: Marcel Dekker.

ROSENBLOOM, DAVID H. and JAMES CARROLL, 1990. *Toward Constitutional Competence: A Casebook for Public Administrators.* Englewood Cliffs, NJ: Prentice Hall.

ROSSELL, CHRISTINE H., 1990. *The Carrot or the Stick for School Desegregation Policy: Magnet Schools or Forced Busing.* Philadelphia: Temple University Press.

STRAUSSMAN, JEFFREY, 1986. "Courts and Public Purse Strings: Have Portraits of Budgeting Missed Something?" *Public Administration Review,* vol. 46, pp. 345–351.

U.S. Department of Commerce, 1988. *1987 Census of Governments.* Washington, D.C.: U.S. Government Printing Office.

WASBY, STEPHEN L., 1981. "Arrogation of Power or Accountability: 'Judicial Imperialism' Revisited." *Judicature,* vol. 65, no. 4, pp. 208–219.

WISE, CHARLES, 1989. "Liability of Public Officials." In James Perry, ed., *Handbook of Public Administration* San Francisco: Jossey Bass. pp. 585–601.

WOOD, ROBERT C., 1982. "Professionals at Bay: Managing Boston's Public Schools." *Journal of Policy Analysis and Management,* vol. 1, no. 4, pp. 1–15.

WOOD, ROBERT C., 1990. *Remedial Law— When Courts Become Administrators.* Amherst, MA: The University of Massachusetts Press.

COURT CASES

Brown v. *Board of Education,* 1954. 347 U.S. 483

Davis v. *Michigan Dept. of Treasury,* 1989. 109 S.Ct. 1500

Griffin v. *Prince Edward County.* 1964. 377 U.S. 218

Jenkins v. *Missouri,* 1984. 593 F. Supp. 1485

Jenkins v. *Missouri,* 1985. 639 F. Supp. 19

Jenkins v. *Missouri,* 1986. 807 F.2d 657

Jenkins v. *Missouri,* 1987. 672 F. Supp. 400

Jenkins v. *Missouri,* 1987. 838 F.2d 260

Jenkins v. *Missouri,* 1988. 855 F.2d 1295

Jenkins v. *Missouri,* 1988. 862 F.2d 677

Jenkins v. *Missouri,* 1989. 898 F.2d 65

Jenkins v. *Missouri,* 1990. 900 F.2d 1174

Jenkins v. *Missouri,* - Court Orders: January 5, 1989; April 3, 1990; January 25, 1990

Milliken v. *Bradley,* 1974. 418 U.S. 717

Milliken v. *Bradley,* 1977. 433 U.S. 267

Missouri v. *Jenkins,* 1990. 110 S.Ct. 1651

Moses Lake Homes v. *Grant County,* 1961. 365 U.S. 744

Swann v. *Charlotte-Mecklenburg Board of Education,* 1971. 402 U.S. 1

SECTION 3

Federalism and Intergovernmental Relations

Federalism and intergovernmental relations are central features of public administration in the United States. Neither is fixed or stable; rather, both are fluid. Historically, federalism has gone through several stages. At the founding, the states were viewed as the most important units for domestic policymaking and implementation. Eventually, as the industrial revolution took hold after the Civil War, this "state centered" federalism was replaced by "dual federalism" in which both the national government and states were deeply involved in domestic matters, but in separate spheres. For example, under dual federalism, the federal government played a greater role in regulating interstate commerce than ever before, but matters, such as public education, that were not administered across state lines were viewed as the domain of the states. Today, we think of federalism in terms of the *interdependence* of the states and national government. Here powers and responsibilities overlap and are often shared. For instance, the national government may issue regulations for occupational health and safety but rely on the state governments for their enforcement. The issue of whether an aspect of commerce crosses state lines is far less important than the impact of economic practices on the economy and society as a whole. The reach of the federal government extends even to regulation of the crops grown and consumed by a single farmer in a single state.[1] Similarly, federal minimum wage and hours regulations have been applied to state employees. Nowadays, a very common practice is for the federal government to establish mandates for state administrative implementation. Many state and local administrators are overseen, if not directly supervised, by federal administrators.

Interdependent federalism creates new challenges and opportunities for public administration. Constitutionally, legally, politically, economically, and administratively it is messy. Interdependence makes it impossible to compartmentalize policies and responsibilities neatly according to level of government. Practically speaking, the central issue is how will federal administrators, on the one side, and state and local administrators, on the other, work together in a host of shared areas of responsibility such as edu-

---

[1] *Wickard* v. *Filburn*, 317 U.S. 111 (1942).

cation, agriculture, employment, safety, health, housing, emergency relief, general welfare, and transportation?

The two selections in this section go a long way in helping to organize our thoughts about federalism, intergovernmental relations, and U.S. public administration. In "Federalism, Intergovernmental Relations, and Intergovernmental Management: Historical Reflections and Conceptual Comparisons," Deil S. Wright compares three contemporary ways of looking at the division of labor between the national and state governments. He notes that the units involved, authority relations, means of conflict resolution, values, politics, and leading actors involved in determining what the relationships among governmental units will be like depend on whether these relationships follow the patterns of traditional federalism, intergovernmental relations, or intergovernmental management. Notably, in Wright's analysis these three approaches coexist. Each will be more or less relevant to any particular area of policy implementation.

Martha Derthick's "American Federalism: Madison's Middle Ground in the 1980s," assesses contemporary federalism in terms of the constitutional and functional relationships between the national and state governments. Her analysis calls attention to the fiscal and juridical aspects of federalism. She concludes that although the power of the federal government vis-à-vis that of the states has grown dramatically since the founding period, the states remain vigorous and necessary in our public administration.

10. Federalism, Intergovernmental Relations, and Intergovernmental Management: Historical Reflections and Conceptual Comparisons

Deil S. Wright

History invites but it neither commands nor compels people to follow what it teaches. Similarly, history, according to La Rochefoucauld, never embraces more than a small part of reality. Two themes of choice (or selectivity) and partiality pose special challenges for this particu-

SOURCE: "Federalism, Intergovernmental Relations, and Intergovernmental Management: Historical Reflections and Conceptual Comparisons" by Deil S. Wright, *Public Administration Review:* 50 (March/April 1990). Reprinted by permission of the American Society for Public Administration.

lar article, which carves out and attempts to digest a specific slice of administrative reality as it presently exists on the American political landscape. The specific scene of the larger picture (or play) sketched here is sufficiently complex and involved, both historically and currently, that it cannot be enclosed by a single term or concept. Instead, as the lengthy title indicates, three concepts are relevant to the focus of this necessarily selective and inherently partial discussion.

To the extent that one overarching

theme does encompass this study, it is best described as an effort to review and analyze the administrative complexities of multijurisdictional relationships in the U.S. political system. The nature of these relationships have evolved over successive eras, periods, or phases.[1] Hence, the historical invitation approaches an imperative, especially in the anniversary context of this article. While history can provide the needed root(s) for contemporary understanding, without analysis and interpretation history offers little or limited fruit. Therefore, the historical reflections provided in the first part of this article subsequently give way to a systematic comparative effort. The comparisons center on the conceptual trilogy incorporated in the title: (1) federalism (FED), (2) intergovernmental relations (IGR), and (3) intergovernmental management (IGM).

THE ROOTS OF FED, IGR, AND IGM

It is common and appropriate to trace the origins and character of federalism (FED) to the framers at the Philadelphia Convention and especially to Madison and his collaborators in *The Federalist*.[2] An alternate and perhaps more appropriate origin point for an administratively oriented entry to the topic, however, is Woodrow Wilson's classic essay on administration.[3] The attention and significance that Wilson accorded FED in his oft-noted essay is regularly overlooked.[4] Two themes, (1) effectiveness and (2) administrative responsibility, were prominent in Wilson's analysis and are reflected in the following quotations.

1. Our duty is, to supply the best possible life to a *federal* organization, to systems within systems: To make town, city, county, state, and federal governments live with a like strength and an equally assured healthfulness,

keeping each unquestionably its own master and yet making all interdependent and co-operative, combining independence with mutual helpfulness. The task is great and important enough to attract the best minds.[5]

2. This interlacing of local self-government with federal self-government is quite a modern conception. . . .

The question for us is how shall our series of governments within governments be so administered that it shall always be to the interest of the public officer to serve not his superior alone but the community also with the best efforts of his talents and soberest service of his conscience?

How shall this be done alike for the local part and for the national whole?[6]

The first passage conveys Wilson's vision of a strong and healthy set of interdependent "systems" of governance. It is remarkably contemporary and could be comfortably inserted into a recent presidential speech or a report of the U.S. Advisory Commission on Intergovernmental Relations (ACIR). His phraseology also suggests that Wilson perceived (perhaps dimly) what has, since the 1930s, been called *intergovernmental relations* (IGR).

In the second excerpt Wilson makes a direct link between FED and administration through the issue of administrative responsibility. For Wilson FED was clearly linked to the question: To whom and in what way are public administrators (officials) responsible? The administrator is, according to Wilson, subject not only to the claims of his or her hierarchical (or intergovernmental) superior, but also "the community" as well. It would not be an inaccurate or inappropriate reading to substitute "the public interest" for "the community" in Wilson's text, especially given the time and context of his 1887 article. Such a substitution calls to mind the exchange a half century later (1940–1941) between Friedrich and Finer over the nature of administrative responsibility and of how a public administrator could and should serve the public interest.[7]

The Friedrich-Finer debate occurred not only in close proximity to the "new federalism" of the New Deal.[8] It also coincided with a new concept that had a significant link with a major public administration issue. IGR was the conceptual innovation; the issue was the politics-administration dichotomy.

Writing in 1939–1940, coterminous with the beginnings of American Society for Public Administration (ASPA) and *Public Administration Review (PAR)*, G. Homer Durham focused attention on "Politics and Administration in Intergovernmental Relations."[9] Durham explored how the new concept of IGR contributed to a revised theory of the politics-administration relationship. He noted that "the growing maze of relationships, legal and extralegal, within the federal system has radically altered any ancient bases-in-fact for such views as the separation of politics from administration."[10]

Durham's own words best convey his approach to blending politics and administration in an interjurisdictional context.

So what of politics and administration in intergovernmental relations? Their interlocking indicates the unreality of checks, balances, and divisions into politics *and* administration. As a guide to a "new theory of the division of powers," the idea of *administrative politics,* or the interrelations of public administrators in what appear to be increasingly more permanent offices with tenure, forms a more realistic concept. Too, with the importance of the Presidency emphasized, the political party emerges as an instrument of policy and consent in a new light. Questions of structure and function in the federal system preclude, under present boundaries and constitutional restrictions, the emergence of a more significant factor than the party in clearly defining the policy-phase of a new "administrative politics."[11] (Italics in the original.)

The emphasis and the confidence reflected in this passage are representative of the period that Newland has called the "founding years" and the "golden era" of public administration.[12] Three factors undergird Newland's claim for the era in which Durham wrote: (1) the accepted primacy of the executive, especially the President, (2) the symbiotic relationship between politics and administration as essential in government, and (3) the presence of a cohesive public administration network that produced a strong sense of community. These elements also formed a firm foundation for an emerging consensus about the character and content of IGR.

The term that Durham suggested, *administrative politics,* did not prosper, but it was clearly indicative of the search for an alternative conceptual framework to capture and characterize the major changes occurring in political, policy, and administrative relationships. The much-discussed separation of administration from politics would soon be demolished. In its place something akin to a continuum of politics-in-administration would emerge.[13]

Durham was unquestionably accurate in viewing IGR, conceptually and operationally, as contributing to the demise of the dichotomy that others subsequently confirmed.[14] Furthermore, his critique of the dichotomy and its connection to FED and IGR should not be underestimated. Dwight Waldo, for example, later (1948) noted: "There is a close similarity between the rigid politics-administration viewpoint and that philosophy of federalism that pictured state and nation moving noiselessly and without friction each in its separate sphere."[15]

Although Durham moved with the intellectual flow in attacking the politics-administration dichotomy, his analysis was not as prescient nor as predictive concerning two other variables he explicitly identified: (1) political party, and (2) professionalism (permanent tenure). Durham anticipated and projected the "importance of the (political) party" as an instrument in producing "a decentralizing of . . . power"[16] In this respect he was a precursor of more extensive developments of the party-as-decentralizer thesis by David Truman,[17] Morton Grodzins,[18] William Riker,[19] and William Buchanan.[20] Decline in party identification, party loyalty, and party efficacy are developments that have raised current questions about the relationship, if any, of the party system to centralizing and decentralizing forces. A 1986 ACIR report, calling for a strengthening and revival of political parties at the grass roots, serves as a reminder of the staying power and pertinence of the issue.[21]

Durham's oblique reference to professionalism touched on another variable whose effect he could, in the late 1930s, only partly perceive. The broad and strong centralizing effects of professionalism were not fully explored and confirmed until later. One subsequent and visible analytic exposition of the force of professionalism on interjurisdictional relations was presented by Beer in his presidential address to the American Political Science Association in 1977.[22] Beer's focus on "representational federalism," put the quietus, if one was needed, on the politics-administration dichotomy. Beer argued that new forms of influence had evolved in the United States, especially since the 1930s, and that the original federal arrangement accommodated them in a way consistent with its historical, flexible, and open-ended character.

Two contemporary structures of interest in Washington, according to Beer, are the "technocrats"[23] and the "topocrats." The former represent the "new professionalism" in national, state, and local governments. They constitute the "professional-bureaucratic complex" of functional program specialists, most easily understood as the vertical linkages forming "picket-fence federalism."[24] The "topocrats" consist of the associations of political and administrative generalists at the state and local levels—governors, state legislators, mayors, county executives, and city managers. They have mobilized on behalf of varied common concerns to make their presence and influence felt in the halls of Congress, the executive branch, and even the judiciary.

The presence of tensions between technocrats and topocrats is hardly new. It had surfaced even as Durham wrote in the late 1930s, but systematic investigation of the cleavages came later in a variety of forms and contexts.[25] The normative issue raised by the cleavage(s) should not be bypassed, however. What has been the effect of these new representational forms on other aspects of the democratic process? Have the technocrats and topocrats caused, as Beer fears, "dilutions of the popular will"? Despite corporate instead of personal representation, Beer concedes that the two entities have added significant strengths to the modern state. He wonders, however, whether "this may be at some cost to free government."[26]

The origin of IGR was closely associated with the demise of the politics-administration dichotomy. It was also connected with the rise of new forms of association and organization that have altered the channels of political representation, policy articulation, and program implementation within the American federal system. Generalist administrators, of the genre about which Harlan Cleveland has spoken so eloquently, have moved to center stage in virtually all aspects of the policy process.[27] Likewise, the managers of specific functional programs, most recently called "policy professionals," have assumed featured roles.[28]

We now turn from this historical review to the task of fitting the roles and functions of these clusters of administrative officials into a broader contextual and comparative framework. For that purpose it is useful to introduce the concept of *intergovernmental management* (IGM).

INTERGOVERNMENTAL MANAGEMENT (IGM)

The concept of federalism has two centuries of U.S. history, tradition, law, and practice behind it. The concept of IGR has a comparatively short half century of application to the American context, and it remains a term that falls somewhat short of either standardized or universal usage. By way of contrast, IGM appeared as a phrase on the public scene only recently—during the 1970s.[29] To date it seems ensconced in the esoteric vocabularies of small, specialized, and even self-interested segments of observer-practitioners of the U.S. governance processes. Among the purposes of this exposition of IGM is the aim to reduce if not remove the mist and mystery surrounding the term. A further intent is to advance the utility of the concept for both analytical and applied purposes.

Woodrow Wilson argued for and actively pursued strategic solutions to issues involving both FED and administrative responsibility.[30] Wilson's confidence in finding clear and constructive solutions to those issues may or may not have been justified, even in his day. Today, however, the complexity, variety, and seemingly intractable nature of interjurisdictional problems appears biased against major, strategic, or dramatic changes in the roles and functions of different political jurisdictions. With some exceptions, many if not most of

the intergovernmental system changes have been modest, gradual shifts that have occurred incrementally. It took near-herculean presidential political efforts in 1981-1982, for example, to produce a noteworthy impact on national-state-local relations.[31] Even then the central proposal of Ronald Reagan's New Federalism, the shifting and sorting out of functions, died aborning.[32]

The emergence of IGM as a concept was associated with three important developments. One was the management-related consequences of national-level policy activism occurring chiefly in the 1960s, but carrying over into the 1970s. A second and related factor was the difficulty in implementing numerous intergovernmental programs, a difficulty that focused prime attention on management problems. A third aspect highlighting IGM has been the gulf or gap between career personnel and political actors. These three developments, quite apart from the political and polarizing effects of "bureaucrat-bashing," have given public management and managers a deserved but not necessarily desired level of visibility.

The emergence of IGM seems indicative of the present modest, marginal, and moderate approach to the resolution of current interjurisdictional issues. Some might even argue that IGM is indicative of the minimalism and myopia prevalent in contemporary American politics, public policy, and public administration.[33] Essays and research under the IGM rubric have blossomed in the past decade, and three defining features have emerged which exemplify its limited (but noteworthy) focus. *Problem solving, coping capabilities,* and *networking* are the three most common terms used in defining IGM. Together they emphasize its implementation focus as well as the centrality of the roles of policy professionals.[34]

Robert Agranoff examined human service delivery programs in the early

1980s and defined IGM as "an emerging concept in the study of affairs between governments, reflecting the increase in public officials who work at the margins between their governments."[35] The activities that constituted IGM in a metropolitan context, according to Agranoff, "in no way lead to fundamental changes in the social structure or resolve complex problems within the metropolitan areas."[36] More broadly, Agranoff argued that the kinds of problems that IGM addresses "are not the type of fundamental solutions that eliminate major social problems nor do they lead to any substantial realignment in the federal system."[37]

The problem-solving focus and implementation emphasis of IGM have been extensively illustrated in articles, essays, and monographs. The more controversial aspects of IGM, however, call for further comment. Only a brief clarification of selected issues can be attempted here.

IGM, with its strong emphasis on the word *management,* has gained modest usage but has also generated significant controversy. Controversy arises when its use suggests a clear hierarchical ordering in the relationships among American political jurisdictions.[38] Stephen Schechter addressed this issue early in the 1980s:

The popular acceptance of intergovernmental management is not a historically discrete occurrence. The starting premise of this article is that "intergovernmental management" (as that term has developed since 1974) is best understood not as a president's pipe dream but as the completion of the twentieth century revolution in public administration first enunciated by Woodrow Wilson. For its adherents, "intergovernmental management" is more than merely compatible with federalism; it is both the natural extension and resuscitating element of the twin commitment to federalism and managerialism in a time of scarcity—both of resources and leadership.[39]

Schechter's concern was not the incompatibility of IGM with federalism "but simply that the *constitutional* relationship between the two has been largely ignored."[40] Elsewhere, Schechter sharply contrasted the different orientations of the terms:

The basic difference between federalism and managerialism, and hence the tension between them, has to do with ends and limits. The end of federalism, in the American system at least, is liberty; the end of managerialism is efficiency. In this sense, the challenge of *public* management consists largely in directing the "gospel of efficiency" to the constitutional ends of limited government.[41]

Sketched on a broader canvas, IGM might be construed as a major manifestation of two important and related organizational forces at work in U.S. political, economic, and social processes.

One of these forces has been called by a political theorist "the age of organization."[42] Major and immense social, political, and administrative organizations, with associated large powers, must be managed. These organizations, their subcomponents, and their members must be enticed, herded, or goaded into action toward some asserted goal.

A second force associated with IGM is the escalation of regulation. The rise in regulation has been traced to a dramatic decline in trust and legitimacy—diminished trust in and among public officials and plummeting legitimacy in the relations between citizens and administrative agencies. Increased litigiousness accompanies and compounds the "regulated society" and highlights the operational aspects of IGM.[43] Thousands of problems arise that must be solved by courts, by administrative appeals units and processes, or by mediation, negotiation, and bargained compromises emerging from specialized, boundary-spanning management skills.

With these issues and contexts as background, this article turns more directly to an exposition and clarification of IGM. It is a concept that captures and to some extent codifies an important dimension of contemporary policy-relevant and politically-significant administrative activity.

COMPARING FED, IGR, AND IGM

One approach to an understanding of IGM is comparative—to contrast it with the related concepts of FED and IGR. Comparisons are made on the basis of several political system features.

Table 10.1 lists six political system features in the left-hand column; the body of the table consists of brief characterizations of how these features are manifested under FED, IGR, and IGM. The system features that form the bases for comparisons are: (1) units involved, (2) authority relationships, (3) means of conflict resolution, (4) values, (5) political quotient, and (6) leading actors/participants. Space constraints limit the amount of attention that can be given to the descriptors contained in the body of the table.

System Features

1.   The types of entities or jurisdictions involved in boundary spanning interactions constitute the first system feature. For FED the primary historical focus has been on national-state relationships with considerably lesser attention devoted to interstate relations. A distinctive feature of IGR has been its extensive interjurisdictional focus. It has commonly included consideration of all possible combinations and permutations

of interaction(s) among every type of U.S. political jurisdiction.[44] A few of these are noted in the second column of Table 10.1.

IGM encompasses all of the jurisdictional interactions included under IGR. Writers, researchers, and practitioners using the IGM concept, however, have employed the term to include two extra-jurisdictional dimensions. One is the politics-in-administration continuum referenced earlier. This takes explicit account of the intrusion of politics into management and *vice versa*.[45]

A second dimension folded into the IGM concept is the mixture of public-private sector relationships. The delivery of public programs and services has increasingly involved third-party intermediaries from the nonprofit, independent, and for-profit sectors. "Contracting out" and "privatization" are two terms that capture some of the extraordinary changes in public administration activity that have been reflected in the concept of IGM.[46]

The addition of these two dimensions or continua to the formal governmental entities involved under FED and IGR adds significantly to system complexity. The added complexity reflects the reality of managing under conditions where there is no sharp demarcation of political versus administrative activities and roles. Furthermore, the involvement of private and nonprofit sector organizations in the conduct of public programs may be relevant, prominent, or even crucial for securing results. This produces a blurring or blending among the public, private, and nonprofit sectors in the conduct of public policy.

2.   Authority relations constitute a second system feature specified in Table 10.1. The pattern of power distribution varies under the three different concepts. In the case of FED, while power may be fragmented and variably clustered, it is ultimately lodged in last-resort cases in the hands of the *national*

government. In IGR the power distribution pattern is posited as less hierarchical; asymmetric relations in terms of power are common, although there may be some persistence in perceived superior-subordinate relationships. Lovell has argued that it is not surprising to find IGR circumstances in which no one is "in charge." Coordination or concerted action may occur in a variety of ways, sometimes more by accident and by informal links than by force or by central direction.[47]

The nature of authority relations in IGM is preponderantly nonhierarchical. The presence and pervasiveness of networks create the presumption of widely if not evenly shared power distribution patterns. There may be varying dependency-autonomy power patterns among specific entities in a network, but across the complete network there is no prime, single, or central source of guidance. The intraorganizational pattern of matrix management is a precedent and analog for interjurisdictional relations.[48]

3. One proposition widely accepted in organization theory is Downs's assertion about interorganizational conflict. Downs argues that every organization operates in an environment in which it is in some degree of conflict with other organizations in that environment.[49] The extensiveness of conflict in political and organizational systems mandates consideration of the means by which conflict is resolved. The particular conflict resolution mechanisms chiefly associated with FED, IGR, and IGM are specified in Table 10.1.

The constitutional base of FED and the prominence of courts as decision units specifying enforceable rules of law are generally acknowledged. Hence the courts and statutes under FED arrangements are significant vehicles of conflict resolution. The popular election of nearly 500,000 public officials in the United States makes elections another important means of conflict resolution (as well

as creation). Additionally, in many states and in most local governments, a variety of referenda elections are held to resolve specific issue conflicts.

Markets, games, and coalitions are three broad categories of structuring competition and resolving conflicts in an IGR context. The literature on IGR games is modest but noteworthy.[50] More extensively and rigorously developed in IGR is the concept of markets. Dating chiefly from the 1950s, the idea of governmental entities operating as firms in a market environment has assumed significant proportions.[51] One need not adopt one or another of the philosophical positions surrounding the public choice approach to make constructive use of a market perspective.[52] Anton has revised and extended the coalitional approach to IGR by relying on "benefits coalitions."[53]

The concepts and behavioral domains of bargaining and negotiation serve as hallmarks for IGM conflict resolution strategies. More specific mechanisms under these rubrics are mediation and dispute settlement processes. Literature on these mechanisms has expanded rapidly in the 1980s.[54]

The problem-solving thrust underlying IGM encourages, perhaps demands, movement toward agreements that involve continued or continuous subsequent interactions among parties to the conflict. This contrasts with court cases under FED which tend toward authoritative termination of interparty contacts. It also differs from markets, games, and coalitions under IGR where contacts may be distant or nonexistent and interparty relations may focus chiefly on assuring that all players abide by some set of prespecified rules.

4. The fourth system feature specified in Table 10.1 is a values component. This feature references the scope, content, and intent the user has in mind when employing one of the three concepts. For FED the value or aim, as men-

Table 10.1 Federalism, Intergovernmental Relations, and Intergovernmental Management: System Features and Illustrative Contrasts between Federalism (FED), Intergovernmental Relations (IGR), and Intergovernmental Management (IGM) (A Framework for Comparative Analysis)

System Features	FED	IGR	IGM
1. Units Involved	National-State, Interstate.	National-State-Local, State-Local, National-Local Interlocal.	IGR units plus: Politics-in-Administration Continuum, Public-Private Sector Mix.
2. Authority Relations	National Supremacy (Contingent Hierarchy).	Perceived Hierarchy (Asymmetric Orientations).	Nonhierarchy Networks (Matrix Management).
3. Means of Conflict Resolution	Laws, Courts, Elections.	Markets, Games, Coalitions.	Bargaining/Negotiation, Dispute Settlement, Coping.
4. Values	Purposes (Mission).	Perspectives (Policy-in-Administration).	Products, Program Results (Management).
5. Political Quotient(s)	High Politics (Partisanship).	Policy Making (Coordination).	Implementation (Problem Solving).
6. Lead(ing) Actors	Elected Politicians.	Administrative Generalists.	Policy Professionals.

tioned by Schechter, may be variously described as liberty, freedom, or constitutional rights. These broad but fundamental values of an ordered society are purposes fostered by FED when viewed as a set of constitutional arrangements. They were values the founding fathers sought and promoted through constitutional "rules of the game."

By way of contrast, IGM posits as an underlying value or end, the notion of achieving specific or concrete program results. Schechter referred to "efficiency" and "managerialism," not necessarily in a favorable light, as the ends or aims of IGM. Clearly, the problem-solving thrust used as one of the defining features of IGM gives the term a results-oriented bias.

For IGR, neither the specific, programmatic, results-focused bent of IGM nor the global, systemwide values of liberty and freedom of FED appear appropriate. Indeed, one reason IGR was coined in the 1930s was the lowered value content and reduced connotative character of the concept. IGR developed and appeared to gain greater usage because of its denotative nature. As a descriptive term, IGR emphasizes an understanding of the images, orientations, or perspectives of the various actors operating between and among political jurisdictions. This predominantly descriptive and analytic nature of IGR is inadequate to convey the results-focused emphasis of IGM.

5. A fifth system feature is indicated by the term "political quotient." The term is intended to convey the popular scope and public visibility of the issues covered under each concept.

The types of issues associated with FED tend to be ones that Bulpitt classified as "high politics" in the United Kingdom.[55] Illustrative of such issues in the United States are those connected with "new federalism" during the Nixon and Reagan Administrations, the "creative federalism" of the Johnson Admin-istration, and similar broad-based, politically-charged policy initiatives. The level of partisanship linked to FED issues is substantial and the locus of decision making on these issues tends to be in Washington, DC. Both the visibility level and the locus for action on these issues come from potent centripetal forces in the political (or social) system. These characteristics promote what might be called a "politics of the center."

If high- and centrally-based politics dominate FED issues, then low-level, implementation-oriented politics characterize IGM activities. Note that politics is not absent from problem-solving and implementation efforts. IGM issues, and the strategies associated with their resolution, simply contain notably lower visibility, more limited scope, and lesser political quotient(s).

IGR matters, on the other hand, are posited as having intermediate levels of politics and partisanship. Advocacy of substantive policy is present, but in a constrained and confined context. Coordination among different and multiple public policies is a valued political aim. Furthermore, IGR and IGM involve state and local (peripheral) entities in the policy process. The type of "politics" present in these arenas might be termed the politics of implementation, the politics of coordination, and the politics of central *and* peripheral participation.

Several factors should be kept in mind when reflecting on the terms and relationships summarized in Table 10.1. First, the elaboration of features identified with each of the three concepts is a matter of analytic emphasis rather than behavioral exclusiveness. The patterns present under FED, for example, are matters of degree and gradations rather than neat or sharp separations from IGR and IGM. Furthermore, the use(s) to which the schematics of Table 10.1 may be put are chiefly for heuristic purposes.

The contrasts and emphases suggested above are aimed at promoting a basic understanding of the different types of phenomena occurring in the U.S. political system. The concepts, categories, and comparisons are not advanced as elements of an explanatory or predictive model. Neither is the framework intended to be normative. Nothing is implied about the desirable or undesirable qualities of FED, IGR, or IGM.

These observations lead directly to another important contextual factor. The framework in Table 10.1 is exploratory and experimental. It is presented here to test its capability to facilitate understanding and interpretation of the broad-ranging and changing relationships in America's political-administrative system(s) over the past half century and more.

Actor Roles

It is both feasible and desirable to pursue these modest heuristic efforts one step further. Table 10.1 identifies a sixth feature for comparing FED, IGR, and IGM at the level of system characteristics—the role(s) of lead(ing) actors. Figure 10.1 uses and extends this system feature by focusing on the varied roles played by major types of actors. Three types of actors are identified by the column headings: popularly elected officials, appointed generalist administrators, and program (functional) managers (policy professionals).

These categories of actors have been identified and analyzed in interjurisdictional literature over the past three or more decades, with Beer offering the sharpest delineation between "topocrats" and "technocrats." Popularly elected officials are distinguished or separated from appointed generalists such as city/county managers, central staff, and nonprogram personnel. Both empirical and impressionistic observations suggest that different interjurisdic-

tional role patterns operate between officials in these two categories. Elected local officials, for example, tend to be the lead persons in making contacts with elected officials in other jurisdictions while appointed generalists tend to contact most often their counterparts in other entities.[56] Similarly, the programmatic professionals or functional managers tend to establish strongest interjurisdictional linkages with like-minded program people in other entities, namely, other policy professionals.[57]

The three categories of officials are cross-classified in relation to several process components associated with FED, IGR, and IGM. Under each concept in Figure 10.1 are explicit or implicit subordinate elements based in part on the elaboration of system features discussed in conjunction with Table 10.1. Thus, politics, purposes, and power are subsidiary components of FED; policy, perspectives, and priorities are components of IGR; programs, projects, and procedures are aspects of IGM.

The cells of the matrix in Figure 10.1 are occupied by symbols of varying size. The broad symbols in the upper left, for example, indicate the large and prominent roles played by elected officials in the components under FED. Likewise, the lower right sector of Figure 10.1 displays large indicators which signify the major and central role played by policy professionals (program managers) in implementation processes. The middle cells of Figure 10.1 highlight the prominence of generalist administrators in the arenas of IGR activities that involve policy, perspectives, and priorities.

The diagonal cells from upper left to lower right *might* be interpreted in a normative or prescriptive sense to be a balanced, appropriate, or "proper" role for each set of actors. Such an interpretation carries the scheme beyond its initial and intended aim. Furthermore, the presence of role extensions, breadth, or spillovers is expected and is indicated by the use of lesser-graded indicators in other cells of each vertical column. That is, elected officials are not restricted in their activities and involvement to the elements listed under FED; they also participate, in a progressively lesser manner and degree, in the elements noted under IGR and IGM. Policy professionals' roles and efforts similarly extend into the activities indicated under IGR and FED.

An added contextual comment serves to conclude this discussion of actor roles and relationships. This formula-tion has clear and acknowledged links to recent efforts by Svara and others to reconceptualize and operationalize the link(s) between politics, policy, and administration.[58] Svara, of course, focuses specifically on city managers (generalist administrators) and their relationships with city councils (elected politicians). He posits a continuum of role differenti-ations among actors in four activity are-nas—mission, policy, administration, and management. The underlying con-ceptual parallels between that frame-work and the one elaborated above should be evident. The chief contrast, of

Figure 10.1
Federalism (FED), Intergovernmental Relations (IGR), and Intergovernmental Management (IGM): Concepts, Actors, and Roles

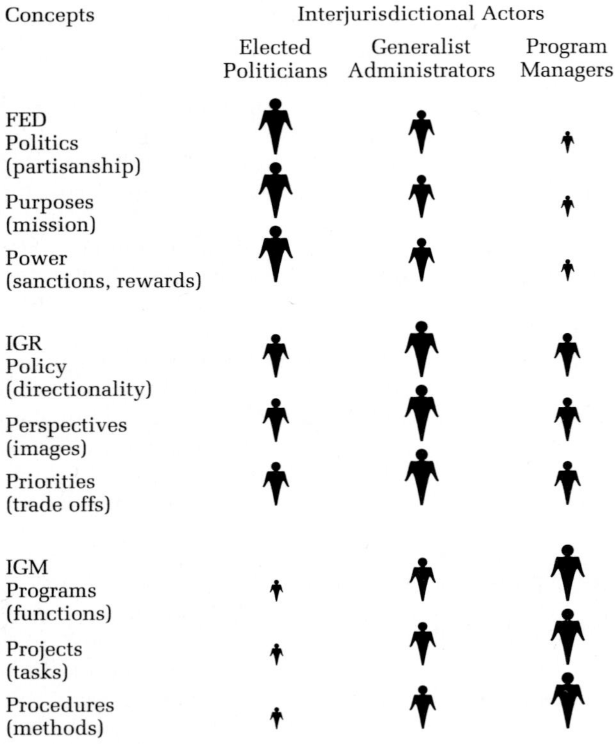

The varying size of the symbols indicates the differing degrees of role involvement.

course, is the more diverse, extended, complex, and uncertain environment of interjurisdictional relationships.

CONCLUDING OBSERVATIONS

All nations of any significant size and consequence confront one of the fundamental problems of governance. How should the competing claims of central and peripheral authority be resolved? The issue is more ancient than the kingly controversies among the 12 tribes of Israel. It is also as current as the latest round of U.S. Supreme Court decisions on state power(s) over abortion, flag burning, and school prayers.

Constitutionally, the issue is commonly framed in legal terms: Which jurisdiction has the authority to do what, with what degree of discretion or autonomy? Administratively, the "basic theoretical question" has been posed by Fesler as "How to relate area and function?"[59] Like the blending of politics and administration, the two questions overlap and are intertwined. The linkage between constitutional arrangements grounded in politics and organizational implementation matters centered around administration is a theme that permeates this article.

The historical origins and emergence of the concepts of FED, IGR, and IGM have been reviewed and sketched briefly. The evolution in usage of the terms reflects the changing patterns of influence and role relationships among and within U.S. political jurisdictions. Power and influence have become notably fragmented and dispersed among actors within a given political jurisdiction. Likewise, authority relationships assume varying shapes among and between political entities—national, state, and local governments.

Increased actor- and entity-based involvement has produced a plethora of participants in the public sector decision-making processes. The resulting complexity has made the tasks of public administration and management at once more demanding and also more difficult. Speaking about "the increasing complexity of the 'implementation structures' within which [public] managers must manage," Peters notes the "increasing degree of fusion between the public and private sectors," as well as "the degree of complexity that exists within the public sector itself."[60] The contrasting aspects of FED, IGR, and IGM typify this public sector complexity and, especially in the case of IGM, the escalated involvement of the private sector.

Greater involvement by the independent and the private sectors is probably not surprising given the scarcity and austerity problems confronting the public sector. The finite character of time, money, and other resources makes scarcity an inherent problem of political and organizational choice. But the fiscal austerity which has prevailed during the past decade has accentuated the importance of connections to other jurisdictions. In some instances the connections have increased based on cooperative ventures; in others they have intensified in a competitive mode. In addition, and especially in fiscal terms, there has been a drop in the degree of dependency on aid from external sources, particularly from the national government.

The onset and continuation of fiscal austerity, sometimes described as cutback management or decrementalism, has prompted some observers to conclude that the United States has moved toward *defacto,* state-oriented, or "fend-for-yourself" federalism.[61] The phrases refer to the relative decline in federal aid coming to state and local governments. The terms also include the rapid as well as the gradual shifts that have occurred in state-local assumption(s) of responsibilities for various functions during the past decade.

Counterposed to these devolution tendencies are movements toward greater regulation.[62] The specifics and the details of centralization through regulation cannot be provided. But the trend in this direction was expressed succinctly by Elazar. He noted that "the American federal system may be passing into a new phase" in which "federal grants no longer set the tone in intergovernmental relations"; instead it is one where "the move seems to be in the direction of new relationships in the field of government regulation."[63]

Most of this regulation emanates from congressionally-enacted and court-approved statutes, with national administrative agencies intimately and crucially involved in regulatory implementation. Within these agencies the role of program (policy) professionals has long been recognized as significant. At the same time there has been a serious question or doubt as to the disposition of the policy professionals to balance program goals with historic FED values. Ostensibly, that balance will now be struck more deliberately.

The formal foundations have been laid for the involvement of program or policy professionals in the process of shaping the future of FED, IGR, and IGM. Executive Order 12612, titled simply "Federalism," was issued on 26 October 1987.[64] This order mandated the creation of a "Federalism Assessment" process within each national executive branch department and agency. This review process requires that in the formulation and implementation of agency policies through regulations, the agency administrators and program managers take into account "fundamental federalism principles" and "federalism policy-making criteria."

The details of the order and the process it creates are beyond the scope and purpose here. It is also too early to judge the impact and consequence(s) of the order. One agency, the U.S. Department of Health and Human Services, indicated that out of 400 legislative proposals emerging annually from its policy formulation processes, about half contained federalism assessment statements.[65]

An important point should not be missed, however. Policy professionals deeply involved in specific program functions are increasingly being asked and/or required to factor their preferences and choices into a broader set of FED, IGR, and IGM value concerns. Those management-based (IGM) preferences and choices are expected to influence significantly the complex configuration of FED and IGR in the 1990s and well past the year 2000.

NOTES

1. Daniel J. Elazar. "The Shaping of Intergovernmental Relations in the Twentieth Century." *The Annals,* vol. 359 (May 1965), pp. 10–22; David B. Walker, *Toward a Functioning Federalism* (Cambridge, MA: Winthrop, 1981); Deil S. Wright, "Intergovernmental Relations: An Analytic Overview," *The Annals,* vol. 416 (November 1974), pp. 1–16.

2. Alexander Hamilton, James Madison, John Jay, *The Federalist Papers* (New York: New American Library, 1961). See also Martha Derthick, "American Federalism: Madison's Middle Ground in the 1980s," *Public Administration Review,* vol. 47 (January/February 1987), pp. 66–74.

3. Woodrow Wilson, "The Study of Administration," *Political Science Quarterly,* vol. 2 (June 1887), pp. 197–222; reprinted in Jay M. Shafritz and Albert C. Hyde, eds., *Classics of Public Administration* (Chicago: The Dorsey Press, 1987), pp. 10–25. Subsequent citations are from the reprinted source.

4. Deil S. Wright, "A Century of the Intergovernmental   Administrative

State: Wilson's Federalism, New Deal Intergovernmental Relations, and Contemporary Intergovernmental Management," in Ralph C. Chandler, ed., *A Centennial History of the American Administrative State* (New York: Macmillan, 1987), pp. 219–260.

5. Wilson, "The Study of Administration," p. 18.

6. *Ibid.,* p. 19.

7. Carl J. Friedrich, "Public Policy and the Nature of Administrative Responsibility," in Carl J. Friedrich and Edward S. Mason, eds., *Public Policy: 1940* (Cambridge, MA: Harvard University Press, 1940), pp. 3–24; Herman Finer, "Administrative Responsibility in Democratic Government," *Public Administration Review,* vol. 1 (Autumn 1941), pp. 335–350.

8. Jane Perry Clark, *The Rise of a New Federalism: Federal-State Cooperation in the United States* (New York: Columbia University Press, 1938), 347 pp.

9. G. Homer Durham, "Politics and Administration in Intergovernmental Relations," *The Annals,* vol. 207 (January 1940), pp. 1–6.

10. *Ibid.,* p. 1.

11. *Ibid.,* p. 6.

12. Chester A. Newland, *Public Administration and Community: Realism in the Practice of Ideals* (McLean, VA: Public Administration Service, 1984), 45 pp.

13. Cheryl Miller Colbert, "An Empirical Analysis of Politics-in-Administration: State Agency and State Agency Head Participation in the Policy Process" (PhD dissertation, University of North Carolina at Chapel Hill, 1983), 270 pp. Colbert locates seven instances where the politics-in-administration continuum appears. See also, James H. Svara, "Dichotomy and Duality: Reconceptualizing the Relationship Between Policy and Administration in Council Manager Cities," *Public Administration Review,* vol. 45 (January/February 1985), pp. 221–232.

14. Four representative statements on the aridity and demise of the politics-administration dichotomy are: Paul H. Appleby, *Policy and Administration* (University: University of Alabama Press, 1949), 173 pp.: Norton Long, "Power and Administration," *Public Administration Review,* vol. 9 (Autumn 1949), pp. 257–264; Wallace Sayre, "Trends in a Decade of Administrative Values," *Public Administration Review,* vol. 11 (Winter 1951), pp. 1–9; Wallace Sayre, "The Premises of Public Administration: Past and Emerging," *Public Administration Review,* vol. 18 (Spring 1958), pp. 102–105.

15. Dwight Waldo, *The Administrative State: A Study of the Political Theory of American Public Administration* (New York: Ronald Press, 1948), p. 128.

16. Durham, "Politics and Administration in Intergovernmental Relations," p. 6.

17. David B. Truman, "Federalism and the Party System," in Arthur W. Macmahon, ed., *Federalism Mature and Emergent* (Garden City, NY: Doubleday, 1955), pp. 115–136.

18. Morton Grodzins, "American Political Parties and the American System," *Western Political Quarterly,* vol. 13 (December 1960), pp. 974–998.

19. William Riker, *Federalism: Origin, Operation, Significance* (Boston: Little, Brown, 1964), 169 pp.

20. William Buchanan, "Politics and Federalism: Party or Anti-Party?" *The Annals,* vol. 359 (May 1965), pp. 107–115.

21. U.S. Advisory Commission on Intergovernmental Relations, *The Transformation in American Politics: Implications for Federalism*

(Washington: U.S. Government Printing Office, 1986), 382 pp. For highlights of the report, see U.S. Advisory Commission on Intergovernmental Relations, "New Relationships in a Changing System of Federalism and American Politics," *National Civic Review,* vol. 75 (November/December 1986), pp. 336–345.

22. Samuel H. Beer, "Federalism, Nationalism, and Democracy in America" *American Political Science Review,* vol. 72 (March 1978), pp. 9–21.

23. *Ibid,* p. 18.

24. Terry Sanford, *Storm Over the States* (New York: McGraw Hill, 1967), p. 80.

25. Edward W. Weidner, "Decision-Making in a Federal System," in Arthur W. Macmahon, ed., *Federalism Mature and Emergent* (Garden City, NY: Doubleday, 1955), pp. 363–383; Edward W. Weidner, *Intergovernmental Relations as Seen by Public Officials* (Minneapolis: University of Minnesota Press, 1960), 162 pp.

26. Beer, "Federalism," p. 20.

27. Harlan Cleveland, "Theses of a New Reformation: The Social Fallout of Science 300 Years After Newton," *Public Administration Review,* vol. 48 (May/June 1988), pp. 681–686. See also, Harlan Cleveland, *The Future Executive* (New York: Harper & Row, 1972), 140 pp.

28. The "policy professionals" category is discussed extensively and perceptively in Paul E. Peterson, Barry G. Rabe, and Kenneth K. Wong, *When Federalism Works* (Washington: Brookings Institution, 1986), 245 pp.

29. Ross Clayton, Patrick Conklin, and Raymond Shapek, eds., "Policy Management Assistance—A Developing Dialogue," *Public Administration Review,* vol. 35 (December 1975, special issue), pp. 693–818; see especially, Ann C. Macaluso,

"Background and History of the Study Committee on Policy Management Assistance," pp. 695–700.

30. Wilson, "The Study of Administration."

31. One noteworthy source for an assessment of the Reagan presidency is John L. Palmer, ed., *Perspectives on the Reagan Years* (Washington: Urban Institute Press, 1986), 215 pp. Others include John L. Palmer and Elizabeth V. Sawhill, eds., *The Reagan Experiment: An Examination of Economic and Social Policies under the Reagan Administration* (Washington: Urban Institute Press, 1982), 530 pp.; John William Ellwood, ed., *Reductions in U.S. Domestic Spending: How They Affect State and Local Governments* (New Brunswick, NJ: Transaction Books, 1982), 337 pp.; Richard P. Nathan and Fred C. Doolittle, *The Consequences of Cuts: The Effects of the Reagan Domestic Program on State and Local Governments* (Princeton, NJ: Princeton Urban and Regional Research Center, 1983), 221 pp.; Lester M. Salamon and Michael S. Lund, eds., *The Reagan Presidency and the Governing of America* (Washington: Urban Institute Press, 1984), 500 pp.; John E. Chubb and Paul E. Peterson, eds., *The New Direction in American Politics* (Washington: Brookings Institution, 1985), 409 pp.

32. Richard S. Williamson, "The 1982 New Federalism Negotiations," *Publius: The Journal of Federalism,* vol. 13 (Spring 1983), pp. 11–32; Timothy J. Conlan, "Federalism and Competing Values in the Reagan Administration," *Publius: The Journal of Federalism,* vol. 16 (Winter 1987), pp. 29–48; and Stephen B. Farber, "The 1982 New Federalism Negotiations: A View from the States," *Publius: The Journal of Federalism,* vol. 13 (Spring 1983), pp. 33–38.

33. Charles H. Levine, "Human Resource Erosion and the Uncertain Future of the U.S. Civil Service: From Policy Gridlock to Structural Fragmentation," *Governance: An International Journal of Policy and Administration,* vol. 1 (April 1988), pp. 115–134; Barbara Ferman, "Slouching Toward Anarchy: The Policymaking/Implementation Gap Revisited," *Governance: An International Journal of Policy and Administration,* vol. 2 (April 1989), pp. 198–212. For opposite (left and right) political stances on the rigidities and inertia in U.S. governmental system(s), see Robert Lekachman, *Visions and Nightmares: America After Reagan* (New York: Macmillian, 1987), 316 pp.; and Charles Murray, *Losing Ground: American Social Policy, 1950–1980* (New York: Basic Books, 1984), 323 pp.

34. Myrna Mandell, "Letters to the Editor: Intergovernmental Management," *Public Administration Times,* vol. 2 (15 December 1979), pp. 2, 6; Daniel J. Elazar, "Is Federalism Compatible with Prefectorial Administration?" *Publius: The Journal of Federalism,* vol. 11 (Spring 1981), pp. 3–22; Stephen L. Schechter, "On the Compatibility of Federalism and Intergovernmental Management," *Publius: The Journal of Federalism,* vol. 11 (Spring 1981), pp. 127–141; Deil S. Wright, "Managing the Intergovernmental Scene: The Changing Dramas of Federalism, Intergovernmental Relations, and Intergovernmental Management," in William B. Eddy, ed., *Handbook of Organizational Management* (New York: Marcel Dekker, 1983), pp. 417–454; Robert Agranoff and Valerie A. Lindsay, "Intergovernmental Management: Perspectives from Human Services Problem Solving at the Local Level," *Public Administration Review,* vol. 43 (May/June 1983), pp. 227–237; Stephen R. Rosenthal, "New Directions for Evaluating Intergovernmental Programs," *Public Administration Review,* vol. 44 (November/December 1984), pp. 491–503; Robert Agranoff, *Intergovernmental Management: Human Services Problem Solving in Six Metropolitan Areas* (Albany: State University of New York Press, 1986), 199 pp.; Robert Agranoff, "Managing Intergovernmental Processes," in James L. Perry, ed., *Handbook of Public Administration* (San Francisco: Jossey-Bass, 1989), pp. 131–147.

35. Agranoff, *Intergovernmental Management,* p. 1.

36. *Idem.*

37. *Ibid.,* p. 2.

38. Elazar, "Is Federalism Compatible with Prefectorial Administration?"; Schechter, "On the Compatibility of Federalism and Intergovernmental Management."

39. *Ibid.,* pp. 127–128.

40. *Ibid.,* p. 129.

41. *Ibid.,* p. 136.

42. Sheldon S. Wolin, *Politics and Vision: Continuity and Innovation in Western Political Thought* (Boston: Little, Brown, 1960), p. 260.

43. James D. Carroll, "The New Juridical Federalism and the Alienation of Public Policy and Administration," *American Journal of Public Administration,* vol. 16 (Spring 1982), pp. 89–106. See also: Michael D. Reagan, *Regulation: The Politics of Policy* (Boston: Little Brown 1987), 241 pp.; U.S. Advisory Commission on Intergovernmental Relations, *Regulatory Federalism: Policy, Process, Impact, and Reform* (Washington: U.S. Government Printing Office, 1984), 326 pp.; Christopher K. Leman and Robert H. Nelson, "The Rise of Managerial Federal-

ism: An Assessment of Benefits and Costs, *Environmental Law,* vol. 12 (Spring 1982), pp. 981–1029; and Margaret Wrightson, "From Cooperative to Regulatory Federalism," *SIAM Intergovernmental News,* vol. 9 (Spring 1986), pp. 1, 5. In her concluding sentence Wrightson makes a telling point about present and future regulatory relationships: "Taken together and projected into the future these trends suggest that the residue of the grand (Reagan) experiment could be a federalism that looks decidedly more regulatory than cooperative" (p. 5).

44. Deil S. Wright, *Understanding Intergovernmental Relations,* 3d ed. (Pacific Grove, CA: Brooks/Cole, 1988), 511 pp.

45. James H. Svara, "Dichotomy and Duality."

46. Hugh Heclo's phrase for the use of intermediaries is "government by remote control." See Hugh Heclo, "Issue Networks and the Executive Establishment," in Anthony King, ed., *The New American Political System* (Washington: American Enterprise Institute, 1978), p. 92. An alternate term is "third-party government." See Lester Salamon, "The Rise of Third-Party Government," *Washington Post,* 29 June 1980, p. C7, where it is noted that "the heart of this change is a shift from direct to indirect or 'third party' government, from an arrangement in which the federal government ran its own programs to one in which it relies primarily on others—states, cities, special districts, banks, nonprofit corporations, hospitals, manufacturers, and others—to carry out its purposes instead." A more extensive development of this thesis is found in Lester M. Salamon, "Rethinking Public Management: Third-Party Government and the Changing Forms of Government Ac-

tion," *Public Policy,* vol. 29 (Summer 1981), pp. 255–275. A similar but more long-term historical analysis is Frederick C. Mosher, "The Changing Responsibilities and Tactics of the Federal Government," *Public Administration Review,* vol. 40 (November/December 1980), pp. 541–548. The use of and controversy surrounding "third-party" participants have expanded considerably since the terms "privatization" and "contracting-out" gained recent prominence. E. S. Savas, *Privatizing the Public Sector: How to Shrink Government* (Chatham, NJ: Chatham House, 1982), 164 pp., and E. S. Savas, *Privatization: The Key to Better Government* (Chatham, NJ: Chatham House, 1987), 308 pp., are two examples of strong advocacy for privatization. Two reflective and more cautionary essays are: Ted Kolderie, "The Two Different Concepts of Privatization," *Public Administration Review,* vol. 46 (July/August 1986), pp. 285–291; and Ronald C. Moe, "Exploring the Limits of Privatization," *Public Administration Review,* vol. 47 (November/December 1987), pp. 453–460. The literature on contracting out is extensive. It has expanded recently as the phrase has become associated with the idea of privatization. See Ruth H. DeHoog, *Contracting Out for Human Services* (Albany: SUNY Albany Press, 1984), 186 pp. An essay that links management and privatization with selected aspects of IGR is James D. Carroll, "Public Administration in the Third Century of the Constitution: Supply-Side Management, Privatization, or Public Investment?" *Public Administration Review,* vol. 47 (January/February 1987), pp. 106–114. An exemplary case study of privatization, implementation, and intergovernmental problem solving in water pollution control efforts is Gerald W. Johnson and John G. Heilman, "Metapolicy Transition and Policy Implementation: New Federalism and Privatization," *Public Administration Review,* vol. 47 (November/December 1987), pp. 468–478.

47. Catherine H. Lovell, "Where We Are in Intergovernmental Relations and Some of the Implications," *Southern Review of Public Administration,* vol. 3 (June 1980), pp. 6–20; Catherine H. Lovell, "Coordinating Grants from Below," *Public Administration Review,* vol. 39 (September/October 1979), pp. 432–439.

48. Stanley M. Davis and Paul R. Lawrence, *Matrix* (Reading, MA: Addison-Wesley, 1977); James E. Webb, *Space Age Management* (New York: McGraw Hill, 1969), 173 pp.

49. Anthony Downs, *Inside Bureaucracy* (Boston: Little Brown, 1967), 292 pp.; see especially chapter 17, "Bureau Territoriality," pp. 211-222.

50. Norton Long, "The Local Community as an Ecology of Games," in Norton Long, ed., *The Polity* (Chicago: Rand McNally, 1962), pp. 139–155; Eugene Bardach, *The Implementation Game: What Happens After a Bill Becomes a Law* (Cambridge, MA: MIT Press, 1977), 323 pp.; Deil S. Wright, "Intergovernmental Games: An Approach to Understanding Intergovernmental Relations," *Southern Review of Public Administration,* vol. 3 (March 1980), pp. 383-403.

51. Vincent Ostrom, Charles M. Tiebout, and Robert Warren, "The Organization of Government in Metropolitan Areas: A Theoretical Inquiry," *American Political Science Review,* vol. 55 (December 1961), pp. 831–842; Robert Warren, "A Municipal Services Market Model of Metropolitan Organization," *Journal of the American Institute of Planners,* vol. 30 (August 1964), pp. 193–203; Vincent Ostrom and Elinor Ostrom, "A Behavioral Approach to the Study of Intergovernmental Relations," *The Annals,* vol. 359 (May 1965), pp. 137-146.

52. Donald B. Rosenthal and James M. Hoefler, "Competing Approaches to the Study of American Federalism and Intergovernmental Relations," *Publius: The Journal of Federalism,* vol. 19 (Winter 1989), pp. 1–24.

53. Thomas J. Anton, *American Federalism and Public Policy: How the System Works* (New York: Random House, 1989), 244 pp.

54. Nancy A. Huelsberg and William F. Lincoln, eds., *Successful Negotiation in Local Government* (Washington: International City Management Association, 1985), 211 pp.; Roger Richman, Orion F. White, Jr., and Michaux Wilkinson, *Intergovernmental Mediation: Negotiations in Local Government Disputes* (Boulder, CO: Westview Press in cooperation with the National Institute of Dispute Resolution, 1986), 173 pp.

55. Jim Bulpitt, *Territory and Power in the United Kingdom: An Interpretation* (Manchester, U.K.: Manchester University Press, 1983), 246 pp.

56. Deil S. Wright, "Intergovernmental Relations in Large Council-Manager Cities," *American Politics Quarterly,* vol. 1 (April 1973), pp. 151–188.

57. Peterson, Rabe, and Wong, *When Federalism Works.*

58. James H. Svara, "Dichotomy and Duality." For a comparative (cross-national) central-government study of politician-bureaucratic (administrator) relationships, see Joel D. Aberbach, Robert D. Putnam, and Bert A. Rockman, *Bureaucrats and Politicians in Western Democracies* (Cambridge, MA: Harvard University Press, 1981), 308 pp., and Joel D. Aberbach and Bert A. Rockman, "Image IV Revisited: Executive and

Political Roles," *Governance: An International Journal of Policy and Administration,* vol. 1 (January 1988), pp. 1–25.

59. James W. Fesler, "The Basic Theoretical Question: How to Relate Area and Function," in Leigh E. Grosenick, ed., *The Administration of the New Federalism: Objectives and Issues* (Washington: American Society for Public Administration, 1973), pp. 4–14. See also, James W. Fesler, *Area and Administration* (University: University of Alabama Press, 1949), 158 pp.

60. B. Guy Peters, *The Politics of Bureaucracy,* 3d. ed. (New York: Longman, 1989), pp. 293–294.

61. S. Kenneth Howard, "DeFacto New Federalism," *Intergovernmental Perspective,* vol. 10 (Winter 1984), p. 4; John Shannon, "Dealing with Deficits: Striking a New Fiscal Balance?" *Intergovernmental Perspective,* vol. 10 (Winter 1984), pp. 5–9;

John Shannon, "The Faces of Fiscal Federalism," *Intergovernmental Perspective,* vol. 14 (Winter 1988), pp. 15–17.

62. Advisory Commission, *Regulatory Federalism.*

63. Daniel J. Elazar, *American Federalism: The View from the States,* 3rd ed. (New York: Harper & Row, 1984), p. 252.

64. Executive Order 12612 (26 October 1987); *Federal Register,* 52:41685–41688 (30 October 1987). One example of an extensive formal effort to implement this executive order is in the U.S. Department of Housing and Urban Development: see *Federal Register,* 53:31926–31940 (12 August 1988).

65. Personal interviews by the author, U.S. Department of Health and Human Services, Office of the Assistant Secretary for Planning and Evaluation (Washington: 11 May 1989).

11.   American Federalism: Madison's Middle Ground in the 1980s

Martha Derthick

"Let it be tried . . . whether any middle ground can be taken, which will at once support a due supremacy of the national authority, and leave in force the local authorities so far as they can be subordinately useful."

So wrote James Madison to Edmund Randolph not long before the constitutional convention.[1] Much of American

SOURCE: "American Federalism: Madison's Middle Ground in the 1980s" by Martha Derthick, *Public Administration Review:* 47 (January/February 1987). Reprinted by permission of the American Society for Public Administration.

constitutional experience has consisted, as did much of Madison's work in Philadelphia, of a search for that middle ground.

At the convention, even partisans of the states conceded that there must be a stronger central government than the Articles of Confederation provided. And even supporters of national supremacy conceded that the states should not be abolished.[2] So the convention settled on a "composition" or "compound republic," as Madison termed it in *The Federalist.*[3] That is, the new government combined features of federal and purely national forms, most obviously in the structure of its legislature, wherein the states were represented, equally, in one house, and the people directly, in proportion to their numbers, in the other.

Eventually, this creation came to be widely regarded as the prototype of federal government, or at least as the most important and successful example of it. K. C. Wheare, writing a basic text on federal government in 1953, began by looking to the Constitution of the United States for his definition. The basic principle, he concluded, "is that of the division of powers between distinct and coordinate governments."[4] In certain matters, for example the coining of money and the making of treaties, the general government was independent of the state governments, whereas the states, in turn, were independent of the general government in other matters.

One wonders if the Founders believed that their "composition" would be stable. Some evidently doubted it. At the outset of the convention, after explaining the distinction between a federal government as it was then understood ("a mere compact resting on the good faith of the parties") and a national one ("having a complete and *compulsive* operation"), Gouverneur Morris seemed to say that the convention must choose one or the other: "He contended that in all communities there must be one supreme power, and one only."[5] "A National Government must soon of necessity swallow [the states] all up," George Read of Delaware predicted.[6] "Mr. Bedford [also of Delaware] contended, that there was no middle way between a perfect consolidation, and a mere confederacy of the States."[7] In 1828, when the composition was nearly 40 years old and under severe strain, Madison seemed uncertain about its prospects but still hopeful. "It will be fortunate if the struggle [between the nation and states] should end in a permanent equilibrium of powers," he wrote.[8]

As the "composition" approaches 200 years of age, it is still not easy to render a simple, indisputable judgment on the outcome. Surely the national government has proved supreme. It got the better of the states in the original contest, as well as in the major tests of subsequent centuries. The nineteenth century, embracing the great debates over nullification and secession and culminating in the Civil War, virtually disposed of the doctrine that the states have the right to decide disputes over the distribution of governmental power. The twentieth century then proceeded to dispose of the original precept that the powers of the national government are confined to those enumerated in a written constitution—a development that was far enough advanced by the end of World War II to cast doubt even then on Wheare's definition.[9]

On the other hand, even now the national government does not operate alone. State governments survive, not as hollow shells (as their detractors often charge and their defenders always fear), but as functioning entities, with their own constitutions, laws, elected officials and independently-raised revenues. Though Congress has pervasively invaded domains once thought exclusively those of the states and though it very much constrains their conduct with commerce clause regulations applying directly to them and with grant-in-aid conditions, on the whole it has refrained from displacing them—apart, that is, from piecemeal preemptions of regulatory functions under the commerce clause, a practice that is well within the bounds of constitutional tradition and indubitably sanctioned by the supremacy clause. As a general rule, when Congress essays new domestic responsibilities it relies on cooperation of the states, with the result that the two levels of government in our federal system are today massively and pervasively intertwined—a fact that is of utmost importance for the conduct of public administration.

As it happens, quite apart from the impending bicentennial of the Constitution, the 1980s are an eminently suitable time for taking stock of the federal system for two reasons. First, because the Reagan era has provided surcease from the passage of expansive new federal legislation, we can pause to appraise the changes that took place between 1965 and 1980, a period marked by numerous innovations in intergovernmental relations. Second, within the Supreme Court and between the Court and the Reagan Administration's second attorney general, a rather heated debate has developed over the importance of federalism and the judicial behavior required to preserve it.

THE PRACTICE OF INTERGOVERNMENTAL RELATIONS: SHARED PROGRAMS

For a student of federalism to make sense of the events of 1965–1980 is no easy task. A great deal happened. Grant-in-aid programs proliferated in the customary categorical pattern and then were revised by the introduction of general revenue-sharing and three broad-based grants—two (for community development and employment and training) which the Nixon Administration designed and a third (social services) that developed unintentionally when several powerful, populous states successfully exploited a loophole in the federal law providing for public assistance grants.[10] As of 1984, following attempts by the Reagan Administration to expand block grants and reduce general revenue-sharing, 20 percent of federal grants were classified as broad-based or general-purpose.

Against the decentralization embodied in less-conditioned grants, however, must be set numerous centralizing acts of Congress that occurred in the same period. Congress replaced several public assistance grant programs with a direct federal program of income support (Supplemental Security Income or SSI) and displayed a heightened willingness to try to make national policy for the remaining category of public assistance, Aid to Families with Dependent Children. It experimented boldly and sometimes irresponsibly with a new grant-in-aid technique, what the Advisory Commission on Intergovernmental Relations has called the "cross-cutting requirement."[11] Employed mainly to prevent discrimination in the use of grants, this technique encompasses in one statutory stroke *all* grant programs or some large class of them, in contrast to Congress's earlier practice of attaching conditions specifically to particular categorical programs.[12]

Related to the "cross-cutting requirement," yet clearly distinguishable from it, is another new and bold grant technique, that which ACIR calls the "crossover sanction."[13] Historically, Congress has confined the sanction of withholding grant funds quite narrowly within grant categories. Withholding would apply only to the activity wherein the recipient's transgression of federal requirements was alleged, but in the 1970s Congress began to threaten sanctions that crossed the boundaries of particular programs. Thus, for example, if states do not meet the pollution control standards of the Clean Air Act, they may be penalized by the withholding of highway aid funds. To assure that the states supplemented federal payments under SSI to the extent that Congress wished, it threatened them with loss of Medicaid grants. Numerous other examples exist. In general, categorical grant-in-aid programs of the 1970s, whether newly enacted or only amended, displayed a much enlarged willingness to intrude in state and local affairs. Statements of federal objectives were often as expansive as grant-in-aid techniques were inventive.

Nor was Congress's inventiveness confined to grant-in-aid programs. In the process of enacting dozens of laws in the 1970s for the regulation of environmental, work-place, and product hazards, Congress repeatedly applied a new technique of intergovernmental relations that has become known as "partial preemption."[14] Very roughly, it is to regulatory programs what the conditioned, categorical grant-in-aid is to spending programs—that is, a way of propounding national objectives and inducing the states to cooperate in pursuing them; the two are often used in tandem. Partial preemption entails the setting of federal regulatory standards but gives the states the option of various forms of participation in the regulatory regime. More often than not, the federal government relies heavily on them for enforcement.

Under the Clean Air Act, for example, Congress sets standards for permissible levels of common pollutants and deadlines for meeting them. States are instructed to adopt implementation plans designed to attain the standards, and the federal Environmental Protection Agency (EPA) reviews the state plans.[15] If a state fails to act or fails to secure EPA's approval of its plan, EPA can develop its own plan for the state. Both the state and federal governments may take action against polluters.

The Surface Mining Control and Reclamation Act uses a similar technique. The act sets forth numerous, detailed performance standards that coal-mining operations must meet. States wishing to assume regulatory responsibility must submit plans for approval by the Office of Surface Mining (OSM) of the Department of the Interior. State laws, regulations, and administrative performance must meet the requirements of the federal act. If a state chooses not to regulate, fails to gain approval

of its plan, or fails to implement the plan satisfactorily, OSM is required to take charge.[16]

As a third example, under the Occupational Safety and Health Act of 1970 the Secretary of Labor is required to promulgate standards, but states may regulate those matters that federal regulations fail to address, and they may also assume responsibility in areas where the federal government has acted if their own standards are "at least as effective" as the federal standards.[17]

The Persistence of State Discretion. From the perspective of the mid-1980s, one can hardly say that the results of this outburst of congressional activity are clear, but it is perhaps not too soon to say that they are clearly ambiguous. Even where the urge to centralize was strongest—in income support and environmental protection programs—state governments retain a great deal of discretion in policy making and freedom from federal administrative supervision. Despite fears of some partisans of the states that they were being turned into mere administrative agents of an overbearing central government, federalism lives. It is manifest in the persistence of interstate differences in program characteristics and in the ineffectiveness of much federal oversight of state administration.

Probably no more striking proof of the persistence of states' individuality exists than the SSI program, in which they are free to supplement the federal minimum payment. Congress in 1973 required supplementation to the extent necessary to hold current recipients harmless against the changes associated with federalization, and some states have also provided optional supplements. Only seven states do not supplement at all, according to a study done in 1984.[18] As of January 1985, the minimum federal payment for an aged individual living alone and having no countable income was $325, but differences in state supplements meant that the actual legal minimum ranged from $325 to a high of $586 in Alaska. Because many recipients have countable income, monthly payments are on average less than these minimums; in August 1985 they ranged from $90.95 per aged recipient in Maine to $252.83 in Alaska.[19]

The persistence of federalism is perhaps even more vividly demonstrated, though, by the administrative features of SSI. Twenty-seven states administer their own supplements. No federal regulations apply to supplements in these states, which remain free to supplement whomever they please in whatever amounts they please. As one would expect, practices vary widely. At an extreme, Illinois continues to calculate an individual budget amount for each of its nearly 30,000 recipients of state supplements.

Nor is the situation vastly different in those 16 states (plus the District of Columbia) that have accepted Congress's offer to have the Social Security Administration administer supplements for them. Eager to get the program under way with the states' cooperation, SSA at the outset agreed to administer a number of variations in supplementation. Variations are permitted among benefit categories, three geographic divisions within a state, and five different living arrangements. One analyst has calculated that there are about 300 different SSI benefits nationally; he counted 158 state-administered variations and 130 federally-administered variations.[20] Perversely, the result of the "national" takeover has been to burden a national administrative agency, the SSA, with many of the accommodations to local circumstances that ordinarily take place through the medium of state administration. The SSA has found this to be a very large burden indeed, as a history of administrative troubles in SSI shows.

In Aid to Families with Dependent Children, which is still basically a state-run program despite prolonged attempts under both Nixon and Carter to achieve a "welfare reform" that would federalize it, interstate payment differences likewise persist, of course. In the second quarter of 1984, the average monthly payment per recipient ranged from $31 in Mississippi to $217 in Alaska. Twenty-three states were providing AFDC-UP—that is, were using welfare to compensate for parental unemployment as well as the absence of an employed adult from the home—but the rest were not.[21] Encouraged by Congress after 1981 to set up work programs for welfare recipients, the states adopted "a flurry of initiatives," according to a report in *The National Journal.* In most states, however, work and training programs were limited to a few counties and to small subgroups of those eligible because of financial, administrative, or geographical constraints.[22] In short, after a decade or more of the most intense effort in Washington to supplant AFDC, the program survived, interstate and even intrastate variations in it remained the norm, and states were quite conspicuously functioning as "laboratories of experiment."

These laboratories were only lightly supervised by federal administrators. Close, detailed supervision of state administration of welfare, which had been attempted by the Bureau of Public Assistance in the years following passage of the Social Security Act, had collapsed by the end of the 1960s, to some extent destroyed by the growth of caseloads, to some extent deliberately abandoned by leaders of the Department of Health, Education and Welfare who believed that the BPA's administrative style had produced too much red tape while failing to contain the caseloads. In the late 1960s, the very detailed guidance developed by the BPA over decades was cancelled in favor of much more general and permissive regulations.[23]

However, in the face of caseloads which continued to mount along with pressures to contain federal spending, the new permissiveness and simplicity did not last long. HEW in the early 1970s initiated an effort to control error rates in AFDC by designing sample studies, setting performance objectives, and manipulating incentives—rewards *and* penalties—in the fashion of new-style management experts and policy analysts rather than old-style social workers, who had had a more patronizing and less scientific approach to dealing with the states. The idea, incorporated in HEW regulations promulgated at the end of 1972, was that the states would be penalized with the loss of federal funds if they had excessive error rates. But thereafter various secretaries of HEW kept postponing sanctions while various subordinates negotiated with one another and with the states over what would be practicable and acceptable. Eventually, 13 states won a judgment from the U.S. District Court in the District of Columbia that the tolerance levels for error set by HEW were arbitrary and capricious. Negotiations resumed, and weak quality control regulations, with which most states would find it easy to comply, were promulgated in 1979.[24] In the Tax Equity and Fiscal Responsibility Act of 1982, Congress set four percent as an allowable error rate in AFDC payments for 1983 and three percent thereafter, with the proviso that the Secretary of Health and Human Services should make no reimbursements for erroneous payments in excess of that rate. However, the Secretary might waive all or part of the reduction in grants if "a State is unable to reach the allowable error rate . . . despite a good faith effort. . . ."[25]

Bargaining and negotiation, not command and obedience, appear to characterize the practice of intergovernmental programs now as in the past, even if the past was far more mindful of a tradition called states' rights. To these negotiations, states bring some newly-acquired strengths that partially offset Congress's diminished sensitivity to their interests, and federal administrative agencies bring some weaknesses of long standing.

State Strengths and Federal Weaknesses. One of the states' strengths consists of organization. Both state and local governments have banded together in various organizations which perform service and lobbying functions on their behalf. When HEW officials were seeking to develop their AFDC quality control program in the 1970s, they negotiated with a group composed of representatives of the National Association of Counties, the National Conference of State Legislatures, National League of Cities/U.S. Conference of Mayors, the National Governors Conference, and the American Public Welfare Association, in which the NGC took the lead. The rise of the "intergovernmental lobby" is well documented, and at least one influential article attributed the passage of general revenue-sharing largely to its existence.[26] A second new-found strength of the states—one not unique to them but widely shared in our society—is their capacity to bring suit. Individually, in *ad hoc* groups or through their formal lobbying organizations, they resort to the courts when they feel that Congress or the executive agencies have transgressed constitutional or statutory bounds.

In general, their constitutionally-based challenges have not succeeded. Courts have found nothing constitutionally impermissible in partial preemptions or the newer grant-in-aid techniques. They typically hold that if a valid national purpose is being served (and under the commerce clause or the power to tax and spend for the general welfare, one always is), and if the states are not being coerced (and under grant-in-aid programs and partial preemptions, the states technically do retain the option of not participating), then the law is valid.

Statutory challenges are another matter, however, as the example of HEW's failed attempt to promulgate strict AFDC quality control regulations shows. Throughout their negotiations with the states, HEW officials in that case were hampered both by intradepartmental differences of view and by a well-founded apprehension over what the courts would permit. Courts are not loathe to find that federal executive agencies have exceeded their statutory authority in promulgating regulations for intergovernmental programs.

Probably the most telling and significant use of the courts' powers of statutory review came in the late 1970s in a set of cases that arose out of the Environmental Protection Agency's promulgation of standards for transportation control plans. Under threat of various civil sanctions, including injunctions, the imposition of receiverships on certain state functions, and fines and contempt citations for state officials, EPA would have required the states to adopt and enforce such measures as parking bans and surcharges, bus lanes, and computerized carpool matching. Three out of four appellate courts which reviewed these regulations found that they had exceeded Congress's intent and strongly hinted that they violated the Constitution as well. The states could be offered the choice of whether to participate in pollution control and could be fully preempted if they chose not to participate, but they could not be ordered to carry out federal regulations.[27]

If negotiation works well for the states, though, it is not just because they are well organized and sometimes victorious in the courts. It is because federal agencies bring serious weaknesses to the bargaining table. Neither of their principal weapons—to withhold funds in grant-in-aid programs, to take charge of enforcement in regulatory programs—is readily usable.

Withholding funds is self-defeating and risks congressional intervention and reprimand. (The HEW officials who struggled with AFDC quality control issues in the 1970s felt under pressure from Congress to do something yet doubted that Congress would come to their defense if they did anything drastic.) Withholding, though occasionally threatened, is rarely used. When issues arise, the contestants negotiate.[28]

The threat to take charge of administration likewise lacks credibility except in isolated cases because federal agencies generally lack the capacity to supersede the states, and everyone knows it. Congress is unwilling to spend the funds or otherwise to bear the onus of creating a large federal bureaucracy; that is why it chooses to rely so heavily on intergovernmental techniques.

Where partial preemption has been employed, giving states the option of assuming responsibility for enforcement and federal agencies' responsibility for approving state plans and supervising their execution, states in general have opted to participate, and federal agencies have in general made the necessary delegations. Among the new regulatory regimes, only that for occupational health and safety remains overwhelmingly a federal responsibility, and that is only because the AFL-CIO successfully challenged the Department of Labor's criteria for delegation in court during the Ford Administration, raising a set of issues that have since remained unresolved. In practice, about half of the states run their own occupational safety and health programs even if the federal government remains nominally in charge almost everywhere.[29]

When state defiance or default requires federal agencies to assume enforcement responsibilities in regulatory programs based on partial preemption, the results are not invariably felicitous. One consequence of the use of partial preemption has been to demonstrate, through various "natural experiments," that federal administration is not necessarily superior to state administration.

In 1981 the Idaho legislature, irritated by the U.S. Environmental Protection Agency (EPA), voted not to fund the state's air quality program, forcing EPA to administer it. Both state and federal officials concluded after a year that the federal takeover caused more problems than it solved. EPA reportedly spent almost five times as much to maintain the Idaho program that year as the state would have spent to do the same job. In another case, Iowa's environmental budget was cut 15 percent in 1982, causing a loss of federal matching funds. The state then returned responsibility for its municipal water-monitoring program to EPA, which managed to conduct only about 15 percent of the inspections formerly performed by the state.[30]

The Office of Surface Mining in 1984 found it necessary to reclaim responsibility from Tennessee and Oklahoma, but nothing in the administrative performance of the federal agency gives grounds for confidence that it can do much better.[31]

A study by the Congressional Research Service in 1983 sought systematically to compare occupational injury rates in states with federally-run programs with those where state agencies remained in charge, in a tentative test of the effectiveness of programs in the two sets. The study concluded that states with state-run programs had a somewhat better performance record.[32] Organized labor has complained that inspections are fewer in states where the Occupational Safety and Health Administration (OSHA) remains responsible for enforcement, although this has not caused it to reexamine its abiding preference for a federal regime. Current failures of federal performance can be blamed on the Republican administration.[33]

The new regulatory regimes are still new enough that one cannot be sure that they have stabilized. The arrival of the Reagan Administration, committed to a sharp reduction in federal spending and a revival of states' rights—or states' responsibilities, as Reagan officials sometimes insist—accelerated delegations to state governments and correspondingly contracted the size and hence administrative capacities of the federal regulatory agencies. Yet it is doubtful that a future change in the election returns would work more than marginal changes in the administrative arrangements that have emerged. Apparently, these arrangements leave much for the states to do and much room for them to negotiate with their federal-agency supervisors over how and how fast to do it.

THE ROLE OF THE COURTS

Insofar as centralization has occurred in the past decade or two, the courts have been at least as influential as Congress, arguably much more so. This is not so much because courts have preferred the national side in overt contests between the national government and the states as because federal courts have aggressively pursued the extension of individual rights with little regard for the effect on the states' prerogatives as governments in their own right.[34]

By steadily enlarging the application of the due process and equal protection clauses of the Fourteenth Amendment, the Supreme Court carried into the late 1960s and early 1970s the vigorous extension of the constitutional rights of individuals begun in the 1950s with *Brown* v. *Board of Education* (or, if one prefers, in 1925 with *Gitlow* v. *New York,* in which the Court first read the Bill of Rights into the Fourteenth

Amendment). Such celebrated cases as *Roe* v. *Wade* (1973), which struck down state laws prohibiting abortion; *Goldberg* v. *Kelly* (1970), which required that a welfare recipient be afforded an evidentiary hearing *before* the termination of benefits; and *Shapiro* v. *Thompson* (1969), which invalidated state residency requirements for welfare applicants, boldly asserted national power at the states' expense.[35]

In the area of voting rights, statutory construction as well as constitutional interpretation has been the Court's route to a radically altered federalism. Since its decision in 1969 in *Allen* v. *State Board of Elections,* the Department of Justice has had power to review municipal annexations, the redrawing of district lines, and the choice of at-large versus district elections in jurisdictions covered by the Voting Rights Act—power that it has used to increase the probability that minority candidates will win office. Such methods of protecting the franchise of blacks and other minorities to whom the law's protection has been extended are far more problematic and intrusive than those contemplated when it was passed in 1965.[36]

Rather less publicized than Supreme Court decisions, yet arguably at least as intrusive, have been the numerous decisions of lower federal courts in the so-called institution cases, in which state governments were ordered to increase their expenditures on facilities for the mentally ill or retarded, criminals, and juvenile detainees. The decrees in these cases have mandated massive and often detailed changes in the operation of institutions and their programs—changes involving the physical condition of the facility, staffing, and quality of services.[37]

In some especially intrusive grant-in-aid programs, notably the Education for All Handicapped Children Act of 1975, Congress has been emboldened by courts. That act requires, as a condition of grants-in-aid, that states have in effect a policy assuring all handicapped children between the ages of 3 and 21 the right to a free appropriate public education and that local educational agencies maintain and annually review an individualized program for each handicapped child. This law built upon federal district court decisions of 1971 in Pennsylvania and 1972 in the District of Columbia.[38]

Where newly-sweeping grant-in-aid conditions have been particularly effective, it has ordinarily been because courts have reinforced and elaborated them, in effect working in tandem with the administrative agency. *Together,* the courts and the Office of Education (and then the Office of Civil Rights, after it was separately constituted) brought about the extraordinary desegregation of Southern schools in the late 1960s. Title VI of the Civil Rights Act of 1964, with a "cross-cutting requirement" which prohibited racial discrimination in the use of federal grants-in-aid, when combined with the grants to elementary and secondary schools that were freshly enacted in 1965, complemented *Brown* v. *Board* and the successor decisions. Also, it was crucially complemented by them. As Gary Orfield notes in his definitive study of the application of Title VI to Southern schools, the decisive federal response came in 1968 in a case involving the schools of New Kent County, Virginia. "Once again the work of black attorneys and the response of the judiciary [created] a shield behind which the administrative techniques of HEW could be effectively employed."[39]

The influence of the courts is shown not just in what they have done, but, less directly, in what they have declined to prevent Congress from doing. For a fleeting moment, in *National League of Cities* v. *Usery* (1976), the Supreme Court seemed willing to revive *and apply* the precept that states' sovereignty imposes some limit on Congress's exercise of the commerce clause. In that decision it held that Congress could not use the Fair Labor Standards Act to regulate the states' determination of their employees' wages and hours.[40] Successor decisions, however, rather than building on *National League of Cities,* led to the repudiation of it in *Garcia* v. *San Antonio Metropolitan Transit Authority* in 1985.[41] While the Court has never said that states' sovereignty imposes *no* limit on Congress's commerce clause powers, it has backed away from trying to define one.

It is little wonder that the Reagan Administration's attempt to construct protection for the states had by late 1985 come to focus on judicial appointments. In its own legislative and administrative choices, the Reagan Administration has been far from consistent in its commitment to strengthening the states. When budget reduction and other objectives have conflicted with that aim, the Administration's devolutionary objectives have often been compromised, as Timothy Conlan has shown in a careful analysis.[42] To that, Reagan officials might well reply that for the preservation of the states as a coordinate element of government, it is the federal bench that matters most.

CURRENT DEBATES

As of the mid-1980s, the value of federalism was very much at issue within the Supreme Court and between the Court and the Reagan Administration's second attorney general. Today's conservatives profess to value the federal principle highly, whereas liberals, in their preoccupation with perfecting individual rights, are either indifferent to questions of government structure or reflexively prefer national to state action.

The current debate, as yet imperfectly joined for lack of a full exposition on either side, appears to turn on essentially the issues which divided federalists and antifederalists 200 years ago. Both sides profess to value liberty and democracy above all. They differ in their judgments of the distribution of governmental power that will best serve those ends.

"A substantive issue like abortion is a matter of public or civic morality," Attorney General Edwin Meese has argued, and "should be decided upon through a free and robust discussion at the level [of government] most appropriate to its determination." In his view, that is the level of state and local government, for "big government does not encourage a sense of belonging. . . . An essential sense of community is far more likely to develop at the local level." A proper understanding of federalism, in this view, would permit such matters as abortion, prayer in the schools, pornography, and aid to parochial schools to be deliberated on by state governments and resolved by the sense of the particular community, there to be incorporated in statutes, rather than being treated at the national level as subjects of constitutional doctrine.[43]

Much as Meese in these remarks argued the superior communal qualities of the states, Justice Lewis F. Powell in a dissent to *Garcia* v. *SAMTA* argued the inferior quality of the federal government's policy processes. Federal laws are drafted by congressional committee staffs and federal regulations, often more important than the laws, by the staffs of agencies, he wrote. A realistic comparison of the operation of the different levels of government, in Powell's view, shows state and local governments to be more accessible and responsive, hence more democratic, than the government based in Washington. That government in the national capital would become remote and alienated from ordinary people was one of the fears of the antifederalists. Their intellectual heirs on the Supreme Court say it has happened.

206 779-2081

Perhaps the most important events in the federal system in the recent past are those which bear on the potential power of such arguments as Meese's and Powell's by affecting either the public's receptivity to them or their plausibility. Even as centralization proceeds—indeed, perhaps because it has proceeded so far—the federal government seems to have suffered a decline in popular esteem. Confidence in its performance dropped sharply in the 1970s, and by the mid-1980s it was doing poorly in polls asking the public to compare it to state and local governments.[44] By contrast, scholarly and journalistic accounts of the performance of state governments uniformly judge it much improved over two or three decades ago, enhanced by legislatures more active, more professional, and better-staffed than formerly—*and* more representative of their constituencies, with ironic thanks to the reapportionment decisions of the Supreme Court.[45]

Governmental competence and perceptions of it aside, all discussions of American federalism must henceforth be altered by what is arguably the most important new social and political datum of our times: the end to Southern exceptionalism. Until now, arguments favoring the states' side in any dispute over federalism suffered fatally from the burden of the South's deviant social system. Whether or not blacks have been successfully integrated into American society (a separate question), there can be little doubt that the South as a region has been integrated. That change, even if achieved very largely by the instrumentalities of the federal government, holds the possibility that the case for the states can at last begin to be discussed on its merits.

That case deserves a more careful contemporary exposition than it has yet received, with due regard for the purposes and expectations of the Founders. The Founders did not make a strong argument for the federal aspects of their "composition." *The Federalist* is "rather inexplicit and ambiguous in its treatment of federalism," for the reason that its authors were at heart nationalists.[46] Madison saw the size of the new republic, not its compound quality, as crucial to the achievement of liberty. His most eloquent and memorable statements were made in support of "extending the sphere."[47] He told the convention that "Were it practicable for the General Government to extend its care to every requisite object without the co-operation of the State Governments, the people would not be less free as members of one great Republic, than as members of thirteen small ones."[48]

Yet Madison's willingness to preserve the states was more than a concession to the fact that their abolition, then as now, was politically unacceptable. Prudent and practical, he thought they would be useful, even if subordinately. He doubted that the national government would be suited to the entire task of governing "so great an extent of country, and over so great a variety of objects."[49]

In this, as in so much else, Madison was very wise. As the burdens of governing grow, the inability or unwillingness of the federal government to bear them alone is manifest.[50] The states therefore remain vigorous, although they are more nearly the subordinately useful governments that Madison anticipated in 1787 than the coordinate ones posited by Wheare's definition.

NOTES

The author is indebted for comments to Wayne Anderson, David R. Beam, Michael D. Reagan, Sarah Ryder, Abigail Thernstrom, and Dwight Waldo.

1. Cited in Irving Brant, *The Fourth President: A Life of James Madison* (Indianapolis: The Bobbs-Merrill Company, 1970), p. 146.

2. "[A] consolidation of the States is not less unattainable than it would be inexpedient," the nationalist Madison wrote, in the same letter to Randolph.

3. The leading statement is No. 39. For an interpretation, see Martin Diamond, "What the Framers Meant by Federalism," in Robert A. Goldwin, ed., *A Nation of States: Essays on the American Federal System* (Chicago: Rand McNally & Co., 1963), pp. 24–41.

4. *Federal Government* (New York: Oxford University Press, 1953), p. 2. Wheare defines the federal principle by reference to the particular features of the United States government, for "The modern idea of what federal government is has been determined by the United States of America," p. 1.

5. *Journal of the Federal Convention Kept by James Madison* (Chicago: Albert, Scott & Co., 1893), p. 74.

6. *Ibid.,* p. 120.

7. *Ibid.,* p. 280.

8. *The Letters and Other Writings of James Madison* (Congress edition: R. Worthington, 1884), vol. III, p. 625.

9. Cf. Edward S. Corwin, "The Passing of Dual Federalism," *Virginia Law Review,* vol. 36 (1950).

10. The Advisory Commission on Intergovernmental Relations (ACIR), in studies of the intergovernmental grant system done in the late 1970s, also counted as block grants those authorized by the Partnership for Health Act of 1966, which had consolidated seven categorical grants, and the Omnibus Crime Control and Safe Streets Act of 1968. See Advisory Commission on Intergovernmental Relations, *Block Grants: A Comparative Analysis* (Washington: ACIR, 1977).

11. Advisory Commission on Intergovernmental Relations, *Regulatory Federalism: Policy, Process, Impact and Reform* (Washington: ACIR, 1984), pp. 8, 71–78.

12. In truth, the technique was not altogether new but had antecedents as old as the Hatch Act, which was amended in 1940 to prohibit partisan political activity by any "officer or employee of any State or local agency whose principal employment is in connection with any activity which is financed in whole or in part by loans or grants made by the United States. . . ." Failure to comply was punishable by the withholding of funds. 54 *Stat.* 767 (1940). Cross-cutting requirements did not become common until the 1960s, however.

13. *Ibid.,* pp. 9, 78–82.

14. *Ibid.,* pp. 9, 82–88. I am much indebted to David R. Beam for enlightenment on the newer techniques of federal influence vis-à-vis the states, derived both from personal conversations and from his work at the ACIR as one of the authors of *Regulatory Federalism*.

15. 84 *Stat.* 1676 (1970). The law says that "Each State . . . shall . . . adopt . . . a plan. . . ."

16. 91 *Stat.* 445 (1977).

17. 84 *Stat.* 1590 (1970).

18. Renato A. DiPentima, "The Supplemental Security Income Program: A Study of Implementation," PhD dissertation (University of Maryland, 1984), p. 80.

19. *Social Security Bulletin,* vol. 48 (October 1985), p. 19, and (November 1985), p. 42. These data published by the federal government cover only those states—slightly more than half of the total—in which the Social Security Administration has responsibility for administering supplemental payments. The SSA lacks comparable data from states that have chosen to administer themselves whatever program of supplementation exists. See the

text, *infra,* for further explanation of federal versus state administration of supplements.

20. DiPentima, *op. cit.,* p. 85.

21. U.S. Department of Health and Human Services, *Quarterly Public Assistance Statistics* (April–June 1984), Tables 7 and 15.

22. Julie Kosterlitz, "Liberals and Conservatives Share Goals, Differ on Details of Work for Welfare," *National Journal* (October 26, 1985), pp. 2418–22.

23. Martha Derthick, *The Influence of Federal Grants: Public Assistance in Massachusetts* (Cambridge: Harvard University Press, 1970), pp. 225–29, and *Uncontrollable Spending for Social Services Grants* (Washington: The Brookings Institution, 1975), pp. 15–24.

24. "Controlling AFDC Error Rates," Kennedy School of Government Case C 14-80-302 (copyright by President and Fellows of Harvard College, 1980).

25. H. Rept. 97-760, p. 79.

26. Donald H. Haider, *When Governments Come to Washington: Governors, Mayors, and Intergovernmental Lobbying* (New York: Free Press, 1974); Samuel H. Beer, "The Adoption of General Revenue Sharing: A Case Study in Public Sector Politics," *Public Policy,* vol. 24 (Spring 1976). The impending demise of general revenue-sharing calls into question the hypothesis that the intergovernmental lobby was responsible for its passage, for there is no reason to suppose that the lobby is less well-organized today than it was in the early 1970s.

27. *Brown* v. *Environmental Protection Agency,* 521 F. 2d 827 (9th Cir., 1975); *Maryland* v. *Environmental Protection Agency,* 530 F. 2d 215 (4th Cir., 1975); *District of Columbia* v. *Train,* 521 F. 2d 971 (D.C. Cir., 1975); *Pennsylvania* v. *Environmental Protection Agency,* 500 F. 2d 246 (3rd Cir., 1974).

28. Cf. Derthick, *The Influence of Federal Grants,* chap. 8. However, the willingness of courts since 1970 to discover private rights of action in federal statutes has to some extent offset the weakness of federal agencies in regard to the use of withholding. As R. Shep Melnick has written, "The private right of action has special significance in joint federal-state spending programs. If an alleged beneficiary could only bring suit against a federal administrator for failing to enforce federal standards, the only relief the court could offer successful plaintiffs would be an injunction cutting off federal funds to the state. . . . But when potential recipients can bring suit against the state for failure to comply with federal requirements, the court can compel the state to pay the plaintiff the money owed. The private right of action, thus, significantly alters the balance of power between the federal government and the states." "The Politics of Partnership," *Public Administration Review,* vol. 45 (November 1985), pp. 656–57.

29. On intergovernmental relations in occupational safety and health, see the oversight hearings held annually by the Subcommittee on Health and Safety of the Committee on Education and Labor, U.S. House of Representatives. The most important titles are: *OSHA Oversight— State of the Agency Report by Assistant Secretary of Labor for OSHA,* 97 Cong. 2 sess. (1983), pp. 212–36; *OSHA Oversight—Staffing Levels for OSHA Approved State Plans,* 98 Cong. 1 sess. (1983); and *Oversight on OSHA: State of the Agency,* 99 COng. 1 sess. (1985), serial no. 99-12.

30. *State of the Environment: An Assessment at Mid-Decade* (Washington: The Conservation Foundation, 1984), p. 458.

31. Rochelle L. Stanfield, "Mine Disaster," *National Journal* (October 12, 1985), p. 2342.

32. U.S. House of Representatives, Committee on Education and Labor, *OSHA Oversight—Staffing Levels for OSHA Approved State Plans,* Hearings before the Subcommittee on Health and Safety, 98 Cong., 1 sess. (1983), pp. 295–327. See also the work of Frank J. Thompson and Michael J. Scicchitano: "State Implementation Effort and Federal Regulatory Policy: The Case of Occupational Safety and Health," *Journal of Politics,* vol. 47 (1985), pp. 686-703, and "State Enforcement of Federal Regulatory Policy: The Lessons of OSHA," *Policy Studies Journal,* vol. 13 (March 1985), pp. 591–598.

33. Michael Wines, "Auchter's Record at OSHA Leaves Labor Outraged, Business Satisfied," *National Journal* (October 1, 1983), pp. 2008–13.

34. For a critique, see Robert F. Nagel, "Federalism as a Fundamental Value: National League of Cities in Perspective," *Supreme Court Review* (1981), pp. 81–109.

35. For a good summary of the Court's use of the Fourteenth Amendment to extend civil liberties, see David Fellman, "The Nationalization of American Civil Liberties," in M. Judd Harmon, ed., *Essays on the Constitution of the United States* (Port Washington, NY: Kennikat Press, 1978), pp. 49–60.

36. Abigail M. Thernstrom, "The Odd Evolution of the Voting Rights Act," *Public Interest* (Spring 1979), pp. 49–76.

37. Gerald E. Frug, "The Judicial Power of the Purse," *University of Pennsylvania Law Review,* vol. 126 (April 1978), pp. 715–794.

38. Erwin L. Levine and Elizabeth M. Wexler, *PL 94-142: An Act of Congress* (New York: Macmillan, 1981), pp. 38–41. In the field of voting rights, statutory amendments and court decisions have interacted to produce the surprisingly far reach of federal action described above. These events are analyzed in detail in a forthcoming book by Abigail M. Thernstrom.

39. Gary Orfield, *The Reconstruction of Southern Education: The Schools and the 1964 Civil Rights Act* (New York: John Wiley and Sons, 1969), p. 262. See also Jeremy Rabkin, "Office for Civil Rights," in James Q. Wilson, ed., *The Politics of Regulation* (New York: Basic Books, 1980), chap. 9.

40. 426 U.S. 833.

41. Slip opinion No. 82-1913, decided February 19, 1985.

42. Timothy J. Conlan, "Federalism and Competing Values in the Reagan Administration," in Laurence J. O'Toole, Jr., ed., *American Intergovernmental Relations* (Washington: CQ Press, 1985), pp. 265–80.

43. Address before the American Enterprise Institute, Sept. 6, 1985.

44. Seymour Martin Lipset and William Schneider, *The Confidence Gap: Business, Labor and Government in the Public Mind* (New York: Free Press, 1968), and Advisory Commission on Intergovernmental Relations, *Changing Public Attitudes on Governments and Taxes: 1984* (Washington: ACIR, 1984).

45. Alan Rosenthal, *Legislative Life: People, Process, and Performance in the States* (New York: Harper & Row, 1981), and William K. Muir, Jr., *Legislature: California's School for Politics* (Chicago: University of Chicago Press, 1982).

46. Martin Diamond, "The Federalist's View of Federalism," in *Essays in Federalism* (Claremont, CA: Insti-

tute for Studies in Federalism, 1961), pp. 21–62. The quotation appears at p. 24. It was left to the anti-federalists to make the case for the states at the time of the founding. See Herbert J. Storing, *What the Anti-Federalists Were For* (Chicago: University of Chicago Press, 1981), chap. 3.

47. The classic statement is contained in *Federalist* No. 10.

48. *Journal,* p. 212.

49. *Ibid.* Later, as the author of the Virginia resolution of 1798 protesting the Alien and Sedition Acts, Madison would find the states to be useful more fundamentally, as a medium for resisting unconstitutional acts of the general government. According to his biographer, Irving Brant, this was an instance of putting "political objectives ahead of abstract thought. . . . He had no desire to exalt state sovereignty, but used it as a weapon. . . ." *James Madison: Father of the Constitution, 1787–1800* (Indianapolis: Bobbs-Merrill, 1950), p. 470. As the experience of even this exceptionally thoughtful and principled man shows, positions on federalism (as perhaps on institutional questions generally), are susceptible to change under the impact of new issues and configurations of interest.

50. Cf. Martha Derthick, "Preserving Federalism: Congress, the States, and the Supreme Court," *The Brookings Review,* vol. 4 (Winter/Spring 1986), pp. 32–37.

SECTION 4

Administrative Organization: Structure and Process

Wallace Sayre observed that public and private organizations are alike "in all unimportant respects."[1] Graham Allison echoes that argument in his selection in this section of the book. The distinction between public and private, however, is only one part of the debate about how organizations differ or are alike. Are all large organizations the same, for example? Are all organizations with the same function similar in other respects? Is a large hospital operated by the federal Veterans' Administration the same type of organization as a large hospital operated by the private sector?

A particularly contemporary perspective of great relevance on the debate is offered by James E. Swiss's discussion of "Adapting Total Quality Management (TQM) to Government." Although TQM has been effective in many business applications, it must be adjusted to fit government because administrative agencies typically provide services rather than products, do not have well defined customers, focus more on inputs than on outputs, and have organizational cultures that make it difficult to focus single-mindedly on anything, including quality alone. In the process of explaining the adjustments TQM will require for wide application in government, Swiss highlights some of the important differences between public and private organizations.

The emphasis on structure and efficiency dominated most early thinking about public organizations. The Scientific Management theorists in the United States such as Luther Gulick and others argued that organizations needed formal, hierarchical, and uniform structures to permit the application of general principles of management. Concepts such as the division of labor, specialization, and span of control added to the strong emphasis on the role of structure in organizational performance. Gulick's acronym POSDCORB (Planning, Organizing, Directing, Staffing, Coordinating, Reporting, and Budgeting) summarized both the simplicity and the generalizability of principles of management in such organizations.[2]

---

[1]Wallace Sayre, "The Triumph of Techniques over Purpose," *Public Administration Review*, 8 (Spring 1948), pp. 134–137.

[2]Luther Gulick, "Notes on the Theory of Organization," in Luther Gulick and L. Urwick, eds., *Papers on the Science of Administration* (New York: Institute of Public Administration, 1937), pp. 3–13.

The problem is, of course, that a large, formally structured organization is not responsive to the environment or to external direction. Particularly in the United States, which relies on a relatively large cadre of political appointees to direct policy and program efforts in public bureaucracies, this insularity became troublesome (see Aberbach and Rockman in Section 2 for additional discussion of this issue). Furthermore, large bureaucratic organizations are designed to be stable; this ability becomes problematic in a political environment demanding change. Two different views on "opening" bureaucracies are presented in the selections dealing with citizen participation in Section 9 and in Michael Lipsky's selection on street-level bureaucracy in this section.

Citizens' and elected officials' dissatisfaction with the performance and responsiveness of public bureaucracies has created consistent calls for change and reform of highly structured public organizations. Many such efforts have targeted the *processes* inside those organizations; information gathering and processing, decision making, financial management and budgeting reforms are common. As the Seidman and Gilmour selection that follows demonstrates, however, reorganization and restructuring reforms have also been frequent. Virtually every president this century has proposed a plan for reorganizing the executive branch of the federal government; in the past one hundred years, a presidential commission or advisory group has proposed structural reforms about every seven years. Jimmy Carter's Civil Service Reform Act of 1978 was unusual because it created both structural and procedural changes. As Seidman and Gilmour demonstrate, still other reforms have attempted to move away from traditional bureaucratic structures to more innovative and flexible organizational types.

There are many other ways to analyze organizations and their performance. Systems analysis, which views organizations as systems in constant interaction with their environment, is very useful for understanding and designing alternatives to rigid hierarchies. Analysts such as Rainey, who bases his work on careful systematic analysis of what organizations do, across sectors and across organizational types, provide a much better understanding of the relationship between critical organizational characteristics and effective performance.[3]

Still other analysts have applied formal mathematical modeling techniques to organizations and their activities. As Jonathan Bendor notes in his selection in this section, the work of William Niskanen was seminal in beginning the application of formal modeling to public bureaucratic organizations and their activities.[4] Recent work in this tradition has produced a distinctly different view of public organizations and their interactions with other key actors in the policy process. A new emphasis on the information that agencies create and control and on the strategic use of that informa-

---

[3]Hal G. Rainey, "Public Management: Recent Research on the Political Context and Managerial Roles, Structures, and Behaviors," *Journal of Management,* 15 (2: 1989), 229–250.

[4]See William Niskanen, *Bureaucracy and Representative Government* (Chicago: Aldine-Atherton, 1971).

tion—generally in budgetary negotiations and decisions—creates a view of public organizations very different from that defined by structural or systems analysts. Principal-agent analysis has also been utilized and is discussed in more depth by Bendor. Bendor provides an apt summary of the application of rational choice models to public administration when he observes that while many such approaches can now be identified in the study of public organizations, there is one critical quality in common: they require analysts to carefully specify assumptions about predicted bureaucratic behavior and to link the analysis to those assumptions. However it emerges, the future analysis of organizational structure, process, and performance will benefit from such additional rigor.

12.   Public and Private Management: Are They Fundamentally Alike in All Unimportant Respects?

Graham T. Allison

My subtitle puts Wallace Sayre's oft quoted "law" as a question. Sayre had spent some years in Ithaca helping plan Cornell's new School of Business and Public Administration. He left for Columbia with this aphorism: public and private management are fundamentally alike in all unimportant respects.

Sayre based his conclusion on years of personal observation of governments, a keen ear for what his colleagues at Cornell (and earlier at OPA) said about business, and a careful review of the literature and data comparing public and private management. Of the latter there was virtually none. Hence, Sayre's provocative "law" was actually an open invitation to research.

Unfortunately, in the 50 years since Sayre's pronouncement, the data base

for systematic comparison of public and private management has improved little. Consequently, when Scotty Campbell called six weeks ago to inform me that I would make some remarks at this conference, we agreed that I would, in effect, take up Sayre's invitation to *speculate* about similarities and differences among public and private management in ways that suggest significant opportunities for systematic investigation.

To reiterate: this paper is not a report of a major research project of systematic study. Rather, it is a response to a request for a brief summary of reflections of a dean of a school of government who now spends his time doing a form of public management—managing what Jim March has labeled an "organized anarchy"—rather than thinking, much less writing.[1] Moreover, the speculation here will appear to reflect a characteristic Harvard presumption that Cambridge either is the world, or is an adequate sample of the world. I say "appear" since as a North Carolinean, I am self-conscious about this parochialism. Nevertheless, I have concluded that the purposes of this

SOURCE: "Public and Private Management: Are They Fundamentally Alike in All Unimportant Respects?" by Graham T. Allison, Proceedings for the Public Management Research Conference, November 19–20, 1979 (Washington, D.C.: Office of Personnel Management, OPM Document 127-53-1, February 1980), pp. 27–38.

conference may be better served by providing a deliberately parochial perspective on these issues—and thereby presenting a clear target for others to shoot at. Finally, I must acknowledge that this paper plagiarizes freely from a continuing discussion among my colleagues at Harvard about the development of the field of public management, especially from Joe Bower, Hale Champion, Gordon Chase, Charles Christenson, Richard Darman, John Dunlop, Phil Heymann, Larry Lynn, Mark Moore, Dick Neustadt, Roger Porter, and Don Price. Since my colleagues have not had the benefit of commenting on this presentation, I suspect I have some points wrong, or out of context, or without appropriate subtlety or amendment. Thus I assume full liability for the words that follow.

This paper is organized as follows:

- Section 1 frames the issue: What is public management?
- Section 2 focuses on similarities: How are public and private management basically alike?
- Section 3 concentrates on differences: How do public and private management differ?
- Section 4 poses the question more operationally: How are the jobs and responsibilities of two specific managers, one public and one private, alike and different?
- Section 5 attempts to derive from this discussion suggestions about promising research directions and then outlines one research agenda and strategy for developing knowledge of and instruction about public management.

SECTION 1

Framing the Issue: What is Public Management

What is the meaning of the term "management" as it appears in Office of *Management* and Budget, or Office of Per-

sonnel *Management?* Is "management" different from, broader or narrower than "administration"? Should we distinguish between management, leadership, entrepreneurship, administration, policymaking, and implementation?

Who are "public managers"? Mayors, governors, and presidents? City managers, secretaries, and commissioners? Bureau chiefs? Office directors? Legislators? Judges?

Recent studies of OPM and OMB shed some light on these questions. OPM's major study of the "Current Status of Public Management Research" completed in May 1978 by Selma Mushkin of Georgetown's Public Service Laboratory starts with this question. The Mushkin report notes the definition of "public management" employed by the Interagency Study Committee on Policy Management Assistance in its 1975 report to OMB. That study identified the following core elements:

1. *Policy Managment* The identification of needs, analysis of options, selection of programs, and allocation of resources on a jurisdiction-wide basis.
2. *Resource Management* The establishment of basic administrative support systems, such as budgeting, financial management, procurement and supply, and personnel management.
3. *Program Management* The implementation of policy or daily operation of agencies carrying out policy along functional lines (education, law enforcement, etc.).[2]

The Mushkin report rejects this definition in favor of an "alternative list of public management elements." These elements are:

- Personnel Management (other than work force planning and collective bargaining and labor management relations)
- Work Force Planning

- Collective Bargaining and Labor Management Relations
- Productivity and Performance Measurement
- Organization/Reorganization
- Financial Management (including the management of intergovernmental relations)
- Evaluation Research, and Program and Management Audit.[3]

Such terminological tangles seriously hamper the development of public management as a field of knowledge. In our efforts to discuss public management curriculum at Harvard, I have been struck by how differently people use these terms, how strongly many individuals feel about some distinction they believe is marked by a difference between one word and another, and consequently, how large a barrier terminology is to convergent discussion. These verbal obstacles virtually prohibit conversation that is both brief and constructive among individuals who have not developed a common language or a mutual understanding of each others' use of terms. (What this point may imply for this conference, I leave to the reader.)

This terminological thicket reflects a more fundamental conceptual confusion. There exists no over-arching framework that orders the domain. In an effort to get a grip on the phenomena—the buzzing, blooming confusion of people in jobs performing tasks that produce results—both practitioners and observers have strained to find distinctions that facilitate their work. The attempts in the early decades of this century to draw a sharp line between "policy" and "administration," like more recent efforts to make a similar divide between "policy-making" and "implementation," reflect a common search for a simplification that allows one to put the value-laden issues of politics to one side (who gets what, when, and how), and focus on the more limited issue of how to perform tasks more efficiently.[4] But can anyone really deny that the "how" substantially affects the "who," the "what," and the "when"? The basic categories now prevalent in discussions of public management—strategy, personnel management, financial management, and control—are mostly derived from a business context in which executives manage hierarchies. The fit of these concepts to the problems that confront public managers is not clear.

Finally, there exists no ready data on what public managers do. Instead, the academic literature, such as it is, mostly consists of speculation tied to bits and pieces of evidence about the tail or the trunk or other manifestation of the proverbial elephant.[5] In contrast to the literally thousands of cases describing problems faced by private managers and their practice in solving these problems, case research from the perspective of a public manager is just beginning.[6] Why the public administration field has generated so little data about public management, my fellow panelist Dwight Waldo will explain. But the paucity of data on the phenomena inhibits systematic empirical research on similarities and differences between public and private management, leaving the field to a mixture of reflection on personal experience and speculation.

For the purpose of this presentation, I will follow Webster and use the term management to mean the organization and direction of resources to achieve a desired result. I will focus on *general managers,* that is, individuals charged with managing a whole organization or multifunctional sub-unit. I will be interested in the general manager's full responsibilities, both *inside* his organization in integrating the diverse contributions of specialized sub-units of the organization to achieve results, and *outside* his organization in relating his organization and its product to external constituencies. I will begin with the simplifying assumption that managers of traditional government organizations are public managers, and managers of traditional private businesses, private managers. Lest the discussion fall victim to the fallacy of misplaced abstraction, I will take the Director of EPA and the Chief Executive Officer of American Motors as, respectively, public and private managers. Thus, our central question can be put concretely: in what ways are the jobs and responsibilities of Doug Costle as Director of EPA similar to and different from those of Roy Chapin as Chief Executive Officer of American Motors?

SECTION 2

Similarities: How Are Public and Private Management Alike?

At one level of abstraction, it is possible to identify a set of general management functions. The most famous such list appeared in Gulick and Urwick's classic *Papers on the Science of Administration.*[7] Gulick summarized the work of the chief executive in the acronym POSDCORB. The letters stand for:

- Planning
- Organizing
- Staffing
- Directing
- Coordinating
- Reporting
- Budgeting

With various additions, amendments, and refinements, similar lists of general management functions can be found through the management literature from Barnard to Drucker.[8]

I shall resist here my natural academic instinct to join the intramural debate among proponents of various lists and distinctions. Instead, I simply offer one composite list (see Table 12.1) that attempts to incorporate the major functions that have been identified for general managers, whether public or private.

These common functions of management are not isolated and discrete, but rather integral components separated here for purposes of analysis. The character and relative significance of the various functions differ from one time to another in the history of any organization, and between one organization and another. But whether in a public or private setting, the challenge for the general manager is to integrate all these elements so as to achieve results.

SECTION 3

Differences: How Are Public and Private Management Different?

While there is a level of generality at which management is management, whether public or private, functions that bear identical labels take on rather different meaning in public and private settings. As Larry Lynn has pointed out, one powerful piece of evidence in the debate between those who emphasize "similarities" and those who underline "differences" is the nearly unanimous conclusion of individuals who have been general managers in both business and government. Consider the reflections of George Shultz (former director of OMB, Secretary of Labor, Secretary of the Treasury; now president of Bechtel), Donald Rumsfeld (former congressman, director of OEO, director of the Cost of Living Council, White House chief of staff, and Secretary of Defense; now president of GD Searle and Company), Michael Blumenthal (former chairman and chief executive officer of Bendix, Secretary of the Treasury, and now vice chairman of Burrows), Roy Ash (former president of Litton Industries, director of OMB; now president of Addressograph), Lyman Hamilton (former budget officer in BOB, high commissioner of

Table 12.1   Functions of General Management

Strategy

1. Establishing Objectives and Priorities for the organization (on the basis of forecasts of the external environment and the organization's capacities).
2. Devising Operational Plans to achieve these objectives.

Managing Internal Components

3. Organizing and Staffing: In organizing the manager establishes structure (units and positions with assigned authority and responsibilities) and procedures (for coordinating activity and taking action); in staffing he tries to fit the right persons in the key jobs.*
4. Directing Personnel and the Personnel Management System: The capacity of the organization is embodied primarily in its members and their skills and knowledge; the personnel management system recruits, selects, socializes, trains, rewards, punishes, and exits the organization's human capital, which constitutes the organization's capacity to act to achieve its goals and to respond to specific directions from management.
5. Controlling Performance: Various management information systems—including operating and capital budgets, accounts, reports and statistical systems, performance appraisals, and product evaluation—assist management in making decisions and in measuring progress towards objectives.

Managing External Constituencies

6. Dealing with "External" Units of the organization subject to some common authority: Most general managers must deal with general managers of other units within the larger organization—above, laterally, and below—to achieve their unit's objectives.
7. Dealing with Independent Organizations: Agencies from other branches or levels of government, interest groups, and private enterprises that can importantly affect the organization's ability to achieve its objectives.
8. Dealing with the Press and Public whose action or approval or acquiescence is required.

*Organization and staffing are frequently separated in such lists, but because of the interaction between the two, they are combined here. See Graham Allison and Peter Stanton, *Remaking Foreign Policy* (Basic Books, 1976), p. 14.

Okinawa, division chief in the World Bank and president of ITT), and George Romney (former president of American Motors, governor of Michigan and Secretary of Housing and Urban Development).[9] All judge public management different from private management— and harder!

Three Orthogonal Lists of Differences. My review of these recollections, as well as the thoughts of academics, has identified three interesting, orthogonal lists that summarize the current state of the field: one by John Dunlop; one major *Public Administration Review* survey of

the literature comparing public and private organizations by Hal Rainey, Robert Backoff and Charles Levine; and one by Richard E. Neustadt prepared for the National Academy of Public Administration's Panel on Presidential Management.

John T. Dunlop's "impressionistic comparison of government management and private business" yields the following contrasts.[10]

1. **Time perspective.** Government managers tend to have relatively short time horizons dictated by political necessities and the political calen-

dar, while private managers appear to take a longer time perspective oriented toward market developments, technological innovation and investment, and organization building.

2. **Duration.** The length of service of politically appointed top government managers is relatively short, averaging no more than 18 months recently for assistant secretaries, while private managers have a longer tenure both in the same position and in the same enterprise. A recognized element of private business management is the responsibility to train a successor or several possible candidates while the concept is largely alien to public management since fostering a successor is perceived to be dangerous.

3. **Measurement of performance.** There is little if any agreement on the standards and measurement of performance to appraise a government manager, while various tests of performance—financial return, market share, performance measures for executive compensation—are well established in private business and often made explicit for a particular managerial position during a specific period ahead.

4. **Personnel constraints.** In government there are two layers of managerial officials that are at times hostile to one another: the civil service (or now the executive system) and the political appointees. Unionization of government employees exists among relatively high-level personnel in the hierarchy and includes a number of supervisory personnel. Civil service, union contract provisions, and other regulations complicate the recruitment, hiring, transfer, and layoff or discharge of personnel to achieve managerial objectives or preferences. By comparison, private business managements have consider-

ably greater latitude, even under collective bargaining, in the management of subordinates. They have much more authority to direct the employees of their organization. Government personnel policy and administration are more under the control of staff (including civil service staff outside an agency) compared to the private sector in which personnel are much more subject to line responsibility.

5. **Equity and efficiency.** In governmental management great emphasis tends to be placed on providing equity among different constituencies, while in private business management relatively greater stress is placed upon efficiency and competitive performance.

6. **Public processes versus private processes.** Governmental management tends to be exposed to public scrutiny and to be more open, while private business management is more private and its processes more internal and less exposed to public review.

7. **Role of press and media.** Governmental management must contend regularly with the press and media; its decisions are often anticipated by the press. Private decisions are less often reported in the press, and the press has a much smaller impact on the substance and timing of decisions.

8. **Persuasion and direction.** In government, managers often seek to mediate decisions in response to a wide variety of pressures and must often put together a coalition of inside and outside groups to survive. By contrast, private management proceeds much more by direction or the issuance of orders to subordinates by superior managers with little risk of contradiction. Governmental managers tend to regard themselves as responsive to many

superiors while private managers look more to one higher authority.

9. **Legislative and judicial impact.** Governmental managers are often subject to close scrutiny by legislative oversight groups or even judicial orders in ways that are quite uncommon in private business management. Such scrutiny often materially constrains executive and administrative freedom to act.

10. **Bottom line.** Governmental managers rarely have a clear bottom line, while that of a private business manager is profit, market performance, and survival.

The *Public Administration Review's* major review article comparing public and private organizations, Rainey, Backoff and Levine, attempts to summarize the major points of consensus in the literature on similarities and differences among public and private organizations.[11] Table 12.2 presents that summary.

Third, Richard E. Neustadt, in a fashion close to Dunlop's notes six major differences between Presidents of the United States and Chief Executive Officers of major corporations.[12]

1. **Time-Horizon.** The private chief begins by looking forward a decade, or thereabouts, his likely span barring extraordinary troubles. The first-term President looks forward four years at most, with the fourth (and now even the third) year dominated by campaigning for reelection. (What second-termers look toward we scarcely know, having seen but one such term completed in the past quarter century.)

2. **Authority** over the enterprise. Subject to concurrence from the Board of Directors which appointed and can fire him, the private executive sets organization goals, shifts structures, procedure, and personnel to suit,

monitors results, reviews key operational decisions, deals with key outsiders, and brings along his board. Save for the deep but narrow sphere of military movements, a President's authority in these respects is shared with well-placed members of Congress (or their staffs); case by case, they may have more explicit authority than he does (contrast authorizations and appropriations with the "take-care" clause). As for "bringing along the Board," neither the Congressmen with whom he shares power or the primary and general electorates which "hired" him have either a Board's duties or a broad view of the enterprise precisely matching his.

3. **Career-System.** The model corporation is a true career system, something like the Forest Service after initial entry. In normal times the chief himself is chosen from within, or he is chosen from another firm in the same industry. He draws department heads et al. from among those with whom he's worked, or whom he knows in comparable companies. He and his principal associates will be familiar with each other's roles—indeed he probably has had a number of them—and also usually with one another's operating styles, personalities, idiosyncracies. Contrast the President who rarely has had much experience "downtown," probably knows little of most roles there (much of what he knows will turn out wrong), and less of most associates whom he appoints there, willy-nilly, to fill places by inauguration day. Nor are they likely to know one another well, coming as they do from "everywhere" and headed as most are toward oblivion.

4. **Media Relations.** The private executive represents his firm and speaks for it publicly in exceptional circumstances; he and his associates judge

Table 12.2   Public Administration Review Research Developments

SUMMARY OF LITERATURE ON DIFFERENCES BETWEEN PUBLIC AND PRIVATE
ORGANIZATIONS: MAIN POINTS OF CONSENSUS
The following table presents a summary of the points of consensus by stating them as
propositions regarding the attributes of a public organization, relative to those of a private
organization

Topic	Proposition
I. Environmental Factors	
I.1. Degree of market exposure (reliance on appropriations)	I.1.a. Less market exposure results in less incentive to cost reduction, operating efficiency, effective performance
	I.1.b. Less market exposure results in lower allocational efficiency (reflection of consumer preferences, proportioning supply to demand, etc.)
	I.1.c. Less market exposure means lower availability of market indicators and information (prices, profits, etc.)
I.2. Legal, formal constraints (courts, legislature, hierarchy)	I.2.a. More constraints on procedures, spheres of operations (less autonomy of managers in making such choices)
	I.2.b. Greater tendency to proliferation of formal specifications and controls
	I.2.c. More external sources of formal influence, and greater fragmentation of those sources
I.3. Political influences	I.3.a. Greater diversity of intensity of external informal influences on decisions (bargaining, public opinion, interest group reactions)
	I.3.b. Greater need for support of "constituencies"—client groups, sympathetic formal authorities, etc.
II. Organization-Environment Transactions	
II.1. Coerciveness ("coercive," "monopolistic," unavoidable nature of many government activities)	II.1.a. More likely that participation in consumption and financing of services will be unavoidable or mandatory. (Government has unique sanctions and coercive powers.)
II.2. Breadth of impact	II.2.a. Broader impact, greater symbolic significance of actions of public administrators. (Wider scope of concern, such as "public interest.")
II.3. Public scrutiny	II.3.a. Greater public scrutiny of public officials and their actions
II.4. Unique public expectations	II.4.a. Greater public expectations that public officials act with more fairness, responsiveness, accountability, and honesty

Table 12.2   (*continued*)

Topic	Proposition
III. Internal Structures and Processes	
III.1. Complexity of objectives, evaluation and decision criteria	III.1.a. Greater multiplicity and diversity of objectives and criteria
	III.1.b. Greater vagueness and intangibility of objectives and criteria
	III.1.c. Greater tendency of goals to be conflicting (more "tradeoffs")
III.2. Authority relations and the role of the administrator	III.2.a. Less decision-making autonomy and flexibility on the part of the public administrators
	III.2.b. Weaker, more fragmented authority over subordinates and lower levels. (1. Subordinates can bypass, appeal to alternative authorities. 2. Merit system constraints.)
	III.2.c. Greater reluctance to delegate, more levels of review, and greater use of formal regulations. (Due to difficulties in supervision and delegation, resulting from III.1.b.)
	III.2.d. More political, expository role for top managers
III.3. Organizational performance	III.3.a. Greater cautiousness, rigidity. Less innovativeness
	III.3.b. More frequent turnover of top leaders due to elections and political appointments results in greater disruption of implementation of plans
III.4. Incentives and incentive structures	III.4.a. Greater difficulty in devising incentives for effective and efficient performance
	III.4.b. Lower valuation of pecuniary incentives by employees
III.5. Personal characteristics of employees	III.5.a. Variations in personality traits and needs, such as higher dominance and flexibility, higher need for achievement, on part of government managers
	III.5.b. Lower work satisfaction and lower organization commitment

(III.5.a. and III.5.b. represent results of individual empirical studies, rather than points of agreement among authors.)

Source: Public Administration Review (March-April, 1976), pp. 236–237.

the exceptions. Those aside, he neither sees the press nor gives its members access to internal operations, least of all in his own office, save to make a point deliberately for public-relations purposes. The President, by contrast, is routinely on display, continuously dealing with the White House press and with the wider circle of political reporters, commentators, columnists. He needs them in his business, day by day, nothing exceptional about it, and they need him in theirs: the TV Network News programs lead off with him some nights each week. They and the President are as mutually dependent as he and Congressmen (or more so). Comparatively speaking, these relations overshadow most administrative ones much of the time for him.

5. **Performance Measurement.** The private executive expects to be judged, and in turn to judge subordinates, by profitability, however the firm measures it (a major strategic choice). In practice, his Board may use more subjective measures; so may he, but at risk to morale and good order. The relative virtue of profit, of "the bottom line" is its legitimacy, its general acceptance in the business world by all concerned. Never mind its technical utility in given cases, its apparent "objectivity," hence "fairness," has enormous social usefulness; a myth that all can live by. For a President there is no counterpart (expect *in extremis* the "smoking gun" to justify impeachment). The general public seems to judge a President, at least in part, by what its members think is happening to them, in their own lives; Congressmen, officials, interest groups appear to judge by what they guess, at given times, he can do for or to their causes. Members of the press interpret both of these and spread a simplified criterion affecting both, the legislative box-score, a standard

of the press's own devising. The White House denigrates them all except when it does well.

6. **Implementation.** The corporate chief, supposedly, does more than choose a strategy and set a course of policy; he also is supposed to oversee what happens after, how in fact intentions turn into results, or if they don't to take corrective action, monitoring through his information system, acting, and if need be, through his personnel system. A President, by contrast, while himself responsible for budgetary proposals, too, in many spheres of policy, appears ill-placed and ill-equipped, to monitor what agencies of states, of cities, corporations, unions, foreign governments are up to or to change personnel in charge. Yet these are very often the executants of "his" programs. Apart from defense and diplomacy the federal government does two things in the main: it issues and applies regulations and it awards grants in aid. Where these are discretionary, choice usually is vested by statute in a Senate-confirmed official well outside the White House. Monitoring is his function, not the President's except at second-hand. And final action is the function of the subjects of the rules and funds; they mostly are not federal personnel at all. In defense, the arsenals and shipyards are gone; weaponry comes from the private sector. In foreign affairs it is the other governments whose actions we would influence. From implementors like these a President is far removed most of the time. He intervenes, if at all, on a crash basis, not through organizational incentives.

Underlying these lists' sharpest distinctions between public and private management is a fundamental *constitutional difference.* In business, the functions of general management are centralized in a single individual: the Chief Executive Officer. The goal is authority commensurate with responsibility. In contrast, in the U.S. government, the functions of general management are constitutionally spread among competing institutions: the executive, two houses of Congress, and the courts. The constitutional goal was "not to promote efficiency but to preclude the exercise of arbitrary power," as Justice Brandeis observed. Indeed, as *The Federalist Papers* make starkly clear, the aim was to create incentives to compete: "the great security against a gradual concentration of the several powers in the same branch, consists in giving those who administer each branch the constitutional means and personal motives to resist encroachment of the others. Ambition must be made to counteract ambition."[13] Thus, the general management functions concentrated in the CEO of a private business are, by constitutional design, spread in the public sector among a number of competing institutions and thus shared by a number of individuals whose ambitions are set against one another. For most areas of public policy today, these individuals include at the federal level the chief elected official, the chief appointed executive, the chief career official, and several congressional chieftains. Since most public services are actually delivered by state and local governments, with independent sources of authority, this means a further array of individuals at these levels.

SECTION 4

An Operational Perspective: How Are the Jobs and Responsibilities of Doug Costle, Director of EPA, and Roy Chapin, CEO of American Motors, Similar and Different?

If organizations could be separated neatly into two homogeneous piles, one public and one private, the task of identifying similarities and differences between managers of these enterprises would be relatively easy. In fact, as Dunlop has pointed out, "the real world of management is composed of distributions, rather than single undifferentiated forms, and there is an increasing variety of hybrids." Thus for each major attribute of organizations, specific entities can be located on a spectrum. On most dimensions, organizations classified as "predominantly public" and those "predominantly private" overlap.[14] Private business organizations vary enormously among themselves in size, in management structure and philosophy, and in the constraints under which they operate. For example, forms of ownership and types of managerial control may be somewhat unrelated. Compare a family-held enterprise, for instance, with a public utility and a decentralized conglomerate, a Bechtel with ATT and Textron. Similarly, there are vast differences in management of governmental organizations. Compare the Government Printing Office or TVA or the police department of a small town with the Department of Energy or the Department of Health and Human Services. These distributions and varieties should encourage penetrating comparisons within both business and governmental organizations, as well as contrasts and comparisons across these broad categories, a point to which we shall return in considering directions for research.

Absent a major research effort, it may nonetheless be worthwhile to examine the jobs and responsibilities of two specific managers, neither polar extremes, but one clearly public, the other private. For this purpose, and primarily because of the availability of cases that describe the problems and opportunities each confronted, consider Doug Costle, Administrator of EPA, and Roy Chapin, CEO of American Motors.[15]

Doug Costle, Administrator of EPA, January 1977. The mission of EPA is prescribed by laws creating the agency and authorizing its major programs. That mission is "to control and abate pollution in the areas of air, water, solid wastes, noise, radiation, and toxic substances. EPA's mandate is to mount an integrated, coordinated attack on environmental pollution in cooperation with state and local governments."[16]

EPA's organizational structure follows from its legislative mandates to control particular pollutants in specific environments: air and water, solid wastes, noise, radiation, pesticides and chemicals. As the new Administrator, Costle inherited the Ford Administration's proposed budget for EPA of $802 million for federal 1978 with a ceiling of 9,698 agency positions.

The setting into which Costle stepped is difficult to summarize briefly. As Costle characterized it:

- "Outside there is a confusion on the part of the public in terms of what this agency is all about: what it is doing, where it is going."
- "The most serious constraint on EPA is the inherent complexity in the state of our knowledge, which is constantly changing."
- "Too often, acting under extreme deadlines mandated by Congress, EPA has announced regulations, only to find out that they knew very little about the problem. The central problem is the inherent complexity of the job that the agency has been asked to do and the fact that what it is asked to do changes from day to day."
- "There are very difficult internal management issues not amenable to a quick solution: the skills mix problem within the agency; a research program with laboratory facilities scattered all over the country and cemented in place, largely by political alliances on the Hill that would frustrate efforts to

pull together a coherent research program."
- "In terms of EPA's original mandate in the bulk pollutants we may be hitting the asymptotic part of the curve in terms of incremental clean-up costs. You have clearly conflicting national goals: energy and environment, for example."

Costle judged his six major tasks at the outset to be:

- assembling a top management team (six assistant administrators and some 25 office heads);
- addressing EPA's legislative agenda (EPA's basic legislative charter—the Clean Air Act and the Clean Water Act—were being rewritten as he took office; the pesticides program was up for reauthorization also in 1977);
- establishing EPA's role in the Carter Administration (aware that the Administration would face hard trade-offs between the environment and energy, energy regulations and the economy, EPA regulations of toxic substances and the regulations of FDA, CSPS, and OSHA, Costle identified the need to build relations with the other key players and to enhance EPA's standing);
- building ties to constituent groups (both because of their role in legislating the agency's mandate and in successful implementation of EPA's programs);
- making specific policy decisions (for example, whether to grant or deny a permit for the Seabrook Nuclear Generating Plant cooling system. Or how the Toxic Substance Control Act, enacted in October 1976, would be implemented: this act gave EPA new responsibilities for regulating the manufacture, distribution, and use of chemical substances so as to prevent unreasonable risks to health and the environment. Whether EPA would require chemical manufacturers to pro-

vide some minimum information on various substances, or require much stricter reporting requirements for the 1,000 chemical substances already known to be hazardous, or require companies to report all chemicals, and on what timetable, had to be decided and the regulations issued);

• rationalizing the internal organization of the agency (EPA's extreme decentralization to the regions and its limited technical expertise).

No easy job.

Roy Chapin and American Motors, January 1977.

In January 1967, in an atmosphere of crisis, Roy Chapin was appointed Chairman and Chief Executive Officer of American Motors (and William Luneburg, President and Chief Operating Officer). In the four previous years, AMC unit sales had fallen 37 percent and market share from over six percent to under three percent. Dollar volume in 1967 was off 42 percent from the all-time high of 1963 and earnings showed a net loss of $76 million on sales of $656 million. Columnists began writing obituaries for AMC. *Newsweek* characterized AMC as "a flabby dispirited company, a product solid enough but styled with about as much flair as corrective shoes, and a public image that melted down to one unshakeable label: loser." Said Chapin: "We were driving with one foot on the accelerator and one foot on the brake. We didn't know where the hell we were."

Chapin announced to his stockholders at the outset that "we plan to direct ourselves most specifically to those areas of the market where we can be fully effective. We are not going to attempt to be all things to all people, but to concentrate on those areas of consumer needs we can meet better than anyone else." As he recalled: "There were problems early in 1967 which demanded immediate attention, and which accounted for much of our time for several months. Nevertheless, we began planning beyond them, establishing objectives, programs and timetables through 1972. Whatever happened in the short run, we had to prove ourselves in the marketplace in the long run."

Chapin's immediate problems were five:

• The company was virtually out of cash and an immediate supplemental bank loan of $20 million was essential.

• Car inventories—company owned and dealer owned—had reached unprecedented levels. The solution to this glut took five months and could be accomplished only by a series of plant shutdowns in January 1967.

• Sales of the Rambler American series had stagnated and inventories were accumulating; a dramatic merchandising move was concocted and implemented in February, dropping the price tag on the American to a position midway between the VW and competitive smaller U.S. compacts, by both cutting the price to dealers and trimming dealer discounts from 21 percent to 17 percent.

• Administrative and commercial expenses were judged too high and thus a vigorous cost reduction program was initiated that trimmed $15 million during the first year. Manufacturing and purchasing costs were also trimmed significantly to approach the most effective levels in the industry.

• The company's public image had deteriorated: the press was pessimistic and much of the financial community had written it off. To counteract this, numerous formal and informal meetings were held with bankers, investment firms, government officials, and the press.

As Chapin recalls "with the immediate fires put out, we could put in place the pieces of a corporate growth plan—a definition of a way of life in the auto industry for American Motors. We felt that our reason for being, which would enable us not just to survive but to grow, lay in bringing a different approach to the auto market—in picking our spots and then being innovative and aggressive." The new corporate growth plan included a dramatic change in the approach to the market to establish a "youthful image" for the company (by bringing out new sporty models like the Javelin and by entering the racing field), "changing the product line from one end to the other" by 1972, acquiring Kaiser Jeep (selling the company's non-transportation assets and concentrating on specialized transportation, including Jeep, a company that had lost money in each of the preceding five years, but that Chapin believed could be turned around by substantial cost reductions and economies of scale in manufacturing, purchasing, and administration).

Chapin succeeded: for the year ending September 30, 1971, AMC earned $10.2 million on sales of $1.2 billion.

Recalling the list of general management functions in Table 1, which similarities and differences appear salient and important?

Strategy. Both Chapin and Costle had to establish objectives and priorities and to devise operational plans. In business, "corporate strategy is the pattern of major objectives, purposes, or goals and essential policies and plans for achieving these goals, stated in such a way as to define what business the company is in or is to be in and the kind of company it is or is to be."[17] In reshaping the strategy of AMC and concentrating on particular segments of the transportation market, Chapin had to consult his Board and had to arrange financing. But the control was substantially his.

How much choice did Costle have at EPA as to the "business it is or is to be in" or the kind of agency "it is or is to be"? These major strategic choices emerged from the legislative process which mandated whether he should be in the business of controlling pesticides or toxic substances and if so on what timetable, and occasionally, even what level of particulate per million units he was required to control. The relative role of the President, other members of the administration (including White House staff, Congressional relations, and other agency heads), the EPA Administrator, Congressional committee chairmen, and external groups in establishing the broad strategy of the agency constitutes an interesting question.

Managing Internal Components. For both Costle and Chapin, staffing was key. As Donald Rumsfeld has observed "the single, most important task of the chief executive is to select the right people. I've seen terrible organization charts in both government and business that were made to work well by good people. I've seen beautifully charted organizations that didn't work very well because they had the wrong people."[18]

The leeway of the two executives in organizing and staffing were considerably different, however. Chapin closed down plants, moved key managers, hired and fired, virtually at will. As Michael Blumenthal has written about Treasury, "if you wish to make substantive changes, policy changes, and the Department's employees don't like what you're doing, they have ways of frustrating you or stopping you that do not exist in private industry. The main method they have is Congress. If I say I want to shut down a particular unit or transfer the function of one area to another, there are ways of going to Congress and in fact using friends in the Congress to block the move. They can also use the press to try to stop you. If I at Bendix wished to transfer a division from Ann Arbor to Detroit because I figured out that we could save money that way, as long as I could do it decently and carefully, it's of no lasting interest to the press. The press can't stop me. They may write about it in the local paper, but that's about it."[19]

For Costle, the basic structure of the agency was set by law. The labs, their location, and most of their personnel were fixed. Though he could recruit his key subordinates, again restrictions like the conflict of interest law and the prospect of a Senate confirmation fight led him to drop his first choice for the Assistant Administrator for Research and Development, since he had worked for a major chemical company. While Costle could resort to changes in the process for developing policy or regulations in order to circumvent key office directors whose views he did not share, for example, Eric Stork, the deputy assistant Administrator in charge of Mobile Source Air Program, such maneuvers took considerable time, provoked extensive infighting, and delayed significantly the development of Costle's program.

In the direction of personnel and management of the personnel system, Chapin exercised considerable authority. While the United Auto Workers limited his authority over workers, at the management level he assigned people and reassigned responsibility consistent with his general plan. While others may have felt that his decisions to close down particular plants or to drop a particular product were mistaken, they complied. As George Shultz has observed: "One of the first lessons I learned in moving from government to business is that in business you must be very careful when you tell someone who is working for you to do something because the probability is high that he or she will do it."[20]

Costle faced a civil service system designed to prevent spoils as much as to promote productivity. The Civil Service Commission exercised much of the responsibility for the personnel function in his agency. Civil service rules severely restricted his discretion, took long periods to exhaust, and often required complex maneuvering in a specific case to achieve any results. Equal opportunity rules and their administration provided yet another network of procedural and substantive inhibitions. In retrospect, Costle found the civil service system a much larger constraint on his actions and demand on his time than he had anticipated.

In controlling performance, Chapin was able to use measures like profit and market share, to decompose those objectives to sub-objectives for lower levels of the organization and to measure the performance of managers of particular models, areas, divisions. Cost accounting rules permitted him to compare plants within AMC and to compare AMC's purchases, production, and even administration with the best practice in the industry.

Managing External Constituencies. As Chief Executive Officer, Chapin had to deal only with the Board. For Costle, within the executive branch but beyond his agency lay many factors critical to the achievement of his agency's objectives: the President and the White House, Energy, Interior, the Council on Environmental Quality, OMB. Actions each could take, either independently or after a process of consultation in which they disagreed with him, could frustrate his agency's achievement of its assigned mission. Consequently, he spent considerable time building his agency's reputation and capital for interagency disputes.

Dealing with independent external organizations was a necessary and even larger part of Costle's job. Since his agency's mission, strategy, authorizations, and appropriations emerged from the process of legislation, attention to Congressional committees, and Congressmen, and Congressmen's staff, and people who affect Congressmen and Congressional staffers rose to the top of Costle's agenda. In the first year, top level EPA officials appeared over 140 times before some 60 different committees and subcommittees.

Chapin's ability to achieve AMC's objectives could also be affected by independent external organizations: competitors, government (the Clean Air Act that was passed in 1970), consumer groups (recall Ralph Nader), and even suppliers of oil. More than most private managers, Chapin had to deal with the press in attempting to change the image of AMC. Such occasions were primarily at Chapin's initiative, and around events that Chapin's public affairs office orchestrated, for example, the announcement of a new racing car. Chapin also managed a marketing effort to persuade consumers that their tastes could best be satisfied by AMC products.

Costle's work was suffused by the press: in the daily working of the organization, in the perception by key publics of the agency and thus the agency's influence with relevant parties, and even in the setting of the agenda of issues to which the agency had to respond.

For Chapin, the bottom line was profit, market share, and the long-term competitive position of AMC. For Costle, what are the equivalent performance measures? Blumenthal answers by exaggerating the difference between appearance and reality: "At Bendix, it was the reality of the situation that in the end determined whether we succeeded or not. In the crudest sense, this meant the bottom line. You can dress up profits only for so long—if you're not successful, it's going to be clear. In government there is no bottom line, and that is why you can be successful if you appear to be successful—though, of course, appearance is not the only ingredient of

success."[21] Rumsfeld says: "In business, you're pretty much judged by results. I don't think the American people judge government officials this way . . . In government, too often you're measured by how much you seem to care, how hard you seem to try—things that do not necessarily improve the human condition . . . It's a lot easier for a President to get into something and end up with a few days of good public reaction than it is to follow through, to pursue policies to a point where they have a beneficial effect on human lives."[22] As George Shultz says: "In government and politics, recognition and therefore incentives go to those who formulate policy and maneuver legislative compromise. By sharp contrast, the kudos and incentives in business go to the persons who can get something done. It is execution that counts. Who can get the plant built, who can bring home the sales contract, who can carry out the financing, and so on."[23]

This casual comparison of one public and one private manager suggests what could be done—if the issue of comparisons were pursued systematically, horizontally across organizations and at various levels within organizations. While much can be learned by examining the chief executive officers of organizations, still more promising should be comparisons among the much larger numbers of middle managers. If one compared, for example, a regional administrator of EPA and an AMC division chief, or two comptrollers, or equivalent plant managers, some functions would appear more similar, and other differences would stand out. The major barrier to such comparisons is the lack of cases describing problems and practices of middle-level managers.[24] This should be a high priority in further research.

The differences noted in this comparison, for example, in the personnel area, have already changed with the Civil Service Reform Act of 1978 and the creation of the Senior Executive Service. Significant changes have also occurred in the automobile industry: under current circumstances, the CEO of Chrysler may seem much more like the Administrator of EPA. More precise comparison of different levels of management in both organizations, for example, accounting procedures used by Chapin to cut costs significantly as compared to equivalent procedures for judging the costs of EPA mandated pollution control devices, would be instructive.

SECTION 5

Implications for Research on Public Management

The debate between the assimilators and the differentiators, like the dispute between proponents of convergence and divergence between the U.S. and the Soviet Union reminds me of the old argument about whether the glass is half full or half empty. I conclude that public and private management are at least as different as they are similar, and that the differences are more important than the similarities. From this review of the "state of the art," such as it is, I draw a number of lessons for research on public management. I will try to state them in a way that is both succinct and provocative:

- First, the demand for performance from government and efficiency in government is both real and right. The perception that government's performance lags private business performance is also correct. But the notion that there is any significant body of private management practices and skills that can be transferred directly to public management tasks in a way that produces significant improvements is wrong.
- Second, performance in many public management positions can be im-

proved substantially, perhaps by an order of magnitude. That improvement will come not, however, from massive borrowing of specific private management skills and understandings. Instead, it will come, as it did in the history of private management, from an articulation of the general management function and a self-consciousness about the general public management point of view. The single lesson of private management most instructive to public management is the prospect of substantial improvement through recognition of and consciousness about the public management function.

Alfred Chandler's prize winning study, *The Visible Hand: The Managerial Revolution in American Business,*[25] describes the emergence of professional management in business. Through the 19th century most American businesses were run by individuals who performed management functions but had no self-consciousness about their management responsibilities. With the articulation of the general management perspective and the refinement of general management practices, by the 1920s, American businesses had become competitive in the management function. Individuals capable at management and self-conscious about their management tasks—setting objectives, establishing priorities, and driving the organization to results—entered firms and industries previously run by family entrepreneurs or ordinary employees and brought about dramatic increases in product. Business schools emerged to document better and worse practice, largely through the case method, to suggest improvements, and to refine specific management instruments. Important advances were made in technique. But the great leaps forward in productivity stemmed from the articulation of the general management point of view and the self-consciousness of managers about their function. (Analogously, at a lower level, the articulation of the salesman's role and task, together with the skills and values of salesmanship made it possible for individuals with moderate talents at sales to increase their level of sales tenfold.)

The routes by which people reach general management positions in government do not assure that they will have consciousness or competence in management. As a wise observer of government managers has written, "One of the difficult problems of schools of public affairs is to overcome the old-fashioned belief—still held by many otherwise sophisticated people—that the skills of management are simply the application of 'common sense' by any intelligent and broadly educated person to the management problems which are presented to him. It is demonstrable that many intelligent and broadly educated people who are generally credited with a good deal of 'common sense' make very poor managers. The skills of effective management require a good deal of uncommon sense and uncommon knowledge."[26] I believe that the most significant aspect of the Civil Service Reform Act of 1978 is the creation of the Senior Executive Service; the explicit identification of general managers in government. The challenge now is to assist people who occupy general management positions in actually becoming general managers.

- Third, careful review of private management rules of thumb that can be adapted to public management contexts will pay off. The 80—20 rule—80 percent of the benefits of most production processes come from the first 20 percent of effort—does have wide application, for example, in EPA efforts to reduce bulk pollutants.

- Fourth, Chandler documents the proposition that the categories and criteria for identifying costs, or calculating present value, or measuring the value added to intermediate products are not "natural." They are invented: creations of intelligence harnessed to operational tasks. While there are some particular accounting categories and rules, for example, for costing intermediate products, that may be directly transferable to public sector problems, the larger lesson is that dedicated attention to specific management functions can, as in the history of business, create for public sector managers accounting categories, and rules, and measures that cannot now be imagined.[27]

- Fifth, it is possible to learn from experience. What skills, attributes, and practices do competent managers exhibit and less successful managers lack? This is an empirical question that can be investigated in a straightforward manner. As Yogi Berra noted: "You can observe a lot just by watching."

- Sixth, the effort to develop public management as a field of knowledge should start from problems faced by practicing public managers. The preferences of professors for theorizing reflects deep-seated incentives of the academy that can be overcome only by careful institutional design.

In the light of these lessons, I believe one strategy for the development of public management should include:

- *Developing a significant number of cases on public management problems and practices.* Cases should describe typical problems faced by public managers. Cases should attend not only to top-level managers but to middle and lower-level managers. The dearth of cases at this level makes this a high priority for development. Cases should examine both general functions of management and specific organizational tasks, for example, hiring and firing. Public management cases should concentrate on the job of the manager running his unit.

- *Analyzing cases to identify better and worse practice.* Scientists search for "critical experiments." Students of public management should seek to identify "critical experiences" that new public managers could live through vicariously and learn from. Because of the availability of information, academics tend to focus on failures. But teaching people what not to do is not necessarily the best way to help them learn to be *doers.* By analyzing relative successes, it will be possible to extract rules of thumb, crutches, and concepts, for example, Chase's "law": wherever the product of a public organization has not been monitored in a way that ties performance to reward, the introduction of an effective monitoring system will yield a 50 percent improvement in that product in the short run. GAO's handbooks on evaluation techniques and summaries suggest what can be done.
- *Promoting systematic comparative research:* management positions in a single agency over time; similar management positions among several public agencies; public management levels within a single agency; similar management functions, for example, budgeting or management information systems, among agencies; managers across public and private organizations; and even cross-nationally. The data for this comparative research would be produced by the case development effort and would complement the large-scale development of cases on private management that is ongoing.
- *Linking to the training of public managers.* Intellectual development of the field of public management should be tightly linked to the training of public managers, including individuals already in positions of significant responsibility. Successful practice will appear in government, not in the university. University-based documentation of better and worse practice, and refinement of that practice, should start from problems of managers on the line. The intellectual effort required to develop the field of public management and the resources required to support this level of effort are most likely to be assembled if research and training are vitally linked. The new Senior Executive Service presents a major opportunity to do this.

The strategy outlined here is certainly not the only strategy for research in public management. Given the needs for effective public management, I believe that a *major* research effort should be mounted and that it should pursue a number of complementary strategies. Given where we start, I see no danger of overattention to, or overinvestment in the effort required in the immediate future.

Any resemblance between my preferred strategy and that of at least one school of government is not purely coincidental.

NOTES

1. In contrast to the management of structured hierarchies, for which the metaphor of a traditional football game in which each team attempts to amass the larger number of points is apt, an organized anarchy is better thought of as a soccer game played on a round field, ringed with goals; players enter and leave the field sporadically, and while there vigorously kick various

balls of sundry sizes and shapes towards one or another of the goals, judging themselves and being judged by assorted, ambiguous scoring systems. See Michael Cohen and James March, *Leadership and Ambiguity* (McGraw-Hill, 1974).

2. Selma J. Mushkin, Frank H. Sandifer and Sally Familton, *Current Status of Public Management: Research Conducted by or Supported by Federal Agencies* (Public Services Laboratory, Georgetown University, 1978), p. 10.

3. *Ibid.*, p. 11.

4. Though frequently identified as the author who established the complete separation between "policy" and "administration," Woodrow Wilson has in fact been unjustly accused. "It is the object of administrative study to discover, first, what government can properly and successfully do, and, secondly, how it can do these proper things with the utmost possible efficiency. . ." (Wilson, "The Study of Public Administration," published as an essay in 1888 and reprinted in *Political Science Quarterly*, December 1941, p. 481.) For another statement of the same point, see Brooks Adams, *The Theory of Social Revolutions* (Macmillan, 1913), pp. 207–208.

5. See Dwight Waldo, "Organization Theory: Revisiting the Elephant," *PAR* (November-December 1978). Reviewing the growing volume of books and articles on organization theory, Waldo notes that "growth in the volume of the literature is not to be equated with growth in knowledge."

6. See *Cases in Public Policy and Management,* Spring 1979 of the Intercollegiate Case Clearing House for a bibliography containing descriptions of 577 cases by 366 individuals from 79 institutions. Current casework builds on and expands earlier efforts of the Inter-University Case Program. See, for example, Harold Stein, ed., *Public Administration and Policy Development: A Case Book* (Harcourt, Brace, and Jovanovich, 1952), and Edwin A. Bock and Alan K. Campbell, eds., *Case Studies in American Government* (Prentice-Hall, 1962).

7. Luther Gulick and Al Urwick, eds., *Papers in the Science of Public Administration* (Institute of Public Administration, 1937).

8. See, for example, Chester I. Barnard, *The Functions of the Executive* (Howard University Press, 1938), and Peter F. Drucker, *Management: Tasks, Responsibilities, Practices* (Harper and Row, 1974). Barnard's recognition of human relations added an important dimension neglected in earlier lists.

9. See, for example, "A Businessman in a Political Jungle," *Fortune* (April 1964); "Candid Reflections of a Businessman in Washington," *Fortune* (January 29, 1979); "A Politician Turned Executive," *Fortune* (September 10, 1979); and "The Ambitions Interface," *Harvard Business Review* (November-December, 1979) for the views of Romney, Blumenthal, Rumsfeld, and Shultz, respectively.

10. John T. Dunlop, "Public Management," draft of an unpublished paper and proposal, Summer 1979.

11. Hal G. Rainey, Robert W. Backoff, and Charles N. Levine, "Comparing Public and Private Organizations," *Public Administration Review* (March-April, 1976).

12. Richard E. Neustadt, "American Presidents and Corporate Executives," a paper prepared for a meeting of the National Academy of Public Administration's Panel on Presidential Management, October 7–8, 1979.

13. *The Federalist Papers,* No. 51. The word "department" has been translated as "branch," which was its meaning in the original papers.

14. Failure to recognize the fact of distributions has led some observers to leap from one instance of similarity between public and private to general propositions about similarities between public and private institutions or management. See, for example, Michael Murray, "Comparing Public and Private Management: An Exploratory Essay," *Public Administration Review* (July-August, 1975).

15. These examples are taken from Bruce Scott, "American Motors Corporation" (Intercollegiate Case Clearing House #9-364-001); Charles B. Weigle with the collaboration of C. Roland Christensen, "American Motors Corporation II" (Intercollegiate Case Clearing House #6-372-350); Thomas R. Hitchner and Jacob Lew under the supervision of Philip B. Heymann and Stephen B. Hitchner, "Douglas Costle and the EPA (A)" (Kennedy School of Government Case #C94-78-216); and Jacob Lew and Stephen B. Hitchner, "Douglas Costle and the EPA (B)" (Kennedy School of Government Case #C96-78-217). For an earlier

exploration of a similar comparison, see Joseph Bower, "Effective Public Management," *Harvard Business Review* (March-April, 1977).

16. U.S. Government Manual, 1978/1979, 507.

17. Kenneth R. Andrews, *The Concept of Corporate Strategy* (Dow Jones-Irwin, 1971), p. 28.

18. "A Politician-Turned-Executive," *Fortune* (September 10, 1979), p. 92.

19. "Candid Reflections of a Businessman in Washington," *Fortune* (January 29, 1979), p. 39.

20. "The Abrasive Interface," *Harvard Business Review* (November-December 1979), p. 95.

21. *Fortune* (January 29, 1979), p. 36.

22. *Fortune* (September 10, 1979), p. 90.

23. *Harvard Business Review* (November-December 1979), p. 95.

24. The cases developed by Boston University's Public Management Program offer a promising start in this direction.

25. Alfred Chandler, *The Visible Hand: the Managerial Revolution in American Business* (Belnap Press of Harvard University Press, 1977).

26. Rufus Miles, "The Search for Identity of Graduate Schools of Public Affairs," *Public Administration Review* (November 1967).

27. Chandler, *op. cit.,* pp. 277–279.

13.   Adapting Total Quality Management (TQM) to Government

James E. Swiss

During the past ten years, total quality management (TQM) has had a major im-

SOURCE: "Adapting Total Quality Management (TQM) to Government" by James E. Swiss, *Public Administration Review:* 52 (July/August 1992). Reprinted by permission of the American Society for Public Administration.

pact on business management practices, and has been adopted by such high profile corporations as General Motors, Motorola, and Xerox (Gabor, 1990). More recently, TQM has begun to spread to many government organizations.[1] TQM has even been endorsed by President Bush, who said, "Reasserting our leadership will require a firm commitment to total quality management and the principle of continuous improvement. . . . Quality improvement principles apply . . . to the public sector as well as private enterprise" (Carr and Littman, 1990, p. 2).

Such enthusiastic endorsements often suggest that TQM can be transferred from the private sector to the public sector with very little modification. These suggestions are mistaken. TQM can indeed have a useful role to play in government, but only if it is substantially modified to fit the public sector's unique characteristics. This article attempts to sketch the adaptations necessary to turn orthodox, business-oriented TQM into a reformed TQM that will succeed in the public sector.

TOTAL QUALITY MANAGEMENT'S BUSINESS BACKGROUND

Total quality management requires adaptation for use in the public sector because it is very much a product of statistical quality control and industrial engineering, and almost all of its early applications were for assembly-line work and other routine processes. TQM was originally developed by an American statistician, W. Edwards Deming, but his approaches were adopted much more enthusiastically in post–World War II Japan than in his native country. When Japanese products such as electronics and automobiles began to outperform and outsell American products, the U.S. business sector started to reemphasize quality, in part by borrowing such Japanese techniques as TQM. There were a number of false starts; for example, many organizations broke off a relatively small piece of TQM—quality circles—and attempted to make them the primary and free-standing technique for achieving quality. However, by the mid-1980s, many U.S. corporations

began to encourage quality through integrated, multifaceted systems.

THE PRINCIPAL TENETS OF (ORTHODOX) TOTAL QUALITY MANAGEMENT

Several related but distinct systems attempt to increase organizational quality. Although Deming-based TQM is not the only quality system,[2] his version, encapsulated in TQM, is by far the most influential and widespread. Because Deming is a synthesizer, TQM contains many of the concepts of other quality management systems, even those not using the term TQM. Accordingly, I will term Deming's TQM the orthodox approach and will discuss its particulars.

TQM is a complicated and demanding system that cannot be completely summarized in a few paragraphs. None the less, many of its most important points can be captured in seven basic tenets.[3] Because TQM was first applied to manufacturing, its tenets sometimes refer to products. However, TQM proponents maintain that a delivered service can be viewed as a product, and, therefore, TQM principles need only minor modifications when applied to business or government services (Kennedy and Young, 1989, p. 87; Deming, 1986, p. xi).

TQM's Primary Tenets

First and foremost, the customer is the ultimate determiner of quality. A product may meet all specifications. However, if it does not provide the customers with the performance they wish—if it is too complex, or expensive, or unattractive—then the quality test has been flunked.

Second, quality should be built into the product early in the production process (upstream) rather than being added on at the end (downstream). Many products and services go through the stages of design, production, inspection, reworking (for products), and then response to consumer complaints. The early, upstream stages of design and production are the crucial ones. If the product or service is designed to be easy to produce, and if those producing it have the training and incentives to maintain consistently high quality, then downstream inspections, reworkings, and responses to consumer complaints are unnecessary. This saves money, but more importantly, it makes the customer much happier. Accordingly, TQM generally opposes mass inspections of products because such inspections provide a safety net that shifts quality responsibilities away from the initial designers and producers.

Third, preventing variability is the key to producing high quality. Slippages in quality arise from too much variation in the product or service. As products and services deviate from a desired norm, their dependability drops rapidly. Deming has said, "If I had to reduce my message for management to just a few words, I'd say it all had to do with reducing variation" (Bryce, 1991, p. 16). Because preventing variability is the most important path to quality, TQM's most important tools are process control charts. Such charts are used to track quality by charting a product's deviation from the optimum; these deviations are then categorized and analyzed.[4]

Fourth, quality results from people working within systems, not individual efforts. When quality slips, it is almost always the system that is wrong, not the people (Carr and Littman, 1990, p. 196; Walton, 1986, p. 92). Because it is the system working through committed people that produces results, it is a grave mistake to focus on individuals. Most of the time, when one individual appears to be performing better than others, the difference in performance is only random variation. Thus today's superior worker is likely to be tomorrow's average one, because a well-working system should lead *all* workers, responding to intrinsic motivators, to perform well.[5] Merit pay and other individually oriented rewards are accordingly misguided and represent a "lottery" (Deming, 1986, p. 110). Because management by objectives (MBO) is so often used for individual measures, it, too, leads the manager astray. All MBO, according to TQM, should be dropped.

One TQM article summarized this approach by saying, "It is worth noting that management by objectives and performance standards works against a quality-supportive organizational culture. Objectives and performance standards focus on individual performance when the individual can seldom control the system within which he or she must work. . . . People become victims or beneficiaries of normal variations built into the system" (Scholtes and Hacquebord, 1988b, p. 47). Another said, "In the Deming view, certain practices are always wrong. Among these are merit pay, incentive programs, the annual review of people, any system that ranks the employees, management by objective . . ." (Aguayo, 1990, p. 131).

Fifth, quality requires continuous improvement of inputs and processes. Quality is not a static attribute; it is a constantly changing target because it represents a delighted (not just satisfied) customer. As the customer's expectations rise, so must the product's quality. What is a high-quality product today will not be one tomorrow. This tenet leads to the principle of *continuous improvement*—every month new ways of improvement must be considered and implemented.

Moreover, this continuous improvement should be directed not at outputs but at the inputs and processes that the manager can directly control. The business manager should stop focusing on the output measure of profits, because profit is a short-term measure that can lead to cutting corners. The manager should focus instead, according to TQM, on improving organizational processes and inputs in order to improve quality, because increased quality will lead to customer loyalty, and long-range profits will inexorably follow (Scholtes and Hacquebord, 1988a, p. 31).

This tenet directly contradicts the rationale of all recent government management reforms. Program budgeting, zero base budgeting (ZBB), MBO, and pay for performance all attempted to move the government manager's focus away from measuring inputs and processes and toward results. TQM urges business managers to move in the opposite direction. Deming, in fact, made elimination of MBO one of his 14 points, and later elaborated: "Focus on outcomes . . . must be abolished, leadership put in its place" (Deming, 1986, p. 54).

Sixth, quality improvement requires strong worker participation. Because quality depends upon the production workers doing it right the first time and upon constant improvement of inputs and processes, which only workers know intimately, worker participation in the ongoing improvement process is crucial. Managers and workers should work together "without fear"—without worrying that each mistake discovered will be punished. They also need to work "without barriers"—using matrix-like structures and quality circles to break down communication barriers between hierarchical levels and between functional units.

Seventh, quality requires total organizational commitment. Quality is achieved only when managers create an organizational culture that focuses on consistently producing quality products and then on improving them every period. If this total commitment flags, quality will drop off rapidly, and the organization will inevitably begin to slip behind competitors.

This requirement for total organizational commitment seems clearer when considered in light of the other TQM tenets already discussed. TQM is an extremely demanding regimen. It requires *all* members of an organization to *constantly* change in order to improve, even after achieving what seems to be a high standard of performance. It requires such high levels of performance that virtually no mistakes are made, and after-the-fact inspections to catch mistakes become unnecessary. Because TQM is so demanding, only an unusually intense and unambiguous organizational culture can keep workers so committed and focused. This organizational culture must be maintained by active and continuous intervention from the top.

ORTHODOX TQM IN GOVERNMENT

In its unmodified or orthodox form, TQM is strikingly ill suited to the government environment. The use of TQM in government has several major problems: insufficient modification for services; insensitivity to the problems of defining governmental customers; inappropriate emphasis on inputs and processes; and demands for top-level intensity that can rarely be met by the governmental culture.

Services vs. Products

TQM was originally designed for routine processes such as manufacturing, yet most government agencies produce services rather than products. Although the problem of applying TQM to business services is widely discussed in the TQM literature (Deming, 1986, pp. 171ff; Ferderber, 1981; King, 1987; Plsek, 1987), solutions are elusive. TQM remains much more difficult to apply to services because services are more labor intensive, and they are often produced and consumed simultaneously. This makes uniformity of output more difficult, and it also means that the consumer will evaluate the service not only on the result but also on the behavior and even the appearance of the person delivering it. If an efficient police officer quickly locates stolen cars but seems ill-groomed or curt, many of his or her customers will not be totally satisfied, despite receiving a high quality output.

Accordingly, quality measures for services are extremely complex. Factor analyses of customer surveys have indicated that overall quality measures for services can be broken into such components as access, communication, competence, courtesy, creativity, reliability, responsiveness, security, tangibles, and understanding (Parasuraman *et al.*, 1985; Cravens *et al.*, 1988; Garvin, 1984, 1988). For many services each of these components must be measured and weighed before it can be determined that a high-quality service has been delivered.

TQM's tenet about reducing variation is also more difficult to apply to services. The quality tracking charts and the concern about the product drift away from the optimum apply much more directly to assembly-line production (e.g., measures of how well the auto door is fitted) than to government services that often have controversial or unclear norms. For example, no clear consensus exists about what processes should be tracked and standardized for a street-level bureaucrat such as a men-

tal health professional or a classroom teacher.

The Problem of Defining the Government Customer

TQM's most important principle is to delight the customer. Accordingly, the single most important question is: Who is the customer? Most discussions of TQM in government pay little or no attention to that question. In business, the company can usually choose its own market niche, and thus define its target customers: luxury car buyers, for example, or price-conscious food purchasers. For many public agencies, on the other hand, defining the customer is a difficult and politically controversial issue. For the Bureau of Land Management (BLM), is the main customer the grazing interests, the mining interests, or the environmentalists? If some combination, how much weight should be given to each? Whether or not BLM is delivering quality services depends entirely upon the answer. Competing clients, with directly contradictory demands, can be found in most government services, from education to health care. Although these battles may be less fierce for those few government services that have routine, uncontroversial missions, they are never totally absent. For example, James Q. Wilson (1989, pp. 122–126) has pointed out the competing clienteles that fight for the outputs of the seemingly noncontroversial postal service.

Moreover, government organizations have obligations to more than their immediate clients. Sometimes the agency's most important customers—the general public—are not only absent but totally inattentive, and yet the agency must risk offending its immediate customers in order to serve the general public. For example, a government agency that oversees banks and treats banks as its customers will greatly damage the public good by keeping banks, in TQM's phraseology, delighted. Yet if the agency puts the taxpaying general public first, it will look in vain for their delighted reaction; the general public will remain resolutely uninterested in the agency's work unless there is a crisis.

This conflict between a program's direct customers (clients) and its ultimate customers (the general public, most of whom are taxpayers) is often very acute for programs that are not universally distributed. The problem arises because any definition of quality is always constrained by cost—a high quality $15,000 car is of course not the same as a high quality $60,000 car. In business this cost constraint does not usually affect customer satisfaction because the buyer of the product is also its recipient, so he or she can choose the appropriate level of cost and quality in order to be delighted. No such balance is likely for nonuniversal government services such as health care, education, or water projects because the buyer is often not the recipient. The buying customers (general taxpayers) will often prefer to minimize costs. At the same time, the direct customers (recipients) of such programs may expect a level of quality that is found only at a very high price, because they do not pay the full cost. No balance between costs and features is likely to please both groups.

The literature on citizen surveys in government has pointed out the difficulty of measuring government performance by public reaction. Generally, public ratings of programs are only tenuously related to objective measures of program performance. Survey results are easily biased by isolated but highly publicized events or by ideological attitudes.[6] Of course, surveys remain useful if viewed as one piece of organizational information, but these survey weaknesses reflect these same inescapable problems of defining customers and of measuring services.

Because government agencies must serve a wide variety of customers who have widely divergent and even contradictory demands and because the general public remains a "hidden customer" with yet additional, often incompatible demands, government agencies often have to deliver a service or product that reflects an uneasy compromise. In such cases, the principle of delighting or even satisfying customers begs too many questions to be a clear or useful goal.[7]

Focusing on Inputs and Processes

Government has traditionally paid relatively little attention to outputs for many reasons: Outputs are politically controversial and difficult to measure; legislators are primarily concerned about inputs such as budgets; bureaucratic prestige often accrues from control of inputs, especially personnel; and legal requirements often demand constant attention to strict procedural rules (Behn, 1982; Wilson, 1989). With all the incentives in government to focus on inputs and processes, there is a constant threat of goal displacement—managers who blindly hew to the minimal legal requirements, or build empires, or put out fires, rather than help the public.

Given this unpromising environment, many public organizations are justifiably proud that over the past 15 years they have implemented results-oriented systems such as MBO performance monitoring systems, and program budgets. Recent surveys show that such systems have been widely installed, that they continue to spread, and that most governmental users rate them a success.[8] Such systems allow many public agencies to now track results, not just processes. Because it is so difficult to determine outputs in the public sector, every success should be savored and nurtured. As already noted, orthodox TQM disputes all this. According to one TQM book, "Many government agencies have difficulty developing performance indicators. This is because they focus on *results indicators* related to final output to external customers, rather than on how processes are performing in making those products and services. Remember, if processes perform as intended, output should be of high quality. You begin by moving away from the concept of results indicators to *process control indicators"* (Carr and Littman, 1990, pp. 61–2).

TQM proponents correctly point out that in business, outputs in the form of quarterly profit reports represent short-term vision and can often lead to goal displacement. They fail to recognize that in the very different world of government, it is stressing inputs and processes that represents short-term business as usual, and therefore focusing on governmental processes is likely to lead to goal displacement. In the public sector, a move toward stressing outputs is in fact usually a move toward the desired longer-range vision.[9]

The Problem of Government Culture

Orthodox TQM depends on an extremely strong organizational culture with an almost single-minded commitment to quality. In order to shape that culture, the managers must be continuously involved in improving management (Walton, 1986, pp. 66, 92; Aguayo, 1990, pp. 92, 117). However, turnover of top-level managers is rapid for many government agencies, and government culture, structured to be open to many outside forces, is almost necessarily weaker than those of business.[10] After summarizing the many disincentives to concentrating on management,[11] one analysis concludes, "What is surprising is that government executives spend any time at all on managing their departments" (Wilson, 1989, p. 217).

ORTHODOX TQM SUMMARIZED

In sum, orthodox TQM can easily do more harm than good because it can encourage a focus on the particularistic demands of direct clients rather than the needs of the more important (but often inattentive) customers, the general public. Orthodox TQM can also cause an organization to neglect or even—if Deming's advice is followed—dismantle such established systems as MBO, program budgets, and performance monitoring systems that set clear output goals and monitor results.[12] Finally, orthodox TQM makes a number of demands for output uniformity and strong, continuous organizational culture that government is intrinsically unable to meet.

Despite all these major problems, a great deal is worth saving in TQM. However, public managers must adapt the system drastically to gain the advantages.

IMPLEMENTING REFORMED TQM IN GOVERNMENT

What would a reformed TQM look like? It would retain orthodox TQM's feedback from clients, its emphasis on tracking performance, and its principles of continuous improvement and participation of the workers.

Client Feedback

Despite the problems in making customer reaction the guiding principle in government management, it is still useful to track the reactions of an agency's immediate clients and to use them as *one* consideration in decisionmaking. TQM provides valuable advice on how to do this.

Tracking Performance

TQM strongly condemns "managing by the numbers." At the same time, one of its major components is quantitative tracking of quality through control charts and other quantitative tools. This performance tracking can make TQM a useful first system for some government agencies. After TQM is implemented, its success can lead to the addition of other quantitative but results-oriented systems, such as program budgeting, MBO, and performance monitoring systems. TQM is likely to be a particularly useful first system for those government workers and managers who have resisted other management systems because they feared such systems would "turn people into numbers." Because TQM emphasizes both intangibles (quality) and people (participation), as well as tracking through numbers, it can be a nonintimidating first step for those who have been put off by the quantitative aspects of other systems.

Continuous Improvement

Each earlier public management innovation was resisted by many workers. Moreover, once the systems were implemented, they were often taken for granted and therefore atrophied over time. For both these reasons, TQM's continuous improvement principle, if internalized by workers and managers, may be its most valuable contribution. The principle suggests that receptivity to new approaches is essential for high performance. If fully accepted, this principle would lessen the resistance to future system innovations and would also decrease the likelihood that they would later stagnate. As a useful side effect, acceptance of this principle would lessen the temptation to oversell future changes, since overselling is often aimed at mitigating resistance.

Worker Participation

Worker participation, now often called empowerment, has been an important management axiom for decades, but it is difficult to put into operation. TQM's quality circles represent a valuable concrete step toward increased participation.

TQM: RELABELING OLD IDEAS?

In all of its forms, TQM incorporates some truly fresh ideas, particularly the new tools for tracking and improving routine government processes. However, because reformed TQM also emphasizes such long-standing managerial principles as worker participation and quantitative output tracking, a natural critique is that reformed TQM is primarily old wine in new bottles. There is a little truth to this critique, but new bottles are often very valuable. For the same reason that people change fashions, ministers change sermons, and organizations change logos, management analysts must periodically change the way they present enduring principles—listener boredom can cause even the best approaches to seem stale over time. If TQM represents a new framework that helps freshen enduring management principles, that can be an additional major advantage.

SUMMARY

Orthodox TQM is ill suited to most government agencies and, in fact, represents a step backwards (away from results) for many of them. Reformed TQM, however, jettisons orthodox TQM's hostility to output goals and measurements, deemphasizes its demands for output uniformity and organizational culture continuity, and sensitizes managers to the dangers of satisfying just an immediate clientele. Yet at the same time, reformed TQM saves the orthodox principles of employee empowerment, continuous improvement, and quantitative tracking of product quality and of client reactions.

If introduced without overselling and with sensitivity to government's unique circumstances, reformed TQM can make a useful contribution to contemporary public management.

NOTES

1. Among the public TQM systems that are discussed in the literature are the city government of Madison, Wisconsin (Sensenbrenner, 1991); the Madison police department (Couper, 1990); the Naval Publications Center (Whitten, 1989); and the Environmental Protection Agency (Cohen and Brand, 1990). The Department of Defense has a new position: Deputy Undersecretary of Defense for Total Quality Management (Keehley, 1991). For a good discussion of the federal history of TQM, see Milakovich (1990). TQM programs within such state governments as Wisconsin, California, Texas, and Florida are mentioned briefly in Carr and Littman (1990).

2. Deming's influence in Japan is reflected by the fact that Japan's most prestigious business award is the Deming Prize (Walton, 1986). Pioneering work in this area has also been done by Deming's mentors, Walter Shewhart and Armand Feigenbaum. Among the most important contemporary quality theorists are Joseph Juran (1989), Kaora Ishikawa, Genichi Taguchi, and Philip Crosby (1979). As noted, Deming is a synthesizer, and so some of the principles of all the above except Crosby are cited and incorporated in his TQM.

3. Deming has summed up his approach in "Fourteen Points" and "Seven Obstacles" (Deming, 1986, chpts. 2 and 3). Because Deming's writings are neither fluid nor tightly structured, other authors have attempted to sum up his thoughts in fewer, clearer points. Among these are Gabor (1990, pp. 18–30), Walton (1986), and Aguayo (1990). The list of tenets given here draws from each of these authors, but reflects a greater emphasis on points most relevant to government mangement. An overview of some of the applications for government managers is contained in Wagenheim and Reurink (1991).

4. The analysis of process charts—distinguishing common causes of variation, which fall within statistical expectations, from special causes, which do not—is central to TQM, but beyond the scope of this discussion. For the same reason, I have also omitted a discussion of the many other statistical and graphical tools of TQM, most of which are very useful. For a good explanation, see Gabor (1990, chap. 2).

5. Deming's belief in the universality and near omnipotence of intrinsic motivators is striking. He has said that in his 60 years of experience he has never met a worker who was not trying his or her hardest (Aguayo, 1990, p. 31). Reflecting his distaste for evaluations and for extrinsic motivators, Deming gives an A to all the students in his university courses (Walton, 1986, p. 91). Not all TQM theorists would endorse those exact views, but almost all (see note 9) would endorse the same practical applications: downplaying output measures, goals, rewards, and ratings.

6. Among the articles that point out the discrepancy between objective output indicators and subjective survey responses are Stipak (1979); Brown and Coulter (1983); and Houghland (1987). On the other hand, Parks (1984) has argued that there are connections, but even he concedes that they are not direct

ones. See also the debate by Stipak and Parks (1984).

7. An extreme example of a misplaced focus on only direct clients was the federal Department of Housing and Urban Development (HUD) in the 1980s. Reed (1982) reported that two of the three criteria on which HUD executive bonuses were based were: (1) "Decisions rarely, if ever, questioned by client groups" and (2) "Decisions consistently praised by affected groups." Because these goals ignore the invisible customer—the general public—in retrospect, they seem to reflect the priorities that led to the massive HUD scandals.

8. These systems are most widespread at the local level. Streib and Poister (1989a) found that by 1988, 66 percent of local governments used program budgeting, 62 percent used MBO, and 67 percent used performance monitoring systems. Larger cities employed all these techniques at even higher rates, and the usage figures represented particularly substantial gains throughout the 1980s for program budgeting and MBO. Over 90 percent of the users characterize these systems as "somewhat" or "very" effective (Streib and Poister, 1989b). Quality circles (before the current TQM drive gained momentum) were used by 32 percent of cities, but only 25 percent of the users rated them as "very effective." TQM proponents would ascribe this low effectiveness rating to the fact that the circles were not part of a broader supporting quality system.

   Although information about usage is not as complete at the state and federal levels, the overall pattern seems similar. A survey of state budgets indicated that they have increasingly incorporated many program budget features (Lee, 1991). At the federal level, program budgeting

never died in the Defense Department (Ferrara and Dunmire, 1988), and MBO has lived on there and in a number of the largest federal departments.

9. Of the main quality approaches, that of Philip Crosby (1979) is the most unlike the Deming-based TQM discussed here, and Crosby seems to see the largest place for goal setting. Nonetheless, the arguments made here about quality systems' maladaptation for government may be strongest for Crosby. His definition of quality is very much specification-based: quality is "conformance to requirements." He espouses "zero defects," an approach with little application to such government functions as school teaching, regulation, and job training. Finally, he deemphasizes the quantitative tools that give substance to TQM's quality exhortations.

10. A praiseworthy attempt to allow each agency to adapt TQM to its particular culture may have motivated OPM's very loose guidelines in implementing federal TQM. However, OPM may have overcompensated. In a thoughtful and interesting critique, Hyde (1991) applauds the lack of rigid guidelines but argues that OPM has been so careful to avoid prescribing specific steps for implementing federal TQM that no clear system is left. He calls for a number of remedies, including much more attention to TQM's means and methodologies. The argument in this article that reformed TQM must retain the quantitative tools of TQM is, I think, in accordance with Hyde's point.

11. The lack of incentives for top political officials to focus on management is well illustrated by the mayor of Madison, Wisconsin, Joseph Sensenbrenner. He was perhaps the elected official most com-

mitted to TQM throughout the 1980s. In an article, he enumerates the many efficiency gains, the increased union support, and the national publicity engendered by TQM, but then states, "But this recognition was not enough to win me a fourth term. Other political factors were more compelling" (Sensenbrenner, 1991, p. 75). Sensenbrenner's case is an illustration that elected officials cannot put their *primary* focus on management matters; their success is usually more closely tied to their political, rather than managerial, skills.

12. Most proponents of output-oriented systems, and particularly of MBO, characterize the systems as participatory, with the subordinates joining the superiors in setting goals and with both parties adjusting the goals jointly as the situation changes. Unilaterally set goals are treated as examples of an improperly functioning system. Within the TQM literature, however, MBO and performance monitoring system goals are usually portrayed as nonparticipatory "quotas" (i.e., Aguayo, 1990, p. 26). Accordingly, output-oriented systems are almost invariably characterized as obstacles, not complements that could potentially be incorporated within a participative TQM system. Thus two pro-TQM authors say of the output-oriented system in the Environmental Protection Agency (EPA), "The actions of one regional program manager provide an example of how to avoid numerical quotas." He placed himself as a buffer between his staff and the EPA's numerical accountability system. He told his staff, "You keep working on improving the process, and don't worry about this quarter's quotas' (Cohen and Brand, 1990, p. 112).

REFERENCES

AGUAYO, RAFAEL, 1990. *Dr. Deming: The American Who Taught the Japanese About Quality.* New York: Lyle Stuart.

BEHN, ROBERT D., 1982. "Policy Analysis and Policy Politics." *Policy Analysis,* vol. 7, pp. 199–226.

BROWN, KARIN AND PHILLIP B. COULTER, 1983. "Subjective and Objective Measures of Public Service Delivery." *Public Administration Review,* vol. 43 (January/February), pp. 50–58.

BRYCE, G. REX, 1991. "Quality Management Theories and Their Application." *Quality,* vol. 30 (January), pp. 15–18.

CARR, DAVID K. AND IAN D. LITTMAN, 1990. *Excellence in Government: Total Quality Management in the 1990s.* Arlington, VA: Coopers & Lybrand.

COHEN, STEVEN AND RONALD BRAND, 1990. "Total Quality Management in the U.S. Environmental Protection Agency." *Public Productivity and Management Review,* vol. 14 (Fall), pp. 99–114.

COUPER, DAVID C., 1990. "Police Department Learns Ten Hard Quality Lessons." *Quality Progress,* vol. 23 (February), pp. 37–40.

CRAVENS, DAVID W. *et al.,* 1988. "Marketing's Role in Product and Service Quality." *Industrial Marketing Management,* vol. 17, pp. 285–304.

CROSBY, PHILLIP, 1979. *Quality Is Free.* New York: New American Library.

DEMING, W. EDWARDS, 1986. *Out of the Crisis.* Cambridge: MIT Press.

FERDERBER, CHARLES J., 1981. "Measuring Quality and Productivity in a Service Environment." *Industrial Engineering,* vol. 13, pp. 38–48.

FERRARA, JOSEPH A. AND DANIEL J. DUNMIRE, 1988. "Bureaucratic Influence of Budget Preparation: A Practitioner's View of Pentagon Budgeting." *Management Science and Policy Analysis,* vol. 5 (Winter), pp. 1–13.

GABOR, ANDREA, 1990. *The Man Who Discovered Quality: How W. Edwards*

Deming Brought the Quality Revolution to America. New York: Times Books.

GARVIN, DAVID A., 1984. "What Does 'Product Quality' Really Mean?" *Sloan Management Review,* vol. 25, pp. 25–43.

————, 1988. *Managing Quality.* New York: Free Press.

HOUGHLAND, JAMES, 1987. "Criteria for Client Evaluation of Public Programs." *Social Science Quarterly* (June).

HYDE, ALBERT C., 1991. "Rescuing Quality Measurement from TQM." *The Bureaucrat,* vol. 19 (Winter), pp. 16–20.

JURAN, JOSEPH, 1989. *Juran on Leadership for Quality.* New York: Free Press.

KEEHLEY, PAT, 1991. "FQI Highlights Quality Management." *Public Administration Times,* vol. 14 (July 1), p. 3.

KENNEDY, DAVID A. AND BARBARA J. YOUNG, 1989. "Managing Quality in Staff Areas." *Quality Progress,* vol. 22 (October), pp. 87–91.

KING, CAROL A., 1987. "A Framework for a Service Quality Assurance System." *Quality Progress,* vol. 20 (September), pp. 27–32.

LEE, ROBERT D., JR., 1991. "Developments in State Budgeting: Trends of Two Decades." *Public Administration Review,* vol. 51 (May/June), pp. 254–262.

MILAKOVICH, MICHAEL E., 1991. "Total Quality Management in the Public Sector." *National Productivity Review* (Spring), pp. 195–213.

PARASURAMAN, A., VALARIE ZEITHAMI, AND LEONARD L. BERRY, 1985. "A Conceptual Model of Service Quality." *Journal of Marketing,* vol. 49 (Fall), pp. 41–50.

PARKS, ROGER B., 1984. "Linking Objective and Subjective Measures of Performance." *Public Administration Review,* vol. 44 (March/April), pp. 118–127.

PLSEK, PAUL E., 1987. "Defining Quality at the Marketing/Development Interface." *Quality Progress,* vol. 20 (June), pp. 28–36.

REED, LEONARD, 1982. "Bureaucrats 2, Presidents 0." *Harper's* (November).

SCHOLTES, PETER R. AND HERO HACQUEBORD, 1988a. "Beginning the Quality Transformation." *Quality Progress,* vol. 21 (July), pp. 28–33.

————, 1988b. "Six Strategies for Beginning the Quality Transformation." *Quality Progress,* vol. 21 (August), pp. 44–48.

SENSENBRENNER, JOSEPH, 1991. "Quality Comes to City Hall." *Harvard Business Review,* vol. 69 (March/April), pp. 64–75.

STIPAK, BRIAN, 1979. "Citizen Satisfaction with Urban Services: Potential Misuse as a Performance Indicator." *Public Administration Review,* vol. 39 (January/February), pp. 46–52.

STIPAK, BRIAN AND ROGER B. PARKS, 1984. "Communications." *Public Administration Review,* vol. 44 (November/December), pp. 551–552.

STREIB, GREGORY AND THEORDORE H. POISTER, 1989a. "Established and Emerging Management Tools: A Twelve-Year Perspective." *The Municipal Yearbook 1989.* Washington, DC: International City Managers Association.

————, 1989b. "Management Tools in Municipal Government: Trends Over the Past Decade." *Public Administration Review,* vol. 49 (May/June), pp. 240–248.

WAGENHEIM, GEORGE D. AND JOHN H. REURINK, 1991 "Customer Service in Public Administration." *Public Administration Review,* vol. 51 (May/June), pp. 263–269.

WALTON, MARY, 1986. *The Deming Management Method.* New York: Praeger.

WHITTEN, SHIRLEY K., 1989. "Award Winning Total Quality at the Naval Publications and Forms Center." *National Productivity Review,* vol. 8 (Summer), pp. 273–286.

WILSON, JAMES Q., 1989. *Bureaucracy.* New York: Basic Books.

14.   Formal Models of Bureaucracy: A Review

Jonathan Bendor

Formal analysis is fairly new in public administration, and there is some skepticism in the field about the intellectual advantages of mathematical methods. This is quite appropriate. As with any new tool, there is a faddishness associated with these methods, and a corresponding danger of goal displacement. A formal model of bureaucracy should be a tool for extending and deepening our knowledge about public organizations. If the underlying ideas are silly, translating them into mathematics will do little good, but if they are promising, deductive reasoning can help us explore their potential: If one believes *A* is a general property of bureaucracies, it would be throwing away information not to work out *A*'s logical implications. This analysis can also increase the falsifiability of our ideas: If *A* implies *B*, but empirically we discover not-*B*, the truth status of *A* is brought into question. Or it may turn out, as Kenneth Arrow discovered about democratic principles, that our informal ideas are logically inconsistent: We thought properties *C* and *D* either describe existing institutions or could describe potential ones, but recasting the ideas into mathematical form reveals this is impossible. Finally, some problems are just too hard to tackle without the aid of formal tools. It is hard to imagine, for example, that Robert Axelrod (1984) would have discovered the robustness of the simple strategy of tit-for-tat in the two-person prisoner's

dilemma without the help of a computer (to put tit-for-tat against many opponents in thousands of rounds of play) and of mathematics (to prove some generic properties of tit-for-tat).

Thus, the advantages of formal reasoning are numerous and genuine. They will endure after the initial burst of enthusiasm for mathematical models has passed, and even after some realistic disillusionment has taken hold.

This chapter is a selective review of recent work on formal models of bureaucracy. Comprehensive coverage has been sacrificed in order to examine selected pieces more intensely than otherwise would have been possible. The first section studies William Niskanen's theory of bureaucracy and its descendants. The second covers principal-agent models. Section 3 focuses on the design of heirarchical institutions. Section 4 examines models based on ideas of bounded rationality.

THE NISKANEN TRADITION

William Niskanen's *Bureaucracy and Representative Government* (1971), an analysis of the bureaucratic causes of governmental growth, was the forerunner of numerous formal models of bureaus. Even today it is probably the single most cited study, and it deserves close attention.

The basic model is designed to examine the budgetary relations between a legislature and an agency. The legislators have a demand for the bureau's output; the more expensive the output, the less they want. The agency is assumed to have one goal—pursuing ever larger budgets. The relationship is an exchange:

SOURCE: "Formal Models of Bureaucracy: A Review" by Jonathan Bendor, *Public Administration: The State of the Discipline,* Naomi Lynn and Aaron Wildavsky, eds. (Chatham: Chatham House, 1990). Reprinted by permission.

The legislature funds the bureau, and in return the agency promises to deliver a specified amount of services. Two assumptions are particularly important in giving the agency the upper hand in the deal. First, it is assumed that the bureau knows the legislature's demand for its services—the maximum the legislature is willing to pay for any amount of output. Second, the agency is not required to reveal a complete cost schedule (i.e., cost as a function of quantity); instead, it can make all-or-nothing offers to the politicians. The only constraint placed on the bureau is that it must deliver the quantity of output it has promised; accordingly, the budget must cover the output's total costs.

These assumptions imply that the agency can offer the legislature a price-output combination that the politicians barely prefer to zero output and budget. In effect, the agency engages in perfect price discrimination: At every point along the demand curve, it charges the maximum price the legislature is willing to pay. Consequently, the bureau's budget is too large, and the politicians realize no gains from the exchange. Assuming that legislative demand represents voters' preferences, bureaucratic output is also excessive. For the socially optimal amount, the cost of the last unit of output just equals its benefit. The bureau, however, will produce past the point where marginal cost equals marginal value. As long as the legislature is willing to pay anything for additional output, the agency will provide it. Thus it produces up to the point where the legislature no longer values its services at all, that is, where the marginal value of output is zero.

It may be that costs rise so steeply that the bureau cannot cover the costs of producing output for which the legislature's marginal value is zero. If so, this solution is infeasible. Instead, the bureau chief will offer to produce the maximum feasible quantity, where costs are just

covered by the budget. (Niskanen calls this second solution the budget- or cost-constrained solution; the first solution is named the demand-constrained result.) As before, for every unit of output the agency charges the maximum price the legislature is willing to pay, hence again the budget is too large, and the legislature does not gain from the exchange. Most important, once again output exceeds the socially optimal amount.

Because some scholars may find Niskanen's demand-supply language unfamiliar, it may be worthwhile to recast his ideas in more familiar terms. Following Romer and Rosenthal (1978), we focus on the logic of a budgetary process marked by agenda control. In their reformulation, the median legislator (M in figure 14.1) has a particular budget that she prefers to all others. Using the standard terminology of spatial models, call this her ideal point. Her preferences are symmetric about this point: Her utility would fall at the same rate if anything higher or lower is appropriated. The bureaucrat wants as large a budget as possible, but he must obtain approval of the median politician. Fortunately, he enjoys the power to manipulate the set of alternatives from which the politician will choose. (In legislatures this is equivalent to a committee offering a bill under a closed rule—the bill cannot be amended on the floor.)

Because the politician dislikes underspending and overspending equally, she is willing, given a choice between no appropriation and one nearly twice as big as her ideal, to settle for the latter, as figure 14.1 indicates. Romer and Rosenthal emphasize that this result is driven by the level of the no agreement appropriation, namely, zero. Should the budget revert to a higher level when the decision makers fail to agree, say the previous year's appropriation (as it might under a continuing resolution), then the agenda setter cannot induce the politician to agree to x; instead, he must settle for y.

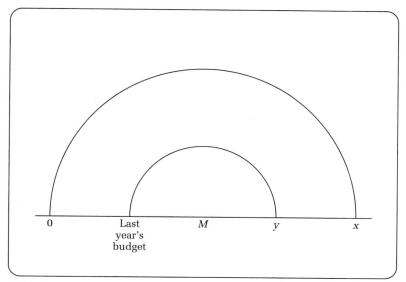

Figure 14.1

The logic of this agenda-setting model is clear; what is problematic is its empirical interpretation. As Miller and Moe (1983) have argued, assuming that bureaus have this kind of power is implausible.* Certainly bureaucrats manipulate the choice sets of their political superiors, but their kind of agenda control derives from expertise: for example, an armed services bureaucrat forwards biased evaluations of proposed weapons systems to the secretary of defense. Thus, this second kind of agenda control is based on asymmetric information, whereas the Niskanen/Romer and Rosenthal kind derives from differential authority, which can occur despite complete information about the set of feasible options and their effects.

The difference between authority-based and information-based agenda

control is clear in Romer and Rosenthal's paper (see also Altfeld and Miller 1984). This distinction is less clear in Niskanen's work because there are inconsistencies between his formal model and the accompanying informal text. As noted, the model assumes authority-based agenda control; in the text he recognizes that bureaucratic influence may depend on superior information.

Why the inconsistency? The explanation is simple: When Niskanen was working on his book in the late 1960s and early 1970s, the technology for modeling games with incomplete and asymmetric information did not exist. Accordingly, he could not translate his informal insights into a formal model. This is not the first or the last time that a scholar, knowing more about a subject than he can formally represent, introduced a slip 'twixt the lip and the cup.

Later on, in *Bureaucracy and Representative Government*, Niskanen (1971) does try to bolster his formal model by introducing a legislative committee that really wields authority-based agenda

*Romer and Rosenthal's interpretation is that the agenda setter is an elected official—specifically, a school board member—and that the final decision makers are voters. This is an empirically reasonable application of the agenda model.

control over the rest of the legislature. This is certainly more reasonable; indeed, such models have received considerable attention from formally inclined students of legislatures in recent years (e.g., Denzau and Mackay 1983; Shepsle and Weingast 1984). Niskanen argues that the self-selection pattern of gaining seats on committees in Congress implies that committee members usually have a high demand for an agency's services. Thus the committee will pose the same take-it-or-leave-it choice to the rest of the legislature as the agency would, and the basic model's results go through unchanged (p. 148).

This justification of the basic model encounters two problems. The first is empirical: Appropriation committees in Congress rarely send their bills out under a closed rule. The second is theoretical: Niskanen's argument presumes that high-demand committees and budget-seeking agencies will collude against the rest of the legislature, but the basis for that collusion and how it is carried out are left opaque. If in the reformulation the only source of influence were authority-based agenda control, collusion would be unnecessary—the committee would not need the agency. In this case, the basic bureaucratic model turns out to have been superfluous; the heart of the process is committee-floor interactions, and overly large budgets are unrelated to bureaucratic supply.

If the agency continues to have influence, presumably it does so because of superior information (Niskanen 1971, 148), for in the reformulation the agency no longer has authority-based agenda control. In this case, collusion is necessary but problematic: Would the agency want to use this expertise to manipulate the committee? Although it is conventional wisdom that budget-seeking bureaus and high-demand committees are allies—these are two of the supports of subgovernments or iron triangles—allies need not have identical preferences

(Mackay and Weaver 1979). By definition, such a committee is oriented toward output; the agency, toward funding. This difference might matter; the committee wants the agency to operate at full efficiency to produce maximum output per dollar, just as a monopolist owner of a private firm wants the firm to operate at maximum technical efficiency. The agency, however, will prefer to function inefficiently if doing so would increase its budget (Munger 1984).

Because of the foregoing problems, modeling in this field has moved toward explicitly endowing the bureau with information-based agenda control. No one now assumes that agencies have authority-based agenda control. An important contribution here was by Miller and Moe (1983). Their fundamental point is that Congress can choose to organize the budgetary process in different ways. Thus, unlike Niskanen's model, which specifies only a single procedure, Miller and Moe compare two sequences. In one specification, the legislature reveals its demand for the agency's services; in the other, it conceals it. In both sequences, Miller and Moe reject the idea that a bureau has authority to set agendas; instead, the agency's influence in the model—not just in the informal story—derives from its superior information about costs. The agency must announce a per unit price schedule; it is forbidden to present take-it-or-leave-it offers. Miller and Moe show that even if the legislature reveals its demand, it always obtains higher net benefits than it does in Niskanen's model. Because the two models are comparable in almost all other respects—linear demand, quadratic costs, and so forth—it is clear that the key difference is dropping authority-based agenda control. Even facing extremely asymmetric information—the bureau knows the true demand function, whereas the legislature relies on the bureau chief's claim concerning cost—the politicians experience net gains. The reason is illustrated in figure 14.2. With the legislature committed to paying a constant amount, *p*, for each unit of output, the bureau cannot price discriminate (announce a supply curve that reproduces the demand curve). Instead, the agency must settle for a budget that is the constant price multiplied by quantity; the shaded rectangle in figure 14.2. Because the median legislator's value of the service is represented by the demand curve, this legislator's net benefits equal the area under the curve minus the budget—the shaded triangle in figure 14.2. Thus "we can now see that these rules of thumb [i.e., assuming constant unit costs] are *rational* in these kinds of budgetary games, regarding their consequences for both the committee and society as a whole. . . . Perhaps surprisingly, then, a legislative rule of thumb adopted entirely in ignorance and not designed to discover true bureaucratic costs is in fact well suited to the pursuit of legislative and social ends" (Miller and Moe 1983, 319–20, emphasis in the original). The advantage of using such a crude heuristic is indeed surprising. The conventional wisdom is

that using rules of thumb generate inferior outcomes, yet Miller and Moe show that remaining committed to the belief that costs increase linearly in output prevents the bureau from manipulating the legislature at will. In some strategic circumstances it may pay to be simple-minded.*

The final major point of the Miller and Moe article is that exploiting asymmetric information is a game two can play. Although bureaucrats know more about supply than politicians do, the latter know more about demand. Therefore Miller and Moe conjecture (p. 321) that the more Congress keeps administrators in the dark about its own preferences, the more the bureaucrats will toe the line and tell the truth. Hence, in their second model, Miller and Moe examine demand-concealing oversight. They conclude that in this circumstance the bureau chief will reveal his true

---

*For a similar argument concerning how the simple decision rules of voters may make them less vulnerable to strategic manipulation by politicians, see Ferejohn (forthcoming).

Figure 14.2

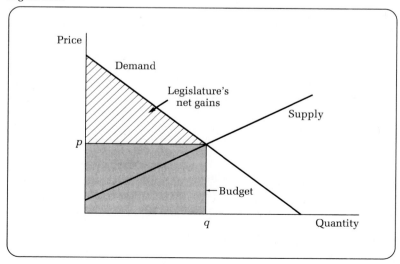

average cost curve (p. 305). Their basic idea that legislators can use their own private information about demand to control bureaucrats in undoubtedly sound; their specific argument, however, is incomplete. In their model, the bureau chief is indifferent to risk: Because he is trying to maximize budgets, he does not care whether he receives budget X for sure or gambles getting 80 percent of X versus 120 percent of X with equal likelihood. Moreover, the bureaucrat's beliefs about demand are not represented in the model. Therefore, it is puzzling why concealing demand would affect his behavior.

Bendor, Taylor, and van Gaalen (1985) explore the Miller and Moe thesis regarding two-sided asymmetric information by filling in the gaps about risk aversion and beliefs. They show that if the bureau chief is made less certain about legislative demand, he communicates more accurate cost information—if he is risk averse. If he is risk neutral, the legislature cannot affect his strategic behavior by concealing its own preferences.

Bendor, Taylor, and van Gaalen (1987b) subsequently show that the above result is not highly general, however. Politicians will not invariably receive better information from bureaucrats (even risk-averse ones) if they obscure their demand for bureaucratic services in an indiscriminate manner. The result in the 1985 paper is valid only for bureaucrats with a certain kind of risk-averse utility function; positing risk aversion by itself is insufficient to generate the expected conclusion.

This negative result indicates that the role of information asymmetry in hierarchical relations is more subtle than it first appears. On reflection, why would we expect that concealing legislative demand would invariably result in greater control over bureaus? If a bureau chief is

risk averse, making his budget less certain, no matter what he does, will of course make him worse off. But that is not the desired effect. What is wanted is to lower the utility of deception, not to lower his utility regardless of how he behaves. Accordingly, in their second paper, Bendor, Taylor, and van Gaalen show that if "the legislature controls the degree of uncertainty in anticipation of the bureau's strategy (i.e., if it increases the uncertainty when the bureau chief requests a big budget but not if he requests a small one), then the bureaucratic response is always the intended one: The bureau is less likely to make inaccurate claims about its program's costs or benefits" (1987b, 23). The essence of this strategy is to reward a risk-averse bureaucrat with a predictable budget if he reveals accurate cost-benefit information and to punish deception, if it is discovered by monitoring, by making his appropriation uncertain.

Once it is recognized that the budgetary process can be reorganized, that it is in large measure a decision variable of the legislature, we see that Niskanen's model is really a *partial equilibrium* theory: The politicians are represented as a passive mechanism—a demand function—rather than as strategic actors in their own right. The bureaucrat takes the demand function as a constraint, optimizing within it. The field exhibits a growing consensus that it is more reasonable to portray all the central decision makers as active, if not fully strategic. Thus a model's predictions must be full equilibrium outcomes; loosely speaking, what happens when everyone is making their best move.

Comments on the Niskanen Tradition

It has been almost twenty years since the publication of *Bureaucracy and Representative Government*. What can be said about the line of research triggered by this work? First, although it is unclear whether our knowledge has accumulated in any simple sense, the techniques of formal modeling have certainly aided systematic inquiry. For example, because Niskanen laid bare his agenda-control assumptions in generating his oversupply result, later researchers could modify this model by dropping this postulate while retaining other features of the model. In addition, a kind of theoretical sensitivity testing became possible as researchers discovered that certain results depended on rather specific assumptions. Thus the process of theoretical trial and error became more rapid as the community of scholars discovered which assumptions were crucial for various conclusions.

Of course, trial and error means discarding some ideas as well as retaining others, and currently it is safe to say that there has been more of the former than the latter. In particular, the old consensus that bureaucratic organization per se leads to oversupply has broken down—among others, see Miller and Moe (1983), Conybeare (1984), and Bendor, Taylor, and van Gaalen (1985). Nevertheless, negative knowledge is knowledge; it is informative to find out that a proposition is less well grounded than one had believed. On the positive side, the field has moved decisively toward models of information-based agenda control, leaving authority-based models to students of legislatures. This kind of progress is probably more difficult in nonmathematical areas of public administration, where it is harder for scholars to modify predecessors' theories because key assumptions have not been explicitly specified.

Second, the growing consensus to model asymmetric information as the foundation of bureaucratic influence will not be paralleled by a convergence on how to represent this asymmetry. Instead, we will see a proliferation of spe-

cialized models with different assumptions about what bureaucrats know that politicians do not (the set of feasible alternatives, the costs and benefits of a known set of alternatives, and so forth). Even within a class of models focusing on, for example, cost uncertainty, the analyses will differ on the precise specification of uncertainty. (Do politicians have unbiased beliefs? Are their beliefs approximated by a normal distribution, a uniform, or any continuous distribution?) We should be prepared for a bewildering thicket of results; it may be a while before general patterns emerge.*

Third, the Niskanen tradition has stayed within a dyadic framework: A bureau and a political superior confront each other. The superior is often labeled a legislature, but the potential multiplicity of decision makers is usually suppressed by taking the median legislator as decisive. This is done to keep the models tractable; as Terry Moe has forcefully argued (1984, 1987), the cost is substantially lessened realism. Conflict among politicians, between and within branches, is a central fact of life for most agencies. Moreover, there are new theoretical arguments (Hammond, Hill, and Miller 1986; Hill 1985), to be examined shortly, showing that crunching legislative politics down to a single dimension dramatically reduces bureaucratic discretion. Therefore, the as-if assumption of a single political superior has serious substantive implications.

Fourth, modelers in this tradition assume a restricted set of bureaucratic ob-

---

*Establishing general patterns will require that scholars in the field acquire greater mathematical sophistication. For example, to show that a bureau is advantaged whenever its political superior becomes less certain about program implementation requires more high-powered mathematics if the superior's beliefs are represented by any continuous distributions than if they are uniformly distributed.

jectives. Simple budget maximization has been the model assumption. There are a few departures from this, such as discretionary budget maximization (Niskanen 1975), but these have been of modest proportions. The idea that administrators may have policy preferences is left to modelers working in the spatial tradition (Calvert, McCubbins, and Weingast 1986; Hill 1985) and to models of search (Bendor, Taylor, and van Gaalen 1987a) that do not fit easily into the traditional supply and demand framework.

Fifth, virtually none of the models in this tradition say anything about implementation. They are basically theories of exchange: The bureau promises to generate a certain quantity of output in return for a budget. How revenues are transformed into programs is rarely analyzed. (Indeed, here the field has experienced some retrogression, for Niskanen devoted a chapter to issues of production.) Implementation questions are finessed by positing that the agency knows that the political superior can perfectly and costlessly observe final output, so it will do whatever it must to generate that amount.

This is an awkward patch job for two reasons. First, as a generation of policy analysts has learned to its sorrow, measuring bureaucratic output is difficult. Output indicators are always imperfect; collecting them is always costly. Ironically, Niskanen acknowledged that the observable output assumption was problematic:

Bureaucrats and their sponsors do not, in fact, talk much about output—in terms of military capability, the value of educational services, the number and condition of the poor, etc. Most of the review process consists of a discussion of the relation between budgets and activity levels, such as the number of infantry divisions, the number of students served, the num-

ber of poor served by a program, etc. The relation between activity level and output is usually left obscure and is sometimes consciously obscured. (1971, 26–27)

Second, even granting the assumption does not resolve all implementation issues, for the output constraint yields determinate predictions about bureaucratic behavior only when it is binding. That is, only when producing the promised quantity means that the bureau must use the minimum-cost technology and allocate the entire budget to production. These conditions need not be satisfied. Consider the simple example of linear demand and constant marginal costs (figure 14.3). If the legislature uses a Miller and Moe rule-of-thumb and stipulates that the budget equals $p \cdot q$, then the budget-maximizing price is the one that makes the percentage change in quantity demanded equal to the percentage change in price. Thus, if the true cost function is below p^*, as it is in figure 14.3, the administrator will want to overstate his costs while promising to deliver q^*, which is feasible. Since the bureau can actually produce at cost c, what does the model predict the bureau will do with the extra funds? No answer is forthcoming because the model has made no claims about bureaucratic preferences for the use of appropriations (preferences for perquisites, desires to appease powerful producer groups by using inefficient technologies, and so forth). Thus, whenever the output constraint is not binding, one needs a model similar to managerial theories of the firm, specifying bureaucratic preferences for resource allocation. Budget maximization does not suffice.

Criticizing a formal model for overly simple assumptions is easy; constructing a superior alternative is another matter. Progress in this field often moves like an amoeba; moving forward in one

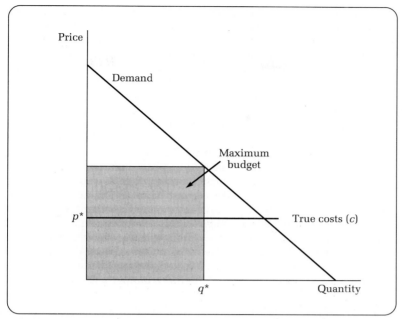

Figure 14.3

direction (replacing an implausible assumption by a more plausible one) is matched by greater simplification in another. The reason, as usual, is analytical tractability.

One could loosen this constraint by realizing the models as simulations, letting the computer crank out the solutions instead of deriving them analytically. A thorough evaluation of simulation models is beyond the scope of this chapter. Briefly, however, it should be noted that simulation is a well established method in behavioral and organizational decision theory (Cohen 1981, 1984; Cohen, March, and Olsen 1972; Crecine 1969; Cyert and March 1963; Levinthal and March 1981). And concerning the specific problems noted above—dyadic analysis, simplified bureaucratic objectives, and neglect of implementation—some recent work (Bendor and Moe 1985, 1986) indicates that computer models can make progress on all these fronts simultaneously.

POLITICAL CONTROL AND PRINCIPAL-AGENT MODELS

Empirical students of bureaucracy have long observed that career officials have programmatic preferences and that agencies, particularly those dominated by a single profession, tend to develop a sense of mission, an orientation toward a particular means as well as ends (Halperin 1974). This mission orientation promotes biased advocacy. As Huntington noted, "The sensitivity of military groups to new program needs depends largely upon service doctrine and service interests. The Air Force was active in pushing strategic deterrence and the Army in innovating European defense since each program was closely related to existing service doctrine. All the services were hesitant in pushing continental defense and limited war, however, which were alien to existing service doctrine" (1961, 288). Because "alleged 'options' are often advocacy in more sophisticated guise, one real choice and two or three straw men" (Destler 1974, 135), students of public administration warned other political scientists not to overemphasize the final policy choices made by political appointees or elected politicians. Instead, scholars should spend more time examining how alternatives are rigged by bureaucrats.

More recently, however, public-choice theorists have pushed the idea of examining stretches of a decision-making sequence one step further. Why stop with the alternative-generating and advice-giving stages? Why not go back further and examine the reward structures established before bureaucratic maneuvering? The basic idea here is that politicians can anticipate the manipulation that Huntington and others have described— they are not so naive as to believe they are being advised by disinterested experts—and they will take steps to reassert control over their more informed subordinates. The analytical point is similar to the criticism directed against Niskanen's basic model: Any theory that represents politicians as the passive targets of agenda manipulation is a partial equilibrium model. Surely the politicians could do better by recognizing the inherent dangers of asymmetric information and taking countermeasures.

This argument undoubtedly has empirical merit. Experienced politicians are suspicious of advice from careerists whom they believe have markedly different policy preferences (Aberbach and Rockman 1976). But these claims of public-choice theorists have been driven as much by the internal logic of equilibrium analysis (why would politicians let themselves be manipulated?) as by evidence. Adding to this momentum, over the last dozen years economists have devoted considerable attention to analyzing problems of control inside firms, problems bearing a strong family resem-

blance to those described by public administrationists. Using the classical rational-choice assumptions in new ways, they have created a class of models known as principal-agent analysis. Ross (1973) is usually cited as the seminal work. See Baiman (1982), Arrow (1985), and Levinthal (1988) for surveys, and Moe (1984) for a clear, nontechnical introduction.

Principal-agent models have two essential components: asymmetric information and conflict of interest. The agent knows something the principal does not, and there is a danger that the agent will exploit this edge strategically. A key question is whether the principal can devise incentives that will induce the agent to act in the principal's interests.

A simple example may clarify the approach. The board of directors of a large firm must decide on a compensation scheme for the head of one of its divisions. The division's profits are a function of the manager's actions (effort) and local variations in the division's operating environment (morale of workers, performance of suppliers, and so forth). Let profit = actions + θ, where θ is a normally distributed random variable representing the local context. The board knows the general form of the profits equation, and it will observe the division's profits, but it cannot observe the manager's day-to-day actions or the local context. (Since it observes profits, if it could also observe the value of θ, it could infer what the manager did, making the control problem trivial.) The board is risk neutral and seeks to maximize the expected net profits of the division: gross profits minus the manager's compensation. Two variables affect the manager's utility: effort, which he dislikes, and money. He is risk neutral in effort, risk averse in money. His utility is additive.

What kind of contract should the board offer? Because the board knows the production function, it can calculate the optimal action the manager should take. Thus it would like to write a contract stipulating that the manager perform that action. But this contract could not be verified, since the board can neither observe the manager nor perfectly infer his action based on the observed outcome. (Low profits could be due to unlucky local context.) And the manager, of course, cannot be trusted to report accurately what he did. Therefore, the contract can be based only on what will be commonly known, the division's profits.

Consider two schemes. In scheme 1, the board gives the manager a percentage of the division's profits. (As in most principal-agent models, it is assumed that the principal, the board, can precommit to a compensation scheme.) This gives the manager an incentive to work hard: He knows that doing so increases the division's expected profits, hence his share. There is a problem, however: This plan makes the manager's income depend on the division's profits, which, due to the unpredictability of θ, is a random variable. Thus the manager's income is itself a random variable. This would not matter were he indifferent to risk; indeed, if that were so, the control problem could be completely eliminated by a contract that gave the stockholders a fixed, lump sum payment every year and the manager the randomly fluctuating remainder. (Such schemes have existed between tenant farmers and landowners.) This arrangement, in effect, internalizes the agency relation, guaranteeing that the manager will act optimally.

It is more empirically plausible, however, to assume that agents are risk averse in income. (A quick check: The reader might ask herself whether she would prefer her current salary with certainty or a fair gamble of double or nothing.) A risk-averse manager prefers that the firm pay him a fixed salary in-

stead of the expected commission of scheme 1. Indeed, he would take somewhat less than the expected commission to make his income certain. The board, being risk neutral, would happily pay the manager that fixed salary, for doing so would increase its expected profits. Therefore, both parties prefer scheme 2—a fixed salary—to scheme 1; hence, the latter is pareto-insufficient. But if the manager is paid a fixed salary, his compensation is not contingent at all on the outcome, so scheme 2 provides no effort incentives. Consequently, in this setting it is impossible to implement a pareto-efficient contract. Pareto-efficient contracts require all risk to be borne by the risk-neutral party, which destroys effort incentives. The problem—headquarters' inability to observe the manager's actions—creates inefficient arrangements.*

Public administrationists may shrug at this analysis. It is, after all, a toy problem. The production function is absurdly simple, and both principal and agent know exactly what it is. Both know the distribution of the disturbance term, θ. The principal knows the agent's utility function. All this poorly approximates real political-control problems. Note, however, that even in

---

*One might conjecture that, over time, the board will infer the manager's actions from the outcomes in an increasingly precise manner, especially if θ is independently and identically distributed over time. This information should allow more efficient arrangements to be supported as Nash equilibria. Radner (1985) shows that for an infinitely repeated game, this conjecture is true in the sense that the less the players discount the future, the closer they can approach a fully efficient contract. In addition to the value of repeated play, the literature has explored two other methods for ameliorating control problems: monitoring—obtaining some (possibly imperfect) indicators of the agent's behavior—and comparing the performance of agents to each other. See Levinthal (1988) for a review of all three.

this toy world the principal and the agent are unable to implement a pareto-efficient contract. The real lesson is to show that even if one assumes the principal knows more than most real-world principals know, control problems emerge nonetheless.

Ironically, whereas economists often use principal-agent models to explore potential control problems, it appears that political scientists often refer to such models to exorcise them and the specter of bureaucratic influence. I cannot document this claim—it is based on comments in conference panels—but my impression is that some scholars believe that these models show that the problem of controlling bureaucrats can be solved by sophisticated politicians, who have only to design appropriate incentives. I believe that this seriously underestimates the empirical difficulties, and wastes principal-agent analysis. It is trivial to show that given enough information about subordinates and sufficiently powerful instruments, politicians can induce bureaucrats to act as they want; it is much more interesting to show how control inefficiencies can emerge despite a principal knowing a great deal.

Currently, it is fair to say that in political science principal-agent models are more talked about than written down. Because these models will become increasingly popular in the formal branches of public administration, specifying their minimal components may be a useful aid to consumers. In the basic principal-agent model, both parties must be active optimizers; representing either as a passive mechanism makes it impossible to depict the essence of the problem—how the agent could strategically exploit asymmetric information and how the boss controls this. There must be some conflict of interest. The boss must suffer from some informational handicap: In some models, he cannot observe the agent's action (often called *moral hazard* or *hidden*

action problems); in others, the agent has information about himself or the task environment that the superior lacks (*adverse selection* or *hidden information* models). Aside from this asymmetry, in the stripped-down models the two actors have homogeneous beliefs. Thus, in the preceding example of the decentralized firm, the board and the manager both knew (or believed) that profits = effort + a disturbance, both knew the distribution of the random variable and the range of values that effort could take on, and both observe the outcome (the amount of profit realized). This implies that in the basic models, the principal already knows what action she would like the agent to take; the problem is in inducing it.* Further, in hidden-action models, it is typically assumed that she knows the agent's utility function, enabling her to predict how the agent would respond to any incentive scheme she may contemplate. Her decision problem is to devise an incentive scheme that maximizes her expected utility—knowing in advance that after the scheme is announced, the agent will act in his own self-interest. The contract must be self-enforcing vis-à-vis the agent: he will only carry out actions that maximize his own expected utility, in the light of the incentives. The principal, however, can pre-commit to what she has promised the agent.† The con-

*Because in the simple moral hazard framework the principal can, in principle, solve the technical optimization problem just as well as the agent can, these models do not capture the phenomenon of asymmetric expertise in the ordinary sense of the word.

†If she could not make legally binding promises, the model would become a prisoner's dilemma: Both sides are better off if they cooperate (establish a relationship) than if they both defect, but each party is tempted to double cross the other. In the basic one-period model, there would be as usual only one solution: Since the agent believes that the boss would defect by not paying him, he would not work.

tract must satisfy a participation constraint: It must yield the agent at least as much expected utility as he can obtain at his next-best opportunity outside the organization in question. Finally, the set of feasible contracts must be specified. (For example, must the agent's wages be positive, or can the principal extract a fine—negative wages—should the outcome fall below a predetermined level?)

If these properties are not specified, mathematically or in words, a reader may be unable to ascertain whether a particular formulation is a genuine principal-agent model. It may instead be an exercise in relabeling, in which hierarchical superiors are called principals and subordinates, agents. Nonmathematically inclined public administrationists have good reason to be suspicious of such exercises, for they may have little content that is genuinely novel.

Alternatively, a formulation may be a genuine agency analysis, but the imprecise specification makes it difficult for readers to figure out how results are derived. It is especially important to state what incentives are feasible, for this assumption strongly influences the agent's optimal behavior. To see this we reconsider the example of the decentralized firm. Assume that the manager's effort can range between zero and 100 and the disturbance term is uniformly distributed between −1 and 1. Contracts with arbitrarily large penalties are legal. The principal, knowing that profits = effort + θ, commits herself to the following deal: As long as profits are at least 99, she will pay the manager a fixed salary of k. (Knowing the agent's preferences and the participation constraint, she has computed k so that the agent's utility of $u(k) - u$ (maximum effort) barely induces him to join the firm.) If profits fall below 99, the principal will extract an exceedingly large fine from the agent. Note the combined effect of unbounded

penalties and a bounded disturbance. Because the principal knows that θ cannot fall below −1, if she observes a profit of 98 she can flawlessly infer that the agent could not have been exerting maximal effort. Since the agent knows this too, he can guarantee that he will not have to pay the fine by pegging his effort at 100. In this informational setting a negative wage is a threat that will never be used; the availability, however, of arbitrarily large penalties enables the principal to arrange a deal that is just as efficient as the one she would establish were she to observe the agent's actions directly. If such penalties were legally or financially impossible, or if there were a significant possibility of an inferential error (the boss mistakenly believing that the agent shirked) or of the boss's double-crossing the agent, this arrangement would not work. (The economist James Mirrlees has shown that even if the disturbance can take on any value, e.g., the normal, this scheme can get arbitrarily close to how well a fully informed superior would do, as long as arbitrarily large penalties are allowed.)

Several pieces in the literature on political control have some, but not all, of the above components of principal-agent models. In particular, it is common for one of the two parties to be represented as a mechanism rather than as a decision maker. In Bendor, Taylor, and van Gaalen (1985), for example, their first model treats the legislature as a demand function plus an exogenously fixed monitoring and penalty system; the bureaucracy is the more active decision maker in that its strategy is endogenously determined. On the other side, Fiorina's models of delegation (1982, 1986) treat the bureaucracy as an exogenously fixed, though noisy, machine that transforms legislative intent into a distribution of outcomes; legislators are the active decision makers. This pattern results from an interaction between academic specialization and the constraints of formal modeling. Most people working on models of political control specialize in either the bureaucracy or the legislature. Like most specialists, they focus on what they know best—their particular institution. In the craft of formal modeling, this means making the better-known institution the active (choosing) figure against the passive ground of its environment, represented as a mechanism or constraint. Such decision-theoretic models are easier to construct than the game-theoretic ones of principal-agent analysis.

I do not mean that decision-theoretic models are useless. On the contrary, these models can yield significant insights. For example, in an analysis of advice giving, Calvert (1985) has proven an interesting result: Under some circumstances, a superior will prefer to listen to the suggestions of more-biased subordinates rather than those of less-biased ones. (The reason: When a subordinate known to be biased against a choice alternative recommends it nonetheless, the odds are good that the option is worthwhile. Thus his advice may contain much information or surprise value, and is potentially valuable.) Though the subordinates in this model are not active decision makers—they are probabilistic black boxes that emit pro or con signals—Calvert's basic result may have implications for how principals select agents, and it may stand up in a fully strategic model.

Recently there have been some attempts by political scientists to construct genuinely bilateral principal-agent models. In Bendor, Taylor, and van Gaalen (1987a), the superior's problem arises from a classical division of labor: The subordinate, who has expertise but no formal authority, designs the set of alternatives; the politician, who has authority but little expertise, makes the final choice. The bureaucrat has programmatic preferences and wants to rig the superior's agenda to boost the odds

that his preferred program will be selected. He does so by allocating more design time to his preferred program. The search for policy alternatives, long considered by behavioral theorists as central to any nonroutine choice process (March and Simon 1958), constitutes agenda manipulation.*

The politician, anticipating the manipulation, controls it in two distinctly different ways. In model 1, the politician cannot pre-commit to anything; instead, she threatens to reject the bureaucrat's options if other policy experts are likely to generate better alternatives. This threat must be credible: It must be in the superior's interest to carry it out should the bureaucrat design unacceptable alternatives. In model 2, she can pre-commit to an incentive scheme, a budgetary schedule that rewards the bureaucrat for designing proposals that benefit the superior. Thus, whereas the second model is a principal-agent analysis, the first model—lacking the necessary property of pre-commitment—is not.

This distinction is not a mere technicality; it is substantively important. In model 1, the superior is sometimes unable to prevent her agenda from being completely rigged, and only under the most fortuitous circumstances does the agency carry out search as a fully informed superior would want. In model 2, once the superior pre-commits to an appropriately conceived budgetary scheme, the bureaucrat plans in an unbiased manner. And the models' results differ in more subtle ways. The technique of comparative statistics (chang-

---

*Search models traditionally have been associated with behavioral theories (Nelson and Winter 1982; Simon 1957). Though most rational-choice models assume that the set of alternatives is exogenously fixed (e.g., in most spatial models of legislatures, proposals—mere points in a policy space—need not be designed), this is not a logical necessity. Optimal-search models have been studied in economics for quite some time.

ing a parameter's value and comparing the new equilibrium to the old equilibrium) show that when the budgetary incentives are in place, changes in the larger environment (such as the quality of options offered by competing specialists) affect the superior's well-being in intuitively expected ways. In model 1, however, these changes can, via the agency's mediating influence, have perverse effects. Thus, model 1 directs our attention to bureaucracy's role in policy formation, whereas model 2 implies we can ignore it. (Indeed, model 2 specifies sufficient conditions for treating the executive branch as a unitary rational actor, in Graham Allison's sense of the phrase.)

The application of principal-agent models to the political control of bureaucracy is in its infancy. Because it builds on the empirically relevant properties of hierarchy (the principal can, within limits, fix the agent's payoff schedule), asymmetric information, and conflicting objectives, and because of its extensive development in the study of the internal organization of the firm, it will be used increasingly by formal modelers of bureaucracy. A few cautions are therefore in order.

The first criticism is the least important. In most of these models, the agent's action is interpreted as effort, which he dislikes. Mechanical transfers of this choice variable to public administration may be inappropriate, particularly if one is studying interactions between politicians and senior administrators. Richard Nixon did not worry that bureaucrats in Health, Education, and Welfare (HEW) were sleeping instead of working; political and programmatic subversion was on his mind.

In part this is a matter of interpretation. The mathematical formalism of principal-agent models typically states only that the agent's choice variable is a real number that varies continuously between an upper and lower bound, and

that his utility decreases monotonically as this variable increases. Effort is a natural interpretation, but it is not the only one. The problem is a bit deeper, however: The formal assumptions may not be the most appropriate representation of politician-bureaucrat relations. In cases of policy conflicts, it is more natural to represent the bureaucrat's choice variable as influencing policy implementation—perhaps picking a point in a policy space, subject to constraints established by his political superiors (Calvert, McCubbins, and Weingast, 1986; Hammond, Hill, and Miller 1986; Hill 1985). In a spatial setting, it is also natural to depict the bureaucrat's utility as being a single-peaked function, with its maximum being his ideal policy. Thus, utility need not decrease steadily in his choice variable. But this does not pose an insuperable barrier to using principal-agent models. Because the essential ingredients of conflicting interests (different ideal points) and asymmetric information (implementation may be hard to observe) are often present, a control problem may still exist: Some of the politicians want the administrator to implement a policy more to their liking than his. At this point, the standard apparatus of agency theory can be brought to bear on the problem: What incentives can the principal(s) deploy to induce the agent to implement the desired policy, how can the principal(s) select, from the set of possible agents, the one that minimizes control problems, and so forth. Therefore, the original Taylorite interpretation of principal-agent models does not seriously constrain their use in public administration.

The second issue concerns the assumption that the principal can precommit to an incentive scheme. The agent, knowing this, can choose without fear that the boss will renege on the deal. This assumption is a good first approximation for firms creating contracts in the shadow of the law. The matter becomes more delicate when the referent is government. Careful attention must be paid to the incentives; if, for example, the agent is to be rewarded by a policy concession, is it plausible to assume that politicians can bind themselves to complex policy decisions? If not, a principal-agent approach is inappropriate; instead, one should construct a model in which the decision makers behave opportunistically, making their best moves at every choice point. But if the reward is a budget, pre-commitment is more plausible. (The President, for example, can at least affirm budgetary figures in a public document.)

In general, the literature has dichotomized the possibility of pre-commitment: Either the principal has unlimited commitment ability or none at all. Neither of these may be a good approximation of governmental control problems. For example, politicians may be able to commit to an appropriation for a single year but not beyond that, or certain policies may be easier to commit to than others. In neither case is commitment an all-or-nothing matter. There has been some progress on developing models of intermediate commitment. In Radner's (1985) repeated-play model, the principal can guarantee a compensation scheme only for a single period. Melumad and Mookherjee (1989) explore the intriguing idea that a principal can augment his commitment abilities by delegating authority to an agent; their work may shed some light on the strategic implications of a partially independent civil service.

Third, almost all these models assume a single principal. This may be a reasonable approximation if one is trying to get some insight into relations well inside a bureaucracy, where one might plausibly assume that the hierarchical pressures on a subordinate are channeled through his immediate superior. Senior bureaucrats, however, often respond to a diverse set of political superiors who may disagree among themselves about the direction the agent should take. We look at models with multiple political superiors next.

Fourth, though principal-agent theory has received little systematic empirical scrutiny, even a casual comparison of its predictions with data indicate problems. Kenneth Arrow has commented in a recent survey, "The theory tends to lead to very complex fee functions. It turns out to be difficult to establish even what would appear to be common-sense properties of monotonicity and the like. We do not find such complex relations in reality. Principal-agent theory gives a good reason for the existence of sharecrop contracts, but it is a very poor guide to their actual terms" (1985, 48). Bengt Holmstrom, a pioneer in this field, notes that results are often very sensitive to a model's assumptions; even the third moment of the disturbance term can matter (1986). Arrow suggests that it is costly to specify complex relations, thus creating a pressure for simple contracts. And the results' hypersensitivity to the fine structure of the assumptions results from the use of classical rationality postulates: Because principal and agent have unlimited powers of computation, they are sensitive to the smallest of changes. It is possible to introduce a cost of writing (and enforcing) contracts into these models; modifying the rationality postulates is a more fundamental change.

Political Control and Multiple Superiors

Most of the preceding works have relied on informational asymmetries as the driving force in causing agency problems. In a stimulating paper, Jeffrey Hill (1985) has shown that bureaucratic discretion—hence control problems—can appear even when information is complete. Problems can arise solely from the legislature's difficulties in reaching stable collective choices. His analysis has been extended by Hammond, Hill, and Miller (1986); the following discussion focuses on the more recent paper.

A simple diagram will help us understand their argument. Figure 14.4 depicts a policy choice facing a legislature. The policy is described by two dimensions, x and y. Each legislator has an ideal policy, points 1, 2, and 3 in the figure. Following the standard Downsian framework, the further away an alternative is from a legislator's ideal, the less she likes it.

Now suppose this mini legislature chooses point r as the policy to be implemented by the agency. (The location of this alternative is immaterial.) The bureau chief, however, has policy preferences of his own: His ideal alternative is point B. The question posed by Hammond, Hill, and Miller is, Can the bureau chief get away with implementing a policy closer to the one he most prefers? The answer is yes, even though the legislature can observe his actions.

Consider point i. Because it is closer to the ideal points of legislators 1 and 2, they prefer it to the bill they helped pass.* Therefore, they will not raise an outcry or conduct oversight hearings when the bureau chief implements policy i. The chief, of course, also prefers the new policy. What he has done is to construct an *implementation coalition* that differs from the legislative coalition, a phenomenon observed by many students of American politics. His discretion derives not from defying legislative intent but from the opportunity to construct new majorities. It is interesting to note that senior bureaucrats in the United States see their roles as having a greater political content than do their European counterparts (Aberbach, Putnam, and Rockman 1981). This role orientation is consistent with experiences of creating implementation coalitions.

---

*For simplicity Hammond, Hill, and Miller assume that the legislators weight the two dimensions equally, so the indifference curves are circles.

Figure 14.4

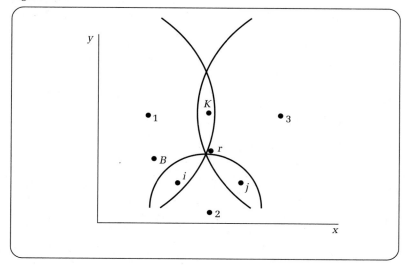

Figure 14.4 illustrates a possibility; it does not establish a general result. Is this possibility an artifact of the example? As Hammond, Hill, and Miller emphasize, the example is not at all peculiar. Social-choice theorists have established that in moderately complex political situations—those in which policies must be described by at least two dimensions—it will almost always be the case that every alternative is vulnerable under majority rule (McKelvey 1976). Refer back to figure 14.4. Even though point r is centrally located, we saw that legislators 1 and 2 prefer point i. Similarly, legislators 2 and 3 prefer alternative j; 1 and 3 prefer K. Thus, latent in the situation are multiple winning coalitions, which the administrator exploits.

The authors show that if the President knows the legislators' ideal points, he can craftily appoint a bureau chief who thereafter, for his own policy reasons, creates an implementation coalition that the chief executive prefers to the legislative coalition. The legislature has the authority to veto an appointment; it will approve the nominee if a majority prefers what he will implement to the status quo. (As usual in the multidimensional setting, such a majority almost always exists.) Thus their spatial model shows how top administrative personnel selections fit into the presidential-congressional game.

These papers, by showing how bureaucrats can influence policy outcomes by colluding with previously latent legislative majorities, are an important contribution to our understanding of political control. The following points remain to be addressed.

First, scholars will disagree over how much influence each side of Pennsylvania Avenue has over appointments. Nevertheless, it is unlikely that any legislature would tolerate an appointee whose ideal policy was outside the legislators' pareto region (the area bounded by the ideal points of the most extreme legislators). Yet, in the authors' diagrammatic examples, the official's ideal is outside this region. Because the administrator will implement a point as close as possible to his ideal point, a policy outlier moves the final outcome farther from the legislative point than would a moderate official. These examples convey an impression of greater administrative influence than is empirically plausible.

Second, the very property of majority rule—the lack of an invulnerable policy—that provides an opening for bureaucratic discretion also makes the authors' predictions less than crystal clear. The model has two stages, concluding with implementation. It appears to yield a determinate prediction: Among all alternatives a majority prefers to the legislative outcome, the bureaucrat implements the policy closest to his ideal. But in the real world policy making never stops, so whatever the administrator implemented this year could be modified the next. And because the property of latent multiple-winning coalitions still holds, legislators who dislike the implementation will be able to find a majority that prefers some new alternative to the one implemented by the agency. Neither paper addresses this issue of equilibrium outcomes (although see Hammond and Miller 1987) or, failing a completely stable outcome, what a statistical distribution of outcomes may look like.

Moreover, since policy making repeats itself over time, politicians may recognize a long-run value in not allowing legislative coalitions to be overturned during implementation, despite a majority's short-run temptation to do so. Hence, one may be able to demonstrate, in the context of a noncooperative game, that it will be an equilibrium strategy for each legislator to support the winning legislative coalition by agreeing to punish the administrator for deviating from legislative intent. (Because typically there are many equilibria in repeated games, however, it should also be possible to show that there are equilibria in which some legislators collude with the agency.)

Third, the results require that the politicians cannot bind themselves to inferior decisions: if the bureau chief implements the bill in a way that makes legislators 1 and 2 better off, they will accept what he has done. (The absence of precommitment means, strictly speaking, that these are not principal-agent models.) This is a substantively important and possibly controversial assumption. On the one hand, the bureau chief's implementation does make the new majority better off, making it easier for these legislators to explain their behavior back home. On the other hand, a bill passed by both chambers and signed by the President has the force of law, so one may contend that the courts will punish administrative deviations from statutory mandate. If the legislators knew in advance that such legal enforcement were guaranteed, in effect they would be precommitted to the policy. An empirically reasonable position is that it is easier for politicians to pre-commit in certain policy arenas than in others (e.g., the Reagan administration discovered that the courts would enforce legislatively established criteria for disability payments) and that the model applies only when pre-commitment is unavailable. The size of the model's domain is, of course, an empirical question.

Fourth, these papers are interesting partly because they demonstrate that agency problems can occur for a quintessentially political reason—the existence of multiple winning coalitions—and despite complete information. Nevertheless, there is something unsettling about the verbal story that accompanies the model. With an unambiguous statute, the administrator is going against the manifest will of Congress, and with complete information, he is doing so in the full light of day. This

is hard to swallow. The authors do present a variant, similar to Hill's original model, that relaxes the complete-information assumption. Following developments in the economic analysis of contracts, they argue that bills will rarely specify all politically relevant contingencies; it is either infeasible (not all contingencies can be foreseen) or too costly to do so. Their model represents this by allowing the legislature to vote on one dimension; the second dimension is left unspecified (see figure 14.5). Since the statute is silent regarding y, the bureau chief has formal discretion to pick any point on x_m. Presumably he will implement the incompletely specified legislation to be closest to his own preferred policy, point V in figure 14.5.

So far, so good. But the authors then argue that the administrator can do still better. Once the legislature recognizes the new dimension, new latent majorities appear. For example, legislators 1 and 2 prefer W to V. (In one dimension, representative 2, as the median voter, could do no better than to support the line x_m.) Therefore, the administrator can get legislators 1 and 2 to go along with an implementation of W. But this raises the same disquieting issue of administrative disregard of legislative intent. Although the bill did not specify everything, it did specify the line x_m. By implementing W, the bureau chief would be flaunting the aspect of the bill that was unambiguous. And again, he would be doing so openly. It seems that the model, ingenious as it is, needs a dose of incomplete information to make it more plausible.

Oversight, Political Control, and Equilibrium Analysis

Although the formal tools of principal-agent theory have diffused slowly into public administration, some of the

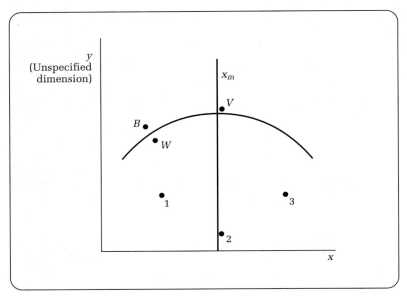

Figure 14.5

ideas have penetrated more quickly. In particular, the concept of equilibrium analysis has influenced how we might think about the political control of bureaucracy, as well as how we should interpret evidence about oversight and control.

Several empirically oriented scholars have observed that legislators do not seem to spend much time overseeing agencies or attempting to influence policy implementation (see Wilson 1980 on regulatory agencies; more generally, see Ogul 1976). These conclusions are plausible enough: Little observed oversight activity suggests little influence.

Yet consider the following sketch of a model of monitoring (McCubbins and Schwartz 1984; Weingast 1984). An administrator either follows legislative intent or implements a program more to his own liking. If he does the former he gets a utility of x. If he does the latter—and his deviation is undiscovered by the legislature—he gets y which exceeds x. With probability p, however,

an interest group or some other affected party (not necessarily the politicians) will discover that he has not carried out legislative intent. If this fire alarm is activated, the legislature ensures that he follows their instructions, and imposes a sanction (such as embarrassing publicity or budget cuts) at a cost s to the administrator.

The bureaucrat, therefore, faces a choice of acting as the perfect agent and getting a sure payoff of x or deviating and getting an expected payoff of $(1 - p)y + p(x - s)$. If $x > (1 - p)y + p(x - s)$, and the bureaucrat perceives this accurately, no alarms go off and the administrator is never grilled on Capitol Hill. Yet by hypothesis we know that this is not because Congress is uninfluential. On the contrary, its sanctions are such an effective deterrent that administrative compliance is assured. Thus, though the model is simple, it reveals an essential point about behavior in equilibrium. As Weingast has stressed, *"The smooth operation of these institutional arrangements (i.e., agency policy equilibrium) involves little direct participation by Congress.* The more effective this system, the less direct and visible the role of Congress in agency decisions" (1984, 157, emphasis in the original). Indeed, the hypotheses that Congress is in complete control and that it exerts no influence are observationally equivalent; both predict that scholars will find no legislative oversight.

The analysis also shows that the arrangement can guarantee administrative compliance even if the underlying chance of direction, p, is small. The value of p denotes the intensity of monitoring. Clearly p could be small—monitoring is casual—yet $x > (1 - p)y + p(x - s)$, if the sanction s is severe enough. (This is essentially an application of Mirrlees's principal-agent theorem.)

Such ideas, enlightening as they are about the logical implications of equilibrium analysis, do not demonstrate that Congress controls the bureaucracy. It is important for scholars not to be swept away by purely mathematical arguments, such as, for any strictly positive p, no matter how small, there exists an s sufficiently large so that $x > (1 - p)y + p(x - s)$. The statement is valid; its empirical implications, however, are less certain, and are limited in several ways. Most obviously, constitutional prohibitions against cruel and unusual punishments limit the magnitude of feasible sanctions in the United States.

There is a more subtle issue. Earlier I stressed that if the sanctions are sufficiently big, they will never be used—in equilibrium, and if the administrator perceives the monitoring and sanction system accurately. Both provisos are important. Suppose the bureaucrat underestimates the sanctions, and believing that s and p are small enough so that $x < (1 - p)y + p(x - s)$, he deviates.

At this point, there are two possibilities: Either he is detected or not. If he is not, what should an outside observer infer about bureaucratic compliance with legislative intent? It is unclear. A Weingastian analysis, buttressed by an accurate assessment of the sanctions, would imply that the bureaucrat would comply (in equilibrium), which is consistent with the fact that no alarm has sounded. But, as stipulated, the bureaucrat has deviated. Now we can probe more deeply into the meaning of equilibrium analysis. The administrator has not complied with legislative intent because he underestimated the penalty for doing so. Eventually his implementation path will be discovered, and he will be sanctioned. Learning what the true penalties are, he will no longer deviate. Thus a complete equilibrium analysis means that not only must an agent's actions be optimal, given his beliefs; in addition his beliefs must be an accurate, or at least unbiased, description of his environment. If his beliefs were biased, he would be making systematic errors. But because systematic errors are correctable, in equilibrium he cannot have biased beliefs. This is a version of the rational expectations hypothesis.

The recent emphasis of equilibrium analysis on actors' beliefs is in some ways a salutary development. In most important organizational situations, payoffs are not common knowledge, so the development of models that can accommodate this fact is potentially significant to students of public administration. In addition, the theorists' insistence that beliefs must be part of equilibrium analysis is a check against some poor methodological practices. Specifically, it is all too easy to defend the rationality postulate from empirical criticism if beliefs are excluded from the analysis. It is virtually guaranteed that any behavior can be rationalized as optimal behavior in the light of some set of beliefs. (I have heard there is an unpublished theorem that proves this.) It has long been known that the rationality postulate is irrefutable unless specific claims are made about the utility function that is being maximized. In a game of incomplete information, however, specifying the content of a utility function does not guarantee falsifiability; beliefs must be specified as well.

The extension of equilibrium analysis to encompass beliefs has a certain logical momentum behind it. It is, however, a purely conceptual analysis of what equilibrium analysis means; it has no empirical content. The statements that our hypothetical administrator will not in equilibrium deviate when $x > (1 - p)y + p(x - s)$, and that with those payoffs no oversight hearings will be observed in equilibrium precisely because the bureaucrat is complying, are not empirical claims about what any particular official is doing. A key empirical question, perhaps the key question, is to establish whether the situation is, in fact, in equilibrium. It is certainly possible that much high-level administrative behavior reflects inaccurate perceptions of one kind or another; hence the behavior is out of equilibrium. Thus the empirical domain of equilibrium analysis may be limited. This does not mean that analysis or even prediction is impossible. It certainly makes both tasks more difficult, however, for they would require empirical work on systematic biases in belief formation and theories of adaptive (disequilibrium) behavior.

One reason why equilibrium analysis in games with incomplete information may have a limited empirical scope is that it is often difficult for decision makers to formulate accurate beliefs. Forming unbiased perceptions of complex issues is not an incidental task, to be completed quickly before the main job of choosing an optimal strategy; it is a major part of the job. Indeed, I have the uncomfortable feeling that what the game theorists have given with one hand—the greater empirical relevance of games with incomplete information—they have taken away with the other—the requirement that decision makers act as perfect Bayesians, fully equipped with Ph.D.s in statistics. The as-if assumption becomes ever more heroic, a polite way of saying increasingly implausible.

THE DESIGN OF HIERARCHICAL INSTITUTIONS

Students of bureaucracy have long suspected that citizens want public organizations to satisfy contradictory criteria. For example, in his cogent essay Herbert Kaufman (1956) argued that Americans have been torn between the values of representativeness, competence, and executive leadership. Recently, these arguments have been recast in a formal framework (Hammond and Miller 1985; Thomas and Hammond 1989). These authors have used the axiomatic approach of social-choice theory by specifying intuitively reasonable criteria that any bureaucratic organization should satisfy and then investigating whether the set of criteria is internally consistent. If a set is inconsistent, the authors have established an impossibility result: One cannot design an institution with the desired qualities. Note how such a result deepens the insights of Kaufman, Simon (1946), and others: It is not merely difficult to design such an organization, it is impossible in principle. If we think about institutional design as a search over a set of alternatives, we see that an impossibility result says that if our stopping rule has the form, "terminate the search once we have discovered an organizational form with properties *a, b, c,*" the search will never end. This is useful information, for it tells us that our aspirations are unrealistic.

To see what is involved, consider one of these impossibility results covered by

Hammond and Miller (1985). Four design criteria are examined: decentralization, universal domain, the pareto property, and acyclicity. *Decentralization* means that the organization delegates authority concerning nonoverlapping sets of alternatives to different experts. *Universal domain* mandates flexibility; the choice process must work on any possible combination of experts' preference orderings over the alternatives at hand. The *pareto criterion* means that if every bureaucrat prefers x to y, the organization itself must rank x over y. *Acyclicity* means that if, at the end of a choice process, the conclusion is that x is better than y and y is better than z, then x must be rated at least as well as z. With some reinterpretation of terms, it can be shown that this case is covered by a result of the social-choice theorist Amartya Sen: No institution can satisfy all criteria.

Hammond and Miller (1985) present four other impossibility theorems. All the results have several principles of administration in common. First, each posits some kind of decentralization as a design criterion. The nature of the decentralization varies: Authority may be distributed horizontally or vertically; jurisdictions may be overlapping or nonoverlapping. The decentralization may even be conditional: Theorem 3 examines a management-by-exception rule (if all subordinates agree on a ranking of options, that fixes the organization's ranking; if not, their superior decides).

Second, each theorem presumes that flexibility is desirable: The universal domain criterion is stipulated as an organizing criterion. Finally, each requires that individual rankings must aggregate to an acyclic organizational ranking. Thus "the proofs of Theorems 1–5 have a key feature: in each case, universal domain allows us to construct a set of preferences which, when aggregated via [the posited structure of authority], violates acyclicity" (Hammond and Miller 1985, 22). As they point out, "At root, decentralization . . . cause(s) trouble because it creates *multiple points of decision-making authority*" (p. 22, emphasis in the original). And because violations appear in the context of several rather different authority structures, it seems there is a deep inconsistency between the general idea of decentralization and other important principles of organizational design.

The theorems are valid, but what is their relevance to bureaucracies? Several objections may be made. The first is that the theorems' appropriate empirical domain includes voters and legislators, who are indeed trying to aggregate individual preferences into a collective choice. It is not sensible to stretch the results to cover bureaucrats; they are not free actors, and bureaucracies as institutions are not established to aggregate individual preferences over alternatives. Judgments, yes; opinions, yes; preferences, no.

But this objection underestimates the generality of Sen's theorem and the other impossibility results. A theorem, like any purely mathematical object, is uninterpreted, referring only to sets, elements of sets, relations (such as orderings) between those elements, and so forth. Thus xPy could be interpreted specifically as "x is preferred to y," but all that the abstract theorem claims is that a relation of ordering obtains between x and y. In some sense, x outranks y; what that sense is depends on the specific application of the theorem. Regarding bureaucracies (and juries and advisory committees), it is indeed more sensible to interpret the ordering as one of judgments—bureaucrat 1 believes that x is a superior alternative to y in terms of some organizational criterion, whereas bureaucrat 2 believes the opposite. This interpretation of institutions aggregating judgments rather than preferences is perfectly appropriate for this theorem, and for social-choice results in general (Sen 1977). Therefore, although Hammond and Miller mainly refer to preferences, in what follows I shall interpret the orderings as judgments.

The second objection concerns the significance of the results. The punch of an impossibility theorem depends on the plausibility of the principles; the less stringent they are, the more surprising the result. In the five results reported by Hammond and Miller, most of the design criteria seem sensible enough, with one exception: universal domain. This is a demanding condition because it requires that an organization's decision process work on any configuration of judgments of individual officials. (Universal domain is also assumed in the most celebrated of all impossibility results, Arrow's theorem on democratic procedures.) This limitless flexibility is tantamount to demanding a kind of perfection, so perhaps it is unsurprising that no institution can pass the test.

Hammond and his colleagues have several replies to this objection. First, we do not yet know how bizarre sets of individual orderings must be in order to create intransitive institutional orderings. Some scholars initially thought Arrow's result was only a mathematical curiosity, and that preference combinations creating majority rule intransitivity were empirically odd. We now know, thanks to a decade of hard work by high powered theorists, that—outside the simple world of unidimensional policy spaces—just the opposite is true: Preference configurations yielding coherent majoritarian choices are extremely special. It is therefore possible that rather tame judgment profiles in the bureaucratic setting will also yield intransitive institutional orderings.

Second, Hammond (1984, 1985) has investigated, via Monte Carlo simulation, the odds that a problematic profile of individual judgments—one necessitating the violation of a principle—will appear in an agency. Although such simulations cannot be completely conclusive, it seems that the more officials whose opinions matter, and the greater the number of alternatives, the greater the probability that the institution's judgment ordering will be intransitive. It should be noted that in these simulations all individual orderings were equally likely, an extreme form of the universal domain property. Empirically, bureaucrats in an agency probably exhibit more homogeneous beliefs due to self-selection and socialization. Judgmental homogeneity within an agency may be purchased at the price of heterogeneity among agencies (Hammond and Miller 1985, 17), however, so the problems may be displaced rather than solved.

A third objection is that the theory's empirical predictions are incorrect: Agencies do not cycle endlessly over different alternatives. This objection rests on the incorrect perception that Hammond and Miller are making unconditional empirical claims about the frequency of indecisive institutional behavior. Their social-choice theorems, however, are not directly about choices; they are about the relation between individual and collective orderings of alternatives. To see the difference, let us consider an example from Hammond (1985, 5) that illustrates another impossibility result. The rules defining the institution are simple. Some decisions are delegated to small groups of subordinates who have expertise. If a group can agree, the matter is settled for the organization; if not, a common superior makes the choice. In this example, subordinates 1 and 2 agree that x is superior to y; since they have jurisdiction over these options, the ranking $xP_o y$ (x is organizationally preferred to y) is established.

Subordinates 3 and 4 do not agree about the relative merits of y and z, so their superior imposes the ordering yP_oz. Finally, because the pair (x, z) was not delegated, the boss has jurisdiction and imposes xP_ox. All together we have $xP_oyP_ozP_ox$: The organization's judgment ordering is cyclic.

But we must be careful to understand precisely what is being stated. The institution's underlying ordering of alternatives is cyclic; we have not predicted that its choice behavior will be cyclic or unstable. Indeed, the relevant impossibility theorem, derived by Thomas and Hammond, makes no direct prediction about the choice behavior of a bureaucracy. Instead, it states one of several principles must give in a situation like this. Empirically, of course, the organization may exhibit decisive behavior: The boss, confronted with the orderings xP_oy and yP_oz, but believing that z is better than x, simply imposes his own views and picks z. This decisiveness does not constitute a counterexample to the Thomas and Hammond result, for the latter did not predict unstable choice behavior. The latent intransitivity of the institution's judgment ordering has not disappeared; it has been evaded by hierarchical fiat.

Concerning empirical theory, we are interested in predicting choices, not latent orderings. An empiricist might say, if the outcome is stable and predictable, who cares if there are latent inconsistencies?* And I think it is fair to say that some of the shock value of the Hammond, Miller, and Thomas work rests on their apparent claim that even hierarchies are vulnerable to choice instability. Such predictions surprise us, for the

common supposition is that hierarchy almost by definition guarantees decisiveness; after all, with a single chief executive, the buck stops here.

Some of the authors' own language promotes this misinterpretation: "Even with a 'boss' who steps in and makes the decisions when the subordinates are in disagreement, organizational preference cycles can still occur" (Hammond 1985, 2). A more careful reading shows that behavioral instability—agencies indecisively cycling over alternatives—is not an implication of the theorems. I would recommend that formal theorists avoid the term *cycles* if they are referring to preference or judgment orderings. In ordinary language, the word connotes choice instability over time.

Although the impossibility results do not make unconditional predictions about choice behavior, they do have empirical content. Since they demonstrate that no agency can simultaneously satisfy principles *a, b,* and *c,* it immediately follows that if a particular bureaucracy has implemented the first two principles, it is not implementing the third. As Hammond and Miller (1985) emphasize, different bureaucracies will exhibit different types of pathologies, that is, violations of different criteria. For example, if agencies make decisive choices, is it because a combination of personnel selection and organizational socialization create sufficiently homogeneous beliefs so that troublesome judgment profiles do not appear (a violation of universal domain)? Or is it due to organizational procedures, such as a bureau chief imposing a choice in the face of underlying judgmental confusion (a violation of decentralization)?

Perhaps surprisingly, then, this most abstract type of theorizing relates directly to much more empirical ways of studying agencies: to social psychological studies of organizational socialization, to behavioral analyses of standard

---

*There are problems with focusing on orderings even for a normative theory of bureaucracy. Sen (1977) has suggested that requiring institutions to produce a complete ordering of alternatives is a bit of a luxury; all we need is that they make choices.

operating procedures, and to sociological studies of the internal authority structure of bureaucracies.

Something along these lines occurred in the study of legislatures. Initially, empirical scholars believed that the McKelvey and Cohen results (on the nonexistence of majority-rule winners) implied a simple unconditional claim that legislative choices are unstable. This was a misinterpretation. These results state that if a certain bare-bones majoritarian procedure is followed, any alternative can almost always be defeated. If A, then B. We do not observe such massive instability: not-B, therefore not-A. Hence these theorems, combined with the empirical observation that legislative choice is relatively stable, have triggered a search for procedures (such as rules about agenda formation) and institutional arrangements (such as committees) that create stability where instability would have otherwise reigned—in Shepsle's (1979) apt phrase, a structure-induced equilibrium.

Just as social-choice theory promoted the new institutionalism in the study of legislatures and emphasized the significance of institutional properties in determining policy choices, so it may for the study of bureaucracy. We may look forward to a rapprochement between formal modelers who understand the importance of fine-grained descriptions of bureaucratic procedures and empiricists who understand the theoretical significance of the procedures and structures they have described. For a stimulating example of this integration of the theoretical and the empirical, see Hammond (1986). This essay also provides a nontechnical introduction to social choice theories of bureaucracy.

MODELS OF BOUNDED RATIONALITY

The preceding models have differed on many counts, but one property they

share: Decision makers are assumed to be perfectly rational. Rational-choice models are spreading throughout political science generally, but there is a special irony associated with their diffusion into public administration; two of the giants of our field, Herbert Simon and James March, have been the main pioneers of models of bounded rationality.

There have been numerous attempts to reconcile the two families of theories, mostly along the line that taking costs of information gathering into account makes apparent differences vanish. Simon, however, would have none of this bland ecumenism, arguing that if a decision maker tries to incorporate costs of information gathering, he is merely adding one more layer of complexity to his decision-making task. Suppose, for example, that an administrator is searching for a choice alternative. Because he hears about alternatives sequentially, there may be a benefit to postponing his selection—something better may turn up. On the other hand, the program constituents are impatient, so, *ceteris paribus,* the administrator prefers to implement sooner rather than later. At this point a modeler can proceed in either of two directions. One could posit that the official satisfices; that is, he has an aspiration level that divides options into acceptable and unacceptable ones. Alternatively, one can assume that the administration uses an optimal acceptance rule. What are the differences? At first glance, there are none. Both decision rules partition the set of all feasible options into two subsets, at least in simple environments.* The rational-choice approach presumes

*If the alternatives are not independent, it may be suboptimal to use the simple rule of accepting alternatives above a certain quality and rejecting those below that level. For an example of less intuitive acceptance policy in a more complex environment, see Bendor, Taylor, and van Gaalen (1987a), property 2f.

that the decision maker behaves as if he knows the probability distribution of future alternatives, discounts them appropriately, and sets his acceptance level to equate the expected marginal benefits of receiving one more alternative with the expected marginal costs. (A Bayesian might posit that the official does not know the true distribution and has only a subjective distribution in his head. This assumption is more plausible, but it leaves unanswered the question of mental calculations and raises the new issue of belief revision.)

Simon was well aware of this interpretation of the search problem. In the appendix to "A Behavioral Model of Rational Choice" (1957), he formalized an optimal search model using as an example a person trying to decide when to accept an offer on his house. Noting the probabilistic information presumed by the rational-choice approach, he said,

> Now the seller who does not have this information, and who will be satisfied with a more bumbling kind of rationality, will make approximations to avoid using the information he doesn't have. First, he will probably limit the planning horizon by assuming a price at which he can certainly sell and will be willing to sell in the nth time period. Second, he will set his initial acceptance price quite high, watch the distribution of offers he receives, and gradually and approximately adjust his acceptance price downward or upward until he receives an offer he accepts—without ever making probability calculations. (Pp. 259–60)

The two approaches differ significantly. They use different assumptions about information available to decision makers, how this information is used, or both. I believe it would be a major methodological error—a self-inflicted wound—to rob ourselves of theoretical

pluralism by ignoring these differences. Indeed, at a time when cognitive psychology has experienced an intellectual renaissance, when experimentalists are examining ever more carefully whether human beings follow the axioms of rational choice, it would be ironic for political scientists to believe that theories of rational choice and theories of limited rationality are equivalent.

Probably more models of boundedly rational choice have been realized as computer programs than as purely mathematical theories whose solutions are worked out by hand. There are several reasons for this. First, there is a natural correspondence between substance and method; a wide variety of adaptive strategies can be easily represented by programming languages. Second, behavioral theorists tend to incorporate more organizational and political complexity in their theories, which renders mathematical models intractable. The following models are, therefore, a sample of the smaller wing of behavioral theory. The sample focuses on three areas that scholars in this tradition have worked on: the effects of experientially driven behavior, models of budgeting, and the role of cognitive heuristics.

Backward-Looking Behavior

Rational-choice models assume that decision makers are relentlessly forward looking.* In contrast, behavioral theo-

*This assumption produces the bizarre prediction that if it is common knowledge that both players are game theoretically rational, they will not cooperate in any round of a prisoner's dilemma that is repeated a known number of times—no matter how long. In general, this assumption makes game theorists agonize over what could happen at the very end of a game. As usual, there is a good idea here—things can fall apart when a relationship is ending—but to assume that people work out their entire strategies by first figuring out what they should do in the last period and then work backward to the pre-

rists emphasize that decision makers are often heavily influenced by experience, by what they have learned.† Does this assumption matter? Two examples show that it can.

First, suppose an administrator has two options, a and b. Neither one is sure to work or doomed to fail; this much he knows. Objectively, the probability that a succeeds is p, the chance that b works is q. We will suppose $p > q$. (They need not sum to one.) These probabilities are constant and independent over time. The decision maker starts off with an initial propensity to try a in the first period,

$$p_1(a),$$

and a similar propensity to try b,

$$p_1(b) = 1 - p_1(a).$$

Over time, he adapts via a simple learning rule: If in period i he tried a and it worked, then his propensity to try a again is strengthened:

$$p_{i+1}(a) = p_i(a) + \alpha(1 - p_i(a)).$$

The parameter α, which represents the rate of learning, is between zero and 1. If a failed, the administrator's propensity to try it is weakened:

$$p_{i+1}(a) = \beta p_i(a)$$

with β also between zero and 1. The equations for alternative b have the same form.

What will the administrator do over the long haul? This is a simple Bush-

Mosteller model of learning, and its properties are well known. A decision maker who learns in this manner will tend, in the long run, to use a over half the time

$$\frac{1 - q}{(1 - p) + (1 - q)}$$

and b the remainder. But this is suboptimal. An expected utility maximizer will, once she or he becomes subjectively certain that $p > q$, use a always. Perhaps surprisingly, even in this simple environment adaptive behavior need not converge to the optimal strategy.

One might object by pointing out that this is an artificial environment. Rarely do decision makers face a choice situation in which the probabilities of success are stationary. If they change, it will generally not be optimal to stick to one alternative because it may pay to experiment. The point is well taken. Specifying optimal behavior in a changing environment is much more difficult, however, and it is not at all clear that adaptive strategies converge to the optimal one in this context either.

For some enlightening extensions of simple learning theory, see Cross (1983). His examples are of economic behavior, but anyone interested in adaptive models will benefit from reading the book.

Second, interorganizational cooperation sometimes has the structure of a prisoner's dilemma: Two section chiefs may be better off helping each other than not, but each may prefer to receive aid and not to endure the cost of giving any. If the situation is repeated over time, Axelrod (1984) has shown that the simple and behaviorally plausible strategy of tit-for-tat (TFT)—cooperate in the first period and thereafter do what your partner did in the previous round—is very robust, doing well in a diverse set of strategic environments. If the players do not discount the future too much, TFT is in Nash equilibrium with itself:

---

sent seems a bit farfetched for long-term matches.

†Again, the differences are real, though incomplete. Dynamic models of rational choice do incorporate learning; the difference is that these models assume decision makers act as perfect Bayesian statisticians in updating their beliefs.

One cannot do better than to play TFT against someone else who is also playing TFT. Note that TFT, like the basic form of reciprocity, is a backward-looking strategy.

Suppose, however, that payoffs are a function of the player's moves plus an exogenous disturbance and that the players observe only their own payoffs, being unable to discriminate between the action of their partner and the disturbance. How does TFT perform in this environment? It can be shown (Bendor 1987) that simple backward-looking strategies do not do well in noisy environments; by failing to discriminate between intended and unintended effects, two players using TFT cannot sustain high levels of cooperation. Indeed, it can be shown that in a wide class of stochastic environments, TFT is no longer in Nash equilibrium with itself. A perfectly rational player, looking forward rather than backward, may try to test the hypothesis that his partner is playing TFT; if the hypothesis continued to be confirmed, and the rational player valued the future sufficiently, he would ignore idiosyncratic fluctuations, maintaining a steady level of cooperation.

Thus, in both a decision context (games against nature) and a strategic setting, experientially driven behavior can be observationally distinguished from future-oriented behavior.

Padgett's Model of Budgeting

The study of budgeting in public organizations has long been the province of behaviorally inclined researchers. Wildavsky's pioneering work in 1964 (3d ed. 1979) drew explicitly on the concept of bounded rationality; interestingly enough, Simon's own thoughts on cognitive limits were partly inspired by some practical problems of resource allocation in several municipal agencies that he encountered in his student days.

For the most sustained effort to construct a nonoptimizing model of budgetary behavior, however, we must turn to the work of John Padgett (1980, 1981).

Padgett's work is impressive. Unlike the foregoing simple adaptive models that depict only one organizational level, Padgett's model grapples with the hierarchical nature of budgeting (Crecine 1970). He demonstrates how fiscal and political constraints from the presidential level (ceilings on departmental totals) can be filtered through the standard operating procedures of the Office of Management and Budget (OMB)—cutting alternative amounts from different programs—and through the attention-focusing patterns of OMB and the departments. Before Padgett, scholars used simulations to analyze how environmental pressures were transmitted by organizational routines (Crecine 1969). To do this in a closed-form mathematical model, one yielding testable predictions about the predicted distribution of budget changes, was quite an achievement.

How executive branch officials search for and test alternatives is one key aspect of the model. This feature is the most purely bureaucratic component of the model and is central to most of the important results. To understand what Padgett has accomplished we must set his work in historical perspective. The standard search metaphor in budgeting had been incrementalism, which clearly derived its justification from bounded rationality: "Incrementalism and other such devices to simplify and speed decisions are inevitable responses to the extra-ordinary complexity of resource allocation in governments of any size" (Wildavsky 1979, 216). But searching in the neighborhood of last year's appropriation is only one way of cutting the decision tree down to size. As both Lindblom (1959) and Wildavsky recognized, there are other rules-of-thumb or heuristics for narrowing search. Clearly, if bounded rationality means anything, it must imply that search is limited; it does not, however, imply that search is always local (incremental).* Nevertheless, partly because dollars provide a natural metric for measuring the geometry of search and partly because political and fiscal constraints typically do mandate small changes, budgetary scholars have concentrated upon the specific heuristic of incrementalism. Accordingly, when Davis, Dempster, and Wildavsky (1974) developed their quantitative models, they represented the then Bureau of the Budget's spring ceiling for a program as a simple linear function of the previous year's obligational authority *(x)*, plus a normally distributed disturbance:

$$Y_{i+1} = \alpha \cdot \chi_i + \varepsilon_{i+1}$$

In this model, incrementalism means that α is close to 1 and that the variance of ε is not too big. This kind of equation is fine for regression analysis, but it is only a rough approximation of the verbal descriptions of Wildavsky and others. Indeed, this specification left the modelers open to the criticism that they viewed budgeting as a mechanical process; the OMB plugs in an α for each program, there is an idiosyncratic pulling and hauling summarized by ε, and that's that.

In this context—a widespread acceptance of verbal descriptions of budgeting informed by ideas of bounded rationality combined with dissatisfaction with their mathematical translation—Padgett's model (1981) is an attempt to close the gap between the verbal and mathematical representations.

In this model, the search of OMB examiners is guided by an overall departmental constraint, *B*, fixed by their superiors. Program submissions at this stage total *A*, so the examiners must find $\Gamma = A - B$ worth of cuts. In every round there is a fixed probability, θ_i, that an examiner's attention will focus on program *i*. This attention probability can vary across the *n* programs; of course

$$\Sigma_{i=1}^{n} \theta_i = 1.$$

Given that an examiner has focused on the ith program, he generates a limited number of salient cut alternatives, anchoring or starting his search at zero cut. (It is assumed that the magnitude of the cut alternatives is distributed exponentially; the parameters of the exponential vary across programs.) The examiner's task is completed when all the cuts he recommends sum to or exceed Γ. Because his attention across programs is governed by a probabilistic process and because he generates alternatives probabilistically, the number of cutting rounds needed to reach the target Γ is a random variable as well.

Note that though the behavior is goal directed, no optimization is posited. The examiner's conduct is well within the limits of rationality as we understand them. Two central premises of bounded rationality are explicitly represented by the mathematical model: Only a limited number of alternatives will be generated, and a simple test will be applied (have I reached Γ?) to end the search. These simple, plausible postulates suffice to yield testable predictions about resource allocation. My only serious reservation about the model pertains to the assumption that the cut alternatives are generated exponentially. As Padgett notes, this is equivalent to positing that the chance a decision maker will perceive a salient alternative

*For example, George Marshall's problem after Pearl Harbor was to decide which integer multiple of the War Department's 1941 appropriation he should request. He probably did not think of many alternatives; however, of those he considered, it is unlikely any were in the neighborhood of the status quo.

within a given dollar interval d is proportional to the size of that interval, or just λd with $\lambda >$ zero. The location of the interval is immaterial. To see concretely what this means, consider the problem of a department secretary trying to decide how much to add to a program. (Since budgets cannot be negative, it is harder to think through the implications of the exponential assumption for cuts.) The exponential hypothesis implies that if the secretary has not perceived a salient alternative in the [0–10 percent] range, then the distribution of salient alternatives in the [10–20 percent] range will be exactly the same, and similarly for [20–30 percent] and so on. (This is the memorylessness property of the exponential.) This seems implausible, for one would expect perceptions of budget increases to become coarser—bigger jumps between alternatives—the farther one moves from the status quo. (The exponential assumption did, however, receive some empirical support [Padgett 1980, 369].)

This is only one objection, and clearly Padgett's work goes a long way toward an adequate mathematical representation of microsearch processes in budgeting.

March and March's Model of Performance Sampling

In terms of the cognitive capabilities attributed to decision makers, the simple models of adaptation and reciprocity described earlier are almost at the opposite spectrum compared to rational-choice models. These simple behavioral models depict decision makers as adaptive machines responding to reinforcement; if something works, one is more inclined to try it again. Obviously this underestimates the cognitive complexity of human beings. As Michael Cohen once remarked to me, in order to construct tractable mathematical models, it seems that scholars postulate either that deci-

sion makers are virtually mindless or have perfect minds. And it is true that the hard middle ground where modelers assume that people are boundedly rational, yet can form complex beliefs and strategies, has been dominated by simulation studies (see especially Cohen 1981, 1984; Taylor 1986).

Empirically, this middle ground is home to cognitive psychologists who have uncovered an interesting variety of heuristics that can produce biased judgments and choices. A sensible strategy for organization theorists is to focus on heuristics that have strong experimental support and are substantively important in bureaucratic decision making. For an unusual effort to analyze the organizational effect of a particular bias—overdependence on small samples—let us consider March and March's (1978) model of performance sampling in educational institutions.

Their basic model is composed of several intuitively plausible components. The performance of school administrators is observed episodically by their superiors. Performance may be either a success or a failure.* After a small number of observations, the organization will make a personnel decision based on the observed proportion of successes. An administrator who has achieved above a cutoff of, for example, 0.80 will be promoted; one who falls below a lower cutoff will be fired. The remainder will be retained, their performance will continue to be sampled, and they may be promoted or fired later on in their careers. Thus the model joins the sampling of a stochastic performance

---

*March and March consider the cases of heterogeneous administrators whose abilities remain constant (some are more able than others, but everyone has a fixed probability of success), of homogeneous administrators who learn over time, and of homogeneous administrators whose probability of success is constant.

process to a pair of aspiration levels. Unlike Simon's (1957) original binary concept of satisficing, in this model the two cutoffs partition performance into three values—unsatisfactory, satisfactory, and superior.

The model has two kinds of implications. The macroimplication, primarily of interest to students of internal labor markets, is that this simple performance-sampling process generates a widely observed distribution of decision times; for a population of officials, the promotion and demotion rates rise at the beginning of appointments and then fall. The microimplication is that overconfidence in small samples "can yield subjectively compelling impressions of causal determinacy" (March and March 1978, 450). (Though March and March do not derive this result formally, it can be easily demonstrated.) Two examples are particularly worth noting:

Hero effect. Within a group of managers of varying abilities, the faster the rate of promotion, the less likely it is to be justified. Performance records are produced by a combination of underlying ability and sampling variation. Managers who have good records are more likely to have high ability than managers who have poor records, but the reliability of the differentiation is small when records are short.

Disappointment effect. On the average, new managers will be a disappointment. The performance records by which managers are evaluated are subject to sampling error. Since a manager is promoted to a new job on the basis of a good previous record, the proportion of promoted managers whose past records are better than their abilities will be greater than the proportion whose past records are poorer. As a result, on the average, managers will do less well in their new jobs than they did in their old

ones, and observers will come to believe that higher level jobs are more difficult than lower level ones, even if they are not. (P. 451)

These effects will appear even when, as in this model, the observations of performance are flawless.

One of the most robust findings of cognitive psychology is that most people are rather poor intuitive statisticians. We see patterns even when evidence is generated by a random process; we place excessive confidence in small samples, particularly when the evidence is concrete and vivid; perhaps most important, we underestimate the effects of sampling bias (Nisbett and Ross 1980, 260). The March and March model (1978) is an important first step in extending this psychological finding to an organizational setting. The decision makers in their world form more complex beliefs about their environments than do the rather primitive actors in the models of adaptation and reciprocity described in the first part of this section. They are not perfect, however. This seems to be a plausible middle range.

CONCLUDING REMARKS

Substance and method, assumptions and formalism, are intertwined in the study of bureaucracy. Take a random sample of political scientists and ask them what they think are the properties of formal models of bureaus. I wager that one would hear two answers: (1) mathematical models and (2) rational-choice assumptions. As we have seen, many prominent examples fit this description. Yet this is an overly narrow interpretation of the formal study of bureaucracy. The one key property, the only key property, is that an analysis be deductive, that one can show that certain conclusions must follow from specified assumptions. If the analysis in question has this property, it is a formal model of bureaucracy, even if the assumptions state that a decision maker acts suboptimally.

This point is elementary; it is also fundamental. I think that our imaginary sample of political scientists would reveal that a premature consensus is forming about the nature of formal models of bureaus. An indicator of this is that some scholars now ask, "What do bureaucrats maximize?" (budgets? utility?), without asking the logically prior question, "Do bureaucrats maximize anything in complex choice situations?" It is as if they think the latter question has already been raised and answered—and answered affirmatively.

This is ironic. It is ironic because Herbert Simon, who pioneered the idea of bounded rationality, has won a Nobel Prize in Economics, the home of deductive theorizing. Simon has shown that it is possible to construct formal models of organizations based on the assumption that individual decision makers have limited computational ability. This line of work has been carried on by James March, Michael Cohen, Roy Radner, John Padgett, Serge Taylor, Robert Axelrod, and Sidney Winter, among others. Individually and collectively, their work constitutes an existence proof that one can analyze deductively with nonmaximizing assumptions.

It is impossible here to examine thoroughly the relative merits of rational-choice theories and behavioral theories. Suffice it to say that I believe that neither approach dominates the other in the sense of being better across all the important criteria that social scientists use to evaluate theories. There are trade-offs. Consider just two criteria: the fruitfulness of the theory in helping us look at familiar phenomena in new ways, and the consistency of the theory with established knowledge in related fields.

Rational-actor models have been quite fruitful. For example, by connecting spatial theories of majority-rule voting

to the classical question of bureaucratic discretion, Hill (1985) has shown how crafty administrators can influence policy outcomes—not by defying the (one and only) legislative majority but by helping to form a new winning coalition. This is an important insight about the problem of the political control of bureaucracy in democracies.

On the second criterion, consistency with knowledge in the related field of cognitive psychology, behavioral theories score better than rational-actor models. There is little doubt that rational-actor theories, whether game theoretic or expected utility maximization, are less consistent with psychologists' understanding of how we think and choose than are behavioral theories. This relative ranking should matter to us. Presumably the reason for assuming perfect rationality is that it allows us to focus our attention on the strategic logic of relations among decision makers rather than focus on the internal intricacies of individual choice. Because this methodological choice reflects the bounded rationality of scientists, behavioral theorists should sympathize with the position. Nevertheless, the simplification is costly. Physicists use ideal gas laws, but they recognize the price they are paying. So should we.

Because no one approach dominates the formal study of bureaus, we should maintain a theoretical pluralism. I am concerned that this pluralism is threatened by a premature consensus on rational-choice assumptions, a consensus that is self-fulfilling. If most formal modelers use rational-choice models, when these models run into empirical difficulties, scholars will tend to patch up the models with ad hoc assumptions rather than move into the uncharted territory of adaptive models. Empirical difficulties will be swept aside as irritating anomalies. Familiar cries will go up: "Optimization models are the only game in town," "You can't beat something with nothing" (i.e., empirical criticism cannot dethrone a theory if no replacement is available); and most important, "We don't know how to construct nonoptimization models." Since the mathematics appropriate for adaptive models are not the same as the mathematics relevant for optimization models, if the field does not invest in behavioral theories now, the odds are good that we will suffer from collective amnesia, forgetting the relevant techniques. And having forgotten how to use screwdrivers, modelers will continue hammering.

This self-fulfilling prophecy will be reinforced by self-selection into the subfield of formal models of bureaus. If Ph.D. students perceive that doing this work requires using theories built on rational-choice foundations, those unwilling to make the necessary tradeoffs will not enter the subfield. Instead, they will do field research or quantitative empirical work that lacks an explicit theoretical base. The result of this self-selection could be two different communities of scholars, sealed off from one another by the reinforcing cleavages of different techniques of inquiry and different substantive assumptions.

To prevent this and to maintain the existing pluralism, we need to expand the mathematical tool kit of students who want to work on formal models of bureaus. This is where the interaction between substance and method is crucial. Requiring a background only of calculus will produce a pool of graduate students predisposed to rational-choice models. Although Newton did not invent the differential calculus to solve utility maximization problems, it is a natural method for that class of problems. Hence, the hammer syndrome would prevail. With only one tool in his kit, a student will be driven by what the formalism is preadapted for.

What, then, in addition to calculus? I would name two major techniques: (1)

probability theory and the allied study of stochastic processes, and (2) computer simulation. Students with a background in probability theory will see, for example, that one can represent the behavior of a bureau searching for a new policy by the sample path of a suitably defined stochastic process, and that the probability of coming up with a satisfactory alternative is the probability that the path enters a specified region of the search space. Similarly, a student with a background in simulation will see that a wide variety of adaptive decision-making strategies can be realized in computer programs. Indeed, as Simon, March, and Cohen have emphasized, computer programs are as natural a formalism for representing rule-governed strategies as calculus is for optimal ones. Students with a background in these techniques, as well as in calculus, will let the problem and their substantive theoretical hunches guide the choice of formalism, rather than let the formalism dictate the content of assumptions.

There would be a second benefit. There are significant complementarities among these techniques. For example, in initially representing the rich complexity of a decision process, a researcher may find simulation most useful. Once he understands the process's central features, he may wish to show that the results hold under more general assumptions than the simulation used. An excellent example of this complementarity is Axelrod's (1984) work on the prisoner's dilemma. Without his simulation tournament, discovering the power of the tit-for-tat strategy would have been much more difficult. But because simulations have to run with specified strategies, this method could not prove that TFT is collectively stable against the invasion of any arbitrary strategy. Therefore, to prove that TFT is collectively stable and under what conditions, Axelrod used purely deductive analysis.

A more general example of complementarity is to examine whether an adaptive process, represented by a simulation or a stochastic process, converges to the equilibrium result of an optimizing model. We would all feel more comfortable in using neoclassical models if we show that a realistic process of learning leads decision makers to optimal alternatives, and does so in real time. Whether or not we get this mental comfort, we will learn a good deal by understanding when convergence does occur and when it does not. I believe this kind of knowledge alone is important enough to warrant maintaining a pluralism of theory and technique in the formal study of bureaus. After all, what does not diverge cannot converge.

It is well to recognize, however, that important disagreements in the field crosscut the arguments over microassumptions. Most prominently, there is a running debate over the extent of bureaucratic influence in national politics. There are those who assert that agencies greatly influence policy outcomes (James Q. Wilson and William Niskanen form an otherwise odd pair), those who assert that Congress subtly controls the bureaucracy (Barry Weingast), and those who have a more pluralist view of institutional influence (Terry Moe). This argument correlates poorly with the rational-choice-behavioral debate: Niskanen, Weingast, and Moe have all constructed rational-choice models, but they have different views on bureaucratic power. This is fortunate because cross-cutting cleavages promote constructive dialogue; reinforcing cleavages foster dogmas. In any event, most students of public administration are probably more interested in macroquestions of influence and power than in the microfoundations of individual choice.

REFERENCES

ABERBACH, JOEL, ROBERT PUTNAM, AND BERT A. ROCKMAN. 1981. *Bureaucrats and Politicians in Western Democracies.* Cambridge, Mass.: Harvard University Press.

ABERBACH, JOEL, AND BERT A. ROCKMAN. 1976. "Clashing Beliefs within the Executive Branch: The Nixon Administration Bureaucracy." *American Political Science Review* 70: 456–68.

ALTFELD, MICHAEL, AND GARY MILLER. 1984. "Sources of Bureaucratic Influence: Expertise and Agenda Control." *Journal of Conflict Resolution* 28:701–30.

ARROW, KENNETH. 1985. "The Economics of Agency." In *Principals and Agents,* edited by John Pratt and Richard Zeckhauser. Boston: Harvard Business School Press.

AXELROD, ROBERT. 1984. *The Evolution of Cooperation.* New York: Basic Books.

BAIMAN, STANLEY. 1982. "Agency Research in Managerial Accounting." *Journal of Accounting Literature* 1:154–213.

BENDOR, JONATHAN. 1987. "In Good Times and Bad: Reciprocity in an Uncertain World." *American Journal of Political Science* 31:531–58.

BENDOR, JONATHAN, AND TERRY MOE. 1985. "An Adaptive Model of Bureaucratic Politics." *American Political Science Review* 79:755–74.

BENDOR, JONATHAN, AND TERRY MOE. 1986. "Agenda Control, Committee Capture, and the Dynamics of Institutional Politics." *American Political Science Review* 80:1187–1207.

BENDOR, JONATHAN, SERGE TAYLOR, AND ROLAND VAN GAALEN. 1985. "Bureaucratic Expertise versus Legislative Authority: A Model of Deception and Monitoring in Budgeting." *American Political Science Review* 79:1041–60.

BENDOR, JONATHAN, SERGE TAYLOR, AND ROLAND VAN GAALEN. 1987a. "Stacking the Deck: Bureaucratic Missions and the Search for Alternatives." *American Political Science Review* 81:873–96.

BENDOR, JONATHAN, SERGE TAYLOR, AND ROLAND VAN GAALEN. 1987b. "Politicians, Bureaucrats, and Asymmetric Information." *American Journal of Political Science* 31:796–828.

CALVERT, RANDALL. 1985. "The Value of Biased Information: A Rational Choice Model of Political Advice." *Journal of Politics* 47:530–55.

CALVERT, RANDALL, MATTHEW MCCUBBINS, AND BARRY WEINGAST. 1986. "Bureaucratic Discretion or Political Control: Process Versus Equilibrium Analysis." Presented at the annual meeting of the American Political Science Association, Washington, D.C.

COHEN, MICHAEL. 1981. "The Power of Parallel Thinking." *Journal of Economic Behavior and Organization* 2:285–306.

COHEN, MICHAEL. 1984. "Conflict and Complexity: Goal Diversity and Organizational Search Effectiveness." *American Political Science Review* 78:435–51.

COHEN, MICHAEL, JAMES MARCH, AND JOHAN P. OLSEN. 1972. "A Garbage Can Model of Organizational Choice." *Administrative Science Quarterly* 17:1–25.

CONYBEARE, JOHN. 1984. "Bureaucracy, Monopoly, and Competition: A Critical Analysis of the Budget-Maximizing Model of Bureaucracy." *American Journal of Political Science* 28:479–502.

CRECINE, JOHN. 1969. *Governmental Problem-Solving.* Chicago: Rand McNally.

CRECINE, JOHN. 1970. *Defense Budgeting: Organizational Adaptation to External Constraints.* Memorandum RM-6121-PR. Santa Monica: Rand.

CROSS, JOHN. 1983. *A Theory of Adaptive Economic Behavior.* New York: Cambridge University Press.

CYERT, RICHARD, AND JAMES MARCH. 1963. *A Behavioral Theory of the Firm.* Englewood Cliffs, N.J.: Prentice-Hall.

DAVIS, OTTO, M.A.H. DEMPSTER, AND AARON WILDAVSKY. 1974. "Toward a Predictive Theory of Government Expenditures: U.S. Domestic Appropriations." *British Journal of Political Science* 4:1–34.

DENZAU, ARTHUR, AND ROBERT MACKAY. 1983. "Gatekeeping and Monopoly Power of Committees: An Analysis of Sincere and Sophisticated Behavior." *American Journal of Political Science* 27:740–61.

DESTLER, I. M. 1974. *Presidents, Bureaucrats, and Foreign Policy.* Princeton, N.J.: Princeton University Press.

FEREJOHN, JOHN. Forthcoming. "Introduction." In *Information and Democracy,* edited by John Ferejohn and James Kuklinski. Champaign: University of Illinois Press.

FIORINA, MORRIS. 1982. "Legislative Choice of Regulatory Forms: Legal Process or Administrative Process?" *Public Choice* 39:33–66.

FIORINA, MORRIS. 1986. "Legislative Uncertainty, Legislative Control, and the Delegation of Legislative Power." *Journal of Law, Economics, and Organization* 2:33–50.

HALPERIN, MORTON. 1974. *Bureaucratic Politics and Foreign Policy.* Washington, D.C.: Brookings Institution.

HAMMOND, THOMAS. 1984. "The Probability of an Organizational Preference Cycle." Presented at the annual meeting of the American Political Science Association, Washington, D.C.

HAMMOND, THOMAS. 1985. "Instability in Hierarchical Decision Making: A Probabilistic Analysis." Presented at the annual meeting of the American Political Science Association, New Orleans, La.

HAMMOND, THOMAS. 1986. "Agenda Control, Organizational Structure, and Bureaucratic Politics." *American Journal of Political Science* 30:379–420.

HAMMOND, THOMAS, JEFFREY HILL, AND GARY MILLER. 1986. "Presidential Appointment of Bureau Chiefs and the 'Congressional Control of Administration' Hypothesis." Presented at the annual meeting of the American Political Science Association, Washington, D.C.

HAMMOND, THOMAS, AND GARY MILLER. 1985. "A Social Choice Perspective on Authority and Expertise in Bureaucracy." *American Journal of Political Science* 29:1–28.

HAMMOND, THOMAS, AND GARY MILLER. 1987. "The Core of the Constitution." *American Political Science Review* 81:1155–74.

HILL, JEFFREY. 1985. "Why So Much Stability? The Role of Agency Determined Stability." *Public Choice* 46:275–87.

HOLMSTROM, BENGT. 1986. "Economic Theories of Organization." Lecture given at the Graduate School of Business, Stanford University.

HUNTINGTON, SAMUEL. 1961. *The Common Defense.* New York: Columbia University Press.

KAUFMAN, HERBERT. 1956. "Emerging Conflicts in the Doctrines of Public Administration." *American Political Science Review* 50:1057–73.

LEVINTHAL, DANIEL. 1988. "A Survey of Agency Models of Organizations." *Journal of Economic Behavior and Organization* 9:153–85.

LEVINTHAL, DANIEL, AND JAMES G. MARCH. 1981. "A Model of Adaptive Organizational Search." *Journal of Economic Behavior and Organization* 2:307–33.

Lindblom, Charles. 1959. "The Science of 'Muddling Through.'" *Public Administration Review* 19:79–88.

McCUBBINS, MATTHEW, AND THOMAS SCHWARTZ. 1984. "Congressional Oversight Overlooked: Police Patrols versus Fire Alarms." *American Journal of Political Science* 28:165–79.

MACKAY, ROBERT, AND CAROLYN WEAVER. 1979. "On the Mutuality of Interests between Bureaus and High Demand Committees: A Perverse Result." *Public Choice* 34: 481–91.

McKELVEY, RICHARD. 1976. "Intransitivities in Multidimensional Voting Models and Some Implications for Agenda Control." *Journal of Economic Theory* 12:472–82.

MARCH, JAMES C., AND JAMES G. MARCH. 1978. "Performance Sampling in Social Matches." *Administrative Science Quarterly* 23:434–53.

MARCH, JAMES G., AND HERBERT A. SIMON. 1958. *Organizations.* New York: Wiley.

MELUMAD, NAHUM, AND DILIP MOOKHERJEE. 1989. "Delegation as Commitment: The Case of Income Tax Audits." *Rand Journal of Economics* 20: 139–63.

MILLER, GARY, AND TERRY MOE. 1983. "Bureaucrats, Legislators, and the Size of Government." *American Political Science Review* 77:297–322.

MOE, TERRY. 1984. "The New Economics of Organization." *American Journal of Political Science* 28:739–77.

MOE, TERRY. 1987. "An Assessment of the Positive Theory of 'Congressional Dominance.'" *Legislative Studies Quarterly* 12:475–520.

MUNGER, MICHAEL. 1984. "On the Mutuality of Interests Between Bureaus and High Demand Review Committees." *Public Choice* 43:211–15.

NELSON, RICHARD, AND SIDNEY WINTER. 1981. *An Evolutionary Theory of Economic Change.* Cambridge, Mass.: Harvard University Press.

NISBETT, RICHARD, AND LEE ROSS. 1980. *Human Inference: Strategies and Shortcomings of Social Judgment.* Englewood Cliffs, N.J.: Prentice-Hall.

NISKANEN, WILLIAM A., JR. 1971. *Bureaucracy and Representative Gov-*

ernment. New York: Aldine-Atherton.

NISKANEN, WILLIAM A., JR. 1975. "Bureaucrats and Politicians." *Journal of Law and Economics* 18:617–44.

OGUL, MORRIS. 1976. *Congress Oversees the Bureaucracy.* Pittsburgh: University of Pittsburgh Press.

PADGETT, JOHN. 1980. "Bounded Rationality in Budgetary Research." *American Political Science Review* 74:354–72.

PADGETT, JOHN. 1981. "Hierarchy and Ecological Control in Federal Budgetary Decision Making." *American Journal of Sociology* 87:75–129.

RADNER, ROY. 1985. "Repeated Principal-Agent Games with Discounting." *Econometrica* 53:1173–98.

ROMER, THOMAS, AND HOWARD ROSENTHAL. 1978. "Political Resource Allocation, Controlled Agendas, and the Status Quo." *Public Choice* 33:27–43.

ROSS, STEPHEN. 1973. "The Economic Theory of Agency: The Principal's Problem." *American Economic Review* 63:134–39.

SEN, AMARTYA. 1977. "Social Choice Theory: A Re-examination." *Econometrica* 45:53–89.

SHEPSLE, KENNETH. 1979. "Institutional Arrangements and Equilibrium in Multidimensional Voting Models." *American Journal of Political Science* 23:27–59.

SHEPSLE, KENNETH, AND BARRY WEINGAST. 1984. "Uncovered Sets and Sophisticated Voting Outcomes with Implications for Agenda Institutions." *American Journal of Political Science* 28:49–74.

SIMON, HERBERT A. 1946. "The Proverbs of Administration." *Public Administration Review* 6:53–67.

SIMON, HERBERT A. 1957. *Models of Man: Social and Rational.* New York: Wiley.

TAYLOR, SERGE. 1986. "Organizational Learning." Manuscript, Graduate School of Business, Stanford University.

THOMAS, PAUL, AND THOMAS HAMMOND. 1989. "The Impossibility of a Neutral Hierarchy." *Journal of Law, Economics, and Organizations* 5:155–84.

WEINGAST, BARRY. 1984. "The Congressional-Bureaucratic System: A Principal-Agent Perspective (with Applications to the SEC)." *Public Choice* 44:147–91.

WILDAVSKY, AARON. 1979. *The Politics of the Budgetary Process.* 3d ed. Boston: Little, Brown.

WILSON, JAMES Q. 1980. "The Politics of Regulation." In *The Politics of Regulation,* edited by James Q. Wilson. New York: Basic Books.

15.   The Critical Role of Street-Level Bureaucrats

Michael Lipsky

Public service workers currently occupy a critical position in American society.

SOURCE: "Toward a Theory of Street-Level Bureaucracy" by Michael Lipsky, *Street-Level Bureaucracy* (New York: Russell Sage Foundation, 1980). Reprinted by permission.

Although they are normally regarded as low-level employees, the actions of most public service workers actually constitute the services "delivered" by government. Moreover, when taken together the individual decisions of these workers become, or add up to, agency policy.

Whether government policy is to deliver "goods"—such as welfare or public housing—or to confer status—such as "criminal" or "mentally ill"—the discretionary actions of public employees are the benefits and sanctions of government programs or determine access to government rights and benefits.

Most citizens encounter government (if they encounter it at all) not through letters to congressmen or by attendance at school board meetings but through their teachers and their children's teachers and through the policeman on the corner or in the patrol car. Each encounter of this kind represents an instance of policy delivery.

Public service workers who interact directly with citizens in the course of their jobs, and who have substantial discretion in the execution of their work are called *street-level bureaucrats* in this study. Public service agencies that employ a significant number of street-level bureaucrats in proportion to their work force are called *street-level bureaucracies.* Typical street-level bureaucrats are teachers, police officers and other law enforcement personnel, social workers, judges, public lawyers and other court officers, health workers, and many other public employees who grant access to government programs and provide services with them. People who work in these jobs tend to have much in common because they experience analytically similar work conditions.[1]

The ways in which street-level bureaucrats deliver benefits and sanctions structure and delimit people's lives and opportunities. These ways orient and provide the social (and political) contexts in which people act. Thus every extension of service benefits is accompanied by an extension of state influence and control. As providers of public benefits and keepers of public order, street-level bureaucrats are the focus of political controversy. They are constantly torn by the demands of service recipi-

ents to improve effectiveness and responsiveness and by the demands of citizen groups to improve the efficacy and efficiency of government services. Since the salaries of street-level bureaucrats comprise a significant proportion of nondefense governmental expenditures, any doubts about the size of government budgets quickly translate into concerns for the scope and content of these public services. Moreover, public service workers have expanded and increasingly consolidated their collective strength so that in disputes over the scope of public services they have become a substantial independent force in the resolution of controversy affecting their status and position.

Street-level bureaucrats dominate political controversies over public services for two general reasons. First, debates about the proper scope and focus of governmental services are essentially debates over the scope and function of these public employees. Second, street-level bureaucrats have considerable impact on people's lives. This impact may be of several kinds. They socialize citizens to expectations of government services and a place in the political community. They determine the eligibility of citizens for government benefits and sanctions. They oversee the treatment (the service) citizens recieve in those programs. Thus, in a sense street-level bureaucrats implicitly mediate aspects of the constitutional relationship of citizens to the state. In short, they hold the keys to a dimension of citizenship.

CONFLICT OVER THE SCOPE AND SUBSTANCE OF PUBLIC SERVICES

In the world of experience we perceive teachers, welfare workers, and police officers as members of separately organized and motivated public agencies. And so they are from many points of view. But if we divide public employees according to whether they interact with citizens directly and have discretion over significant aspects of citizens' lives, we see that a high proportion and enormous number of public workers share these job characteristics. They comprise a great portion of all public employees working in domestic affairs. State and local governments employ approximately 3.7 million in local schools, more than 500,000 people in police operations, and over 300,000 people in public welfare. Public school employees represent more than half of all workers employed in local governments. Instructional jobs represent about two-thirds of the educational personnel, and many of the rest are former teachers engaged in administration, or social workers, psychologists, and librarians who provide direct services in the schools. Of the 3.2 million local government public employees not engaged in education, approximately 14 percent work as police officers. One of every sixteen jobs in state and local government outside of education is held by a public welfare worker.[2] In this and other areas the majority of jobs are held by people with responsibility for involvement with citizens.

Other street-level bureaucrats comprise an important part of the remainder of local government personnel rolls. Although the U.S. Census Bureau does not provide breakdowns of other job classifications suitable for our purposes, we can assume that many of the 1.1 million health workers,[3] most of the 5,000 public service lawyers,[4] many of the employees of the various court systems, and other public employees also perform as street-level bureaucrats. Some of the nation's larger cities employ a staggering number of street-level bureaucrats. For example, the 26,680 school teachers in Chicago are more numerous than the populations of many of the Chicago suburbs.[5]

Another measure of the significance of street-level bureaucrats in public sector employment is the amount of public funds allocated to pay them. Of all local government salaries, more than half went to public education in 1973. Almost 80 percent of these monies was used to pay instructional personnel. Police salaries comprised approximately one-sixth of local public salaries not assigned to education.[6]

Much of the growth in public employment in the past 25 years has occurred in the ranks of street-level bureaucrats. From 1955 to 1975 government employment more than doubled, largely because the baby boom of the postwar years and the growing number of elderly, dependent citizens increased state and local activity in education, health, and public welfare.[7]

Street-level bureaucracies are labor-intensive in the extreme. Their business is providing service through people, and the operating costs of such agencies reflect their dependence upon salaried workers. Thus most of whatever is spent by government on education, police, or other social services (aside, of course, from income maintenance, or in the case of jails and prisons, inmate upkeep) goes directly to pay street-level bureaucrats. For example, in large cities over 90 percent of police expenditures is used to pay for salaries.[8]

Not only do the salaries of street-level bureaucrats constitute a major portion of the cost of public services, but also the scope of public services employing street-level bureaucrats has increased over time. Charity was once the responsibility of private agencies. The federal government now provides for the income needs of the poor. The public sector has absorbed responsibilities previously discharged by private organizations in such diverse and critical areas as policing, education, and health. Moreover, in all these fields government not only has supplanted private organizations but also has expanded the scope of responsibility of public ones. This is evident in increased public expectations for security and public safety, the extension of responsibilities in the schools to concerns with infant as well as postadolescent development, and public demands for affordable health care services.[9]

Public safety, public health, and public education *may* still be elusive social objectives, but in the past century they have been transformed into areas for which there is active governmental responsibility. The transformation of public responsibility in the area of social welfare has led some to recognize that what people "have" in modern American society often may consist primarily of their claims on government "largesse," and that claims to this "new property" should be protected as a right of citizens.[10] Street-level bureaucrats play a critical role in these citizen entitlements. Either they directly provide public benefits through services, or they mediate between citizens and their new but by no means secure estates.

The poorer people are, the greater the influence street-level bureaucrats tend to have over them. Indeed, these public workers are so situated that they may well be taken to be part of the problem of being poor. Consider the welfare recipient who lives in public housing and seeks the assistance of a legal services lawyer in order to reinstate her son in school. He has been suspended because of frequent encounters with the police. She is caught in a net of street-level bureaucrats with conflicting orientations toward her, all acting in what they call her "interest" and "the public interest."[11]

People who are not able to purchase services in the private sector must seek them from government if they are to receive them at all. Indeed, it is taken as a sign of social progress that poor people are granted access to services if they are too poor to pay for them.

Thus, when social reformers seek to ameliorate the problems of the poor, they often end up discussing the status of street-level bureaucrats. Welfare reformers move to separate service provision from decisions about support payments, or they design a negative income tax system that would eliminate social workers in allocating welfare. Problems of backlog in the courts are met with proposals to increase the number of judges. Recognition that early-childhood development largely established the potential for later achievement results in the development of new programs (such as Head Start) in and out of established institutions, to provide enriched early-childhood experiences.

In the 1960s and early 1970s the modal governmental response to social problems was to commission a corps of street-level bureaucrats to attend to them. Are poor people deprived of equal access to the courts? Provide them with lawyers. Equal access to health care? Establish neighborhood clinics. Educational opportunity? Develop preschool enrichment programs. It is far easier and less disruptive to develop employment for street-level bureaucrats than to reduce income inequalities.

In recent years public employees have benefitted considerably from the growth of public spending on street-level bureaucracies.[12] Salaries have increased from inadequate to respectable and even desirable. Meanwhile, public employees, with street-level bureaucrats in the lead, have secured unprecedented control over their work environments through the development of unions and union-like associations.[13] For example, teachers and other instructional personnel have often been able to maintain their positions and even increase in number, although schools are more frequently under attack for their cost to taxpayers. The ratio of instructional personnel in schools has continued to rise despite the decline in the number of school-age children.[14] This development supplements general public support for the view that some street-level bureaucrats, such as teachers and police officers, are necessary for a healthy society.[15]

The fiscal crisis that has affected many cities, notably New York and more recently Cleveland and Newark, has provided an opportunity to assess the capacity of public service workers to hold onto their jobs in the face of enormous pressures. Since so much of municipal budgets consists of inflexible, mandated costs—for debt service, pension plans and other personnel benefits, contractually obligated salary increases, capital expenditure commitments, energy purchases, and so on—the place to find "fat" to eliminate from municipal budgets is in the service sector, where most expenditures tend to be for salaries. While many public employees have been fired during this crisis period, it is significant that public service workers often have been able to lobby, bargain, and cajole to minimize this attrition.[16] They are supported in their claims by a public fearful of a reduced police force on the street and resentful of dirtier streets resulting from fewer garbage pickups. They are supported by families whose children will receive less instruction from fewer specialists than in the past if teachers are fired. And it does not hurt their arguments that many public employees and their relatives vote in the city considering force reductions.[17]

The growth of the service sector represents the furthest reaches of the welfare state. The service sector penetrates every area of human needs as they are recognized and defined, and it grows within each recognized area. This is not to say that the need is met, but only that the service state breaches the barriers between public responsibility and private affairs.

The fiscal crisis of the cities focuses on the service sector, fundamentally challenging the priorities of the service state under current perceptions of scarcity. Liberals have now joined fiscal conservatives in challenging service provision. They do not do so directly, by questioning whether public services and responsibilities developed in this century are appropriate. Instead, they do it backhandedly, arguing that the accretion of public employees and their apparently irreversible demands upon revenues threaten the autonomy, flexibility, and prosperity of the political order. Debates over the proper scope of services face the threat of being overwhelmed by challenges to the entire social service structure as seen from the perspective of unbalanced public budgets.

CONFLICT OVER INTERACTIONS WITH CITIZENS

I have argued that street-level bureaucrats engender controversy because they must be dealt with if policy is to change. A second reason street-level bureaucrats tend to be the focus of public controversy is the immediacy of their interactions with citizens and their impact on people's lives. The policy delivered by street-level bureaucrats is most often immediate and personal. They usually make decisions on the spot (although sometimes they try not to) and their determinations are focused entirely on the individual. In contrast, an urban renewal program might destroy a neighborhood and replace and substitute new housing and different people, but the policy was prolonged, had many different stages, and was usually played out in arenas far removed from the daily life of neighborhood residents.

The decisions of street-level bureaucrats tend to be redistributive as well as allocative. By determining eligibility for benefits they enhance the claims of some citizens to governmental goods and services at the expense of general taxpayers and those whose claims are denied. By increasing or decreasing benefits availability to low-income recipient populations they implicitly regulate the degree of redistribution that will be paid for by more affluent sectors.

In another sense, in delivering policy street-level bureaucrats make decisions about people that affect their life chances. To designate or treat someone as a welfare recipient, a juvenile delinquent, or a high achiever affects the relationships of others to that person and also affects the person's self-evaluation. Thus begins (or continues) the social process that we infer accounts for so many self-fulfilling prophecies. The child judged to be a juvenile delinquent develops such a self-image and is grouped with other "delinquents," increasing the chances that he or she will adopt the behavior thought to have been incipient in the first place. Children thought by their teacher to be richly endowed in learning ability learn more than peers of equal intelligence who were not thought to be superior.[18] Welfare recipients find or accept housing inferior to those with equal disposable incomes who are not recipients.[19]

A defining facet of the working environment of street-level bureaucrats is that they must deal with clients' personal reactions to their decisions, however they cope with their implications. To say that people's self-evaluation is affected by the actions of street-level bureaucrats is to say that people are reactive to the policy. This is not exclusively confined to subconscious processes. Clients of street-level bureaucracies respond angrily to real or perceived injustices, develop strategies to ingratiate themselves with workers, act grateful and elated or sullen and passive in reaction to street-level bureaucrats' decisions. It is one thing to be treated neglectfully and routinely by the telephone company, the motor vehicle bureau, or other government agencies whose agents know nothing of the personal circumstances surrounding a claim or request. It is quite another thing to be shuffled, categorized, and treated "bureaucratically" (in the pejorative sense), by someone to whom one is directly talking and from whom one expects at least an open and sympathetic hearing. In short, the reality of the work of street-level bureaucrats could hardly be farther from the bureaucratic ideal of impersonal detachment in decision making.[20] On the contrary, in street-level bureaucracies the objects of critical decisions—*people*—actually change as a result of the decisions.

Street-level bureaucrats are also the focus of citizen reactions because their discretion opens up the possibility that they will respond favorably on behalf of people. Their general and diffuse obligation to the "public interest" permits hope to flourish that the individual worker will adopt a benign or favorable orientation toward the client. Thus, in a world of large and impersonal agencies that apparently hold the keys to important benefits, sanctions, and opportunities, the ambiguity of work definitions sustains hope for a friend in court.

This discussion helps explain continued controversy over street-level bureaucracies at the level of individual service provision. At the same time, the peculiar nature of government service delivery through street-level bureaucrats helps explain why street-level bureaucracies are apparently the primary focus of community conflict in the current period, and why they are likely to remain the focus of such conflict in the foreseeable future. It is no accident that the most heated community conflicts since 1964 have focused on schools and police departments, and on the responsiveness of health and welfare agencies and institutions.[21] These are the sites of the provision of public benefits and sanctions. They are the locus of individual decisions about and treatment of citizens, and thus are primary targets of protest. As Frances Fox Piven and Richard Cloward explain:

> . . . people experience deprivation and oppression within a concrete setting, not as the end product of large and abstract processes, and it is the concrete experience that molds their discontent into specific grievances against specific targets. . . . People on relief [for example] experience the shabby waiting rooms, the overseer or caseworker, and the dole. They do not experience American social welfare policy. . . . In other words, it is the daily experience of people that shapes their grievances, establishes the measure of their demands, and points out the targets of their anger.[22]

While people may experience these bureaucracies as individuals, schools, precinct houses, or neighborhood clinics are places where policy about individuals is organized collectively. These administrative arrangements suggest to citizens the possibility that controlling, or at least affecting, their structures will influence the quality of individual treatment. Thus we have two preconditions for successful community organization efforts: the hope and plausibility that individual benefits may accrue to those taking part in group action and a visible, accessible, and blamable collective target.[23]

Community action focused on street-level bureaucracies is also apparently motivated by concerns for community character. The dominant institutions in communities help shape community identity. They may be responsive to the dominant community group (this has been the traditional role of high schools in Boston) or they may be unresponsive and opposed to conceptions of community and identity favored by residents, as in the case of schools that neglect the Spanish heritage of a significant minority. Whether people are motivated by specific grievances or more diffuse concerns that become directed at community institutions, their focus in protesting the actions of street-level bureaucracies may be attributed to the familiarity of the agency, its critical role in community welfare, and a perception at some level that these institutions are not sufficiently accountable to the people they serve.

Finally, street-level bureaucrats play a critical role in regulating the degree of contemporary conflict by virtue of their role as agents of social control. Citizens who receive public benefits interact with public agents who require certain behaviors of them. They must anticipate the requirements of these public agents and claimants must tailor their actions and develop "suitable" attitudes both toward the services they receive and toward the street-level bureaucrats themselves. Teachers convey and enforce expectations of proper attitudes toward schooling, self, and efficacy in other interactions. Policemen convey expectations about public behavior and authority. Social workers convey expectations about public benefits and the status of recipients.

The social control function of street-level bureaucrats requires comment in a discussion of the place of public service workers in the larger society. The public service sector plays a critical part in softening the impact of the economic system on those who are not its primary beneficiaries and inducing people to accept the neglect or inadequacy of primary economic and social institutions. Police, courts, and prisons obviously play such a role in processing the junkies, petty thieves, muggers, and others whose behavior toward society is associated with their economic position. It is a role equally played by schools in socializing the population to the economic order and the likely opportunities for different strata of the population. Public support and employment programs expand to ameliorate the impact of unemployment or reduce the incidence of discontent; they contract when employment opportunities improve. Moreover, they are designed and implemented to convey the message that welfare status is to be avoided and that work, however poorly rewarded, is preferable to public assistance. One can also see the two edges of public policy in the "war on poverty" where the public benefits of social service and community action invested neighborhood institutions with benefits for which potential dissidents could compete and ordinary citizens could develop dependency.[24]

What to some are the highest reaches of the welfare state are to others the furthest extension of social control. Street-level bureaucrats are partly the focus of controversy because they play this dual role. Welfare reform founders on disagreements over whether to eliminate close scrutiny of welfare applications in order to reduce administrative costs and harassment of recipients, or to increase the scrutiny in the name of controlling abuses and preventing welfare recipients from taking advantage. Juvenile corrections and mental health policy founder on disputes over the desirability of dismantling large institutions in the name of cost effectiveness and rehabilitation, or retaining close supervision in an effort to avoid the costs of letting unreconstructed "deviants" loose. In short, street-level bureaucrats are also at the center of controversy because a divided public perceives that social control in the name of public order and acceptance of the status quo are social objectives with which proposals to reduce the role of street-level bureaucrats (eliminating welfare checkups, reducing parole personnel, decriminalizing marijuana) would interfere.

Public controversy also focuses on the proper kind of social control. Current debates in corrections policy, concerning automatic sentencing and a "hard-nosed" view of punishment or more rehabilitative orientations, reflect conflict over the degree of harshness in managing prison populations. In educational practice the public is also divided as to the advisability of liberal disciplinary policies and more flexible instruction or punitive discipline and more rigid, traditional approaches. The "medicalization" of deviance, in which disruptive behavior is presumed cause for intervention by a doctor rather than a disciplinarian, is another area in which there is controversy over the appropriate kind of social control.

From the citizen's viewpoint, the roles of street-level bureaucrats are as extensive as the functions of government and intensively experienced as daily routines require them to interact with the street ministers of education, dispute settlement, and health services. Collectively, street-level bureaucrats absorb a high share of public resources and become the focus of society's hopes for a healthy balance between provision of public services and a reasonable burden of public expenditures. As individuals, street-level bureaucrats represent the hopes of citizens for fair and effective treatment by government even as they are positioned to see clearly the limitations on effective intervention and the constraints on responsiveness engendered by mass processing.

NOTES

1. These definitions are analytical. They focus not on nominal occupational roles but on the characteristics of the particular work situations. Thus not every street-level bureaucrat works for a street-level bureaucracy [for example, a relocation specialist (a type of street-level

bureaucrat) may work for an urban renewal agency whose employees are mostly planners, builders, and other technicians]. Conversely, not all employees of street-level bureaucracies are street-level bureaucrats (for example, file clerks in a welfare department or police officers on routine clerical assignments).

The conception of street-level bureaucracy was originally proposed in a paper prepared for the Annual Meeting of the American Political Science Association in 1969. "Toward a Theory of Street-Level Bureaucracy." It was later revised and published in Willis Hawley and Michael Lipsky, eds., *Theoretical Perspectives on Urban Politics* (Englewood Cliffs, N.J.: Prentice-Hall, 1977), pp. 196–213.

2. U.S. Bureau of the Census, Public Employment in 1973, Series GE 73 No. 1 (Washington, D.C.: Government Printing Office, 1974), p. 9. Presented in Alan Baker and Barbara Grouby, "Employment and Payrolls of State and Local Governments, by Function: October 1973," *Municipal Year Book, 1975* (Washington, D.C.: International City Managers Association, 1975), pp. 109–112, table 4/3. Also, Marianne Stein Kah, "City Employment and Payrolls: 1975," *Municipal Year Book, 1977* (Washington, D.C.: International City Managers Association, 1977), pp. 173–179. These figures have been adjusted to represent full-time equivalents. For purposes of assessing public commitments to providing services, full-time equivalents are more appropriate statistics than total employment figures, which count many part-time employees.

3. Jeffry H. Galper, *The Politics of Social Services* (Englewood Cliffs, N.J.: Prentice-Hall, 1975), p. 56.

4. Lois Forer, *Death of the Law* (New York: McKay, 1975), p. 191.

5. *New York Times,* April 4, 1976, p. 22.

6. Baker and Grouby, "Employment and Payrolls of State and Local Governments."

7. *New York Times,* July 10, 1977, p. F13.

8. Of four cities with populations over one million responding to a *Municipal Year Book* survey, the proportion of personnel expenditures to total expenditures in police departments averaged 94 percent and did not go beyond 86 percent. Cities with smaller populations showed similar tendencies. These observations are derived from David Lewin, "Expenditure, Compensation, and Employment Data in Police, Fire and Refuse Collection and Disposal Departments," *Municipal Year Book, 1975,* pp. 39–98, table 1/21. However, the variation was much greater in the less populous cities because of smaller base figures and the fact that when cities with smaller bases make capital investments, the ratio of personnel to total expenditures changes more precipitously.

That public expenditures for street-level bureaucracies go to individuals primarily as salaries may also be demonstrated in the case of education. For example, more than 73 percent of all noncapital education expenditures inside Standard Metropolitan Statistical Areas goes toward personal services (i.e., salaries). See Government Finances, Number 1, Finances of School Districts, 1972 U.S. Census of Government (Bureau of the Census, Social and Economic Statistics Administration, U.S. Department of Commerce), table 4.

9. Many analysts have discussed the increasing role of services in the economy. See Daniel Bell, *The Coming of the Post-Industrial Society: A Venture in Social Forecasting* (New York: Basic Books, 1973); Alan Gart-

ner and Frank Reissman, *The Service Society and the Consumer Vanguard* (New York: Harper & Row, 1974); Victor Fuchs, *The Service Economy* (New York: Columbia University Press, 1968). On transformations in public welfare, see Gilbert Steiner, *Social Insecurity* (Chicago: Rand McNally, 1966), chap. 1; on public safety, see Allan Silver, "The Demand for Order in Civil Society," in David Bordua, ed., *The Police: Six Sociological Essays* (New York: John Wiley, 1967), pp. 1–24.

10. Charles Reich, "The New Property," *Yale Law Journal,* vol. 73 (April, 1964): 733–787.

11. Carl Hosticka, "Legal Services Lawyers Encounter Clients: A Study in Street-Level Bureaucracy" (Ph.D. diss., Massachusetts Institute of Technology, 1976), pp. 11–13.

12. See Frances Piven's convincing essay in which she argues that social service workers were the major beneficiaries of federal programs concerned with cities and poor people in the 1960s. Piven, "The Urban Crisis: Who Got What and Why," in Richard Cloward and Frances Piven, *The Politics of Turmoil* (New York: Vintage Books, 1972), pp. 314–351.

13. J. Joseph Loewenberg and Michael H. Moskow, eds., *Collective Bargaining in Government* (Englewood Cliffs, N.J.: Prentice-Hall, 1972). A. Laurence Chickering, ed., *Public Employee Unions* (Lexington, Mass.: Lexington Books, 1976); and Margaret Levi, *Bureaucratic Insurgency* (Lexington, Mass.: Lexington Books, 1977).

14. The decline is a function of the lower birthrate and periodicity in the size of the school-age population originally resulting from the birth explosion following World War II. See Baker and Grouby, *Municipal Year Book, 1975,* pp. 109ff., on serviceability ratios.

15. This perspective remains applicable in the current period. However, in reaction to this tendency, programs that would eliminate service mediators and service providers, such as negative income taxation and housing allowances, have gained support. Fiscal scarcity has brought to public attention questions concerning the marginal utility of some of these service areas.

16. Consider the New York City policemen who, in October 1976, agreed to work overtime without pay so that a crop of rookie patrolmen would not be eliminated. *New York Times,* October 24, 1976, p. 24.

17. There can be no better illustration of the strength of the organized service workers and their support by relevant interests than the New York State Assembly's overriding of Gov. Hugh Carey's veto of the so-called Stavisky bill. This legislation, written in a period of massive concern for cutting the New York City budget, required the city to spend no less on education in the three years following the fiscal collapse than in the three years before the crisis, thus tying the hands of the city's financial managers even more. *New York Times,* April 4, 1976, p. E6; April 18, 1976, p. E6.

18. The seminal work here is Robert Rosenthal and Lenore Jacobson, *Pygmalion in the Classroom* (New York: Holt, Rinehart and Winston, 1968).

19. Martin Rein, "Welfare and Housing," Joint Center Working Paper Series, no. 4 (Cambridge, Mass.: Joint Center for Urban Studies, Spring, 1971, rev. Feb. 1972).

20. On the alleged importance of bureaucratic detachment in processing clients see Peter Blau, *Exchange and Power in Social Life* (New York: John Wiley, 1964), p. 66.

21. See National Advisory Commission on Civil Disorders, *Report* (New

York: Bantam, 1968); Peter Rossi et al., *Roots of Urban Discontent* (New York: John Wiley, 1974).

22. Frances Fox Piven and Richard Cloward, *Poor People's Movements* (New York: Pantheon, 1977), pp. 20–21.

23. Michael Lipsky and Margaret Levi, "Community Organization as a Political Resource," in Harlan Hahn, ed., *People and Places in Urban Society* (Urban Affairs Annual Review, vol. 6) (Newbury Park, Calif.: Sage Publications, 1972), pp. 175–199.

24. See James O'Connor's discussion of "legitimation" and his general thesis concerning the role of the state service sector, in O'Connor, *The Fiscal Crisis of the State* (New York: St. Martin's, 1973). On social control functions in particular policy sectors see Samuel Bowles and Herbert Gintis, *Schooling in Capitalist America* (New York: Basic Books, 1976); Frances Fox Piven and Richard Cloward, *Regulating the Poor* (New York: Pantheon, 1971); Galper, *The Politics of Social Services;* Richard Quinney, *Criminology* (Boston: Little, Brown, 1975); Ira Katznelson, "Urban Counterrevolution," in Robert P. Wolff, ed., *1984 Revisited* (New York: Alfred Knopf, 1973), pp. 139–164.

SECTION 5

Public Personnel Systems

Nothing is more central to public administration than the employees of public organizations and the legal, management, and compensation systems that govern their organizational lives. The quality of public employees and public employment has been a concern throughout the history of the United States although, as many have noted, the role of administration per se is not addressed in the Constitution. Thomas Jefferson, for example, fretted that the composition of the small federal work force in his presidency did not accurately reflect the composition of the citizenry. Later, the emphasis on partisan affiliation rather than personal qualifications as the most important criterion for federal employment created a call for reform. The subsequent move from patronage to a fledgling merit system was one of the most important developments in the history of the federal personnel system.

The Pendleton Act was passed in 1883; although it covered only about 10 percent of the federal work force at time of passage, its provisions for admission to the federal service based on competitive examination created the framework for the civil service systems we know today. As the Ingraham and Rosenbloom selection that follows demonstrates, the simplicity of the early merit principles—equal access, entrance by competitive exam, and neutral administration free from partisan political intrusion—has been replaced by a complex set of principles, guidelines, rules, and regulations. The complexity and constraints of the federal civil service system led President Jimmy Carter to advocate his Civil Service Reform Act of 1978 by declaring that there "was no merit in the merit system!" Many other analyses of civil service systems have found that the rigid centralization and the removal of many personnel responsibilities from line managers have contributed to systems that are often counterproductive and ineffective. In both the federal government and in many states (as the selection by Joel Douglas aptly demonstrates) the role of labor unions and collective bargaining both complicates and attenuates civil service systems even further. While there continues to be widespread support for the fundamental principles of merit, the systems which now surround them are coming under increasing attack. Some states, such as Florida and Virginia, have dramatically altered their state civil service systems or are considering doing so.

At the federal level, classification and compensation systems have been the target of recent reforms or proposals for reform. Compensation became particularly problematic because the uniform national pay scale for many civil service jobs created significant gaps between public and private sector pay scales in many parts of the country. Recruiting for federal jobs became difficult and nearly impossible for scientific and technical occupations. Passage of the Federal Employees Pay Comparability Act of 1991 was one response to these problems. The National Academy of Public Administration has urged that federal classification activities also be reviewed and greatly simplified. Reforms such as pay for performance are other efforts to increase the discretion and flexibility available to managers in the federal service.

As Ingraham and Rosenbloom observe in the excerpts from "The State of Merit," however, recruiting and rewarding are only one part of total public service responsibilities. Many democratic objectives are also entwined in public personnel systems. Perhaps the most significant of these is the objective of representativeness, or the view that, to the maximum extent possible, public organizations' employees should reflect the composition of society and the citizens served by the organization. Equal Employment Opportunity and Affirmative Action policies are efforts to meet these objectives. The increasingly diverse work force of the future projected by demographic trends and forecasts will cast the need for internally diverse public organizations in bold relief.

Still another peculiarly public issue in personnel is political appointees and their relationship to the career bureaucracy. Initially intended to give the president the ability to provide policy and program direction to the executive branch, the presidential appointment system has become a rather controversial part of the federal service. Franklin Roosevelt used the appointment authority when he created New Deal agencies; Dwight Eisenhower created Schedule C Authority by Executive Order so that he would have greater appointment ability in "policy sensitive" areas; every president since Richard Nixon has devised a strategy to tighten control of career bureaucrats by political appointees. But there are problems and some appear intractable. Political appointees often lack the policy and program expertise necessary to achieve presidential objectives inside the agencies; many lack requisite management skills as well. Most significantly, however, many appointees stay in position for very short periods of time. They do not learn enough about either the policies or the organizations they theoretically head to effectively manage change.

Perry and Wise discuss another crucial issue: motivation and commitment in the public service. For many years, motivation of public employees was considered primarily in terms of private sector research and patterns. This produced significant inconsistencies and gaps in knowledge about the public work force and in incentives created for it. Compensation provides one important example. As the National Commission on the Public Service and others have observed, a long-standing tenet of public sector compensation was that pay levels could be somewhat lower than those of the private sector because employees derived satisfaction from "public service." On the other hand, reforms such as pay for performance were clearly based on the assumption that financial incentives were important—and perhaps the most important—incentives for public employees. The structure of motivations and incentives in the public service is not well understood; it ranks high on the research agenda for the future. Perry and Wise summarize critical issues; their analysis is very useful in better understanding how public personnel systems both constrain and support public employees.

These issues represent only one part of the many that confront public personnel systems today. Decreasing budgets and other large scale organizational changes, total quality management and the emphasis on better serving those who receive public services, and nearly constant demands for more flexible and innovative public management systems create a turbulent environment for personnel systems created many years ago. Understanding these influences and issues, and effectively meeting the challenges they present, will be an enormous task. It must be successfully accomplished, however, if public personnel systems are to fulfill their role in government.

16. The State of Merit in the Federal Government

*Patricia W. Ingraham and
David H. Rosenbloom
with the research assistance of
John P. Knight*

> The merit system, by raising the character and capacity of the subordinate service, and by accustoming the people to consider personal worth and sound principles, rather than selfish interest and adroit management as the controlling elements of success in politics, has also invigorated national patriotism, raised the standard of statesmanship, and caused political leaders to look more to the better sentiments and the higher intelligence for support.
> —*The Eaton Report to President Rutherford B. Hayes, 1879*

SOURCE: "The State of Merit in the Federal Government" by Patricia W. Ingraham and David H. Rosenbloom. Reprinted by permission of Chatham House Publishers, Inc.

THE PROBLEM

For over one hundred years, the American civil service has been guided by merit principles. Those principles, underpinning a system intended to protect federal employment and employees from partisan politics, were simple and direct: fair and open competition for federal jobs, admission to the competitive service only on the basis of neutral examinations, and protection of those in the service from political influence and coercion. The system that has grown from these principles, however, is not simple and direct. Today, rules and regulations related to federal personnel administration fill thousands of pages. Today, the federal government's merit system *does not work.* These procedures have created a system in which the recruitment, testing, and hiring of employees is often conducted independently of those who will manage and be responsible for the employees' performance. The personnel function is often viewed independently—indeed, often in isolation—from management concerns and priorities. Many continue to define merit only in terms of entrance to the federal service through centralized neutral and objective examinations, but in a diverse and complex society, tests alone are not an accurate measure of merit. It is abundantly clear that the construction and administration of such examinations create as many problems as they solve. Many federal managers argue that the time spent trying to understand the system overshadows whatever benefits the merit system provides.

In 1978, President Jimmy Carter declared that there was "no merit in the merit system." Others have argued that there is no system in the merit system. Incremental laws and procedures, accumulating over a one-hundred-year period, have created a jerrybuilt set of rules and regulations whose primary emphasis is on negative control of federal personnel, rather than on a positive affirmation of merit and quality in the federal service. The design of a system intended to screen large numbers of applicants for a limited number of positions is outdated and inappropriate for contemporary

technology and the changing demographics of the twenty-first century. The elimination of the discriminatory Professional and Administrative Career Examination (PACE) in 1982 demonstrated how entrance procedures should not look, but failed to specify how they should. The gradual accretion of often conflicting objectives, rules, and regulations has created, not a coherent national system of merit, but a confusing maze of procedure. At the same time, the long-term effectiveness of the federal government rests on the ability to recruit and retain a quality workforce. The many restrictive components of the contemporary merit system severely inhibit that ability. Merit has come to signify a narrow and negative focus on positions and jobs, rather than competence, accountability, and effective public service.

It is not the intent of this chapter to propose or endorse specific reforms, although there are many. Instead, the purpose is to describe the disjointed evolution and current state of the federal merit system—the status quo from which future reforms must proceed. Very clearly, those reforms cannot build on a clear and coherent foundation, for no such foundation exists. Future reforms, therefore, must address fundamental questions: What does "merit" mean for contemporary federal personnel administration?[1] What are the critical components of a merit system for the future? Is it possible to replace rules and regulations with flexibility and discretion for federal personnel, but still to ensure accountability and responsiveness to the public and to elected officials? Without this fundamental analysis, current proposals for reform may only contribute to the system's baggage; the ability of the federal government to be an effective and competitive employer will not be addressed.

THE ORIGINS

The passage of the Pendleton Act in 1883 began the process of creating a civil service based on merit for the American national government. Strongly anchored in the experience of the British civil service, the American system nonetheless reflected uniquely American politics and government. The public excesses of the patronage system were viewed as a national disgrace and as a serious burden on the presidency. The assassination of President James Garfield by a demented office seeker dramatically demonstrated the problem. The glut of office seekers in Washington and their constant demands on the president and his staff created other problems; they reportedly led President Abraham Lincoln to request, when he contracted smallpox, that all the office seekers be sent to him, for "now I have something I can give to each of them."[2]

The passage of the legislation reflected political realities as well. There were strong civil service leagues in many states. They had successfully placed personnel reform on the agenda for the 1882 congressional elections. The support expressed for reform in those midterm elections ensured that it would become a national issue. Political demands, however, were tempered by a serious constitutional question: Did the creation of a centralized personnel system and Civil Service Commission violate the powers of both the president and Congress over personnel matters?[3]

The dilemma posed by the political need to act and questions of constitutional legitimacy produced a classically political solution: The initial legislation covered only 10 percent of the federal workforce. But Congress granted the president power to include additional federal employees in the classified civil service by Executive Order. Patronage would be controlled, but slowly. Van Riper notes, "If the act permitted an orderly retreat of parties from their prerogatives of plunder, it made possible as well the gradual administrative development of the merit system."[4]

At the heart of the new merit system was one fundamental principle: Admission to the classified civil service would be *only* through open competitive examinations. Unlike the British system, which relied on formal academic training, the American system hailed the practical American spirit; the examinations would focus on common sense, practical information, and skills. The examination system would be designed to provide all who desired federal employment a fair, equal, and objective opportunity to enter the civil service. The act created decentralized Boards of Examiners to administer the tests and specified that they "be so located as to make it reasonably convenient and inexpensive for applicants to attend before them."[5]

The American system also differed from its British heritage in its definition and treatment of neutrality. Very clearly, political neutrality was to be a hallmark of the new classified civil service. The need for a competent civil service that would serve either political party well was widely accepted. At the same time, neither members of Congress, the president, nor the reformers were willing to commit to the British tradition of an elite higher civil service whose members were active participants in policy debates. Policy participation was not viewed as a legitimate administrative function. For the American civil service, neutrality was a protection against politics, but also an exclusion from policy. Herbert Kaufman offered the following assessment: "the civil service was like a hammer or a saw; it would do nothing at all by itself, but it would serve any purpose, wise or unwise, good or bad, to which any user put it."[6]

THE GROWTH OF THE CLASSIFIED SERVICE

The origins of the merit system in the federal government are important for a number of reasons. First, because the system had a purposefully limited beginning, growth could, and did, occur in an unplanned and unpredictable way. Second, the system was formed in a way designed to gather the largest possible number of applicants for a limited number of government jobs. The "fair and open competition" principle was interpreted from the outset to be national competition for what were then largely Washington-based jobs (postmasters were not included in the original legislation). The system was, in short, designed to be a screening system and was based on the fundamental assumption that there would be many more job seekers than jobs. Further, since most positions would be in Washington, centralizing the personnel function within the Civil Service Commission made good sense. Third, despite the emphases on objective merit and free and open competition, the Pendleton Act included provisions whose intent and impact was to attenuate those emphases. The act specifically noted, for example, that veterans were to continue to be given preference in federal hiring, a practice that had been formally established in 1865. In addition, the Pendleton Act reaffirmed the nation's commitment to a geographically "representative" federal workforce, an emphasis first articulated during George Washington's presidency. Merit, veterans' preference, and geographic representativeness did not necessarily coincide, even in 1883. In the ensuing years, veterans' groups, in particular, have often pursued objectives clearly at odds with those of federal personnel experts and managers.

Finally, the provision for presidential determination of increased coverage did not remove politics from the development of the civil service system; instead, it ensured that the growth of "merit" would be dependent on political cycles. Presidents who chose to extend the merit system often came under attack from their own parties for doing so; each extension of civil service coverage meant fewer patronage appointments and fewer payoffs for party loyalty. As a result, commitment by presidents to merit and the classified civil service fluctuated dramatically in the early years. Generally, presidents such as Theodore Roosevelt (also a former civil service commissioner) who succeeded a president of their own party found advancing merit to be somewhat easier than those who did not. President William McKinley, for example, included 1700 additional employees in the classified service by Executive Order, but also exempted about 9,000 employees through rollback and new exemption procedures.[7] Woodrow Wilson took the reins of a federal government that had been controlled for sixteen years by Republicans. Despite his association with the National Civil Service Reform Association, the Wilson administration was under intense pressure for patronage. President Wilson said of this pressure, "The matter of patronage is a thorny path that daily makes me wish I had never been born."[8]

Congress, too, retained a keen interest in patronage. As new governmental tasks and functions were approved, Congress could choose to place the jobs created outside the classified service. From the time of the first Wilson term to the New Deal, that option was often pursued. It was pushed to new heights— this time at presidential initiative—in Franklin Roosevelt's New Deal. The experience of the civil service in the New Deal years is treated differently by different analysts; Van Riper, for example, offers an exceedingly harsh assessment. More pragmatically, Kaufman notes that Franklin Roosevelt managed to "kill two birds with one stone," when he "put into effect all of the programs and projects he considered vital for the welfare of the country. And he excepted the positions in these agencies from the classified service, thus enabling him to fill many of the patronage demands threatening the merit system."[9] In any case, prior to Roosevelt's election in 1932, approximately 80 percent of federal employees were in the competitive civil service. By 1936, that proportion had declined to about 60 percent.[10]

The percentage of the federal workforce under merit protection gradually increased during and after World War II. That time period also saw notable efforts to bring cohesion to the previously haphazard development of the civil service system. The Ramspeck Act in 1940, for example, gave the president the authority to eliminate existing exemptions, including those created by the Pendleton Act. By 1951, about 87 percent of total federal employment was in the classified service.[11] The percentage expanded still further throughout the 1960s and 1970s, so that, by 1980, well over 90 percent of the federal workforce was covered by civil service laws and regulations.

THE GROWTH IN COMPLEXITY

The Pendleton Act itself contained the seeds for the disjointed growth, internal contradictions, and enormous complexity of the American merit system. The very limited initial coverage and the presidential power to extend merit created "blanketing in" procedures. As each new group of employees was thus included in the system, employees who had been appointed by patronage became members of the merit system. As the Civil Service Commission noted, "Although the practice represents a deviation from the merit principle, it makes future appointments to the 'blanketed in' positions subject to merit

rules."[12] In addition, the provisions for veterans' preference flatly repudiated the merit principles that applied to everyone else in the competitive system. It was not until 1953, for example, that veterans were required to achieve a passing score on the competitive examinations before having their five- or ten-point veterans' preference added.[13] All other applicants, of course, were not considered for federal employment if they failed the examination.

HIRING

There were other deviations from merit principles. Almost from the beginning, the Civil Service Commission divided the classified civil service into "competitive" (competitive exam required), "noncompetitive" (noncompetitive exam required) and "excepted" (no exam required). Schedule A authority, which exempted from examination some positions that were technically within the classified service, formalized these distinctions. Until 1910, all noncompetitive and excepted categories were lumped under Schedule A authority. In 1910, Schedule B was created to include all noncompetitive positions. In 1953, an Executive Order from President Dwight Eisenhower removed confidential and other policy-sensitive positions from Schedule A and placed them in the newly created Schedule C, whose intent was to permit the president greater numbers of political appointees in policy-sensitive posts (as well as in other lower-level positions, such as chauffeurs and receptionists).[14] Although Schedule A authority is now used primarily for appointing in specialized professions such as law and accounting, Schedule B authority became the primary vehicle for federal hiring in the period immediately following the abolition of PACE. Because federal hiring during this period was limited to a few major agencies with the greatest employment needs, most federal agencies had no systematic hiring authority available to them and little, if any experience with Schedule B. In 1985, one of the last years of heavy reliance on Schedule B, 98 percent of all appointments under the authority were made by nine of the twenty-one largest departments and agencies.[15] The use of Schedule C, although fairly limited initially, has also expanded in the past twenty years, primarily at upper grade levels.[16]

It is also important to consider the large number of special authorities under which federal agencies now hire. Reliance on such authorities (as well as on Schedule B) was necessitated by the abolition of the Professional and Administrative Career Examination (PACE) in 1982. PACE, which replaced the earlier Federal Service Entrance Examination (FSEE), had provided a single centralized means of recruitment and entry for many federal jobs. When PACE was abolished with no replacement, it became necessary for the Office of Personnel Management (OPM) and the many federal agencies to fall back on existing limited authorities and to use them for purposes for which most had never been intended.

Temporary appointment authority, intended to simplify hiring and separation, as well as to limit the expansion of government, is one such special authority. Temporary appointments have increased substantially in both numbers and duration in recent years, particularly since 1984, when the OPM permitted expansion of their use. Of equal significance, methods of appointing to temporary positions have increased dramatically. At the present time in the federal government, there are *thirty-five* ways to appoint to temporary positions alone.[17] Part-time appointments are an additional option; they, too, are not consistently made through competitive examination procedures.

Direct-hire authority was created for hard-to-hire occupations such as engineers, nurses, and scientists. Direct-hire appointments are made on the basis of unassembled examinations. In 1989, a new direct-hire authority was created for Vietnam veterans. The Outstanding Scholar authority permits on-the-spot hiring of college graduates who have completed four-year degrees with a GPA of 3.5 or better. Simplified hiring procedures also exist for affirmative-action hires, for returned Peace Corps volunteers, and for students enrolled in the Cooperative Education Program, among others. A precise and current list of the many authorities available to federal employers is difficult because the OPM has not updated and distributed such a list since 1980. It is important to note, however, that in 1989, 45 percent of federal career appointments were made under provisions that delegated either examining or hiring authority (or, in some cases, both) to the individual agencies. Another 25 percent were direct-hire appointments in hard-to-hire occupations, while about 15 percent were specialized mid- to senior-level appointments for which there was no register. Only about 15 percent of the appointments were made through "traditional" civil service procedures; that is, through centralized examination or from central registers administered by OPM.[18]

Finally, the federal merit hiring "system" is made more complex by the inclusion of entire agencies (FBI, CIA, Postal Service) in excepted authorities and by the creation of separate but parallel merit systems in others (TVA, for example). The Foreign Service operates with a separate system; so too does the Public Health Service. In some organizations, such as the Department of Health and Human Services and the State Department, more than one system is in place.

In 1978, major civil service reform legislation was passed. A centerpiece of

Carter administration domestic policy, the Civil Service Reform Act of 1978 (CSRA) was intended to simplify federal personnel policy through decentralization and delegation, as well as to increase the accountability and responsiveness of federal employees through performance appraisal and evaluation. CSRA created financial incentives linked to performance for top career executives and mid-level managers. The act created the Senior Executive Service (SES) in an effort to make the senior management cadre of the federal career service more flexible and more responsive. It codified federal labor-management practices for the first time, reaffirmed the federal government's commitment to representativeness and affirmative action, and provided new protection for whistleblowers. The act abolished the Civil Service Commission and replaced it with the Office of Personnel Management, the Merit Systems Protection Board, and the Federal Labor Relations Authority. These new institutions were to be leaders in shaping a new and more coherent federal personnel and human resource management strategy.

Because CSRA was the first comprehensive reform of the civil service in nearly a hundred years, expectations for improvements were high. In fact, however, many of those expectations have not been met.[19] This is due to a modest understanding and shallow level of support for many of the reforms; the new political environment of the Reagan administration also had a profound impact on many of the primary implementation activities. The budgetary cutbacks in the early years of the Reagan administration accompanied implementation of critical components of the reform. Much of the political rhetoric accompanying proposed policy changes was directed at the career bureaucracy: the "permanent government." Morale was very low. Delegation, decentralization, and simplifi-

cation proceeded in fits and starts; attention was again paid to this issue only because the abolition of PACE removed the major central means of recruiting and testing for the federal service.

Most significantly, however, for all its emphasis on greater clarity and simplicity in the federal merit system, the Civil Service Reform Act did not replace the tangle of procedures related to federal personnel practices. In many respects, it merely added another layer of complexity and confusion to an already complex system. Decentralization and delegation of recruiting and hiring, for example, is not simplification if 6,000 pages of rules, regulations, and guidelines remain in effect. The ability to understand and monitor such a system is extremely difficult, and probably impossible in the absence of any central guiding principles and objectives. The ability to understand and manage effectively in such a system is made even more difficult when other characteristics of the federal personnel system are considered.

CLASSIFICATION AND COMPENSATION

Classification of federal employees was formally authorized in 1923 with the passage of the Classification Act. This legislation not only classified positions according to duties and responsibilities but also assigned salary levels to those positions. It therefore established in law the principle of nationally uniform compensation levels. The act was passed shortly after the Budget and Accounting Act of 1921, and clearly fell under the umbrella of the economy and efficiency movement so prevalent in government at that time. Van Riper notes that "the Bureau of the Budget [created by the 1921 act] tended to emphasize economy at the expense of almost everything else. But the pressing need for careful estimates of personnel and personnel costs, if any budget was to really mean anything, stimulated further concern with the standardization . . . of federal wages and functions."[20]

The administration of the new act was supervised by a newly created Personnel Classification Board.

In addition, the act established in law the American principle of "rank in job," rather than the European practice of "rank in person." This meant that the salary or wages for each job was determined solely by the position and by the necessary qualifications for that position, not by the personal qualifications of the person filling the position (although presumably they matched fairly closely). Finally, the act institutionalized the very specialized nature of the American civil service. The jobs to be classified were narrow and specific; again, in keeping with the economy and efficiency movement, flexibility and discretion were limited whenever possible.

Although an analysis of the Classification Act's effectiveness in 1929 indicated that it had not created a "consistent and equitable system of . . . pay for positions involving the same work,"[21] there was no additional reform in this area until 1949. There were, however, fairly consistent calls for change during that twenty-year period. The Commission of Inquiry on Public Service Personnel noted in 1935, for example, that "the most obvious fault to be found with all classifications made on the American plan is their complexity—the great number of classes and occupational hierarchies that are set up. What seem to be the most trifling differences in function or difficulty are formally recognized and duly defined. . . ." The commission noted further that "classifications of such complexity are to be condemned because of the fetters that they place upon department heads in the management of their business."[22]

The Ramspeck Act extended the Civil Service Commission's authority for classification to the entire field service in 1940; in 1945 a presidential order directed the commission to begin that task. By that time, the commission was responsible for about half of the total federal civil service positions.[23] The complexity of the federal personnel system was now much in evidence. The absence of a comprehensive wage-and-salary policy had become a notable problem. The final report of the first Hoover Commission detailed the issues related to pay and personnel and concluded: "Probably no problem in the management of the Government is more important than that of obtaining a capable and conscientious body of public servants. Unfortunately, personnel practices in the federal government give little room for optimism that these needs are being met."[24]

In 1949, at least partially in response to Hoover Commission recommendations, the Classification Act of 1949 was passed. The act created the "supergrade" system, which preceded the Senior Executive Service, and simplified the occupational series by merging the previous five into two. The Classification Act of 1949 is important for another reason: It marked an early point on what has now come to be considered the "cycle" of centralization and decentralization in federal personnel policy. Excessive centralization of classification activities was perceived to be a major cause of an overly rigid and slow system. As a result, the 1949 act delegated classification authority for positions below the supergrades back to the agencies. It gave the Civil Service Commission postaudit review authority for those delegations. With other authority such as examining still residing with the Civil Service Commission, with very limited experience in classification activity at the agency level, and with extensive central regulations and procedures still governing the activity, however, this delegation set the precedent for others to follow. Authority was gradually pulled back into the commission until, when the Civil Service Reform Act of 1978 was written, excessive centralization was again perceived to be the problem.

Despite the centrality of classification activities to federal personnel policy and pay, classification has not been thoroughly analyzed since before the passage of the 1949 act. In the intervening forty years, the procedures and regulations associated with classification—most notably the classification and qualification standards[25]—have become seriously outdated and burdensome. The Merit Systems Protection Board recently found, for example, that *63 percent* of the white-collar classification standards currently in use were issued before 1973.[26] In addition, for the 1982–84 period, OPM declared a moratorium on writing new classification standards and the problem was exacerbated. Because grade levels flow directly from classification and qualification standards (or they *should*), the link between these standards and pay is immutable. Obsolescent standards inevitably influence the ability to determine fair pay for an occupation or grade. There are more than 900 occupations in the federal classified service and over 30 different pay systems. The links between the two cannot be ignored in reform, and simplification or total redesign of federal classification schemes is also necessary.

The Civil Service Reform Act of 1978, which did not address the issue of pay, did give the Office of Personnel Management authority to delegate classification activities to the agencies. It did so, however, without addressing or eliminating the plethora of rules and regulations that had accumulated over the years and without directly reforming the Classification Act of 1949. As noted earlier, this failure to address the procedural "baggage" added yet another layer of complexity to a very murky system. To date,

OPM has limited such delegation to a very small number of demonstration projects. "Reform" of classification and qualification standards has occurred primarily through efforts to write "generic" standards, which provide greater flexibility. Without a fundamental reexamination of classification procedures, however, other efforts at personnel and pay reform necessarily remain somewhat tangential to change.

TRAINING AND DEVELOPMENT

Training and development of the federal workforce has had a somewhat checkered history. Although a limited number of agencies created education and training programs for their employees, general direction and support was clearly lacking until the passage of the Government Employees Training Act of 1958. Indeed, Van Riper notes that, before 1940, "the excess of applicants compared to available jobs had suggested to both Congress and many administrators that extensive in-service training programs were essentially wasteful."[27] The very limited supply of labor during World War II mandated that federal personnel policy include provisions for training and retraining of federal personnel. At the end of the war, however, many of these activities were cut back or eliminated. The training void was duly noted by the first Hoover Commission and, partially in response to the Hoover Report, President Truman directed the Civil Service Commission to attack what the commission itself called the "curse of excessive specialization."[28] By most accounts, this attack garnered only modest results.

During the presidency of Dwight Eisenhower, whose military training convinced him of the benefits of the enterprise, training began to achieve more credibility. In Eisenhower's first term, the Federal Training Policy Statement was issued. This directive advocated formulation of training plans and emphasis on employee development opportunities. The Civil Service Commission was given lead responsibility for these training efforts. In 1958, during the second Eisenhower term, his administration followed up with the Government Employees Training Act of 1958. Although passage of the act involved intense political negotiation, this act legitimized the training function and provided funds for training and centralized training programs. In its 1974 report, *Biography of an Ideal,* the Civil Service Commission argued that the provisions of the 1958 act "make the training function in the United States Government the envy of even the most advanced of nations."[29] That statement was undoubtedly an exaggeration in 1974; it is clearly not accurate today.

Like much else in the federal personnel system, training and development have not grown in a systematic and coherent way. Despite the provisions of the 1958 act (which has never been revisited), training has remained a fairly low priority. In times of budget cuts and constraints, training costs are often the first to be eliminated from the budget. In its report to the National Commission on the Public Service, the Task Force on Education and Training said, "There are significant shortcomings in federal government human resource policies. Government agencies spend far too little on training of all kinds and concentrate their efforts on meeting narrow, short-term needs. The area of greatest concern is the plainly inadequate attention paid to the development of management and executive leadership in the civil service."[30]

The Civil Service Commission and, later, the Office of Personnel Management, did not develop a government-wide training strategy until Constance Newman assumed the directorship of OPM in the Bush administration. Financial support for training at both central and agency levels remains very limited.

At the same time, the need for training and retraining has never been more clear. The demographics of the twenty-first century, changing skill demands, and dramatic technological progress all point to new development needs. Merit and competence are inextricably intertwined.

THE COURTS AND THE MERIT SYSTEM

In the 1970s and 1980s, the federal judiciary played a substantial role in defining and redefining the merit system. The Supreme Court, in particular, has been an ardent supporter of two historical tenets of merit: (1) depoliticization of the public service, and (2) assuring that operational definitions and applications of merit in public personnel administration are strongly job related.

Depoliticization

A major goal of the merit system has been to remove partisan politics from public personnel management. George William Curtis, a leading nineteenth-century civil service reformer, noted that the merit system made it possible to take "the whole non-political public service out of politics."[31] The effort had two prongs: to prohibit public employees from taking an active part in partisan political management and campaigning, and to eliminate patronage hiring and dismissal from the public service. The Supreme Court has embraced both elements of depoliticization.

The effort to remove public employees from partisan politics has been most generally embodied in the first and second Hatch Acts (1939 and 1940) and in various state and local equivalents. The first Hatch Act applies only to federal employees; it prohibits them from using their "official authority or influence for the purpose of interfering with or affecting the result of an election," or from taking an "active part in political management or political campaigns." The second Hatch Act applies similar restrictions to state and local government employees whose positions are at least partially funded by the federal government. These measures carve out a legal and political status for public employees that is remarkably different from that of ordinary citizens. While partisan political participation is considered virtuous for citizens generally, it is simply illegal for public employees. Not surprisingly, both acts have been subject to challenge in the courts on the grounds that they violate the First and Fourteenth Amendment rights of public employees. They have also been attacked for vagueness because both acts lack a comprehensive definition of the activities they proscribe.

The constitutional arguments against the Hatch Acts and similar political neutrality statutes have filled volumes of law reviews and many court briefs. In 1973, however, the Supreme Court seemed to put the constitutional issues to rest in an opinion that strongly supported depoliticization of the public service and afforded Congress great latitude in seeking to achieve that end. In U.S. *Civil Service Commission* v. *National Association of Letter Carriers (NALC)*,[32] the Court held:

> We unhesitatingly reaffirm . . . that Congress . . . has the power to prevent [federal employees covered by the first Hatch Act] from holding a party office, working at the polls and acting as party paymaster for other party workers. . . . Our judgment is that neither the First Amendment nor any other provision of the Constitution invalidates a law barring this kind of partisan political conduct by federal employees.
>
> Such a decision on our part would no more than confirm the judgment of history, a judgment made by this country over the last century that it is

in the best interests of the country, indeed essential, that federal service should depend upon meritorious performance rather than political service.

The *NALC* decision effectively allows Congress to take virtually any reasonable steps to remove the federal service from partisan political activity. The Court went even further in supporting depoliticization when, in *Elrod* v. *Burns* (1976),[33] it ruled patronage dismissals from ordinary public-service positions *unconstitutional.*

Elrod concerned the constitutionality of patronage dismissals from the Cook County, Illinois, Sheriff's Office. The discharged employees claimed that their First and Fourteenth Amendment rights to freedom of belief and association had been violated. A majority of the Supreme Court's justices agreed that the dismissals were unconstitutional, but the Court was unable to reach a majority opinion as to precisely why.

The issue was more fully clarified in *Branti* v. *Finkel* (1980),[34] in which the Court came close to "constitutionalizing" merit. In assessing the patronage dismissal of two public defenders in Rockland County, New York, Justice John Paul Stevens, speaking for the Court's majority, reasoned that patronage dismissals are unconstitutional unless "the hiring authority can demonstrate that that party affiliation is an appropriate requirement for the effective performance of the public office involved." As Justice Lewis Powell argued in dissent, however, the only logical alternative to a patronage system is one that is merit oriented: "Many public positions previously filled on the basis of membership in national political parties now must be staffed in accordance with a constitutionalized civil service standard that will affect the employment practices of federal, state and local governments."

An important aspect of the *Branti* ruling is that the Court reasoned that merely labeling positions "policy making" or "confidential" is not enough to justify patronage dismissals from them. In practice, this means that some traditional public personnel classifications, such as "excepted" and "exempt," will no longer be synonymous with "at the pleasure" of the political official at the head of an agency or government.

In sum, the Supreme Court has been very sympathetic to the nineteenth-century civil service reformers' ideal of taking politics out of the public service and the public service out of politics. It has declared that patronage dismissals will generally be unconstitutional and has held that the Constitution can easily accommodate restrictions on public employees' partisan political activities. At the same time, it must be noted that Congress has recently raised questions about the overall utility of the Hatch Act and about its infringement on the rights of public employees. Each of the last several sessions has seen the introduction of legislation intended to roll back Hatch provisions. Those in favor of reform argue that federal employees are severely disadvantaged by the inability to participate in politics on their own behalf. Those opposing reform argue that continued political restrictions on federal employees are essential to maintaining any semblance of a merit system. It is important to note that the strength of the proreform group has increased recently; in fact, some observers predicted reform of the Hatch Acts before the end of 1990.[35] The Supreme Court's view of such legislation, should it pass, could be an important redefinition of merit.

Making Sure That the Merit System Assures Merit

A second aspect of the judiciary's involvement in public personnel administration has concerned the very meaning of *merit*. Here, too, the thrust of judicial activity has been two pronged.

All merit systems afford covered employees protection against arbitrary, capricious, illegal, or unconstitutional dismissals. These same systems provide for dismissals in the interests of the efficiency of the public service. During the aftermath of the loyalty-security programs of the late 1940s and early 1950s, the federal judiciary began to look more closely at the government's claims that particular dismissals promoted efficiency. In *Board of Regents* v. *Roth* (1972),[36] the Supreme Court held that public employees are constitutionally entitled to procedural due process protection when dismissals abridged their constitutional rights or liberties, damaged their reputations, seriously impaired their future employability, or infringed upon a property interest, such as tenure, in their jobs. By 1985, the Court had expanded the application of due process considerably. In *Cleveland Board of Education* v. *Loudermill*,[37] it found that a public employee had a "property right" in a job because the Ohio civil service statute made him a "classified civil service" employee, who was entitled to retain his position "during good behavior and efficient service."

Constitutional due process in dismissals from the civil service does not necessarily require elaborate procedures. It does require that the government, as employer, state its reasons for the dismissal and allow the public employee to try to rebut its claims. Once the record contains each side's perspective, review by an administrative official or a court is generally possible. Unsubstantiated claims that dismissals will promote efficiency have been vulnerable to successful challenge. Thus, where there is a merit system, the government cannot simply purport that dismissals serve efficiency objectives; it must demonstrate conclusively that they do so.

The federal judiciary has also sought to assure that merit systems yield merit by requiring, under some circumstances, that standard civil service examinations be strongly job related. In a series of cases beginning in the early 1970s, the courts have held that employment practices having a negative impact on the employment interests of members of minority groups and women are illegal unless they are valid in the sense of being job related.[38] These rulings have been under the Civil Rights Act of 1964, as amended, and the Constitution's equal protection clause (limited to the public sector). There have been numerous instances in which public agencies have been unable to demonstrate sufficient job relatedness to make the practices at issue legally or constitutionally acceptable. One remedy that the judiciary may impose in such cases is quota hiring from among qualified minority-group members for a limited period of time, as in *United States* v. *Paradise* (1987).[39]

These cases have forced public-sector jurisdictions to rethink their definitions and applications of merit principles and to attempt to eliminate cultural bias in their hiring and promotional procedures. In *Johnson* v. *Santa Clara County* (1987),[40] the Supreme Court accepted a broad definition of merit that included an effort to establish a socially representative workforce. It specifically embraced the principle that exam scores do not have to be the sole determinant in promotions. Instead, jurisdictions are free to consider a range of factors, including sex and minority-group status. In *Johnson,* the Court noted that merit systems can be flexible because "there is rarely a single, 'best qualified' person for a job. An effective personnel system will bring before the selecting official several fully-qualified candidates who each may possess different attributes that recommend them for selection."[41]

Thus the federal judiciary and the Supreme Court have strengthened two aspects of the merit system. They have protected depoliticization by upholding

regulations prohibiting federal employees from engaging in partisan political activity. They have required depoliticization by finding that patronage dismissals from the public service will generally be unconstitutional. The courts have also strengthened the merit system by requiring that dismissals, selections, and promotions done in the name of merit actually embody merit.

THE MERIT SYSTEM AND MERIT PRINCIPLES

This, then, is the procedural and legal environment of the contemporary federal "merit system." The remarkable growth of complexity in both the environment and the system has been reflected in restatements of the underlying principles: Not surprisingly, there are more merit principles today than there were in 1883. After a long period of formal silence about what the merit principles actually ensured, they have been enunciated in legislation twice in the past twenty years. In 1970, the Intergovernmental Personnel Act formally listed the merit principles for the first time:

1. Hiring and promoting employees on the basis of relative ability, with open consideration for initial appointment.
2. Providing fair compensation.
3. Retaining employees on the basis of performance, correcting inadequate performance and separating those whose inadequate performance cannot be corrected.
4. Training employees as needed for high quality performance.
5. Assuring fair treatment of applicants and employees in all aspects of personnel administration without regard to political affiliation, race, color, national origin, sex, or religious creed, and with proper regard for their privacy and constitutional rights as citizens.

6. Protecting employees against partisan political coercion; and prohibiting use of official position to affect an election or nomination for office.[42]

It is worth noting that the Intergovernmental Personnel Act, by using the lever of federal funding, applied these merit principles to state and local governments, just as the second Hatch Act had earlier prohibited state and local employees from partisan political activity.

In 1978, the principles were restated and somewhat redefined again in the Civil Service Reform Act. Now there were nine, much more complex, principles:

1. Recruitment should be from qualified individuals from appropriate sources in an endeavor to achieve a workforce from all segments of society, and selection and advancement should be determined solely on the basis of relative ability, knowledge and skills, after fair and open competition that assures that all receive equal opportunity.

2. All employees and applicants for employment should receive fair and equitable treatment in all aspects of personnel management without regard to political affiliation, race, color, religion, national origin, sex, marital status, age, or handicapping condition, and with proper regard for their privacy and constitutional rights.

3. Equal pay should be provided for work of equal value, with appropriate consideration of both national and local rates paid by employers in the private sector, and appropriate incentives and recognition should be provided for excellence in performance.

4. All employees should maintain high standards of integrity, conduct, and concern for the public interest.

5. The federal workforce should be used efficiently and effectively.

6. Employees should be retained on the adequacy of their performance, inadequate performance should be corrected, and employees should be separated who cannot or will not improve their performance to meet required standards.

7. Employees should be provided effective education and training in cases in which such education and training would result in better organizational and individual performance.

8. Employees should be (a.) protected against arbitrary action, personal favoritism, or coercion for partisan political purposes, and (b.) prohibited from using their official authority or influence for the purpose of interfering with or affecting the result of an election or a nomination for election.

9. Employees should be protected against reprisal for the lawful disclosure of information that the employee reasonably believes evidences (a.) a violation of any law, rule, or regulation, or (b.) mismanagement, a gross waste of funds, an abuse of authority, or a substantial and specific danger to public health and safety.[43]

Whatever else might be said about the merit principles as we near the year 2000, they are no longer simple and straightforward. Even the principles without their baggage do not provide clear guidance to the federal manager or personnel director who seeks to ensure merit within the overarching objective of effective service delivery. Further, the principles themselves now contain conflicting purposes and objectives. They are more comprehensive, but they are much, much more confusing.

COPING WITH THE MERIT SYSTEM

How do federal managers deal with the constraint, confusion, and complexity of merit as it exists today? In an effort to examine this question, staff members of the National Commission conducted a series of interviews with personnel directors and others in agencies that have made extensive and recent use of existing hiring procedures. Representatives from different agencies, different regions of the country, and central and field offices were interviewed to determine whether and where differences in attitudes toward merit existed. Many persons interviewed requested confidentiality. To honor those requests, no persons or agencies are identified in this chapter. In the interviews, commission staff focused on entrance to the federal service, rather than on promotion once inside.

Two findings from our interviews are paramount: first, there continues to be remarkable support for the merit *principles*. Second, there is almost unanimous dissatisfaction with the merit *system*. Furthermore, although there is strong support for reforming and removing what many refer to as the "procedural baggage" of the merit system, there is a continuing awareness of the potential for political and other abuse of the merit system and for the need for some protection of career employees and positions. There was, nonetheless, a very strong conviction that federal personnel directors and other federal managers, left on their own, would actively pursue merit. One group of managers said, "If the slate were clean, most of the agencies, most of the time, would create procedures that make good sense. Those procedures that they would re-create would look like the merit principles."[44]

Other managers affirmed this commitment, but emphasized that both the definition of merit and the means of pursuing it need to be examined. Arguing that managers must focus on purpose, not problems, one personnel director said, "The merit system has come to be a way of life, but we must remember that the principles are the basis."[45] Another noted that merit "is confused and it is

struggling, but it is there. The system, however, is beyond repair; it needs to be totally rethought. Delegating bad procedures to us does not solve problems; we need to go back to the fundamental principles and guidelines."[46]

The central agency personnel directors interviewed were unanimous in their assessment that the basic design of the current merit system is not appropriate for either current or future recruiting and hiring needs. One director said, "The days of national recruiting are over; the reality is that if you waste the time advertising nationwide, you lose the opportunity to hire the people you really need."[47] Representatives of an agency noted for its innovation and foresight in relation to personnel summarized the situation in these terms: "the goal is to find the best person for the job. The principles are fundamental and they shape the process, but you cannot control merit in a centralized way. . . . The system is arcane and archaic and we have not done a good job of articulating the new realities."[48]

The interviews uncovered strong differences between central agency staff and field staff in relation to the status of merit. The view of the merit system as archaic and procedure bound was echoed in the field office interviews, but those interviews reflected serious concerns about protecting merit as well. One manager put it in the following terms, "The merit system has little credibility . . . only a few remaining bureaucrats and a few conscientious managers are keeping it from being totally disregarded."[49] Another manager said, "Until merit is defined as something other than test scores, we will continue to reach merit goals, but the quality of the workforce and the quality of the work, will go steadily down."[50]

Underlying many of these concerns is the conviction that while the merit system does not work well or consistently anymore, no coherent replacement or direction has been advanced. Without that replacement and additional guidance, field managers fear replacing even an unworkable system. Indeed, a recent report of the General Accounting Office found that in the face of extensive decentralization and inadequate central-to-field communication, many field managers simply did not know how they were supposed to operate in relation to merit. There has been virtually no systematic monitoring of field experience and precedent; GAO found that even keeping adequate records was problematic.[51]

Overall, then, while there continues to be strong support for the fundamental principles of merit, dissatisfaction with and confusion about the current system is high. Further, the split between central agency personnel and field personnel in terms of how well agencies are coping in the current environment is cause for concern. The inability, or unwillingness, of central personnel to trust and train other personnel in their own agencies is damning evidence of the problems with merit today. The problem highlighted by National Commission interviews has been noted elsewhere. A recent MSPB survey reported that "personnel specialists view delegation of authority from agency personnel offices to line managers somewhat less favorably than they view delegation from OPM to agencies. Whereas 83 percent of respondents believe that delegation of authorities from OPM to agency personnel offices can lead to improved personnel management, only 60 percent believe the same is true of delegation from personnel offices to line management."[52]

It may be that, lacking confidence in field managers, central agency personnel have failed to take the responsibility of decentralization and delegation seriously. The same may be said of the Office of Personnel Management. The ensuing lack of reporting and monitoring is a serious deficiency that needs to be correct-

ed. A more accurate record of experience with decentralized merit is necessary for effective reform. In addition, the need for training and education—about the new environment, the new accountability, and the new responsibility—is very clear. It must be given high priority.

CONCLUSIONS AND RECOMMENDATIONS

Today, neither the essential definition of merit nor fundamental merit principles is clear. Merit cannot mean, as one would assume from examining the system, excessive constraint and blind obedience to a nearly unintelligible maze of procedure. No manager or personnel director can work consistently or effectively in a system defined by over 6,000 pages of rules and regulations. One hundred years of accumulated rules and regulations are the baggage of merit. They do not clarify and define; they obscure. The current system essentially assumes that public managers must be coerced into meritorious behavior; there is no presumption that, left to their own skills and conscience, members of the federal service will nonetheless pursue quality and effective service.

The basic components of the system continue to reflect demographic realities of the late nineteenth century. For many federal agencies, many occupations, and many regions of the country, the contemporary reality is that personnel systems cannot screen out potential employees, but must gather them in. Demographic projections for the next twenty years demonstrate very clearly that to be competitive in these activities, the federal government must be flexible, aggressive, and innovative. The current system is set up precisely to discourage such qualities.

Key components of the current system have not been reexamined for many years. Classification and training are leading examples. A crazy quilt of rules and regulations, patched together as new needs and demands appeared over the past hundred years, provides false assurance that important protections are in place. Rhetoric creates both complacency about the status quo and an unnecessarily negative view of the career civil servants the system is intended to protect.

Today, it is inconceivable that a major nation could govern well, resolve social and economic problems, or play an effective global role in the absence of a strong civil service that is well integrated into its political institutions and culture. Throughout the world, national civil services are being reformed and restructured. Virtually everywhere, government is considered a tool for formulating and implementing public policies. But as Alexander Hamilton noted two centuries ago in *The Federalist Papers,* "the true test of a good government is its aptitude and tendency to produce a good administration."

Good government in the United States requires much better public administration. There is no doubt that public personnel administration, always the cornerstone of public administration, must be redesigned—or perhaps designed for the first time—if the United States is to meet the challenges of the present and the future. There is no "quick fix" for the civil service and public administration. There is a dramatic need to decide, for the first time in over a hundred years, what kind of public service the American national government needs and deserves. Proceeding from that base, future reforms must provide the map and the tools for a new system.

NOTES

1. Throughout this chapter, "merit" is defined primarily in terms of entrance to the federal service. Very clearly, promotion and protection of employees' rights are also part of the merit mosaic. Both, however, are worthy of separate treatment.

2. Civil Service Commission, *Biography of an Ideal* (Washington, D.C.: CSC, 1974), 28.

3. Paul P. Van Riper, *History of the United States Civil Service* (Evanston, Ill.: Row, Peterson, 1958), 106.

4. Ibid, 105.

5. The Civil Service Act of 1883 (Pendleton Act), *Statutes at Large of the United States of America,* vol. 20, p. 403, sec. 3.

6. Herbert Kaufman, "The Growth of the Federal Personnel System," in The American Assembly, *The Federal Government Service* (New York: Columbia University Press, 1954), 36.

7. Stephen Skrowronek, *Building a New American State: The Expansion of National Administrative Capacities, 1877–1920* (New York: Cambridge University Press, 1982), 70–71.

8. Woodrow Wilson, quoted in Van Riper, *History of Civil Service,* 234.

9. Herbert Kaufman, "Growth of Federal Personnel System," 39. For Van Riper's dissenting view, see Van Riper, *History of Civil Service,* chap. 13.

10. See the Civil Service Commission, *Biography of an Ideal,* 66.

11. See the discussion of the Ramspeck Act and its implementation in Van Riper, *History of Civil Service,* 344–46.

12. Civil Service Commission, *Biography of an Ideal,* 49.

13. Ibid., 89.

14. Van Riper, *History of Civil Service,* 207.

15. Merit Systems Protection Board, *In Search of Merit: Hiring Entry Level Federal Employees* (Washington, D.C.: MSPB, September 1987), i.

16. The greatest increase occurred in the Carter presidency; the elevated levels from that administration were increased still further under Presi-

dent Reagan. See Patricia W. Ingraham, "Building Bridges or Burning Them? The President, the Appointees and the Bureaucracy," *Public Administration Review,* September/October 1987, 425–35.

17. This number is based on research conducted by the U.S. Navy, Office of Civilian Personnel.

18. Data from the U.S. Office of Personnel Management, Office of Career Entry.

19. For extensive discussion of CSRA, see Patricia W. Ingraham and David Rosenbloom, Co-Editors, "Symposium on Ten Years of Civil Service Reform," *Policy Studies Journal,* Winter 1989.

20. Van Riper, *History of Civil Service,* 298.

21. Ibid., 304.

22. Lucius Wilmerding, Jr., *Government by Merit* (New York: McGraw-Hill, 1935), 57.

23. See Van Riper, *History of Civil Service,* 426–27.

24. *Final Report of the First Hoover Commission,* in *Basic Documents of American Public Administration, 1776–1950,* ed. Frederick C. Mosher (New York: Holmes and Meier, 1976), 210.

25. Standards are the tools actually used to describe a job and the necessary qualifications for it. The Merit Systems Protection Board notes that "typically, each occupation is covered by a standard that describes the work of the occupation at various grade levels . . . to function, the classification process must bring together three elements—position descriptions, classification standards, and human judgment—to arrive at appropriate conclusions. . . . OPM's qualification standards determine what skills are needed and evaluate whether candidates who apply are basically qualified to perform the work." Merit Systems Protection Board, *OPM's Classification and Qualification Systems: A Renewed Emphasis, A Changing Perspective* (Washington, D.C.: MSPB, November 1989), 6–7.

26. Ibid., 12.

27. Van Riper, *History of Civil Service,* 380.

28. Ibid., 432.

29. Civil Service Commission, *Biography of an Ideal,* 97.

30. Task Force on Education and Training, National Commission on the Public Service, *Investment for Leadership: Education and Training for the Public Service* (Washington, D.C., 1989), 120.

31. George William Curtis, *The Situation* (New York: National Civil Service Reform League, 1886), 17.

32. 413 U.S. 548 (1973).

33. 427 U.S. 347 (1976).

34. 445 U.S. 507 (1980).

35. For a full discussion of the issues surrounding Hatch reform, see chap. 2 of this book.

36. 408 U.S. 564 (1972).

37. 470 U.S. 532 (1985).

38. See David H. Rosenbloom, "What Every Public Personnel Manager Should Know about the Constitution," in *Public Personnel Administration,* ed. Steven Hays and Richard Kearney (Englewood Cliffs, N.J.: Prentice-Hall, 1990), 49–52, for a brief recent analysis.

39. 94 L. Ed.2d 203 (1987).

40. 94 L. Ed.2d 615 (1987).

41. 413 U.S. 548 (1973).

42. This summary of the principles contained in the Intergovernmental Personnel Act is taken from Civil Service Commission, *Biography of an Ideal,* 99–100.

43. P.L. 95–454, 13 October 1978, Civil Service Reform Act of 1978, Title I.

44. Personal interview, National Commission on the Public Service staff, February 1990.

45. Ibid.

46. Personal interview, National Commission on the Public Service staff, March 1990.

47. Ibid.

48. Personal interview, National Commission on the Public Service staff, February 1990.

49. Telephone interview, National Commission on the Public Service staff, December 1989.

50. Ibid.

51. General Accounting Office, *Federal Recruiting and Hiring* (Washington, D.C.: GAO, May 1990).

52. Merit Systems Protection Board, *Federal Personnel Management Since Civil Service Reform* (Washington, D.C.: MSPB, November 1989), 10.

17. The Motivational Bases of Public Service

James L. Perry and Lois Recascino Wise

The past two decades have brought enormous changes in the environment for public service. Beginning in the mid-1960s, public confidence in American institutions began a two-decade decline.[1] Nowhere is the decline in public trust more apparent than in government. At the start of this last decade of the twentieth century, only one in four Americans expressed confidence in government to "do what is right."

The decline in public trust has precipitated a "quiet crisis" in the federal civil service.[2] The recent report of the National Commission on the Public Service, more commonly referred to as the Volcker Commission after its chair, Paul Volcker, the former chairman of the Federal Reserve Board, recited a litany of shortcomings in the federal personnel system.[3] Although no comparable evidence is available on the status of state

SOURCE: "The Motivational Bases of Public Service" by James Perry and Lois Wise, *Public Administration Review:* 50 (May/June 1990). Reprinted by permission of the American Society for Public Administration.

and local government civil service systems, they no doubt have suffered problems similar to those experienced at the federal level.

In the face of these long-term trends and their associated consequences, political leaders have begun to call for a rebirth of the public service ethic. The 1988 presidential race was the first in over a decade in which bureaucrat bashing was not one of the favorite pastimes of the candidates. President Bush has been joined in his call for a renewal of interest in public service by other prominent public servants, including former Secretary of State George Shultz and former Comptroller General Elmer B. Staats.[4]

Calls for a recommitment of Americans to values associated with government service, among them personal sacrifice and duty to the public interest, raise practical questions about the power of these values to stimulate and direct human behavior. At their core, calls for a renewal of public service motivation assume the importance of such motivations for an effective and efficient public service. Those who advocate using public service motivation as the primary steering mechanism for bureaucratic behavior perceive that it is essential for achieving high levels of performance.

At least two developments of recent years, one intellectual and one practical, call into question the strength of a public service ethic. One is the rise of the public choice movement, which is predicated on a model of human behavior that assumes that people are motivated primarily by self interest.[5] According to this view, because self interest is at the root of human behavior, incentives, organizations, and institutions must be designed to recognize and to take advantage of such motivations. A related development, this one arising within government, is the growing popularity of monetary incentive systems, especially at top organizational levels.[6] Extrinsic rewards controlled by one's supervisor are now seen as a major means for directing and reinforcing managerial and executive behavior. These related trends stand in opposition to the view that public service motives energize and direct the behavior of civil servants.

The present study seeks to clarify the nature of public service motivation and to identify and evaluate research related to its effects on public employee behavior. The article reviews existing literature about public service motivation to identify the phenomena more precisely. It then discusses the implications of public service motivation for behavior in public organizations. Needs for future research are discussed in conclusion.

THEORIES OF PUBLIC SERVICE MOTIVATION

Public service is often used as a synonym for government service embracing all those who work in the public sector. But public service signifies much more than one's locus of employment. For example, Elmer Staats has written: "'Public service' is a concept, an attitude, a sense of duty—yes, even a sense of public morality."[7] Staats' observation reflects both the breadth and depth of meaning that has been associated with the idea of public service.

Public service motivation may be understood as an individual's predisposition to respond to motives grounded primarily or uniquely in public institutions and organizations.[8] The term "motives" is used here to mean psychological deficiencies or needs that an individual feels some compulsion to eliminate. Following Knoke and Wright-Isak, this discussion recognizes that these motives may fall into three analyically-distinct categories: rational, normbased, and affective.[9] Rational motives involve actions grounded in individual utility maximization. Norm-based motives refer to actions generated by efforts to conform to norms. Affective motives refer to triggers of behavior that are grounded in emotional responses to various social contexts.

The motivational characteristics of public service have drawn the attention of scholars dating to the beginnings of the field of public administration. The concern that motives affect the quality and content of public outputs is equally long. The most prominent stream of research on public service motivation historically has focused on attitudes of citizens and various elites toward government employment. Most recognizable among these contributions is Leonard White's *The Prestige Value of Public Employment in Chicago* and Kilpatrick, Cummings, and Jennings', *The Image of the Federal Service.*[10] Although prestige is a factor that influences the attractiveness of public sector jobs, it does not set apart the motivational bases of public service from other sectors of employment. Early incentive theorists identified prestige as an incentive derived from the size and growth of an organization.[11]

Despite obvious differences in extrinsic rewards, other research has looked comparatively at motivation levels of public and private managers and generally has found few differences in overall measures of motivation.[12] However, this research has not identified what other motives public employment serves to compensate for its limited appeal to traditional rational motives. Do specific motives exist that are associated with public service primarily or exclusively, and, if there are, what are they?

Rational

Little of the literature on public service motivation acknowledges that some of the motives unique to public service are rational in nature; motives are usually treated as wholly altruistic. A strong case can be made, however, that public service motivation is sometimes grounded in individual utility maximization.

In a recent article, Steven Kelman posed the question: "What are the distinctive advantages that might draw people to government?"[13] One of his answers was that public servants are drawn to government to participate in the formulation of good public policy. Although Kelman associates an individual's desire to participate in the formulation of good public policy with the norm of public spirit, it is likely to appeal to many civil servants in more rational terms. *Participation in the process of policy formulation* can be exciting, dramatic, and reinforcing of an individual's image of self importance. Rawls asserts that a greater realization of self emanates from "skillful and devoted exercises of social duties."[14] Someone drawn to the public sector to participate in policy making may therefore be satisfying personal needs while serving social interests.

Anthony Downs argued that some civil servants are motivated by *commitment to a public program because of* *personal identification* with the program.[15] He offered Billy Mitchell and the military use of aircraft as an example of such a motivational base, but other examples such as J. Edgar Hoover and Hyman Rickover come readily to mind. Rickover, for example, was so dedicated to the nuclearization of the U.S. Navy that, even in the face of opposition to his amassing influence and power, he remained at his post well beyond normal retirement age.

A related rational motive that for many individuals may not be served outside of government is *advocacy for a special interest*. Individuals may be drawn to government or pursue particular courses of action within government because of their belief that their choices will facilitate the interests of special groups. One of the arguments frequently found in the literature on representative bureaucracy is that a widely representative bureaucracy facilitates inclusion of a range of policy perspectives in a society.[16] Such an argument assumes that one motive prevalent in pluralistic societies is an individual's conscious or unconscious advocacy for special interests.

Norm-Based

Frederickson and Hart have argued that one of the primary reasons why American public administration has had difficulty coping in recent years is its excessive and uncritical reliance upon the values of business administration.[17] Careerism has displaced idealism as a guide for bureaucratic behavior, although there are some notable exceptions to this trend.

One of the most commonly identified normative foundations for public employment is *a desire to serve the public interest*.[18] Downs argues that the desire to serve the public interest is essentially altruistic even when the public interest is conceived as an individual's personal opinion. Others may disagree with

Down's interpretation of public interest but still agree that the norm is integral to most conceptions of public service motivation.[19] The role of values such as nationalism and loyalty to country in shaping a career dedicated to public service is reflected in the life of Louis Brownlow. In recounting Brownlow's career on the one-hundredth anniversary of his birth, Barry Karl described a man fully dedicated to the profession of serving the public and totally disinclined from making any personal gains from his work.[20] In *Private Lives of Public Servants,* Kenneth Lasson describes a physician who was similarly motivated. The physician, who joined the Food and Drug Administration to protect the public from inadequately tested drugs, provided the following reflection about his motivations: "I realize, intellectually, that I have accomplished far more in my years at Food and Drug than I could have in private practice. When I helped take 'MER/29' off the market I did more good than a lifetime of seeing individual patients."[21]

A desire to serve the public interest is only one value integral to the construct of public service motivation. Bruce Buchanan, citing Frederick Mosher's classic, *Democracy and the Public Service,* argues that the public service ethic involves a unique sense of *loyalty to duty and to the government as a whole.*[22] Buchanan speculates that this norm derives from the state's sovereign power and the role of public employees as nonelected trustees of portions of this power. Similarly, Heclo has argued that the extent to which public policies are responsive to citizens' preferences is significantly affected by the public bureaucracy.[23]

A related normative anchor for public administrators flows from the concept of *social equity.*[24] Social equity involves activities intended to enhance the well-being of minorities who lack political and economic resources. Frederickson

argues that the obligations of public administrators are threefold: to provide services efficiently and economically while enhancing social equity. He suggests that the inclusion of social equity among the values served by public administrators helps to define the political nature of public administration roles.

Affective

As noted above, some public employees may be motivated by a commitment to a public program because of personal identification with a program. In many instances, however, *commitment to a program* may emanate *from a genuine conviction about its social importance.* The sources of commitment to a program may be difficult to distinguish in practice, but they are conceptually distinct. Luther Gulick captured the distinction in referring to what he termed "the nobility of the great objectives of the public service." He believed that motives derived from service to society would be more lasting than those based on the profit motive.[25]

Frederickson and Hart suggest that the central motive for civil servants should be the *patriotism of benevolence.* They define patriotism of benevolence as "an extensive love of all people within our political boundaries and the imperative that they must be protected in all of the basic rights granted to them by the enabling documents."[26] They go on to suggest that the patriotism of benevolence combines love of regime values and love of others. Although Frederickson and Hart argue that the patriotism of benevolence represents a particular moral position, it also may be understood to describe an emotional state. In fact, the type of moral "heroism" envisioned by Frederickson and Hart may be attainable only through an emotional response to humankind, which brings with it a willingness to sacrifice for others.

Of course, people are a mix of motives, exhibiting combinations of values over a lifetime and focusing on different motives at various points in their careers. Personal or environmental factors might account for changes in individual motives, but clearly an individual can switch among public service motives as well as away from these stimuli altogether. For example, Robert Caro's autobiography of Robert Moses traces his progression from the norm-based motives of a civil service reformer to the rational motives of a power broker. Describing the failure of Moses' attempts to reform the New York City civil service and the lesson that power makes dreams come true that he drew from it, Caro writes:

> The net result of all his work was nothing. There was no civil service standardization. . . . Convinced he was right, he had refused to soil the white suit of idealism with compromise. He had really believed that if his system was right—scientific, logical, fair—and if it got a hearing, the system would be adopted. . . . But Moses had failed in his calculations to give certain factors due weight. He had not sufficiently taken into account greed. He had not sufficiently taken into account self-interest. And, most of all, he had not sufficiently taken into account the need for power.[27]

To summarize, a variety of rational, norm-based, and affective motives appear to be primarily or exclusively associated with public service. This is not to say that all public employees are driven by these needs. Public service motivation is seldom identified with individual utility maximization, but motives such as participation in the process of policy formulation, commitment to a public program because of personal identification with it, and advocacy for

special or private interests are essentially rational in nature. Public service motivation is most commonly associated with particular normative orientations—a desire to serve the public interest, loyalty to duty and to the government as a whole, and social equity. The affective aspects of public service motivation have been relatively neglected and may be the least important component of the overall concept. However, motives such as patriotism of benevolence seem to be grounded in an individual's emotional state.

BEHAVIORAL IMPLICATIONS OF PUBLIC SERVICE MOTIVATION

Of what significance is the public service motivation construct? Although theory has not been well developed, the literature on public administration has contended that what has historically been called the public service ethic and what is defined more formally in the present study as public service motivation has significant behavioral implications. The level and type of an individual's public service motivation and the motivational composition of a public organization's workforce have been posited to influence individual job choice, job performance, and organizational effectiveness. Some of the potential behavioral implications of public service motivation can be summarized in propositional form.

1. *The greater an individual's public service motivation, the more likely the individual will seek membership in a public organization.*

The general attraction-selection framework implied by this proposition has broad acceptance and has received substantial empirical support.[28] It presumes that organizations with certain properties attract and/or select employees with particular personal attributes. These personal attributes, in turn, influence how employees react to the organization. Thus, the proposition suggests that the greater the strengths of rational, norm-based, and affective public service motives are to an individual, the more likely the individual is to seek public organizations as environments in which to satisfy these needs.

Although evidence indicates that public organizations attract different types of individuals than do private organizations, only limited research attention has been given to issues surrounding the individual-organization match.[29] Available empirical research on the attraction-selection framework involving public organizations provides moderate support for a public service motivation-membership relationship. A comparative study of sectoral choice by Blank found that although clear correlations exist between wages and sectoral choice, sectoral choice involves more than wage comparisons.[30] Among Blank's conclusions was that highly educated and more experienced workers are far more likely to choose the public sector, offsetting lower wages with rewards arising from the characteristics of their jobs.

In two studies comparing graduate students about to enter or reenter the profit and nonprofit sectors of the economy, Rawls and his associates found that nonprofit entrants valued helpfulness (working for the welfare of others), cheerfulness, and forgiveness (willing to pardon others) more highly than students bound for the private sector. Nonprofit entrants placed less value on a comfortable life and economic wealth.[31] These empirical findings are strongly supportive of the relationship in proposition one.

Further theoretical support for the proposition is provided by Albert Hirschman. In *Shifting Involvements,* Hirschman described a cycle of collective behavior that shifts over time be-

Table 17.1   Public Service Motives

Rational
Participation in the process of policy formulation.
Commitment to a public program because of personal identification.
Advocacy for a special or private interest.

Norm-Based
A desire to serve the public interest.
Loyalty to duty and to the government as a whole.
Social equity.

Affective
Commitment to a program from a genuine conviction about its social importance.
Patriotism of benevolence.

tween two ends of a public-private continuum.[32] The spectrum is associated with public affairs or civic involvement at one end and private interests at the other. Hirschman argues that shifts along the continuum are products of factors that both pull masses of people into public or private affairs, such as exceptional economic conditions, and, when preferences change, push individuals away from such activities.

The theory is applicable to decisions by individuals about whether to join and remain with public organizations. Hirschman argues that shifting involvements represent preference changes resulting from disappointments experienced in pursuing either public or private interests. It follows that if individuals are drawn to public organizations because of expectations they have about the rewards of public service but those expectations go unfulfilled, they are likely either to revise their preferences and objectives or to seek membership in organizations compatible with their interests. Thus, public service motivation should be understood as a dynamic attribute that changes over time and, therefore, may change an individual's willingness to join and to stay with a public organization.

Collectively perceived frustrations associated with public life or, conversely, with the perceived moral bankruptcy of private pursuits can produce a similar phenomenon on a larger scale. Dramatic shifts in the attractiveness of government service since the early 1960s could be attributed to the types of collective behavior posited by Hirschman's model.[33] More generally, the literature on "the image of public service"[34] often identifies the push and pull factors contributing to mass shifts in preferences for or frustrations with government service that influence recruitment and retention of members.

In their classic book, *Organizations,* March and Simon posit that organizations depend on individuals to make two broad sets of decisions on behalf of the organization: to participate and to perform. Proposition one posited a direct relationship between membership or the decision to participate and public service motivation. Although the evidence is less compelling, proposition two suggests a similar relationship between public service motivation and the decision to perform.

2. *In public organizations, public service motivation is positively related to individual performance.*

Systematic empirical evidence about the relationship between public service motivation and performance does not exist, but other research regarding the effects of motivational factors on individual performance can be drawn upon to support this proposition. The connection between job characteristics and work performance, which is based on the research of Turner and Lawrence, has been examined by a number of different researchers.[35] The expectation is that individuals will be motivated to perform well when they find their work meaningful and believe that they have responsibility for the outcomes of their assigned tasks. Among the job characteristics that contribute to performance motivation are autonomy, task identity, and perceived task significance. It can be argued that these are the attributes that individuals with public service motives derive from public sector employment. For individuals with high levels of public service motivation, significant tasks include those that provide opportunities to address questions of social equity, to express loyalty to country, to advocate a valued special interest, or to pursue social programs.

Public service motivation is likely to be positively related to an individual's organizational commitment. Individuals who are highly committed are likely to be highly motivated to remain with their organizations and to perform. In addition, because committed employees are likely to engage in spontaneous, innovative behaviors on behalf of the organization, such employees are likely to facilitate an organization's adjustment to contingencies. In some instances, public service motivation, by inducing high levels of commitment, may produce negative outcomes. Individuals motivated by public service may carry their commitment beyond reasonable boundaries. Extreme commitment could lead to fanatical behavior, suspension of individual judgment, and the like, i.e., the syndrome that Schein termed "failures of socialization."[36]

3. *Public organizations that attract members with high levels of public service motivation are likely to be less dependent on utilitarian incentives to manage individual performance effectively.*

The question of what sort of motives serve as the principal motivational bases in public organizations is integrally related to the way incentive systems are structured. As a general rule, the incentives that organizations provide are likely to be most effective if they are contingent on the motives of individual members. Thus, organizations whose members are motivated primarily by rational choice are likely to find utilitarian incentives most effective. Organizations whose members are motivated by norm-based and affective considerations must rely more heavily on normative and affectual incentives.

Utilitarian incentives, if maintained at a satisfactory level, are not likely to be critical determinants of outputs where individuals identify with the tasks or mission of the organization. Thus, public organizations that attract employees with high levels of public service motivation will not have to construct incentive systems that are predominantly utilitarian to energize and direct member behavior. Where public service motivation is absent, individual utilitarian benefits may be the most effective incentives. In those instances in which organizational leadership incorrectly matches incentives to motives, the organization is unlikely to reach its maximum potential performance.

The great risk in the current trend of treating the public service like private enterprise is that it fails to acknowledge unique motives underlying public sector employment and the critical linkage between the way a bureaucracy operates in an administrative state and the advancement of social and democratic values. Current crises of ethics and accountability among politically-appointed senior managers in government may be an outgrowth of the idea that management in the public sector is not unique.[37] At the same time, declines in the advancement of social goals may be linked to the emphasis on business management techniques in government. As others have demonstrated, these trends are not unique to the American scene.[38]

Rainey's comparative research on incentives provides empirical support for proposition III. Rainey compared the responses of middle managers in public agencies and private profit-making corporations on a series of scales measuring incentive structures, organizational goal clarity, and individual role characteristics.[39] He found that public managers perceived a weaker relationship between performance and extrinsic rewards. It would have been reasonable to expect differences on scales measuring organizational goal clarity and motivation, but Rainey found no differences. He speculated that different incentives in public organizations act as alternatives to the constrained extrinsic incentive structure and positively influence motivation and effort. In support of this interpretation, he found a comparatively stronger relationship between expected timeliness, quantity and quality of work, and sense of meaningful public service for public sector managers. In a study of public and private managers in Atlanta, Georgia, Baldwin replicated Rainey's results, finding no differences in levels of expressed motivation.[40]

RESEARCH IMPLICATIONS

This study suggests several areas where future research might be focused. An obvious priority is that more research needs to be conducted to explore and test the propositions above and to refine understanding of the behavioral implications of public service motivation. Within this context, an understanding of the way values and incentive structures shift over time is a critical ingredient for developing an understanding of cyclical swings in the popularity of public sector employment.

A second research need is the development of measurement methods that facilitate better understanding of how public service motivation contributes to organizational commitment and performance. A necessary component of efforts to advance understanding of the different aspects of public service motivation is a system for defining and measuring public service motives. The available literature does not provide operational indicators of these motives that can be used in research. Development of a psychometric instrument capable of measuring an individual's public service motivational structures along with a model that operationalizes the linkages between individual values, organizational environment and task structure, and outcome (such as commitment, performance, and job satisfaction) is a critical next step.

A third research priority has a greater applied emphasis: how can public service motives be instilled in potential recruits for government service? The problem of transferring to young people the motives of public service has been addressed by statespersons and researchers. Certainly, the image of the public service is a critical ingredient.[41] The public bureaucracy cannot serve as the 'whipping boy' for politicians and the public and still attract large numbers of excellent young people into its ranks. Some would argue that highly competitive rates of pay are a critical element for a prestigious public sector,[42] but high rates of pay may not attract individuals with high levels of public service motivation.

National initiatives may serve as a catalyst for activating public service motivation. A charismatic leader or collective action can effectively transmit a call for public service. Current discussion in the U.S. Congress has focused on legislation that would provide public service opportunities for young people. These programs are intended to develop normative and affective bases of public service motivation. One idea is to provide a public service experience as a component of high school education. Another approach is to make financial aid for college contingent on public service.

Socialization or inculcation of motives, as Chester I. Barnard labeled it, can also be achieved through managerial techniques both in the pre-entry and entry stages of organizational membership.[43] The identification of common motives and the development of nationalistic motives are the techniques upon which military recruitment and training are based. Similarly, recent college graduates were recruited into a leading edge computer development company by a combination of incentives presented during the job interview process. The chance to participate in an important project, to create a prototype, was a key incentive for young engineers, but they were also attracted by the description of autonomy in job structure and the idea that only the best engineers would be offered jobs.[44]

CONCLUSION

This review suggests that while a crisis in government service is widely recognized, understanding the motives of public servants and the way to stimulate public service motivation are, at best, at a preliminary stage. The popular notion that management in government is not different from private business or industry runs counter to the development and advancement of a theory of public service motivation. The field lacks a clear definition of the different motives that people experience as well as a theoretical context for linking these motives to motivational strategies and incentive structures. Further, a more sophisticated understanding of the effects of cyclical factors on the value of public service employment is fundamental to the development of a working model. Finally, the relationship between individual value structures and the conduct of government remains a critical concern for administrative states where democracy is largely implemented by the bureau-cracy.

NOTES

1. Seymour Martin Lipset and William Schneiders, *The Confidence Gap* (Baltimore, MD: The Johns Hopkins University Press, 1987).
2. Charles H. Levine with the assistance of Rosslyn S. Kleeman, "The Quiet Crisis of the Civil Service: The Federal Personnel System at the Crossroads," Occasional Paper No. 7 (Washington: National Academy of Public Administration, December 1986).
3. *Report of the National Commission on the Public Service* (Washington: National Commission on the Public Service, March 1989).
4. George Schultz, "Public Service in America," (Washington: United States Department of State, Bureau of Public Affairs, Office of Public Communication, January 1989); and Elmer B. Staats, "Public Service and the Public Interest," Public Administration Review, vol. 48 (March/April 1988), pp. 601–605.
5. One of the first and most prominent statements of the public choice perspective is William A. Niskanen, Jr., *Bureaucracy and Representative Government* (Chicago: Aldine-Atherton, 1971).
6. See, among others, Peter Smith Ring and James L. Perry, "Reforming the Upper Levels of the Bureaucracy: A Longitudinal Study of the Senior Executive Service," *Administration and Society,* vol. 15 (May 1983), pp. 119–144; James L. Perry, "Merit Pay in the Public Sector: The Case for a Failure of Theory," *Review of Public Personnel Administration,* vol. 7 (Fall 1986), pp. 57–69; James L.

Perry, Beth Ann Petrakis, and Theodore K. Miller, "Federal Merit Pay, Round II: An Analysis of the Performance Management Recognition System," *Public Administration Review,* vol. 49 (January/February 1989), pp. 29–37.
7. Staats, "Public Service and the Public Interest," p. 601.
8. For an earlier call for research on public service motivation, see Hal G. Rainey, "Reward Preferences Among Public and Private Managers: In Search of the Service Ethic," *American Review of Public Administration,* vol. 16 (Winter 1982), pp. 288–302.
9. David Knoke and Christine Wright-Isak, "Individual Motives and Organizational Incentive Systems," *Research in the Sociology of Organizations,* vol. 1 (1982), pp. 209–254.
10. Leonard D. White, *The Prestige Value of Public Employment (Chicago: University of Chicago Press, 1929); Franklin P. Kilpatrick, Milton C. Cummings, Jr., and M. Kent Jennings,* The Image of the Federal Service (Washington: The Brookings Institution, 1964).
11. Herbert A. Simon, *Administrative Behavior,* 2d ed. (New York: Free Press, 1957), p. 116.
12. See, for example, Hal G. Rainey, "Public Agencies and Private Firms: Incentive Structures, Goals, and Individual Roles," *Administration and Society,* vol. 15 (August 1983), pp. 207–242, and J. Norman Baldwin, "Are We Really Lazy," *Review of Public Personnel Administration,* vol. 4 (Spring 1984), pp. 80–89.
13. Steven Kelman, "'Public Choice' and Public Spirit", *The Public Interest,* no. 87 (Spring 1987), pp. 80–94.
14. John Rawls, *A Theory of Justice* (Cambridge, MA: Belknap Press, 1971).
15. Anthony Downs, *Inside Bureaucracy* (Boston: Little Brown, 1967).

16. Kenneth John Meier, "Representative Bureaucracy: An Empirical Analysis," *The American Political Science Review,* vol. 70 (June 1975), pp. 526–542.

17. H. George Frederickson and David K. Hart, "The Public Service and the Patriotism of Benevolence," *Public Administration Review,* vol. 45 (September/October 1985), pp. 547–553.

18. See, for example, Anthony Downs, *Inside Bureaucracy.*

19. Gary L. Wamsley, Charles T. Goodsell, John A. Rohr, Camilla M. Stivers, Orion F. White, and James F. Wolf, "The Public Administration and the Governance Process: Refocusing the American Dialogue," in Ralph Clark Chandler, ed., *A Centennial History of an American Administrative State* (New York: The Free Press, 1987), pp. 291–317.

20. Barry D. Karl, "Louis Brownlow," *Public Administration Review,* vol. 39 (November/December 1979), pp. 511–516.

21. Kenneth Lasson, *Private Lives of Public Servants* (Bloomington: Indiana University Press, 1978), pp. 81–133.

22. Bruce Buchanan II, "Red Tape and the Service Ethic: Some Unexpected Differences Between Public and Private Managers," *Administration and Society,* vol. 4 (February 1975), pp. 423–444, and Frederick C. Mosher, *Democracy and the Public Service* (New York: Oxford University Press, 1968).

23. Hugh Heclo, *A Government of Strangers: Executive Politics in Washington* (Washington: Brookings Institution, 1977).

24. H. George Frederickson, "Toward a New Public Administration," *Toward a New Public Administration: The Minnowbrook Perspective* (Scranton, PA: Chandler Publishing, 1971), pp. 309–331.

25. Stephen K. Blumberg, "Seven Decades of Public Administration: A Tribute to Luther Gulick," *Public Administration Review,* vol. 41 (March/April 1981), pp. 245–248.

26. Frederickson and Hart, "The Public Service and the Patriotism of Benevolence," *supra.*

27. Robert A. Caro, *The Power Broker: Robert Moses and the Fall of New York* (New York: Knopf, 1974), p. 85.

28. Greg R. Oldham and J. Richard Hackman, "Relationships Between Organizational Structure and Employee Reactions: Comparing Alternative Frameworks," *Administrative Science Quarterly,* vol. 26 (March 1981), pp. 66–83.

29. See James L. Perry and Lyman W. Porter, "Factors Affecting the Context for Motivation in Public Organizations," *Academy of Management Review,* vol. 7 (January 1982), pp. 89–98.

30. Rebecca M. Blank, "An Analysis of Workers' Choice Between Employment in the Public and Private Sectors," *Industrial and Labor Relations Review,* vol. 38, (January 1985), pp. 211–224.

31. James R. Rawls, Robert A. Ullrich, and Oscar Tivis Nelson, Jr., "A Comparison of Managers Entering or Reentering the Profit and Nonprofit Sectors," *Academy of Management Journal,* vol. 18 (September 1975), pp. 616–623.

32. Albert O. Hirschman, *Shifting Involvements: Private Interest and Public Action* (Princeton, NJ: Princeton University Press, 1982).

33. *Idem.*

34. See, for example, Marc Holzer and Jack Rabin, "Public Service: Problems, Professionalism, and Policy Recommendations," *Public Productivity Review,* no. 43 (Fall 1987), pp. 3–12.

35. Arthur N. Turner and Paul R. Lawrence, *Industrial Jobs and the*

Worker (Cambridge, MA: Harvard Graduate School of Business Administration, 1965); Clifford Hurston, "Job Reconstruction in Progress," *Management World,* vol. 17 (March/April 1988), p. 19; Y. Fried and G. R. Ferris, "The Validity of the Job Characteristics Model: A Review and Meta-analysis," *Personnel Psychology,* vol. 40 (Summer 1987), pp. 287–322.

36. Edgar H. Schein, "Organizational Socialization and the Profession of Management," *Industrial Management Review,* vol. 9 (Winter 1968), pp. 1–15.

37. See Candace Hetzner, "Lessons for America One Hundred Years After Pendleton," *Public Productivity Review,* no. 43 (Fall 1987), pp. 15–30, and Frederickson and Hart, "The Public Service and the Patriotism of Benevolence."

38. Patricia W. Ingraham and B. Guy Peters, "The Conundrum of Reform: A Comparative Analysis," *Review of* *Public Personnel Administration,* vol. 8 (Summer 1988), pp. 3–16.

39. Hal G. Rainey, "Public Agencies and Private Firms: Incentive Structures, Goals, and Individual Roles," *supra.*

40. J. Norman Baldwin, "Are We Really Lazy," *supra.*

41. Marc Holzer and Jack Rabin, "Public Service: Problems, Professionalism and Policy Recommendations," *Public Productivity Review,* no. 43 (Fall 1987), pp. 3–13.

42. Twentieth Century Fund, *The Government's Managers: Report of the Twentieth Century Fund Task Force on the Senior Executive Service* (New York: Priority Press, 1987).

43. Chester I. Barnard, *The Functions of the Executive* (Cambridge, MA: Harvard University Press, 1938), pp. 150–152.

44. Tracy Kidder, *The Soul of a New Machine* (New York: Avon Books, 1981).

18.   State Civil Service and Collective Bargaining: Systems in Conflict

Joel M. Douglas

THE NATURE OF THE CONFLICT

The relationship between collective bargaining legislation and state civil service merit systems (CSMS)[1] has generated challenges and obstacles for public personnel administration. Questions remain as to the impact of collective bargaining on preexisting CSMS and the continued authority of public managers

SOURCE: "State Civil Service and Collective Bargaining: Systems in Conflict" by Joel Douglas, *Public Administration Review:* 51 (March/April 1992). Reprinted by permission of the American Society for Public Administration.

to unilaterally prescribe the terms and conditions of employment. CSMS continue to regulate traditional personnel functions; however, states with public employee unions negotiate fringe benefits, compensation programs, time-and-attendance standards, union membership requirements, and labor and management grievance procedures. In some jurisdictions, labor relations systems (LRS), along with conventional CSMS, serve as integral components of public personnel administration. In others, there are jurisdictional clashes, functional overlap and election of forum questions.

Disagreements persist as to the ability of CSMS and LRS to coexist. Many observers rely on conventional wisdom and lack empirical data to substantiate their positions regarding the dominance of one system over the other. Proponents of civil service submit that CSMS are robust healthy organizations and remain the only means to properly staff the bureaucracy. Supporters of LRS claim that civil service has been unable to adapt to recent pressures confronting personnel systems.

The purpose of this article is to explore the statutory relationship between state CSMS and LRS, to verify the existence of conflicting systems, and to ascertain if one prevails. If CSMS are statutorily protected by direct reference or by limits on the scope of bargaining, then it may be argued that the perception of the diminished status of merit systems is false. If the legislation indicates the subjugation of CSMS and broad-scale support for LRS by declaring the supremacy of collective bargaining agreements (CBA) or, by permitting negotiations on subjects that traditionally had been reserved to CSMS, then such observations would be warranted.[2]

This study is statutorily based, structural in design, and does not include or account for bargaining relationships that voluntarily exceed legislated scope of bargaining mandates, administrative rulings, or Public Employment Relations Board (PERB) promulgated case law. The primary questions addressed are to what extent, and in what manner, have labor relation systems been accommodated with preexisting civil service merit systems. The research was limited to states where employees bargain pursuant to either comprehensive legislation or laws pertaining to only state employees.

The evolution of CSMS as unilateral, centralized personnel systems with control over merit rules and regulations, and almost every facet of the employ-

ment relationship, remained virtually unchallenged until the mid-1960s, when public-sector collective bargaining legislation began to emerge. The extensive unionization of public employees was not predicted in either size or intensity. That this period of growth occurred at a time when private-sector union membership was in a period of decline, further documents the uniqueness of this phenomena. As of 1990, public-sector collective bargaining legislation covering state employees, either as part of a generic bill or one limited specifically to them, had been enacted in 28 states. Over 6.3 million public employees, accounting for 37 percent of the public-sector work force, were reported to be represented for the purpose of collective bargaining.[3]

Many CSMS were not adaptable to this new labor relations environment. During this period of collective bargaining growth, tension between civil service and union advocates was evident. Unlike organized labor, civil service has a narrow constituency that has remained relatively passive-reactive. The political strength of public-sector unions was largely responsible for the passage of collective bargaining legislation and other structural changes in the organization, implementation and delivery of personnel services. This is not meant to suggest that the erosion of CSMS can be attributed solely to the growth of unionization; however, the increase in collective bargaining played a major role in this development.[4]

Confrontation between CSMS and LRS over control of specific subject areas has been litigated in several forums, including administrative agencies, state legislatures, courts, and public employment relations boards. One of the more contentious areas of disagreement occurred over the scope of bargaining. Public sector legislation delineates scope as: (1) mandatory subjects that must be bargained, (2) prohibited subjects that may not be bargained, and (3) permissive subjects that may be bargained. Without a statutory ban, the parties in a unionized relationship are free to negotiate those subjects that they believe constitute the whole of the employment relationship. It is within the "permissive" category that most litigation about scope occurs.[5] Unions, employers, and CSMS often have diverse perspectives and claims. CSMS may contend that topics viewed by management as nonmandatory or prohibited, or perceived by unions as mandatory, were traditionally reserved to the civil service and are still under its exclusive province. Demands to enlarge the scope of bargaining and negotiate permissive and/or prohibited subjects, thereby making inroads into managerial prerogatives, have been made by unions. Employers have argued that a topic is prohibited and attempted to remove it from bargaining and potential union control. Scope remains a complex area that reflects several problems addressed in this article.

REVIEW OF THE LITERATURE

The literature on civil service is voluminous, yet there is a paucity of empirical research on the association between CSMS and LRS. The research, reflecting a time-based orientation, is divided into three approaches: accommodation, conflict, and synthesis.

Accommodation

Those writing before the widespread advent of public-sector labor relations suggested that accommodation between traditional CSMS and the newly developing collective bargaining model was necessary; yet, they left no doubt as to the supremacy of the former. Researchers in this category are the most numerous; however, the majority of their work was done in the 1960s and early 1970s before the emergence of public-sector unionization. They envisioned labor relations as a personnel task to be performed within the overall umbrella of CSMS and not deserving special consideration.

The U.S. Civil Service Commission, in the *U.S. Civil Service Commission: A Biography of an Idea,* acknowledged the existence of employee-management relations problems. Included was the need to preserve merit, to keep it and all other public policy issues outside of negotiations, and to clarify the legal framework of bargaining.[6] Others suggested that accommodation was possible, and there was no " . . . inherent pervasive conflict between collective bargaining decisions and merit rules, but rather, diverse impacts on merit administration resulting in some instances in a strengthening and in other instances in a weakening of traditional merit rules."[7] The continuation of merit in collective bargaining, without conflicting with union goals, was urged by some. There were those who maintained that, if certain areas were excluded from the scope of bargaining (i.e., the merit principle) and if CSMS's unilateral authority were limited to items deemed essential to merit implementation, the two systems might coexist.[8] A former president of the American Federation of State, County and Municipal Employees (AFSCME) noted that there was not an "either-or" relationship between CSMS and collective bargaining and suggested that each had its respective place within the labor relations model. In support of this position, he cited AFSCME's international constitution commitment to the promotion of civil service legislation and a career service.[9]

Conflict

Those who foresaw friction between the two systems wrote during the 1970s, a period when public-sector bargaining

RESEARCH DESIGN

Scope of bargaining parameters, statute revocation, and primacy of legislation procedures were examined and the following provisions identified for review:

1. statutorily protected CSMS;
2. subjects reserved exclusively to CSMS and not within the scope of bargaining;
3. statutorily protected LRS and/or CBA that supersede existing CSMS; and
4. subjects reserved exclusively as management rights and not within the scope of bargaining

These categories are not mutually exclusive. For example, a statute might express a philosophical commitment to the merit system and at the same time remove subjects from CSMS jurisdiction, declaring them to be within the scope of bargaining and negotiable. The legislative scope of bargaining with respect to subjects reserved to CSMS or declared a management right, is shown in Table 18.1, and statewide public-sector labor relations legislation for state employees is reported in Appendix 1 [see page 274]. No assessment was made as to the appropriateness of the scope of bargaining determinations or whether a bias was reflected.

The federal government's LRSs were not included in this study. The limited scope of bargaining in the federal sector, as well as other distinguishing features, including the ban against bargaining over salary and other economic issues, creates a model different from state labor relations systems, and, in an attempt to standardize the research, the federal model was excluded.

The lack of impact studies that quantify system effectiveness created a problem in research design and program evaluation. Without documenting civil service or labor relations competency, the strength of either was difficult to ascertain with precision. This article presents a static analysis and may be used as a resource by those seeking a quantified approach. No attempt was undertaken to analyze the behavior and values of legislatures that created a CSMS/LRS framework; however, the data and analysis should be of assistance to policy-makers. Further research in the form of case studies is needed to ascertain the relationship between CSMS/LRS in any specific jurisdiction. This article is limited to the public-sector as there is no private-sector corollary.

was rapidly growing and becoming more established. They acknowledged the existence of conflict, urged reexamination of both systems, and addressed the problems associated with imposing collectively bargained employee's rights on CSMS. Limits on unilateral actions by civil service commissions have diminished to a condition referred to by one observer as "management by itself."[10] Another researcher contrasted CSMS and LRS and referred to labor relations as "the greatest personnel 'add-on' of all times" and noted that the add-on has the potential to develop into the "central thrust of public personnel administration. . . ."[11] Dependent upon one's viewpoint, the add-on may constitute a threat or promise to the system.

The differences between collective bargaining and merit principles focus on the creation of a bilateral employment philosophy and ". . . the extent to which the terms of employment will be based upon collective as distinguished from individual considerations."[12]

The appearance of a proposed Model Public Personnel Administration Law in 1970 fueled the debate concerning the role of collective bargaining within public personnel administration.[13] It recommended the (1) legitimatizing of public-sector collective bargaining, (2) abolishing the Civil Service Commission, and (3) merit system coverage for all public employees. Writing in support of the model law, the former director of the National Civil Service League recommended the passage of state and local government collective bargaining laws, although he cautioned that negotiations be prohibited over the law itself.[14] Opposing the model law, the director of a state civil service commission noted that if collective bargaining were authorized, it "can overcome our merit systems and deliver them into the hands of the union bosses and the politicians."[15]

Synthesis

Those who wrote in the 1980s were aware of the tensions between civil service and collective bargaining and predicted the development of LRS as the dominant model. They argued that the presence of a unionized work force required a sharper delineation of responsibilities and increased authority for CSMS in limited areas.[16] An analysis of Michigan's CSMS and LRS addresses the need for a mechanism to resolve legal conflict between the two.[17] A study

of public-sector labor relations in California noted the emergence of a policy that supports a "limited form of negotiation between employing governments and their employees with respect to compensation and employment conditions."[18]

The literature in the field illustrates the ambiguity concerning the relationship between CSMS and LRS. Most writers acknowledge the existence of difficulties in the administration and delivery of personnel services when the two systems conflict. There is no unanimity regarding structural or programmatic solutions.

LEGISLATIVE DEVELOPMENTS

A content analysis was conducted of all statewide public-sector labor relations laws enacted through 1990. Statutes were identified as either free standing or as amendments to existing civil service legislation. Each was examined in its entirety to determine coverage—encompassing all public workers or specifically limited to state employees (see box).

The outcome of labor relations systems frequently depend upon the legislative, legal, and administrative rules that develop the bargaining framework. There is no national public sector collective bargaining statute; each state and political subdivision is free to enact their own legislation. Consistency among public-sector labor relations legislation is not imperative and variety and experimentation have occurred.[19] Some states have enacted comprehensive collective bargaining statutes while others have limited the process to specific occupational groups. State employees bargain collectively pursuant to legislation in 28 states while in others, they may informally negotiate, but without statutory protection.[20]

Two additional categories of quasi labor relations statutes—grievance procedures and payroll deduction plans—

were noted in the research. Legislated, as opposed to negotiated, employee grievance procedures were found in seven states. In some, they supplemented statewide LRS; in others, the reason for their enactment was less clear.[21] Nine states provided for payroll deduction plans, which employees may use to support employee associations or unions.[22] Nonbargaining states are listed in this study for comparative purposes.

Four categories of treatment concerning the statutory relationship between collective bargaining legislation and civil service systems are evident upon examination.

Statutorily Protected CSMS within Comprehensive Labor Relations Statutes

In this category, CSMS are protected by legislative guarantees to the continuation of, and adherence to, merit systems. This method, found in nine statutes, reaffirms merit principles and systems. Statutorily protected systems are more difficult to erode and/or eliminate. The degrees of protection vary from broad-scale philosophical encouragement to requirements for civil service commissioners to be politically neutral. Some statutes combine these concepts with scope-of-bargaining restrictions and are discussed in the following section, while others treat the issues separately.

Philosophical commitments to merit systems and to strengthening them within collective bargaining parameters are found in Alaska[23] and California.[24] The California statute, however, appears to be weakened by a provision mandating the supremacy of collective bargaining legislation over CSMS for the administration of employer-employee relations. Hawaii forbids the parties from agreeing "to any proposal which would be inconsistent with merit principles. . . ."[25] Maine requires that the obligation to bargain "shall not be construed to be in derogation of or contravene the spirit and intent of the merit system principles and personnel laws."[26] A provision against the erosion of CSMS is found in Vermont.[27]

New Jersey protects existing CSMS, and the rights deriving from it, by guaranteeing the continuation of civil service laws or regulations to civil service employees who may choose unionization.[28] Inconsistencies between collective bargaining legislation and CBAs, and municipal home-rule charters, are precluded in Pennsylvania.[29] Washington permits public employers to refuse to bargain over subjects previously delegated to any CSMS or local personnel board.[30] New Hampshire provides that "Nothing herein shall be construed to diminish the authority of the state personnel commission. . . ."[31] Although not a collective bargaining statute, the Utah State Employees Grievance Procedure requires that members of the state Personnel Review Board maintain a philosophical and sympathetic commitment to merit principles.[32]

Selected Topics Reserved to CSMS and not Subject to Collective Bargaining

CSMS may be statutorily protected by designating certain topics as under their exclusive domain and not within the scope of bargaining. This approach limits the negotiation process. If the topics reserved to CSMS are deemed essential to the employment relationship, then it may be argued that LRS play a subordinate role. Conversely, if the topics are ancillary and the fundamentals of the employment relationship are collectively bargained, then the function of CSMS is weakened. Caution should be exercised when comparing scope of bargaining limitations with subjects that are actually negotiated.

Appointments, conduct of exams, grading of examinations, grievances, hiring and selection, performance rating, position classification, promotion, and retirement have been identified in one or more states as legislatively excluded from the scope of bargaining and deemed under the exclusive jurisdiction of CSMS. These subjects are itemized into three groupings: (1) preemployment procedures and requirements, (2) position classification, and (3) performance appraisal. The preemployment hiring process is one traditionally viewed as a unilateral right of the employer. Topics in this category include initial appointments, the conduct and grading of civil service examinations, and the ranking of candidates for selection. Position classification, a subject fundamental to merit principles, is another area statutorily cited as reserved to CSMS and not bargainable. Performance appraisal and rating has customarily been associated with civil service rules and regulations and is considered essential to the maintenance of an efficient work force. Although an appeals procedure challenging performance evaluations may be negotiable under the "impact theory," the use of ratings is not.

Ten states have enacted legislation which reserve enumerated subjects to CSMS and remove them from the scope of bargaining. New Hampshire restricts bargaining over the policies and procedures of merit system principles, the grading of merit examinations, and matters ". . . relating to recruitment, examination, appointment and advancement under conditions of political neutrality. . . ."[33] Kansas designates subjects which may/may not be contained in the "Memorandum of Agreement." Reserved to civil service are the authority " . . . to conduct and grade merit examinations and to rate candidates in the order of their relative excellence, from which appointments or promotions may be made. . . ."[34] Iowa removes subjects from the scope of bargaining which might ". . . dimin-

ish the authority and power" of CSMS to perform its functions. Included are retirement systems and the authority to ". . . recruit employees, prepare, conduct and grade examinations, rate candidates in order of their relative scores for certification for appointment or promotion or for other matters of classification. . . ."[35]

Ohio identifies certain preemployment practices as not appropriate subjects for negotiations, including "the conduct and grading of civil service examinations, the ratings of candidates, the establishment of eligible lists from the examinations and the original appointments from the eligible lists. . . ."[36] Maine removes " . . . rules and regulations for personnel administration" that pertain to the "initial probationary status" from the obligation to bargain.[37] Connecticut reserves to CSMS selected preemployment merit principles. These subjects, cited as "Prohibited Acts of Employees and Employee Organizations," include the right to ". . . establish, conduct and grade merit examinations and to rate candidates in order of their relative excellence. . . ."[38] Other states that have reserved certain topics to CSMS and exempt from the scope of bargaining include New York, Vermont, and Wisconsin.

Statutorily Protected CBA Supersede Existing CSMS

Supremacy of CBA over CSMS in "choice of law" or other conflict matters is found in nine statutes. In these situations, the labor contract is statutorily protected, presumed superior, and preempts preexisting civil service law. Although it is arguable that absent these provisions the CBA would still take precedence over conflicting CSMS, this is the clearest method of legislating civil service inferiority and demonstrates substantial union political strength. Contractual supremacy is provided in several ways. CBA may (1) take precedence over all aspects of civil service, (2) be restricted only to enumerated subjects, or (3) be limited to employment relationships that provide for grievance arbitration.

The most direct contract supremacy provision is found in Hawaii where the statute provides for the CBA to take precedence over conflicting legislation, including ". . . all contrary local ordinances, executive orders, legislation rules, or regulations adopted by the State, a county or any department or agency thereof, including the departments of personnel services or the civil service commission."[39] Florida provides that the merit system shall not be repealed by the enactment of a labor relations statute. However in the event of conflict between CSMS and LRS, the former does not apply.[40] Similar language is found in Illinois where, in the event of conflict between CSMS and LRS, the negotiated CBA ". . . shall prevail and control."[41] Discretion is minimal in these provisions as contractual supremacy is mandated.

Several states provide for labor contract supremacy with respect to limited subjects. Maine provides that demotion, lay-off, reinstatement, suspension, removal, discharge, and discipline are under the terms of the LRS when the CBA provides for binding grievance arbitration.[42] In Wisconsin, the labor agreement shall ". . . supersede such provisions of civil service and other applicable statutes related to wages, hours and conditions of employment. . . ."[43] If a conflict arises in Massachusetts over matters within the scope of bargaining, the ". . . terms of the collective bargaining agreement shall prevail."[44] CBA preeminence over CSMS and state personnel boards of review is mandated in Ohio for ". . . wages, hours and terms and conditions of public employment . . . "and in situations where there are contractual grievance and binding

arbitration procedures. However, in conflicts involving civil rights, affirmative action, unemployment or worker's compensation, retirement or residency requirements, these laws prevail over the CBA.[45]

Other states have enacted provisions that protect limited segments of the labor relations process if they conflict with CSMS. Washington limits CBA supremacy to conflicts arising over union security provisions.[46] Michigan provides that the labor relations legislation ". . . shall be deemed to apply in so far as the power exists in the legislature to control employment by the state or the emoluments thereof."[47] The New York statute, while not protecting labor agreements per se, mandates that state PERB receive immunity from interference by the state civil service commission. PERB staff who, by nature of their employment, are considered exempt employees, are afforded the privileges and protections of civil service law.[48]

Subjects Statutorily Designated as Exclusively a "Management Right" and not Subject to Collective Bargaining

The removal of topics from the scope of bargaining and declaring them to be a management right not subject to the negotiations process creates a category that signifies dissatisfaction with both CSMS and LRS. Many of these subjects were at one time under civil service jurisdiction. By legislatively reserving them to management, a statutory constraint has been created that, while strengthening employers, weakens both civil service and LRS. This approach represents an attempt to statutorily protect civil service and limit what employees can negotiate. It theoretically maintains bureaucratic control over unions and protects the taxpayer from employee organizations that might otherwise use their political influence to obtain demands.[49] The method used to designate management rights is either a prohibition on the scope of bargaining or a ban on jurisdictions entering into compulsory agreements.

Management-rights subjects are found in 11 statutes. Most reaffirm the authority of public employers to determine agency mission and set performance standards. Florida specifies the right of public employers to " . . . exercise control over its organization and operations, take disciplinary action for proper cause, and relieve its employees from duty because of lack of work"; however, employees or their union may initiate grievances.[50] The management rights provision in Illinois restricts employers from negotiating topics of "inherent managerial policy," except when they affect "wages, hours and terms and conditions of employment as well as the impact thereon. . . ."[51] Montana delineates certain subjects as management prerogatives and prescribes that collective bargaining shall not be construed as a limit on legislative authority with respect to ". . . appropriations for salary and wages, hours, fringe benefits, and other conditions of employment."[52] Nebraska forbids any jurisdiction from entering into a "compulsory agreement" with public employees on a variety of topics, including "grievances, labor disputes, rates of pay, hours of employment or conditions of work."[53] The meaning of this provision is unclear with respect to the requirement to bargain the terms and conditions of employment.

The Ohio law, one of the most detailed in this category, contains a three-part scope of bargaining provision. The first section sets forth the terms and conditions of employment that may be bargained, and the second delineates subjects reserved to CSMS. The third identifies topics reserved as management rights and excluded from the scope of bargaining, unless the public employer otherwise agrees to negotiate.

Due to the comprehensiveness of this provision, it is set forth below in detail for illustrative purposes.

1. Determine matters of inherent managerial policy which include, but are not limited to areas of discretion or policy such as the functions and programs of the public employer, standards of services, its overall budget, utilization of technology, and organizational structure;
2. Direct, supervise, evaluate, or hire employees;
3. Maintain and improve the efficiency and effectiveness of governmental operations;
4. Determine the overall methods, process, means, or personnel by which governmental operations are to be conducted;
5. Suspend, discipline, demote, or discharge for just cause, or lay off, transfer, assign, schedule, promote, or retain employees;
6. Determine the adequacy of the work force;
7. Determine the overall mission of the employer as a unit of government;
8. Effectively manage the work force.[54]

Other states that have legislatively designated subjects as management rights and beyond the scope of bargaining are Illinois, Iowa, Kansas, Minnesota, New Hampshire, and Vermont.

ANALYSIS OF LEGISLATION

The data reflect a variety of attempts at preserving state CSMS while at the same time encouraging the development of LRS. Statewide collective bargaining statutes requiring negotiations and execution of written CBA are evidence of the legislative response to the demand of public employees to alter the nature and structure of employment relationships. In every situation, LRS superseded, but did not replace, existing

CSMS. The failure of state legislatures to implement termination procedures for CSMS or to successfully integrate LRS and CSMS has resulted in numerous problems, including duplicative services, discussed in the next section. No one collective bargaining model emerges as dispositive, yet certain commonalties are evident. CSMS have been derogated by the widespread existence of LRS; however, on the macro level, it is difficult to quantify to what extent.[55] Collective bargaining legislation was not enacted in a vacuum. The 28 statutes included in this study enable state employees to embark upon new forms of governance and bilateral negotiations as to the terms and conditions of employment. The system that previously regulated the employment relationship was CSMS; if it had remained viable in terms of fulfilling its historical mission, then collective bargaining legislation would have been unnecessary.

An examination of the statutes reinforces the position of the LRS advocates. Approximately one-third of the 28 states have enacted provisions expressing support for the continuation or preservation of merit systems; however, the strength of these cannot be determined. Three of the states, Hawaii, Maine, and Washington, also provide for the supremacy of LRS over CSMS when conflicts occur thereby raising questions as to the extent of the continuation of the merit system. It is arguable that the strongest allegiance to CSMS is found in states where the following three conditions are met: (1) a statutory commitment to merit, (2) subjects have been removed from the scope of bargaining and reserved to CSMS, and (3) certain topics have been designated as management rights not subject to bargaining. Only two state statutes, New Hampshire and Vermont, contain all of these criteria. Five states— Iowa, Kansas, New Hampshire, Ohio, and Vermont—have designated subjects as either reserved to CSMS or as a man-

agement right and therefore not bargainable. That so few states have protected civil service in this manner is illustrative of diminished support for that system.

The attempt to integrate collective bargaining statutes within state civil service merit systems is contradictory. CSMS do not evolve into LRS; certain fundamental characteristics inherent in each militate against juxtapositioning. Merit principles based on individualism, open competitive examinations, fitness and efficiency, probationary evaluation periods, and a politically neutral bureaucracy, form the cornerstone of civil service. Although merit principles may be acknowledged and supported by unions, they are not, nor can they be, the building blocks of unionism. The union is an instrument rooted in collectivism, designed to counterbalance the employer and ensure equality and uniform treatment of employees. As long as the determination of merit and fitness possess subjective elements, they cannot be considered legitimate union objectives. These characteristics are associated with both public-sector and private-sector unions, but the absence of CSMS in the private sector minimizes the difficulty.

The doctrine of exclusive primary jurisdiction, the rule specifying the agency charged with responsibility for issuing initial decisions, has been ignored. There is no evidence to document the revocation of existing civil service statutes in favor of more recent LRS legislation. In two states, Ohio and Illinois, which enacted collective bargaining laws during the 1980s, CSMS were not eliminated. Where language supportive of maintaining CSMS is found in collective bargaining legislation, the enforceability of such provisions remains unclear. Support for merit systems is a relatively safe position for policy-makers to assume, but, whether CSMS are stronger because of stated legislative commitment is debatable. Furthermore, such pledges may be hyperbole at best as the incompatibility of the systems may be beyond repair.

Subjects identified in the reserved-to-CSMS category relate to preemployment issues; however, in those jurisdictions where strong LRS exist and the subject is negotiable, there appears to be a practice of leaving these tasks to civil service. Other topics cited as reserved to CSMS are performance rating, position classification, and promotion. Although unions are aware of the importance of these issues, they have been unable to make substantial headway negotiating these subjects into CBAs. Nine states have legislatively removed subjects from the scope of bargaining and reserved them to CSMS.

The structural pattern between civil service and labor relations legislation is consistent. In every state, the civil service statute predates the collective bargaining law. Whereas administrative law principles suggest that the more recent legislation applies, few have a legislative commitment to that effect. Contract supremacy clauses reinforce the position of those who argue that LRS have replaced CSMS as the primary force within public personnel. It is arguable that statutory contractual supremacy is indicative of union political strength and that silence is a matter of individual lawmakers' convenience; without an examination of the legislative history of each act, this point is unknown.

Legislative silence on the scope of negotiations reflects a policy of allowing issues to be litigated. Designating them as a management right eliminates the risk of erosion through collective bargaining. Eleven states have enacted provisions whereby enumerated subjects are reserved as a management right, including traditional civil service functions such as recruitment, hiring, selection, transfer, and promotion. Granting control over preemployment functions to management and not civil service is considered more detrimental to CSMS than LRS because most unions are willing to forego negotiations for workers not yet hired. Their primary concern remains negotiating and protecting benefits and job security for the existing rank and file. The statutory designation of management-right subjects has been at the expense of civil service and further weakens that system. It is difficult to ascertain from a legislative analysis whether the employer actually performs the tasks reserved to it, or if CSMS continues to be the vehicle to implement and administer the process. It is unknown if the removal of topics from civil service control is a transfer of function from what may be perceived as one arm of management to another. An analysis of each jurisdiction's scope-of-bargaining case law is necessary to further assess this issue. Table 18.1 identifies those subjects statutorily removed from the scope of negotiations and reserved to CSMS or designated as a management right.

Topics previously under the exclusive control of CSMS and now categorized as nonmandatory subjects of bargaining continue to have an impact on the terms and conditions of employment. "Impact bargaining," the requirement to bargain the effect of implementing nonmandatory subjects on the terms and conditions of employment, is commonplace and permits a broader range of bargaining than might have been originally intended. Topics included under impact bargaining are often contested and litigation frequently occurs. States that statutorily constrain the scope of bargaining may raise false employee expectations while deterring union political strength. Scope limits may be critical to the preservation of civil service or management rights yet weaken collective bargaining.

Causal inferences should be questioned when assessing the deterioration of CSMS. One might question if the passage of LRS legislation weakened civil

Table 18.1 Subjects Statutorily Removed from the Scope of Bargaining, by State

Number	Subject	Reserved by State to Civil Service	Reserved by State as Management Right
1.	Appointments	CT, IA, KS, ME, NH, OH, WI	
2.	Direction of employees		FL, IA, IL, KS, MN, MT, OH, PA
3.	Discipline		FL, KS, OH
4.	Efficiency/operations		IA, KS, MT, OH, VT
5.	Emergency actions		MT, VT
6.	Examinations/conduct	CT, IA, KS, ME, NH, OH, WI	IL
7.	Examinations/grading	CT, IA, KS, ME, NH, OH	IL
8.	Grievances	MA, NH, NY	NE
9.	Hiring/selection	NH, VT, WI	IA, IL, KS, MN, MT, OH, PA
10.	Mission/goal/determinant		FL, IL, OH
11.	Organization's structure		IL, MN, NH, OH, PA
12.	Performance rating	CT, IA, KS, ME, OH	
13.	Position classification	ME, NY, VT, WI	MT
14.	Promotion	CT, IA, KS, ME, NH, OH, WI	IL, KS, MT, OH, PA
15.	Retention		IL, KS, MT, OH, PA
16.	Retrenchment/layoffs		IA, KS, MT, OH
17.	Retirement systems	IA	
18.	Staffing		KS, MT
19.	Technological changes		MN, NH, OH, PA
20.	Transfer		IL, KS, MT, OH, PA, WI

service or was the system so infirm that it was beyond resuscitation. Causality is difficult to measure in this study; however, it is evident that the collective bargaining legislation did little, if anything, to strengthen CSMS. At best, the legislation appears to reflect a tacit understanding to allow CSMS to continue within the parameters of LRS. The best causality evidence would be case studies on the relationship between the two systems.

THE EMERGENCE OF DUAL PERSONNEL SYSTEMS

The research suggests the emergence of dual personnel systems (DPS), which may be defined as shared systems that attempt to integrate competing elements of CSMS and LRS. They are found in states where collective bargaining laws have been enacted as an addition, or part of, civil service legislation, and where the scope of bargaining is broad. The development of DPS is evidenced by the widespread enactment of public-sector collective bargaining statutes. This has resulted in the creation of an inconsistent legislative framework, one which is difficult to implement and might not accurately reflect existing personnel policy and practice. The task of uniting collective bargaining statutes within existing CSMS has been largely ignored.

DPS may exist as the result of competition between CSMS, LRS, and public employers, over control of subjects designated as management rights. Employee promotions are illustrative of this conflict. In some jurisdictions, this subject is considered within the purview of CSMS, while in others it may either be

Appendix 1   Labor Relations Legislation for State Employees

State	Statute	Date
Alabama	No comprehensive statute	N/A
Alaska	Collective Bargaining in Public Employment Act	1972
Arizona	State Employees: Payroll Deductions Act	1983
Arkansas	State Employees: Payroll Deductions Act	1983
California	Collective Bargaining: State Employee Organizations Act	1971
Colorado	State Employees' Grievance Procedure Act	1973
Connecticut	State Employee Relations Act	1965
Delaware	Public Employees' Right to Bargain and Organize Collectively Act	1965
Florida	Public Employee Relations Act	1974
Georgia	Strikes by State Employees Act	1982
Hawaii	Collective Bargaining in Public Employment Act	1970
Idaho	No comprehensive statute	N/A
Illinois	Public Labor Relations Act	1983
Indiana	No comprehensive statute	N/A
Iowa	Public Employment Relations Act	1974
Kansas	Public Employee Labor Relations Act	1971
Kentucky	No Comprehensive Statute	N/A
Louisiana	Public Employees: Dues Checkoff	1966
Maine	State Employees Labor Relations Act	1969
Maryland	No comprehensive statute	N/A
	State Employees' Grievance Procedure	1977
Massachusetts	Collective Bargaining by Public Employees Act	1973
	State Employee Grievance Procedures	1965
Michigan	Public Employment Relations Act	1978
Minnesota	Public Employment Labor Relations Act	1971
Mississippi	No comprehensive statute	N/A
Missouri	Collective Bargaining by Public Employees Act	1967
Montana	Collective Bargaining for Public Employees Act	1973
Nebraska	Public Employee Bargaining Act	1967
Nevada	State Employees: Checkoff	1981

reserved as a management right or negotiated between the parties. The issue may be further aggravated if the CBA contains promotion criteria rooted in seniority contradicting the CSMS requirement of promotions based on fitness and competitive exams. Another seniority related issue could occur as political subdivisions consolidate services, thereby requiring the dovetailing of seniority lists. Would civil service requirements prevail over negotiated agreements?

Confusion over primary and concurrent jurisdiction, scope of bargaining, and election of forum is commonplace. Questions of a substantive nature regarding employee classification status and procedural questions, once within the exclusive jurisdiction of state civil service commissions, may be now litigated in multiple forums. If CSMS have traditionally exercised control over employee time-and-attendance procedures and the parties subsequently collectively bargain alternate systems, which forum controls? If union demands for wage increases are met with employer support for employee reclassification, can it still be said that position classification remains outside the scope of bargaining?[56] Disputes over performance ratings, licensing and credentialing, public safety training, certification requirements, and performance ratings may also arise when both CSMS and LRS simultaneously attempt regula-

Appendix 1   Labor Relations Legislation for State Employees (Cont.)

State	Statute	Date
New Hampshire	Public Employee Labor Relations Act	1975
New Jersey	Employer-Employee Relations Act	1968
	Public Employees: Dues Deduction	1981
New Mexico	Labor Management Relations in the Classified Service Act	1978
New York	Public Employees' Fair Employment Act	1967
North Carolina	Public Employee Membership in Labor Unions Act	1981
	State Employees: Checkoff	1981
North Dakota	No comprehensive statute	N/A
	Public Employee Dispute Mediation Act	1969
Ohio	Public Employee Bargaining Act	1983
Oklahoma	No comprehensive statute	N/A
Oregon	Collective Bargaining Public Employment Act	1975
Pennsylvania	Public Employee Relations Act	1970
Rhode Island	Collective Bargaining by State Employees Act	1958
South Carolina	State Employees' Grievance Procedure	1982
South Dakota	Public Employees' Unions Act	1969
Tennessee	No comprehensive statute	N/A
	State Employees' Dues Deductions	1980
Texas	Public Employee Collective Bargaining Ban Act	1947
	Public Employees: Checkoff	1967
Utah	No comprehensive statute	N/A
	State Employees' Grievance Procedure	1979
	Public Employees: Checkoff	1969
Vermont	State Employee Labor Relations Act	1969
Virginia	Strikes by State Employees Act	1970
	State Employees' Grievance Procedure	1982
Washington	Public Employees' Collective Bargaining Act	1967
	Union Security Agreements—State Employees Act	1977
West Virginia	State Employees: Checkoff	1982
Wisconsin	State Employment Labor Relations Act	1966
Wyoming	No comprehensive statute	N/A

tion.[57] This study does not recommend the creation of a national public-sector scope-of-bargaining standard; however, these examples are illustrative of the wide range of diversity that exists.

The function of civil service as an impartial arbiter has been called into question. In most unionized jurisdictions, the role of the civil service commission has been diminished and their traditional unilateral rule-making authority reduced to an appellate capacity. Some employees and unions view CSMS as an arm of the administration and not a neutral body and have characterized it as an employer liability in the bargaining process. Concurrent jurisdiction exists either as a theoretical position or at the tolerance of the union. Some unions may support CSMS for a variety of reasons, including using it as a means of limiting management rights. In those jurisdictions where CSMS have authority over some aspect of the terms and conditions of employment, i.e., retirement and health care benefits, unions might perceive a greater opportunity to effect their goals by lobbying a weakened CSMS in lieu of negotiating with an adversarial employer.[58]

DPS have damaged civil service merit systems and while they continue, this research supports the contention that, for state employees, LRS, more than CSMS, have become the primary forces in human resource policy formulation and implementation. Although CSMS retain their legislative basis, in unionized states they have become supporting players and no longer possess a monopoly over public personnel administration. Inconsistent personnel policies have created problems beyond the unionization question. Policymakers must reassess the delivery of human resource services within the parameters of a unionized employment relationship and consider legislation to alleviate the DPS problem. Although it may have been expedient not to address the issue when public sector unionism was in its early stages, avoidance is no longer a viable policy.

In states where collective bargaining laws have been implemented, civil service merit systems have become tired institutions, are in a period of decline, and may be at the twilight of their existence. This is evidenced by the widespread diffusion of its authority and the emergence of strong labor relations systems. In some jurisdictions, the collective bargaining agreement has become a central component of the personnel function. Bilateralism has replaced unilateralism in the decisionmaking process. The problems identified as characteristic of dual personnel systems are political in nature and will remain as long as policymakers see no advantage to change. Living with dual personnel systems is an option widely followed yet not recommended. Collective bargaining does not fit within civil service merit systems. The task ahead is the enactment of statutory revocation provisions for state civil service merit systems that conflict with labor relations systems and the preservation of merit principles within the context of collective bargaining.[59]

NOTES

1. Within the context of this article, civil service systems are defined as statutorily enacted personnel rules and regulations designed to implement merit principles such as recruitment and selection on the basis of knowledge, skills and ability, nondiscrimination, and testing. Characteristics of CSMS include independent bipartisan commissions, government-wide central personnel agency responsibilities, control of the examining function, and enforcing rules pertaining to staffing the bureaucracy. The terms "civil service" and "civil service merit systems" are used interchangeably throughout this article.

2. In addition to being an academic, the author has been a practicing labor relations neutral for over 25 years and has served as a mediator, fact-finder, or arbitrator in hundreds of public-sector labor disputes. The idea for this project grew out of the author's dual experiences as academic/practitioner. The approach used in this article focused on structure, legislation, and administrative law. It is acknowledged that behavior may not be determined from this strategy and there may be other methods of examining this problem; however, they are beyond the parameters of this undertaking.

   Anonymous referees expressed concern that this is not the best available method to ascertain the nature of public-sector labor relations. I agree. However, the primary purpose of this research is to discern the statutory relationship between CSMS and LRS. No attempt was made to distinguish between jurisdictions which have long-standing, mature collective bargaining relationships or where unionization is a relatively new phenomena.

3. U.S. Department of Labor, *Current Wage Developments* (February 1990). These estimates do not represent union membership but only those employees covered by collective bargaining agreements.

4. It is arguable that the decrease in CSMS effectiveness contributed to the development of LRS. This theory may be correct; however, in the absence of any supporting documentation, it remains untested. One is reminded of the statement by Frederick Mosher when he wrote about the relationship between civil service and collective bargaining. "The founders of civil service did not bargain on collective bargaining." *Democracy and the Public Service* (New York: Oxford University Press, 1968), p. 176.

5. Permissive bargaining may occur over subjects that have been classified as neither illegal nor mandatory. The parties are free to bargain these topics if they desire but cannot negotiate them to the point of impasse or strike. Employers may seek to bargain permissive management-rights subjects in exchange for a tradeoff. However, within the context of this article, permissive bargaining is of little concern.

6. *U.S. Civil Service Commission, Biography of an Idea: A History of the Federal Civil Service* (Washington: U.S. Government Printing Office, 1973). For earlier studies of civil service, see Paul Van Riper, *History of the United States Civil Service* (Evanston: Row, 1958), and Leonard D. White, *Government Career Service* (Chicago: University of Chicago Press, 1935).

7. Raymond D. Horton, David Lewin, and James W. Kuhn, "Some Impacts of Collective Bargaining on Local Government: A Diversity Thesis." *Administration and Society,* vol. 7(4) (1976), pp. 497–516.

8. I. B. Helburn and N. D. Bennett, "Public Employee Bargaining and the Merit Principle." *Labor Law Journal,* vol. 23 (1972), pp. 618–629.

9. Jerry Wurf, "Merit: A Union View." *Public Administration Review,* vol. 34, (1974), pp. 431–434.

10. David T. Stanley, *Managing Local Government Under Union Pressure* (Washington: The Brookings Institution, 1972).

11. Chester A. Newland, "Public Personnel Administration: Legalistic Reforms vs. Effectiveness, Efficiency and Economy." *Public Administration Review,* vol. 36 (September–October 1976), p. 532.

12. Frederick C. Mosher, *Democracy and the Public Service* (New York: Oxford University Press, 1968), p. 176.

13. "Model Public Personnel Administration Law," 6th Law (Washington: *National Civil Service League,* 1971).

14. Jean Couturier, "The Model Public Personnel Administration Law: Two Views," *Public Personnel Review,* vol. 32(4) (1971), pp. 202–210.

15. Harold E. Forbes, "The Model Public Personnel Administration Law: Two Views," *Public Personnel Review,* vol. 32(4) (1971), pp. 210–214.

16. Charles Feigenbaum, "Civil Service and Collective Bargaining: Conflict or Compatibility," *Public Personnel Management,* May/June (1974), pp. 244–252.

17. Fred Hustad, "The Legal Conflict Between Civil Service and Collective Bargaining in Michigan," *Public Personnel Review,* vol. 31 (October 1970), pp. 269–272.

18. Winston W. Crouch, *Organized Civil Servants* (Berkeley: University of California Press, 1978).

19. For complete text of statewide public-sector collective bargaining legislation, see *Topical Law Reports—Public Employee Bargaining* (Washington, D.C., Commerce Clearing House, vol. I-III, 1990).

20. Most of the occupation-specific statutes cover police and firefighters.

21. Suggestions have been made that legislated employee grievance procedures are part of a union avoidance policy. Establishing these programs in a nonunion environment enables employers to weaken union organizing drives by granting employees a benefit frequently associated with unionized employment relationships. Another reason for the existence of these processes may be found in federal grant requirements that mandate employee grievance systems in order to qualify for funding.

22. While it is arguable that payroll deduction plans provide a neutral employee benefit, they may also be construed as a means of union development.

23. Alaska, Public Employment Relations Act, ch. 113, L. 1972, sec. 23.40.070.

24. California, Collective Bargaining State Employee Organizations (George Brown Act), sec. 3528–3536, ch. 10.5, div. 4, Title 1, ch. 254, L. 1971 352.

25. Hawaii, Collective Bargaining in Public Employment Act 75, L. 1984, sec. 15, 215(7).

26. Maine, State Employees Labor Relations Act, ch. 9-B, Title 26, Maine Revised Statutes, sec. 979 D, E(2).

27. Vermont, State Employee Labor Relations Act, sec. 904, ch. 27, Title 3, Vermont Statutes Annotated.

28. New Jersey, Employer-Employee Relations Act, ch. 103, L. 1982.

29. Pennsylvania, Public Employee Relations Act, P.L. 563, no. 195, ch. 19, Title 43, Pennsylvania Statutes Annotated, sec. 703.

30. Washington, Public Employees' Collective Bargaining Act, ch. 41.56, Title 41, Revised Code of Washington (1976), sec. 41.56.100.

31. New Hampshire, Public Employee Labor Relations Law, sec. 1–16, ch. 273–A, New Hampshire Revised Statutes Annotated, 1985, sec. 273–A:3, III.

32. Utah, State Employees Grievance Procedure, ch. 139, L. 1979, sec. 67-19-20(2).

33. See note 31.

34. Kansas, Public Employee Labor Relations Act, ch. 345., L. 1981, Kansas Statutes Annotated, sec. 75–4330.

35. Iowa, Public Employment Relations Act, ch. 1037, L. 1978, sec. 9.

36. Ohio, Public Employee Bargaining Law, ch. 4117, Ohio Revised Code, S.B. 133, sec. 4117.08(B).

37. See note 26 at sec. 979–p, E(1).

38. Connecticut, State Employee Relations Act, Public Act 472, L. 1981 and Public Act 83–318, L. 1983, Sec. 3 (sec. 5–272(d)).

39. See note 25 at sec. 89–19.

40. Florida, Public Employee Relations Act, ch. 447, L. 1984, sec. 447.601.

41. Illinois, Public Labor Relations Act, Public Act 83–1012, L. 1983, sec. 15(a).

42. See Maine, note 26 at sec. 961–973, ch. 9–A, sec. 969.

43. Wisconsin, State Employment Labor Relations Act, ch. 111, subchapter V, L. 1981, sec. 111.93(3).

44. Massachusetts, Collective Bargaining By Public Employees, ch. 539, L. 1983, sec. 7 para. 19, 412(7).

45. See note 36 at sec. 4117–10.

46. See note 30 at sec. 41.56.122(1).

47. Michigan, Public Employment Relations Act, Michigan Compiled Laws, sec. 423.3, Act 18, L. 1976, also sec. 423.204a.

48. New York, Public Employees' Fair Employment Act, ch. 392, L. 1967, sec. 205.6.

49. For an analysis of the union bargaining power argument and the need to protect the public from unions, see Wellington and Winter,

The Unions and the Cities (Washington, D.C.: The Brookings Institution, 1971). Arguing against the imposition of the private-sector bargaining model to the public sector, they submit that if it were done, it would result in other political groups being disadvantaged (p. 2).

50. See note 40.

51. See note 41 at sec. 4.

52. Montana, Collective Bargaining for Public Employees, Revised Code of Montana, ch. 31, Title 39, L. 1979.

53. Nebraska, Public Employee Bargaining, Revised Statutes of Nebraska, L.B. 204, L. 1981.

54. See, note 36 at sec. 4117.08 (C)(1).

55. Supporters of CSMS may claim that the indictment of civil service contained here exceeds the stated proofs and that the collective bargaining statutes do not specifically erode that longstanding system. Arguments articulating this position may be fashioned by citing statutes that appear supportive of CSMS or are silent as to LRS dominance. Yet, what is critical to an understanding of the issues raised here is that the very existence of widespread collective bargaining legislation may be the best evidence available to support the claim that LRS, and not CSMS, are the dominant factor in those 28 states where state employees bargain pursuant to statute.

　　In addition to the articles cited in the review of the literature, support for the theories advanced in this article are found in several public administration books. For example, Richard J. Stillman notes: "Finally, the real loser with the advent of public service unions into the internal dynamics of bureaucratic policymaking has been the underlying philosophy and practices of the century-old civil subsystem. Concepts such as merit selection, open competitive exams, nonpartisan civil service boards, and 'color blind' promotions based upon individual competence have yielded in many areas to union concerns about seniority, 'closed shop' union membership, and third-party mediation of disputes by those outside civil service." *The American Bureaucracy* (Chicago: Nelson Hall, 1987, p. 153).

56. While serving as a fact-finder for the State of New York PERB, I was involved in a labor dispute in which position classification became part of the collective bargaining process. In an impasse between a state agency and a union representing over 10,000 employees, compensation emerged as a major point of resistance. The union demanded a 9 percent increase while the state offered 4 percent. A strike appeared imminent and was averted when the state civil service commission unexpectedly announced the reclassification of the job title in which the majority of the unit served. The newly reclassified pay grade resulted in an increase of approximately 5 percent. The union claimed that they had won increases of 9 percent while the employer submitted that they never exceeded their original 4 percent offer, and the civil service reclassification was incidental to bargaining.

57. Pursuant to a CBA between the state of New York and the Civil Service Employees Association, a joint labor-management committee was established to adjudicate complaints over employee performance evaluations and ratings even though a CSMS appeals procedure existed. The committee's charge was to adjudicate employee complaints from those rated less than satisfactory and denied performance increments. The author served as the neutral chair of the committee for a

period of three years until such time that the union withdrew their support for the program. See contractual clauses pertaining to Committee on Work Environment and Productivity (CWEP) in *Collective Bargaining Agreements between State of New York and Civil Service Employees Association* (1978–1981).

58. Employers have suggested to the author that they have used CSMS as a means of circumventing the CBA when the issue of classification and promotion are raised. Seeking to promote employee "A" instead of more senior employee "B" they can challenge union seniority claims by appealing to CSMS that the senior employee is less then qualified. The opposite argument can be raised by unions.

59. A bill to amend the civil service law by abolishing the Department of Civil Service and State Civil Service Commission and " . . . transferring the functions, powers and duties heretofore exercised by them to the department of personnel services and the merit protection commission . . ." was introduced in the New York State Assembly. (See Assembly Bill No. 11879, June 5, 1990.)

SECTION 6

Budgeting

With the possible exception of public personnel, no aspect of U.S. public administration is as controversial and perplexing as budgeting. The federal deficit and taxation are staples of electoral politics and media attention. The issues are many. There are no acceptable simple answers to any of the following questions. How should budgets be constructed? Should expenditures be categorized by programs ("Star Wars"), performance (defense), objects (such as military hardware), or results (peace)? How should they be made; that is, what are the appropriate roles for the executive, legislature, legislative committees, administrative agencies, budgeting agencies (such as the Office of Management and Budget and the Congressional Budget Office), and the courts? When should a budget be balanced, in deficit or in surplus? What accounting procedures will be used? Which taxes are fairest? Most efficient? How much governmental spending and taxation are too much? Indeed, even the distinction between public investment and waste is often in dispute, as when one legislator's effort to help his or her constituents is viewed by others as pork barrel spending.

Ever since the 1910s, American public administration has sought to develop theories and methods of budgeting that would win answers to these and other questions. Vast improvements in the theory and practice of public budgeting have been made. However, ultimately the politics of budgeting is so pervasive that controversy inevitably continues. Despite a great deal of effort, new techniques, and theories, the question posed in our first selection by V. O. Key, Jr., one of this century's great American political scientists, remains perplexing: "On what basis shall it be decided to allocate x dollars to activity A instead of activity B?" Responses abound. Some argue that decisions should be made on the basis of cost-benefit and cost-effective analysis. Others favor greater control by the elected executive, whereas still others favor turning decisions over to the public insofar as feasible. In practice, throughout most of the post–World War II era budget decisions have been made by incremental adjustments to the previous year's budget. Recently, however, incrementalism has been strained by the extent to which governmental outlays have become fixed by earlier policy commitments.

In the second selection, "The Political Economy of Efficiency: Cost-Benefit Analysis, Systems Analysis, and Program Budgeting," Aaron Wildavsky gives what may be the "permanent" answer to Key's question—

"politics." He argues that budgeting is necessarily suffused with political choices and that " . . . economic rationality, however laudable in its own sphere, ought not to swallow up political rationality. . . ."

In "Why Does Government Grow?" James Buchanan, a Nobel Prize laureate in economics, considers the politics of budgeting in a more fundamental sense. He asks the basic question, "Do governments expand in direct response to the demands of ordinary people for more and better public-service programs? Or do governments operate independently of the people, producing results that may not be related to the wishes of the citizens and which, on balance, do the people more harm than good?" Drawing on available evidence and argumentation, Buchanan concludes that ". . . the motivational structure of the governmental bureaucracy [is] the primary source for that part of governmental growth that does not represent response to the demands of citizens for goods and services." He proposes that one way of "reducing excessive governmental spending might be aimed at the motivational structure of bureaucracy rather than at aggregate budgetary or tax levels." This can be accomplished by application of the following principle: "Governmental financing of goods and services must be divorced from direct governmental provision or production of these goods and services." In short, he views privatization, or the private provision of such goods and services through government financing, as the key to stopping excessive governmental spending "in its tracks."

The call for privatization by Buchanan and others has had a substantial impact on public administration at all governmental levels in the United States. The Reagan and Bush administrations broadly favored it, as have many states and municipalities. However, the practice of privatization remains controversial. Which governmental functions should be provided by private organizations? Trash collection? Education? Incarceration? Dispute resolution? Defense? Not all voters, interest groups, and analysts of government are as anxious as Buchanan to remove government from the direct provision of services. They worry about how effective and costly the monitoring of contracts will be, corruption, lack of competition among private firms seeking government contracts, and the tendency of private organizations to engage in "creaming," that is, providing service where it is easiest, rather than doing so universally (private schools and the equivalent of first class mail services, such as Federal Express, provide examples).

In the last selection, "Budget Theory and Budget Practice: How Good the Fit?", Irene Rubin sounds a cautionary note. Theories about budgeting, no matter how appealing, can be off the mark. Rubin examines how normative and descriptive budget theories have fared in the face of political and economic change. She concludes that the normative theories promoted by reformers seeking to use the budget as a decision-making tool for more efficient government have been quite successful. For all their remaining obscurity, budgets are now much clearer, more coherent documents than they were at the beginning of the twentieth century. Rubin notes that nevertheless a number of problems remain, most visibly at the federal level where efforts at deficit reduction have faltered. Descriptive budget theory, by contrast, has had difficulty. Rubin writes: "Incrementalism, which was intended not only as a normative theory but also as a descriptive theory, was dominant and in many ways inadequate. It prevented many budgeters from seeing the changing budget reality in front of them and theorizing about it. As a result, theory and practice grew unacceptably far apart." In particular, incrementalism failed to grapple adequately with the extent to which the budget was fixed on the spending side by entitlements and becoming so on the revenue side by public demands for tax limitations. It also failed to analyze the extent to which budgeting had been centralized in the office of the elected executive in some governments, but not in others. Incredibly, incrementalism had also continued to assert "that policy issues were not dealt with in the budget process"—even after observation suggested otherwise. However, Rubin concludes that now "budgeters have regained the ability to see what is in front of them, and they are beginning to recapture the ability to theorize from what in fact is there. The field is poised for a mushrooming of descriptive theory over the next few years." Normative theory, by contrast, has become fixated on the need to curb national spending and appears to be less effectual than in the past. Taken together, the selections in this section provide a rich overview of the major questions raised by public budgeting. They efficiently capture its full complexity and import.

19.   The Lack of a Budgetary Theory

V. O. Key, Jr.

On the most significant aspect of public budgeting, i.e., the allocation of expenditures among different purposes so as to achieve the greatest return, American budgetary literature is singularly arid. Toilers in the budgetary field have busied themselves primarily with the organization and procedure for budget preparation, the forms for the submission of requests for funds, the form of the budget document itself, and like questions.[1] That these things have deserved the consideration given them cannot be denied when the unbelievable resistance to the adoption of the most rudimentary essentials of budgeting is recalled and their unsatisfactory condition in many jurisdictions even now is observed. Nevertheless, the absorption of energies in the establishment of the mechanical foundations for budgeting has diverted attention from the basic budgeting problem (on the expenditure side), namely: On what basis shall it be decided to allocate x dollars to activity A instead of activity B?

Writers on budgeting say little or nothing about the purely economic aspects of public expenditure. "Economics," says Professor Robbins, "is the science which studies human behavior as a

SOURCE: "The Lack of Budgetary Theory" by V. O. Key, Jr., *American Political Science Review,* Vol. 34, December 1940. Reprinted by permission of the American Political Science Foundation.
[1]See A. E. Buck, *Public Budgeting* (New York, 1929); J. Wilner Sundelson, *Budgetary Methods in National and State Governments* (New York State Tax Commission, Special Report No. 14, 1938); *ibid.,* "Budgetary Principles," *Political Science Quarterly,* Vol. 50, pp. 236–263 (1935).

relationship between ends and scarce means which have alternative uses."[2] Whether budgetary behavior is economic or political is open to fruitless debate; nevertheless, the point of view and the mode of thought of the economic theorist are relevant, both in the study of and action concerning public expenditure. The budget-maker never has enough revenue to meet the requests of all spending agencies, and he must decide (subject, of course, to subsequent legislative action) how scarce means shall be allocated to alternative uses. The completed budgetary document (although the budget-maker may be quite unaware of it) represents a judgment upon how scarce means should be allocated to bring the maximum return in social utility.[3]

In their discussions of the review of estimates, budget authorities rarely go beyond the question of how to judge the estimates for particular functions, i.e., ends; and the approach to the review of the estimate of the individual agency is generally directed toward the efficiency with which the particular end is to be achieved.[4] Even in this sort of review, budget-makers have developed few standards of evaluation, acting, rather, on the basis of their impressionistic judgment, of a rudimentary cost accounting, or, perhaps, of the findings of administrative surveys. For decisions on the requests of individual agencies, the techniques have by no means reached perfection.[5] It is

sometimes possible to compute with fair accuracy whether the increased efficiency from new public works, such as a particular highway project, will warrant the capital outlay. Or, given the desirability of a particular objective, it may be feasible to evaluate fairly precisely alternative means for achieving that end. Whether a particular agency is utilizing, and plans to utilize, its resources with the maximum efficiency is of great importance, but this approach leaves untouched a more fundamental problem. If it is assumed that an agency is operating at maximum efficiency, the question remains whether the function is worth carrying out at all, or whether it should be carried out on a reduced or enlarged scale, with resulting transfers of funds to or from other activities of greater or lesser social utility.

Nor is there found in the works of the public finance experts much enlightenment on the question herein considered. They generally dispose of the subject of

[2]Lionel Robbins, *An Essay on the Nature and Significance of Economic Science* (2nd ed., London, 1935), p. 16.

[3]If the old saying that the state fixes its expenditures and then raises sufficient revenues to meet them were literally true, the budget officer would not be faced by a problem of scarcity. However, there is almost invariably a problem of scarcity in the public economy—to which all budget officers, besieged by spending departments, will testify.

[4]See Buck, *op. cit.,* Chap. 11.

[5]The development of standards for the evaluation of the efficiency of performance of

particular functions—entirely apart from the value of the functions—is as yet in a primitive stage. Such standards, for budgetary purposes at least, require cost accounting, which implies a unit of measurement. A standard of comparison is also implied, such as the performance of the same agency during prior fiscal periods, or the performance of other agencies under like conditions. In the absence of even crude measurement devices, budgetary and appropriating authorities are frequently thrown back upon the alternative of passing on individual items—three clerks, two messengers, seven stenographers, etc.—a practice which often causes exasperation among operating officials. Although our knowledge of budgetary behavior is slight, the surmise is probably correct that questions of the efficiency of operation in achieving a particular end are generally hopelessly intermingled with the determination of the relative value of different ends. Operating officials often shy away from experimentation with devices of measurement, but it may be suggested that measures of the efficiency of performance should tend to divert the attention of budgetary and appropriating officials from concern with internal details to the pivotal question of the relative value of services.

expenditures with a few perfunctory chapters and hurry on to the core of their interest—taxation and other sources of revenue. On the expenditure side, they differentiate, not very plausibly, between productive and unproductive expenditure; they consider the classification of public expenditures; they demonstrate that public expenditures have been increasing; and they discuss the determination of the optimum aggregate of public expenditure; but they do not generally come to grips with the question of the allocation of public revenues among different objects of expenditure.[6] The issue is recognized, as when Pigou says: "As regards the distribution, as distinct from the aggregate cost, of optional government expenditure, it is clear that, just as an individual will get more satisfaction out of his income by maintaining a certain balance between different sorts of expenditure, so also will a community through its government. The principle of balance in both cases is provided by the postulate that resources should be so distributed among different uses that the marginal return of satisfaction is the same for all of them. . . . Expenditure should be distributed between battleships and poor relief in such wise that the last shilling devoted to each of them yields the same real return. We have here, so far as theory goes, a test by means of which the distribution of expenditure along different lines can be settled."[7] But Pigou dismisses the subject with a paragraph, and the discussion by others is not voluminous.[8]

The only American writer on public finance who has given extended attention to the problem of the distribution of expenditures is Mabel Walker. In her *Municipal Expenditures,* she reviews the theories of public expenditure and devises a method for ascertaining the tendencies in distribution of expenditures on the assumption that the way would be pointed to "a norm of expenditures consistent with the state of progress at present achieved by society." While her method would be inapplicable to the federal budget,[9] and would probably be of less relevance in the analysis of state than of municipal expenditures, her study deserves reflective perusal by municipal budget officers and by students of the problem.[10]

Literature skirting the edges of the problem is found in the writings of those economists who have concerned themselves with the economic problems of the socialist state. In recent years, a new critique of socialism has appeared.[11] This attack, in the words of one who attempts to refute it, is ". . . more subtle and technical than the previous ones, based on the supposed inability of a socialist community to solve purely economic problems. . . . What is asserted is that, even with highly developed technique, adequate incentives to activity, and rational control of population, the economic directors of a socialist commonwealth would be unable to balance against each other the worthwhileness of different lines of production or the relative advantages of different ways of producing the same good."[12] Those

[6]See, for example, H. L. Lutz, *Public Finance.*

[7]*A Study in Public Finance* (London, 1928), p. 50. See also E. R. A. Seligman, "The Social Theory of Fiscal Science," *Political Science Quarterly,* Vol. 41, pp. 193–218, 354–383 (1926), and Gerhard Colm, "Theory of Public Expenditures," *Annals of the American Academy of Political and Social Science,* Vol. 183, pp. 1–11 (1930).

[8]For a review of the literature, see Mabel L. Walker, *Municipal Expenditures.* (Baltimore, 1930), Chap. 3.

[9]In this connection, see C. H. Wooddy, *The Growth of the Federal Government, 1916–1932* (New York, 1934).

[10]In the field of state finance, a valuable study has been made by I. M. Labovitz, in *Public Policy and State Finance in Illinois* (Social Science Research Committee, University of Chicago. Publication pending).

[11]See F. A. von Hayek (ed.), *Collectivist Economic Planning* (London, 1935).

[12]H. D. Dickinson, "Price Formation in a Socialist Community," *Economic Journal,*

who believe this problem not insoluble in a socialist economy set out to answer the question: "What is the proper method of determining just what commodities shall be produced from the economic resources at the disposal of a given community?"[13] One would anticipate from those seeking to answer this question some light on the problems of the budget-maker in a capitalist state. But they are concerned only with the pricing of state-produced goods for sale to individuals in a socialist economy. Professor Dickinson, for example, excludes from his discussion goods and services provided in a socialist economy "free of charge to all members of society, as the result of a decision, based on other grounds than market demands, made by some authoritative economic organ of the community."[14] That exclusion removes from consideration the point at issue. Nevertheless, the critics of socialist theory do at least raise essentially the same problem as that posed in the present discussion; and their comment is suggestive.

Various studies of the economics of public works touch the periphery of the problem concerning the allocation of public expenditures. The principal inquiries have been prosecuted under the auspices of the National Resources Plan-

ning Board and its predecessor organizations. These reports, however, are concerned in the main with the question of how much in the aggregate should be spent, and when, in order to function as the most effective absorber of the shocks incidental to cyclical fluctuations. Two studies, by Arthur D. Gayer and John M. Clark, deal with public works outlays as stabilizers of the economic order and with related matters.[15] These works suggest factors relevant in the determination of the total amount of the capital budget; but in them the problem of selection among alternative public works projects is not tackled. In another study, the latter issue is approached by Russell V. Black from a rich background of city planning experience, and he formulates a suggestive but tentative set of criteria for the selection and programming of public works projects.[16]

Planning agencies and professional planners have been more interested in the abstract problem of ascertaining the relative utility of public outlays than has any other group. The issue is stated theoretically in a recent report: "The problem is essentially one of the development of criteria for selecting the objects of public expenditure. As a larger and larger proportion of the national income is spent for public purposes, the sphere of the price system with its freedom of choice of objects of expenditure is more and more restricted. Concurrently, the necessity for developing methods by which public officials may select ob-

---

Vol. 43, pp. 237–250. See also, E. F. M. Durbin, "Economic Calculus in a Planned Economy," *Economic Journal*, Vol. 46, pp. 676–690 (1936), and A. R. Sweezy, "The Economist in a Socialist Economy," in *Explorations in Economics; Notes and Essays Contributed in Honor of F. W. Taussig* (1936), pp. 422–433.

[13]F. M. Taylor, "The Guidance of Production in a Socialist State," *American Economic Review*, Vol. 19, pp. 1–8 (1929).

[14]*Op. cit.*, p. 238. Of Soviet Russia, Brown and Hinrichs say: "In a planned economy, operating if necessary under pressure to accomplish a predetermined production, the decision with regard to major prices is essentially a political one." "The Planned Economy of Soviet Russia," *Political Science Quarterly*, Vol. 46, pp. 362–402 (1931).

[15]J. M. Clark, *Economics of Planning Public Work* (Washington, Government Printing Office, 1935); A. D. Gayer, *Public Works in Prosperity and Depression* (New York, National Bureau of Economic Research, 1935). See also the essay by Simeon E. Leland in National Resources Committee, *Public Works Planning* (Washington, Government Printing Office, 1936).

[16]*Criteria and Planning for Public Works* (Washington, National Resources Board, mimeographed, 1934). See especially pp. 165–168.

jects of expenditure which will bring the greatest utility or return and most accurately achieve social aspirations becomes more pressing. In a sense, this constitutes the central problem of the productive state. If planning is to be 'over-all' planning, it must devise techniques for the balancing of values within a framework that gives due regard both to the diverse interests of the present and to the interests of the future."[17] Planning agencies have not succeeded in formulating any convincing principles, either descriptive or normative, concerning the allocation of public funds, but they have, within limited spheres, created governmental machinery facilitating the consideration of related alternative expenditures. The most impressive example is the Water Resources Committee (of the National Resources Planning Board) and its subsidiary drainage-basin committees.[18] Through this machinery, it is possible to consider alternatives in objectives and sequences of expenditure—questions that would not arise concretely without such machinery. Perhaps the approach toward the practical working out of the issue lies in the canalizing of decisions through the governmental machinery so as to place alternatives in juxtaposition and compel consideration of relative values. This is the effect of many existing institutional arrangements; but the issue is rarely so stated, and the structure of government, particularly the federal-state division, frequently prevents the weighing of alternatives.

It may be argued that for the best performance of individual public functions a high degree of stability in the amount of funds available year after year is desirable, and that the notion that there is, or needs to be, mobility of resources as among functions is erroneous. Considerable weight is undoubtedly to be attached to this view. Yet over periods of a few years important shifts occur in relative financial emphasis on different functions of government. Even in minor adjustments, the small change up or down at the margin may be of considerable significance. Like an individual consumer, the state may have certain minimum expenditures generally agreed upon, but care in weighing the relative utility of alternative expenditures becomes more essential as the point of marginal utility is approached. Moreover, within the public economy, frictions (principally institutional in character) exist to obstruct and delay adjustments in the allocation of resources in keeping with changing wants probably to a greater extent than in the private economy.

Efforts to ascertain more precisely the relative "values" of public services may be thought fruitless because of the influence of pressure groups in the determination of the allocation of funds. Each spending agency has its clientele, which it marshals for battle before budgetary and appropriating agencies.[19] And there are those who might contend that the pattern of expenditures resultant from the interplay of these forces constitutes

---

[17]National Resources Committee, *The Future of State Planning* Washington, Government Printing Office, 1938), p. 19. Mr. J. Reeve has called my attention to the fact that the problem of allocation of public expenditures has come to be more difficult also because of the increasingly large number of alternative purposes of expenditure.

[18]For an approach to the work of the Water Committee in terms somewhat similar to those of this paper, see National Resources Committee, *Progress Report*, December, 1938, pp. 29–36. For an example of the work, see National Resources Committee, *Drainage Basin Problems and Programs, 1937 Revision* (Washington, Government Printing Office, 1938).

[19]See E. B. Logan, "Group Pressures and State Finance," *Annals of the American Academy of Political and Social Science*, Vol. 179, pp. 131–135 (1935), and Dayton David McKean, *Pressures on the Legislature of New Jersey* (New York, 1938), Chap. 5.

a maximization of return from public expenditure, since it presumably reflects the social consensus on the relative values of different services. If this be true, the more efficient utilization of resources would be promoted by the devising of means more accurately to measure the political strength of interests competing for appropriations. That the appropriation bill expresses a social consensus sounds akin to the mystic doctrine of the "general will." Constantly, choices have to be made between the demands of different groups; and it is probably true that factors other than estimates of the relative political strength of contending groups frequently enter into the decisions. The pressure theory suggests the potential development in budget bureaus and related agencies of a strong bureaucracy strategically situated, and with a vested interest in the general welfare, in contrast with the particularistic drives of the spending agencies.

It is not to be concluded that by excogitation a set of principles may be formulated on the basis of which the harassed budget official may devise an automatic technique for the allocation of financial resources. Yet the problem needs study in several directions. Further examination from the viewpoints of economic theory and political philosophy could produce valuable results. The doctrine of marginal utility, developed most finely in the analysis of the market economy, has a ring of unreality when applied to public expenditures. The most advantageous utilization of public funds[20] resolves itself into a matter of value preferences between ends lacking a common denominator.

As such, the question is a problem in political philosophy; keen analyses in these terms would be of the utmost importance in creating an awareness of the problems of the budgetary implementation of programs of political action of whatever shade. The discussion also suggests the desirability of careful and comprehensive analyses of the budgetary process. In detail, what forces go into the making of state budgets? What factors govern decisions of budgetary officials? Precisely what is the rôle of the legislature? On the federal level, the field for inquiry is broader, including not only the central budgetary agency, but departmental budget offices as well. Studies of congressional appropriating processes are especially needed.[21] For the working budget official, the implications of the discussion rest primarily in a point of view in the consideration of estimates in terms of alternatives—decisions which are always made, but not always consciously. For the personnel policy of budget agencies, the question occurs whether almost sole reliance on persons trained primarily in accounting and fiscal procedure is wise. The thousands of little decisions made in budgetary agencies grow by accretion into formidable budgetary documents which from their sheer mass are apt often to overwhelm those with the power of final decision. We need to look carefully at the training and working assumptions of these officials, to the end that the budget may most truly reflect the public interest.[22]

---

[20]This matter is really another facet of the problem of the determination of the "public interest" with which E. P. Herring grapples in *Public Administration and the Public Interest*.

[21]For such studies, useful methodological ideas might be gleaned from Professor Schattschneider's *Politics, Pressures, and the Tariff*.

[22]Helpful comments by I. M. Labovitz and Homer Jones on a preliminary draft of this paper are hereby acknowledged.

20.   The Political Economy of Efficiency: Cost-Benefit Analysis, Systems Analysis, and Program Budgeting

Aaron Wildavsky

"The encroachment of economics upon politics is not difficult to understand. Being political in perspective is viewed as bad; having the perspective of the economist is acclaimed as good. As a discipline, economics has done more with its theory, however inadequate, than has political science. Under some conditions economists can give you some idea of what efficiency requires. It is a rare political scientist who would even concern himself with political rationality. Economists claim to know and work to defend their interests in efficiency: political scientists do not even define their sphere of competence. Thus the market place of ideas is rigged at the start."

There was a day when the meaning of economic efficiency was reasonably clear.

An objective met up with a technician. Efficiency consisted in meeting the objective at the lowest cost or in obtaining the maximum amount of the objective for a specified amount of resources. Let us call this "pure efficiency." The desirability of trying to achieve certain objectives may depend on the cost of achieving them. In this case the analyst (he has graduated from being a mere technician) alters the objective to suit available resources. Let us call this "mixed efficiency." Both pure and mixed efficiency are limited in the sense that they take for granted the existing structure of the political system and work within its boundaries. Yet the economizer, he who values efficiency most dearly, may discover that the most efficient means for accomplishing his ends cannot be secured without altering the machinery for making decisions. He not only alters means and ends (resources and objectives) simultaneously but makes them dependent on changes in political relationships. While he claims no special interest in or expertise concerning the decision apparatus outside of the market place, the economizer pursues efficiency to the heart of the political system. Let us call this "total efficiency." In this vocabulary, then, concepts of efficiency may be pure or mixed, limited or total.

A major purpose of this paper is to take the newest and recently most popular modes of achieving efficiency—cost-benefit analysis, systems analysis, and program budgeting—and show how much more is involved than mere economizing. *Even at the most modest level of cost-benefit analysis, I will try to show that it becomes difficult to maintain pure notions of efficiency. At a higher level, systems analysis is based on a mixed notion of efficiency. And program budgeting at the highest levels*

SOURCE: "The Political Economy of Efficiency: Cost-Benefit Analysis, Systems Analysis, and Program Budgeting," by Aaron Wildavsky, *Public Administration Review:* 26 (December 1966). Reprinted by permission of the American Society for Public Administration.

leaves pure efficiency far behind its over-reaching grasp into the structure of the political system. Program budgeting, it turns out, is a form of systems analysis, that is, political systems analysis.

These modes of analysis are neither good for nothing nor good for everything, and one cannot speak of them as wholly good or bad. It is much more useful to try to specify some conditions under which they would or would not be helpful for various purposes. While such a list could not be exhaustive at this stage, nor permanent at any stage (because of advances in the art), it provides a basis for thinking about what these techniques can and cannot do. Another major purpose of this paper, therefore, is to describe cost-benefit and systems analysis and program budgeting as techniques for decision-making. I shall place particular stress upon what seems to me the most characteristic feature of all three modes of analysis: the aids to calculation designed to get around the vast areas of uncertainty where quantitative analysis leaves off and judgment begins.

COST-BENEFIT ANALYSIS

. . . One can view cost-benefit analysis as anything from an infallible means of reaching the new Utopia to a waste of resources in attempting to measure the unmeasureable.[1]

[1] A. R. Prest and R. Turvey, "Cost-Benefit Analysis: A Survey," *The Economic Journal,* Vol. LXXV, December, 1965, pp. 683–75. I am much indebted to this valuable and discerning survey. I have also relied upon:
Otto Eckstein, "A Survey of the Theory of Public Expenditure Criteria," in *Public Finances: Needs, Sources, and Utilization,* National Bureau of Economic Research (New York, Princeton University Press, 1961), pp. 439–504.

Irving K. Fox and Orris C. Herfindahl, "Attainment of Efficiency in Satisfying De-

The purpose of cost-benefit analysis is to secure an efficient allocation of resources produced by the governmental system in its interaction with the private economy. The nature of efficiency depends on the objectives set up for government. In the field of water resources, where most of the work on cost-benefit analysis has been done, the governmental objective is usually postulated to be an increase in national income. In a crude sense, this means that the costs to whomever may incur them should be less than the benefits to whomever may receive them. The time streams of consumption gained and foregone by a project are its benefits and costs.

The aim of cost-benefit analysis is to maximize "the present value of all benefits less that of all costs, subject to specified restraints."[2] A long view is taken in that costs are estimated not only for the immediate future but also for the life of the project. A wide view is taken in that indirect consequences for others—variously called externalities, side-effects, spillovers, and repercussion effects—are considered. Ideally, all costs and benefits are evaluated. The usual procedure is to estimate the installation costs of the project and spread them over time, thus making them into something like annual costs. To these costs are added

mands for Water Resources," *American Economic Review,* May, 1964, pp. 198–206.

Charles J. Hitch, *On the Choice of Objectives in Systems Studies* (Santa Monica, The RAND Corporation, 1960).

John V. Krutilla, "Is Public Intervention in Water Resources Development Conducive to Economic Efficiency," *Natural Resources Journal,* January, 1966, pp. 60–75.

John V. Krutilla and Otto Eckstein, *Multiple Purpose River Development* (Baltimore, Johns Hopkins Press, 1958).

Roland N. McKean, *Efficiency in Government Through Systems Analysis with Emphasis on Water Resources Development,* (New York, 1958).
[2] Prest and Turvey, *ibid.,* p. 686.

an estimate of annual operating costs. The next step involves estimating the average value of the output by considering the likely number of units produced each year and their probable value in the market place of the future. Intangible, "secondary," benefits may then be considered. These time streams of costs and benefits are discounted so as to obtain the present value of costs and benefits. Projects whose benefits are greater than costs may then be approved, or the cost-benefit ratios may, with allowance for relative size, be used to rank projects in order of desirability.

Underlying Economic and Political Assumptions

A straightforward description of cost-benefit analysis cannot do justice to the powerful assumptions that underlie it or to the many conditions limiting its usefulness. The assumptions involve value judgments that are not always recognized and, when recognized, are not easily handled in practice. The limiting conditions arise partly out of the assumptions and partly out of severe computational difficulties in estimating costs, and especially benefits. Here I can only indicate some major problems.

Cost-benefit analysis is based on superiority in the market place,[3] under competitive conditions and full employment, as the measure of value in society. Any imperfection in the market works against the validity of the results. Unless the same degree of monopoly were found throughout the economy, for example, a governmental body that enjoys

monopolistic control of prices or outputs would not necessarily make the same investment decisions as under free competition. A similar difficulty occurs where the size of a project is large in comparison to the economy, as in some developing nations. The project itself then affects the constellation of relative prices and production against which its efficiency is measured. The assumption based on the classical full employment model is also important because it gives prices special significance. Where manpower is not being utilized, projects may be justified in part as putting this unused resource to work.

The economic model on which cost-benefit analysis depends for its validity is based on a political theory. The idea is that in a free society the economy is to serve the individual's consistent preferences revealed and rationally pursued in the market place. Governments are not supposed to dictate preferences nor make decisions.

This individualist theory assumes as valid the current distribution of income. Preferences are valued in the market place where votes are based on disposable income. Governmental action to achieve efficiency, therefore, inevitably carries with it consequences for the distribution of income. Projects of different size and location and composition will transfer income in different amounts to different people. While economists might estimate the redistributive consequences of various projects, they cannot, on efficiency grounds, specify one or another as preferable. How is this serious problem to be handled?

Benefit-cost analysis is a way of trying to promote economic welfare. But whose welfare? No one knows how to deal with interpersonal comparisons of utility. It cannot be assumed that the desirability of rent supplements versus a highway or dam can be measured on a single utility scale. There is no scientific way to compare losses and gains among

---

[3]In many important areas of policy such as national defense it is not possible to value the product directly in the market place. Since benefits cannot be valued in the same way as costs, it is necessary to resort to a somewhat different type of analysis. Instead of cost-benefit analysis, therefore, the work is usually called cost-effectiveness of cost-utility analysis.

different people or to say that the marginal loss of a dollar to one man is somehow equal to the gain of a dollar by another. The question of whose utility function is to prevail (the analyst versus the people involved, the upstream gainers versus the downstream losers, the direct beneficiaries versus the taxpayers, the entire nation or a particular region, and so on) is of prime importance in making public policy.

The literature on welfare economics is notably unable to specify an objective welfare function.[4] Ideally, actions would benefit everyone and harm no one. As an approximation, the welfare economist views as optimal an action that leaves some people better off and none worse off. If this criterion were applied in political life, it would result in a situation like that of the Polish Diet in which anyone who was damaged could veto legislation. To provide a way out of this impasse, Hicks and Kaldor proposed approval of decisions if the total gain in welfare is such that the winners could compensate the losers. But formal machinery for compensation does not ordinarily exist and most modern economists are highly critical of the major political mechanism for attempting to compensate, namely, log-rolling in Congress on public works projects.[5] It is a

very imperfect mechanism for assuring that losers in one instance become winners in another.

Another way of dealing with income distribution is to accept a criterion laid down by a political body and maximize present benefits less costs subject to this constraint. Or the cost-benefit analyst can present a series of alternatives differing according to the individuals who pay and prices charged. The analyst must not only compute the new inputs and outputs, but also the costs and benefits for each group with whom the public authorities are especially concerned. No wonder this is not often done! Prest and Turvey are uncertain whether such a procedure is actually helpful in practice.[6]

Income redistribution in its most extreme form would result in a complete leveling or equality of incomes. Clearly, this is not what is meant. A more practical meaning might be distributing income to the point where specific groups achieve a certain minimum. It is also possible that the operational meaning of income redistribution may simply be the transfer of some income from some haves to some have nots. Even in the last and most minimal sense of the term it is by no means clear that projects that are inefficient by the usual economic criteria serve to redistribute income in the desired direction. It is possible that some inefficient projects may transfer income from poorer to richer people. Before the claim that certain projects are justified by the effect of distributing income in a specified way can be accepted, an analysis to show that this is what actually happens must be at hand.

Since the distribution of income is at stake, it is not surprising that beneficia-

[4]A. Bergson, "A Reformulation of Certain Aspects of Welfare Economics," *Quarterly Journal of Economics*, February, 1938; N. Kaldor, "Welfare Propositions and Interpersonal Comparisons of Utility," *Economic Journal*, 1939, pp. 549–52; J. R. Hicks, "The Valuation of Social Income," *Economics*, 1940, pp. 105–24; I. M. D. Little, *A Critique of Welfare Economics* (Oxford, 1950); W. J. Baumol, *Welfare Economics and the Theory of the State* (Cambridge, 1952); T. Scitovsky, "A Note on Welfare Propositions in Economics," *Review of Economic Studies*, 1942, pp. 98–110; J. E. Meade, *The Theory of International Economic Policy*, Vol. II: *Trade and Welfare* (New York, 1954).

[5]For a different view, see James M. Buchanan and Gordon Tullock, *The Calculus of Consent: Logical Foundations of Constitu-

tional Democracy* (Ann Arbor, University of Michigan Press, 1962).

[6]Prest and Turvey, *op. cit.*, p. 702. For a contrary view, see Arthur Maas, "Benefit-Cost Analysis: Its Relevance to Public Investment Decisions," Vol. LXXX, *The Quarterly Journal of Economics*, May, 1966, pp. 208–226.

ries tend to dominate investment decisions in the political arena and steadfastly refuse to pay for what they receive from government tax revenues. They uniformly resist user charges based on benefits received. Fox and Herfindahl estimate that of a total initial investment of three billion for the Corps of Engineers in 1962, taxpayers in general would pay close to two-thirds of the costs.[7] Here, greater use of the facilities by a larger number of beneficiaries getting something for nothing inflates the estimated benefits which justify the project in the first place. There may be a political rationale for these decisions, but it has not been developed.

In addition to redistributing income, public works projects have a multitude of objectives and consequences. Projects may generate economic growth, alleviate poverty among some people, provide aesthetic enjoyment and opportunities for recreation, improve public health, reduce the risks of natural disaster, alter travel patterns, affect church attendance, change educational opportunities, and more. No single welfare criterion can encompass these diverse objectives. How many of them should be considered? Which are susceptible of quantification? The further one pursues this analysis, the more impassable the thicket.

Limitations in the Utility of Cost-Benefit Analysis

One possible conclusion is that at present certain types of cost-benefit analysis are not meaningful. In reviewing the literature on the calculus of costs and benefits in research and development, for example, Prest and Turvey comment on "the uncertainty and unreliability of cost estimates . . . and . . . the extraor-

dinarily complex nature of the benefits. . . ."[8]

Another conclusion is that one should be cautious in distinguishing the degree to which projects are amenable to cost-benefit analysis.

. . . When there are many diverse types of benefits from a project and/or many different beneficiaries it is difficult to list them all and to avoid double counting. This is one reason why it is so much easier to apply cost-benefit analysis to a limited purpose development, say, than it is to the research and development aspects of some multi-purpose discovery, such as a new type of plastic material. . . . It is no good expecting those fields in which benefits are widely diffused, and in which there are manifest divergences between accounting and economic costs or benefits, to be as cultivable as others. Nor is it realistic to expect that comparisons between projects in entirely different branches of economic activity are likely to be as meaningful or fruitful as those between projects in the same branch. The technique is more useful in the public-utility area than in the social-services area of government.[9]

If the analysis is to be useful at all, calculations must be simplified.[10] The multiple ramifications of interesting activities can be taken into account only at the cost of introducing fantastic complexities. Prest and Turvey remark of one such attempt, that "This system . . . requires knowledge of all the demand and supply equations in the economy, so is scarcely capable of application by road engineers."[11] They suggest omitting

---

[7]Irving K. Fox and Orris C. Herfindahl, "Attainment of Efficiency in Satisfying Demands for Water Resources," *American Economic Review,* May, 1964, p. 200.

[8]Prest and Turvey, *Op. Cit.,* p. 727.
[9]*Ibid.,* pp. 729, 731.
[10]David Braybrooke and Charles Lindblom, *A Strategy for Decision* (New York, 1963).
[11]Prest and Turvey, *op. cit.,* p. 714.

consideration where (1) side effects are judged not terribly large or where (2) concern for these effects belongs to another governmental jurisdiction.[12]

If certain costs or benefits are deemed important but cannot be quantified, it is always possible to guess. The increasing use of recreation and aesthetic facilities to justify public works projects in the United States is disapproved by most economists because there can be a vast, but hidden, inflation of these benefits. For example, to attribute the same value to a recreation day on a reservoir located in a desert miles from any substitute source of water as to a day on an artificial lake in the heart of natural lake country is patently wrong. Economists would prefer to see recreation facilities listed in an appendix so that they can be taken into account in some sense, or, alternatively, that the project be presented with and without the recreation facilities, so that a judgment can be made as to whether the additional services are worth the cost.[13]

Economists distinguish between risk, where the precise outcome cannot be predicted but a probability distribution can be specified, and uncertainty, where

one does not even know the parameters of the outcomes. The cost-benefit analyst must learn to live with uncertainty, for he can never know whether all relevant objectives have been included and what changes may occur in policy and in technology.

It is easy enough to cut the life of the project below its expected economic life. The interest rate can be raised. Assumptions can be made that costs will be higher and benefits lower than expected. All these methods, essentially conservative, are also highly arbitrary. They can be made somewhat more systematic, however, by sensitivity analysis in which length of life, for instance, is varied over a series of runs so that its impact on the project can be appraised.

Lessening uncertainty by hiking the interest or discount rate leads to greater difficulties, for the dominance of "higher" criteria over economic analysis is apparent in the frustrating problem of choosing the correct interest rate at which to discount the time streams of costs and benefits essential to the enterprise. Only an interest rate can establish the relationship between values at different periods of time. Yet people differ in preferences for the present versus the intermediate or long-run value. Moreover, the interest rate should also measure the opportunity cost of private capital that could be used to produce wealth elsewhere in the economy if it had not been used up in the form of tax income spent on the project under consideration. Is the appropriate rate the very low cost the government charges, the cost of a government corporation like TVA that must pay a somewhat higher rate, the going rate of interest for private firms, or an even higher rate to hedge against an uncertain future? As Otto Eckstein has observed, " . . . the choice of interest rates must remain a value judgment."[14]

[12]*Ibid.*, p. 705.

[13]See Jack L. Knetch, "Economics of Including Recreation as a Purpose of Water Resource Projects," *Journal of Farm Economics,* December, 1964, p. 1155. No one living in Berkeley, where "a view" is part of the cost of housing, could believe that aesthetic values are forever going to remain beyond the ingenuity of the quantifier. There are also costs and benefits, such as the saving and losing of human life, that can be quantified but can only be valued in the market place in a most peculiar (or ghoulish) sense. See Burton Weisbrod, *The Economics of Public Health; Measuring the Economic Impact of Diseases* (Philadelphia, 1961), for creative attempt to place a market value on human life. Few of us would want to make decisions about public health by use of this criterion, not at least if we were the old person whose future social value contribution is less than his cost to the authorities.

[14]Otto Eckstein, *op. cit.,* p. 460.

If the efficiency of a project is insensitive to interest costs, then these costs can vary widely without mattering much. But Fox and Herfindahl discovered that if Corps of Engineer projects raised their interest (or discount) rate from 2⅝ to 4, 6, or 8 per cent, then 9, 64, and 80 per cent of their projects, respectively, would have had a benefit-cost ratio of less than unity.[15] This single value choice among many has such large consequences that it alone may be decisive.

The Mixed Results of Cost-Benefit Analysis

Although cost-benefit analysis presumably results in efficiency by adding the most to national income, it is shot through with political and social value choices and surrounded by uncertainties and difficulties of computation. Whether the many noneconomic assumptions and consequences actually result in basically changing the nature of a project remains moot. Clearly, we have come a long way from pure efficiency, to verge upon mixed efficiency.

Economic analysts usually agree that all relevant factors (especially nonmarket factors) cannot be squeezed into a single formula. They therefore suggest that the policy maker, in being given the market costs and benefits of alternatives, is, in effect, presented with the market value he is placing on nonmarket factors. The contribution of the analyst is only one input into the decision, but the analyst may find this limited conception of his role unacceptable to others. Policy makers may not want this kind of input; they may want *the* answer, or at least an answer that they can defend on the basis of the analyst's legitimized expertise.

The dependence of cost-benefit analysis on a prior political framework does not mean that it is a useless or trivial ex-

ercise. Decisions must be made. If quantifiable economic costs and benefits are not everything, neither would a decision-maker wish to ignore them entirely. The great advantage of cost-benefit analysis, when pursued with integrity, is that some implicit judgments are made explicit and subject to analysis. Yet, for many, the omission of explicit consideration of political factors is a serious deficiency.

The experience of the Soil Conservation Service in lowering certain political costs may prove illuminating. For many years the Service struggled along with eleven major watershed projects involving big dams, great headaches, and little progress. Because the watersheds were confined to a single region, it was exceedingly difficult to generate support in Congress, particularly at appropriations time. The upstream-downstream controversies generated by these projects resulted in less than universal local approval. The SCS found itself in the direct line of fire for determining priorities in use of insufficient funds.

Compare this situation with the breakthrough which occurred when SCS developed the small watershed program. Since each facility is relatively inexpensive, large numbers can be placed throughout the country, markedly increasing political support. Agreement on the local level is facilitated because much less land is flooded and side payments are easier to arrange. A judicious use of cost-benefit analysis, together with ingenious relationships with State governors, places the choice of priorities with the States and yet maintains a reasonable level of consistency by virtue of adherence to national criteria. Errors are easier to correct because the burden of calculation has been drastically reduced and experience may be more easily accumulated with a larger number of small projects.

Consider the situation in which an agency finds it desirable to achieve a ge-

[15]Fox and Herfindahl, *op. cit.*, p. 202.

ographical spread of projects in order to establish a wider base of support. Assume (with good reason) that cost-benefit criteria will not permit projects to be established in some states because the value of the land or water is too low. One can say that this is just too bad and observe the agency seeking ways around the restriction by playing up benefits, playing down costs, or attacking the whole benefit cost concept as inapplicable. Another approach would be to recognize that federalism—meaning, realistically, the distribution of indulgences to State units—represents a political value worth promoting to some extent and that gaining nation-wide support is important. From this perspective, a compromise solution would be to except one or two projects in each State or region from meeting the full requirement of the formula, though the projects with the highest benefit-cost ratio would have to be chosen. In return for sacrificing full adherence to the formula in a few instances, one would get enhanced support for it in many others.

Everyone knows, of course, that cost-benefit analysis is not the messiah come to save water resources projects from contamination by the rival forces of ignorance and political corruption. Whenever agencies and their associated interests discover that they cannot do what they want, they may twist prevailing criteria out of shape: Two projects may be joined so that both qualify when one, standing alone, would not. Costs and benefits may be manipulated, or the categories may be so extended that almost any project qualifies. On the other hand, cost-benefit analysis has some "good" political uses that might be stressed more than they have been. The technique gives the responsible official a good reason for turning down projects, with a public-interest explanation the Congressman can use with his constituents and the interest-group leader with his members.

This is not to say that cost-benefit analysis has little utility. Assuming that the method will continue to be improved, and that one accepts the market as the measure of economic value, it can certainly tell decision makers something about what they will be giving up if they follow alternative policies. The use of two analyses, one based on regional and the other on national factors, might result in an appraisal of the economic costs of federalism.

The burden of calculation may be reduced by following cost-benefit analysis for many projects and introducing other values only for a few. To expect, however, that the method itself (which distributes indulgences to some and deprivations to others) would not be subject to manipulation in the political process is to say that we shall be governed by formula and not by men.

Because the cost-benefit formula does not always jibe with political realities—that is, it omits political costs and benefits—we can expect it to be twisted out of shape from time to time. Yet cost-benefit analysis may still be important in getting rid of the worst projects. Avoiding the worst where one can't get the best is no small accomplishment.

SYSTEMS ANALYSIS

The good systems analyst is a "chochem," a Yiddish word meaning "wise man," with overtones of "wise guy." His forte is creativity. Although he sometimes relates means to ends and fits ends to match means, he ordinarily eschews such pat processes, preferring instead to relate elements imaginatively into new systems that create their own means and ends. He plays new objectives continuously against cost elements until a creative synthesis has been achieved. He looks down upon those who say that they take objectives as given, knowing full well that the apparent solidity of the objective will dissipate during analysis and that, in any case, most people do not know what they want because they do not know what they can get.

Since no one knows how to teach creativity, daring, and nerve, it is not surprising that no one can define what systems analysis is or how it should be practiced. E. S. Quade, who compiled the RAND Corporation lectures on systems analysis, says it "is still largely a form of art" in which it is not possible to lay down "fixed rules which need only be followed with exactness."[16] He examined systems studies to determine ideas and principles common to the good ones, but discovered that "no universally accepted set of ideas existed. It was even difficult to decide which studies should be called good."[17]

Systems analysis is derived from operations research, which came into use during World War II when some scientists discovered that they could use simple quantitative analysis to get the most out of existing military equipment. A reasonably clear objective was given, and ways to cut the cost of achieving it could be developed, using essentially statistical models. Operations research today is largely identified with specific techniques: linear programming; Monte Carlo (randomizing) methods; gaming and game theory. While there is no hard and fast division between operations research and systems analysis, a rough separation may perhaps be made. The less that is known about objectives, the more they conflict, the larger the number of elements to be considered, the more uncertain the environment, the more likely it is that the work will be called a systems analysis. In systems analysis there is more judgment and intuition and less reliance on quantitative methods than in operations research.

Systems analysis builds models that abstract from reality but represent the crucial relationships. The systems analyst first decides what questions are relevant to his inquiry, selects certain quantifiable factors, cuts down the list of factors to be dealt with by aggregation and by eliminating the (hopefully) less important ones, and then gives them quantitative relationships with one another within the system he has chosen for analysis. But crucial variables may not be quantifiable. If they can be reduced to numbers, there may be no mathematical function that can express the desired relationship. More important, there may be no single criterion for judging results among conflicting objectives. Most important, the original objectives, if any, may not make sense.

It cannot be emphasized too strongly that a (if not the) distinguishing characteristic of systems analysis is that the objectives are either not known or are subject to change. Systems analysis, Quade tells us, "is associated with that class of problems where the difficulties lie in deciding what ought to be done— not simply how to do it—and honors go to people who . . . find out what the problem is"[18] Charles Hitch, the former Comptroller of the Defense Department, insists that:

> . . . learning about objectives is one of the chief objects of this kind of analysis. We must learn to look at objectives as critically and as professionally as we look at our models and our other inputs. We may, of course, begin with tentative objectives, but we must expect to modify or replace them as we learn about the systems we are studying—and related systems. The feedback on objectives may in some cases be the most important result of our study. We have never undertaken a major system study at RAND in

---

[16]E. S. Quade, *Analysis for Military Decisions* (Chicago, 1964), p. 153.

[17]*Ibid.*, p. 149.

[18]*Ibid.*, p. 7.

which we are able to define satisfactory objectives at the beginning of the study.[19]

Systems analysts recognize many good reasons for their difficulties in defining problems or objectives. Quade reaches the core: "Objectives are not, in fact, agreed upon. The choice, while ostensibly between alternatives, is really between objectives or ends and nonanalytic methods must be used for a final reconciliation of views."[20] It may be comforting to believe that objectives come to the analyst from on high and can be taken as given, but this easy assumption is all wrong. "For all sorts of good reasons that are not about to change," says Hitch, "official statements of national objectives (or company objectives) tend to be nonexistent or so vague and literary as to be non-operational."[21] Objectives are not only likely to be "thin and rarified," according to Wohlstetter, but the relevant authorities "are likely to conflict. Among others there will be national differences within an alliance and within the nation, interagency, interservice, and intraservice differences. . . ."[22]

Moreover, even shared objectives often conflict with one another. Deterrence of atomic attack might be best served by letting an enemy know that we would respond with an all-out, indiscriminate attack on his population. Defense of our population against death and destruction might not be well served by this strategy,[23] as the Secretary of Defense recognized when he recommended a city-avoidance strategy that might give an enemy some incentive to spare our cities as well. Not only are objectives large in number and in conflict with one another, they are likely to engender serious repercussion effects. Many objectives, like morale and the stability of alliances, are resistant to quantification. What is worth doing depends on whether it can be done at all, how well, and at what cost. Hence, objectives really cannot be taken as given; they must be made up by the analyst. "In fact," Wohlstetter declares, "we are always in the process of choosing and modifying both means and ends."[24]

Future systems analysts are explicitly warned not to let clients determine objectives. A suggestive analogy is drawn with the doctor who would not ignore a patient's "description of his symptoms, but . . . cannot allow the patient's self diagnosis to override his own professional judgment."[25] Quade argues that since systems analysis has often resulted in changing the original objectives of the policy-maker, it would be "self-defeating to accept without inquiry" his "view of what the problem is."[26]

I have stressed the point that the systems analyst is advised to insist on his own formulation of the problem because it shows so closely that we are dealing with a mixed concept of efficiency.

Adjusting objectives to resources in the present or near future is difficult enough without considering future states of affairs which hold tremendous uncertainty. Constants become variables; little can be taken for granted. The rate of technological progress, an opponent's estimate of your reaction to his latest series of moves based on his reaction to yours, whether or not atomic war will occur, what it will be like, whether

---

[19]Charles J. Hitch, *op. cit.*, p. 19.
[20]E. S. Quade, *op. cit.*, p. 176.
[21]Charles J. Hitch, *op. cit.*, pp. 4–5.
[22]Albert Wohlstetter, "Analysis and Design of Conflict Systems," in E. S. Quade, *op. cit.*, p. 121.
[23]See Glenn H. Snyder, *Deterrence and Defense* (Princeton, 1961).

[24]Wohlstetter in Quade, *op. cit.*, p. 122.
[25]E. S. Quade, *op. cit.*, p. 157. Quade attempts to soften the blow by saying that businessmen and military officers know more about their business than any one else. But the import of the analogy is clear enough.
[26]*Ibid.*, pp. 156–57.

we shall have warning, whether the system we are working on will cost anything close to current estimates and whether it will be ready within five years of the due date—on most of these matters, there are no objective probabilities to be calculated.

An effective dealing with uncertainty must be a major goal of systems analysis. Systems analysis is characterized by the aids to calculation it uses, not to conquer, but to circumvent and mitigate some of the pervasive effects of uncertainty. Before a seemingly important factor may be omitted, for example, a sensitivity analysis may be run to determine whether its variation significantly affects the outcome. If there is no good basis for calculating the value of the factor, arbitrary values may be assigned to test for extreme possibilities. Contingency analysis is used to determine how the relative ranking of alternatives holds up under major changes in the environment, say, a new alliance between France and Russia, or alterations in the criteria for judging the alternatives, such as a requirement that a system work well against attacks from space as well as earth. Contingency analysis places a premium on versatility as the analyst seeks a system that will hold up well under various eventualities even though it might be quite as good for any single contingency as an alternative system. Adversary procedures may be used to combat uncertainty. Bending over backwards to provide advantages for low ranking systems and handicaps for high ranking systems is called a fortiori analysis. Changing crucial assumptions in order to make the leading alternatives even, so that one can judge whether the assumptions are overly optimistic or pessimistic, is called break-even analysis.[27] Since all these methods add greatly to the burden of calculation, they must be used with some discretion.

A variety of insurance schemes may also be used to deal with uncertainty. In appraising what an opponent can do, for instance, one can assume the worst, the best, and sheer inertia. In regard to the development of weapons, insurance requires not one flexible weapon but a variety of alternatives pursued with vigor. As development goes on, uncertainty is reduced. Consequently, basic strategic choice involves determining how worthwhile paying for the additional information is by developing rival weapons systems to the next stage. The greater the uncertainty of the world, the greater the desirability of having the widest selection of alternative weapons to choose from to meet unexpected threats and opportunities. Alchian and Kessel are so wedded to the principle of diversified investment that they "strongly recommend this theorem as a basic part of systems analysis."[28]

As a form of calculation, systems analysis represents a merger of quantitative methods and rules of thumb. First, the analyst attempts to solve the problem before he knows a great deal about it. Then he continuously alters his initial solution to get closer to what he intuitively feels ought to be wanted. Means and ends are continuously played off against one another. New objectives are defined, new assumptions made, new models constructed, until a creative amalgam appears that hopefully defines a second best solution, one that is better than others even if not optimal in any sense. In the famous study of the

"More than any single thing, the skilled use of a fortiori and break-even analyses separate the professionals from the amateurs." They think that convincing others that you have a good solution is as important as coming up with one.

[27]Herman Kahn and Irwin Mann, *Techniques of Systems Analysis* (Santa Monica, The RAND Corporation, 1957), believe that

[28]Armen A. Alchian and Reuben A. Kessel, *A Proper Role of Systems Analysis* (Santa Monica, RAND Corporation, 1954), p. 9.

location of military bases conducted by Albert Wohlstetter and his associates at the RAND Corporation, widely acknowledged as a classic example of systems analysis, Wohlstetter writes:

> The base study . . . proceeded by a method of successive approximations. It compared forces for their efficiency in carrying a payload between the bases and targets without opposition either by enemy interceptors or enemy bombers. Then, it introduced obstacles successively: first, enemy defenses; then enemy bombardment of our bombers and other elements needed to retaliate. In essence, then, the alternative systems were tested for their first-strike capability and then they were compared for their second-strike capacity. And the programmed system performed in a drastically different way, depending on the order in which the opposing side struck. In the course of analyzing counter-measures and counter-counter-measures, the enemy bombardment turned out to be a dominant problem. This was true even for a very much improved overseas operating base system. The refueling base system was very much less sensitive to strike order. It is only the fact that strike order made such a difference among systems contemplated that gave the first-strike, second-strike distinction an interest. And it was not known in advance of the analysis that few of the programmed bombers would have survived to encounter the problem of penetrating enemy defenses which had previously been taken as the main obstacle. The analysis, then, not only was affected by the objectives considered, it affected them.[29]

The advantage of a good systems study is that by running the analysis

through in theory on paper certain disadvantages of learning from experience may be avoided.

If the complexity of the problems encountered proved difficult in cost-benefit analysis, the burdens of calculation are ordinarily much greater in systems analysis. Many aspects of a problem simply must be put aside. Only a few variables can be considered simultaneously. "Otherwise," Roland McKean tells us, "the models would become impossibly cumbersome, and . . . the number of calculations to consider would mount in the thousands."[30] Formulas that include everything may appear more satisfactory but those that cannot be reduced "to a single expression are likely to convey no meaning at all. . . ."[31] Summing up their experience, Hitch and McKean assert that:

> . . . analyses must be piecemeal, since it is impossible for a single analysis to cover all problems of choice simultaneously in a large organization. Thus comparisons of alternative courses of action always pertain to a part of the government's (or corporation's) problem. Other parts of the over-all problem are temporarily put aside, possible decisions about some matters being ignored, specific decisions about others being taken for granted. The resulting analyses are intended to provide assistance in finding optimal, or at least good, solutions to sub-problems: in the jargon of systems and operations research, they are suboptimizations.[32]

Although admitting that much bad work is carried on and that inordinate

[29]Albert Wohlstetter in E. S. Quade, *op. cit.*, pp. 25–26.

[30]R. N. McKean, "Criteria," in E. S. Quade, *op. cit.*, p. 83.
[31]E. S. Quade, *op. cit.*, p. 310.
[32]Charles J. Hitch and Roland N. McKean, *The Economics of Defense in the Nuclear Age* (Cambridge, Harvard University Press, 1961), p. 161.

love of numbers and machines often get in the way of creative work,[33] practitioners of systems analysis believe in their art. "All of them point out how the use of analysis can provide some of the knowledge needed, how it may sometime serve as a substitute for experience, and, most importantly, how it can work to sharpen intuition."[34] Systems analysis can increase explicitness about the assumptions made and about exclusions from the analysis. The claim is that systems analysis can be perfected; sheer intuition or unaided judgment can never be perfect.

Yet there is also wide agreement that systems analysts "do philosophy,"[35] that they are advocates of particular policy alternatives. What Schelling calls "the pure role of expert advisor" is not available for the analyst who "must usually formulate the questions themselves for his clients."[36] Beyond that, Wohlstetter argues that systems analysts can perform the function of integrating diverse values. New systems can sometimes be found that meet diverse objectives.[37] The politician who gains his objectives by inventing policies that also satisfy others, or the leader of a coalition who searches out areas of maximum agreement, performs a kind of informal systems analysis.

All these men, however, work within the existing political structure. While cost-benefit analysis may contain within it implicit changes in existing govern-

mental policies, it poses no direct challenge to the general decision-making machinery of the political system. Program budgeting is a form of systems analysis that attempts to break out of these confines.

PROGRAM BUDGETING

It is always important, and perhaps especially so in economics, to avoid being swept off one's feet by the fashions of the moment.[38]
So this new system will identify our national goals with precision . . .[39]

On August 25, 1965, President Johnson announced that he was asking the heads of all Federal agencies to introduce "a very new and revolutionary system" of program budgeting. Staffs of experts set up in each agency would define goals using "modern methods of program analysis." Then the "most effective and the least costly" way to accomplish these goals would be found.[40]

Program budgeting has no standard definition. The general idea is that budgetary decisions should be made by focusing on output categories like governmental goals, objectives, end products or programs instead of inputs like personnel, equipment, and maintenance. As in cost-benefit analysis, to which it owes a great deal, program budgeting lays stress on estimating the total financial cost of accomplishing objectives. What is variously called cost-effectiveness or cost-utility analysis is employed in order to select "alternative approaches to the achievement of a benefit already determined to be worth achieving."[41]

---

[33]See Hitch on "Mechanitis—putting . . . machines to work as a substitute for hard thinking." Charles Hitch, "Economics and Operations Research: A Symposium. II," *Review of Economics and Statistics,* August, 1958, p. 209.

[34]E. S. Quade, *op. cit., p.* 12.

[35]*Ibid.,* p. 5.

[36]T. C. Schelling, "Economics and Operations Research: A Symposium. V. Comment," *Review of Economics and Statistics,* August, 1958, p. 222.

[37]Albert Wohlstetter in E. S. Quade, *op. cit.,* p. 122.

[38]Prest and Turvey, *op. cit.,* p. 684.

[39]David Novick, Editor, *Program Budgeting* (Cambridge, Harvard University Press, 1965), p. vi.

[40]*Ibid.,* pp. v–vi.

[41]Alan Dean, quoted in D. Novick, *ibid.,* p. 311.

Not everyone would go along with the most far-reaching implications of program budgeting, but the RAND Corporation version, presumably exported from the Defense Department, definitely does include "institutional reorganization to bring relevant administrative functions under the jurisdiction of the authority making the final program decisions." In any event, there would be "information reporting systems and shifts in the power structure to the extent necessary to secure compliance with program decisions by the agencies responsible for their execution."[42] Sometimes it appears that comprehensiveness—simultaneous and complete examination of all programs and all alternatives to programs every year—is being advocated. Actually, comprehensiveness has been dropped (though not without regret) because "it may be too costly in time, effort, uncertainty, and confusion."[43] There exists considerable ambivalence as to whether decisions are implicit in the program categories or merely provide information to improve the judgment of governmental officials.

Programs are not made in heaven. There is nothing out there that is just waiting to be found. Programs are not natural to the world; they must be imposed on it by men. No one can give instructions for making up programs. There are as many ways to conceive of programs as there are of organizing activity,[44] as the comments of the following writers eloquently testify:

It is by no means obvious . . . whether a good program structure should be based on components of specific end objectives (e.g., the accomplishment of certain land reclamation targets), on the principle of cost separation (identifying as a program any activity the costs of which can be readily segregated), on the separation of means and ends (Is education a means or an end in a situation such as skill-retraining courses for workers displaced by automation?), or on some artificially designed pattern that draws from all these and other classification criteria.[45]

Just what categories constitute the most useful programs and program elements is far from obvious . . . If one puts all educational activities into a broad package of educational programs, he cannot simultaneously include school lunch programs or physical education activities in a Health Program, or include defense educational activities (such as the military academies) in the Defense Program. . . . In short, precisely how to achieve a rational and useful structure for a program budget is not yet evident.[46]

In much current discussion it seems to be taken for granted that transportation is a natural program category. But that conclusion is by no means obvious.[47] A first question one might ask is whether, given their nature, health activities merit a separate, independent status in a program budget. The question arises because these activities often are constituents of, or inputs into, other activities whose purpose or goal orientation is the dominating one. Outlays by the Department of De-

[42]R. N. McKean and N. Anshen in D. Novick, *ibid.,* pp. 286–87. The authors say that this aspect of program budgeting is part of the general view adopted in the book as a whole.

[43]Arthur Smithies in *ibid.,* p. 45.

[44]A look at the classic work by Luther Gulick and Lyndall Urwick, *Papers on the Science of Administration* (New York, Columbia University Press, 1937), reveals considerable similarity between their suggested bases of organization and ways of conceptualizing programs.

[45]N. Anshen in D. Novick, *op. cit.,* pp. 19–20.

[46]G. A. Steiner in *ibid.,* p. 356.

[47]A. Smithies in *ibid.,* p. 41.

fense for hospital care, for example, though they assist in maintaining the health of one segment of the population, are undertaken on behalf of national defense, and the latter is their justification.[48]

The difficulties with the program concept are illustrated in the space program. A first glance suggests that space projects are ideally suited for program budgeting because they appear as physical systems designed to accomplish different missions. Actually, there is a remarkable degree of interdependence between different missions and objectives—pride, scientific research, space exploration, military uses, etc.—so that it is impossible to apportion costs on a proper basis. Consider the problem of a rocket developed for one mission and useful for others. To apportion costs to each new mission is purely arbitrary. To allocate the cost to the first mission and regard the rocket as a free good for all subsequent missions is ludicrous. The only remotely reasonable alternative—making a separate program out of the rocket itself—does violence to the concept of programs as end products. The difficulty is compounded because the facilities that have multiple uses like boosters and tracking networks tend to be very expensive compared to the items that are specific to a particular mission.[49] Simple concepts of programs evaporate upon inspection.

Political realities lie behind the failure to devise principles for defining programs. As Melvin Anshen puts it, "The central issue is, of course, nothing less than the definition of the ultimate objec-

tives of the Federal government as they are realized through operational decisions." The arrangement of the programs inevitably affects the specific actions taken to implement them. "Set in this framework," Anshen continues, "the designation of a schedule of programs may be described as building a bridge between a matter of political philosophy (what is government for?) and . . . assigning scarce resources among alternative governmental objectives."[50]

Because program budgeting is a form of systems analysis (and uses a form of cost-benefit analysis), the conditions that hinder or facilitate its use have largely been covered in the previous sections. The simpler the problem, the fewer the interdependencies, the greater the ability to measure the consequences of alternatives on a common scale, the more costs and benefits that are valued in the market place, the better the chances of making effective use of programs. Let us take transportation to illustrate some of the conditions in a specific case.

Investments in transportation are highly interdependent with one another (planes versus cars versus trains versus barges, etc.) and with decisions regarding the regional location of industry and the movements of population. In view of the powerful effects of transportation investment on regional employment, income, and competition with other modes of transport, it becomes necessary to take these factors into account. The partial equilibrium model of efficiency in the narrow sense becomes inappropriate and a general equilibrium model of the economy must be used. The combination of aggregative models at the economy-wide level and inter-region and inter-industry models that this approach requires is staggering. It is precisely the limited and partial character of cost-effectiveness analyses, taking so much for granted and

[48]Marvin Frankel in *ibid.,* pp. 219–220. I have forborne citing the author who promises exciting discussion of the objectives of American education and ends up with fascinating program categories like primary, secondary, and tertiary education.

[49]See the excellent chapter by M. A. Margolis and S. M. Barro, *ibid.,* pp. 120-145.

[50]*Ibid.,* p. 18.

eliminating many variables, that make them easy to work with for empirical purposes. Furthermore, designing a large-scale transportation system involves so close a mixture of political and economic considerations that it is not possible to disentangle them. The Interstate Highway Program, for example, involved complex bargaining among Federal, State, and local governments and reconciliation of many conflicting interests. The development of certain "backward" regions, facilitating the movement of defense supplies, redistribution of income, creating countervailing power against certain monopolies, not to mention the political needs of public officials, were all involved. While cost-utility exercises might help with small segments of the problem, J. R. Meyer concludes that, "Given the complexity of the political and economic decisions involved, and the emphasis on designing a geographically consistent system, it probably would be difficult to improve on the congressional process as a means of developing such a program in an orderly and systematic way."[51]

On one condition for effective use—reorganization of the Federal government to centralize authority for wide-ranging programs—proponents of program budgeting are markedly ambivalent. The problem is that responsibility for programs is now scattered throughout the whole Federal establishment and decentralized to State and local authorities as well. In the field of health, for example, expenditures are distributed among at least twelve agencies and six departments outside of Health, Education, and Welfare. A far greater number of organizations are concerned with American activities abroad, with natural resources and with education. The multiple jurisdictions and overlapping responsibili-

ties do violence to the concept of comprehensive and consistent programs. It "causes one to doubt," Marvin Frankel writes, "whether there can exist in the administrative echelons the kind of overall perspective that would seem indispensable if Federal health resources are to be rationally allocated."[52] To G. A. Steiner it is evident that "The present 'chest of drawers' type of organization cannot for long be compatible with program budgeting."[53] W. Z. Hirsch declares that "if we are to have effective program budgeting of natural resources activities, we shall have to provide for new institutional arrangements."[54] Yet the inevitable resistance to wholesale reorganization would be so great that, if it were deemed essential, it might well doom the enterprise. Hence, the hope is expressed that translation grids or crossover networks could be used to convert program budget decisions back into the usual budget categories in the usual agencies. That is what is done in Defense, but that Department has the advantage of having most of the activities it is concerned with under the Secretary's jurisdiction. Some program analysts believe that this solution will not do.

Recognizing that a conversion scheme is technically feasible, Anshen is aware that there are "deeply frustrating" issues to be resolved. "The heart of the problem is the fact that the program budget in operation should not be a mere statistical game. Great strategic importance will attach to both the definition of program structure and content and the establishment of specific program objectives (including magnitude, timing, and cost)."[55] The implications of program budgeting, however, go far beyond specific policies.

---

[51]J. R. Meyer in *ibid.*, p. 170. This paragraph is based on my interpretation of his work.

[52]M. Frankel, *ibid.*, p. 237.
[53]*Ibid.*, p. 348.
[54]*Ibid.*, p. 280.
[55]Ibid., pp. 358–59.

It will be useful to distinguish between policy politics (which policy will be adopted?), partisan politics (which political party will win office?), and system politics (how will decision structures be set up?). Program budgeting is manifestly concerned with policy politics, and not much with partisan politics, although it could have important consequences for issues that divide the nation's parties. *My contention is that the thrust of program budgeting makes it an integral part of system politics.*

As presently conceived, program budgeting contains an extreme centralizing bias. Power is to be centralized in the Presidency (through the Budget Bureau) at the national level, in superdepartments rather than bureaus within the executive branch, and in the Federal government as a whole instead of State or local governments. Note how W. Z. Hirsch assumes the desirability of national dominance when he writes: "These methods of analysis can guide Federal officials in the responsibility of bringing local education decisions into closer harmony with national objectives."[56] G. A. Steiner observes that comprehensiveness may be affected by unrestricted Federal grants-in-aid to the states because "such a plan would remove a substantial part of Federal expenditures from a program budgeting system of the Federal government."[57] Should there be reluctance on the part of State and local officials to employ the new tools, Anshen states "that the Federal government may employ familiar incentives to accelerate this progress."[58] Summing it up, Hirsch says that "It appears doubtful that a natural resources program budget would have much impact without a good deal of centralization."[59]

Within the great Federal organizations designed to encompass the widest ramifications of basic objectives, there would have to be strong executives. Cutting across the subunits of the organization, as is the case in the Department of Defense, the program budget could only be put together by the top executive. A more useful tool for increasing his power to control decisions vis-a-vis his subordinates would be hard to find.[60]

Would large-scale program budgeting benefit the Chief Executive? President Johnson's support of program budgeting could in part stem from his desire to appear frugal and also be directed at increasing his control of the executive branch by centralizing decisions in the Bureau of the Budget. In the case of foreign affairs, it is not at all clear whether it would be preferable to emphasize country teams, with the budget made by the State Department to encompass activities of the other Federal agencies abroad, or to let Commerce, Agriculture, Defense, and other agencies include their foreign activities in their own budgets. Program budgeting will unleash great struggles of this kind in Washington. An especially intriguing possibility is that the Bureau of the Budget might prefer to let the various agencies compete, with the Bureau coordinating (that is, controlling) these activities through a comprehensive foreign affairs program devised only at the Presidential level.

Yet is it not entirely clear that Presidents would welcome all the implications of program budgeting. It is well and good to talk about long-range planning; it is another thing to tie a President's hands by committing him in advance for five years of expenditures. Looking ahead is fine but not if it means

---

[56]*Ibid.*, p. 206.
[57]*Ibid.*, p. 347.
[58]*Ibid.*, p. 365.
[59]*Ibid.*, p. 280.

[60]See my comments to this effect in *The Politics of the Budgetary-Process* (Boston, 1964), p. 140. For discussion of some political consequences of program budgeting, see pp. 135–142.

that a President cannot negate the most extensive planning efforts on grounds that seem sufficient to him.[61] He may wish to trade some program budgeting for some political support.

In any event, that all decisions ought to be made by the most central person in the most centralized body capable of grabbing hold of them is difficult to justify on scientific grounds. We see what has happened. First pure efficiency was converted to mixed efficiency. Then limited efficiency became unlimited. Yet the qualifications of efficiency experts for political systems analysis are not evident.[62]

We would be in a much stronger position to predict the consequences of program budgeting if we knew (a) how far toward a genuine program budget the Defense Department has gone and (b) whether the program budget has fulfilled its promise. To the best of my knowledge, not a single study of this important experiment was undertaken (or at least published) before the decision was made to spread it around the land. On the surface, only two of the nine program categories used in the Defense De-

partment appear to be genuine programs in the sense of pointing to end purposes or objectives. Although strategic retaliation and continental defense appear to be distinct programs, it is difficult to separate them conceptually; my guess is that they are, in fact, considered together. The third category—general purpose forces—is presumably designed to deal with (hopefully) limited war anywhere in the world. According to Arthur Smithies, "The threat is not clearly defined and neither are the requirements for meeting it. Clearly this program is of a very different character from the other two and does not lend itself as readily to analysis in terms either of its components or of its specific contribution to defense objectives."[63]

What about the program called airlift and sealift? These activities support the general purpose forces. Research and development is carried on presumably to serve other defense objectives, and the same is true for the reserve forces.

No doubt the elements that make up the programs comprise the real action focus of the budget, but these may look less elegant when spread into thousands of elements than they do in nine neat

---

[61]See William H. Brown and Charles E. Gilbert, *Planning Municipal Investment: A Case Study of Philadelphia* (Philadelphia, University of Pennsylvania Press, 1961), for an excellent discussion of the desire of elected officials to remain free to shift their commitments.

[62]It may be said that I have failed to distinguish sufficiently between planning, programming, and budgeting. Planning is an orientation that looks ahead by extending costs and benefits or units of effectiveness a number of years into the future. Programming is a general procedure of systems analysis employing cost-effectiveness studies. In this view program budgeting is a mere mechanical translation of the results of high level systems studies into convenient storage in the budgetary format. No doubt systems studies could be done without converting the results into the form of a program budget. This approach may have a lot to be said for it and it appears that it is the one that is generally followed in the Department of Defense in its

presentations to Congress. But if the systems studies guide decisions as to the allocation of resources, and the studies are maintained according to particular program categories and are further legitimatized by being given status in the budget, it seems most unlikely that programming will be separated from budgeting. One is never sure whether too much or too little is being claimed for program budgeting. If all that program budgeting amounts to is a simple translation of previous systems studies into some convenient form of accounting, it hardly seems that this phenomenon is worth so much fuss. If the program categories in the budget system are meaningful, then they must be much more than a mere translation of previously arrived at decisions. In this case, I think that it is not my task to enlighten the proponents of program budgeting, but it is their task to make themselves clear to others.

[63]A. Smithies in Novick, *op. cit.*, p. 37.

rows. When one hears that hundreds of program elements are up for decision at one time,[64] he is entitled to some skepticism about how much genuine analysis can go into all of them. Part of the argument for program budgeting was that by thinking ahead and working all year around it would be possible to consider changes as they came up and avoid the usual last minute funk. Both Hitch[65] and Novick[66] (the RAND Corporation expert on defense budgeting) report, however, that this has not worked out. The services hesitate to submit changes piecemeal, and the Secretary wants to see what he is getting into before he acts. The vaunted five year plans are still in force but their efficacy in determining yearly decisions remains to be established.

One good operational test would be to know whether the Department's systems analysts actually use the figures from the five year plans in their work or whether they go to the services for the real stuff. Another test would be whether or not the later years of the five year projections turn out to have any future significance, or whether the battle is really over the next year that is to be scooped out as part of the budget. From a distance, it appears that the services have to work much harder to justify what they are doing. Since McNamara's office must approve changes in defense programs, and he can insist on documentation, he is in a strong position to improve thinking at the lower levels. The intensity of conflict within the

Defense Department may not have changed, but it may be that the disputants are or will in the future be likely to shout at a much more sophisticated level. How much this is due to McNamara himself, to his insistence on quantitative estimates, or to the analytic advantages of a program budget cannot be determined now. It is clear that a program budget, of which he alone is master, has helped impose his will on the Defense Department.

It should also be said that there are many notable differences between decision-making in defense and domestic policy that would render suspect the transmission of procedures from one realm to the other. The greater organizational unity of Defense, the immensely large amounts of money at stake, the extraordinarily greater risks involved, the inability to share more than minimal values with opponents, the vastly different array of interests and perceptions of the proper roles of the participants, are but a few of the factors involved.

The Armed Services and Appropriations Committees in the defense area, for example, are normally most reluctant to substitute their judgment on defense for that of the President and the Secretary of the Department. They do not conceive it to be their role to make day to day defense policy, and they are apparently unwilling to take on the burden of decision. They therefore accept a budget presentation based on cavernous program categories even though these are so arranged that it is impossible to make a decision on the basis of them. If they were to ask for and to receive the discussion of alternative actions contained in the much smaller program elements on which McNamara bases his decisions, they would be in a position to take the Department of Defense away from its Secretary.

There is no reason whatsoever to believe that a similar restraint would be shown by committees that deal with do-

[64]See U.S. House Appropriations Committee Subcommittee on Department of Defense Appropriations for Fiscal 1965, 88th Congress, 2nd Session, IV, p. 133. McNamara asserted that some 652 "subject issues" had been submitted to him for the fiscal 1965 budget.

[65]Charles Hitch, *Decision Making for Defense* (Berkeley, University of California Press, 1965).

[66]Novick, *op. cit.,* p. 100.

mestic policies. It is at least possible that the peculiar planning, programming, and budgeting system adopted in Defense could not be repeated elsewhere in the Federal establishment.

POLITICAL RATIONALITY *this is good*

These considerations

Political rationality is the fundamental kind of reason, because it deals with the preservation and improvement of decision structures, and decision structures are the source of all decisions. Unless a decision structure exists, no reasoning and no decisions are possible. . . . There can be no conflict between political rationality and . . . technical, legal, social, or economic rationality, because the solution of political problems makes possible an attack on any other problem, while a serious political deficiency can prevent or undo all other problem solving. . . . Nonpolitical decisions are reached by considering a problem in its own terms, and by evaluating proposals according to how well they solve the problem. The best available proposal should be accepted regardless of who makes it or who opposes it, and a faulty proposal should be rejected or improved no matter who makes it. Compromise is always irrational; the rational procedure is to determine which proposal is the best, and to accept it. In a political decision, on the other hand, action never is based on the merits of a proposal but always on who makes it and who opposes it. Action should be designed to avoid complete identification with any proposal and any point of view, no matter how good or how popular it might be. The best available proposal should never be accepted just because it is best, it should be deferred, objected to, discussed, until major opposition disappears. Compro-

mise is always a rational procedure, even when the compromise is between a good and a bad proposal.[67]

We are witnessing the beginning of significant advances in the art and science of economizing. Having given up the norm of comprehensiveness, economizers are able to join quantitative analysis with aids to calculation of the kind described by Lindblom in his strategy of disjointed incrementalism.[68]

Various devices are employed to simplify calculations. Important values are omitted entirely; others are left to different authorities to whose care they have been entrusted. Here, sensitivity analysis represents an advance because it provides an empirical basis to justify neglect of some values. Means and ends are hopelessly intertwined.

The real choice is between rival policies that encapsulate somewhat different mixes of means and ends. Analysis proceeds incrementally by successive limited approximations. It is serial and remedial as successive attacks are made on problems. Rather than waiting upon experience in the real world, the analyst tries various moves in his model and runs them through to see if they work. When all else fails, the analyst may try an integrative solution reconciling a variety of values to some degree, though meeting none of them completely. He is always ready to settle for the second or third best, provided only that it is better than the going policy. Constrained by diverse limiting assumptions, weakened by deficiencies in technique, rarely able to provide unambiguous measures, the systems, cost-benefit, and program analysis is

---

[67]Paul Diesing, *Reason in Society* (Urbana, 1962), pp. 198, 203–4, 231–32.

[68]Braybrooke and Lindblom, *op. cit.* See also Lindblom, *The Intelligence of Democracy* (New York, 1965).

nonetheless getting better at calculating in the realm of efficiency. Alas, he is an imperialist at heart.

In the literature discussed above there appears several times the proposition that "the program budget is a neutral tool. It has no politics."[69] In truth, the program budget is suffused with policy politics, makes up a small part of President Johnson's partisan politics, and tends towards system politics. How could men account for so foolish a statement? It must be that they who make it identify program budgeting with something good and beautiful, and politics with another thing bad and ugly. McKean and Anshen speak of politics in terms of "pressure and expedient adjustments," "haphazard acts . . . unresponsive to a planned analysis of the needs of efficient decision design." From the political structure they expect only "resistance and opposition, corresponding to the familiar human disposition to protect established seats of power and procedures made honorable by the mere facts of existence and custom."[70] In other places we hear of "vested interests," "wasteful duplication," "special interest groups," and the "Parkinson syndrome."[71]

Not so long ago less sophisticated advocates of reform ignored the political realm. Now they denigrate it. And, since there must be a structure for decision, it is smuggled in as a mere adjunct of achieving efficiency. Who is to blame if the economic tail wags the political dog? It seems unfair to blame the evangelical economizer for spreading the gospel of efficiency. If economic efficiency turns out to be the one true religion, maybe it is because its prophets could so easily conquer.

It is hard to find men who take up the cause of political rationality, who plead the case for political man, and who are primarily concerned with the laws that enable the political machinery to keep working. One is driven to a philosopher like Paul Diesing to find the case for the political:

> . . . the political problem is always basic and prior to the others. . . . This means that any suggested course of action must be evaluated first by its effects on the political structure. A course of action which corrects economic or social deficiencies but increases political difficulties must be rejected, while an action which contributes to political improvement is desirable even if it is not entirely sound from an economic or social standpoint.[72]

There is hardly a political scientist who would claim half as much. The desire to invent decision structures to facilitate the achievement of economic efficiency does not suggest a full appreciation of their proper role by students of politics.

A major task of the political system is to specify goals or objectives. It is impermissible to treat goals as if they were known in advance. "Goals" may well be the product of interaction among key participants rather than some "deus ex machina" or (to use Bentley's term) some "spook" which posits values in advance of our knowledge of them. Certainly, the operational objectives of the Corps of Engineers in the Water Resources field could hardly be described in terms of developing rivers and harbors.

Once the political process becomes a focus of attention, it is evident that the principal participants may not be clear about their goals. What we call goals or objectives may, in large part, be opera-

[69]M. Anshen in D. Novick, *op. cit.,* p. 370.
[70]*Ibid.,* p. 289.
[71]*Ibid.,* p. 359.

[72]Paul Diesing, *op. cit.,* p. 228.

tionally determined by the policies we can agree upon. The mixtures of values found in complex policies may have to be taken in packages, so that policies may determine goals as least as much as general objectives determine policies. In a political situation, then, the need for support assumes central importance. Not simply the economic, but the *political* costs and benefits turn out to be crucial.

A first attempt to specify what is meant by political costs may bring closer an understanding of the range of requirements for political rationality.[73] Exchange costs are incurred by a political leader when he needs the support of other people to get a policy adopted. He has to pay for this assistance by using up resources in the form of favors (patronage, logrolling) or coercive moves (threats or acts to veto or remove from office). By supporting a policy and influencing others to do the same, a politician antagonizes some people and may suffer their retaliation. If these hostility costs mount, they may turn into reelection costs—actions that decrease his chances (or those of his friends) of being elected or reelected to office. Election costs, in turn, may become policy costs through inability to command the necessary formal powers to accomplish the desired policy objectives.

In the manner of Neustadt, we may also talk about reputation costs, i.e. not only loss of popularity with segments of the electorate, but also loss of esteem and effectiveness with other participants in the political system and loss or ability to secure policies other than the one immediately under consideration. Those who continually urge a President to go all out—that is, use all his resources on a wide range of issues— rarely stop to consider that the price of success in one area of policy may be defeat in another. If he loses popularity with the electorate, as President Truman did, Congress may destroy almost the whole of his domestic program. If he cracks down on the steel industry, as President Kennedy did, he may find himself constrained to lean over backwards in the future to avoid unremitting hostility from the business community.

A major consequence of incurring exchange and hostility costs may be undesirable power-redistribution effects. The process of getting a policy adopted or implemented may increase the power of various individuals, organizations and social groups, which later will be used against the political leader. The power of some participants may be weakened so that the political leader is unable to enjoy their protection.

The legitimacy of the political system may be threatened by costs that involve the weakening of customary political restraints. Politicians who try to suppress opposition, or who practice election frauds, may find similar tactics being used against them. The choice of a highly controversial policy may raise the costs of civic discord. Although the people involved may not hate the political leader, the fact that they hate each other may lead to consequences contrary to his desires.

The literature of economics usually treats organizations and institutions as if they were costless entities. The standard procedure is to consider rival alternatives (in consideration of price policy or other criteria), calculate the differences in cost and achievement among them, and show that one is more or less efficient than another. This typical way of thinking is sometimes misspecified. If the costs of pursuing a policy are strictly economic and can be calculated directly in the market place, then the procedure should work well. But if the costs include getting one or another organization to change its policies or procedures, then these costs must also be taken into

---

[73]I am indebted to John Harsanyi for suggestions about political rationality.

account.[74] Perhaps there are legal, psychological, or other impediments that make it either impossible or difficult for the required changes to be made. Or the changes may require great effort and result in incurring a variety of other costs. In considering a range of alternatives, one is measuring not only efficiency but also the cost of change.

Studies based on efficiency criteria are much needed and increasingly useful. My quarrel is not with them as such, at all. I have been concerned that a single value, however important, could triumph over other values without explicit consideration being given these others. I

would feel much better if political rationality were being pursued with the same vigor and capability as is economic efficiency. In that case I would have fewer qualms about extending efficiency studies into the decision-making apparatus.

My purpose has not been to accuse economizers of doing what comes naturally. Rather, I have sought to emphasize that economic rationality, however laudible in its own sphere, ought not to swallow up political rationality—but will do so, if political rationality continues to lack trained and adept defenders.

---

[74]In the field of defense policy, political factors are taken into account to the extent that the studies concentrate on the design of feasible alternatives. In the choice of overseas basing, for example, the question of feasibility in relation to treaties and friendly or unfriendly relationships with other countries is

considered. Thus it seems permissible to take into account political considerations originating outside of the country, where differences of opinions and preferences among nations are to some extent accepted as legitimate, but apparently not differences internal to the American policy.

---

21.   Why Does Government Grow?

James M. Buchanan

The explosive growth of government at all levels today is alarming. Even people who do not examine the simple statistics should be increasingly concerned about higher and higher taxes levied in support of governmental programs that become less and less efficient in providing benefits of real value. If a forward look is attempted, the picture seems horrendous. In a decade governments will be using up more than one-half of each dollar of national income generat-

ed, and well over a third of gross national product will be expended through governmental channels. The propensity of government to seize upon and to spend additional dollars of the income growth that the national economy generates cannot be questioned. But as the share of government in the economy grows, can the private and nongovernmental sector continue to provide the means of satisfying government's voracious appetite?

The need to understand why government grows so rapidly seems urgent. If alarm about the current spending explosion is to lead to effective political countermeasures, if the explosion is to be stopped or even slowed

SOURCE: James Buchanan, "Why Does Government Grow?" in *Budgets and Bureaucrats* edited by Thomas E. Borcherding. Durham: Duke University Press, 1977. Reprinted with permission of the publisher.

down, we must have some understanding, some explanation, of why it is occurring. We must explain the institutional and political processes that produce the results that we see, results that seem fully desirable only to the bureaucrats on the expanding public payrolls.

The research project undertaken by members of the staff of the Center for the Study of Public Choice, Virginia Polytechnic Institute and State University, and under the sponsorship of the Foundation for Research in Economics and Education, has such explanation as its primary objective. Preliminary results of this research are reported in detail in the following papers; this paper provides a summary overview.

Government growth clearly has a momentum all its own, quite independent of general growth in the national economy. Economists have devoted much attention to isolating the sources of economic growth, but, surprisingly, they have paid almost no attention to the problem of determining why governments' share in the national economy continues to increase.

Because of this relative neglect, the research here must be treated as exploratory and provisional. There are no widely accepted paradigms or models upon which specific hypotheses might be constructed and tested. Features of several models will appear in the papers attached, and no single and inclusive explanatory theory emerges full-blown from our efforts. Further research is clearly needed here, and if our preliminary results can stimulate this, one subsidiary purpose will have been accomplished. More importantly, if political leaders and their advisers can be informed of the significance as well as the difficulty of getting answers to the basic question posed, the first step toward corrective countermeasures may be closer than current observation suggests.

What Government Spending, When, and How?

Before we discuss explanations of why government grows, however, some disaggregation is in order. We must look, even if briefly, at the historical record. Growth in total government spending and taxation may exert differing effects with differing mixes among levels of government. Furthermore, growth rates that might be currently observed may be viewed quite differently if they are believed to be temporary phenomena than if they represent long-term patterns. Finally, growth in aggregate governmental activity, even at one level, may depend for its effects on just how this activity is organized, on just what functions are expanding within the public sector.

Borcherding's paper on the record of a century of public spending provides a historical perspective. Significant results emerge from the data presented for the period 1870 through 1970. In the nineteenth century the public sector, overall, was expanding, but it was growing less rapidly than national income. And equally, if not more, important, within the public sector itself decentralization was occurring, with local government spending expanding relative to that of the states, and with state-local spending combined expanding relative to that by the federal government. Both of these results turned around in this century. The twentieth century is characterized by both an increasing governmental share in the national economy and an increasing portion of this public-sector share occupied by the federal government. Centralization *and* growth have occurred, a much more fearsome pair than the converse, growth with decentralization.

Somewhat surprisingly perhaps, within the governmental budget itself, there has been no dramatic shift in spending patterns over the century. Transfers have increased slightly relative to resource-using expenditures, and notably during the 1960s. Furthermore, this element of spending seems most likely to rise during ensuing decades. And, notably, the United States pattern differs from that in other Western nations largely in the relatively smaller share of transfer expenditures undertaken.

The nineteenth century record suggests clearly that an increasing governmental share is not a necessary and inevitable accompaniment to national economic development. The explosion in taxation and public spending that we live with is a twentieth century phenomenon, and the pattern that was changed before can be reversed. Government need not grow more rapidly than the national economy; there is no such relationship written in our stars.

This is not to suggest that a reversal of the trend established over many decades will be easy to accomplish, even if the institutional means are discovered, the political leadership emerges, and the public support is mobilized. Simple and straightforward projections of current trends yield fearful results, as Jacobe's paper demonstrates for the federal government alone. This remains true regardless of the time period used for the basis of projection. As a supplemental note of pessimism, the record suggests that almost every projection of government growth made during the years since World War 2 has been woefully inaccurate, and always on the side of under- rather than overestimation. It is time to become concerned.

Government "By the People"? or Government "Against the People"?

Do governments expand in direct response to the demands of ordinary people for more and better public-service programs? Or do governments operate independently of the people, producing results that may not be related to the wishes of the citizens and which, on balance, do the people more harm than good? These questions get at the very heart of democracy, and they may not seem directly connected to problems of taxation and spending. But until they are answered, no progress at all can be made toward explaining government growth. In a democratic decision model, any explanation for observed high rates of growth in taxation and spending must be grounded on the demands of the citizens. Why do people want governmental agencies to do so much for them, things which they might do better privately?

Why are the people willing to pay onerous taxes for governmental programs? Are those goods and services normally offered by governments characteristically those that become relatively more important as income rises through time? Does the shift from a production to a service economy necessarily embody an expanded role for government? Does increasing population in general, and increasing concentration of this population in particular, generate pressures on governments to supply relatively more services and the private sector relatively less? Does the relatively lower productivity of resources used by governments generate the paradoxical pattern of relatively expanding governmental spending? These subsidiary questions, and more, will be discussed directly or indirectly in the research papers. These questions emerge from a "government by the people" or democratic model of politics. As the questions might indicate, and as the research results support, some part of the overall expansion in the public sector of the national economy can be satisfactorily explained in this way.

But not all. Resort to a quite different and nondemocratic model of the political structure leads to quite different subsidiary questions, the answers to which yield further explanatory potential. Are the people misled into thinking that their taxes are low and that public spending benefits are high? Do they operate under a set of fiscal illusions? If they do, what are the institutions and instruments that foster these illusions, and what individuals and groups find it advantageous to maintain these institutions? Where does the political party, the aspiring politician, the working bureaucrat fit into the picture? What motivates the men who must provide the human bridge between "the people"—those who pay the taxes—and "the people"—those who may secure benefits from governmental programs? Are these two sets of people necessarily equivalent? Or is government increasingly becoming a means of making transfers among groups? What is the role of the political entrepreneur in all this? What are the effects of allowing bureaucrats to vote? Is not this a direct conflict of interest?

Once again, each of these subsidiary questions will be discussed, directly or indirectly, in the research papers here. Note, however, that such questions as these emerge only in a model that is nondemocratic in its essentials, a model that offers an explanation of observed results in terms of a perversion of the true demands of the people.

Neither of these two contrasting models of politics will be proved appropriate or inappropriate here. Any plausibly adequate explanation of the expansion of the governmental sector in the modern American economy requires both models, or some mixture of the two. Without doubt, some considerable part of the observed growth in the public sector, at all levels, is directly traceable to the demands of the citizenry, genuine demands for more services accompanied by an increased willingness to shoulder the tax burdens required for financing. But, once this is acknowledged, there can also be little doubt but that a significant and remaining part of the observed growth in the public sector can be ex-

plained only by looking at the motivations of those who secure direct personal gains from government expansion, gains that are unrelated to the benefits filtered down to the ordinary citizens.

The two contrasting models of politics provide a helpful means of presenting the research results in summary form. But they do more than that. The means toward checking the expansion of taxation and spending may depend critically on our ability to separate the two forces at work. Blunderbuss attempts to cut back on public spending programs, willy-nilly, and without recognition that such attempts may be subverted by the bureaucracy, may backfire. If the bureaucracy retains power to allocate general spending cuts among functions, it will, of course, direct the cuts to those areas that are most sensitive, those most in demand by the people. If we adopt the norm that government programs should be directly responsive to the demands of the citizenry, whether we might personally agree with the citizenry or not, but that government should not offer an instrument of enrichment for self-serving bureaucrats, the prospect for checking the expansion in the public sector may lie not so much in direct spending or taxing limitations but, instead, in structural-procedural reforms within the governmental structure itself. Rules that allow for more contracting out and for less direct provision by governments may do more toward reducing tax burdens than budgetary limits. Changes in pay schedules for teachers may produce more education at less cost more effectively than changes in the size of the educational budget at any governmental level.

RESPONSIVE GOVERNMENT

Inflation, Population, and Public Spending

The most obvious explanatory elements in the growth of gross public spending can be covered briefly and without detail. Defined in current dollar magnitudes, total spending, both for the private and the public sectors of the economy, increases as inflation occurs. Even when the gross figures are reduced to real terms, to dollars of constant purchasing power, however, we still are faced with the task of explaining more than 4300 percent increase in aggregate government spending over the years of this century.

One of the first explanations suggested is population growth. To what extent can we "explain" the growth of government as a direct consequence of the population increase over the period? Borcherding's computations suggest that some 25 percent of the increase in real spending by governments might be explained by population, on the presumption that the goods and services supplied by political units are demanded in the same fashion as those supplied in the private sector. That is to say, if there are really no net efficiency gains to be secured through providing the goods and services jointly through governments, we can then "explain" up to 25 percent of the increase in this way. But, somewhat paradoxically, if such efficiencies do not exist, there is no argument for having the goods provided by governments at all. Goods and services had as well be provided and supplied through ordinary markets. On the other hand, if there are clear net efficiency gains to be made through the joint-supply properties of governments, the explanatory potential for population increase falls below the 25 percent figure noted.

The Services Economy and Income Elasticity of Demand

In either case, our major explanatory task remains before us. What causes the growth in real government spending per capita?

As the general development in the national economy has taken place, there has been a pronounced shift in employment away from production and trade and into the services sector. Since government output is heavily weighted by services, this underlying shift in the structure of the economy would, in itself, explain some of the relative increase in the size of the public sector. When Borcherding examines the data, however, he finds that, even within the services sector, government has increased its relative share in employment. As with population increase, there remains much more to explain.

The growth in income itself will, of course, explain a large share of spending growth in absolute terms. But income will explain some of the relative increase in the government's share only if it can be demonstrated that the goods and services supplied publicly are those for which individuals' demands are highly responsive to income shifts, more responsive than for nongovernmental goods, considered as a package. If the income elasticity of demand is high, to slip into economists' jargon here, there will be a more than proportionate increase in demand consequent on an increase in incomes. Borcherding's estimates suggest that governmentally supplied goods and services possess no such characteristic features, and that the responsiveness in demand to income change is, if anything, somewhat less than that which characterizes private spending. We must look elsewhere for our explanation.

The Public Productivity Paradox

Most of us who use governmental services do not need to be informed that productivity is low relative to that in the nongovernmental sector. Anyone who doubts this statement need only call on his personal experience with the mails during the last Christmas holiday season. And Spann examines the data and he finds that for the five-year period 1962–67 there was no net increase in productivity in the state-local services covered in his study. If anything, productivity may have slightly declined over that period. Earlier work by Professor William Baumol of Princeton University suggested that extremely low rates of productivity growth are characteristic features of the goods and services that governments have traditionally supplied. We need not argue here about whether the relatively low productivity in government employment is inherent in the technology of the goods and services supplied or stems from the motivation system for employees in government. The facts are that, for whatever reason, we witness the phenomenon of increasing productivity in the private sector of the economy alongside stationary or even declining productivity in the public sector.

This unbalanced relationship between rates of productivity increase for the two sectors insures that, in real terms, the relative costs of goods and services supplied governmentally increase. In order to maintain a labor force, wages and salaries in the public sector employments will have to be roughly equivalent to wages and salaries obtainable in the private sector. But the latter, wages and salaries in the market sector, will tend to increase as productivity increases, without necessarily causing an increase in the prices of private-sector output. When governmental employers find it necessary to offer matching wages and salaries, but without the accompanying increase in productivity, the unit costs of goods and services supplied governmentally must rise relative to the costs of market-produced goods and services. To the individual demanders, and consumers, of governmental goods and services the "prices" of these, measured in units of privately produced goods that are given up, must increase.

With an increase in relative price, quantity demanded normally is expected to go down, other things remaining the same. This first principle of economic theory remains valid here. But even though price increases and quantity demanded decreases (if all other determinants of demand should remain unchanged), the buyer or demander may still *spend more* on the good than before. And since we measure the size of the public or governmental sector by total spending, there is nothing really inconsistent about the low productivity in this sector being one of the important causal factors in the growth of spending for goods and services supplied by this sector. The importance of this factor might be more accurately estimated if we did, in fact, have good measures for governmental output in physical terms. Lacking this, we must make do with what we have, and the evidence suggests that this effect, stemming from the combination of low productivity growth and a relatively low price elasticity of demand for publicly supplied goods and services, does add significantly to our explanation of government growth.

Urbanization and Congestion

As population has increased, and as the structure of the national economy has changed, urbanization has taken place. This increases the economic interdependence among persons, and with this the potential for conflict, because of common use of resources that have not historically been assigned as private property. With urbanization comes congestion in all its forms, and this opens up a role for governments in mitigating the evils if not eliminating them. One part of the hypothesis here can scarcely be questioned. More governmental action is required as congestion increases, and congestion is directly related to the concentration of people in space. But the type of governmental action suggested may not, and need not, give rise to large increases in government budgets. To reduce congestion, corrective regulatory measures may be in order (e.g., zoning, traffic controls, emission and effluent standards, etc.). These may require only nominal budgetary outlays.

On the other hand, increases in incomes that accompany urbanization should reduce economic interdependencies of the positive sort and thus should reduce the need for governmental action. In very poor communities, citizens may find it essential to join forces through governmental units to provide common facilities (e.g., swimming pools). As communities, and individuals, become richer, however, each family can afford to provide its own facilities. This should be a force working toward a reduction rather than an increase in the relative share of government in the economy.

Borcherding examines the evidence empirically. He finds that there is little or no explanatory value in urbanization as a cause for government growth.

Growth of Responsive Government

Any or all of the reasons discussed above might explain why governments would grow, even in an "ideal democracy," where the demands of the people are transmitted directly into observed budgetary outcomes. As we have indicated, a large part of any total explanation must take these demand-increasing influences into proper account. Borcherding attempts to make quantitative estimates, and he concludes that perhaps as much as one-half to two-thirds of the real growth in per capita government spending can be explained satisfactorily by combining all of the elements discussed to this point. As he puts it in his paper, all of these factors combined explain why we might observe an aggregate governmental sector spending about one-fifth of gross national product (GNP), but they do not help us in going beyond this and in explaining why we observe government spending more than one-third of GNP.

The gap that remains after we have exhausted all of the economic elements that might reflect genuine demands of the people for expanded governmental services is a large one. More importantly, this gap is the margin for potential correction, the margin for reduction that might be accomplished with net benefits to most of the citizenry. We need not, in fact, be greatly concerned if governmental growth could somehow be limited to the rates required to allow responsible and responsive adjustment to the demand-increasing factors. We become properly concerned when observed rates of increase clearly exceed these limits, in the current instance by as much as one-third. It is this margin that must be tackled with corrective measures, and, therefore it is essential that our analysis extend beyond those factors treated in part 1.

EXCESSIVE GOVERNMENT

Tax Consciousness and Fiscal Illusions

We need to introduce elements of a non-democratic model of politics. We must search for reasons why budgetary results are not those desired by the citizens for whom spending programs are alleged to be undertaken, why these results are uniformly in the direction of excessively large outlays. Our research must examine possibilities of breakdowns in the transmission of individuals' demands through the political-fiscal process, including the possibility that the transmission institutions may be deliberately perverted by self-seeking politicians and bureaucrats who succeed in isolating themselves from the discipline imposed by the electoral process.

Perhaps the most significant finding in the unpublished 1972 survey of California citizens' attitudes conducted under the supervision of Professor W. C. Stubblebine for the Foundation for Research in Economics and Education concerns the failure of citizens to estimate properly the true tax costs of various state-local spending programs. These costs are underestimated, sometimes by a factor of two-thirds. The people who pay taxes do not realize how much they pay, and they think that they secure government goods and services at bargain prices. Suppose that we know the cost of an automobile to be $3000 and that we ask a buyer how much he paid. If he tells us $1000, we should indeed be amazed at his ignorance, and we should predict that he would foolishly spend too much on cars. Yet this is roughly what the situation is with respect to individuals' indirect "purchases" of governmental goods and services through the whole political budgetary process.

This prompts our research into the sources for such illusions. Why does the average citizen underestimate the costs of public services? In his paper Goetz suggests several parts of an answer, and details need not be elaborated here. Relatively large amounts of state-local taxes are at least partially concealed in the final market prices of goods and services. The consumer looks at the retail price of a good, and he rarely breaks this down into the "true price" and "tax" components. Income taxes, which have become increasingly important at the state level, and which (along with payroll taxes) dominate the federal revenue structure, are largely withheld at the income source. Withholding has the effect of making the individual unaware that he is paying for a slice of government before he has the opportunity to pay for anything else. He concerns himself with his net or take-home paycheck, and his consciousness of a tax obligation comes home to him only on tax accounting day in March or April of each year. With the property tax, traditionally the mainstay

of local governmental revenue systems, the relatively high awareness of the taxpayer is reduced by the inclusion of tax obligations in monthly mortgage payments. And, for renters, property taxes are equivalent to excise taxes; they show up imbedded in rents.

Economists always return to a central principal, TANSTAAFL, "there ain't no such thing as a free lunch," by which they mean that someone must pay, even if a good seems to be costless to those who consume it. Many fiscal institutions have "free lunch" features built into them and foster the notion that some monies are free. The federal government's program of grants to states and localities increased dramatically in the 1960s. Recipient governments, as represented by their politicians, treat federal grants as if these are, in fact, free monies. The elementary fact that individuals who live in California are also federal taxpayers is lost in the shuffle between Washington and Sacramento.

Fortunately, the national economy continues to grow. National income goes up year by year. This growth insures that the base of taxation increases. From this it follows that, even without changes in tax rates, revenues collected will rise through time. Legislators, whether in the Congress or in the state assemblies, again treat this automatic revenue increase as free money, to be used for new spending programs if desired. Goetz estimates that only a third of the increase in state-local revenues is generated by new taxes and by increased tax rates. Two-thirds of the increase stems from the automatic increase in collections consequent on income growth in the economy.

Although we have included this brief treatment of fiscal illusions under nondemocratic models of politics, we should note that fiscal instruments that generate illusions may be chosen by the people. Taxpayers may, in fact, prefer to fool themselves (as witness Governor

Reagan's unsuccessful fight to keep the California income tax on a nonwithholding basis). Even in a tolerably working democracy, individuals may be reluctant to accept tax instruments that will produce rational budgetary choices. This is a democratic dilemma; rational behavior in selecting among taxes may guarantee irrational budgetary results. All of this may be acknowledged, yet the primary explanation for the persistence of illusions may lie in the behavior of those who find it in their private interests to insure irrational budgetary outcomes.

Politics for Profit

Politicians are politicians because they want to be. They are no more robots than other men. Yet the politician who would do nothing other than reflect the preferences of his constituents would in fact, be robot-like in his behavior. Few, if any, politicians are so restricted. They seek office because they seek "profit," in the form of "political income," which will normally be obtained only if their behavior is not fully in accord with the desires of electoral majorities. Those men who are attracted to politics as a profession are likely to be precisely those who have considerable interest in promoting their own version of good government, along with those who see the potential opportunities for direct and indirect bribes, and those who evaluate political office as means toward other ends.

The electoral process offers, at best, a crude disciplinary check on those who depart too much from constituency preferences. Elections are held only at periodic intervals. Information is poor, and citizens have relatively little private interest in securing more. As a result, almost any politician can, within rather wide limits, behave contrary to the interests of his constituents without suffering predictable harm. If he departs far

from these preferences, he may fail to be reelected. But if the stakes are high, if the potential gains to him in "political income" are sufficiently large, reelection may be willingly sacrificed. Bush et al. explore several of these possibilities in one of his papers.

If the behavior of politicians in seeking and securing "political income" while holding elective office does nothing but create some slack between the working of practical government and an idealized drawing-board model, there would be no cause for concern here. But if this behavior of politicians biases results consistently in the direction of larger governments, it becomes relevant for our purpose. The presence of such biases seems clearly established. Even such a straightforward item as the legislative salary level is directly related to budgetary size. It is much easier to justify a legislative salary increase item in a ten- than in a six-billion-dollar budget. It is much easier to increase legislative salaries for an assembly that meets for six months each year than for an assembly that meets for two months each biennium.

If we introduce the opportunities for potential bribes, whether these be illegal or sub rosa, it is equally clear that these opportunities increase, perhaps exponentially, with growth in governmental size. If, however, governments are excessively large for satisfying constituency demands, or at least for satisfying the preferences of the required majority of constituents, why do not political entrepreneurs find it profitable to appeal to those who would benefit, in the net, from budgetary reductions? Why should platforms based on tax reduction, and spending reduction, not be observed? Why should those legislators, and coalitions of legislators, who seek indirect bribes not seek out those who might benefit from reductions in governmental size? The basic reason is that taxes are more general than spending programs.

Spending projects tend to be concentrated so as to provide benefits to particular groups whereas taxes tend to be levied generally on all those who qualify in terms of a defined base. Furthermore, incumbent politicians, elected on a tax-and-spend program are becoming increasingly difficult to displace. The increasing costs of entry into politics serve to maintain incumbents in elected office. The analysis does not suggest that new political entrepreneurs appealing to those who seek limits on governmental growth must fail in their efforts. It suggests only that the task of this type of political entrepreneur is much more difficult than that faced by the aspiring, and especially incumbent, politicians who can appeal to specific constituency demands for new and expanded projects.

Conflict of Interest

When he became Deputy Secretary of Defense in 1969, David Packard was required to dispose of holdings in a company that maintained an interest in defense contracts. Conflict-of-interest rules have been rigorously applied to high-level governmental appointees during the last decade. Given this, it is perhaps somewhat surprising that the obvious conflict of interest presented by the extension of the voting franchise to members of the vast governmental bureaucracy, at all levels, has scarcely been noted. As Bush and Denzau, and Borcherding, Bush, and Spann remark in their papers, almost no one has analyzed this particular problem. And, unfortunately for our purposes, it seems that the initial disenfranchisement of bureaucrats located in the District of Columbia was not related to the conflict of interest discussed here. Even the Hatch Act, which did seek to reduce overt political activity of bureaucrats, is now under fire in the courts, and it may well be jettisoned if some federal judge decides that he likes his bureaucrat neighbor.

We must be specific. Why is there an obvious conflict of interest present when bureaucrats are allowed to vote in elections organized by the jurisdiction that employs them? Bureaucrats are no different from other persons, and, like others, they will rationally vote to further their own interests as producers when given the opportunity. Clearly their interests lie in an expanding governmental sector, and especially in one that expands the number of its employees. Salaries can be increased much more readily in an expanding agency than in a declining or stagnant one. Promotions are much more rapid in an organization that is increasing in size than in one that is remaining stable or declining in size. From this it follows directly that bureaucrats will vote for those politicians and parties that call for overall governmental expansion rather than for their opposites. This introduces yet another bias in voting outcomes, a bias that grows increasingly important as the sheer size of the bureaucracy grows.

Perhaps this conflict of interest need not be of major concern, even now, if all eligible voters chose to exercise their options. The nonbureaucrat, however, has relatively little private, personal interest in voting, per se, unless the alternatives involve issues that directly influence his well-being. He votes largely out of some sense of duty or obligation to democratic forms, and when voting is costly he may not vote at all. Often he does not; only fifty-five percent of eligible voters participated in the 1972 presidential election.

Things are quite different with the bureaucrat. He will have a much greater interest in exercising his franchise, because his own well-being is directly related to electoral outcomes. And, to the extent that a relatively larger proportion of bureaucrats vote, their individual votes have more value in determining outcomes than might be indicated from a simple head count. Bush et al. examine the data on voting behavior and find that the conflict-of-interest hypothesis is corroborated. From the data they compute a power index for bureaucrats which allows us to place effective weights on their votes, and indirectly to measure the bias that their exercise of the franchise introduces.

Education for the People or Education for the Educators?

We bring our discussion down to concrete terms if we look at one part of the bureaucracy. Educational outlays make up more than 40 percent of combined state and local budgetary expenditures. In his two research papers, Staaf carefully examines the data on recent changes in educational organization and asks: Have the changes been implemented for the benefit of the taxpaying public or for the benefit of those educators who make the organizational decisions? The evidence suggests that the changes have been designed to benefit the members of the educational bureaucracy. The taxpaying public has found itself burdened with significantly higher costs without getting demonstrable improvements in the quality of educational services.

The consolidation of school districts is a case in point. Major consolidation reduced the number of districts from 117,000 in 1940 to 18,000 in 1970. This change took place despite the absence of data suggesting that consolidation facilitates superior educational quality. Why, then, did it occur? How can we explain the institutional change? Once we look at the motivational structure within the educational bureaucracy the answer emerges. Consolidation is desired by educators because salary levels and promotion prospects, and notably those for educational administrators, depend directly on district size.

A by-product of consolidation is a reduction in the competitiveness among local school systems, and an increase in monopoly control of local education. One objective of the educational bureaucracy is to shield itself from competitive pressures, pressures that must work for efficiency in terms of results desired by the final consumers of education, even if not by those educators who supply it.

The absence of effective competition, the difficulty in defining output, and the absence of cost-reducing motivation in the governmental sector—these allow cost-increasing institutions to become imbedded in the bureaucratic structure. Staaf looks in one paper at data on teacher salary levels. He finds that salaries depend largely on educational attainment (higher degrees or work toward higher degrees) and on years of teaching experience. Salaries are unrelated to student achievement, and the data indicate that there is little or no relationship between these salary-making variables and achievement of students. Apparently, students do equally well under teachers who have attained only minimal levels of training and who are not experienced as they do under highly educated teachers with long years of experience. These results suggest that education, as a public service, is being purchased inefficiently in almost all jurisdictions. But what person or group in the education bureaucracy has any motive for changing the pattern? Quite the opposite. School system administrators find their own salaries to be related directly to the number of teachers with experience and with higher degrees. The cost-increasing features feed on themselves.

But why don't experience and training matter? Surely experience in teaching should lead to better teaching and surely education has some positive value. Staaf explains the paradox by examining the behavioral situation in which teachers find themselves. Since their rewards are not related in any way to the final output that they produce, which should be measurable in student achievement, teachers have no personal incentive to perform well. They are not so much bad teachers, as they are teachers who have no reason to be good.

Private Provision of Public Goods and Services: Reducing Spending (and Taxes) Without Reducing Benefits

Aspiring politicians who seek to dislodge incumbents from elective office often refer to major cost-savings that might be introduced by greater efficiencies in spending, cost-savings that may be utilized to provide additional goods without the necessity of imposing new taxes. The public accepts most of these arguments for what they are, and it does not expect the pattern of governmental growth to be changed much regardless of which politician or political party gains power. When we look carefully at the institutional structure of government, however, at the internal motivational system at work in the bureaucracy, the prospect of securing dramatic efficiency gains becomes exciting. If major institutional changes could be made, government budgets could be slashed (along with taxes) without reducing either the quantity or the quality of goods and services enjoyed by the final consumer, the taxpaying citizen.

But a shift in approach would be required to accomplish this. *Governmental financing of goods and services must be divorced from direct governmental provision or production of these goods and services.* There may be fully legitimate arguments for governmental financing but little or no argument for governmental provision. Through the simple device of introducing private provision under governmental financing, the growth in public spending may, figuratively speaking, be stopped in its tracks.

Why should this make so much difference? Why should private contractors be able to supply the same quality of goods and services at substantially lower costs? The motivational differences between the private firm, whose managers can secure direct monetary rewards from cost-savings, and the bureaucratic agency are clear enough, even without supporting empirical evidence. But the facts themselves are dramatic. Spann examines the results of the various studies that have compared the costs of private and public provision of similar services. Scottsdale, Arizona, gets its fire protection from a private firm at one-half the cost of the same quality protection under governmental provision. Monmouth County, New Jersey, has its garbage collected by private contractors at two-thirds of the cost of doing it publicly. These are examples of what might be achieved by widespread introduction of private provision under governmental financing. The introduction of educational vouchers, with the education being supplied to families by private firms, might produce higher quality education at substantially lower costs. Even if parental choices through full voucher schemes should not be accepted, the willingness of local governments to purchase education through performance contracting with private firms offers substantial potential for cost reduction.

Such institutional changes may do much toward checking excessive government growth. But even the widespread introduction of the private provision of goods and services that are governmentally financed may not remove the basic bureaucratic influences in democratic decisions. Persons employed by private firms which supply goods on contract to governments may behave similarly to persons who work directly for governments.

CONCLUSIONS

We started out to explain why governments grow so rapidly. We end by zeroing in on the motivational structure of the governmental bureaucracy as the primary source for that part of governmental growth that does not represent response to the demands of citizens for goods and services. The policy implication is that attempts to reduce excessive governmental spending might be aimed at the motivational structure of bureaucracy rather than at aggregate budgetary or tax levels. On the other hand, if the bureaucracy is considered to be so firmly entrenched and its institutions so rigid that direct attack would be futile,

alternative means may be required. It may prove possible to force through the internal structural changes that might be suggested by the analysis only if aggregate budget and tax limits are imposed on legislative bodies, at the constitutional level. Legislators respond to many constituencies, including that of the bureaucracy. And until the legislator is forced by constitutional restrictions to face up to the inherent conflict between the interests of the citizenry and those of the bureaucracy, he may continue to take the route which, to him, seems that of least resistance. This route has been, until now, that of allowing government budgets (and taxes) to grow.

22.   Budget Theory and Budget Practice: How Good the Fit?

Irene S. Rubin

Theory in budgeting, like much of public administration, has been of two kinds, descriptive and normative. Descriptive theory is based on close observation or participation in public sector activities. Theorists describe trends, sequences of events, and infer causes, paying attention to local variations as well as uniformities across cases. Normative theory—advice—may be based on a much narrower range of observations than descriptive theory and its proposed solutions may be based on values rather than observations. If the explanatory power of the descriptive theory is too weak, or if the advice of normative theory is not adopted by public officials or is adopted

and abandoned because it does not work, the gap between theory and practice may become unacceptably wide.

An examination of the gap between budget theory and practice requires separate examination of the success over time of normative and descriptive budget theory. This article is therefore divided into two parts, one on normative theory and one on descriptive theory. In each part, the past, present and likely future of the relationship between theory and practice is outlined. Where the analysis indicates deterioration of the relationship, suggestions are made on how the relationship might be improved.

THE CONTENT OF NORMATIVE BUDGET THEORY

Normative budget theory dates back at least to the turn of the century. Lively

SOURCE: "Budget Theory and Budget Practice: How Good the Fit?" by Irene Rubin, *Public Administration Review:* 50 (March/April 1990). Reprinted by permission of the American Society for Public Administration.

budgeting debates took up whole issues of journals in a variety of social science disciplines. The practical advice reformers gave about accounting and budget exhibits was supported by a theory of government and the way budgeting relates to the state. Individual theorists differed on particulars, but the executive budget reform proposals[1] were generally based on a federalist model of government. Reformers looked longingly back at Hamilton's financial authority and across at the political systems of England, Switzerland and Germany.[2] They wanted a stronger, more independent executive, more like the Prime Minister in a parliamentary form of government, and less role for parties and party caucuses; generally they sought a smaller role for legislators. Their concern for the growth of government spending often led them to recommend that the legislature in general, and Congress in particular, give up the option of increasing executive-branch recommendations of the executive. These proposals led to debate on the role of the budget process in a democracy.[3]

While many reformers were concerned to limit the growth of government and the access of special interests, it mattered to them how it was to be done. They looked at the evolution of line-item controls that legislative bodies had devised to control machines, especially in New York City, and they argued that although effective in achieving their purpose, they hamstrung the executive and created less efficient government.[4] It was not only spending control the reformers were after, but efficient government. They specifically rejected line item budgets and detailed appropriations in favor of lump sum appropriations that allowed better management.

The program for achieving the reformers' goals included not only the expansion of the power of the executive to formulate policy and review proposals but also new budget formats to convey decision-making information about programs to the legislature and the public for their review. Public accountability was an important theme in this reform literature, and it could only be achieved by improving the quality of budget information and publicizing that information. The public as well as the legislature should understand what the government was doing and how much it was spending to achieve particular goals.

These reformers did not argue that new services should not be included in the budget, only that the cost for doing so should be the lowest possible commensurate with the quality of services demanded. They therefore advocated cost accounting (with its program budgeting implications) and detailed performance budgets based on unit costs. The assumption was that when such information was made public, there would be an outcry if one city's park services cost much more than another's.[5]

The budget reformers at the turn of the century also emphasized the role of planning in the budget. They argued that budgets must contain a work plan and provide funding for future as well as current needs. Some of the reformers went further and argued that budget planning was a way of finding and responding to unmet needs in the community. Otho Cartwright, for example, argued that he would go further than his fellow budget advocates in arguing for a state law that would provide the means to ask the public what its needs were. He argued that members of the public should be allowed to present their case to the proper government authority. He envisioned civic societies that would advocate particular policies, such as more industrial safeguards or better sanitation in the schoolhouses.[6]

While there was considerable variation in the scope of planning advocated by the early reformers, they agreed that planning was inherent in budgeting.

Some of the reformers explicitly linked city planning and budgeting, arguing that poor planning for growth and inadequate sewers, streets, and tunnels cost more money in the end and were inefficient. They implied that a vision of the future city, which would bring order out of chaos, had to be linked to the budget and plans for capital and service spending.[7]

Budget planning meant at the least choosing particular target levels of service by activity and figuring out in advance what it would cost in personnel and supplies to accomplish those specific goals. The reformers rejected a model of budgeting that allowed the departments to ask for what they wanted instead of requesting what they needed to accomplish particular tasks. They were convinced that there was much waste in government and that expenditures could be cut back without losing much in the way of services. They did not think that changes could be implemented only at the margins. They told stories of cutting departmental budgets in half while improving services.[8]

Paralleling these early budget reformers were the public economists, who advocated some of the same kinds of reforms, but from a different theoretical perspective. While the budget reformers emphasized both the need to run government like a business and the constitutional basis for their reforms, the public economists based their arguments on what they perceived as rational choices and optimization of decision making. Both groups emphasized the need to get the most from each dollar, but the public economists were less concerned with cost accounting and management and more concerned with choices between options, laying out the options carefully and choosing between them on carefully specified grounds.

Over the years, many specific budget reforms have been formulated and advocated, then adopted, rejected, or modified. Many of these reforms have the same goals or purposes as those of the reformers of the early 1900s. Program budgeting, for example, and its explanation of what government is trying to accomplish at what cost, addresses specific concerns raised by the early reformers; the linking of planning to programming in the Planning Programming, Budgeting System (PPBS) was also foreshadowed many years earlier. Performance budgets, with their varied emphasis on measuring demands and workloads or efficiency and unit costs, also reflect earlier concerns. The idea of determining desired service levels, associating costs with each one, and budgeting for only desired levels of service is the heart of Zero-Based Budgeting (ZBB) and Target-Based Budgets, but it was also part of the early reformers' attempts to judge what was needed versus what was wanted and to get out of the budget waste that had accumulated over the years. Current models of budgeting for outcomes perfectly express the activist, efficiency, and accountability goals of the early reformers. Management by objectives links the specific annual goals of the city to work loads and the personnel evaluation system, an elaboration of the old reformers' goals.

Normative Theory and Practice

How successful has this normative theory and its specific offspring been? Evaluations of budget reforms, both specifically and generically, have often been negative. The reformers urged wide public participation in budgeting, with open hearings, advertisements, public presentation of budget exhibits, and budgets that were explanatory to the average person. Such participation was either short lived or did not materialize. Calls for a consolidated budget that explained to the public the range of programs and types of spending have dimmed in the face of continuing fragmentation, multiyear budgets, off-budget accounts, and different types of spending. Specific reforms, such as Management by Objectives (MBO), PPB, and ZBB have been evaluated and declared to be failures.[9]

More generically, the incrementalists argued that many reforms required comprehensive evaluation of programs and specific delineation of spending for specific purposes, which would have negative effects. A great number of programs could not be compared at one time, and the effects of making spending clearer would undoubtedly be more conflict. They disapproved of the idea of bringing the public more into the budgeting process for fear of increased and conflicting demands. They argued that budgeting should not be reformed.[10]

A review of the literature suggests that budgeters have underestimated the success of normative theory for a variety of reasons. One reason is that once a reform has been widely adopted, people tend to forget the role of normative theory in bringing the changes about. The federal government, most of the states, and nearly all cities with over 10,000 population have adopted the executive-budget model. Other kinds of recommendations, such as keeping enterprise funds separate, setting rates for public enterprises so as not to make a profit, and using the modified accrual basis of accounting have become accepted budgetary practices. The distinction between the detailed budget presentation of the President to Congress and the lump sum appropriation of Congress in its approved budget was suggested by the budget reformers, and it has been the dominant pattern in the federal government for many years. The idea that budgets should be tools for public accountability, and therefore should be easy to read, has been widely accepted and often inventively implemented.[11]

Even more recent and controversial recommendations for budget reform like zero-based budgeting, program budgeting, management by objectives, and performance budgeting have been far more successful than many people in public administration have thought. Some studies suggested that many budget reforms were fads that had few or no lasting effects; in some cases they changed the budget formats but not the decision making.[12]

Some of the most discouraging of the evaluations have been at the federal level. But there is only one federal government, it is highly complex and unusual, and it is not typical of the state or local governments or of public budgeting in general. Historically, state and local governments have often innovated first and successfully and then the innovation has spread to the federal government. That such innovation should be judged essentially by what happens in the federal government seems unjustifiable. Budget innovations have been much more widely adopted and implemented at state and local levels, especially in the past decade.

Other reasons that success with normative budgeting has been underestimated are that evaluators looked too quickly to find consequences and tried to find the innovation in the exact form in which it was introduced. "The absorptive character of government, gradually adapting and incrementally augmenting its activities, suggests that change may more easily be measured on a time scale congenial to a forester or a geologist than to a Congress or a White House in a hurry."[13] Many of the innovations were clumsy when introduced, so that public administrators adopted and then adapted them, piecing together parts of reforms that suited their environments. Consequently, if one looked right away for the impacts of a specific budget innovation, one was likely to see fumbling implementation or even evasion of key provisions, but if one looked a decade or more later, one was likely to see a blending of pieces of different reforms that were functioning well in some places.

The reforms were often oversold, leading to the inevitable claim that they could not deliver. "In order for major reform legislation to become law, exaggerated claims are made for its future performance."[14] If one claims that a budget reform will reduce the federal deficit and the federal deficit remains, the reform appears to have failed, even if a variety of more modest improvements were made. Evaluations that examine the evolution of goals over time and evaluate outcomes on a scale of achievement have found budget innovations moderately successful.[15]

Normative Theory and Practice on the State and Local Levels

At the municipal level in the United States, many proposed budget reforms have been adopted in whole or in part and have been adapted to the needs and capacities of the local communities. Sometimes it has taken cities many years to implement the changes because they did not have the necessary information base, accounting system, or staff time. Sometimes the reform has been interrupted or delayed, or even lost, but budget changes can occur gradually. The direction of the change is obvious when looked at over the period of a decade or more.

One study of a national sample of cities compared a 1976 International City Management Association survey with a study using the same survey instrument in 1982 and 1983. Over that time period, the change in reported budget sophistication was dramatic. The use of program, zero base, or target budgeting had increased from 50 percent to 77 percent of the sample; the use of MBO increased from 41 percent to 59 percent; and performance monitoring was up from 28 percent to 68 percent. About two thirds of the sample reported they used program budgeting, while a third reported using either ZBB or Target-Based Budgeting, which is a form of ZBB. The number of cities reporting that they had tried and dropped these innovations was not negligible, but it was still quite low. Reports of effectiveness varied by specific technique, but the ones which reported the most widespread adoption, such as program budgeting, were considered effective by about 44 percent of the respondents. Only performance measurement among the widely adopted tools got generally low ratings for effectiveness.[16]

A more recent study looked at the same budget practices in 1987 and found little additional use of these techniques but considerable stability in the numbers of users. The authors concluded that these tools "have become staples rather than fads in public management."[17] All of these studies do not include very small cities and so exaggerate somewhat the overall rate of usage. Still for cities with over 25,000 in population, the use of these tools remains high and constant.

Cross-sectional studies on self-reported data are useful, especially when done at intervals with the same instrument, but they leave one wondering whether those who reported them meant ZZB or MBO. Did it mean that the city went through all the information gathering and analysis implied in the process or that a vague statement of goals was added to the budget before each program? Nor is it clear from these studies if cities are gradually adding to existing reforms in a logical way so that one builds on the next or if they are modifying existing practices to be less threatening or more effective. To answer some of these questions, a mini-panel study was designed, looking at the budgets of 15 cities across the country over approximately 10 years, from about 1977 to about 1987. The smallest of the cities was about 40,000 population.[18]

Briefly, the results confirm the cross sectional data. In 1977 nine cities out of the 15 had relatively straightforward line-item budgets; ten years later, only five cities had straight line item budgets. There was increasing use of some form of performance measures, although the definition and measures of performance were not stable either across departments or across time. The use of ZZB or Target-Based Budgeting was low but stable: two out of the fifteen used zero based or target based budgeting at the beginning and at the end of the period. The most dramatic change was in MBO. In 1977 none of the cities used this technique as part of the budget format, but by 1987, four of the 15 were using it. From the budgets themselves it appears that some of the cities were using the formats more seriously as part of their decision-making process than others. And some cities included a variety of formats not specifically named.

To get a sense of smaller cities and the most recent data, 12 municipal budgets from suburban Dupage County, Illinois, were examined. Sizes ranged from 6,700 to 90,000 population. One had no real budget (which is legal under Illinois law), six had straight line-item budgets, the others had some combination of program budgets with goals and objectives statements, or program budgets with MBO and performance measures. Cities of 14,000 and smaller population were much more likely to have straight line-item budgets. This is not really surprising, as their municipal operations are likely to be much simpler, and staff and council are much more likely to know each other and the programs intimately without the help of management controls and informative budgets.

It is clear from reading these budgets that in most cases the budget process itself has changed, not only the format. For example, in Hanover Park, a village of about 32,000 population, the President and the Board of Trustees first set forth their goals for the year, and then the departments' objectives are set and supporting goals are established. The process lasts over six months. In the budgets, the departments and boards list their previous year's objectives, which ones they obtained on time and which ones are still ongoing, and then describe their objectives for the next budget year. In Bensenville, population about 16,000, the budget introduction lists the goals and objectives for the city for the upcoming year: these include both potential service expansions and possible mergers and reorganizations of service delivery. The year's tasks include an evaluation of a neighborhood survey of citizen satisfaction with services and redesign of the city's handling of complaints. Each department lists concrete and extensive objectives and goals in the budget.

The most dramatic of the budgets from Dupage County is that of Downers Grove, population about 43,000. That budget combines program budgeting, line-item controls, and an MBO system. The system was developed over more than a decade. It has been combined with a five-year financial plan to create what the manager calls "results budgeting." The five-year plan is an integrated long-range operating budget and capital improvement plan. It describes where the city is headed and what the financial requirements will be. Portions of the plan appear in the annual budget. The City Manager, Kurt Bressner, argues, "The importance of integrating the MBO system into the budget cannot be overstated. Through this step, the desired results are directly linked to the resources necessary to achieve them."[19] This is exactly what the budget reformers of the early 1900s were trying to achieve. Many cities have pieces of this integrated system, and they seem to be moving in this direction, even though they do not have it all assembled yet.

This is not to say that no simple line-item budgets exist out there. Commission cities, of which only a few remain in the whole country, tend to budget in a line-item and highly decentralized fashion, but as an outdated and largely abandoned reform, commission cities are not typical of future trends. Small cities, counties, and some rural cities still budget with simple line items with no explanation, but they probably do not need much more sophistication.

The response of state governments has been similar to that of the cities. More than half the states make use of program budgets, performance reporting and monitoring, program analysis, program evaluation, and forward year projections of revenue and expenditure. Seventy-four percent of the states report using program budgeting; 38 percent of the users report that it is highly effective, and 62 percent report that it is somewhat effective. ZBB is used by fewer states, 20 as opposed to 37 that use program budgeting, but the proportion of those reporting effectiveness is about the same. Performance monitoring is fairly widespread, but a lower percentage of states that report such monitoring consider it highly successful. Nevertheless, a high proportion consider it somewhat effective. Most of these budget innovations have been hybridized and adapted, using parts of some and parts of other reforms.[20]

What is equally interesting are the reforms that now seem to represent the state of the art.[21] Increasingly, planning is merging with budgeting. The result is multiyear budgeting, which is not just a projection of budget numbers but a corporate plan which includes statements of policy, underlying assumptions, and goals for the community.[22] In drawing up the plans, consideration is given to unmet needs, changes in the community, anticipated growth, and changing technology. Perhaps more common in rapidly growing and changing communi-

nities, these plans are the local adaptations of PPBS, home grown, to fit the local need. Even when no corporate long-term plan exists, there is often a capital long-term plan with the explicit goal of creating a preapproved list of priorities in which the first year of the plan pops out as a section of the next year's budget.

The recent integration of MBO with the budget implies that goal setting, personnel evaluation, work loads, and budget are being integrated in some budgets. The program manager in essence promises to do so much work and gets so much budget to do it. When integrated with the budget, this work load data gives the citizen a good look at exactly what his or her money is doing. MBO has the advantage of linking the budget with the personnel evaluation system, and hence it is more than a plan or report.

What budget reform has not yet generally achieved at the local level is good cost accounting and good performance budgeting. Cost accounting has sometimes become political. When a particular service is sorted out for a cost analysis, councilmembers may view the service as too expensive and try to use cost accounting to make it politically vulnerable. Or a manager may try to make a program look less expensive through cost accounting to defend it from its detractors. Cost accounting does not have the appearance of a neutral skill that can help save money. With respect to performance measures, departments have resisted what appears to them to be unfair evaluations. The department heads often fear, with some justification, that low efficiency ratings will be blamed on them and the council will take away resources from them in a misguided effort to increase efficiency. Since departments seldom have complete control over what are viewed as departmental outcomes—such as dollar losses for fires—department heads fear that they will be blamed for such things as a rash of arson fires, regardless of the quality of their work. Nevertheless, some elements of performance budgeting have crept into municipal budgets, even if they are not yet working to everyone's satisfaction.

In short, contemporary budgeting at the state and local levels reflects many of the practices recommended by budget theory, and it continues to evolve. Public administration has clearly been successful in proposing reforms that are attractive to practitioners when those reforms have appeared to have the capacity to solve budgetary problems. The reforms have not always worked to everyone's satisfaction, but the relation between normative budget theory and budget practice has been close, especially at state and local levels.

Normative Theory and Practice at the Federal Level

In recent years the record at the federal level has not been as strong. Budget reformers had a major hand in designing the executive budget process in 1921, and reform ideas were evident in the redesign of congressional budgeting in 1974. But reform ideas played little role in the 1985 deficit reduction act known as Gramm-Rudman-Hollings.

The 1974 reform emphasized the role of professional budget staff to enable Congress to have sufficient information to make budget decisions. It also emphasized the importance of having overall budget targets and ways of setting and enforcing budget priorities. These were two persistent themes in the reform literature.

By contrast, the Gramm-Rudman-Hollings deficit reduction act set up a variety of across-the-board cuts—with many of the most popular entitlement programs exempted—that would automatically be invoked if the normal budget process could not achieve a specified target for deficit reduction. Where previous budget reforms had tried to include entitlement programs to bring them into budget scrutiny and to make them part of budget tradeoffs, Gramm-Rudman-Hollings exempted them; where previous budget reforms had striven to make thoughtful comparisons among competing programs, Gramm-Rudman-Hollings cut across the board.

The Gramm-Rudman-Hollings deficit reduction law was often referred to as a bad idea whose time had come.[23] The reported intent of the law was to make the mandatory cuts so distasteful to both Democrats and Republicans that they would join together to make a proper budget that would reduce the deficit below the trigger level for the automatic cuts. Instead, the law has worked to enhance the incentives to make deficits look smaller than they are (to get below the trigger level) by using "smoke and mirrors." Senator James Exon has argued, "Rather than force action, the Gramm-Rudman process fakes action. . . . After two years of operation, Gramm-Rudman has not worked."[24]

It was not just Gramm-Rudman-Hollings that suggested that normative theory was not working at the federal level; many other budget reform proposals of the past few decades have not worked well at the federal level. Part of the reason seems to be the size and complexity of the federal government. Putting together a citywide list of priorities coming from a half dozen or even a dozen city departments is a massive task but not an impossible undertaking. Putting together a priority list of programs in one department of the complexity of the federal Health and Human Services without an agreed upon set of criteria for such a ranking may well be impossible or so difficult as to overwhelm any advantage the process might have produced.

Another problem has been that reform proposals have not kept up well with the increased complexity of the federal budget over the years. Parts of the federal budget receive continuing appropriations that are semi-permanent and do not go through annual budget review. Many capital projects such as weapons systems are authorized for expenditure over a period of years, and the matter of what part has been spent or remains to be spent clouds the logic of an annual comprehensive review. Reformers' programs have included consolidated annual budgets with explicit comparison between major categories of spending, but the reality of federal budgeting today is multiple budgets, and parts of the budget are multiyear.[25] More important, some compelling reasons exist for the increased complexity, and it is not likely to go away any time soon. The result is that many old reform proposals no longer make much sense.

Other reform proposals have been taken as far as they usefully can be taken. For years, the reform proposal for assuring balanced budgets was increasingly to strengthen the power of the chief executive over the budget. In the states, for example, the governors have been given stronger and stronger budget vetoes. But the reform has probably already gone too far, contributing to an atrophy of legislatures, and the trend for the past 10 to 20 years has been back in the other direction, to give legislatures more balanced responsibilities over budget matters.[26] It has become increasingly clear that legislatures are not necessarily more profligate than governors and that Congress is not historically more likely to spend than the President.[27] Some executives are more prone to spending, and some legislatures are more prone to spending. A reform that purports to control spending by giving the executive more and legislatures less spending power seems wrong-headed.[28]

Part of the problem of the recent failure of budget reform at the federal level has been the focus on trying to reduce the size of the deficit through reforming budget processes or legislating discipline. A budget reform can help carry out the goals of politicians once they have made up their minds, but it cannot make up their minds. Public administration may have been asking budget reform to do the impossible.

Some of the increasing complexity of the budget that has made federal reforms so difficult has affected state and local levels as well. Capital projects may sprawl across years. Budgets at all levels are likely to contain a variety of resources, including loan guarantees, loans and revolving funds, contracts, insurance, grants, subsidies, and direct service delivery. The problems of exaggerated executive budget power are more extreme at the state and local level than they are at the national level. As a result, many traditional bits of reform advice are becoming less relevant at all levels of government.

IMPROVING THE RELATIONSHIP BETWEEN NORMATIVE THEORY AND PRACTICE

How can the relationship of normative budget theory and practice be improved in the coming years? First, a better understanding is needed of what the budget process and format can and cannot do so that reform proposals will be realistic. Greater clarity is required about the difference between being idealistic, asking for budgets to be completely transparent, for example, and suggesting budget reforms as solutions to broader problems that such reforms may influence only marginally. The former is an important part of public administration; the latter at best makes budget reform look impotent, and at worst, detracts attention from more likely solutions.

Second, reconsideration is needed to what accountability means and how to achieve it in budgets that allocate multiple resources on a multiple year basis. For example, what does "consolidated" mean in such a budget? One does not want to add tax expenditures to outlays—they are different kinds of numbers and they do not meaningfully add. One does not want to include the balances in trust funds to offset the deficit, as the United States government now does, when those funds can never be spent to reduce that deficit. So some parts of the budget should remain separate; full consolidation in the context of different types of expenditures and expenditure restrictions should not be a goal.

However, openness and clarity of presentation are more urgent in this context of multiyear and multisource budgets than they were when budgets were simpler. The completeness of the budget takes on increasing importance. Are the costs of tax breaks adequately represented? How are the costs of loans presented? Are various subsidies reported? How? What about the shifting of costs through regulation of the economy? How are unfunded liabilities being reported, where, and with what accuracy? In short, what is not in the budget that should be? This avenue of budget reform needs to be continued and applied more widely at state and local levels.

The appropriate level of budgetary secrecy must be reexamined. Openness of budget decision making to the public also opens the budget process to interest groups; is that an adequate argument for closing budget decisions? To what extent have procedures been created or endorsed to close deliberations to the public and press while still keeping them open to interest groups? One could argue, for example, that the federal black budget for security agencies is a secret only from the American public and not from foreign powers. Can budget processes be prescribed that buffer decision makers somewhat from interest groups and still keep them open and accountable to the public?

What level of secrecy is justified and at what potential and actual cost? The tendency has been to create budget systems that are closed on the executive side and open on the legislative side; as budget power has shifted overwhelmingly toward the executive branch, what has been the impact on public accountability and democratic government? Is the trend toward greater balance between the legislature and the executive gradually solving the problem of accountability, or is the legislature going to become more isolated or insulated as it regains more budget power?

Third, indicators are needed to give early warning when various processes or interests are getting out of balance, with potentially serious and unwanted consequences on the budget. Perhaps indicators need to flash a warning when the budget estimates have become too rosy. Governments need to avoid the extremes of centralization or decentralization, of executive or legislative dominance, of openness and secrecy. Perhaps a need exists to measure and monitor the swings, to give early warning of needed adjustments. It would also be useful to monitor the budget process itself for signs of excessive strain and potential future collapse. How much stress can the process take? How much delay is too much? What does failure of the budget process look like?

Fourth, balance needs to be struck between precontrols and postcontrols in budget implementation. How effective have various measures to evaluate programs been with respect to the budget? Are program audits or even financial audits used in the preparation of new budgets? Is there a way to make such audits more useful, more accessible to more people? Varied controls are at governments' disposal now, but how many are too many? Budget practice is alert to the possibility of giving agencies too much autonomy, but how should governments guard against the inefficiencies of giving them too little? This was a problem that bothered the early reformers, but normative budgeting has not yet worked out a good set of answers.

If ways can be recommended to improve accountability in complex budgets, the link between taxpayers and public decision makers can be strengthened. If ways can be recommended to public officials to explain what they are doing and how well they are doing it, perhaps the anti-government flavor of tax revolts can be moderated. The match between theory and practice may also be improved if budgeters learn to give conditional rather than absolute advice. It is necessary to learn when particular reforms are likely to work and when they have outlived their usefulness. If reform can be reconceptualized, reaching for a new set of ideals beyond reducing the deficit and even beyond traditional goals of increased efficiency and fiscal control, budgeters will have a better chance of affecting the future of budget practice.

THE HISTORICAL LINKAGE BETWEEN DESCRIPTIVE THEORY AND PRACTICE

If, in normative theory, budgeters were more successful than they knew, in descriptive theory, scholarly evaluation may have been overly optimistic. Incrementalism, which was intended not only as a normative theory but also as a descriptive theory, was dominant and in many ways inadequate. It prevented many budgeters from seeing the changing budget reality in front of them and theorizing about it. As a result, theory and practice grew unacceptably far apart.

At the national level, Aaron Wildavsky's well known study, *The Politics of the Budgetary Process,* emphasized the role of agencies in the budget process, assumed their desire for growth, and discussed their strategies in dealing with the congressional review process, especially the appropriations committees. That book came out in 1964 and was updated at intervals until 1984. The author gave up the framework and wrote a new book, *The New Politics of the Budgetary Process,* published in 1988. Two years after Wildavsky's 1964 book, Richard Fenno's blockbuster, *The Power of the Purse: Appropriations Politics in Congress,* was published. This book is still treated as a classic, and together they framed the incrementalist assumptions about budgeting at the national level. They emphasized the centrality of a legislatively dominated budget, the importance of agencies in the process, the decentralization of the process, and the lack of comparison between alternatives for spending. The incrementalist model argued that no major changes in budgets from year to year and hence that few choices of policy consequence were being made in the context of the budget.

These assumptions may have seemed more descriptive in the 1960s than later, but even then they left major elements out of the picture. The entitlement programs had been created during the Great Depression of the 1930s, the U.S. Office of Management and Budget (OMB) had become an office in the Executive Office of the President in 1939; and Presidents had certainly taken on policy roles in budget formation from time to time. But the incrementalist model left out these features, and others did not fill in the blanks for years.

At the state level, Thomas Anton wrote a detailed case study of budgeting in Illinois,[29] published in 1966, describing the role of all the major budget actors and concluding that no one, not even the governor, had much policy input. He described the budget process as relatively unchanging, despite the recent evolution of budgeting before the period of his study. Budgeting continued to change dramatically after his study. By 1970, the governor had a centralized office of budgeting, which became a major tool in imposing the governor's priorities on the budget, and the revised state constitution gave the governor a reduction veto, increasing his power over the budget enormously. But Anton never revised the study, and no one else wrote as comprehensive a study of state budget politics in Illinois. The 1960s and 1970s were periods of major change and reform in state budgeting, but the incrementalists seemed to ignore most of it.[30]

At the local level, Arnold Meltsner did one of the Oakland, California, studies on the politics of local revenue, published in 1971.[31] This study described Oakland as having little autonomy over taxes and being constrained by public opposition to taxes that resulted in fragmented revenues and low property taxes. He described the citizens as being generally uninterested in government, and he concluded that budgeting presented few policy issues for public reaction. Though he undoubtedly captured some element of revenue processes common at the local level, he missed many of them and perhaps inadvertently suggested that what he said about Oakland was typical of other cities across time.

These studies were followed for many years with quantitative studies of budgetary outcomes that seemed to reaffirm that budgets changed little and did not involve policy choices. These models focused attention on the difference between last year's budget and this year's and the size of the increment for different departments or programs. They made assumptions about the definition of the base budget, because the theory divided all budgets into unquestioned bases and sometimes superficially examined increments. Zero-based budgets and in fact any kind of budget tradeoffs were explicitly rejected by the incre-

mental modelers. Even those who wished to disprove the incrementalists' assumptions and conclusions followed the incrementalists' hypotheses in order to disprove them.

Though there have always been a few dissenters, incrementalist theory dominated budgeting literature for close to two decades, and it focused attention away from phenomena that did not fit the theory. Only when something dramatic happened, such as a constitutional crisis or a major reform, did attention shift to describing what had happened.

For example, incrementalism postulates a decentralized budget process, which focused attention away from the actual level of centralization and coordination of the budget process. Congressional budget reforms in 1974 eventually forced attention to the issue, but those focusing on it had to work outside the theory of incrementalism. It was not until 1980 that Allen Schick's (nonincrementalist) comprehensive description of the causes and functioning of the 1974 Budget and Impoundment Control Act was published.[32] That study brought home a fact that should have been obvious much sooner, that the level of centralization of budget processes varies, and that theory needs to describe and explain that variation.

Due to the incrementalist model, budgeters did not focus for many years on the role of the budget office as a policy formulator. Incrementalism argued that budgeting does not really deal with policy, that policy is dealt with somewhere else. The changing role of OMB at the national level ultimately forced attention on the issue, but theory did not direct attention there.[33]

Incrementalism assumes that moderate revenue growth will create a positive increment to be distributed among the departments and agencies. It did not deal with the possibility of frozen or declining revenues. The deep recession of 1974–1975, Proposition 13 in California, and expansion of the tax limitation movement in the later 1970s culminated in major federal cuts of the early 1980s under President Reagan, giving budgeters pause. These environmental changes brought about startlingly obvious changes in budgeting. A large number of studies were done documenting and trying to explain what was happening outside the context of incrementalist theory. By the early 1980s, budgeters were beginning to theorize about what it all meant.[34] One conclusion was that budgeting was both top down and bottom up, and the balance changed over time in response to environmental changes. More broadly, it meant both that the level of resource availability affected budgeting and that budget behavior was conditional and not absolute.[35] It also meant the budget base was not inviolable and that cuts were often not across the board.[36]

The budget reforms of 1974 in Congress were precipitated in part by a constitutional crisis about who had control over spending, Congress or the President. This issue focused attention on the historical evolution of the location and balance of budget power.[37] Debate about the success of the 1974 congressional budget reform helped to focus attention on the issue of what such budgetary changes were accomplishing, and hence focused attention on previous historical reforms, their circumstances, and their outcomes.[38] When this focus was blended with the realization that budgeting varied in the degree of top-down emphasis and also varied with resource levels, the outcome was the beginning of a reformulated budget theory that emphasized historical conditions and developments over time.[39] Incrementalism had been static, arguing that changes in budgeting were few. The theory examined changes from one year to the next, downplaying major historical changes. That mold has now been broken, and budgeting has a much more self-conscious concern with change.

Similarly, incrementalist theory directed attention away from issues of budget tradeoffs for many years. When the issue was finally addressed, it tended to be at least initially by nonbudgeters, many of whom were outside public administration completely. This literature was primarily quantitative, often comparative, and generally at the national level. Many authors tried to prove statistically that tradeoffs had to occur in the budget process. Even at the local level, where the level of discretion in spending is often small, budget tradeoffs occur over time.[40]

At the local level, the lack of adequate descriptive theory has been acute. The most important omission has been the neglect of the linkage between municipal policy making and budgetary decisions. Incrementalism blocked the view for many years by asserting that policy issues were not dealt with in the budget process. Recent observation suggests otherwise.

Most major policy issues decided at city hall involve budgetary decisions, and most are made in the context of budgetary decision making. Will businesses be subsidized at the expense of homeowners, or will single-family homeowners be subsidized at the expense of apartment buildings? Will the poor or the "well to do" bear the greater burden of taxation? What range of services will the city provide, and to whom? What work will be done on what projects, and how much money will be allocated to the capital as opposed to the operating budget? How will the city deal with requests for grants, loans, or subsidies from social service providers, builders, or merchants? These issues routinely come up in the budget process. They do not always come up directly in the hearings between the departments and the budget office, however, which may have misled incrementalists into thinking that such decisions were not part of the budget process.

Policy decisions of varying scope occur with some regularity. For example, for the last few years cities have been wrestling with how to cope with the loss of General Revenue Sharing. In Dekalb, Illinois, the resulting debate forced a confrontation between social services and so-called basic services. The city decided to increase taxes to replace the lost revenues. The tax increase that was decided on was regressive and grouped earmarked capital funding with social services as the beneficiaries of the tax.[41] It is difficult to imagine a more far-reaching discussion on the priorities of the city and on definitions of need, equity, and balance between group interests. Two years later, De Kalb's city council was struggling with a choice of making appropriations for economic development (expansion) or absorbing the costs of drainage problems for existing homeowners, a problem that was being exaggerated by economic development at the city's margins. Again, this is a common policy issue raised in the context of the budget, requiring resolution in the budget through choice of projects and funding alternatives.

Other policy-laden decisions occur at intervals or at periods of city growth or decline. The time span of the observer has to be long enough to see these events, or the observer has to be lucky enough to come across them. Cities, for example, examine their revenues at intervals. They tend to set up commissions to explore a variety of options and to make recommendations. When the city goes for a new tax or a tax increase, it is a time of public accounting, a time when the city has to demonstrate that it is well run and that it is doing what the citizens want it to do. This is a decidedly nonincremental part of municipal decision making, and it has been undertheorized.

A second issue that has been relatively ignored because of the incrementalists' focus on departmental autonomy and legislative budgets is the amount of centralized executive review of the budget proposal, the amount of policy input from the executive and the legislature in the formation of the proposal, and the level and timing of the involvement of the council in decision making. In many cities, perhaps half, the budget process begins with a meeting between the executive and the council to discuss budget priorities. These priorities are then reflected in the budget that the executive proposes. Such a model implies that the departments are given guidance on what to emphasize in their proposals, and that the departments follow such guidance. This is not the only model of the budget process, but it is an important one, and, with its emphasis on central control and cooperation between the legislature and the executive, it is outside the realm of much budget theory. It happens, but what does it mean?

Municipal budgeting looks incremental only in the sense that revenues tend to increase slowly, and most changes occur at the margins. This is not a very significant discovery, since it would not be reasonable to expect that cities would terminate their fire departments and instead, double their police departments. Reorganizations—shifting and merging functions, emphasizing some tasks at the expense of others—occur with considerable frequency but are not easily detected in an incremental analysis of budget totals. Detection requires a perspective that goes inside the departments. In short, many nonincremental decisions are part of the municipal budget process and have been relatively unexplored.

The history of the relationship between descriptive theory and practice in budgeting suggests a worsening of the relationship from the middle 1960s until the early 1980s, followed by a rapid improvement. Continued accumulation of good descriptive studies is needed to encourage budgeters to theorize about trends and causation. More descriptive theory is needed. Openness and variety should be the guiding principles: explore everything that might be relevant. Explore the relationship between budgeting and society and the link between budget processes and democracy. Look at trends over time; try to link changing environmental conditions, budget processes, and budget outcomes. Budget theory has been too restrictive about what is important for far too long. Budgeting is complex, and no simple theory will ever be adequate to describe it.

SUMMARY AND CONCLUSION

The relationship between budget theory and practice has been different, depending on whether one was looking at normative or descriptive theory. On the normative side, budget theory has generally been more successful than imagined; that is, it has set attractive goals that have often been a guide for behavior. On the side of descriptive or even predictive theory, budget theory has been much weaker, often unable to see the phenomena in plain view to theorize about their meaning.

Projecting to the near future, successes in normative theory may be limited unless budget theory can formulate some recommendations that address the complexity of modern multifunction, multisource, multiyear budgets. By contrast, descriptive research has improved enormously in recent years, and the near future for descriptive theory looks bright.

Budgeters have regained the ability to see what is in front of them, and they are beginning to recapture the ability to theorize from what in fact is there. The field is poised for a mushrooming of descriptive theory over the next few years. The match between descriptive theory and practice will almost certainly improve over the next decade. Unfortu-

nately, recent proposals for reform have often been attempts to curb the deficit or curb the level of national spending. The result has been a series of unrelated, and sometimes worn-out proposals, many of which have little potential for success. But perhaps the growth in descriptive theory will suggest some useful reforms.

NOTES

1. For a definition and well known exposition of the arguments for an executive budget, see Frederick A. Cleveland, "The Evolution of the Budget Idea in the United States," American Academy of Political and Social Science, *The Annals,* vol. 62 (November 1915), pp. 15–35.

2. For the theoretical underpinnings of this reform, see particularly Henry Ford Jones, "Budget Making and the Work of Government," American Academy of Political and Social Science, *The Annals,* vol. 62 (November 1915), pp. 1–14.

3. One elegant version of this argument appears in Edward A. Fitzpatrick's *Budget Making in a Democracy* (New York: MacMillan, 1918). He opens his book with a quote from Gladstone, "Budgets are not merely affairs of arithmetic, but in a thousand ways go to the root of prosperity of individuals, the relation of classes and the strength of kingdoms" (p. vii).

4. The argument that New York City had overdone budget controls through excessively detailed line items is made by Henry Bruére, "The Budget as an Administrative Program," *The Annals,* vol. 62 (November 1915), pp. 176–191. Fitzpatrick emphasizes this failure in drawing up his proposals for a more reformed and effective legislature and better information in the budget format for legislators to review. See Fitzpatrick, chs. 5 and 6.

5. See, for example, Paul T. Beisser, "Unit Costs in Recreational Facilities," *The Annals,* vol. 62 (November 1915), pp. 140–147.

6. Otho Grandford Cartwright, "County Budgets and Their Construction," *The Annals,* vol. 62 (November 1915), pp. 229–230.

7. See, for example, J. Harold Braddock, "Some Suggestions for Preparing a Budget Exhibit," *The Annals,* vol. 62 (November 1915), p. 157. He waxes rhapsodic on the relationship between city planning and budgeting. "It means that the great distributive function of our economic life is to be articulated with the other great function, production, in agreement with the dominant principle of the day—efficiency."

8. For one such example, see Tilden Abramson, "The Preparation of Estimates and the Formulation of the Budget—The New York City Method," *The Annals,* vol. 62 (November 1915), p. 261.

9. Allen Schick, "A Death in the Bureaucracy: The Demise of Federal PPB," *Public Administration Review,* vol. 33 (March/April 1973), pp. 146–156, and Richard Rose, "Implementation and Evaporation: The Record of MBO," *Public Administration Review,* vol. 37 (January/February 1977), pp. 64–71. For a negative pronouncement on ZBB, see Allen Schick, "The Road from ZBB," *Public Administration Review,* vol. 38 (March/April 1978), pp. 177–180.

10. Arnold Meltsner and Aaron Wildavsky, "Leave City Budgeting Alone! A Survey, Case Study, and Recommendations for Reform," in John P. Crecine, ed., *Financing the Metropolis: Public Policy in Urban Economics,* vol. 4, Urban Affairs Annual Reviews (Beverly Hills, CA: Sage, 1970), pp. 311–358.

11. For example, Elgin, Illinois, lists each year all the interfund transfers, where they came from, where they went to, and for what reason. (This is an innovation I would recommend for many other cities.) Budget issues are described for each program before the numbers are presented. The Town of Windsor, Connecticut, has a budget that reports demand data, such as the number of fire incidents per year over a five-year period and the reported crime rate over a decade. This data outlines the basis on which a budget is formulated. Windsor's extremely clear program layout describes the functions of each program, describes any changes, and discusses key issues. Program narratives tell the reader what specific issues the program is dealing with each year and why.

12. Thomas Lauth in his article, "Zero-Based Budgeting in Georgia: The Myth and the Reality," *Public Administration Review,* vol. 38 (September/October 1978), pp. 420–430, argues that those who expected Zero Based Budgeting to eliminate programs were disappointed, that budgeting remained incremental, and that ZBB took place in that context. Allen Schick makes a similar point for the federal level in "The Road from ZBB," *Public Administration Review,* vol. 38 (March/April 1978), pp. 177–180.

13. Rose, *op. cit., supra,* p. 64.

14. Howard Shuman, *Politics and the Budget* (Englewood Cliffs, NJ: Prentice Hall, 1984), p. 276.

15. See, for example, David Sallack and David Allen, "From Impact to Output: Pennsylvania's Planning-Programming-Budgeting System in Transition," *Public Budgeting and Finance,* vol. 7 (Spring 1987), pp. 38–50. Another example of this

type of analysis is in Shuman, *Politics and the Budget,* chapter 10. Rudolph Penner and Alan Abramson, *Broken Purse Strings: Congressional Budgeting, 1974–88* (Washington: The Urban Institute, 1988), evaluate the 1974 Budget Impoundment and Control Act of 1974 over a 14-year period, with careful evaluation of what the original goals of the Act were for those who designed it, rather than some of the claims later made for it. They argue, as others have argued, that the reform was neutral in terms of aims to increase or decrease spending, and hence the law cannot reasonably be judged on failure to curtail spending. They claim some successes and some failures of the reform over time.

16. Theodore Poister and Robert P. McGowan, "The Use of Management Tools in Municipal Government: A National Survey," *Public Administration Review,* vol. 44 (May/June 1984), pp. 215–223.

17. Theodore Poister and Gregory Streib, "Management Tools in Municipal Government: Trends over the Past Decade," *Public Administration Review,* vol. 49 (May/June 1989), p. 242.

18. The cities are New York City; Pittsburgh, Pennsylvania; Baltimore, Maryland; San Antonio, Texas; Durham, North Carolina; Cambridge, Massachusetts; Tucson, Arizona; Wichita, Kansas; South Bend, Indiana; Amarillo, Texas; Baton Rouge, Louisiana; Victoria, Texas; Oklahoma City, Oklahoma; Spokane, Washington; and Grand Forks, North Dakota. These cities were chosen on three criteria, range of size, distribution across the country, and the availability of sample budgets ten years apart. There may have been some bias in the sample, as cities with better budgets may have

been more eager to send a sample to an archive.

19. The quotation is from Downers Grove's 1989–1990 budget introduction.

20. Stanley Botner, "The Use of Budgeting/Management Tools by State Governments," *Public Administration Review,* vol. 45 (September/October 1985), pp. 616–620.

21. Sixty percent of respondents in the 1987 Georgia State Survey said they had used strategic planning. Seventy percent reported using some form of financial trend monitoring, and 68 percent reported using multiyear revenue and expenditure forecasts. Poister and Streib, *op. cit., supra,* p. 242.

22. The author served as consultant to such a planning process in 1988–1989 for the city of Warrenville, population about 9,000. A fictionalized version of the process is described in a teaching case written by this author, "Dollars, Decisions, and Development," in *Managing Local Government,* James Banovetz, ed., the International City Management Association, 1990.

23. Lance LeLoup, Barbara Luck Graham, and Stacey Barwick, "Deficit Politics and Constitutional Government: The Impact of Gramm-Rudman-Hollings," *Public Budgeting and Finance,* vol. 7 (Spring 1987), pp. 100–101.

24. This quote is from Penner and Abramson, *op. cit. supra,* p. 76; they cite their source as Hedrick Smith, *The Power Game: How Washington Works* (New York: Random House, 1988), p. 667.

25. For a good discussion of the level of complexity in recent federal budgeting and its implications for public budgeters, see Naomi Caiden, "Shaping Things to Come: Super-Budgeters as Heroes (and Heroines)

in the Late-Twentieth Century," in Irene Rubin, ed., *New Directions in Budget Theory* (Albany: SUNY Press, 1988), pp. 43–58.

26. For a discussion of this historical trend and specific examples, see Irene Rubin, *The Politics of Public Budgeting: Getting and Spending, Borrowing and Balancing* (Chatham, NJ: Chatham House, 1990).

27. For a good summary of the evidence with respect to the federal level, see Norman Ornstein, "The Politics of the Deficit," in Phillip Cagan, *Essays in Contemporary Economic Problems: The Economy in Deficit, 1985* (Washington: The American Enterprise Institute, 1985) pp. 311–334. R. Douglas Arnold has been instrumental in debunking the argument that the tendency of a Member of Congress to support pork projects has increased and is causing increases in federal spending. Such spending has decreased as a proportion of the budget in recent years. "The Local Roots of Domestic Policy," in Thomas Mann and Norman Ornstein, eds., *The New Congress* (Washington: The American Enterprise Institute, 1981), pp. 250–287. For a summary of the argument that governors may be expansionist or tightfisted, see Aaron Wildavsky, *Budgeting, A Comparative Theory of Budgetary Processes,* 2d ed. (New Brunswick, NJ: Transaction Press, 1986), pp. 229–236.

28. Evidence from the states is not supportive of the argument that more and more powerful executives mean less expenditure per capita. States without line-item vetoes for the governors do not spend more per capita than states that have such enhanced executive budget powers. Benjamin Zycher, "An Item Veto Won't Work," *Wall Street Journal,* 24 October 1984. Line-item and reduction vetoes often do not reduce expenditures, but rather substitute the governor's proposals and wishes for those of the legislature. See, for example, Calvin Bellamy, "Item Veto: Dangerous Constitutional Tinkering," *Public Administration Review,* vol. 49 (January/February 1989), pp. 46–51. See also Glenn Abney and Thomas Lauth, "The Line-Item Veto in the States: Instrument for Fiscal Restraint or an Instrument for Partisanship," *Public Administration Review,* vol. 45 (May/June 1985), pp. 372–377.

29. Thomas Anton, *The Politics of State Expenditures in Illinois* (Urbana: University of Illinois Press, 1966).

30. S. Kenneth Howard is an exception to this generalization. He wrote about the budgetary changes in the states in the 1970s but remained pretty much in the incrementalist framework. See *Changing State Budgeting* (Lexington, KY: Council of State Governments, 1973).

31. Arnold Meltsner, *The Politics of City Revenue* (Berkeley: University of California Press, 1971).

32. Allen Schick, *Congress and Money: Budgeting, Spending and Taxing* (Washington: The Urban Institute Press, 1980).

33. One of the first pieces to call attention to the changing role of OMB from one of neutral competence to one of more political loyalty was Hugh Heclo's "OMB and the Presidency—the problem of neutral competence," *Public Interest,* vol. 38 (Winter 1975), pp. 80–98. Interest was stimulated in OMB by the role it played under President Nixon when he began to deal with the Watergate scandal and OMB took over micromanaging the agencies. Larry Berman's history of OMB, *The Office of Management and Budget and the Presidency, 1921–1979* (Princeton, NJ: Princeton University Press, 1979) was written in the same vein.

But the majority of articles on the policy role of OMB were written in response to the dramatic increase in political role of the office under President Reagan and Budget Director David Stockman. See, for example, Chet Newland, "Executive Office Policy Apparatus: Enforcing the Reagan Agenda," in Lester Salamon and Michael S. Lund, eds., *The Reagan Presidency and the Governing of America* (Washington: The Urban Institute Press, 1984), pp. 135–180, and Bruce Johnson, "From Analyst to Negotiator: the OMB's New Role," *Journal of Policy Analysis and Management,* vol. 3 (Summer 1984), pp. 501–515.

34. One landmark article was published in 1982 by Barry Bozeman and Jeffrey Straussman, "Shrinking Budgets and the Shrinkage of Budget Theory," *Public Administration Review,* vol. 42 (November/December 1982), pp. 509–515. Bozeman and Straussman contended that top-down budgeting had characterized the three previous administrations but that budgeters had not theorized about it, in part because incrementalism limited their view. While casting aside large chunks of the incrementalist model, Bozeman and Straussman added to budget theory several key themes, especially that budgeting has both top-down and bottom-up elements and that the emphasis on each changes with the environment.

35. See Allen Schick, "Budgetary Adaptations to Resource Scarcity," in Charles Levine and Irene Rubin, eds., *Fiscal Stress and Public Policy* (Beverly Hills, CA: Sage, 1980), pp. 113–134.

36. The literature suggests that cuts often begin in places that are difficult to see, such as in delayed maintenance or delayed capital projects. Money is gathered up which is not yet spent so that new hires are delayed or the slots eliminated, and purchases not yet made are cancelled. The result of this kind of decision rule is anything but across the board; it impacts some agencies much more heavily than others. Sometimes what started out as an across-the-board cut affected only some agencies when others were able to mobilize political support to prevent cuts. For some examples and rudimentary theory for the local level, see Charles Levine, Irene Rubin, and George Wolohojian, *The Politics of Retrenchment* (Beverly Hills, CA: Sage, 1981).

37. This literature grew up outside of the incrementalist model. See, for example, Louis Fisher, *Presidential Spending Power* (Princeton, NJ: Princeton University Press, 1975), and James Sundquist, *The Decline and Resurgence of Congress* (Washington: Brookings, 1981).

38. See, for example, the work of Charles Stewart on congressional budget reforms of the post-civil war era and their consequences, *The Design of the Appropriation Process in the House of Representatives, 1865–1921* (Cambridge, England: Cambridge University Press, 1989).

39. Some excellent historical work on municipal budgeting and finance has been published recently. See, for example, Terrence McDonald, *The Parameters of Urban Fiscal Policy: Socioeconomic Change and Political Culture in San Francisco, 1860–1906* (Berkeley: University of California Press, 1986), and Terrence McDonald and Sally K. Ward, eds., *The Politics of Urban Fiscal Policy* (Beverly Hills, CA: Sage, 1984). Budgeting during the Great Depression is still relatively unexplored, but one exciting exception is Jeff Mirel, "The Politics of Educa-

tional Retrenchment in Detroit, 1929–1935," *History of Education Quarterly,* vol. 24 (Fall 1984), pp. 323–358.

40. On tradeoffs in New York City's budgets, see Charles Brecher and Raymond Horton, "Community Power and Municipal Budgets," in Irene Rubin, ed., *New Directions in Budget Theory* (Albany: SUNY Press, 1988), pp. 148–164. Most of the literature that calls itself "tradeoffs" is in political science. See, for example, Bruce Russett, "Defense Expenditures and National Well Being," *American Journal of Political Science,* vol. 76 (December 1982), pp. 767–777. In public administration, tradeoffs are considered in evaluations of ZBB and other budget processes that create explicit targets for spending for various parts of the budget.

41. This case is described in greater detail in Irene Rubin, *The Politics of Public Budgeting, supra,* ch. 1.

Decision Making

In the opening chapter of his classic book, *Administrative Behavior* (1945), Herbert Simon noted that "although any practical activity involves both 'deciding' and 'doing,' it has not commonly been recognized that a theory of administration should be concerned with the processes of decision as well as the processes of action."[1] Simon, who received a Nobel Prize in economics, went on to argue that "the task of 'deciding' pervades the entire administrative organization quite as much as does the task of 'doing'— indeed, it is integrally tied up with the latter. *A general theory of administration must include principles of organization that will insure correct decision-making,* just as it must include principles that will insure effective action"[2] (emphasis added). By elevating decision making to a central concern of public administrative organization, *Administrative Behavior* revolutionized the field.

Twenty years later, in an article on "Administrative Decision Making" (included here), Simon accurately noted that "There is no need, at this late date, to justify the study of organization and administration in terms of the decision-making process, for decision-making concepts and language have become highly popular in writing about administration." That said, what are the main approaches to analyzing decision making that had developed? Simon identifies several.

One branch of decision making studies can be broadly categorized as "operations research." Here, the emphasis is on using quantitative techniques to analyze, clarify, and even prescribe decision making. A second used experiments to learn more about how individuals and groups make decisions. Another line of development has focused on persuasion and evocation. Finally, some researchers have viewed decisions from a structural perspective. This approach rests on the premise that "a decision is not a simple, unitary event, but the product of a complex social process generally extending over a considerable period of time." The structural approach encourages the use of computer simulations that can potentially predict how people will decide under varying conditions, as well as in repetitive and nonrepetitive situations.

---

[1]Herbert Simon, *Administrative Behavior* 2d ed. (New York: Free Press, 1957), p. 1.
[2]*Ibid.*

Charles Lindblom's "The Science of 'Muddling Through'" has also become a classic. It maps out two approaches to decision making: (1) rational-
comprehensive and (2) successive limited comparisons. The first seeks to
establish ends and the means toward their attainment with a high degree of
rationality. The second, among other characteristics, looks at ends and
means together, and promotes incrementalism, or limited steps toward
some general policy goal. Lindblom's article is so rich that these two models have been treated as theoretical, normative, and descriptive. In fact,
their comparison is even about the nature of political systems. In order to
achieve a degree of comprehensiveness, the successive limited comparisons model ("muddling through") requires participation by interest groups
and individuals in governmental decision making. It promotes pluralism,
whereas the rational comprehensive approach does not. Lindblom concludes that public administrators ought not be apologetic for relying so
heavily on muddling through in practice. In his view, " . . . it will be superior to any other decision-making method available for complex problems
in many circumstances, certainly superior to a futile attempt at superhuman comprehensiveness."

For all its virtues, muddling through is not perfect. It is possible to take
a series of limited steps only to arrive, irreversibly, in a place one does not
want to be. A well-known example is the Bay of Pigs invasion of Cuba in
1961 by a force of Cuban exiles trained by the United States.[3] Although the
force was created as a contingency, its very existence eventually became
politically problematic. There appeared to be no desirable way either to
maintain it or disband it. Consequently, the pressure to use it against Cuba
became more substantial. In "Mixed Scanning Revisited," Amitai Etzioni
discusses a corrective for this defect of muddling through.

Mixed scanning " . . . is akin to scanning by satellites with two lenses:
wide and zoom. Instead of taking a close look at all formations, a prohibitive task, or only at the spots of previous trouble, the wide lenses provide
clues as to the places to zoom in, looking for details." For instance, units of
the Executive Office of the President, such as the Council of Economic Advisors, can obtain the "big picture" while other agencies can deal with the
problems of specific industries or sectors of the economy. Etzioni elaborates
upon the mixed scanning model and discusses its development and use in
the field.

Read broadly, the selections in this section indicate that discussions
about the choice of decision making processes are inevitably also debates
about organizational design and political institutions. Decision making
processes are strongly related to matters of centralization/decentralization,
pluralism, and representation.

---

[3]For a review from President John F. Kennedy's perspective, see Theodore Sorenson,
Kennedy (New York: Harper and Row, 1965), esp. p. 296.

23.   Administrative Decision Making

Herbert A. Simon

There is no need, at this late date, to justify the study of organization and administration in terms of the decision-making process, for decision-making concepts and language have become highly popular in writing about administration.[1] This paper will describe some of the progress that has been made over the past quarter century, employing this approach, toward deepening our scientific knowledge—what new facts have been learned about human behavior in organizations, what new scientific procedures for ascertaining facts, what new concepts for describing them, and what new generalizations for explaining them. This progress extends both to descriptive and normative matters: to the pure science of administration, and its application to the practical business of managing.

To satisfy limits on this journal's space, your patience and my time, the account will be highly selective. Only a few notable and significant advances have been selected; others for which equally plausible claims might be made are ignored. A frequent practice in the social sciences is to bemoan our present ignorance while making optimistic predictions about future knowledge. It is a pleasure to survey an area of social science where, by contrast, we can speak without blushing about our present knowledge—indeed, where only a small sample of the gains in knowledge that have been achieved in the past quarter century can be presented.

OPERATIONS RESEARCH AND MANAGEMENT SCIENCE

One obvious answer to the question "What's new?" is the spectacular development in the normative theory of decision making that goes under the labels of "operations research" and "management science." Through these activities, many classes of administrative decisions have been formalized, mathematics has been applied to determine the characteristics of the "best" or "good" decisions, and myriads of arithmetic calculations are carried out routinely in many business and governmental organizations to reach the actual decisions from day to day. A number of sophisticated mathematical tools—linear programming, queuing theory, dynamic programming, combinatorial mathematics, and others—have been invented or developed to this end.

Like all scientific developments, this one has a long intellectual history, and did not spring, full-grown, from the brow of Zeus. Nevertheless, the state of the art today is so remarkably advanced beyond its position before World War II that the difference of degree becomes one of kind.[2]

The quantitative decision-making tools of operations research have perhaps had

SOURCE: "Administrative Decision Making" by Herbert Simon, *Public Administration Review:* 25 (March 1965). Reprinted by permission of the American Society for Public Administration.

[1] The term "decision-making" occurred three times in the titles of articles in the first fifteen volumes of the *Public Administration Review*—that is, through 1955; it occurred ten times in the next eight volumes, or about six times as often per annum as in the earlier period.

[2] Some notion of the state of proto-operations-research just before World War II, as it applied to municipal administration, can be obtained from Ridley and Simon, *Measuring Municipal Activities* (Chicago: International City Managers' Association, first edition, 1938).

more extensive application in business than in governmental organizations. It is worth recalling, however, that many of these tools underwent their early development in the American and British military services during and just after the Second World War (where the terms "operations research" and "operations analysis" were coined). Among the inventors of linear programming, for example, were Tjalling Koopmans, seeking, as statistician with the Combined Shipping Adjustment Board, a means for scheduling tanker operations efficiently; and George B. Dantzig and Marshall K. Wood, in the Office of the Air Force Controller, who used as one of their first (hypothetical) programming problems the scheduling of the Berlin Airlift.

Operations research, particularly in its governmental applications, has retained close intellectual ties with classical economic theory, and has sought to find effective ways of applying that theory to public budgeting and expenditure decisions. This has been a central preoccupation of the RAND Corporation effort, as exemplified by such works as Charles J. Hitch and Roland N. McKean, *The Economics of Defense in the Nuclear Age.*[3] In the past several years, Hitch, as Controller of the Department of Defense, and a number of his former RAND associates have played major roles in bringing the new tools to bear on Defense Department budget decisions. Thus, while the quarter century begins with V. O. Key's plaint about "The Lack of a Budgetary Theory,"[4] it

ends with a distinct revitalization of the whole field of public expenditure theory, and with a burgeoning of new analytic tools to assist in allocating public resources.

OPTIMALITY AND ALL THAT

In many ways the contributions of operations research and management science to decision-making theory have been very pragmatic in flavor. The goal, after all, is to devise tools that will help management make better decisions. One example of a pragmatic technique that has proved itself very useful, and has been rapidly and widely adopted over the past five years, is the scheduling procedure variously called PERT, or critical path scheduling. This technique does not use any very deep or sophisticated mathematics (which may account partly for the speed of its adoption), but is mainly an improvement of the common sense underlying the traditional Gantt Chart.

Contrasting with this pragmatic flavor, advances in operations research have been paralleled by developments in the pure theory of rational choice—a theory that has reached a very high level of mathematical and logical elegance and rigor. Among these developments per-

---

[3]Cambridge: Harvard University Press, 1960.

[4]*American Political Science Review,* December 1940, p. 1142. Labels have an unfortunate tendency to compartmentalize knowledge. Thus, the literature of "budgeting" has been only partly informed by the literature on "decision making," and vice versa, and both of these have sometimes been isolated from the economics literature on resources

allocation and public expenditure theory. Variants on the same basic sets of ideas are rediscovered each generation: "measurement of public services," "program budgeting," "performance budgeting," "engineering economy," "cost-benefit analysis," "operations analysis." What is genuinely new in this area in the past decade is the power and sophistication of the analytic and computational tools. Some impression of these tools may be gained from the Hitch and McKean book previously mentioned; from Roland N. McKean, *Efficiency in Government Through Systems Analysis* (Wiley, 1958); Arthur Maass, *et. al., Design of Water Resource Systems* (Harvard U. Press, 1962); or Allen V. Kneese, *The Economics of Regional Water Quality Management* (Johns Hopkins U. Press, 1964), and the references cited therein.

haps the most important are: (1) rigorous, formal axiom systems for defining the concept of utility in operational terms, (2) extension of the theory of rational choice to encompass the maximization of expected utility under conditions of uncertainty, (3) extension of the theory to repeated choices over time—dynamic optimization, and (4) extension of the theory to competitive "gaming" situations. These formal advances have had an important influence, in turn, on directions of work in theoretical statistics (statistical decision theory, Bayesian statistics), and on the kinds of models that are preferred by operations researchers—or at least by the theorists among their number.[5]

An evaluation of these contributions on the pure theory of rational choice would return a mixed verdict. On the positive side, they have provided enormous conceptual clarification for discussions of "rationality." For example, it has always been unclear what rationality meant in a pure outwitting or bargaining situation, where each party is trying to outguess, and perhaps bluff, the other. If the theory of games, due to von Neumann and Morgenstern, did not solve this problem for all situations, it at least made painfully clear exactly what the problem is.

On the negative side, fascination with the pure theory of rational choice has sometimes distracted attention from the problems of decision makers who possess modest calculating powers in the face of a world of enormous complexity. (In the real world, the calculating powers of electronic computers as well as men must be described as "modest.") A normative theory, to be useful, must call only for information that can be obtained and only for calculations that can be performed. The classical theory of rational choice has generally ignored these information-processing limitations. It has assumed that rationality was concerned with choice among alternatives that were already specified, and whose consequences were known or were readily calculable. It has assumed, also, comparability of consequences—that is, a practically measurable utility index.

Since these conditions, on which the classical theory rests, are so seldom satisfied in the real world, great interest attaches to procedures that make less heroic assumptions about the "givens" and the knows; and there is considerable progress in devising less-than-optimal decision procedures for situations where the optimum is unknown and practically undiscoverable. These procedures, often called *heuristic methods,* are distinguishable from optimizing techniques in three respects: they grapple, as most optimizing techniques do not, with the problems of designing and discovering alternatives, as well as with choosing among given alternatives; they frequently "satisfice," or settle for good-enough answers in despair at finding best answers; they commonly do not guarantee the qualities of the solutions they provide, and often do not even guarantee they will find a solution. The second and third of these characteristics are, of course, not virtues, but are the price that must be paid for extending our theory and tools for decision making to the wide range of real-world situations not encompassed by the classical models.

By way of illustration, a common problem of business and governmental management involves locating a system of warehouses over a country so that products can be distributed from production points to ultimate users as economically as possible. Attempts to for-

---

[5]Since I have discoursed at length on these matters elsewhere, I shall be brief here. See "Theories of Decision Making in Economics and Behavioral Science," 49 *American Economic Review* 253-283. (June 1959), and Part IV of *Models of Man* (Wiley, 1957).

mulate the warehousing problem so that the optimizing methods known as linear programming can be used have failed because the computations become too lengthy. However, heuristic techniques have been applied successfully to find "good" solutions to the problem where "best" solutions are unattainable.[6]

It is traditional to observe, in any discussion of the modern decision-making tools, that knowledge of these tools runs far in advance of application, and that the domain of application has been limited largely to decisions that are well-structured or "programmed," and quantitative in character. The warehousing problem described above has both of these characteristics. Whether this limitation on applications is inherent or temporary is a more controversial question. One of the important tasks before us now is to see how far we can go in extending the applicability of the new decision-making tools to areas that are ill-structured, and qualitative, calling for "judgment," "experience," and even "creativity." To do this, we shall presumably have to understand what "judgment," "experience," and "creativity" are, a topic discussed later.

EXPERIMENTS ON DECISION MAKING

A second area of significant advance has been in applying the experimental method to the investigation of decision making. This has been done both by arranging for experiments on live real-world organizations—on the model of the Hawthorne experiments—and/or by bringing organizations, or organizationoid systems into the laboratory. For obvious reasons, the latter has been done more often than the former.

The first volume of the *Public Administration Review* contained a report of a large-scale field experiment on the decision-making processes of social workers,[7] but similar experiments have been exceedingly rare in the succeeding twenty-five years. One of the few other examples to which I can refer is the study done in the Prudential Life Insurance Company by the Survey Research Center of the University of Michigan.[8] Either researchers on organizations decided that the information attainable from field experiments was not worth the trouble and cost of carrying out such experiments, or they found it difficult to secure the cooperation of business and governmental organizations in arranging such experiments—or both. Whatever the reason, field experiments have not been an important procedure for learning about organizational decision making.

In a few cases researchers have tried to import relatively sizeable organizations into the laboratory—hence, their studies lie on the boundary line between field and laboratory experiments. The Systems Research Laboratory of the RAND Corporation, for example, studied decision making by simulating, under controlled conditions, an entire air defense control center and associated early warning stations, manned on a full-time basis over a period of several months by a staff of some thirty subjects. While the studies conducted by the Systems Research Laboratory had as their direct outgrowth a major Air Force training program, the laboratory proved less tractable as a setting for obtaining data for testing theories of the decision-making process, and there has

---

[6] Alfred A. Kuehn and Michael J. Hamberger, "A. Heuristic Program for Locating Warehouses," *Management Science,* July 1963.

[7] Herbert A. Simon and William R. Divine, "Human Factors in an Administrative Experiment," 1 *Public Administration Review* 485-492. (Autumn 1941).

[8] N. C. Morse and E. Reimer, "Experimental Change of a Major Organizational Variable," 52 *Journal of Abnormal and Social Psychology* 120-129. (1955).

been no subsequent rash of studies of this kind.[9]

In contrast to the dearth of field experiments and large-scale laboratory experiments, laboratory experimentation with relatively small groups has been a thriving enterprise. Several examples of methodological advances in the art of small-group experimentation can be mentioned. Fred Bales, with his interaction process analysis, developed a scheme of data processing useful for studying the interaction of task-oriented and social-system oriented behavior in small problem-solving groups. Alex Bavelas devised a small-group task that permitted the experimenter to alter the decision-making process by opening or closing particular channels of communication between members of the group. In succeeding years, the Bales coding scheme and the Bavelas small-group task have both been used in a substantial number of studies, manipulating a great many different independent variables. Both have proved exceedingly valuable in permitting the cumulation of comparable knowledge from a whole series of experiments carried out by different investigators in different laboratories.

It is impossible to summarize here, or even to reference, the numerous contributions to the substantive knowledge of decision making that have been contributed by the small-group experiments. A single example will convey the flavor of such work. Cyert and March were able to produce bias in the estimates of members of a simulated organization by creating partial conflict of interest among them, but showed that under certain circumstances this bias did not affect organizational performance.[10]

New knowledge about organizational decision making can be obtained from appropriately planned experiments on individuals as well as from small-group experiments. Andrew Stedry, for example, has tested in this way theories about how budget controls affect behavior in organizations.[11] The series of studies of influence processes carried out at Yale by the late Carl Hovland and his associates belong in the same category.[12]

PERSUASION AND EVOCATION

Mention of the Yale research on influence processes marks a good point in our discussion to turn to several substantive developments in the theory of decision making. The notion that a decision is like a conclusion derived from a set of premises has been a useful metaphor for analyzing the decision-making process. Following the metaphor a step further, we can view each member of an organization as "inputting" certain premises, and "outputting" certain conclusions, or decisions. But each member's conclusions become, in turn, the inputs, that is to say, the premises, for other members. For one person to influence another involves inducing him to use appropriate premises in his decision making.

What happens in an organization, or in any kind of social system, when there are conflicting premises pushing a particular decision in different directions? Much of the research on influence processes has been aimed at answering this question. In much of this research, influence has been conceived as a kind of "force," so that when several influences are brought to bear simultaneously, the outcome is interpreted as a "resultant" of the impinging forces. Per-

[9]Robert L. Chapman, *et al.,* "The System Research Laboratory's Air Defense Experiments," 5 *Management Science* 250-269. (April 1959).
[10]Richard M. Cyert and James G. March, *The Behavioral Theory of the Firm* (Prentice-Hall, 1963), pp. 67–77.

[11]*Budget Control and Cost Behavior* (Prentice-Hall, 1960), Chapter 4.
[12]See the Yale Studies in Attitude and Communication, edited by Hovland and Rosenberg, and published by the Yale University Press.

suasion is then a process of exerting such a force.

An important advance in understanding decision making has been to complement the notion of persuasion with the notion of evocation. When we want someone to carry out a particular action, we may think of our task as one of inducing him to *accept* latent decision premises favorable to the action that he already possesses. Thus, writing about food will often make a reader hungry, but we would hardly say that we had "persuaded" him that he was hungry; it would be better to say that we had "reminded" him.

Processes of persuasion play their largest role in decision making in conflict situations—where the issue is already posed, and the alternatives present. This is the framework within which most of the Yale studies on attitude change were carried out. It is also the framework for the important and well-known study of *Voting* by Berelson, Lazarsfeld, and McPhee.[13]

On the other hand, in studies of decision making where the focus of attention of the participants is one of the main independent variables, the evoking processes take on larger importance. The recent study of the Trade Agreements Act renewal, by Raymond Bauer, Ithiel Pool, and Lewis Dexter indicates that these processes played a major role in deciding the issue.[14] The authors describe the setting of their study thus (p. 5): "We are interested in the sources of information for each of these populations, the bases of its attitudes on the trade issue, *and the circumstances which lead some individuals to take active roles in the making of policy.*" (Emphasis supplied.) They demonstrate convincingly that the behavior of particular Congressmen on the trade issue depended as much on the alternative claims on their time and attention as on the distribution of interests of their constituents.

To the extent that the mechanism of evocation is important for decision making, many new ways arise in which organizational arrangements may affect behavior. As example, one of the findings of the study just mentioned (p. 229) can be cited:

> In summary, we would suggest that most significant of all to an understanding of what communication went out from business on foreign trade was neither self-interest nor ideology, but the institutional structure which facilitated or blocked the production of messages. Whether a letter to a congressman would get written depended on whether organization facilitated it, whether the writer's round of daily conversations would lead up to it, whether a staff was set up to produce it, and whether the writer conceived writing this letter to be part of his job.

Evoking mechanisms take on special prominence wherever dynamic change is occurring. Studies of the diffusion of innovations show that the timing of adoption of an innovation depends critically on the means for getting people to attend to it.[15] From every point of view, the new knowledge gained about evoking and attention-directing processes is a major substantive advance in our understanding of organizational decision making.

---

[13]University of Chicago Press, 1954.

[14]*American Business and Public Policy: The Politics of Foreign Trade* (Atherton Press, 1963).

[15]See J. Coleman, E. Katz, and H. Menzel, "Diffusion of an Innovation Among Physicians," 20 *Sociometry* 253-270. (1957); also, H. A. Simon and J. G. March, *Organizations* (Wiley, 1957), Chapter 7.

THE STRUCTURE OF DECISIONS

A decision is not a simple, unitary event, but the product of a complex social process generally extending over a considerable period of time. As noted, decision making includes attention-directing or intelligence processes that determine the occasions of decision, processes for discovering and designing possible courses of action, and processes for evaluating alternatives and choosing among them. The complexity of decision making has posed grave difficulties in its study and description, difficulties only now being overcome by recent methodological innovations.

Traditionally, a decision-making process was captured and recorded by the common-sense tools of the historian using everyday language. The notion that a decision might be viewed as a conclusion drawn from premises—a notion mentioned earlier—introduced a modicum of system into the description of decision making. According to this view, in order to record a decision-making process it was necessary to discover the sources of the decision premises, and the channels of communication they followed through the organization to the point where they became the raw materials of decision.

Studies that adopted this general approach to the description of decisions, while remaining within the traditional case-study framework, became increasingly frequent during the period under discussion. One example is Herbert Kaufman's excellent study of *The Forest Ranger,* aimed at analyzing "the way their decisions and behavior are influenced within and by the Service."[16] Another is the study by the Carnegie Tech group of the influence of accounting information on operating decisions in large companies.[17]

The method of these studies is best described as "systematized common sense." The decision premise concept provides an ordering and organizing principle; it reduces somewhat the subjectivity of the description and the dangers of observer bias; but it falls far short of allowing complete formalization of the description. And it cannot, of course, solve the problem of how to validate generalizations with data from single cases.

The invention of the modern digital computer radically changed the situation. As gradually became apparent to those who came into contact with computers, the computer is a device that is capable of making decisions. (One demonstration of this is its use to implement the analytic decision-making schemes introduced by operations research.) Hence, a language suitable for describing the processes going on in computers might well be appropriate for describing decision making in organizations. At least the notion appeared to be worth a trial: to equate "decision premise" with the concepts of data input and program of instructions in a computer, and to equate the concept of a conclusion with the concept of the output of a computer program.

An early, and rather primitive, attempt to describe an organization decision-making process in computer programming terms appeared in 1956.[18] In this study the authors recounted the steps taken by a business firm to reach a decision about the installation of an electronic computer. They then showed how this sequence of events could be explained by a program composed of an organized system of relatively sim-

---

[16]Johns Hopkins U. Press, 1960, p. 4.

[17]*Centralization versus Decentralization in Organizing the Controller's Department* (New York: The Controllership Foundation, 1954). The study is summarized in John M. Pfiffner and Frank P. Sherwood, *Administrative Organization* (Prentice-Hall, 1960), Chapter 21.

[18]R. M. Cyert, H. A. Simon, and D. B. Trow, "Observation of a Business Decision," 29 *Journal of Business* 237-248. (1956).

ple and general information-gathering, searching, problem-solving, and evaluating processes. Of particular interest was the fact that the decision examined in this study was not a highly structured, quantitative one, but one that called for large amounts of professional and administrative judgment.

Encouraging results from early studies of this kind raised hopes that it might be possible to use computer programming languages formally as well as informally to construct theories of organizational decision making, and to test those theories by simulating the decision process on the computer. Computer programs seeking to explain several kinds of organizational decision-making situations have, in fact, been constructed, and have shown themselves adequate to simulate important aspects of the human behavior in these situations. The decisions that have been simulated in this way to date are still relatively simple ones, but they encompass behavior that would generally be regarded as professional, and as involving judgment. Two of the best-developed examples are a simulation of a department store buyer and a simulation of a bank trust investment officer.[19]

I am not aware that any single comparable simulation of a decision-making process in the area of public administration has yet been carried out, but it appears that several are under way in current research. Perhaps the most likely target for initial attempts is public budgeting. If we examine the strategies described in recent empirical studies, like those of Wildavsky,[20] we will see that

they can be rather directly translated into components of computer programs.

Parallel with these simulations of administrative decision making there has been a considerable exploration of individual thinking and problem solving processes, also using computer simulation as the tool of theory formulation and theory testing.[21] Today, we have a considerable specific knowledge on how human beings accomplish complex cognitive tasks. We have reasons for optimism, too, that this body of knowledge will increase rapidly, for in the digital computer language we have an analytic tool and a means for accurate expression whose powers are commensurate with the complexity of the phenomena we wish to describe and understand.

LANDMARKS AND NEW ROADS

These, then, are some of the more prominent landmarks along the road of decision-making research over the past twenty-five years. On the normative side, the analytic tools of modern operations research have secured an important place in the practical work of management. Their role in everyday decision making promises to be much enlarged as present techniques are supplemented by new heuristic approaches.

On the side of the pure science of administration, there have been equally fruitful developments. The experimental method, in the small-group laboratory, can now be used to study a wide range of decision-making behaviors that are relevant to organizations. We have introduced the concept of evocation into our theories of influence, and have used it to gain new understanding of the decision-making process in changing environments. Finally, the modern digital com-

---

[19]Descriptions of these two simulations may be found in Chapters 7 and 10, respectively, of Cyert and March, *Behavioral Theory of the Firm,* op cit.

[20]Aaron Wildavsky, *The Politics of the Budgetary Process* (Little, Brown and Company, 1964).

[21]For a survey, and numerous examples, see Edward Feigenbaum and Julian Feldman, *Computers and Thought* (McGraw-Hill, 1963).

puter, a powerful new tool, has provided both a language for expressing our theories of decision making and an engine for calculating their empirical implications. Theories can now be compared with data of the real world of organizations.

The attention-directing mechanisms so important in decision making also have played their part in determining the particular developments sampled in this paper. Another scientist, with a different set of research concerns, would choose a different sample. The fact that even one such sample exists shows how far we have come during the past twenty-five years toward understanding human behavior in organizations.

24.   The Science of "Muddling Through"

Charles E. Lindblom

Suppose an administrator is given responsibility for formulating policy with respect to inflation. He might start by trying to list all related values in order of importance, e.g., full employment, reasonable business profit, protection of small savings, prevention of a stock market crash. Then all possible policy outcomes could be rated as more or less efficient in attaining a maximum of these values. This would of course require a prodigious inquiry into values held by members of society and an equally prodigious set of calculations on how much of each value is equal to how much of each other value. He could then proceed to outline all possible policy alternatives. In a third step, he would undertake systematic comparison of his multitude of alternatives to determine which attains the greatest amount of values.

In comparing policies, he would take advantage of any theory available that generalized about classes of policies. In considering inflation, for example, he would compare all policies in the light of the theory of prices. Since no alternatives are beyond his investigation, he would consider strict central control and the abolition of all prices and markets on the one hand and elimination of all public controls with reliance completely on the free market on the other, both in the light of whatever theoretical generalizations he could find on such hypothetical economies.

Finally, he would try to make the choice that would in fact maximize his values.

An alternative line of attack would be to set as his principal objective, either explicitly or without conscious thought, the relatively simple goal of keeping prices level. This objective might be compromised or complicated by only a few other goals, such as full employment. He would in fact disregard most other social values as beyond his present interest, and he would for the moment not even attempt to rank the few values that he regarded as immediately relevant. Were he pressed, he would quickly admit that he was ignoring many related values and many possible important consequences of his policies.

As a second step, he would outline those relatively few policy alternatives that occurred to him. He would then compare them. In comparing his limited number of alternatives, most of them familiar from past controversies, he would

SOURCE: "The Science of 'Muddling Through'" by Charles E. Lindblom, *Public Administration Review:* 19 (Spring 1959). Reprinted by permission of the American Society for Public Administration.

not ordinarily find a body of theory precise enough to carry him through a comparison of their respective consequences. Instead he would rely heavily on the record of past experience with small policy steps to predict the consequences of similar steps extended into the future.

Moreover, he would find that the policy alternatives combined objectives or values in different ways. For example, one policy might offer price level stability at the cost of some risk of unemployment; another might offer less price stability but also less risk of unemployment. Hence, the next step in his approach—the final selection—would combine into one the choice among values and the choice among instruments for reaching values. It would not, as in the first method of policy-making, approximate a more mechanical process of choosing the means that best satisfied goals that were previously clarified and ranked. Because practitioners of the second approach expect to achieve their goals only partially, they would expect to repeat endlessly the sequence just described, as conditions and aspirations changed and as accuracy of prediction improved.

BY ROOT OR BY BRANCH

For complex problems, the first of these two approaches is of course impossible. Although such an approach can be described, it cannot be practiced except for relatively simple problems and even then only in a somewhat modified form. It assumes intellectual capacities and sources of information that men simply do not possess, and it is even more absurd as an approach to policy when the time and money that can be allocated to a policy problem is limited, as is always the case. Of particular importance to public administrators is the fact that public agencies are in effect usually instructed not to practice the first method. That is to say, their prescribed functions

and constraints—the politically or legally possible—restrict their attention to relatively few values and relatively few alternative policies among the countless alternatives that might be imagined. It is the second method that is practiced.

Curiously, however, the literatures of decision-making, policy formulation, planning, and public administration formalize the first approach rather than the second, leaving public administrators who handle complex decisions in the position of practicing what few preach. For emphasis I run some risk of overstatement. True enough, the literature is well aware of limits on man's capacities and of the inevitability that policies will be approached in some such style as the second. But attempts to formalize rational policy formulation—to lay out explicitly the necessary steps in the process—usually describe the first approach and not the second.[1]

The common tendency to describe policy formulation even for complex problems as though it followed the first approach has been strengthened by the attention given to, and successes enjoyed by, operations research, statistical decision theory, and systems analysis. The hallmarks of these procedures, typical of the first approach, are clarity of objective, explicitness of evaluation, a high degree of comprehensiveness of overview, and, wherever possible, quantification of values for mathematical analysis. But these advanced procedures remain largely the appropriate techniques of relatively small-scale problem-solving where the total number of variables to be considered is small and value problems restricted. Charles Hitch, head of the Economics Division of RAND Corporation, one of the leading centers for application of these techniques, has written:

I would make the empirical generalization from my experience at RAND and elsewhere that operations research is the art of sub-optimizing, i.e., of solving some lower-level problems, and that difficulties increase and our special competence diminishes by an order of magnitude with every level of decision making we attempt to ascend. The sort of simple explicit model which operations researchers are so proficient in using can certainly reflect most of the significant factors influencing traffic control on the George Washington Bridge, but the proportion of the relevant reality which we can represent by any such model or models in studying, say, a major foreign-policy decision, appears to be almost trivial.[2]

Accordingly, I propose in this paper to clarify and formalize the second method, much neglected in the literature. This might be described as the method of *successive limited comparisons.* I will contrast it with the first approach, which might be called the rational-comprehensive method.[3] More

impressionistically and briefly—and therefore generally used in this article— they could be characterized as the branch method and root method, the former continually building out from the current situation, step-by-step and by small degrees; the latter starting from fundamentals anew each time, building on the past only as experience is embodied in a theory, and always prepared to start completely from the ground up.

Let us put the characteristics of the two methods side by side in simplest terms. (See Figure 24.1).

Assuming that the root method is familiar and understandable, we proceed directly to clarification of its alternative by contrast. In explaining the second, we shall be describing how most administrators do in fact approach complex questions, for the root method, the "best" way as a blueprint or model, is in fact not workable for complex policy questions, and administrators are forced to use the method of successive limited comparisons.

FIGURE 24.1

Rational-Comprehensive (Root)	Successive Limited Comparisons (Branch)
1a. Clarification of values or objectives distinct from and usually prerequisite to empirical analysis of alternative policies.	1b. Selection of value goals and empirical analysis of the needed action are not distinct from one another but are closely intertwined.
2a. Policy-formulation is therefore approached through means-end analysis: First the ends are isolated, then the means to achieve them are sought.	2b. Since means and ends are not distinct, means-end analysis is often inappropriate or limited.
3a. The test of a "good" policy is that it can be shown to be the most appropriate means to desired ends.	3b. The test of a "good" policy is typically that various analysts find themselves directly agreeing on a policy (without their agreeing that it is the most appropriate means to an agreed objective).

4a. Analysis is comprehensive; every important relevant factor is taken into account.	4b. Analysis is drastically limited:
	  i) Important possible outcomes are neglected.
	  ii) Important alternative potential policies are neglected.
	  iii) Important affected values are neglected.

5a. Theory is often heavily relied upon.	5b. A succession of comparisons greatly reduces or eliminates reliance on theory.

INTERTWINING EVALUATION AND EMPIRICAL ANALYSIS (1B)

The quickest way to understand how values are handled in the method of successive limited comparisons is to see how the root method often breaks down in its handling of values or objectives. The idea that values should be clarified, and in advance of the examination of alternative policies, is appealing. But what happens when we attempt it for complex social problems? The first difficulty is that on many critical values or objectives, citizens disagree, congressmen disagree, and public administrators disagree. Even where a fairly specific objective is prescribed for the administrator, there remains considerable room for disagreement on subobjectives. Consider, for example, the conflict with respect to locating public housing, described in Meyerson and Banfield's study of the Chicago Housing Authority[4] disagreement which occurred despite the clear objective of providing a certain number of public housing units in the city. Similarly conflicting are objectives in highway location, traffic control, minimum wage administration, development of tourist facilities in national parks, or insect control.

Administrators cannot escape these conflicts by ascertaining the majority's preference, for preferences have not been registered on most issues; indeed, there often are no preferences in the absence of public discussion sufficient to bring an issue to the attention of the electorate. Furthermore, there is a question of whether intensity of feeling should be considered as well as the number of persons preferring each alternative. By the impossibility of doing otherwise, administrators often are reduced to deciding policy without clarifying objectives first.

Even when an administrator resolves to follow his own values as a criterion for decisions, he often will not know how to rank them when they conflict with one another, as they usually do. Suppose, for example, that an administrator must relocate tenants living in tenements scheduled for destruction. One objective is to empty the buildings fairly promptly, another is to find suitable accommodation for persons displaced, another is to avoid friction with residents in other areas in which a large influx would be unwelcome, another is to deal with all concerned through persuasion if possible, and so on.

How does one state even to himself the relative importance of these partially conflicting values? A simple ranking of them is not enough; one needs ideally to know how much of one value is worth sacrificing for some of another value. The answer is that typically the administrator chooses—and must choose—directly among policies in which these values are combined in different ways. He cannot first clarify his values and then choose among policies.

A more subtle third point underlies both the first two. Social objectives do not always have the same relative values. One objective may be highly prized in one circumstance, another in another circumstance. If, for example, an administrator values highly both the dispatch with which his agency can carry through its projects and good public relations, it matters little which of the two possibly conflicting values he favors in some abstract or general sense. Policy questions arise in forms which put to administrators such a question as: Given the degree to which we are or are not already achieving the values of dispatch and the values of good public relations, is it worth sacrificing a little speed for a happier clientele, or is it better to risk offending the clientele so that we can get on with our work? The answer to such a question varies with circumstances.

The value problem is, as the example shows, always a problem of adjustments at a margin. But there is no practicable way to state marginal objectives or values except in terms of particular policies. That one value is preferred to another in one decision situation does not mean that it will be preferred in another decision situation in which it can be had only at great sacrifice of another value. Attempts to rank or order values in general and abstract terms so that they do not shift from decision to decision end up by ignoring the relevant marginal preferences. The significance of this third point thus goes very far. Even if all administrators had at hand an agreed set of values, objectives, and constraints, and an agreed ranking of these values, objectives, and constraints, their marginal values in actual choice situations would be impossible to formulate.

Unable consequently to formulate the relevant values first and then choose among policies to achieve them, administrators must choose directly among alternative policies that offer different marginal combinations of values. Somewhat paradoxically, the only practicable way to disclose one's relevant marginal values even to oneself is to describe the policy one chooses to achieve them. Except roughly and vaguely, I know of no way to describe—or even to understand—what my relative evaluations are for, say, freedom and security, speed and accuracy in governmental decisions, or low taxes and better schools than to describe my preferences among specific policy choices that might be made between the alternatives in each of the pairs.

In summary, two aspects of the process by which values are actually handled can be distinguished. The first is clear: evaluation and empirical analysis are intertwined; that is, one chooses among values and among policies at one and the same time. Put a little more elaborately, one simultaneously chooses a policy to attain certain objectives and chooses the objectives themselves. The second aspect is related but distinct: the administrator focuses his attention on marginal or incremental values. Whether he is aware of it or not, he does not find general formulations of objectives very helpful and in fact makes specific marginal or incremental comparisons. Two policies, X and Y, confront him. Both promise the same degree of attainment of objectives $a, b, c, d,$ and e. But X promises him somewhat more of f than does Y, while Y promises him somewhat more of g than does X. In choosing between them, he is in fact offered the alternative of a marginal or incremental amount of f at the expense of a marginal or incremental amount of g. The only values that are relevant to his choice are these increments by which the two policies differ; and, when he finally chooses between the two marginal values, he does so by making a choice between policies.[5]

As to whether the attempt to clarify objectives in advance of policy selection is more or less rational than the close intertwining of marginal evaluation and empirical analysis, the principal difference established is that for complex problems the first is impossible and irrelevant, and the second is both possible and relevant. The second is possible because the administrator need not try to analyze any values except the values by which alternative policies differ and need not be concerned with them except as they differ marginally. His need for information on values or objectives is drastically reduced as compared with the root method; and his capacity for grasping, comprehending, and relating values to one another is not strained beyond the breaking point.

RELATIONS BETWEEN MEANS AND ENDS (2B)

Decision-making is ordinarily formalized as a means-ends relationship:

means are conceived to be evaluated and chosen in the light of ends finally selected independently of and prior to the choice of means. This is the means-ends relationship of the root method. But it follows from all that has just been said that such a means-ends relationship is possible only to the extent that values are agreed upon, are reconcilable, and are stable at the margin. Typically, therefore, such a means-ends relationship is absent from the branch method, where means and ends are simultaneously chosen.

Yet any departure from the means-ends relationship of the root method will strike some readers as inconceivable. For it will appear to them that only in such a relationship is it possible to determine whether one policy choice is better or worse than another. How can an administrator know whether he has made a wise or foolish decision if he is without prior values or objectives by which to judge his decisions? The answer to this question calls up the third distinctive difference between root and branch methods: how to decide the best policy.

THE TEST OF "GOOD" POLICY (3B)

In the root method, a decision is "correct," "good," or "rational" if it can be shown to attain some specified objective, where the objective can be specified without simply describing the decision itself. Where objectives are defined only through the marginal or incremental approach to values described above, it is still sometimes possible to test whether a policy does in fact attain the desired objectives; but a precise statement of the objectives takes the form of a description of the policy chosen or some alternative to it. To show that a policy is mistaken one cannot offer an abstract argument that important objectives are not achieved; one must instead argue that another policy is more to be preferred.

So far, the departure from customary ways of looking at problem-solving is not troublesome, for many administrators will be quick to agree that the most effective discussion of the correctness of policy does take the form of comparison with other policies that might have been chosen. But what of the situation in which administrators cannot agree on values or objectives, either abstractly or in marginal terms? What then is the test of "good" policy? For the root method, there is no test. Agreement on objectives failing, there is no standard of "correctness." For the method of successive limited comparisons, the test is agreement on policy itself, which remains possible even when agreement on values is not.

It has been suggested that continuing agreement in Congress on the desirability of extending old age insurance stems from liberal desires to strengthen the welfare programs of the federal government and from conservative desires to reduce union demands for private pension plans. If so, this is an excellent demonstration of the ease with which individuals of different ideologies often can agree on concrete policy. Labor mediators report a similar phenomenon: the contestants cannot agree on criteria for settling their disputes but can agree on specific proposals. Similarly, when one administrator's objective turns out to be another's means, they often can agree on policy.

Agreement on policy thus becomes the only practicable test of the policy's correctness. And for one administrator to seek to win the other over to agreement on ends as well would accomplish nothing and create quite unnecessary controversy.

If agreement directly on policy as a test for "best" policy seems a poor substitute for testing the policy against its objectives, it ought to be remembered that objectives themselves have no ultimate validity other than they are agreed upon. Hence agreement is the test of "best" policy in both methods. But where the root method requires agreement on what elements in the decision constitute objectives and on which of these objectives should be sought, the branch method falls back on agreement wherever it can be found.

In an important sense, therefore, it is not irrational for an administrator to defend a policy as good without being able to specify what it is good for.

NONCOMPREHENSIVE ANALYSIS (4B)

Ideally, rational-comprehensive analysis leaves out nothing important. But it is impossible to take everything important into consideration unless "important" is so narrowly defined that analysis is in fact quite limited. Limits on human intellectual capacities and on available information set definite limits to man's capacity to be comprehensive. In actual fact, therefore, no one can practice the rational-comprehensive method for really complex problems, and every administrator faced with a sufficiently complex problem must find ways drastically to simplify.

An administrator assisting in the formulation of agricultural economic policy cannot in the first place be competent on all possible policies. He cannot even comprehend one policy entirely. In planning a soil bank program, he cannot successfully anticipate the impact of higher or lower farm income on, say, urbanization—the possible consequent loosening of family ties, possible consequent eventual need for revisions in social security and further implications for tax problems arising out of new federal responsibilities for social security and municipal responsibilities for urban services. Nor, to follow another line of repercussions, can he work through the soil bank program's effects on prices for agricultural products in foreign markets and consequent implications for foreign relations, including those arising out of economic rivalry between the United States and the U.S.S.R.

In the method of successive, limited comparisons, simplification is systematically achieved in two principal ways. First, it is achieved through limitation of policy comparisons to those policies that differ in relatively small degree from policies presently in effect. Such a limitation immediately reduces the number of alternatives to be investigated and also drastically simplifies the character of the investigation of each. For it is not necessary to undertake fundamental inquiry into an alternative and its consequences; it is necessary only to study those respects in which the proposed alternative and its consequences differ from the status quo. The empirical comparison of marginal differences among alternative policies that differ only marginally is, of course, a counterpart to the incremental or marginal comparison of values discussed above.[6]

Relevance as Well as Realism

It is a matter of common observation that in Western democracies public administrators and policy analysts in general do largely limit their analyses to incremental or marginal differences in policies that are chosen to differ only incrementally. They do not do so, however, solely because they desperately need some way to simplify their problems; they also do so in order to be relevant. Democracies change their policies almost entirely through incremental adjustments. Policy does not move in leaps and bounds.

The incremental character of political change in the United States has often been remarked. The two major political parties agree on fundamentals; they offer alternative policies to the voters only on relatively small points of difference. Both parties favor full employment, but they define it somewhat differently; both favor the development of water power resources, but in slightly different ways; and both favor unemployment compensation, but not the same level of benefits. Similarly, shifts of policy within a party take place largely through a series of relatively small changes, as can be seen in their only gradual acceptance of the idea of governmental responsibility for support of the unemployed, a change in party positions beginning in the early 1930s and culminating in a sense in the Employment Act of 1946.

Party behavior is in turn rooted in public attitudes, and political theorists cannot conceive of democracy's surviving in the United States in the absence of fundamental agreement on potentially disruptive issues, with consequent limitation of policy debates to relatively small differences in policy.

Since the policies ignored by the administrator are politically impossible and so irrelevant, the simplification of analysis achieved by concentrating on policies that differ only incrementally is not a capricious kind of simplification. In addition, it can be argued that, given the limits on knowledge within which policy-makers are confined, simplifying by limiting the focus to small variations from present policy makes the most of available knowledge. Because policies being considered are like present and past policies, the administrator can obtain information and claim some insight. Nonincremental policy proposals are therefore typically not only politically irrelevant but also unpredictable in their consequences.

The second method of simplification of analysis is the practice of ignoring important possible consequences of possible policies, as well as the values attached to the neglected consequences. If this appears to disclose a shocking shortcoming of successive limited comparisons, it can be replied that, even if the exclusions are random, policies may nevertheless be more intelligently formulated than through futile attempts to achieve a comprehensiveness beyond human capacity. Actually, however, the exclusions, seeming arbitrary or random from one point of view, need be neither.

Achieving a Degree of Comprehensiveness

Suppose that each value neglected by one policy-making agency were a major concern of at least one other agency. In that case, a helpful division of labor would be achieved, and no agency need find its task beyond its capacities. The shortcomings of such a system would be that one agency might destroy a value either before another agency could be activated to safeguard it or in spite of another agency's efforts. But the possibility that important values may be lost is present in any form of organization, even where agencies attempt to comprehend in planning more than is humanly possible.

The virtue of such a hypothetical division of labor is that every important interest or value has its watchdog. And these watchdogs can protect the interests in their jurisdiction in two quite different ways: first, by redressing damages done by other agencies; and, second, by anticipating and heading off injury before it occurs.

In a society like that of the United States in which individuals are free to combine to pursue almost any possible common interest they might have and in which government agencies are sensitive to the pressures of these groups, the system described is approximated. Almost every interest has its watchdog. Without claiming that every interest has a sufficiently powerful watchdog, it can be argued that our system often can assure a more comprehensive regard for the values of the whole society than any attempt at intellectual comprehensiveness.

In the United States, for example, no part of government attempts a comprehensive overview of policy on income distribution. A policy nevertheless evolves, and one responding to a wide variety of interests. A process of mutual adjustment among farm groups, labor unions, municipalities and school boards, tax authorities, and government agencies with responsibilities in the fields of housing, health, highways, national parks, fire, and police accomplishes a distribution of income in which particular income problems neglected at one point in the decision processes become central at another point.

Mutual adjustment is more pervasive than the explicit forms it takes in negotiation between groups; it persists through the mutual impacts of groups upon each other even where they are not in communication. For all the imperfections and latent dangers in this ubiquitous process of mutual adjustment, it will often accomplish an adaptation of policies to a wider range of interests than could be done by one group centrally.

Note, too, how the incremental pattern of policy-making fits with the multiple pressure pattern. For when decisions are only incremental—closely related to known policies, it is easier for one group to anticipate the kind of moves another might make and easier too for it to make correction for injury already accomplished.[7]

Even partisanship and narrowness, to use pejorative terms, will sometimes be assets to rational decision-making, for they can doubly insure that what one agency neglects, another will not; they specialize personnel to distinct points of view. The claim is valid that effective rational coordination of the federal administration, if possible to achieve at all, would require an agreed set of values[8]—if "rational" is defined as the practice of the root method of decision-making. But a high degree of administrative coordination occurs as each agency adjusts its policies to the concerns of the other agencies in the process of fragmented decision-making I have just described.

For all the apparent shortcomings of the incremental approach to policy alternatives with its arbitrary exclusion coupled with fragmentation, when compared to the root method, the branch method often looks far superior. In the root method, the inevitable exclusion of factors is accidental, unsystematic, and not defensible by any argument so far developed, while in the branch method the exclusions are deliberate, systematic, and defensible. Ideally, of course, the root method does not exclude; in practice it must.

Nor does the branch method necessarily neglect long-run considerations and objectives. It is clear that important values must be omitted in considering policy, and sometimes the only way long-run objectives can be given adequate attention is through the neglect of short-run considerations. But the values omitted can be either long-run or short-run.

SUCCESSION OF COMPARISONS (5B)

The final distinctive element in the branch method is that the comparisons, together with the policy choice, proceed in a chronological series. Policy is not made once and for all; it is made and remade endlessly. Policy-making is a process of successive approximation to some desired objectives in which what is desired itself continues to change under reconsideration.

Making policy is at best a very rough process. Neither social scientists, nor politicians, nor public administrators yet know enough about the social world to avoid repeated error in predicting the consequences of policy moves. A wise policy-maker consequently expects that his policies will achieve only part of what he hopes and at the same time will produce unanticipated consequences he would have preferred to avoid. If he proceeds through a *succession* of incremental changes, he avoids serious lasting mistakes in several ways.

In the first place, past sequences of policy steps have given him knowledge about the probable consequences of further similar steps. Second, he need not attempt big jumps toward his goals that would require predictions beyond his or anyone else's knowledge, because he never expects his policy to be a final resolution of a problem. His decision is only one step, one that if successful can quickly be followed by another. Third, he is in effect able to test his previous predictions as he moves on to each further step. Lastly, he often can remedy a past error fairly quickly—more quickly than if policy proceeded through more distinct steps widely spaced in time.

Compare this comparative analysis of incremental changes with the aspiration to employ theory in the root method. Man cannot think without classifying, without subsuming one experience under a more general category of experiences. The attempt to push categorization as far as possible and to find general propositions which can be applied to specific situations is what I refer to with the word "theory." Where root analysis often leans heavily on theory in this sense, the branch method does not.

The assumption of root analysts is that theory is the most systematic and economical way to bring relevant knowledge to bear on a specific problem. Granting the assumption, an unhappy fact is that we do not have adequate theory to apply to problems in any policy area, although theory is more adequate in some areas— monetary policy, for example—than in others. Comparative analysis, as in the branch method, is sometimes a systematic alternative to theory.

Suppose an administrator must choose among a small group of policies that differ only incrementally from each other and from present policy. He might aspire to "understand" each of the alternatives—for example, to know all the consequences of each aspect of each policy. If so, he would indeed require theory. In fact, however, he would usually decide that, *for policy-making purposes,* he need know, as explained above, only the consequences of each of those aspects of the policies in which they differed from one another. For this much more modest aspiration, he requires no theory (although it might be helpful, if available), for he can proceed to isolate probable differences by examining the differences in consequences associated with past differences in policies, a feasible program because he can take his observations from a long sequence of incremental changes.

For example, without a more comprehensive social theory about juvenile delinquency than scholars have yet produced, one cannot possibly understand the ways in which a variety of public policies—say on education, housing, recreation, employment, race relations, and policing—might encourage or discourage delinquency. And one needs such an understanding if he undertakes the comprehensive overview of the problem prescribed in the models of the root method. If, however, one merely wants to mobilize knowledge sufficient to assist in a choice among a small group of similar policies—alternative policies on juvenile court procedures, for example—he can do so by comparative analysis of the results of similar past policy moves.

THEORISTS AND PRACTITIONERS

This difference explains—in some cases at least—why the administrator often feels that the outside expert or academic problem-solver is sometimes not helpful and why they in turn often urge more theory on him. And it explains why an administrator often feels more confident when "flying by the seat of his pants" than when following the advice of theorists. Theorists often ask the administrator to go the long way round to the solution of his problems, in effect ask him to follow the best canons of the scientific method, when the administrator knows that the best available theory will work less well than more modest incremental comparisons. Theorists do not realize that the administrator is often in fact practicing a systematic method. It would be foolish to push this explanation too far, for sometimes practical decision-makers are pursuing neither a theoretical approach nor successive comparisons, not any other systematic method.

It may be worth emphasizing that theory is sometimes of extremely limited helpfulness in policy-making for at least two rather different reasons. It is greedy for facts; it can be constructed only through a great collection of observations. And it is typically insufficiently precise for application to a policy process that moves through small changes. In contrast, the comparative method both economizes on the need for facts and directs the analyst's attention to just those facts that are relevant to the fine choices faced by the decision-maker.

With respect to precision of theory, economic theory serves as an example. It predicts that an economy without money or prices would in certain specified ways misallocate resources, but this finding pertains to an alternative far removed from the kind of policies on which administrators need help. On the other hand, it is not precise enough to predict the consequences of policies restricting business mergers, and this is the kind of issue on which the administrators need help. Only in relatively restricted areas does economic theory achieve sufficient precision to go far in

resolving policy questions; its helpfulness in policy-making is always so limited that it requires supplementation through comparative analysis.

SUCCESSIVE COMPARISON AS A SYSTEM

Successive limited comparisons is, then, indeed a method or system; it is not a failure of method for which administrators ought to apologize. None the less, its imperfections, which have not been explored in this paper, are many. For example, the method is without a built-in safeguard for all relevant values, and it also may lead the decision maker to overlook excellent policies for no other reason than that they are not suggested by the chain of successive policy steps leading up to the present. Hence, it ought to be said that under this method, as well as under some of the most sophisticated variants of the root method—operations research, for example—policies will continue to be as foolish as they are wise.

Why then bother to describe the method in all the above detail? Because it is in fact a common method of policy formulation, and is, for complex problems, the principal reliance of administrators as well as of other policy analysts.[9] And because it will be superior to any other decision-making method available for complex problems in many circumstances, certainly superior to a futile attempt at superhuman comprehensiveness. The reaction of the public administrator to the exposition of method doubtless will be less a discovery of a new method than a better acquaintance with an old. But by becoming more conscious of their practice of this method, administrators might practice it with more skill and know when to extend or constrict its use. (That they sometimes practice it effectively and sometimes not may explain the extremes of opinion on "muddling through," which is both praised as a highly sophisticated form of problem-

solving and denounced as no method at
all. For I suspect that in so far as there
is a system in what is known as "muddling through," this method is it.)

One of the noteworthy incidental consequences of clarification of the method
is the light it throws on the suspicion an
administrator sometimes entertains that
a consultant or adviser is not speaking
relevantly and responsibly when in fact
by all ordinary objective evidence he is.
The trouble lies in the fact that most of
us approach policy problems within a
framework given by our view of a chain
of successive policy choices made up to
the present. One's thinking about appropriate policies with respect, say, to
urban traffic control is greatly influenced by one's knowledge of the incremental steps taken up to the present. An
administrator enjoys an intimate knowledge of his past sequences that "outsiders" do not share, and his thinking
and that of the "outsider" will consequently be different in ways that may
puzzle both. Both may appear to be talking intelligently, yet each may find the
other unsatisfactory. The relevance of
the policy chain of succession is even
more clear when an American tries to
discuss, say, antitrust policy with a
Swiss, for the chains of policy in the
two countries are strikingly different
and the two individuals consequently
have organized their knowledge in quite
different ways.

If this phenomenon is a barrier to
communication, an understanding of it
promises an enrichment of intellectual
interaction in policy formulation. Once
the source of difference is understood, it
will sometimes be stimulating for an administrator to seek out a policy analyst
whose recent experience is with a policy chain different from his own.

This raises again a question only
briefly discussed above on the merits of
likemindedness among government administrators. While much of organization theory argues the virtues of common values and agreed organizational
objectives, for complex problems in
which the root method is inapplicable,
agencies will want among their own
personnel two types of diversification:
administrators whose thinking is organized by reference to policy chains
other than those familiar to most members of the organization and, even more
commonly, administrators whose professional or personal values or interests
create diversity of view (perhaps coming
from different specialties, social classes,
geographical areas) so that, even within
a single agency, decision-making can be
fragmented and parts of the agency can
serve as watchdogs for other parts.

NOTES

1. James G. March and Herbert A.
Simon similarly characterize the literature. They also take some important steps, as have Simon's recent articles, to describe a less heroic model
of policy-making. See *Organizations*
(John Wiley and Sons, 1958), p. 137.
2. "Operations Research and National
Planning—A Dissent," 5 *Operations
Research* 718 (October, 1957). Hitch's
dissent is from particular points
made in the article to which his
paper is a reply: his claim that operations research is for low-level problems is widely accepted.

For examples of the kind of problems to which operations research is
applied, see C. W. Churchman, R. L.
Ackoff and E. L. Arnoff, *Introduction
to Operations Research* (John Wiley
and Sons, 1957); and J. F. McCloskey
and J. M. Coppinger (eds.), *Operations Research for Management,* Vol.
II (The Johns Hopkins Press, 1956).
3. I am assuming that administrators
often make policy and advise in the
making of policy and am treating decision making and policy-making as
synonymous for purposes of this
paper.

4. Martin Meyerson and Edward C. Banfield, *Politics, Planning and the Public Interest* (The Free Press, 1955).

5. The line of argument is, of course, an extension of the theory of market choice, especially the theory of consumer choice, to public policy choices.

6. A more precise definition of incremental policies and a discussion of whether a change that appears "small" to one observer might be seen differently by another is to be found in my "Policy Analysis," 48 *American Economic Review* 298 (June, 1958).

7. The link between the practice of the method of successive limited comparisons and mutual adjustment of interests in a highly fragmented decision-making process adds a new facet to pluralist theories of government and administration.

8. Herbert Simon, Donald W. Smithburg, and Victor A. Thompson, *Public Administration* (Alfred A. Knopf, 1950), p. 434.

9. Elsewhere I have explored this same method of policy formulation as practiced by academic analysts of policy ("Policy Analysis," 48 *American Economic Review* 298 [June, 1958]). Although it has been here presented as a method for public administrators, it is no less necessary to analysts more removed from immediate policy questions, despite their tendencies to describe their own analytical efforts as though they were the rational-comprehensive method with an especially heavy use of theory. Similarly, this same method is inevitably resorted to in personal problem-solving, where means and ends are sometimes impossible to separate, where aspirations or objectives undergo constant development, and where drastic simplification of the complexity of the real world is urgent if problems are to be solved in the time that can be given to them. To an economist accustomed to dealing with the marginal or incremental concept in market processes, the central idea in the method is that both evaluation and empirical analysis are incremental. Accordingly I have referred to the method elsewhere as "the incremental method."

25. Mixed Scanning Revisited

Amitai Etzioni

An article on mixed scanning as a "third" approach to decision making, published in the *Public Administration Review* (December 1967) which was awarded the William Mosher Award, generated a steady stream of discussion,

SOURCE: "Mixed Scanning Revisited" by Amitai Etzioni, *Public Administration Review*: 46 (January/February 1986). Reprinted by permission of the American Society for Public Administration.

criticisms, and applications but very little empirical research. The approach was developed in contrast to rationalist models of decision making and to incrementalism. Rationalist approaches were held to be Utopian because actors cannot command the resources and capabilities required by rationalist decision making. Incrementalism was shown to overlook opportunities for significant innovations and to ignore the empirical fact that incremental decisions are often, in effect, made within the context of fundamental decisions. For example, once the U.S. embraced the Truman Doctrine after World War II, and decided to contain the USSR (rather than either allow it to expand or have the U.S. attempt to free countries within the Soviet Bloc), numerous incremental decisions were made in Greece, Turkey, and Iran. However, these were implemented and guided by the fundamental context-setting decision and cannot be properly understood without taking into account the basic decision.

MIXED SCANNING: DEFINITION AND ILLUSTRATIONS

Mixed scanning is a hierarchical mode of decision making (Goldberg, 1975, p. 934) that combines higher order, fundamental decision making with lower order, incremental decisions that work out and/or prepare for the higher order ones. The term scanning is used to refer to search, collection, processing, and evaluation of information as well as to the drawing of conclusions, all elements in the service of decision making. Mixed scanning also contains rules for allocation of resources among the levels of decision making and for evaluation, leading to changes in the proportion of higher versus lower levels of scanning based on changes in the situation.

For example, chess players, unable to review all the options (Haynes, 1974, pp. 7–8) and seeking to do better than merely think one or two steps ahead, running from trouble or toward a seeming opportunity, divide their time and psychic energy between first deciding among fundamental approaches ("ready to attack" vs. "need to further develop the forces"; "attack on the queen, or —king, side") and then examining in detail options only within the chosen approach. (In effect, this form of scanning may take place on more than two levels; e.g., choosing a major strategy, a sub-strategy, and then examining in detail some options within that substrategy.) Rules for allocation are illustrated in chess when the game must be completed within a given time period. Players will then engage in less higher-level scanning, i.e., allot it less time, as the game progresses, although it may be granted "extra" time if the strategy followed runs into difficulties.

This approach is less demanding than the full search of all options that rationalism requires, and more "strategic" and innovative than incrementalism. It was suggested in the 1967 publication that it is both empirically supported, in that the most effective decision makers are expected to use mixed scanning, and the most suitable, i.e., normative correct, approach.

Mixed scanning, it was suggested in the original publication, is akin to scanning by satellites with two lenses: wide and zoom. Instead of taking a close look at all formations, a prohibitive task, or only at the spots of previous trouble, the wide lenses provide clues as to places to zoom in, looking for details. In the years that passed a new technology was developed which applies the "double-lens" approach of mixed scanning, Decision Information Discipline System (DIDS). The system provides computer graphic displays of geodata, usually in the form of a map. The system has a zoom capacity that allows its users to zero in instantaneously on subunits (or subsets of variables), for example states within the USA and counties within the states. Wallace (1983) studied the 10 uses of the system as instances of mixed scanning. In one case a wide scan established that some areas were losing population although they were in parts of the county that by general trends should have been experiencing population growth. The zoom revealed these to be places in which military bases were being closed. In four, possibly five, of the 10 cases the approach led to what

Wallace calls "unexpected" findings (p. 318). The broad scanning was more economical than detailed (zoom-in) scanning of all counties. At the same time, the zoom-in scanning of counties, singled out by the broad scanning, prevented the loss of information that would have ensued if only broad scanning would have taken place.

OPERATIONALIZATION

A significant part of the works that followed spelled out the mixed-scanning model in programmatic terms, terms that can be used as a guide for decision makers, as a starting point for a computer program, and as a basis for research designs. Etzioni (1968, pp. 286–288) started this elaboration:

a. *On strategic occasions* (for definition see d below) (i) list all relevant alternatives that come to mind, that the staff raises, and that advisers advocate (including alternatives not usually considered feasible).

(ii) Examine briefly the alternatives under (i) (for definition of "briefly" see d below), and reject those that reveal a "crippling objection." These include: (a) utilitarian objections to alternatives which require means that are not available, (b) normative objections to alternatives which violate the basic values of the decision-makers, and (c) political objections to alternatives which violate the basic values or interests of other actors whose support seems essential for making the decision and/or implementing it.

(iii) For all alternatives not rejected under (ii), repeat (ii) in greater though not in full detail (for definition of scale see d).

(iv) For those alternatives remaining after (iii), repeat (ii) in still fuller detail (see d). Continue until only one alternative is left, or randomize the choice among those remaining (and

ask the staff in the future to collect enough information to differentiate among all the alternatives to be reviewed).

b. *Before implementation* (i) when possible, fragment the implementation into several sequential steps (an administrative rule).

(ii) When possible, divide the commitment to implement into several serial steps (a political rule).

(iii) When possible, divide the commitment of assets into several serial steps and maintain a strategic reserve (a utilitarian rule).

(iv) Arrange implementation in such a way that, if possible, costly and less reversible decisions will appear later in the process than those which are more reversible and less costly.

(v) Provide a time schedule for the additional collection and processing of information so that information will become available at the key turning points of the subsequent decisions, but assume "unanticipated" delays in the availability of these inputs. Return to more encompassing scanning when such information becomes available and before such turning points.

c. *Review while implementing.* (i) Scan on a semi-encompassing level after the first sub-set of increments is implemented. If they "work," continue to scan on a semi-encompassing level after longer intervals and in full, over-all review, still less frequently.

(ii) Scan more encompassingly whenever a series of increments, although each one seems a step in the first direction, results in deeper difficulties.

(iii) Be sure to scan at set intervals in full, over-all review even if everything seems all right, because: (a) a major danger that was not visible during earlier scanning but becomes observable now that it is closer might loom a few steps (or increments) ahead; (b) a better strategy might now be possible although it was ruled out in earlier rounds (see if one or more of the crippling objections was removed, but also look for new alternatives not previously examined); and (c) the goal may have been realized and, therefore, need no further incrementation. If this occurs, ask for new goal(s), and consider terminating the project.

d. *Formulate a rule for the allocation of assets and time among the various levels of scanning.* The rule is to assign "slices" of the available pie to (i) "normal" routines (when incrementing "works"); (ii) semi-encompassing reviews; (iii) over-all reviews; (iv) initial reviews when a whole new problem or strategy is considered; (v) a time "trigger," at set intervals, to initiate more encompassing reviews without waiting for a crisis to develop; and (vi) an occasional review of the allocation rule in the over-all review, and the establishment of the patterns of allocation in the initial strategic review.

Janis and Mann (1977, p. 37) introduced a major improvement of the program. They point out that while in the initial scanning, all those options that have no "crippling objections" are held over for closer scanning, which amounts to a "quasi-satisficing" approach, "each time the surviving alternatives are reexamined, the testing rule might be changed in the optimizing direction by raising the minimum standard (from crippling objections to more minor objections)."

They also expanded the range of decision making to which mixed scanning may be applied: "Although intended for policy makers, the same program, with minor modifications, could be applied to an individual's work-task decisions and to personal decisions involving career, marriage, health or financial securi-

ty" (1977, p. 38). For such applications, they indicated, step a(i) must be modified: the staff and advisers would be replaced by family or friends.

Starkie (1984, p. 75) concurs with Etzioni that a mere accumulation of numerous incremental changes is not expected to yield the equivalent of a contextual or fundamental decision, because the incrementalist model provides no guide lines for the accumulation; it is likely to be random or scattered. In contrast, in mixed scanning, the fundamental decisions provide such guidance. Starkie correctly points out that Etzioni's suggestion that an "incremental 'creep' followed by a sudden change when existing policies are no longer sustainable by modification alone" is but one possible pattern of a combination of incremental and fundamental decisions; incrementation may *follow* a fundamental decision, just as readily as the other way around. Chadwick (1971) relates the various methods of decision making to different purposes and techniques of decision making. He sees rationalism as related to attempts to explore the long range; and sees its techniques as either normative forecasting or exploration and simulation; that is, lacking in empirical content. He sees the purpose of mixed scanning as the "provision of alternative sets of action policies," using evaluation, the design methods, and something he calls "planning balance sheet" (p. 340). No details are provided concerning these techniques and Chadwick's endorsement of mixed scanning "as a highly acceptable meta-procedure" is based on his judgment that it is flexible but not on an empirical study. Wright (1977) follows a similar tack.

How a fundamental decision can be told from an incremental decision properly concerned several who examined the mixed-scanning model. Lee (1979, p. 486) agrees with the basic approach, to wit "it is more rational in practice to be selective and systematic about a number of feasible options than to 'rationally' examine all the choices." He adds, however, that the theory "does not tell us at what point the selection ceases to be rational." Cates (1979, p. 527) writes: "my problem is trying to identify a big or little decision. Appearances are deceiving." (See also, Falcone, 1981.)

On the other hand, Alexander (1972, p. 327) does not experience this difficulty: he finds that an example Braybrooke and Lindblom use to show how a policy is determined by incremental decisions, the 1940 "state of emergency" declared by F. D. Roosevelt prior to U.S. entry into World War II, was in effect an incremental step implementing his prior fundamental decision, to involve the United States in the war, one way or another.

One way to differentiate between incremental and fundamental decisions is *relative* size. For example, Fenno (1966) used the fact that Congress tends to make only 10 percent or less changes in the budgets of numerous federal agencies, each year, to argue that it is only incrementing. Ten percent or less may amount to billions of dollars but in the context may be considered small or incremental. Etzioni, in turn, used the same rule of thumb, i.e., 10 percent or less is marginal, to show that many of the actual decisions made were nonincremental: 211 out of the 444 decisions Fenno studied (12 years, 37 agencies) were actually changes of 20 percent or larger, within one year; 24 decisions entailed a budget change of 50 percent or more; seven—100 percent or more (Etzioni, 1968, p. 289). Other changes were small, but only following a major change. For example, the U.S. defense budget increased at the beginning of the Korean War from 5.0 percent of the Gross National Product in 1950 to 10.3 in 1951.

Another way to distinguish between incremental and fundamental decisions is to check for a nestling relationship. If an incremental decision requires or draws on a contextual decision, this is the fundamental one. For example R&D review committees that authorize funds for federal projects act incrementally if they review each project, of which there are many, on its own merits. They engage in mixed scanning if they first form some guidelines as to what lines of research they wish to promote and heed these when they render specific decisions. Indeed, some projects, that do not qualify by the criteria chosen, may not need to be reviewed in detail at all.

POSITIVE AND NORMATIVE

All three approaches to decision making are not only positive, in the sense that they claim to describe the ways decision makers actually act, but also normative approaches in that they prescribe how effective decisions ought to be made. Alexander (1972) would add here, "under the given circumstances," because he does not believe that there is one appropriate decision-making strategy for all circumstances. Janis and Mann (1977, p. 38) suggest that different types of decision makers will find different strategies suitable to their divergent personalities and levels of education and training. In contrast, I hold that these situational and actor differences will be reflected in the relative investment among the various scanning levels. For instance, those with less education will tend to invest less in higher scanning. However, no actor, under any realistic circumstances, can abide by the rationalist approach. And, all actors under all but highly unlikely circumstances would lose by merely incrementing, although if the situation is very stable and the actors happen to use the best strategy to begin with, the damage would be smaller than under other circumstances.

Parkinson (1980) applies the mixed-scanning approach in an attempt to develop a new policy-making model for the educational system in Ohio, superior to the existing one. The approach used in the educational system before Parkinson's endeavor was relatively incremental; contextual considerations were neglected (1980, p. 161). Following the mixed-scanning approach, Parkinson developed a model that defines policy first on a broad level and then evaluates policy on an incremental level. To incorporate the mixed-scanning approach, Parkinson suggested that there is a need to establish a meta policy group with the capability to maintain broad perspectives needed for longer range planning. "The collection and maintenance of broad policy information and its ready availability to all would enlarge the policy view to incorporate more than the current preoccupation with immediacy—that is solving the problems of the moment—without destroying the need for individuals and groups to research and provide information on specific policy issues which are of particular interest to themselves" (1980, p. 169). Parkinson's study is normative in that it is prescriptive; he did not study the results of shifting to the mixed-scanning model he favored in his study.

Hackett (1980) offers a model for the use of power by administrators. Much of his work does not concern mixed scanning but the way "assets" (resource, personality) are converted into intraorganizational power. However one of the major components of his power model is the use of mixed scanning. He integrates it into his model by tying sweeps of scanning to the development of plans to deploy or "activate" the administrator's power assets. Thus, for example, if scanning reveals a loss of cooperation, power assets have to be deployed to regain cooperation (or to force one's way), or, presumably, to modify one's approach (1980, p. 102; see also p. 14).

Seen in a wider perspective, differences in normative models tie to differences in general world views. Rationalists tend to be philosophically attuned to *laissez faire* classical liberal and libertarian perspectives. They are also highly optimistic in that they see the individual decision maker as highly self-reliant and able. In that sense they are also highly optimistic, utilitarian, and Utopian (Bradley, 1973, pp. 297-298). Incrementalists favor conserving the status quo, because they are blind to opportunities for radical departures (Dror, 1969) or to major reforms. They are also highly pessimistic about human capacity to know and to act sensibly.

Mixed scanning is most compatible with a progressive, innovative viewpoint. It assumes a capacity of the actors to adapt to changing circumstances, even major changes, including the structure of the actors themselves. Revolutionary changes, which entail a breakdown of the old regime and the rise from the ashes of a new one, may occur in a poorly scanning actor but, under most conditions, can be avoided by proper scanning *if* the findings of the scanning undertaken are heeded and proper adaptations are made. At the same time the hyperoptimism of fine-tuned planning and rationalist models is avoided. (Indeed, Dyson, 1975, p. 160, reports that the model "stimulated S.P.D. intellectuals." The S.P.D. referred to is the German Social Democratic Party.) As Bradley (1973, p. 298) puts it: "Mixed-scanning seeks to avoid the most serious problems of both the overly rationalistic model and the excessively pragmatic model. . . . Normatively, it provides for the standing and predictability, which at least in the long run, is necessary to a decent society as well as acceptance of needed major innovations. . . ."

Others have questioned whether mixed scanning avoids the twin traps. Hanna (1980) depicted incrementalism as compatible with market economies and those who champion them; rational planning as reflecting "value authoriza-tionism," and mixed scanning as "ignor-ing normative issues." He does not pro-vide the reasons for reaching this conclusion. Smith and May (1980, p. 153) pose a more serious challenge:

> But in fact it is not clear that the unre-alistic and conservative shortcomings would actually be avoided. They might merely be confined or moved to different sectors of the decision mak-ing process. There is no guarantee that within these confines they might not even be accentuated. We would need to examine mixed scanning in prac-tice before we could judge. Other is-sues are side-stepped. For example Et-zioni retains the presumption that decision makers can summarize and rank their values, at least ordinarily. As we have mentioned, it has been ar-gued with conviction that values are ordered only in contexts of specific choice.

Indeed, whether or not values can be "summarized" is an empirical question which unfortunately has not been stud-ied, at least in this context.

STRUCTURAL FACTORS

The original article (Etzioni, 1967) and the following elaboration (Etzioni, 1968) stressed the role of structural factors. Decisions are not made in a vacuum; they are deeply affected by the position and relative power of the decision mak-ers and their relation to one another.

Rationalism assumes an all-powerful actor, as reflected in the notion that ac-tors ought to set their goals and set about implementing them, without ask-ing about their place in various power hierarchies or the strategies needed to deal with them. For instance, a subordi-nate may need to act differently than a high ranking executive. Incrementalism is most compatible with the acceptance of existing power relations. As Bradley (1973, p. 298) put it: "The unorganized, and others who lack control over ade-quate decision-making resources, have no role to play in the game of partisan mutual adjustment." (Mutual adjust-ment is usually associated with incre-mentalism.) Mixed scanning sensitizes the decision maker to taking into ac-count *other* actors; one of the major fac-tors scanning encompasses is the pos-ture of other actors and the relations among them.

The structural element received little attention in the more than 50 publica-tions that deal with mixed scanning, possibly due to a widespread tendency to treat decision making as a disembod-ied strategy. (A full list of references is available from the author.) Wimberly and Morrow (1981), one of the few who examined this factor, concluded that in-crementalism leans toward consensus whereas rationalism tends toward opti-mization and hence to disregard of consensus. Mixed scanning is viewed as seeking to provide a "compromise" of the two approaches. The authors see mixed scanning as "involved" and "time consuming" (p. 504) but deem these features as unavoidable if both the need to scan sufficiently, not to overlook a major opportunity, without being burdened down with insurmount-able details, are to be attended to. They hence conclude that mixed scanning is "most suitable for the full range of deci-sions" (p. 506).

A structural point was made by Snort-land and Stanga (1973) when they ap-plied mixed scanning to the relations among courts. The higher courts (like higher ranking executives) attempt to re-serve for themselves the fundamental decisions and expect the lower courts to increment. When the lower courts deal with incremental cases in contexts the higher courts have not passed on, this becomes "a matter of concern" for the higher ones.

A similar relationship has been observed between federal agencies and other agencies and private agents. Cardinal (1973) explored a specific act from a mixed-scanning viewpoint; namely the National Environmental Policy Act of 1969, focusing on its implementation. Special attention is paid to Section 4332(c) that provides for an institutionalization of the scanning levels. The "generalist policy leadership is seen as coming from the EPA . . . to be the primary line agency to create and complement policies. . ." (p. 469). Detailed implementation and related incremental decisions are often left to other agencies: states, localities, or corporations.

Berry (1974, pp. 358-359) examines what he calls "community relations" under different decision-making strategies, specifically in the context of the relations between Comprehensive Health Planning Agencies and their councils. The rationalists' plan, he finds, is "technically sophisticated" and hence requires a "rather stable" environment. This, in turn, requires council members who are technically competent *and* "following approval of this document [the master plan] community reaction and debate would be discouraged. . . ." Incrementalism requires a high level of consensus building; hence great attention must be paid to a council that is based upon fair representation. Mixed scanning requires deep public awareness of the *fundamental* decisions and of the main alternative schemes. (But, by implication, less involvement in incremental decisions.)

SOME EVIDENCE

Snortland and Stanga (1973, pp. 1021–1031) applied mixed scanning to the study of the law. First they found the model applied to the Constitution.

The second phase of the incorporation of the Bill of Rights provides an illus-

tration of mixed-scanning. While the first phase proceeded absent-mindedly, the second involved fundamental decisions by the Court within a mixed-scanning framework of both fundamental and bit decision. *Mapp v. Ohio,* and certainly *Gideon v. Wainwright,* appear to represent major and conscious fundamental decisions to incorporate provisions of the Bill of Rights into the fourteenth amendment. Within a few years after these decisions, the Court virtually completed the process of incorporation by incremental decision-making. The Court did not adopt Justice Black's position, which called for immediate and complete incorporation. Rather, the Court made a fundamental choice on the incorporation question, but ensured that the process could be halted if it proved to be deleterious to the administration of criminal justice. The Court retained the freedom to reevaluate this major policy decision and to retrench, if necessary. This is precisely the process that is prescribed by the mixed-scanning model.

Snortland and Stanga show the relevance of mixed scanning to two major Supreme Court decisions: *Miranda* and *Brown.* In the case of *Miranda,* the context setting decision involved both formulating guidelines and selecting the incrementing case. In the case of *Brown,* the fundamental decision both followed and set the context to incremental ones.

The Court clearly was aware that its first decision on interrogations and confessions after *Escobedo* would be an important one. The case takes on an even greater significance, in terms of mixed-scanning, when it is realized that *Miranda* and the companion cases "were as representative of police interrogation situations as *Escobedo* had been unique." *Miranda* involved not only a conscious decision of a fundamental question but also a selection of cases that would encourage a broad application of the new policy to interrogation and confession cases.

. . . The *Brown* decision provides a useful example of the application of the mixed-scanning model. *Brown* was preceded by a series of cases that strongly eroded the "separate but equal" doctrine. Because of the incremental nature of these cases, the outcome in *Brown* should have been a surprise to no informed observer. Yet it is clear that *Brown* was a major policy decision of fundamental importance. It was not an incremental decision, although it is likely, as Shapiro suggests, that the Court had already resolved to outlaw segregation. Many aspects of racial discrimination were left unanswered by *Brown*. The questions were to be worked out incrementally, as is shown by the second *Brown* decision.

Many additional detailed points made by the two authors cannot be recaptured here.

Wiseman (1979) examined the design and development of planning processes used within the Scottish health service. Various decision-making approaches are examined and "for reasons set out below, a mixed-scanning approach was felt to be most relevant" (p. 104). The subject of the study is the Scottish Home Health Department (SHHD) that encompasses 15 district health boards and a headquarters that contains an administrative and a planning unit. Before reorganization, the focus of the study, the SHHD was "very much geared to the administration and management of existing health services and the development of policies was mainly undertaken in response to external stimuli" (p. 105). Issues arose on an ad hoc basis, with no systematic evaluations of the situation, and decision making was largely one of

incrementalism, although sporadic and futile attempts to introduce rationalisms occurred. For example, an attempt was made to use management science techniques for manpower planning purposes. Disappointment with the results of this approach led to a search for a more effective approach.

. . . A rational comprehensive approach was rejected at an early stage because of the limited planning resources available, the complexities of a changing environment, the multiple interests and the multiple accountability of individuals within the health service. On the other hand, there was also a desire to introduce more rationality and more balance into policy-making than had been possible in the past. This inevitably meant searching for a middle course which would improve on past practice. A mixed-scanning approach was proposed which embodied three key components (Wiseman, 1979, p. 107).

The first element was the introduction of a scanning process, whose purpose was to review from time to time "what had been happening, to identify and where possible anticipate major issues for possible detailed attention and in general to provide an overview on which the future directions for the development of health services could be considered" *(ibid.)*. To ensure that the process would not be rationalistic it was agreed that "the review process would consider the field of health services in broad terms but not in depth and would not attempt to produce detailed policies or plans for any one specific aspect" *(ibid.,* p. 107).

The second element was a selection procedure, to sort out which of the fundamental issues identified by the review process would be subject to detailed study and planning, taking into account the limited resources. The third element entailed detailed planning of the relatively small subset of issues selected for incrementalization. Wiseman (1979, p. 104) reports that the plan was implemented but provides no observations on its effectiveness. (Two other publications, Wiseman, 1978 and 1980, deal with the same effort but provide no more detail on the outcome of the introduction of mixed scanning.)

Berry (1974, pp. 351–353) suggests briefly how mixed scanning can be applied to a variety of situations, including the decision of an owner of several newspapers in small communities of whether or not to include a given additional town in his chain, and the use of sudden changes in death or morbidity data to initiate various levels of scanning by public health authorities (scope of search depends on the relation of departure of the data from the established norms). Berry proceeds to suggest the amount of resources and time various approaches to decision making require: The rationalist approach requires "maximum time and funds before action"; incremental—least; mixed scanning relatively few funds but more than incrementalists and "moderate time"; the radical approach is as taxing and time consuming as the rationalist ones (p. 356).

Deshler (1974) trained 56 educational administrators in mixed scanning and observed their behavior both before and after the training and attained information from them by the use of questionnaires and interviews. He found that practically all those studied scanned broadly "naturally," before they were exposed to mixed scanning (p. 89). However, before they were introduced to mixed scanning about half limited their scanning to local issues, ignoring state and federal ones; and most tended to scan downward, not upward, and internally and not externally. Mixed scanning enhanced the scope of their scans upward and outward. It also decreased

their tendency to attach the label of "excellent" to whatever was established practice and enhanced their tendency to consider alternatives. "The process enables you to think about the issue in greater depth. It removes your tunnel vision. It stimulates cross-disciplinary thinking, and opens up new areas for consideration" interviewers told Deshler (Deshler, 1974, p. 101).

DeVall, Bolas, and Kang (1976) compared the three approaches to the decision making in their study of the utilization of applied social research in 240 projects. They developed a measure of "overall policy impact" based on interviews with policy makers. (The measure has five elements the correlations among which were examined. For details see *ibid.*, appendix B.) Testing next showed that the rationalist approach, defined as explicitly, fully spelled-out "policy norms," has a poor policy impact. The impact was 12.56 when the norms were clearest; 13.40 when they were unclear; and 19.07 when they were not explicitly indicated.

Incrementation, operationalized as adjusting closely the policy research to the "ongoing, day-to-day processes of decision making" showed considerable policy impact (highest, 17.60). Mixed scanning was operationalized as full scanning, rather than merely diagnosing the problem or merely identifying policy goals—also encompassing implementation options. It was associated with the most intense use of the applied social research. The policy impact reading was 23.67.

CONCLUSION

Mixed scanning seems to have an intuitive appeal to a fair number of scholars and action-oriented students of decision making. The ways it might be operationalized for the purpose of research or implementation have been clarified over the years, and the essential difference between fundamental and incremental decisions seems not to pose great difficulties. The links between the three different approaches of decision making and various intra- and interorganizational power structures, as well as between power approaches versus consensus building, have been explored. However, it remains to be empirically substantiated if, indeed, rational models are more suitable for totalitarianism or high-power approaches (e.g., master planning); incrementalism to highly pluralistic, special-interest dominated polities; and mixed scanning to systems that combine a balanced commitment to the collectivity with pluralism (Etzioni, 1984). The alternative hypothesis would be that rationalism does not work even for highly centralized systems (as the recent changes in USSR and China suggest) and that incrementalism reinforces the weakness of pluralism without a collective framework. All may require mixed scanning albeit using different mixtures of higher and lower levels of scanning.

Above all, mixed scanning is still very short of case studies and quantitative studies of situations in which decision-making strategies were changed from either rationalist or incrementalist ones to mixed scanning. More needs to be known of the results in terms of effectiveness and of the factors that hindered or fostered the use of mixed scanning.

BIBLIOGRAPHY

ALEXANDER, ERNEST R., "Choice in a Changing World," *Policy Sciences,* vol. 3 (September 1972), pp. 325–337.

BERRY, DAVID E., "The Transfer of Planning Theories to Health Planning Practice," *Policy Sciences,* vol. 5 (September 1974), pp. 343–361.

BRADLEY, MICHAEL, "Decision-Making for Environmental Resources Management," *Journal of Environmental Management,* vol. 1 (1973), pp. 289–302.

CARDINAL, THOMAS E., "Comment—The National Environmental Policy Act of 1969 and Its Implementation: A Socio-Political-Legal Look at the 'New' Environmental Planning," *Journal of Urban Law,* vol. 50 (1973), pp. 465–485.

CATES, CAMILLE, "Beyond Muddling: Creativity," *Public Administration Review,* vol. 39 (November/December 1979), pp. 527–532.

CHADWICK, GEORGE F., *A Systems View of Planning* (New York: Pergamon Press, 1971).

DESHLER, JOHN DAVID, "Utilizing Mixed-Scanning as a Strategy for Administrative Decision-Making," Ph.D. dissertation (University of California, Los Angeles, 1974).

DEVALL, MARK VAN, CHERYL BOLAS, AND TAI S. KANG, "Applied Social Research in Industrial Organizations: An Evaluation of Functions, Theory, and Methods," *Journal of Applied Behavioral Science,* vol. 12 (April/May/June 1976), pp. 158–177.

DROR, Y., "Muddling Through—Science or Inertia?" In Amitai Etzioni, ed., *Readings on Modern Organization* (Englewood Cliffs, N.J.: Prentice-Hall, 1969).

DYSON, K. H. F., "Improving Policy-Making in Bonn: Why the Central Planners Failed," *The Journal of Environmental Management,* vol. 1 (May 1975), pp. 289–302.

Etzioni, AMITAI, "Mixed Scanning: A 'Third' Approach to Decision Making," *Public Administration Review,* vol. 27 (December 1967), pp. 385–392.

ETZIONI, AMITAI, *The Active Society: A Theory of Societal and Political Processes* (New York: The Free Press, 1968).

ETZIONI, AMITAI, *Capital Corruption* (New York: Harcourt, Brace, Jovanovich, 1984).

FALCONE, DAVID, "Health Policy Analysis: Some Reflections on the State of the Art," *Policy Studies Journal,* vol. 9 (Special Issue, No. 1, 1981), pp. 188–197.

FENNO, RICHARD F., *The Power of the Purse* (Boston: Little, Brown, 1966).

GOLDBERG, M. A., "On the Inefficiency of Being Efficient," *Environment and Planning,* vol. 7 (December 1975), pp. 921–939.

HACKETT, JOHN ALLEN, "A Theoretical Model for the Predictive Analysis of Power," Ph.D. dissertation (George Peabody College for Teachers, Vanderbilt University, 1980).

HANNA, ALLAN ALEXANDER, "Settlement and Energy Policy in Perspective: A Theoretical Framework for the Evaluation of Public Policy," Ph.D. dissertation (University of Western Ontario, 1980).

HAYNES, PAUL A., "Towards a Concept of Monitoring," *Town Planning Review,* vol. 45 (January 1974), pp. 6–29.

JANIS, IRVING, AND LEON MANN, *Decision Making* (New York: The Free Press, 1977).

LEE, KENNETH, "Health Care Planning, Policies, and Incentives," *Futures* (December 1979), pp. 482–490.

PARKINSON, GEOFFREY WILLIAM, "Policy-Making at the State Level for K-12 Education," Ph.D. dissertation (Ohio State University, 1980).

SMITH, GILBERT AND DAVID MAY, "The Artificial Debate Between Rationalist and Incrementalist Models of Decision Making," *Policy and Politics,* vol. 8 (April 1980), pp. 147–161.

SNORTLAND, NEIL E. AND JOHN E. STANGA, "Neutral Principles and Decision-Making Theory: An Alternative to Incrementalism," *The George Washington Law Review,* vol. 41 (July 1973), pp. 1006–1032.

STARKIE, DAVID, "Policy Changes, Configurations, and Catastrophies," *Policy and Politics,* vol. 12 (January 1984), pp. 71–84.

WALLACE, DORIS NADINE, "An Exploratory Study of the Utility of the Decision Information Display System for Decision Making and Policy Analysis," Ph.D. dissertation (American University, 1983).

WIMBERLEY, TERRY AND ALLYN MORROW, "Mulling Over 'Muddling Through' Again," *International Journal of Public Administration,* vol. 3 (1981), pp. 483–508.

WISEMAN, COLIN, "Selection of Major Planning Issues," *Policy Sciences,* vol. 9 (February 1978), pp. 71–86.

WISEMAN, COLIN, "Strategic Planning in the Scottish Health Service—A Mixed Scanning Approach," *Long Range Planning,* vol. 12 (February 1979), pp. 103–113.

WISEMAN, COLIN, "Policy-Making for the Scottish Health Services at National Level," *Scottish National Yearbook 1980* (1980), pp. 135–160.

WRIGHT, KEVIN, "An Exchange Strategy for the Interface of Community-Based Corrections into the Service System," *Human Relations*, vol. 30 (October 1977), pp. 879–897.

Public Policy and Public Administration

For many years, public administrators were seen as neutral implementors of public policies shaped and designed elsewhere in the democratic process. Since the 1960s, with the growth of public policy analysis, both the policy process itself and the role of public administration in it have been reevaluated.

Initially, the analysis of public policy focused on the nature and components of the policy process. Other important work analyzed the differences between types of policy; Theodore Lowi, for example, identified four different policy arenas in American domestic policies. In this early work, the role of public administration was considered to be quite limited; implementation was the purview of bureaucratic organizations and actors; other policy activities—defining the problem, getting the problem on the policy agenda, designing and passing a legislative solution—were reserved for the executive, the legislature, and the citizenry. As the selections by Sabatier and Mazmanian, and by Bendor and his colleagues demonstrate, however, more critical and rigorous analysis of the bureaucratic role in policy demonstrates it to be much more extensive and significant throughout the policy process than originally thought.

Another important emphasis in policy analysis has been on rationalizing the policy process and its outcomes. Proceeding from the premise that politics is messy and imprecise, recent proponents of public policy analysis argue that the introduction of rigorous analytical methodologies and decision tools will dramatically improve both the definition of public problems and the identification of alternative solutions to them. Further, it is argued that more rational decision processes will be more efficient, but also more responsive to citizen needs and preferences. This version of public policy analysis values objectivity and neutrality; it is based on an abiding belief in technical analysis and abilities. The application of economic theories and analytical techniques, rather than those more traditionally associated with political science and public administration, accompanied the recent growth of this type of policy analysis. Jenkins-Smith provides a succinct summary of this perspective; his conclusion that policy analysis can play a significant role in creating and managing more effective public programs endorses the need for greater rigor in analysis throughout the policy process.

While this tradition continues to be quite strong, another has begun to supplement it. Reflecting some disenchantment with the ability of technical analysis to address complex problems, some scholars have started to analyze the actual use of policy analysis in policy decisions and have found its utility to be mixed. Paul Light's analysis of social security forecasting, for example, finds that very sophisticated analytical techniques produced essentially inaccurate information. Further, he finds that, while the technical analysis provided a rationale for policy choice, the decision was heavily informed by politics. In this setting, policy analysis becomes just one more bargaining chip in political decision making.

Still other analysts have argued that previous efforts at analysis focused too much on implementation of policy and on outcomes of policy, but not enough on the design of policy. The ability to understand increasingly complex public problems, to understand causal linkages between problem and proposed solutions, and to improve the theoretical foundation, as well as the quality and relevance of information available for analysis, have become recent focal points. These analysts suggest that the often documented policy failures or limited successes are not due to improper or faulty implementation. They argue, instead, that the correct policy solution was not matched to the problem, or that the problem was never correctly defined.

Through it all, the central role of politics has begun to emerge once again. All analysis, it is clear, is ultimately fed into the political process. In many cases, expert analysis becomes only one more information chip in political bargaining; the hoped-for rationalization of the process is overwhelmed by the political arena. Further, competing analyses often suggest dramatically different solutions to the same problem. Again, selective choice of information and analysis is political. In a democratic society, elected officials appropriately utilize expert analysis as they see fit.

All of these developments have been significant for public administration and public administrators. The rational policy analysis paradigm, with its emphasis on careful—and narrow—problem definition and weighing of alternative solutions, stands in direct contrast to both politics and administration as usual. As Jenkins-Smith notes in the selection that follows, ". . . the use of analysis . . . is seen by its proponents as in tension with the norms and practice of American politics, and as providing the vehicle for reform in both the policies selected and the procedures for selecting them." In this context, public administrators are seen as both part of the problem and part of the solution. Bureaucratic decision making, with traditional emphasis on incremental, reactive choice, is to be reformed. On the other hand, public bureaucracies provide one natural home for policy analysts and their activities. Further, evaluation of past programs and policies is an important part of policy analytic activities. Public bureaucracies play a crucial part in clarifying program goals and objectives and in providing program activity data. They also, of course, have a major stake in the outcomes of the evaluation effort. In many cases, public agencies both implement and evaluate the programs for which they are responsible; in these cases it is essential to have analytical capabilities inside the organization.

The study of public policy and policy analysis is now a well established part of political science and public administration. The perspectives provided by a public policy focus are invaluable, even if sometimes uncomfortable, for public sector employees and organizations. The "What difference does it make?" questions that policy analysis asks are at the heart of why public organizations exist: to deliver services, or to monitor service delivery by others, so that citizens are served efficiently, effectively, and equitably by their tax dollars.

26.   The Policy Analysis Paradigm

Hank C. Jenkins-Smith

What is it that is praised and criticized as policy analysis? How can it be characterized in a way that renders examination of the implications of its use for American politics—if not a straightforward exercise—at least a manageable problem? What are the characteristics of the analysis and advice provided that make it distinctive from, for example, the prescriptions for the Good Polity in the writings of the ancient Greek theorists? Perhaps no definitive characterization is available, for the scope and content of policy analysis remain matters of extensive debate among both theorists and practitioners.[1] Yet if analysts are not in full agreement on the uses to which they are to put their tools, an examination of the core methods and techniques of policy analysis indicates that there exists, if not unanimity on its characterization, at least a set of characteristics that, owing to their force, clarity, and deep grounding in the theories underlying policy analysis, may be called a "dominant paradigm" in the field.[2]

For purposes of this chapter, the primary techniques of policy analysis are accepted at face value, as are the definitions of value, public interest, and decision criteria from which those tech-

SOURCE: "The Policy Analysis Paradigm" by Hank C. Jenkins-Smith, *Democratic Politics and Policy Analysis* (Pacific Grove, CA: Brooks/Cole, 1990). Reprinted by permission.

[1]Illustrative of the divergence of views on the characterization of policy analysis are the reflections of Aaron Wildavsky in *Principles for a Graduate School of Public Policy*, (Berkeley, CA: University of California at Berkeley, 1977), and those of Mark Moore in "Statesmanship in a World of Particular Substantive Choices," in *Bureaucrats, Policy Analysts, Statesmen: Who Leads?*, ed. Robert Goldwin (Washington, DC: American Enterprise Institute, 1980), pp. 20–36. Wildavsky, in particular, seems to celebrate the myriad of approaches taken to policy analysis in the various schools of public policy, and purposefully leaves the content of his own approach open-ended.

[2]I am, of course, not the first to speak of a dominant paradigm in policy analysis: see Aaron Wildavsky, *Speaking Truth to Power*, (Boston: Little, Brown, 1979). Also see his "The Political Economy of Efficiency: Cost–Benefit Analysis, Systems Analysis, and Program Budgeting," *Public Administration Review*, 26(2) (December 1966), pp. 292–310.

niques are derived. The intent is not to erect a "straw man," but rather to address the *normative and logical implications* of policy analysis as derived from the primary analytical techniques. Many, perhaps most, policy analysts embrace these implications, but more important for our purposes is that the key "threats" and "promises" of policy analysis for democratic government are typically cast in terms of the implications of policy analytical techniques. To understand the dialogue between proponents and critics of policy analysis, it is critical that the underlying normative bases of analysis be teased out of the technical core of analysis. Even more, assessment of the threats and promises of policy analysis, and its place in American policy making, requires that these normative bases and their implications be made explicit.

In the sections that follow, the core of the policy analytic approach—the conception of choice grounded in utility theory and employing the criterion of economic efficiency—is described in some detail. In addition, the origins and techniques for application of the efficiency criterion are given sufficient attention to illustrate the normative basis and implications of efficiency as the primary grounding principle in policy analysis.[3] The more technical elements of the descriptions of efficiency and its development are reserved for the exhibits in this chapter.

[3]Though the primacy of the efficiency principle in policy analysis, and its basis in theory, may seem obvious to some readers, recent attempts to come to grips with the apparent tensions between democratic politics and the principles of efficiency have neglected the theoretical idea of efficiency altogether. See for example, Douglas Yates' *Bureaucratic Democracy* (Cambridge, MA: Harvard University Press, 1982), and M. E. Hawkesworth's *Theoretical Issues in Policy Analysis* (Albany, NY: SUNY Press, 1988).

CHARACTERIZING POLICY ANALYSIS

I have argued that efficiency analysis and the efficiency criterion of choice make up the core of policy analysis. For that reason, much of what policy analysts learn and do, and much of the substantive knowledge employed, is deliberately excluded from the characterization of policy analysis made here. This exclusion may appear to doom this characterization of policy analysis to inaccuracy because policy analysis appears to be eclectic: it makes use of techniques developed in the fields of economics, mathematics, statistics, operations research, and systems dynamics, among others, to provide decision makers with advice in the formulation of public policy. In applying those techniques, the analyst may draw on knowledge from fields such as sociology, political science, welfare economics, law, organization theory, the physical and biological sciences, and elsewhere. Policy analysis must take the analyst wherever the policy issue leads, making analysis the multidisciplinary activity par excellence.[4]

Despite the apparent cacophony of activities involved in policy analysis, the logic of analysis imposes an order on these activities and bends them to a uniform purpose: to determine which policy (if any) provides the largest net gains in social welfare. Examining how social welfare is defined and how it is estimated will take up much of this chapter. At heart the procedure is derived from the model of rational individual decision making, wherein the

[4]See Martin Landau, "The Proper Domain of Policy Analysis," *American Journal of Political Science*, vol. 21 (May 1977), p. 419; and Duncan MacRae, Jr. and Dale Whittington, "Policy Analysis as an Applied Social Science Discipline," *Administration and Society*, 6(4) (February 1975), pp. 363–388.

individual, with a given set of preferences, limited resources, and using the knowledge at his or her disposal, takes the action likely to maximize his or her individual utility.[5] Thus, in the style of the rational decision maker, the policy analyst is to use a range of analytical techniques and multiple fields of knowledge to engage in a number of distinct procedures or steps, including: (1) identifying the "problem" to be resolved, (2) specifying the goal(s) to be sought through public policy, (3) identifying or inventing the available policy alternatives, (4) estimating the effects of each of the alternatives, both favorable and unfavorable, (5) imputing values in a single, commensurable metric to those effects, and (6) choosing the "best" policy alternative according to an explicit decision rule.[6] The techniques and fields employed are thus intended to be steps in a rational procedure for making public choice. If, as is typically the case, the government policy is to result in some change in human condition or behavior, the analyst requires knowledge about that condition or behavior. In addition, the analyst may require behavioral models that indicate the change likely to result from government action. Furthermore, where problems are more complex, the analyst may employ more sophisticated quantitative models to determine the relationship between various possible government actions and the desired policy outcomes. All of these activities, however, are steps in the direction of discovering— among the options available—the policy that best serves "society's" interests. It therefore follows that the criterion that determines the best or optimal choice serves as both the logical and normative core of policy analysis: logical because it indicates what knowledge is required and what techniques are applicable, and normative because it prescribes the best policy.

In the analysis of the optimal allocation of things valued in society (which is the quintessential problem of policy analysis), the problem is generally conceived by policy analysts as being concerned with two components: one concerns the attainment of an equitable *distribution* of valued things in society, and the other concerns the attainment of an *efficient* satisfaction of individual wants given the distribution of valued things.[7] Each of these components provides criteria that may serve as the normative core of policy analysis. Yet, from the standpoint of the policy analytic

[5]For a development of the assumption of rationality in individual choice, see William H. Riker, and Peter C. Ordeshook, *An Introduction to Positive Political Theory* (Englewood Cliffs, NJ: Prentice Hall, 1973), Chapter 2, and Herbert Simon, *The Science of the Artificial* (Cambridge, MA: MIT Press, 1969). For an introduction to the application of the rational choice approach to public decision, see Edith Stokey and Richard Zeckhauser, *A Primer for Policy Analysis* (New York: W. W. Norton and Co., 1978), Chapter 3.

[6]Many such lists of steps are enumerated in the policy analysis literature, each quite similar to the list presented here. See, for example, Stokey and Zeckhauser, *A Primer of Policy Analysis,* pp. 5–6; David Nachmias, *Public Policy Evaluation: Approaches and Methods* (New York: St. Martins Press, 1979) pp. 12–18; Alice Rivlin, *Systematic Thinking for Social Action* (Washington, DC: Brookings Institution, 1971), pp. 3–5. The Graduate School of Public Policy at the University of California at Berkeley propounds a version of the above list called the "eightfold path," which seeks to give somewhat greater emphasis to the role of analysis in *creating* policy alternatives. For a critique of this restrictive "problem solving" approach, see Martin Rein and Sheldon White, "Policy Research: Belief and Doubt," in *Policy Analysis*, 3(2) (Spring 1977), pp. 239–271.

[7]A still broader conception of "public sector management" adds economic stabilization as a further relevant concern. See Richard Musgrave, *The Theory of Public Finance* (New York: McGraw-Hill, 1959), Chapter 1.

framework, equity criteria suffer from the lack of a solid analytical basis and from a lack of consensus on the appropriate formulation of such criteria, while the efficiency criterion is well grounded in the analytical framework and provides a normative standard that is both well understood and widely accepted.

Limitations on the use of equity criteria. Normative criteria based on the distribution of values in society are necessarily derived from a conception of distributive justice.[8] Such criteria must address how scarce valuables are to be allocated among groups or individuals. Policy analysts, borrowing from mainstream welfare economics and working from a strictly individualistic utilitarian framework, have typically declined to propose an explicit normative standard for the distribution of value. In an evolution to be described later in this chapter, analysts have become heirs to a tradition that has concluded that, given the limits of what can be "objectively" and unambiguously identified as "improvements" in social welfare, analysts can say little regarding the superiority of one efficient distribution of values over another. The techniques and methods employed in policy analysis thus give analysts no independent *analytical* base from which to propound the supremacy of any distribution of values.

Given the lack of a criteria of distributive justice readily derived from the dominant analytical framework, should analysts seek to employ a distributive criterion they must rely for their normative standard on some source outside that framework. As a practical matter, many competing distributional criteria are available for use in public policy formulation, and an impartial analyst is left in a position of attempting to display the expected results of the policies that would be optimal under some range of contending standards.[9] Furthermore, though the analyst may be unable to assess the competing standards on grounds of distributive justice from within the analytic framework, he or she is able to assess the effects of each of the equity standards in terms of the efficiency of the distribution of values that results. The analyst is able to specify, for example, the effects that a given scheme of redistribution of wealth may have on the work incentives of the participants.[10] But perhaps most illustrative of the favored place of efficiency relative to equity criteria is the argument that analysts should treat redistribution of wealth as a "good," like other goods, that can be val-

---

[8] There are numerous theories of distributive justice that could provide a normative criterion for policy analysis. One of the most widely known of such theories can be found in John Rawls' *A Theory of Justice* (Cambridge, MA: Harvard University Press, 1971), which stands as a justification of the redistributive social programs of the 1960s and early 1970s. An opposing criterion, providing for a much more restricted role for government, can be found in Robert Nozick's *Anarchy, State and Utopia* (New York: Basic Books, 1974.)

[9] The complexity and ambiguity resulting from inclusion of such standards may also restrict the breadth of applicability of policy analysis. Thus Duncan MacRae, Jr., and Dale Whittington argue in a very perceptive article that "The price of formal rationality [traditional benefit—cost analysis] is that some wrong decisions will be made. The price of substantive rationality [in which appropriate social equity considerations are made] may be that no expert advice at all will be available for some of these decisions." See their "Assessing Preferences in Cost–Benefit Analysis: Reflections on Rural Water Supply Evaluations in Haiti," *Journal of Policy Analysis and Management,* vol. 7, no. 2 (Winter 1988), pp. 246–263; p. 260.

[10] Perhaps the most thorough, though still inconclusive, study of this nature is contained in Joseph A. Pechman and P. Michael Timpane, eds., *Work Incentives and Income Guarantees: The New Jersey Negative Income Tax Experiment* (Washington, DC: Brookings Institution, 1975).

ued.[11] If the value of an increment of redistribution can be determined by, for example, determining people's "willingness-to-pay" for it, redistribution can be included like any other good provided by government within the framework of an efficiency analysis. In this way, assuming that the hurdles in the way of discovering how much people value redistribution could be overcome, equity criteria would be subsumed under the criteria of efficiency.[12]

In response to attempts to integrate equity concerns into the framework of efficiency, a number of practitioners and theorists have countered that such attempts will necessarily result in disagreement and may discredit the use of policy analysis altogether. One widely used text in policy analysis contends that, if policy analysts attempt to mingle equity and efficiency analyses through employment of such techniques as distributional weights or

other equity criteria, then the result of analyses will necessarily be arbitrary. The weights chosen

> [w]ill vary with the political climate and are likely to cause squabbles among economists themselves, and between economists and the public. To the extent that economists did not reject the principle of employing such weights but participated in the struggle to establish one set of weights rather than another, cost–benefit analysis as a technique could become discredited.[13]

Others have held that attempts to collapse equity concerns together with efficiency concerns, in order to make them commensurable, merely cloud the issue and bury personal judgment and bias under an impenetrable thicket of numbers.[14] The implication is that policy analysts should do what they know how to do, efficiency analysis, and leave the equity concerns of policy to others.

To recapitulate, equity criteria concerning the distribution of values are external to the dominant framework of policy analysis; given the lack of consensus on appropriate equity criteria, analysts are limited to assessing and displaying the results of equity criteria supplied by others, or to reviewing the efficiency implications of various equity criteria—or at most, barring technical difficulties, the analyst may reduce the equity criteria to a component of efficiency analysis. To many analysts the difficulties of including equity consider-

---

[11] According to A. Myrick Freeman, III, "Under plausible assumptions about individuals' utility functions, namely interdependence, it can be shown that individuals could increase their utility by contributing to government enforced tax and transfer systems." "Project Evaluation and Design with Multiple Objectives," *Public Expenditure and Policy Analysis*, eds. Robert H. Haveman and Julius Margolis, 2nd ed. (Chicago: Rand McNally, 1977), p. 242.

[12] When offering this technique for analysis of distributional programs, it is usual for the proponent of the method to rely on the valuation of elected officials, rather than on the public at large, to determine the value of redistribution as a good. See Freeman, ibid. Also see Harold M. Hochman and James D. Rogers, "Pareto Optimal Redistribution," in *American Economic Review*, 59(no. 4) (September 1969), pp. 542–557; and Otto Eckstein, "A Survey of Public Expenditure Criteria," in the Universities National Bureau for Economic Research's *Public Finances: Needs, Sources, and Utilization* (Princeton, NJ: Princeton University Press, 1961), pp. 439–504.

[13] E. J. Mishan, *Cost–Benefit Analysis*, 3rd ed. (Boston: George, Allen and Unwin, 1982).

[14] See, for example, Otto Eckstein, "A Survey of Public Expenditure Criteria," p. 449, and Peter O. Steiner, "The Public Sector and the Public Interest," in Haveman and Margolis, *Public Expenditure and Policy Analysis*, pp. 62–64.

ations suggest that such considerations be left to others.

Efficiency analysis suffers far less from such limitations. As shall be described below, efficiency analysis falls squarely within the tradition of policy analysis as it has developed from the utilitarian theorists of the eighteenth century. Though disputes remain, the basic criteria of efficiency are widely agreed upon among economists and policy analysts, eliminating the necessity to choose among competing normative standards. Because the concept of efficiency is well defined, and because a broad consensus exists on the proper formulation of an efficiency criterion, no "outside" specification of the criterion from clients is required. Moreover, it is the concept of efficiency that ties together the disparate elements of analysis; it imposes a logic on the collection of data, valuation of outcomes, and comparison of and selection among alternatives. Finally, the conception of efficiency provides a coherent normative standard that can be applied, in the abstract at least, across the full range of activities in which government engages. It is with little exaggeration, therefore, that the concept of efficiency can be said to provide the logical and normative core of policy analysis.

DEVELOPMENT OF UTILITY THEORY

The concept efficiency did not spring forth, fully formed, from the brow of Zeus. Rather, the concept has evolved over the past two centuries, beginning as a key element of a reformist (and quite radical) political movement and undergoing transformation toward an ever more technical and "content-free" analytical concept. Yet the current form owes much to its early makeup, and the place accorded efficiency analysis in policy making is much in line with the early vision.

Central to the concept of efficiency is the theory of utility developed by economists from foundations first laid by Jeremy Bentham late in the eighteenth century. Bentham declared the "season of fiction" to be at an end and called for enlightened formulation of public policy based on the principles of utility.[15] According to Bentham, an experience provides utility when it produces "benefit, advantage, pleasure, good, or happiness," or when it prevents "mischief, pain, evil, or unhappiness."[16] All individual behavior could be understood as the pursuit of utility, based on a hedonistic calculus designed to maximize pleasure and minimize pain. The value of an act or experience was to be defined in terms of the pleasures and pains it brought to individuals; individuals were thus the ultimate arbiters of value.

For Bentham the concept of utility was rich in substantive content. The chief dimensions of utility were (1) intensity, (2) duration, (3) certainty or uncertainty, and (4) propinquity or remoteness. Also important were fecundity (meaning the likelihood that the pleasure or happiness would be followed by more of the same) and purity (meaning the likelihood that the pleasure would *not* be followed by pain).[17] Bentham lists no less than twenty-six categories of pleasures and pains making up the "simple" roots of utility to which all specific pains and pleasures can be reduced, including (but not limited to) sense, wealth, skill, amity, good name,

---

[15]In Jeremy Bentham, *Fragment on Government,* in *The Collected Works of Jeremy Bentham,* eds. J. H. Burns and F. Rosen (New York: Oxford University Press, 1983), pp. 393–501; p. 441.

[16]In Jeremy Bentham, *Introduction to the Principles of Morals and Legislation,* eds. J. H. Burns and H. I. A. Hart (London: Athlone Press, 1970), p. 12. Utility generally is discussed on pp. 11–16.

[17]Ibid., pp. 38–41.

power, piety, benevolence, and association.[18]

Having named the categories and dimensions of utility, Bentham then specified the factors influencing the quantity of utility that an individual would derive from a particular experience. While the sources of pain and pleasure may be common to all men, the amounts of utility received by individuals from a given source will not be uniform. Bentham argued that an individual would gain utility based upon his or her "quantum" of sensibility, a factor that varies from person to person. The quantum of sensibility, in turn, is affected by a host of factors—primarily education—that serve to "bias" the sensibilities of both body and mind.[19]

Much like economists who followed him, Bentham employed money as a common metric in the measurement of pleasures. He argued as follows: imagine two pleasures, between which one is indifferent, one of which may be purchased with money and the other not. Because one is indifferent between them, the pleasures must be equal.

> But the pleasure produced by the possession of money, is as the quantity of money that produces it: money is therefore the measure of this pleasure. But the other pleasure is equal to this; the other pleasure therefore is the money that produces this: therefore money is also the measure of that other pleasure.[20]

Furthermore, while money can be used to value pleasures, the value of money itself *decreases* as the amount of money held increases—a phenomenon later dubbed the decreasing marginal utility of money. As Bentham argued, ". . . the quantity of happiness produced by a particle of wealth (each particle being of the same magnitude) will be less and less at every particle . . ."[21]

For Bentham, the development and use of utility theory in the formulation of public policy rested on an unresolved ambiguity. On one hand, Bentham held that it would be impossible to determine with any exactitude the quantity of utility that an individual obtained from an experience or to compare the gains or losses of utility of any two individuals. On the other hand, unless one *could* compare the utilities of individuals the utility calculus would provide little aid to the formulation of public policy. The solution, for Bentham, was simply to *assume* utilities to be comparable. The assumption was justified as providing a useful tool for legislators that would be, at worst, far better than any basis for legislation that failed to take utility into account. In the words of Bentham's disciple, Etienne Dumont,

> Differences of character are inscrutable; while the diversity of circumstances is such that they are never the same for two individuals. Unless, therefore, we begin by eliminating these two considerations, it will be impossible to arrive at any general conclusions. But, although any one of our propositions may be found false or inexact when applied in a given case, this should not lead us to doubt their theoretical accuracy or their

---

[18]Ibid., Chapter 5. Especially intriguing is Bentham's catalog of the types of pleasures to be gained from viewing a country scene in the footnote in ibid. on pp. 49–50.

[19]Ibid., pp. 51–69.

[20]Elie Halevy, *La Formation du radicalisme philosophique* (Paris: Germer Bailliere, 1901), p. 410, as cited in George Stigler, "The Development of Utility Theory," in his *Essays in the History of Economics* (Chicago: University of Chicago Press, 1965), pp. 66–155.

[21]In Jeremy Bentham, *Works of Jeremy Bentham* (Edinburgh: Tait, 1843), vol. 3, p. 229, as cited by Stigler, "The Development of Utility Theory," p. 73.

practical utility. It is sufficient to justify our propositions if (a) they approach more nearly to the truth than any others that can be substituted for them, and (b) they can be employed more conveniently than any others as the basis for legislation.[22]

Based on his elaborate utility calculus, Bentham called for the state to employ legislation to pursue "the greatest good for the greatest number."[23] By this Bentham meant the establishment of public policy that would increase the sum of the utilities of the individuals that make up society. An illustrative example employing his calculus concerns the distribution of wealth in society. Based on his conception of the diminishing marginal utility of money, Bentham determined that the greatest aggregate utility from the wealth of society would be obtained by evening out the distribution of wealth; gains in utility from giving money to the poor would more than offset losses in utility from taking money from the rich. On further reflection, however, Bentham determined that the loss of utility sustained from weakening the security of property, resulting from taxing the rich, would offset any gains made through the redistribution of wealth. Therefore the utility calculus could not support legislation to equalize wealth in society.[24]

A central weakness in Bentham's calculus was its inability to compare the utilities of different individuals in prescribing legislation for the greatest good. Could we be sure that the loss of utility due to weakening the security of property would outweigh the gains to be had from a more equal distribution of wealth if we were unable to compare the respective gains and losses sustained by different individuals? Alternatively, could we even be sure that a more equal distribution of wealth would result in larger aggregate utility? Might not the rich have had sufficient opportunity to partake of education and other factors affecting their "sensibilities" to pain and pleasure such that their loss would be felt far more acutely than the gains of the poor, notwithstanding the diminishing marginal utility of money? The utility theorists following Bentham struggled with the problem presented by the incomparability of individual utilities and generally rejected Bentham's contention that utilities could be assumed comparable.

Building from foundations laid by Bentham, utility theorists have broadened and generalized the theory of utility, effectively purging it of the substantive form and content specified by Bentham. Late in the nineteenth century, political economists Stanley Jevons, Leon Walras, and Carl Menger, among others, altered Bentham's formulations to focus on the satisfaction to be obtained from the possession of individual goods.[25] Among these early theorists the concept of diminishing marginal utili-

[22]Etienne Dumont, *Bentham's Theory of Legislation,* trans. by Charles Atkinson (London: Oxford University Press, 1914), p. 134.

[23]In Burns and Rosen, eds., *The Collected Works of Jeremy Bentham,* passim.

[24]In Dumont, *Bentham's Theory of Legislation,* pp. 157–162. One observer ties the early rise of policy analysis to the activities of Benthamite reformers in nineteenth century Britain, when Bentham's techniques were applied to health care issues. See Rudolf Klein's "The Rise and Decline of Policy Analysis: The Strange Case of Health Policymaking in Britain," *Policy Analysis,* 2(3) (Summer 1976), pp. 459–475.

[25]The primary works are, Stanley Jevons, *Theory of Political Economy,* 4th ed. (London: Macmillan, 1911), Leon Walras, *Elements d'économie politique pure* (Paris: Pichon and Durand-Auzais, 1926), and Carl Menger, *Grundsatze der Volkswirtschaftslehre* (Vienna: Braumuller, 1871). For a lucid summary of the contributions of these "early marginalists" see Stigler, *The Development of Utility Theory.* Also see Jacob Oser and William C. Blanchfield, *The Evolution of Economic Thought,* 3rd ed. (New York: Harcourt, Brace, Jovanovich, 1975), pp. 220–241.

ty—holding that the increment of utility gained from possession of an added unit of a good declines as the number of units possessed increases—was deemed a general law of utility.[26] Furthermore, most early marginal utility theorists held total utility of the individual to be derived from simple summation of the utilities gained from the goods possessed by the individual.

This formulation, however, ignored complementary and substituting goods that, when consumed, change the utility to be gained by consumption of other goods. This problem led theorists to specify a more general formulation of the individual's "utility function," that would allow for utilities to be affected by such relationships among goods.[27] The general utility function eliminated the need to assume diminishing marginal utility for consumption of individual goods in order to assure equilibrium in economic trades; indeed, diminishing marginal utility was shown to be neither a necessary nor sufficient condition for achievement of equilibri-

um conditions.[28] Still later developments of utility theory, based on the concept of indifference schedules (see Exhibit 26.2), took a further leap toward generality; the conception of individual utility itself that had underlaid the development of utility theory was abandoned as too "metaphysical" and restrictive. As Vilfredo Pareto wrote early in this century,

> The entire theory [now] rests on a fact of experience, that is to say, on the determination of the quantities of goods which constitute combinations that are equivalent for the individual. The theory of economic science thus acquires the rigor of rational mechanics; it deduces its results from experience, without the intervention of any metaphysical entity.[29]

The development of utility theory has thus been marked by a progressive development away from the substantively grounded, limited theory of utility proposed by Jeremy Bentham; successively, interpersonal comparisons of utility, additive individual utility functions, the requirement of diminishing marginal utility, and even the "metaphysical" conception of utility itself have been shed in favor of increasingly general propositions. Yet, despite the increasing generality of the theory, the prescriptive "legislative" role of utility theory envisioned by Bentham has been preserved.[30] That prescriptive role is embodied in the concept of economic efficiency.

---

[26]For these theorists the measure of utility gained from the last unit of the good obtained, the so-called "marginal unit," must be equal to the money value of the price paid for it. Prices, in turn, were seen simply as the rate of exchange by which the good under consideration could be traded for other goods. Utility maximizing individuals would spend their available resources such that the gain in utility from expenditure of the last dollar would be the same for all types of goods; that is, utility is maximized when:

$$MU_1 = MU_2/P_2 = MU_3/P_3 = \ldots = MU_n/P_n$$

where MU_2 is the utility gained from possession of the last unit of good 2, and P_2 is the price or exchange rate of good 2 for good 1. It was assumed that, should the price of one good fall relative to all others, more of that good would be purchased—becoming the familiar law of demand in economics.

[27]Francis Edgeworth developed the more general utility function in *Mathematical Psychics* (London: Kegan Paul, 1881).

[28]Stigler, *The Development of Utility Theory*, pp. 98–100.

[29]Vilfredo Pareto, *Manuale di economia politica* (Milan: Piccola Biblioteca Scientifica, 1919), pp. 160, 169, as cited in Stigler, *The Development of Utility Theory*, p. 126.

[30]Bentham would surely be quite comfortable with the modern concept of "hedonic damages," applied by economists in death-related lawsuits. The idea is to measure the "value of life" that stems from the joys of living; what is the dollar loss attributable to the

THE CONCEPT OF EFFICIENCY

Efficiency analysis is applicable whenever one regards a system in which individuals seek cooperatively to satisfy their wants. Thus it is equally applicable (in principle) to political and economic systems. It is assumed at the outset that the system is made up of individuals, and that each of these individuals has an ordinally ranked set of wants or "preferences." "Society" is thus strictly an aggregation of individuals, and social welfare is no more or less than the aggregation of the welfare of the individuals that make up the society. As stated by a leading economist,

> [I]n Western economics, economic welfare is almost always related to individual welfare; it is postulated that there can be no welfare other than what accrues to individuals. This is a rejection of the organic theory of the state: the state as an entity enjoys no welfare, only the people that compose it.[31]

The normative heart of the concept of efficiency derives straight from Bentham: a social system or policy ought to be designed to maximize the satisfaction of individual wants, subject to certain limitations on the analyst's ability to specify what constitutes an "improvement" in overall want satisfaction. Thus efficiency analysis, like Bentham's calculus of pleasure and pain, is based solidly on an individualistic and utilitarian view of human activity.

The problem addressed by efficiency analysis concerns the opposition of individual wants and the limited means available to satisfy those wants. An economic or political system can be regarded as a mechanism for adjusting the myriad of competing individual wants to available means. The question asked by efficiency analysis is, how well does a particular system (method for making choices) or policy (a given choice or set of choices) for the allocation of society's resources satisfy individual wants? The answer is necessarily limited because of the premise that each individual holds a possibly unique schedule of preferences; without omniscience it is impossible to determine whether satisfaction of one individual's wants adds more to total well-being (or social welfare) than would satisfaction of some other individual's wants. Rather than confront the problem of the incomparability of individual utilities directly, the criterion of efficiency provides a way around this problem.

In a society of limited resources, and in which individuals compete for those resources in order to satisfy wants, improvement of a single individual's well-being can occur either (1) without reduction (and perhaps with improvement) in the well-being of others, or (2) with a concomitant decrease in the well-being of others. In the latter case, due to the assumed incomparability of individual utilities, it is impossible to determine whether society as a whole is made better by the change. In the former case, when one person's gain is not offset by the losses of others, the sum of the individuals' welfare can unambiguously be said to have increased. This represents a clear-cut increase in the efficiency with which wants are satisfied.

Pareto optimality. The strict criterion of efficiency, often called Pareto optimality, is met when a system allocates re-

---

ending of a person's life? One guru of hedonic damages, Stanley V. Smith, argues that the value of a life may be as high as $12 million, but puts the "reasonable" range at between $500,000 and $3.5 million. See Paul M. Barrett, "Price of Pleasure: New Legal Theorists Attach a Dollar Value to the Joys of Living," *Wall Street Journal,* vol. CXIX, no. 114 (December 12, 1988) p. A-1.

[31]Eckstein, "A Survey of Public Expenditure Criteria," p. 441.

sources in such a way that no further re-allocation of goods can increase any individual's utility without diminishing the utility of others. Put otherwise, all individuals are made as well-off as possible to the point that any increase in the well-being of one must decrease the well-being of someone else. If at any time any individual can be made better-off without reducing the well-being of others, the system is not operating strictly efficiently.[32] A given policy is efficient in this strict sense if it increases the well-being of at least one individual without diminishing that of others. It is important to note that there exists no uniquely efficient allocation of resources; beginning from any less than optimal distribution of wealth, movement toward efficiency can be achieved by distributing the added increment of well-being in countless ways among the members of society. Thus, many Pareto optimal solutions exist, differing according to the distributions of goods achieved.

A more thorough and somewhat more technical description of Pareto efficient solutions is provided in Exhibit 26.1.

The Kaldor-Hicks criterion. Unbending application of the strict Pareto optimality criterion would impose rather severe restrictions on government action: no

action, no matter how beneficial it might be to the community as a whole, could be taken that diminished the well-being of even one individual. In the extreme, even an action required to maintain the viability of the community (say, maintenance of law and order) would violate the criterion if any person, on the basis of his or her own assessment of the effect of the action on his or her utility, determined that the action would leave them worse off than would no action at all. But clearly much of government action does just that: policies of income redistribution, progressive taxation, use of eminent domain for the construction of highways and dams, and price-support programs for agricultural products, to name just a few, improve the lot of some at the expense of others. The applicable criterion, then, would be one that would allow assessments of the efficiency of policies that do increase the welfare of some at the expense of others.

The use of such a criterion would seem to run up against the problem of the comparison of individual utilities—the problem avoided through the use of the strict criterion of efficiency—because one must weigh the gains of some in society against the losses of others. The solution takes the form of a weak criterion of efficiency, sometimes called "Kaldor-Hicks criterion."[33]

The Kaldor-Hicks criterion allows redistributions that increase *net* welfare such that those who gain from the distribution could compensate those who lose, restoring the losers to their prior level of well-being, while the winners retain enough of their gains to be better-off than they would have been without the redistribution. In this case individu-

---

[32]The development of the concept of efficiency in this chapter refers primarily to efficiency in exchange among consumers. It is important to also recognize the application of efficiency in production: briefly, in economic terms, efficiency in production means production on the "production possibilities frontier"—meaning the maximum output given the available material inputs and technology—at the point at which the marginal rate of transformation of one good into another is equal to the ratio of the prices of those goods. See Michael Intriligator, *Mathematical Optimation and Economic Theory,* 2nd ed. (Englewood Cliffs, NJ: Prentice-Hall, 1971), pp. 178–189. Also see Robert Y. Awh, *Microeconomics: Theory and Applications* (New York: John Wiley & Sons, 1976), pp. 161–210.

[33]This discussion draws heavily from the classic paper by J. R. Hicks, "The Foundations of Welfare Economics," *The Economic Journal,* 49(196) (December 1939), pp. 696–712.

als' utilities need not be compared; as long as a common value of the good redistributed is available, such as the money value of the gains and losses to the individuals involved,[34] it is possible to determine just how much of the improvement to the gainers must be given in compensation to the losers to assure that no one is worse off than they would have been without the redistribution. Thus, the criterion specifies that a system that results in an allocation of goods from which subsequent redistribution could result in *net* increases in social well-being is not efficient. Furthermore, in the comparison of policies, the relevant criterion is: which policy option serves to create the largest net gain in social well-being?

Although the Kaldor-Hicks criterion requires that a policy result in net gains in social well-being, it does not require that the gains actually be redistributed in a manner that offsets the losses of those harmed by redistribution. The principle requires only that such a compensation *could* have been made, and that net social gains be left over. It is enough to show that, in the aggregate, sufficient value has been created to more than offset the losses entailed. No guidance is offered by the criterion as to whether or how compensation should be made; such decisions are beyond the scope of efficiency analysis and must be made on the basis of other criteria.

[34]Specification of gains and losses to different individuals in money terms does not directly imply a comparison of individual utilities because one need not assume that the value of an added (or subtracted) dollar is the same for all individuals. Because money *does* measure the relative market value of whatever is gained or lost in terms of all other goods that have prices, once the money value of a loss is specified it is known how much money compensation is required to increase the losers' ability to obtain enough other goods to compensate for the original loss.

The Kaldor-Hicks criterion is the central normative standard in the policy analysis paradigm. The criterion is applied most widely as the decision rule for benefit-cost analysis. Benefit-cost analysis is essentially concerned with whether a policy generates more social benefits than social costs, and if so, what level of program expenditure provides optimal results. The steps in benefit-cost analysis include:

1. identification of the project or projects to be evaluated;
2. determination of all impacts, favorable and unfavorable, present and future, on all of society;
3. valuation of those impacts, either directly through market values or indirectly through shadow price estimates;
4. calculation of the net benefit—total value of positive impacts less total value of negative impacts; and
5. application of the decision rule: selection of the project that produces the largest net social benefits.[35]

The decision rule employed is a straightforward application of the Kaldor-Hicks criterion; if gains in social well-being are in excess of losses incurred, those who gain from the program could compensate those who lose and still retain net benefits, and the program should be undertaken. Still another widely used technique, cost-effectiveness analysis, is a truncated form of efficiency analysis. This technique asks only which policy achieves a given objective at least cost, or which one achieves most of a desired objective at a fixed cost. These techniques, and the methods of estimation and projection that make them possible, constitute the primary tools of the trade for the public

[35]See, e.g., Stokey and Zeckhauser, *A Primer for Policy Analysis,* pp. 136–138. Also see Mishan, *Cost-Benefit Analysis,* passim.

policy analyst. At its core, then, policy analysis as generally practiced is applied efficiency analysis.

EFFICIENCY AND MARKET PRICES

The use of competitive market prices has come to be one of the cornerstones of efficiency analysis in public policy. The reasons for the affinity of market analysis and public policy are several: ideological persuasion surely plays a part along with technical and theoretical reasons.[36] The chief theoretical link of competitive markets to efficiency analysis, however, lies in the Pareto efficient properties of free market outcomes.

One of the earliest and most important applications of utility theory was termed the "theorem of maximum satisfaction," holding that competitive market allocations of value will be Pareto efficient.[37] In brief, the theorem states that utility maximizing consumers will adjust consumption patterns such that the ratio of the gains in utility for possession of the last unit (marginal utility) of any two

goods is equal to the ratio of the prices of those goods.[38] Because consumers face common prices, the ratio of the marginal utilities for any two goods will be the same for all persons.[39] This is precisely the condition in which consuming individuals will, through voluntary market exchange, have achieved a Pareto optimal allocation of available goods.[40] Thus Leon Walras could proclaim:

> Production in a market governed by free competition is an operation by which the [productive] services may be combined in products of appropriate kind and quantity to give the greatest possible satisfaction of needs within the limits of the double condition that each service and each product have only one price in the market, at which supply and demand are

---

[36]An eloquent case for greater reliance on "voluntary" means of production and exchange on libertarian grounds can be found in Freidrich A. Hayek, *The Road to Serfdom* (Chicago: University of Chicago Press, 1972) and *Individualism and Economic Order* (Chicago: University of Chicago Press, 1948). Another libertarian defense of greater reliance on markets and less on collective action can be found in Nozick, *Anarchy, State and Utopia.* An alternative and less dogmatic justification for markets is made by Arthur Okun, *Equality and Efficiency: The Big Tradeoff,* (Washington, DC: Brookings Institute, 1975). Here the productive force of the market, which has "proved to be an efficient organizer of production in practice as well as in theory," is raised in defense of markets (p. 50).

[37]See Walras, *Elements d'économie,* p. 231, as described in Stigler, *The Development of Utility Theory,* pp. 94–97. The discussion of efficiency is paraphrased from that provided by James M. Henderson and Richard E. Quandt in *Microeconomic Theory* (New York: McGraw-Hill, 1958), pp. 87–88.

[38]Assuming that consumers face common prices for n available goods, and each acts to maximize utility by purchase of those goods within a limited budget, each consumer will contrive to purchase each of the n goods until the ratio of the gains in utility for possession of the last unit ("marginal utility") of any two goods is equal to the ratio of the *prices* of those two goods. That is to say: $(\delta U_m/\delta x_i)/(\delta U_m/\delta x_1) = p_i/p_1$, where U_m is total utility of person m, x, is the quantity of good i consumed, and p_1 is the price of good j.

[39]This can be expressed as: $(\delta U_m/\delta x_i)/(\delta U_m/\delta x_1) = (\delta U_n/\delta x_i)/(\delta U_n/\delta x_1)$, where m and n are any two consumers, and i and j are any two goods.

[40]Note that this condition is equivalent to the consumers' condition that the indifference curves (which are often called "marginal rates of substitution") are tangent in the Edgeworth diagrams discussed in exhibit 26–1; for a given distribution of the two "goods," the ratios of the marginal utilities of guns and butter for Ron and Jim (shown by the *slopes* of their indifference curves) were the same only when the curves were tangent. When the curves were tangent, Ron and Jim were on the Pareto "contract curve"; no subsequent improvement could be made in the well-being of either party without reducing that of the other. A symmetrical proof exists for the Pareto optimality of free markets for the production of goods and services by competitive firms. See Henderson and Quandt, ibid.

equal, and that the prices of the products are equal to their costs of production.[41]

Pareto's conditions for the theorem of maximum satisfaction have, of course, been extended; it is now recognized that all significant costs and benefits of a good must be captured by its price (e.g., the price must cover the costs incurred by pollution generated in producing or consuming the good), information about all significant aspects of the good must be freely available, and it must be costless for participants to make trades in the market.[42]

The Pareto optimal quality of competitive price gives it a special role in the valuation of goods produced and resources utilized in public programs. Market price indicates the efficient valuation of a good, in money terms, relative to other goods in the economy. The valuation of all such goods in terms of money is, of course, necessary in order to be able to compare the costs and benefits of public policy in a common metric. However, a difficulty arises for those frequent cases in which no market price exists for the various benefits and costs of the policy: how are policy analysts to compare the value of goods that are not priced—or that are not believed to have competitive prices in the market? For example, how would the analyst compare the value of reduced risk of deaths in auto accidents with that of the increased costs of travel time resulting from the imposition of the 55 mile per hour speed limit, neither of which "goods" are directly priced in the market? Alternatively, how would an analyst quantify the benefits—or more likely the costs—of allocation schemes for petroleum products during periods in which oil supplies are disrupted, as they were in the 1973 and 1979–1980 "oil crises"?

The answer is through the use of "shadow prices." When no market price is available for the goods and resources under consideration, or when available prices are not deemed to meet the requirements of the perfectly competitive market, shadow price estimates of competitive market prices are to be used. As stated by one economist:

> The basic question asked by the analyst when he searches for shadow price is: what would the users of the public output be willing to pay? The analyst tries to simulate a perfect and competitive market for the public output, estimate the price which would have resulted, and accept this as the shadow price.[43]

Thus the analyst estimates what individuals *would* have been willing to pay for the good had it been available in a competitive market, using such estimating techniques as: (1) interpolation from the prices of similar goods, (2) treatment of the good provided by the public program as intermediate to the production of other goods that have market prices, and valuation of the intermediate good according to its marginal contribution to the final goods, and (3) estimating the value of the good created by the public program to be equal to the reduction in costs to society that would result from existence of the good.[44] Using such tech-

[41]Walras, *Elements d'économie,* p. 231, as cited in Stigler, *The Development of Utility Theory,* p. 97.

[42]See Otto A. Davis and Morton I. Kamien, "Externalities, Information, and Alternative Collective Action" in Haveman and Margolis, *Public Expenditure,* pp. 82–104. Also see Kenneth Arrow, "The Organization of Economic Activity: Issues Pertinent to the Choice of Market Versus Nonmarket Allocation," ibid., pp. 67–81.

[43]Julius Margolis, "Shadow Prices for Incorrect or Nonexistent Market Values," ibid., p. 204.

[44]Ibid., pp. 213–219.

niques to calculate shadow prices for goods and resources without competitive market prices is a crucial step in the application of the Kaldor-Hicks criterion through benefit–cost analysis. Benefit–cost analysis thus attempts to work from market prices, or estimated market prices, in order to assure that the resources used and benefits produced by public programs are valued as they would be under an efficient allocation of resources.

Another important market-based technique employed in valuation of public policy options involves the calculation of expected changes in "economic surplus" attributable to the option. Economic surplus is composed of two elements: (1) the value to consumers of the good in excess of what they must pay to get it, and (2) the difference between the price a producer receives for a good and the actual costs of production. Whenever a policy affects price, consumer demand, or production costs, economic surplus is altered. In part the alteration reflects transfers of surplus between groups of producers and consumers; it also reflects net changes in the amount of economic surplus generated. These net changes are treated as equivalent to changes in social benefits because of the policy, and can thus be used to indicate the dollar value to society of a particular policy option. A more detailed description of this technique is provided in Exhibit 26.2.

In addition to the central role of market prices in the valuation of goods and resources in benefit–cost analysis, markets are used as guides to determination of the *appropriateness* of government action. If competitive markets generate an efficient allocation of resources, government should "intervene" into such allocations only when the market deviates in some way from the purely competitive model. Among the conditions most prone to arise as reasons for government action are the following:[45]

1. the industry faces ever increasing returns to scale;
2. relevant market information is not believed to be freely available to producers and consumers;
3. the existence of "public goods," meaning goods for which consumption by one person does not exclude consumption by others. Lighthouses and national defense are familiar examples;
4. there are significant "spillover" costs or benefits from production and consumption; and
5. one or more actors in a market are believed to hold "monopoly power."

When the first condition arises, as for example may be true for transmission of electricity or provision of local telephone service, it is least costly to limit the number of providers. Because this may create monopoly power conditions, it has been usual for government to regulate such industries. Occurrence of the second condition is particularly a problem when (a) the market information is difficult to understand and (b) the consequences of misinformation can be disastrous, as is true with respect to the purchase of pharmaceuticals. Sales of drugs are, accordingly, regulated. Where the third condition arises, the private market will not provide the public good in optimal amounts. In such cases, the government typically provides the good, as with national defense. The fourth condition occurs whenever production of goods imposes costs or provides benefits not captured by the price of the good. The various forms of pollution are

[45]Taken from Davis and Kamien, "Externalities, Information, and Alternative Collective Action," Haveman and Margolis, *Public Expenditure and Policy Analysis*. Also see Arrow, "The Organization of Economic Activity," ibid.

the most celebrated examples, as illustrated by the acid rain debate now in progress. Fifth, when a buyer or seller holds "market power" he or she is able to unilaterally alter the price of the good. U.S. antitrust laws are specifically designed to limit occurrences of such conditions, and regulations are designed to limit abuse when monopoly conditions are unavoidable.[46]

In all these cases, then, the appropriateness of government action is justified by some "failure" in the market. The growth of the literature on market failure over the past century has, from the perspective of efficiency analysis, *increased* the range of legitimate government intervention into the allocation of goods and services as the known sources of market failure have proliferated.[47] In more recent years, however, more attention has been given to the perceived failure of government action—particularly the failure of regulation—to improve the situation when markets fail.[48] Just as the development of understanding of market failure *increased* the scope of appropriate government action, the literature on "government failure" suggests that the perceived scope for intervention in the interest of efficiency has narrowed once again.

---

[46]For the best and most exhaustive treatment of market failure, see David L. Weimer and Aiden R. Vining, *Policy Analysis: Concepts and Practice* (Englewood Cliffs, NJ: Prentice-Hall, 1989), chapter 3.

[47]For a few of the better known works on this area, see: F. H. Knight, "Some Fallacies in the Interpretation of Social Cost," *Quarterly Journal of Economics,* vol. 38 (1924), pp. 582–606. A. A. Young, "Pigou's Wealth and Welfare," *Quarterly Journal of Economics,* vol. 27 (1913), pp. 672–686. T. Scitovsky, "Two Concepts of External Economics," *Journal of Political Economy,* vol. 62 (1954), pp. 143–151. R. H. Coase, "The Problem of Social Cost," *Journal of Law and Economics,* vol. 3 (1960), pp. 1–44. K. A. Arrow, "The Organization of Economic Activity," *Public Expenditure and Policy Analysis.*

[48]See, for example, Roger G. Noll, *Reforming Regulation: An Evaluation of the Ash*

EFFICIENCY CRITERION: PRESCRIPTION OF THE PARADIGM

I have argued that the dominant paradigm of policy analysis finds its roots in utility theory, as developed from the utility calculus of Jeremy Bentham and as employed in the analysis of the efficiency of public policies. Efficiency is employed as a metavalue; efficiency is the pursuit of value maximization—and takes as given the particular values pursued by citizens or public officials. I have also argued that the frequent usage of the theory of competitive markets in policy analysis stems largely, though perhaps not exclusively, from the Pareto efficient properties of the purely competitive market. The use of such techniques as benefit-cost analysis derive from the more general concept of efficiency; benefit-cost analysis is an application of the Kaldor-Hicks criterion, declaring a policy efficient if it generates net social benefits.

How well does the content of the curriculum in public policy analysis schools bear out this argument? In a broad review of public policy curricula, a leading scholar noted that among the "subset of existing arts and sciences and professional fields" from which the policy curriculum was synthesized, foremost was

. . . microeconomics, the intellectual source of the optimization techniques introduced with such apparent success into [Secretary] Robert McNamara's Defense Department—and subsequently blessed by [President] Lyndon

---

Council Proposals (Washington, DC: Brookings Institute, 1971); Charles Wolf, *Markets or Governments: Choosing Between Imperfect Alternatives* (Cambridge, MA: MIT Press, 1988); and Weimer and Vining, op. cit., chapter 4. For recent criticism of specific governmental programs and regulations, see any issue of *Regulation,* published by the American Enterprise Institute, Washington, DC.

Johnson as a resource for the government as a whole.[49]

Regarding specific curricular content, microeconomics—and benefit-cost analysis—are clearly central: in a nationwide survey of public policy programs, microeconomics was found to be a required core course in all but a very few. Many schools add a specific required course in benefit–cost analysis or "applied microeconomics."[50] In evaluating the role of microeconomics in public policy programs, the reviewer argued that:

> Through its normative focus on efficiency, microeconomics teaches the student to seek opportunities for resource allocations that can, at least potentially, make everyone better-off.[51]

The content of the most widely used textbooks on public policy analysis further bears out the prominence of efficiency analysis: the discussion of efficiency, of benefit-cost analysis, and their application to policy problems generally take up the bulk of such texts.[52] The empirical evidence thus supports the argument that efficiency analysis and its application constitute the core of the policy analysis paradigm.

This should not be taken to say that efficiency provides the only criterion employed in analysis—indeed, as I will point out later, in practice analysts sometimes ignore efficiency altogether. What is argued here is simply that efficiency analysis is deeply imbedded in the *approach* and the techniques of policy analysis, and that the relatively undisputed definition and centrality of the efficiency criterion make it the essential and most prominent characteristic of the policy analysis paradigm. For these reasons, while analysis in practice frequently departs from the prescription of the paradigm, the prescription itself serves as the basis for the claims made on behalf of analysis and for much of the criticism leveled at analysis.

POLICY ANALYSIS AND POLITICS IN TENSION

The policy analysis paradigm is itself a partial political theory. Deriving its conception of value from radically individualistic utilitarianism, the paradigm adopts the efficiency criterion—maximization of net gains in social (i.e., aggregated individual) welfare—as the central guide for choice of public policy. Other bases of value, such as rights or equity, are either reduced to the terms of efficiency or act as parameters within which the efficiency criterion is employed. Within such limits, the approach and technique of analysis are designed to accurately translate citizen preferences into public policy. Because these elements of the paradigm are explicitly political, in that they bear fundamentally on the allocation of value in society, the paradigm has strong implications for the appropriate form and process of government.

One proponent of the policy analysis paradigm has described at some length

---

[49]Donald Stokes, "Political and Organizational Analysis of the Policy Curriculum," *Journal of Policy Analysis and Management,* vol. 6, no. 1 (Fall 1986), pp. 45–55; pp. 45–46.

[50]Lee S. Friedman, "Public Policy Economics: A Survey of Current Pedagogical Practice," *Journal of Policy Analysis and Management,* vol. 6, no. 3 (Spring 1987), pp. 503–520. The survey was of all degree-granting public policy programs that were institutional members of the Association for Public Policy Analysis and Management.

[51]Ibid., p. 518.

[52]See, for example, Weimer and Vining, *Policy and Analysis: Concepts and Practice,* Stokey and Zeckhauser, *A Primer;* and Nachmias, *Public Policy Evaluation: Approaches and Methods.* A leading text that takes an "alternative approach," Garry Brewer and Peter deLeon's *The Foundations of Policy Analysis* (Pacific Grove, CA: Brooks/Cole, 1983), still gives prominent place to these concepts—despite the explicit alternative spin.

the ideal form of government appropriate to full implementation of the policy analysis paradigm.[53] All participants would know and agree to all ultimate objectives of policy maximization of citizen welfare and would be able to make necessary trade-offs among objectives. Full information would be obtained by participants, involving benefit–cost analyses of all options, resulting in a shifting of resources among programs to assure that the marginal benefits of such programs remain equal. Most importantly, the makers of public decisions must be provided with proper incentives to maximize social welfare; the legislative process should resemble a "smoothly functioning market system." In legislatures as in markets, the full set of costs and gains of any decision—as these are experienced by individual citizens—would be brought to bear on the decisionmaker.

> Considering legislative decisions, this implies the need for a political process in which the full set of impacts of a decision on all citizens—the poor and minority groups as well as those with vested power—be somehow registered with decision makers.[54]

The overall attempt is to create institutions and processes that serve to better map the preferences of *all* citizens into public policy. Much of the recent effort to reform the budgetary process, such as the institutionalization of Planning, Programming, Budgeting System (PPBS),[55]

Zero Based Budgeting (ZBB), and more recently Executive Order 12291, which calls for systematic benefit–cost analysis of all "major" regulations,[56] has sought to implement pieces of this ideal of government.

The urge for institutions and processes that better map citizen preference into public policy leads to considerable friction between the ideals of the policy analysis paradigm and perceptions of American politics-as-usual. Because politics in practice often appears resistant to the application of analysis, proponents of the policy analysis paradigm tend to view politics with some disdain. One policy analyst, lamenting the minimal attention given policy analysis in Congress, writes:

> In short, because of the characteristics of the legislative process and the structural characteristics of Congress itself, objective policy analysis does not automatically find a warm reception in the legislative branch. Except in unusual circumstances, analysis directed at isolating policy alternatives that serve the general interest will fail to dominate the power and pleas of special interest advocates. *Without major reform of the operation of Congress,* the probability is not high that an increased flow of analytic studies directed at Congress will play a significant role in improving legislative decisions.[57]

Nonetheless, policy analysis is seen by many as a partial corrective to the de-

[53]See Robert H. Haveman, "Policy Analysis and the Congress: An Economist's View," *Policy Analysis,* 2(2) (Spring 1976), pp. 235–250. Also see Roland McKean, "The Unseen Hand in Government," *American Economic Review,* vol. 55 (June 1965), pp. 496–505.
[54]Haveman, "Policy Analysis," p. 239.
[55]See Allen Schick, "The Road to PPB: The Stages of Budget Reform," in *Perspectives on Budgeting,* ed. Allen Schick (Washington, DC: American Society for Public Administration, 1980), pp. 46–67.

[56]See William West, "Institutionalizing Rationality in Regulatory Administration," *Public Administration Review,* 43(4) August 1983, pp. 326–334, and V. Kerry Smith, ed. *Environmental Policy Under Reagan's Executive Order: The Role of Benefit–Cost Analysis* (Chapel Hill, NC: University of North Carolina Press, 1984).
[57]Haveman, "Policy Analysis," p. 248. Emphasis added.

ficiencies of politics as practiced. In the words of two proponents of the policy analysis paradigm:

One of the great virtues of the benefit-cost approach is that the interests of individuals who are poorly organized or less closely involved are counted. (This contrasts with most political decision making procedures.) Even when pushed by powerful interest groups, projects whose benefits do not outweigh their costs will be shown to be undesirable. The benefits and costs accruing to all—to the highway builders, the environmentalists, the "little people," the users and providers of services, the taxpaying public—will be counted on a dollar-for-dollar basis. Benefit–cost analysis is a methodology with which we pursue efficiency and which has the effect of limiting the vagaries of the political process.[58]

The use of analysis, then, is seen by its proponents as in tension with the norms and practice of American politics, and as providing the vehicle for reform in both the policies selected and the procedures for selecting them.[59]

[58]Stokey and Zeckhauser, *A Primer,* p. 151.
[59]Several observers see in the policy paradigm considerable *antipathy* to politics in general. According to these observers, proponents of analysis have adopted the notion implicit in the "end of ideology" euphoria of the 1960s that the messy business of politics can be replaced by objective *management* of public issues. See James B. Rule, "The Problem with Social Problems," *Politics and Society,* 2(2) (Fall 1971), pp. 47–56; Sylvia Fries, "Expertise Against Politics: Technology as Ideology on Capitol Hill," *Science, Technology and Human Values,* vol. 43 (Spring 1983), pp. 6–15; and Max Nieman, "The Ambiguous Role of Policy Analysis and an Illustrative Look at Housing Policy" (paper presented at the annual meeting of the Western Political Science Association, Sacramento, CA, April, 1984).

Out of these tensions grow both the promise of the policy analysis paradigm as an enhancement of democratic characteristics of American politics, and the perceived threats to the norms and operation of American politics. The promise is that, through widespread utilization of techniques based on the criterion of efficiency in the formulation of public policy, we will achieve a better translation of the preferences of citizens into public policies. Needless to say, that promise holds considerable democratic appeal. Critics, however, argue that should the proponents of the policy analysis paradigm be successful in working their reforms, dire threats to norms and operation of democratic politics will be realized. . . .

EXHIBIT 26.1
EFFICIENCY IN VOLUNTARY EXCHANGE

The concept of Pareto efficiency . . . can be illustrated with the use of a device called the Edgeworth diagram. The diagram represents the changes in ordinally ranked levels of utility of two (or more) individuals, originally endowed with some quantity of two kinds of goods (or bundles of goods), when the goods are exchanged (or reallocated). Adequate description of the diagram requires a brief digression into the geometric method of depicting ordinal rankings of utility in a two-product "utility space."[60]

Imagine for illustrative purposes an individual who gains well-being from the possession of two kinds of goods. Both goods are "private goods": possession and consumption of the good by

[60]For a description of the formal theory underlying the concepts discussed in the following paragraphs, see W. Hildenbrand and A. P. Kirman, *Introduction to Equilibrium Analysis: Variations on Themes by Edgeworth and Walras* (New York: American Elsevier, 1976), especially Chapter 1.

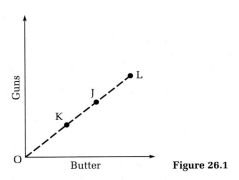

Figure 26.1

one individual excludes possession and consumption of the good by other individuals. The goods can take any form (tangible, intangible, discrete, continuous, or whatever) as long as they exist in limited supply and can be possessed in various quantities; for now assume them to be guns and butter—though resalable presidential pardons and religious indulgences would do just as well. Our individual (call him Jim) gains some level of utility from any combination of guns and butter and generally prefers more of either good to less. The quantities of guns and butter can be shown, as in Figure 26.1, in a two-dimensional space with guns represented on the vertical axis and butter on the horizontal axis.[61] Utility within the space is represented ordinally by distance from the origin; any mix of goods in the space, say point *J,* provides more utility than would a mix anywhere on the ray between the origin and point *J.* Thus *J* provides more utility than *K,* but less than *L.*

Jim is assumed to be able to compare the utility he receives from any two combinations of guns and butter. In comparing two points in the space, Jim will be able to tell whether one or the other points is preferred, or whether he is "indifferent" between them. Using these comparisons, it would be possible to find all those combinations of guns and butter that would provide Jim with the same level of utility as would point *J;* we would say Jim is indifferent among all these points. Connecting all these points creates an "indifference curve," as shown in Figure 26.2. For the sake of clarity, the indifference curves shown are convex to the origin. In practical terms, this means that Jim prefers some mix of guns and butter to an extreme case of all one and none of the other. Furthermore, if Jim is indifferent between two mixes, he will prefer the average of the two to either one of them. While this assumption seems valid in many cases, one need not assume strict convexity of indifference curves to derive many of the basic results of the theory of consumer behavior. All mixes of goods below and to the left of the indifference curve are inferior (for Jim) to those on the curve; all those above and to the right are preferable to those on the curve. As indicated in Figure 26.2, Jim could assemble a number of indifference curves of varying distances from the origin, thus creating an "indifference map" of his pref-

Figure 26.2

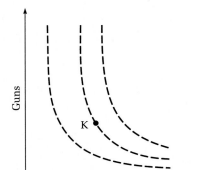

[61]To be precise, figure 26.1 is the northeast quadrant of a Cartesian space, representing the area in which the values for both coordinates are equal to or greater than zero.

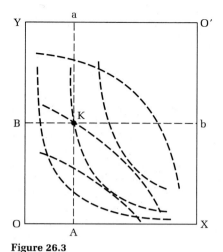

Figure 26.3

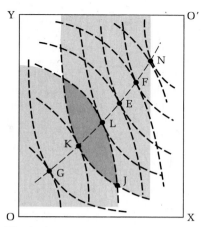

Figure 26.4

erences among the full range of possible mixes of guns and butter.

In Figure 26.3 we introduce a second actor, Ron, who also values possession of guns and butter, and we limit the availability of guns and butter. As before, Jim's preferences are represented by indifference curves that are convex to the origin (point *O*). But now Ron's preferences are shown as well, originating from the upper right corner in Figure 26.3 (point *O′*). Ron's preferences are represented in the same manner as Jim's, except that his indifference map has been rotated 180 degrees and superimposed on top of Jim's. Because the availability of guns and butter is now fixed, the distance *OX* (or *YO′*) represents the total supply of butter, while *OY* (or *XO′*) shows the total supply of guns. Any point in the space thus represents a potential distribution of the total supply of guns and butter between Jim and Ron. For example, point *K* in Figure 26.3 shows a distribution in which Jim has *OA* butter and *OB* guns while Ron has *O′a* butter and *O′b* guns.

Turning back to the question of efficiency, how can it be determined if a particular distribution of guns and butter between Jim and Ron is efficient?

Beginning from point *J* in Figure 26.4, Jim will prefer any mix of guns and butter above or to the right of the indifference curve on which *J* is a point, as shown by the area shaded by vertical lines. Ron, on the other hand, will prefer any point below or to the left of the indifference curve on which *J* is a point, as shown by the horizontal shading. The overlap of these two areas, the "lens" made by the two interfacing indifference curves, shows the set of redistributions of guns and butter that will improve the position of one or both persons while making neither worse off. Point *K*, for example, improves Ron's position while leaving Jim indifferent to his prior position. Likewise, point *L* improves Jim's position while leaving Ron as well-off as he was before but no better. Thus, point *J* is "Pareto inefficient" because it can be improved upon without making anyone worse off. Any redistribution to a point in the lens will increase efficiency.

Notice that, should the initial distribution of guns and butter be at point *E*, no redistribution could be made that would not diminish the well-being of either Jim or Ron. Such a point is "Pareto efficient." Pareto efficient points will occur where Jim's and Ron's indifference curves are tangent, such as points *E, F, G,* and *N.*[62] Were all such points identified and connected, they would form the "contract line," the set of points from which no cooperative improvement could be made. In an efficient system of distribution, allocations would always be on the contract line; an efficient policy will always move the participants into the lens area as shown in Figure 26.4.

. . . Given an initial inefficient distribution of valued things, there are many possible efficient reallocations that could be made. Referring again to Figure 26.4, beginning from distribution *J, any* reallocation that moved onto the contract line between points *K* and *L* would provide an efficient solution. On the basis of the efficiency criterion alone, however, there is no way to determine whether one of these solutions is superior to another; according to Edgeworth, the exact placement on the contract line will be determined by "higgling dodges and designing obstinacy, and other incalculable and often disreputable accidents."[63] Furthermore, the efficiency criterion takes no account of the initial starting position; such "endowments" of wealth are taken as given. In Figure 26.4, point *N* is just as efficient—though perhaps not as egalitarian—as point *L.*

The usefulness of the Edgeworth diagram stems from its illustration of the meaning of efficiency in very general terms. The strict criterion of efficiency would hold that a reallocation of things of value should be undertaken if the new distribution resulted in placement in the lens of increased efficiency—or better still, on the contract line. The criterion says nothing about which of the possible efficient allocations should be made. A movement away from the contract line is ruled out as inefficient. Thus, movement in Figure 26.4 from point *L* to point *J* violates the efficiency criterion, though it may well satisfy some other criterion for public decision making.

EXHIBIT 26.2
ECONOMIC SURPLUS IN EFFICIENCY ANALYSIS

One of the more widespread uses of market theory in efficiency analysis involves the concept of "economic surplus," initially developed by Alfred Marshall to assess gains or losses in the utility of consumers and producers resulting from changes in market conditions.[64] Building from the works of earlier utility theorists, Marshall argued that changes in utility derived from market operations could be analyzed by estimating market supply-and-demand relationships and assessing how changes in these relationships affect "consumers' surplus" and "producers' surplus."

In the theory of competitive markets, price is assumed to be set by the cost of producing the last unit of the good (referred to as the "marginal cost") for which a purchaser can be found. Utility, for a given consumer, is assumed to be represented by the amount of money that consumer is willing to pay to get a

---

[62] Technically, the slope of the indifference curve at any point shows the "marginal rate of substitution" of guns for butter at a given point while utility is held constant. Where the two persons' indifference curves are tangent, their marginal rates of substitution are equal. In this situation the two persons' *relative* valuation of the two goods, for very small changes in the mix of goods held, are equal. This condition characterizes the outcome of an efficient allocation of valued things.

[63] Francis Edgeworth, *Mathematical Psychics* (London: Keegan Paul, 1881), p. 46, as cited in George Stigler, *Essays in the History of Economics* (Chicago: University of Chicago Press, 1965), pp. 104–105.

[64] See Alfred Marshall, *Principles of Economics* (London: Macmillan, 1890).

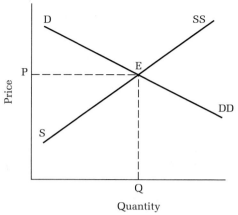

Figure 26.5

unit of the good. The area under the demand curve thus represents the total utility that consumers would gain from consumption of the good.

Assuming that the quantity of the good demanded increases as the price drops, as shown by demand curve *DD* in Figure 26.5, and that price is set competitively at price *P*, all purchasers but the very last one (the one who buys the "*Q*th" good) would have been willing to pay more than the competitive price rather than go without the good. All consumers but the one who buys the *Q*th good can thus be said to gain a "surplus" of utility over and above the price paid for the good. In Figure 26.5 this surplus is represented by the triangle *PDE*—the area under the demand curve and above price.

Producers of the good, on the other hand, can make added profit from producing more of the good as long as the price received for the good is greater than the "marginal cost" of producing the next unit. Thus, assuming that marginal costs rise as more of the good is produced, as shown by supply curve *SS* in Figure 26.5, producers of all but the last unit (the *Q*th unit) will receive a price higher than was required to in-

duce them to produce it. Area *SPE*, below price and above the marginal cost (supply) curve, represents this "surplus" of value to producers. Together consumers' and producers' surplus are referred to as *economic surplus*, representing the value provided to society by production and consumption of the goods in excess of the costs of production of the goods. The policy concern, applying the potential Pareto criterion, is to take those actions that result in *net* increases in economic surplus.

Use of Marshall's concept of economic surplus in efficiency analysis can be illustrated by example. Imagine a country that has long forbidden import of a commodity—say corn—with the result that domestic farmers produce corn in the quantity price relationship shown by supply curve *SS* in Figure 26.6. Domestic demand *DD* results in market equilibrium at *E* with price *P*. Now imagine that the restrictions on corn imports are removed, resulting in a new total corn supply curve *SS′*, as shown in Figure 26.6. New equilibrium price *P′* and quantity *Q′* would result. In view of the new domestic situation, is the government policy of permitting imports of corn efficient?

Consumers' surplus has grown from an original amount *PDE* to *P′DE′*, an increase of *P′PEE′*. Domestic producers' surplus, however, has declined from *SPE* to *SP′K*, a decline of *P′PEK*. Clearly, employing the strict Pareto optimality criteria, the change could not be called efficient. But using the Kaldor-Hicks criterion, consumers would be able to pay producers *P′PEK* and *still* have a net gain of area *KEE′*. Thus, by the Kaldor-Hicks criterion, the policy is efficient.

Armed with these tools, the utility theorist would be able to assess whether a government-induced change in price, demand, or supply would result in a net increase or decrease in economic surplus. Later theorists have significantly revised Marshall's initial

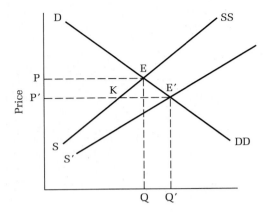

Figure 26.6

formulation; in particular, it is now recognized that the demand curve used to assess the effects of changes in prices must also reflect changes in the marginal utility of money due to the fact that changes in price will alter the real income of consumers.[65] Numerous technical criticisms of the approach have been made, primarily contending that we lack adequate measures of the effect of price changes on the consumer's marginal utility of money.[66] Despite ongoing theoretical disputes over the validity of economic surplus analysis as a

measure of changes in social utility,[67] economic surplus is among the most widely employed bases of efficiency analysis. Perhaps in the end, Bentham's reasoning in justifying his own utility calculus will be revived for economic surplus:

It is sufficient to justify our propositions if (a) they approach more nearly to the truth than any others that can be substituted for them; and (b) they can be employed more conveniently than any other as the basis of legislation.[68]

[65]J. R. Hicks was responsible for this adjustment of the theory, and thus the "Hicksian income compensated demand curve" replaces the "Marshallian demand curve" in most modern analyses. See J. R. Hicks, *A Revision of Demand Theory* (London: Clarendon Press, 1956).

[66]For criticisms of the use of economic surplus see Paul A. Samuelson, *Foundations of Economic Analysis* (Cambridge, MA: Harvard University Press, 1947) and I. M. D. Little, *A Critique of Welfare Economics* (London: Clarendon Press, 1957).

[67]Defenders of the use of utility theory include Allen Herberger, "Monopoly and Resource Allocation," *American Economic Review,* vol. 54, (May 1954), pp. 77–87; R. D. Willig "Consumers' Surplus Without Apology," *American Economic Review,* vol. 66, (September 1976), pp. 589–597; and Jerry A. Hausman, "Exact Consumers' Surplus and Deadweight Loss" (unpublished manuscript, June 1980).

[68]Etienne Dumont, *Bentham's Theory of Legislation,* trans. by Charles Atkinson (London: Oxford University Press, 1914), p. 134.

27.   Social Security and the Politics of Assumptions

Paul C. Light

Every governmental decision involves assumptions about how the world works today and how it will work tomorrow. Assumptions help Congress and the president interpret the past, understand the present, and most importantly, predict the future. They help governments define the size of problems and narrow the range of solutions. If the assumptions are accurate, they can form the basis of careful, almost rational decisions. If not, they can become the target of skillful political manipulation and sabotage. Moreover, assumptions are an increasingly important product of government. Census data, labor projections, fertility forecasts, budget estimates, and the like often form the bases for private sector decisions.[1]

Because uncertainty always exists, governments often must choose between competing assumptions of the future. Foreign policy makers must decide whether the Soviets are basically evil or somewhat more humane; Social Security experts must decide whether the future looks rosy or pessimistic; health specialists must decide whether cost inflation is caused by new technologies or wasteful overutilization. Because no clear answers exist, all must use assumptions; and the choice of one set of assumptions over another can have a dramatic impact on virtually every stage of the policy-making process.

Assumptions shape estimates of the basic problems, definitions of the potential solutions, legislative and political

SOURCE: "Social Security and the Politics of Assumptions" by Paul C. Light, *Public Administration Review*: 45 (May/June 1985). Reprinted by permission of the American Society for Public Administration.

support, and final implementation. In 1976, for example, the U.S. defense establishment changed its basic assumption about Soviet military spending. Instead of spending an estimated 6-8 percent of Gross National Product on defense, the Soviets were now assumed to be spending 11-13 percent. Because no change was made in the corresponding assumptions about Soviet industrial capacity, however, the new forecast concluded that the Soviets were producing twice as much overnight, all attributable to the new assumption. One key participant in the process ultimately used the new figures to argue "Why the Soviet Union Thinks It Could Fight and Win a Nuclear War."

Other examples abound. In 1977, President Jimmy Carter adopted a pessimistic forecast of future energy consumption and declared the "moral equivalent of war." He was wrong. In 1981, President Ronald Reagan and his budget director, David Stockman, used highly optimistic assumptions to show a slight budget surplus by 1984. They also were wrong. Between 1981 and 1983, the estimated four-year budget deficit jumped by $1.4 trillion, with 60 percent of the increase traced to the failure of the economic assumptions. According to the 1983 economic forecast by the Office of Management and Budget, a 1 percent increase in that year's inflation figures would boost expenditures by $50 billion over five years, while a 1 percent lower rate of growth would cut revenues by $47 billion over the same period. Indeed, budget forecasts have become a caricature of the mistakes inherent in predicting the economic future.

Yet, despite the obvious importance of

underlying assumptions, they are often neglected by students of public policy and administration alike. Assumptions are often accepted as a "given," as if no choice is involved. This article reflects an effort to raise the study of assumptions as important to an understanding of how government works and how policy makers decide. Here, assumptions are defined as the underlying bases for forecasts and estimates. Assumptions should be seen as the inputs of the forecasting process.

SOCIAL SECURITY ASSUMPTIONS

Social Security may offer the best opportunity to study the role of assumptions in an indexed federal system. Over the past decade, the basic economic and demographic forecasts used in framing the policy debate have been more often wrong than right. Those mistakes have had lasting impacts. In 1977, for example, Carter and Congress based a Social Security rescue bill on what quickly proved to be overly optimistic economic assumptions. At that point in history, little reason was seen to expect the double-digit inflation and economic stagflation that came just two years later. At the time, the assumptions were neither too optimistic nor too pessimistic; they were the best guesses available. Looking back, they simply failed to anticipate the depth of the economic crisis. Carter was not wrong to claim that his rescue bill would keep the system solvent for 50 years. The problem was that his image of the future never came true.

Those mistakes would not have mattered but for the indexing of benefits to inflation in the mid-1970s. Because benefits grow automatically each year, the only way that Carter and Congress could tell if their repairs would work was to predict the future. And they were wrong. If benefits had not been indexed,

there would have been no need to predict. Congress would have retained its discretion over benefit increases. Ironically, Republicans had pushed for indexing as a way to keep costs down, but they later led the fight to cut the cost-of-living adjustment (COLA) because their assumptions were wrong.

With Social Security on automatic pilot, it became increasingly important to build accurate predictions of the future. Legislators could make the "right" choices only if they knew what was coming far down the road. Moreover, because little room for error was present in the trust fund reserves, accurate assumptions were critical for keeping the system afloat during lean years. Nevertheless, as the demand for accuracy grew, the world became more uncertain. As one Congressional Budget Office aide lamented in 1982, "We don't know who'll be in office in 1984. We don't know whether the Federal Reserve Board will give into pressure to expand the money supply. We don't know if the Middle East will blow up."

Nevertheless, it is not enough simply to admit that the future is cloudy. Government must make predictions. However, instead of giving a single "best guess" of the future, the Social Security Administration (SSA) has often provided multiple estimates. From 1976 to 1980, SSA provided three different scenarios each year. In 1981, under intense pressure from the Reagan White House, SSA provided five (including a new "Worst-Case" designed to sell deep benefit cuts to Congress). In 1982 and 1983, the critical years for the recent rescue effort, SSA provided four different sets of predictions: (1) optimistic, labeled Alternative I, (2) mildly optimistic, Alternative II-A, (3) intermediate or best-guess, Alternative II-B, and (4) pessimistic, Alternative III. Though the actuaries never advertise their forecasts as anything but rough scenarios, the assumptions carry such precision that policy makers often take them as clear predictions of the future. The choice of one over the others could change both the size of the then-coming Social Security crisis, as well as the savings from each potential solution. By simply changing the underlying assumptions, of course, problems could be made to appear and disappear, grow and shrink at will.

Separately, each assumption involves a specific future event or condition. What will unemployment be in the year 2015? What will inflation be in the year 2033? What will happen to birth rates in the next four decades? The major difference between Social Security and other economic assumptions is the time frame. Whereas most economic forecasts cover only the next five years or so, Social Security assumptions cover the next 75 years.

Together, economic and demographic assumptions create a picture of the future that can be used to predict how a program such as Social Security will fare over time. Some assumptions, particularly about inflation, predict how much Social Security will spend in future benefits. Other assumptions, particularly about unemployment and wage growth, predict how much Social Security will raise in taxes. Still other assumptions, particularly about fertility, predict how many workers will be supporting how many retirees. When merged together in a computer, these different assumptions generate a specific forecast of Social Security income and outgo years into the future. By changing one or more of the underlying assumptions, actuaries and other political participants can alter the final forecast.

THE WORLD ACCORDING TO SSA

By the early 1980s, assumptions had emerged as one key for controlling the Social Security agenda. As an OMB official noted after the Social Security compromise was signed and sealed in 1983, "Only a handful of people know how important the economic assumptions really are. If you can get your opponents to accept your data, then the rest of the argument will be on your terms. You become the one who says what works and what doesn't. A change of a percentage point here and there can have tremendous impact. It's like stacking a deck in a card game."[2]

Despite increased public and private competition over most economic assumptions, SSA maintained a monopoly over the Social Security estimates at the start of the 1980's. That was not to say that SSA had some magic in predicting the future. Rather, most other forecasters were unwilling to put their reputations or energy into 75-year predictions. Unfortunately, most SSA actuaries were not trained in economic forecasting, either in the short- or long-term. Further, until the automatic indexing of benefits, the actuaries never had to predict the future. They could merely hold the economy constant into the future. None of the key economic indicators would change from year to year.

With the change to indexing in 1972, the actuaries had to switch from static to dynamic assumptions. Benefits were going to increase automatically every year into the future. To keep the system going, the actuaries had to start predicting the future, anticipating economic booms and busts. To make estimates of outgo, they had to predict inflation; to make estimates of income, they had to predict wage growth and unemployment. Because the system was now on automatic pilot, they had to pinpoint any coming crisis. Then they would have to tell Congress and the president what to do. Yet, could they predict an uncertain future under increasing political and economic pressure? That they developed more sophisticated and sensitive models is to their credit; that the future remained unpredictable is beyond their blame. Nevertheless, they continued to produce yearly forecasts, built on cloudy assumptions. Congress and the president, in turn, continued to use the forecasts to design major policy reforms.

The question, of course, was whether the forecasts were right. Accuracy would determine whether anybody listened and whether the repairs would work.

The Image

That accuracy was based on four basic views of the world. First, all of the economic forecasts at SSA showed a world that always got better. No matter how bad inflation or unemployment was at the start of a forecast, the future always improved. This optimism may have been a fact of human nature. After all, no one wants to predict that the world will collapse tomorrow. Indeed, some SSA actuaries argue that optimistic forecasts have a self-fulfilling quality, as if simply wishing for a healthy economy would make it come true. Though these same actuaries will admit that overly optimistic forecasts led legislators astray on Carter's rescue bill, they still believe in the power of positive thinking.

Second, the forecasts showed a world without economic cycles. The actuaries acknowledged the presence of such cycles, but they still gave the forecasts a veneer of steady trends over time. They simply assumed that the economic shocks would balance over the decades. However, at least in the short term, it made a great deal of difference whether the boom came first or second. If the boom came before the bust, the Social Security trust fund would be able to lay in a margin of safety for the bad times; if the bust came before the boom, the program might not even make it to the good days ahead. The timing of economic cycles had become critical in figuring how much to raise and when to do it.

Third, the forecasts showed a world that could be understood and predicted. The underlying belief that the world can be known far into the future is essential for building long-range forecasts. Though the estimates were never advertised as anything more than sketches of what might happen, they were often used as the final word on what would happen. And the actuaries were partially to blame. Instead of giving ballpark figures, the SSA forecasts contained precise numbers far into the future. As one Treasury Department aide remarked, "Sometimes I look at the estimates and wonder how they picked a 1.7 percent growth figure for 2015 instead of a 1.5 or a 2.3. How do they know? The answer is that they don't and they can't. But they have to build something in. It's an artificial forecast."

Fourth, despite the actuaries' optimism, the forecasts had begun to show a world in deep trouble by the early 1980s. "Each new forecast substitutes what was thought to be a good year with another bad one," a Treasury Department staffer noted. "The performance of the economy has been so bad that even the bad estimates are good. So when you take that good year and replace it with a bad year, you lose a little more of the trust fund balance. . . . We've been stumbling from one crisis to another."

These four patterns added up to a world that would steadily improve from an ever worsening crisis. Each year's forecast was always worse than the last but showed an eventual upturn. Each cloud had a silver lining. It was a form of "pessimistic optimism."

The Reality

It is not particularly difficult to check the actuaries' predictions against reality; one simply has to look at actual economic performance. For the most part, the recent predictions have been very wrong, even for the year in which they were published. From the mid-1970s to the early 1980s, they underestimated inflation, overestimated wage growth, and underestimated unemployment. The further out in time the assumptions move, the more inaccurate they become. Yet, policy makers must use those longer-term assumptions for building legislation. In 1983, for example, the assumptions had to cover the 1983–1990 period. Even given the range of guesses between Alternatives I and II, the forecasts were much too optimistic. Recent predictions for real wage growth (wage growth minus inflation), the most important assumption for short-term forecasts, are contrasted with the actual performance in Table 27.1. In 1975, for example, the optimistic assumption for real wage growth in 1976 was 1.4 percent; the actual experience was 2.8 percent.

In theory, of course, the optimistic estimate was designed to give a rosy view of the world. If that was the goal, Alternative I did the job. Not once in past years had true economic performance come close to the optimistic prediction. In theory, the intermediate estimate, now called Alternative II-B, was designed to be the actuaries' best guess of what would happen, the most likely prediction of the future. If that was the goal, Alternative II-B did not succeed. Except for 1976, the intermediate estimate was far too optimistic. Moreover, in theory, the pessimistic estimate was designed to give an overly gloomy view of the world. If that was the goal, Alternative III did not work, either. Even the most pessimistic estimates were too optimistic!

It is more difficult to assess the accuracy of the long-term estimates. In an unpublished survey of 380 practicing actuaries outside of government, the General Accounting Office found that there is more pessimism in the discipline as a whole than in SSA. More than 70 percent of the actuaries surveyed believed the long-term CPI rate was too

high; 60 percent believed the long-term real wage growth was too high; and 63 percent believed the fertility rate was too high. In short, outside actuaries, trained in the same methodology as the SSA actuaries, saw the assumptions as overly optimistic.

The actuaries had several responses to their declining accuracy. First, their reports became longer, offering more explanations as a defense against error. Between 1976 and 1983, the annual forecast report doubled in size, from 58 pages to 120 pages. Second, and more important, the actuaries began to spread their assumptions over a larger range of possibilities. Slowly, the distance between optimism and pessimism increased. The distance between the optimistic and pessimistic assumption about inflation, for example, doubled over a five-year period. This pattern is summarized for real wage growth in Table 27.2. As an SSA aide acknowledged, "We've learned the hard way to have significant variation among the estimates. Starting in the mid-1970s, we have built greater distance between the alternatives. It's a way of creating greater accuracy." In short, the actuaries expanded their predictions to cover more numbers on the economic roulette wheel. Only in 1981 and 1982 did actual economic performance fall within the range of the SSA predictions—for the first time in nearly five years of forecasting—landing between Alternatives II-B and III. This success was almost entirely the result of the greater spreads. The actuaries bet more numbers and finally won.

Turning Points

Unfortunately, the errors had already affected two crucial turning points in the 1970s, leading to serious legislative mistakes. The first came in 1972, with indexing of Social Security to inflation. SSA's best guess showed 15 percent inflation and 122 percent real wage

Table 27.1 SSA Real Wage Growth Assumptions and Actual Experience, 1976–1983

Years:	1976	1977	1978	1979	1980	1981	1982	1983	1984	1985	1986	1987	1988	1989	1990
Actual Experience	2.8	0.3	0.6	−2.3	−4.5	−0.1	−0.2	1.2	—	—	—	—	—	—	—
Optimistic Assumption (I)															
1976	1.4	2.5	4.1	4.1	4.1	2.8	2.9	3.1	2.5	2.5	2.5	2.5	2.5	2.5	2.5
1977		2.4	2.9	3.3	2.5	2.4	2.7	1.8	1.8	2.0	2.1	2.4	2.5	2.5	2.5
1978			1.1	2.4	2.6	2.6	2.4	2.0	2.0	2.0	2.9	3.0	3.1	3.1	2.8
1979				−1.0	1.3	2.2	1.3	2.6	2.6	2.7	2.3	2.7	2.7	2.9	2.6
1980					−4.3	0.9									
1981						−0.1									
1982							1.9	1.4	2.9	2.8	1.7	1.9	2.2	2.3	3.0
1983*								1.8	1.9	1.6					3.1
1984									2.2	1.7					2.2
Intermediate Assumption (II-B)															
1976	1.4	2.5	3.4	3.0	2.7	2.2	2.4	2.4	2.0	2.0	2.0	2.0	2.0	2.0	2.0
1977		2.4	2.7	2.5	2.4	2.3	1.9	1.5	1.4	1.3	1.4	1.7	2.0	2.0	2.0
1978			1.1	1.8	2.2	2.2	1.9	1.3	1.2	1.3	1.0	1.1	1.3	1.5	1.8
1979				−1.1	0.6	2.5	0.2	0.7	0.6	0.7	0.9	1.3	1.4	1.5	1.4
1980					−4.6	−0.2									
1981						−0.9									
1982							−0.3	0.2	0.7	0.3	0.8	1.3	1.3	1.4	1.5
1983 (February, preliminary)								0.2	1.1	0.4					1.3
1983 (June, final)								1.5	0.2	0.2	0.9	1.1	1.4	1.5	1.6
1984									1.2	0.8					1.6
Pessimistic Assumption (III)															
1976	1.4	2.0	2.4	1.9	1.9	1.6	1.8	2.0	1.5	1.5	1.5	1.5	1.5	1.5	1.5
1977		2.4	2.2	0.5	2.3	1.9	1.4	1.2	1.1	1.2	1.1	1.3	1.5	1.5	1.5
1978			1.1	1.4	0.3	1.0	0.9	0.3	0.2	0.5	0.6	0.3	0.5	0.7	1.0
1979				−1.1	−0.2	1.9	−1.6	0.0	0.7	0.4	0.3	0.7	0.8	1.1	0.8
1980					−6.7	−2.0									
1981 (III)						−1.1									
1981 (Worst-Case)						−2.2	−2.6	−1.3	1.1	0.7	0.2				
1982							−0.9	−2.3	−1.8	0.0	0.1	0.7	0.9	1.1	1.0
1983 (February, preliminary)								−1.0	−0.7	−0.7					
1983 (June, final)								0.6	−1.8	−0.3	0.4	0.4	0.9	1.1	1.2
1984									−0.1	−0.7					1.3

*No preliminary estimate made in 1983.
Source: Board of Trustees of the Federal Old-Age and Survivors Insurance and Disability Insurance Trust Funds, Annual Reports, 1975–1984.

Table 27.2   Distances Between Assumptions of Real Wage Growth, 1976–1984

Year	Optimistic and Intermediate*	Intermediate and Pessimistic	Optimistic and Pessimistic
1976 forecast for 1977	0.0	0.5	0.5
1977 forecast for 1978	0.2	0.5	0.7
1978 forecast for 1979	0.6	0.4	1.0
1979 forecast for 1980	0.7	0.8	1.5
1980 forecast for 1981	1.1	1.8	2.9
1981 forecast for 1982	1.1	1.8	2.9
1982 forecast for 1983	1.2	2.5	3.7
1983 (February) for 1984	0.8	1.8	2.6
1983 (June) for 1984	1.7	2.0	3.7
1984 for 1985	0.9	1.5	2.4

*The intermediate forecast for 1981–1984 is the Alternative II-B path.

growth for the 1973–1977 period. The actual experience was 41 percent inflation and 1 percent real wage growth. Looking at the predictions, Republicans had seen the automatic COLA as a way of controlling costs. They had been misled by the assumptions.

The second turning point came in 1977, with passage of Carter's rescue bill. SSA's best guess showed 28 percent inflation and 13 percent real wage growth for the 1978–1982 period. The actual experience was 60 percent inflation and a negative 7 percent real wage growth. Looking at the predictions, Democrats had thought a series of tax increases would be more than enough to take the system into the next century. Once again, Congress had been misled by the forecasts.

Were the mistakes important? The answer is clearly yes. Once benefits were automatically tied to inflation, accurate assumptions became critical for making legislative decisions. In this large, old program, tiny mistakes in assumptions could create massive deficits. With the Social Security trust fund skating from check to check with barely one month's reserve, seemingly trivial errors in inflation or wage estimates could lead to a major crisis in very short order. And that is exactly what happened in 1980.

THE SOURCES OF ERROR

Four sources of error were present in the Social Security assumptions: the environment, technique, assumption drag, and politics. If they could be corrected, the predictions would improve, lending greater confidence to the occasional repairs. If they could not be corrected, Congress and the president would face more surprises.

1. The Social and Economic Environment

The most important source of error was an unpredictable world itself. No one predicted the high rates of inflation and low rates of growth that occurred in the 1970s; not SSA, OMB, or the private forecasters. "If I had made those kinds of predictions," an SSA actuary argued, "I would have been practicing in an asylum." The Social Security assumptions of the 1970s were simply not far out of line with the then-conventional wisdom about the future. And because the past is the starting point for any forecast, the process works only if history repeats itself. Unfortunately, as Stockman reported, "I'm beginning to believe that history is a lot shakier than I ever thought it was. . . . In other words, I think there are more random elements, less determinism, and more discretion in the course of history than I ever believed before."[3]

Most of these errors involved unknowns—whether election-year benefit increases, wars, economic busts, oil embargoes, medical breakthroughs, or whatever. The actuaries could not predict a 1973 Arab oil embargo that no one else foresaw. They could not predict a 1979 economic bust that no one else forecast. It was difficult to criticize SSA for errors that were beyond predictive experience. Indeed, as one top SSA actuary noted, "The long and short of it is that I can't predict the future. No one can. We know that any specific estimate we make will be wrong."[4] Looking back over the first decades of Social Security, however, these were exactly the kinds of problems that provided both the growth and crisis in the program.

2. Technique

A second source of error was technique. Several problems characterized the methods used in forecasting the future at SSA. One rested on the world-without-cycles view mentioned earlier. Because the assumptions did not allow for boom or bust, the forecasts were most inaccurate at the start and finish of an economic cycle. At the end of a recovery, for example, the actuaries were likely to be overly optimistic about the next few years, even though the economy might be slipping into a recession. At the end of a recession, they were likely to be overly pessimistic, even though recovery might be just around the corner.

The actuaries were well aware of the problem and occasionally experimented with cyclical forecasts. Unfortunately, presidential staffs became quite concerned when SSA actuaries started predicting recessions. According to one actuary, "We had a very bad year in 1982. Everything dragged down. The Treasury

Department guys wanted us to build in a slow recovery as far out as possible. What we wanted to do was put in an explicit cycle, with a recession somewhere out around 1986 or 1987. They obviously won."

Another technical error came from the lack of an SSA economic model. According to a White House aide, "The actuaries sit down and shoot for good (Alternative II), mediocre (Alternative II-B), and poor (Alternative III) scenarios. They don't particularly care if the estimates are accurate, just that they show the different possible outcomes." The process worked from the top down, not from some economic theory up. Nor were their economic assumptions checked by some standard model to make sure that the predictions could actually occur in the real world. As one OMB aide argued, "A lot of results surprise the actuaries because they don't know what's happening in their own models. What they do is set each number independently of the others. They do inflation one place; tax rates another; benefit increases still another. The problem is that all the variables interact. They load all this stuff into a computer and get some numbers, but they don't have any meaning."

These technical errors were complicated by the lack of state-of-the-art computing facilities at SSA. Even if the actuaries had had some theory of how the economy works, their computers could not handle the analysis. The actuaries were but one set of clients at SSA among many who needed computer time. Despite repeated promises of improvement, the computer system remained antiquated, often unavailable for routine forecasting, and slow.

3. Assumption Drag

A third source of error in the SSA estimates came from assumption drag.[5] "The problem with all of these estimates," a Health and Human Services

Department official said, "is that they're out of date almost as soon as the ink is dry." Because the SSA forecasts were prepared in the spring but published in June, they were out of date by the following winter. At best, SSA had data only from the final quarter of the preceding year in drafting its forecast. But, the economy had demonstrated a remarkable ability to change quickly in recent years, leading to serious gaps between the initial forecasts, final publication of the reports, and actual use on Capitol Hill. To draft more timely assumptions, however, SSA needed better computer equipment, a stronger model of the economy, and a more predictable world.

4. Politics

As accuracy continued to drop over the late 1970s, the Social Security assumptions were subject to increasing manipulation. Since no way existed to predict economic performance very far into the future, why not use the assumptions to support the president's program? If, as Stockman argued, "none of us really understands what's going on with all these numbers," why not build a set of assumptions to fit the president's political needs? If, as Stockman also argued, "all the conventional estimates just wind up as mud . . . as absurdities," why not cast them in the president's image of the world?

In fact, that is precisely what recent administrations have done to the Social Security assumptions. In 1981, for example, Stockman used optimistic economic projections to sell his budget cuts on Capitol Hill but pessimistic assumptions to design Social Security reform. Senator Bill Bradley spotted the difference in Senate Finance Committee hearings on the Reagan budget in 1981. "We have two sets of books in which there are different sets of economic assumptions. One of the sets is the budget of this ad-

ministration upon which all the spending cuts are based. . . . That set says there will be unemployment of 6.6 percent. . . . Then we have the pessimistic assumptions for the Social Security trust fund. . . . That set says the unemployment will be 9.7 percent in 1983, not 6.6 percent. So this is your classic case where you can't have it both ways."[6] Economic assumptions were being drafted less to predict the future and more to sell administration programs.

The Social Security forecasting process was actually well designed for that kind of political sabotage. Under the forecasting timetable at SSA, the actuaries made a preliminary forecast early in each calendar year, submitting the tentative estimates to the secretaries of Health and Human Services, Treasury, and Labor, and only then starting the negotiating process toward a final agreement. Plenty of time was available for Congress and the president to influence the assumptions.

Given the impact of assumptions on the size of the Social Security crisis and the dollar-for-dollar returns on each solution, the actuaries often had to bargain with Congress and the president over competing views of the world in the early 1980s. Even small changes in fertility and real wage growth could have very large impacts on the short- and long-term deficit predictions. And since the economy was changing on an almost daily basis, confusion existed over which estimates (optimistic to pessimistic) to use and when to update them. In dealing with the White House, much of the conflict focused on the first years of the forecasts. "The first couple of years are the toughest," an actuary explained. "The politicos want to have the best picture on the short term. If you've got a budget before Congress, you don't want those old actuaries to come in and show your figures to be wrong. So those first years are where most of the battles come. . . . Let's say those estimates are often plausible but not probable." Yet those estimates are the key for setting the short-term targets.

THE POLITICS OF ASSUMPTIONS

Consider three recent examples of political influence in the Social Security forecasting process.

Fertility (1977)

The first example comes from the Carter administration and involves a change in the 1977 fertility assumption. Fertility remains the single most important factor for predicting far into the future. After a decade of steep declines in the birth rate, the SSA actuaries had changed the fertility assumption in 1974 to 1.9 births per woman. That meant there would be fewer "assumed" children to support their parents in the next century, increasing the size of the predicted long-term Social Security crisis. When Carter came into office in 1977, the fertility assumption was pushed back up to 2.1 births, even though actual rates fell to 1.77 that year. The change created the image of a smaller Social Security crisis, and meant there would be more "assumed" children to support their parents. Democrats would not have to cut benefits to solve the coming deficits. Though the change was only two-tenths of a percent, it had a dramatic impact on the Social Security forecasts. Yet, as one administration participant remembered, "We had to argue that the population would at least replace itself, that we would not stay below zero population growth for long."

New Estimates (1981)

The second example of political influence comes from the Reagan administration—with a series of changes in the 1981 economic assumptions, the most

important factor for predicting the immediate future. Most of the political pressure centered on Stockman's 1981 budget forecast, designed to sell the president's program on Capitol Hill. Traditionally, SSA had used the president's annual economic forecasts as the basis for the intermediate Social Security projections. After all, the president's forecast was supposed to be the best guess of the future. In 1981, however, Stockman's forecast was seen as so rosy that SSA decided it belonged in the optimistic Social Security projections.

The White House was incensed with this decision. SSA would merely confirm what the Democrats were saying: that the budget forecast promised far more than it could deliver. Moreover, wasn't SSA part of the executive branch? In theory, the president had the final power over the Social Security forecasts. He could order SSA to use Stockman's assumptions for the intermediate projections. And he did. He could also order SSA to create a new "worst-case" assumption to sell major benefit cuts to Congress. And he did. That new forecast would be so negative that Congress simply could not ignore the coming crisis.

SSA also had some power. The actuaries could refuse to sign their own report. And they did. They could refuse to testify on Capitol Hill. And they did. Without their support, the White House would be accused of openly rigging the Social Security forecasts, thereby tampering with the program. The White House would have to persuade the actuaries to give in. In the negotiations that followed the actuaries finally struck a bargain: they would prepare a worst-case forecast if the White House would allow two intermediate estimates. The president's budget would be labeled Alternative II-A, while the actuaries' best guess would be labeled Alternative II-B. Only then would the actuaries add a worst-case estimate.

It was a good bargain for SSA. "We had always wanted a way to get around the president's budget forecast anyway," an SSA participant noted, "and this was the perfect way to do it. Presidential budgets have been getting more unrealistic over the past few years. We didn't want to throw out the baby with the bath water."

Thus, the 1981 report contained five different estimates of the Social Security future. Alternative I (more optimistic than normal), Alternative II-A (the president's budget), Alternative II-B (the actuaries' most realistic scenario), Alternative III, and finally the new worst-case forecast. Little wonder some members of Congress were confused.

Compromising Estimates (1982–1983)

The third example involves the 1982–1983 forecasts. The 1982 estimates appear to be overly pessimistic, while the preliminary 1983 estimates appear to be more optimistic. According to the participants, the two sets of assumptions reflect the competing pressures of defining problems and selling solutions. The 1982 assumptions reflected the administration's concern that Congress might not undertake serious reform. The assumptions were more pessimistic to create pressure on Congress.

By the time SSA started drafting the 1983 forecasts, however, a Social Security compromise was in hand. The package had been negotiated in January

and reflected intense bargaining between the White House and Congress. It was a fragile agreement, built on sacrifices by both sides. Liberals agreed to benefit cuts and federal employee coverage, while conservatives agreed to tax increases and limited general revenues. Once the bargaining was over, the participants waited for a preliminary report from SSA. The dilemma was clear: if the new estimates showed too much economic improvement, liberals might abandon the package as unnecessary and cruel; if the estimates showed too much economic decline, conservatives might abandon the package as inadequate. The dilemma was complicated by the fact that liberals and conservatives were using different estimates. Liberals had been using the intermediate estimates as a defense against benefit cuts, arguing that a small tax increase might be enough. Conservatives had been using the pessimistic estimates as a lever in favor of benefit cuts, arguing that even a large tax increase would not work.

Thus, as SSA prepared the 1983 estimates, there was considerable pressure to help the intermediate and pessimistic estimates reach their own compromise. As one SSA aide remarked at the time, "We ought to try to make the numbers come out on this, even if it means playing around a little. If we have to go back into the package for any reason, we'll be in trouble." Table 27.3 shows how SSA solved the dilemma in setting the targets for the short-term crisis. The projected

Table 27.3 Projected Short-Term Deficits Under Competing Forecasts

Assumption	Deficit (billions)			Estimated Compromise Savings
	1982	1983	Change	
Intermediate II-B	$ 59	$112	+$57	$168
Pessimistic III	$214	$212	−$ 1	$180

Sources: National Commission on Social Security Reform memoranda; Trustees Reports; House Ways and Means Committee documents.

savings under the compromise are also included in the table.

With the estimated savings under the Social Security rescue proposal at $168 billion under the intermediate and $180 billion under the pessimistic, the February 1983 estimates provided considerable support for passage. Comparing 1982 and 1983, had the intermediate-B forecast improved as fast as the pessimistic (about 1 percent), liberals would have been hard pressed to support the package; they only would have needed $70 billion, slightly less than the amount raised by tax increases in the package. Had the pessimistic estimate deteriorated as fast as the intermediate (about 90 percent), conservatives would have had ample evidence that the package was not enough; it would have been approximately $200 billion short. How did the SSA assumption-builders achieve this remarkable compromise? The answer is by letting the pessimistic estimate improve much faster than the intermediate fell. The distance between the intermediate-B and pessimistic estimates narrowed significantly between the 1982 and February 1983 estimates. The spread closed from 2.5 percent on real wage growth in 1982 to 1.8 percent in early 1983, a compromise of 25 percent of the distance.

Patterns of Politics

The choice of one set of assumptions over another often rests on what each side wants to do. On Social Security, for example, conservatives were on the offensive, looking for major benefits cuts. They used pessimistic assumptions to define the size of the coming crisis. The larger the problem, the greater the need for some benefit cuts. Yet conservatives also used optimistic assumptions to define the impact of benefit cuts on the elderly. The smaller the impact, the greater the potential for congressional passage. Further, if conservatives could define the size of the problem with one set of assumptions but the range of solutions with another, they might win deeper benefit cuts from liberals. Whereas tax revenues did not change under pessimistic or optimistic assumptions, the impact of COLA cuts varied widely with the assumptions used.

Liberals, in contrast, used optimistic assumptions to define the size of the problem but pessimistic assumptions to attack the proposed benefit cuts. Since liberals were on the defensive, trying to protect their program against cuts, they needed a small problem to stop or delay congressional action. If the crisis was modest and temporary, why panic? Yet liberals also used pessimistic assumptions to show how deeply the benefit cuts might go. These patterns of offense and defense are summarized in Table 27.4.

The problem in the battle over assumptions was that liberals and conservatives often switched back and forth between optimism and pessimism, de-

Table 27.4   The Patterns of Assumption

	Offense	Defense
	Attack Social Security	Defend Social Security
For defining the problems	Use PESSIMISTIC	Use OPTIMISTIC
For selling, attacking the solutions	Use OPTIMISTIC	Use PESSIMISTIC

pending on their political needs. Both sides also moved back and forth in time, picking older or newer estimates to support their legislative positions. In early 1983, for example, liberals continued to use the year-old 1982 forecasts because the inflation figures made their COLA cuts look bigger. Conservatives, by contrast, used the newer estimates because the inflation figures made the cuts smaller. The use of different assumptions by the same side could only heighten public confusion about Social Security. Overly pessimistic assumptions about impending bankruptcy created unnecessary fears about collapse, while overly optimistic assumptions about long-lasting repairs created lower confidence when the rescues did not work.

As predictive accuracy dropped, the political games increased. With no way to predict the future and with great pressure to adopt some kind of assumptions. Congress and the president began to select their estimates on the basis of political payoffs, not accuracy.

II-B OR NOT II-B

Some of these sources of error could be controlled, others could not. Because the world was likely to change, it was impossible to predict very far into the future. Even with highly sophisticated econometric models, some with thousands of equations and dozens of separate indicators, private forecasters did not do very well at forecasting even the coming year or two, let alone 75 years. The SSA actuaries did not stand a much better chance, even if they had new computers, new models, and a more acceptable methodology. "Our inability to predict the economy for one year," Stockman reluctantly concluded in 1983, "should be evident after the experience that we've gone through."[7]

The failure of the Social Security forecasts in the late 1970s had serious im-

pacts on Congress and the president. Certainly, no one could use the estimates as objective predictions of reality. No one could build a rescue bill based on a single set of assumptions. Though some were more inaccurate than others, none could be trusted from year to year. Because it was impossible to choose assumptions on the basis of a track record, politics began to play a greater role in defining the future. Rational analysis was impossible without accurate tools.

Clearly, no one had a monopoly on truth in the 1970s and early 1980s. Without accurate forecasts, Congress and the president had to add a new step to the debate. Before they could even talk about problems and solutions, they had to agree on base-line assumptions. This assumption-building process became a key opportunity for stalemate. Not only was it too complicated for the public to understand, it was beyond the grasp of many legislators. The failure of technical analysis created a new chance for delay and confusion as each side fought to defend its vision of the future.

If no one could predict the future, how could Congress and the president make the right choices on Social Security? One answer was to put the program on a diet of stabilizers and fail-safes; that is, to build in mechanisms to protect the Social Security system from adverse economic conditions: change the COLAs, build in automatic triggers for emergency transfers of general revenues or taxes, and so forth. A second answer was simply to unindex the program; that is, return the discretion over benefit increases to Congress and the president. Because these two answers were politically expensive and technically questionable, the legislative builders had to decide whether to plan for the best or the worst that could happen—whether to put Social Security on a pessimistic footing or let the program move forward on a less severe outlook. Even here, however, it was a political issue. "The reason no one uses truly pessimistic forecasts," an SSA aide argued, "is because we don't know if we could get Congress to commit the kinds of funds or cuts to answer pessimistic forecasts. Think about the tax rates and benefit cuts needed to insulate that program against really bad economic performance."

Thus, one reason even the pessimistic forecasts are often optimistic is that government simply cannot plan for the worst that might happen. Indeed, planning for the worst case might actually make it happen. Imagine raising payroll taxes high enough to cover the poorest economic performance; then imagine how many jobs might be lost and how many businesses might close. It could be a self-fulfilling prophecy. Yet the risks of not planning for the worst are obvious: the program could collapse, public confidence could sink even further. As a result, most legislators are willing to plan for something less than the best, but not the absolute worst.

CONCLUSION

This article has addressed the importance of assumptions in the policy-making process. At least for Social Security, the battle over economic and demographic assumptions proved critical both for setting the targets for the rescue and for measuring the range of alternatives.[8] Even with new computer systems and a formal econometric model, it is not clear that the predictions could have been—or will now be—more accurate. Yet, Congress and the president will continue to rely on the assumptions for making choices, if only because little else can be done with an indexed program. Whether SSA should continue to offer such precision in the forecasts is open to question. By providing such detailed figures, SSA built an artificial veneer of accuracy that simply cannot exist in a forecast covering 75 years into the future.

NOTES

1. Much of this article is drawn from the author's interviews surrounding the 1983 Social Security rescue. Those interviews were conducted while the author was an American Political Science Association Congressional Fellow with Rep. Barber B. Conable, Jr., and involved more than 100 respondents contacted several times over the rescue period. Because those interviews were confidential, those quoted are not identified by name.
2. As with most of the interviews, this respondent was promised confidentiality as a condition of the conversation.
3. Greider, "The Education of David Stockman," *The Atlantic,* vol. 248 (December 1981), p. 39.
4. Francisco R. Bayo, deputy chief actuary for long-range program estimates, quoted in the *National Journal,* vol. 16 (June 23, 1984), p. 1216.
5. See William Ascher, *Forecasting* (Baltimore: The Johns Hopkins University Press, 1978), for an excellent discussion of the topic.
6. Greider, *op. cit.,* p. 38.
7. David Stockman, "Face the Nation," CBS News, Transcript (February 6, 1983).
8. See Paul Light, *Artful Work: The Politics of Social Security Reform* (New York: Random House, 1985), for a more detailed summary of the impact of the assumptions on the ongoing debate.

28.   The Conditions of Effective Implementation: A Guide to Accomplishing Policy Objectives

Paul Sabatier and Daniel Mazmanian

The capacity of public policy to alter social behavior is a complex process that should be seen in historical perspective. In any specific policy area, the basic policy orientation often remains fairly constant over time, with change coming in small increments as a result of adjustments made by relevant agencies, interest groups, and legislative committees.[1] In this paper, however, we examine the conditions under which a statute or other major policy action (such as an appellate court decision) that seeks to alter significantly the historical evolution of policy can actually achieve its objectives.

The bulk of the literature on policy implementation that has developed over the past decade is generally quite pessimistic about the ability of important policy initiatives actually to effect the desired social changes. Studies of Title I of the Elementary and Secondary Education Act of 1965, efforts to create jobs in Oakland, California, under the Public Works and Economic Development Act of 1965, the 1970 Clean Air Amendments, the New Towns In-Town program, and the Comprehensive Employment and Training Act (CETA) of 1973

have all concluded that these programs have had only very limited success in achieving their stated objectives.[2] In fact, a recent review of federal social programs suggests that such programs must be altered to fit within the constraints of local political systems if they are to be implemented at all.[3]

On the other hand, some federal statutes—most notably the 1966 Voting Rights Act and the 1964 Civil Rights Act—have been effectively implemented.[4] In addition, a recent study indicates that the California legislation creating the Bay Conservation and Development Commission has been quite successful in drastically reducing the historical trend of dredging and filling in San Francisco Bay.[5]

SOURCE: "Effective Implementation" by Paul Sabatier and Daniel Mazmanian in *Policy Analysis:* 5 (Fall 1979). Copyright © 1979 by the Regents of the University of California. Reprinted by permission.

[1] In such cases, policy implementation is relatively unproblematic, as change is incremental and there is a high degree of consensus among the major actors. See A. Lee Fritschler, *Smoking and Politics,* 2d ed. (Englewood Cliffs, N.J.: Prentice Hall, 1975), ch. 1; and Charles Lindblom, *The Intelligence of Democracy* (New York: Macmillan Co., 1964).

[2] Jerome Murphy, "Title I of FSEA: The Politics of Implementating Federal Education Reform," *Harvard Educational Review* 41 (1971): 35–63; Milbrey McLaughlin, *Evaluation and Reform: Title I* (Cambridge, Mass.: Ballinger Publishing Co., 1975); Jeffrey Pressman and Aaron Wildavsky, *Implementation* (Berkeley and Los Angeles: University of California Press, 1973); Henry Jacoby and John Steinbruner, *Clearing the Air* (Cambridge, Mass.: Ballinger Publishing Co., 1973); Charles Jones, *Clean Air* (Pittsburgh: University of Pittsburgh Press, 1975); Martha Derthick, *New Towns In-Town* (Washington, D.C.: Urban Institute, 1972); Carl Van Horn, "Implementing CETA: The Federal Role," *Policy Analysis* 4 (Spring 1978): 159–83.

[3] Paul Berman, "The Study of Macro- and Micro-Implementation," *Public Policy* 26 (Spring 1978): 172–79.

[4] See Harrell Rodgers and Charles Bullock, *Law and Social Change* (New York: McGraw Hill, 1972), and *Coercion to Compliance* (Lexington, Mass.: D.C. Heath, 1976).

[5] Gerald Swanson, "Coastal Zone Management from an Administrative Perspective: A

Clearly some programs are much more able than others to fulfill their legal mandates. The purpose of this paper is to identify and explain a set of five (sufficient and generally necessary) conditions under which a policy decision that seeks a substantial (non-trivial) departure from the status quo can achieve its policy objectives. Recognizing, however, that all of these conditions are probably seldom met in practice, we also suggest a number of strategies available to legislators and other policy formulators for overcoming specific deficiencies. Our objective throughout the paper is to maximize the congruence among policy objectives, the decisions of the implementing agencies, and the actual impacts of those decisions.

The paper is addressed to two different audiences: scholars interested in developing a general theory or conceptual framework of the implementation process (in which respect our work builds upon the earlier efforts of people like Van Meter and Van Horn, Bardach, Hargrove, Williams, and Berman), and policy formulators (such as legislators) and their staffs who wish to estimate the implementability of various policy alternatives and to understand the manner in which they can structure the implementation process so as to maximize the probability that statutory objectives will be attained.[6] For this purpose, it is important that the proposed framework provide not only a clear understanding of what is crucial but also distinguish those factors under the control of policy formulators from those over which policy formulators have only a very limited influence.[7]

One final introductory note: We feel that the literature on policy implementation has become unduly fragmented, both between types of policies—with some authors limiting their scope to social (distributive) programs, while others are concerned only with regulatory policies—and between types of policy-making institutions, with very little integration between studies of the implementation of legislative and judicial decisions. While such fragmentation can be partially attributed to scholars' traditional caution concerning the generalizability of their conclusions, it is nevertheless inimical to the heuristic value of comparative studies and to the norm that theories should apply to as wide a range of phenomena as possible. Therefore we shall throw modesty to the wind and argue that our framework applies to all governmental programs that seek to change some target group's behavior, either as an end in itself or as a means to

Case Study of the San Francisco Bay Conservation and Development Commission," *Coastal Zone Management Journal* 2 (1975): 81–102. For another example, see Robert Johnston, Seymore Schwartz, and Thomas Klinkner, "Successful Plan Implementation: The Growth Phasing Program of Sacramento County," *AIP Journal* (October 1978): 412–23.

[6] See Donald Van Meter and Carl Van Horn, "The Policy Implementation Process: A Conceptual Framework," *Administration and Society* 6 (February 1975): 445–88; Eugene Bardach, *The Implementation Game* (Cambridge,

Mass.: MIT Press, 1977); Erwin Hargrove, *The Missing Link* (Washington, D.C.: Urban Institute, 1975); Walter Williams and Richard Elmore, eds., *Social Program Implementation* (New York: Academic Press, 1976); Berman, "Macro- and Micro-Implementation"; Martin Rein and Francine Rabinovitz, "Implementation," working paper no. 43 (Cambridge, Mass.: Joint Center for Urban Studies, 1977); Harold Luft, "Benefit Cost Analysis and Public Policy Implementation," *Public Policy* 24 (Fall 1976): 437–462.

[7] See Victor Nielsen, "Input-Output Models and the Non-Use of Policy Analysis" (Paper presented at the 1974 Annual Meeting of the Western Political Science Association, Denver, Colo., April 1974); James Coleman, "Problems of Conceptualization and Measurement in Studying Policy Impacts," in *Public Policy Evaluation,* Sage Yearbooks in Politics and Public Policy, vol. 2, ed. Kenneth Dolbeare (Beverly Hills, Calif.: Sage, 1975), pp. 24–26.

some desired end-state. At the very least our framework applies to traditional regulatory programs governing private behavior, attempts to change the behavior of private actors through the conditional disbursement of funds, and attempts to change the behavior of field-level public officials (such as school boards, teachers, police) through legal directives or the conditional disbursement of funds. Moreover, although our focus throughout is on the implementation of statutes, the framework also applies to appellate court decisions.[8]

THE CONDITIONS OF EFFECTIVE POLICY IMPLEMENTATION

It is our contention that a statute or other major policy decision seeking a substantial departure from the status quo will achieve its objectives under the following set of conditions:

1. The program is based on a sound theory relating changes in target group behavior to the achievement of the desired end-state (objectives).
2. The statute (or other basic policy decision) contains unambiguous policy directives and structures the implementation process so as to maximize the likelihood that target groups will perform as desired.
3. The leaders of the implementing agencies possess substantial managerial and political skill and are committed to statutory goals.
4. The program is actively supported by organized constituency groups and by a few key legislators (or the chief

executive) throughout the implementation process, with the courts being neutral or supportive.
5. The relative priority of statutory objectives is not significantly undermined over time by the emergence of conflicting public policies or by changes in relevant socioeconomic conditions that undermine the statute's "technical" theory or political support.

The conceptual framework underlying this set of conditions has been presented elsewhere in greater detail and is based upon a (proto) theory of public agencies that views them as bureaucracies with multiple goals that are in constant interaction with interest (constituency) groups, other agencies, and legislative (and executive) sovereigns in their policy subsystem.[9]

Before elaborating on each of these conditions, we should note that obtaining target group compliance is obviously much more difficult in some situations than in others. The greater the difficulty, the greater the legal and political resources that must be marshalled if compliance is to be achieved. In the terms of our framework, the required "strength" (or degree of bias) of the last four conditions is a function of several factors, including the amount of change required in target group behavior, the orientation of target groups toward the mandated change, and the diversity in proscribed activities of target groups. In other words, the greater the mandated change, the more opposed the target groups, and

[8]For an excellent comparative analysis of the ability of legislatures and appellate courts to structure the implementation process, see Lawrence Baum, "Implementation of Legislative and Judicial Policies: A Comparative View," in *Effective Policy Implementation,* ed. Daniel Mazmanian and Paul Sabatier (Lexington, Mass.: Lexington Books, 1980).

[9]Paul Sabatier and Daniel Mazmanian, *The Implementation of Regulatory Policy: A Framework of Analysis* (Davis, Calif.: Institute of Governmental Affairs, 1979); and Paul Culhane, "Bureaucratic Politics Theory and the Open Systems Metaphor" (Paper presented at the 1978 Annual Meeting of the Southwestern Political Science Association, Houston, Texas, April 1978).

the more diverse their proscribed activities, the greater must be the degree of statutory structuring, the skill of implementing officials, the support from constituency groups and sovereigns, and the stability in socioeconomic conditions if statutory objectives are to be attained. Within this context, the set of five conditions should always be sufficient to achieve policy objectives. Moreover, each condition is probably necessary if the change sought is substantial and requires five to ten years of effort; in easier situations, however, it may be possible to omit one of the last three conditions.

Condition 1: The program is based on a sound theory relating changes in target group behavior to the achievement of the desired end-state (objectives).

Most basic policy decisions are based upon an underlying causal theory that can be divided into two components—the first relating achievement of the desired end-state(s) back to changes in target group behavior, the second specifying the means by which target group compliance can be obtained.[10] Both the "technical" and the "compliance" components must be valid for the policy objective(s) to be attained.

At this point, we are concerned only with the former ("technical") component, as the remaining four conditions

[10] For related discussions, see Berman, "Macro- and Micro-Implementation," p. 163; and Pressman and Wildavsky, *Implementation,* "Preface." In principle, a valid technical component should *(a)* incorporate all major factors directly contributing to the problem within the purview of the program and *(b)* correctly relate each of these factors to the desired end-state(s). Leonard Goodwin and Phyllis Moen, for example, suggest that one of the major reasons for dissatisfaction with American welfare policy is that, at any point in time, it has addressed only a very limited subset of the factors affecting income disabilities and thus has had little effect on the overall problem ("On the Evolution and Implementation of Welfare Policy," in *Effective Policy Implementation,* ed. Mazmanian and Sabatier).

in our framework relate primarily to the latter. In particular, we wish to emphasize that target group compliance—and the costs involved in obtaining it—may be wasted if not correctly linked to the desired end-state. For example, the "technical" component of the theory underlying the 1970 Clean Air Amendments relates air quality levels back to emissions from various stationary and mobile sources (the target groups). It assumes that human activities are the major source of air pollutants and that pollutant emissions from various sources within an air basin can be related, via diffusion models, to air quality levels at specific locations. To the extent that nonhuman sources, such as volcanoes, constitute a major emission source or that little is known about pollutant interaction and transport in the atmosphere, target group compliance with legally prescribed emission levels will not achieve air quality objectives (or will do so only very inefficiently). Moreover, the administrative and other costs involved in obtaining compliance are likely to be resented—with a corresponding decline in political support for the program—to the extent that promised improvements in air quality are not at least approximated. In short, an invalid technical component has both direct and indirect effects on the (non)achievement of policy objectives.

We should note, however, that there are some programs for which target group compliance can be interpreted as the policy objective. In such instances, the absence of any explicit attempt to link target group behavior to some subsequent end-state means that the first of our five conditions would not apply (as the underlying "technical" component deals directly with that linkage). For example, the goal of desegregation policy in the South could be construed as the elimination of dual schools—in which case the compliance of local target groups (school boards) would be tantamount to successful implementation. Insofar, however, as the goal of desegregation was not simply the elimination of dual schools but also the improvement of black children's reading scores, the "technical" assumption that unified schools improve reading scores would have to be valid for the policy objective to be attained.

Condition 2: The statute (or other basic policy decision) contains unambiguous policy directives and structures the implementation process so as to maximize the likelihood that target groups will perform as desired.

This is the condition most under the control of policy formulators (such as legislators). Unfortunately, its importance has often been overlooked by behaviorally oriented social scientists. For these reasons, we will briefly examine its constituent parts.

(a) The policy objectives are precise and clearly ranked, both internally (within the specific statute) and in the overall program of implementing agencies. Statutory objectives that are precise and clearly ranked in importance serve as an indispensable aid in program evaluation, as unambiguous directives to implementing officials, and as a resource available to supporters of those objectives both inside and outside the implementing agencies.[11] For example,

implementing officials confronted with objections to their programs can sympathize with the aggrieved party but nevertheless respond that they are only following the legislature's instructions. Clear objectives can also serve as a resource to actors outside the implementing institutions who perceive discrepancies between agency outputs and those objectives (particularly if the statute also provides them formal access to the implementation process, such as via citizen suit provisions).

While the desirability of unambiguous policy directives within a given statute is normally understood, it is also important that a statute assigned for implementation to an existing agency clearly indicate the relative priority that the new directives are to play in the totality of the agency's programs. If this is not done, the new directives are likely to undergo considerable delay and be accorded low priority as they struggle for incorporation into the agency's operating procedures.[12]

---

[11]For general discussions of the importance of unambiguous objectives as requisites of program evaluation and as political resources, respectively, see Leonard Rutman, ed., *Evaluation Research Methods* (Beverly Hills, Calif.: Sage, 1977), ch. 1; and Theodore Lowi, *The End of Liberalism* (New York: W. W. Norton, 1969).

We would like to suggest that the clarity and consistency of statutory objectives be conceptualized along the following ordinal scale: (1) Ambiguous objectives. These include both meaningless injunctions to regulate "in the public interest" and mandates to balance potentially conflicting objectives—such as air quality and industrial employ-

ment—without establishing priorities among them. (2) Definite "tilt." This involves a relatively clear ranking of potentially conflicting, rather general objectives—such as to improve air quality even if it results in some unemployment. (3) Qualitative objectives. These involve a rather precise qualitative mandate—for example, to protect air quality so as to maintain the public health, including that of susceptible populations. Note that this qualitative objective is considerably more precise than that under a "tilt." (4) Quantitative objectives, such as to reduce automotive emissions from 1970 levels 90 percent by 31 December 1975. Clearly, the last objective constitutes a greater resource to proponents of change than the first.

[12]For examples in which vague and/or inconsistent objectives have hampered the achievement of behavioral change, see Murphy, "Title I of ESEA," pp. 38–44; Richard Weatherly and Michael Lipsky, "Street Level Bureaucrats and Institutional Innovation: Implementing Special Education Reform," *Harvard Educational Review* 47 (May 1977): 180–96; Pressman and Wildavsky, *Implementation,* pp. 25–26, 71–77, 87–90; and Richard Johnson, *The Dynamics of Compliance*

(b) The financial resources provided to the implementing agencies are sufficient to hire the staff and conduct the technical analyses involved in the development of regulations, the administration of permit/service delivery programs, and the monitoring of target group compliance. Although this condition is fairly obvious, ascertaining what constitutes "sufficient" resources presents enormous difficulties in practice. As a general rule, however, a threshold level of funding is necessary for there to be any possibility of achieving statutory objectives, and the level of funding above this threshold is (up to some saturation point) proportional to the probability of achieving those objectives. Financial resources are perhaps particularly problematic in labor-intensive service delivery programs and in regulatory programs with a high scientific or technological component, where implementing agencies often lack the funds to engage in the research and development necessary to examine critically the information presented by target groups and, in some cases, to develop alternative technologies.[13]

(c) Implementation is assigned to agencies supportive of statutory objectives that will give the new program high priority. Any new program requires implementing officials who are not merely neutral but also sufficiently committed and persistant to develop new regula-

tions and standard operating procedures and to enforce them in the face of resistance from target groups and from public officials reluctant to make the mandated changes.[14]

Thus it is extremely important that implementation be assigned to agencies whose policy orientation is consistent with the statute and which will accord the new program high priority. This is most likely when a new agency is created with a clear mandate after an extensive political struggle, as the program will necessarily be its highest priority and the creation of new positions opens the door to a vast infusion of statutory supporters. Alternatively, implementation can be assigned to a prestigious existing agency that considers the new mandate compatible with its traditional orientation and is looking for new programs. In addition to selecting generally supportive agencies, a statute can sometimes stipulate that top implementing officials be selected from social sectors that generally support the legislation's objectives.[15] Even if this cannot be done

---

[14]For reviews of the reasons for bureaucratic resistance to change, see Richard Elmore, "Organizational Models of Social Program Implementation," *Public Policy* 26 (Spring 1978): 199–216; Herbert Kaufman, *The Limits of Organizational Change* (University, Ala.: University of Alabama Press, 1971); and Anthony Downs, *Inside Bureaucracy* (Boston: Little, Brown and Co., 1967), ch. 13, 14, 16, and 19.

[15]For example, several studies of state and regional land use agencies have shown that local elected officials are generally more likely than appointees of state officials to approve proposed developments—thereby suggesting that a land use statute can significantly affect the probable policy orientation of the implementing agency through the distribution of appointees from these two categories. See Edmond Costantini and Kenneth Hang, *The Environmental Impulse and Its Competitors* (Davis, Calif.: Institute of Governmental Affairs, 1973), pp. 55–58; and Judy Rosener with Sally Russell and Dennis Brehn, *Environmental vs. Local Control*, mimeographed (Irvine: University of California, 1977).

(Evanston, Ill.: Northwestern University Press, 1967), pp. 58–59. In contrast, clear standards facilitated implementation of the 1965 Bay Conservation and Development Act (Swanson, "Coastal Zone Management," pp. 81–102).

[13]This has, for example, been a substantial constraint on the acquisition of information concerning off-shore petroleum resources and in the development of low-emission motor vehicles. See U.S., Senate, Committee on Interior, *Hearings on the Energy Information Act,* 93d Cong., 2d sess., 1974; and Jacoby and Steinbruner, *Clearing the Air,* ch. 3–4.

through legislation, legislative supporters can often play a critical role in the appointment of non-civil-service personnel within the implementing agencies.

In practice, however, the choice of implementing agencies and officials is often severely constrained. In many policy areas (such as education) there is little option but to assign implementation to existing agencies that may well be hostile or whose personnel may be so preoccupied with existing programs that any new mandate tends to get lost in the shuffle. In addition, most positions within any governmental agency are occupied by career civil servants who are often resistant to changes in existing procedures and programs and only moderately susceptible to the sanctions and inducements available to political appointees. In fact, the generally limited ability of policy formulators to assign implementation to agency officials committed to its objectives probably lies behind many cases of suboptimal correspondence of policy outputs with statutory objectives.[16]

(d) The statute (or other basic policy decision) provides substantial hierarchical integration within and among implementing agencies by minimizing the number of veto/clearance points and by providing supporters of statutory objectives with inducements and sanctions sufficient to assure acquiescence among those with a potential veto. Surely one of the dominant themes in the implementation literature is the difficulty of obtaining coordinated action within any given agency and among the numerous semiautonomous agencies involved in most implementation efforts. The problem is particularly acute in federal statutes that rely on state and local agencies for carrying out the details of program delivery and for which some field-level implementors and/or target groups display considerable resistance toward statutory directives. Thus one of the most important attributes of any statute (or other basic policy decision) is the extent to which it hierarchically integrates the implementing agencies. To the extent the system is only loosely integrated, there will be considerable variation in the degree of behavioral compliance among implementing officials and target groups—as each responds to the incentives for modification within its local setting—and thus a distinctly suboptimal attainment of statutory objectives.[17]

The degree of hierarchical integration among implementing agencies is determined by the number of veto/clearance points involved in the attainment of statutory objectives and the extent to which supporters of statutory objectives are provided with inducements and sanctions sufficient to assure acquiescence among those with a potential veto. Veto/clearance points involve those occasions in which an actor has the capacity (quite apart from the question of legal authority) to impede the achievement of statutory objectives.[18]

---

[16]See, for example, Murphy, "Title I of FSEA," pp. 35–63; Pressman and Wildavsky, *Implementation,* ch. 3–5; Bardach, *Implementation Game,* ch. 5; Rodgers and Bullock, *Coercion to Compliance,* ch. 2; N. Milner, *The Court and Local Law Enforcement: The Impact of Miranda* (Beverly Hills, Calif.: Sage, 1971); and Hugh Heclo, *A Government of Strangers* (Washington, D.C.: Brookings, 1977), ch. 3–6.

[17]See Elmore, "Social Program Implementation," pp. 199–216; Berman, "Macro- and Micro-Implementation," pp. 166–79; Rodgers and Bullock, *Coercion to Compliance;* Pressman and Wildavsky, *Implementation,* ch. 5; Frederick Lazin, "The Failure of Federal Enforcement of Civil Rights Regulations in Public Housing, 1963–1971: The co-optation of a Federal Agency by Its Local Constituency," *Policy Sciences* 4 (September 1973): 263–74.

[18]This is a slightly more restrictive notion of veto/clearance point than that used by Pressman and Wildavsky (*Implementation,*

Resistance from specific veto points can be overcome, however, if the statute provides sufficient sanctions and/or inducements to convince role occupants (whether implementing officials or target groups) to alter their behavior. In short, if these sanctions and inducements are great enough, the number of veto points can delay—but probably never ultimately impede—behavioral compliance by target groups.[19] In practice, however, the compliance incentives are usually sufficiently modest that the number of veto/clearance points becomes extremely important. As a result, the most direct route to a statutory objective—such as a negative income tax to provide a minimum income—is often preferable to complex programs administered by numerous semiautonomous bureaucracies.[20]

  (e) *The decision rules of implementing agencies are supportive of statutory objectives.* In addition to providing un-ambiguous objectives, generally supportive implementing officials, few veto points, and adequate incentive for compliance, a statute (or other basic policy decision) can further bias the implementation process by stipulating the formal decision rules of the implementing agencies. The decisions of implementing agencies are likely to be consistent with statutory objectives to the extent, for example, that the burden of proof in permit/licensing cases is placed on the applicant and that agency officials are required to make findings fully consistent with statutory objectives. In addition, a statute can assign authority to make final decisions within implementing institutions to those subunits most likely to support statutory objectives. Finally, when multimembered commissions are involved, the statute can stipulate the majority required for specific actions. In the case of regulatory agencies that operate primarily through the granting of permits or licenses, decision rules that make the granting of a permit contingent upon substantial consensus, such as a two-thirds majority, are obviously conducive to stringent regulation.

  (f) *The statute (or other basic policy decision) provides ample opportunity for constituency (interest) groups and sovereigns supportive of statutory objectives to intervene in the implementation process through, for example, liberal rules of standing to agency and judicial proceedings and requirements for periodic evaluation of the performance of implementing agencies and target groups.* While a statute can take steps to assure that implementing officials are generally supportive of statutory objectives and that the decision process involving implementing agencies and target groups contains few veto points, adequate incentives for compliance, and supportive formal rules, we nevertheless contend that implementing officials can-

---

ch. 5). In calculating the total number of such points, one must add those involved in the development of general rules and operating procedures, in the disposition of specific cases, and in the enforcement of those decisions. One must also consider the possibility that implementing agencies are not given adequate legal authority to achieve mandated objectives. Thus any purely cooperative arrangements needed with other agencies must also be included in the number of veto points; in such cases, of course, the implementing agencies are likely to possess very few incentives to induce compliance, and thus the system can be said to be poorly integrated.

[19]For an example of the ability of sanctions to bring about behavioral compliance over the strong resistance of target groups (in this case, southern school officials), see Rodgers and Bullock, *Coercion to Compliance,* pp. 36–45.

[20]For discussions of the advantages of simplicity, see Pressman and Wildavsky, *Implementation,* ch. 7; Bardach, *Implementation Game,* pp. 250–53; and Charles Schultze, *The Public Use of Private Interest* (Washington, D.C.: Brookings, 1977).

not necessarily be trusted to act in a manner consistent with statutory objectives. What is also required is constant oversight and intervention from supportive constituency groups and legislative (and executive) sovereigns.

A statute (or other basic policy decision) can take a number of steps to maximize the probability of such intervention. First, it can require opportunities for public input at numerous stages in the decision process of implementing agencies and even require that the agencies take positive steps to assure the participation of unorganized potential beneficiaries. Second, it can provide for liberal rules of standing to appeal agency decisions to the courts. For example, the citizen suit provisions of the 1970 Clean Air Amendments have been used on several occasions to compel the U.S. Environmental Protection Agency to carry out statutorily mandated provisions that it had failed, for one reason or another, to do.[21] Third, requirements for periodic reporting of agency performance to legislative and executive sovereigns and for evaluation studies by prestigious independent organizations (such as the National Academy of Sciences) are conducive to external oversight of the implementing agencies and probably to the achievement of statutory objectives.[22]

In sum, a carefully formulated statute (or other basic policy decision) should be seen as a means by which legislators and other policy formulators can structure the entire implementation process and maximize the probability that the policy outputs of the implementing agencies and the behavior of target groups (whether outside or inside those agencies) will be consistent with statutory objectives. This requires, first, that they develop unambiguous policy objectives and incorporate a valid technical theory linking target group compliance with the desired impacts. In order to maximize the probability of such compliance, they should then assign implementation to supportive agencies, provide implementing officials with adequate financial resources, hierarchically integrate the implementation process through minimizing veto points and providing sufficient incentives to overcome resistance, bias the formal decision rules of implementing agencies, and provide opportunities for outsiders to participate in the implementation process and to evaluate accurately agency (and target group) performance.

But a statute, no matter how well it structures implementation, is not a sufficient condition for assuring target group compliance with its objectives. Assuring sufficient compliance to actually achieve those objectives normally takes at least three to five, and often ten to twenty, years. During this period, there are con-

---

[21] See Bruce Kramer, "Economics, Technology, and the Clean Air Amendments of 1970: The First Six Years," *Ecology Law Quarterly* 6 (1976): 161–230; and Marc Mihaly, "The Clean Air Act and the Concept of Nondegradation: Sierra Club v. Ruckelshaus," *Ecology Law Quarterly* 2 (Fall 1972): 801–36. For general discussions of legal standing, see Karen Orren, "Standing to Sue," *American Political Science Review* 70 (September 1976): 723–41; and Kenneth Stewart, "Environmental Law: Standing to Sue," 30 *Vanderbilt Law Review* (1977): 1271–95.

[22] While these mechanisms can increase the probability of favorable oversight, they are certainly not cure-alls. Evaluation studies by prestigious external sources are likely to aid

implementation effectiveness because of the difficulties of agencies to evaluate critically their own programs (see Rodgers and Bullock, *Coercion to Compliance,* ch. 6, and Murphy, "Title I of ESEA," pp. 42–44). Nevertheless, there are a wide variety of reasons why both agencies and legislatures conduct evaluation studies—only some of them relating to improving program performance (see Martin Rein and Sheldon White, "Policy Research: Belief and Doubt," *Policy Analysis* 3 [Spring 1977]: 239–71).

stant pressures for even supportive agency officials to lose their commitment, for supportive constituency groups and sovereigns to fail to maintain active political support, and for the entire process to be gradually undermined by changing socioeconomic forces. In short, while a statute can go a long way toward assuring successful implementation, there are additional conditions that must be fulfilled if its objectives are to be attained.

Condition 3: The leaders of the implementing agencies possess substantial managerial and political skill and are committed to statutory objectives.

As already indicated, legislators and other policy formulators can take a number of important steps—both in the drafting of a statute and in the subsequent appointment of non-civil-service personnel—to increase substantially the probability that the leaders of implementing agencies will be supportive of statutory objectives. In practice, however, statutory levers are often somewhat limited (except where creation of a new agency is feasible), and the process of appointing political executives is heavily dependent upon the wishes of the chief executive and important legislators—several of whom may well not be committed to implementation of the basic policy decision. In short, the support of top implementing officials is sufficiently important and problematic to warrant being highlighted as a separate condition for successful implementation.

Moreover, policy support is essentially useless if not accompanied by political and managerial skill in utilizing available resources. Political skill involves the ability to develop good working relationships with sovereigns in the agency's subsystem, to convince opponents and target groups that they are being treated fairly, to mobilize support among latent supportive constituencies, to present the agency's case adroitly through the mass media, and so forth. Managerial skill involves developing

adequate controls so that the program is not subject to charges of fiscal mismanagement, maintaining high morale among agency personnel, and managing internal dissent in such a way that dissidents are convinced they have received a fair hearing.[23]

Finally, there is some evidence that maintaining high morale, commitment, and perhaps even skill becomes increasingly difficult over time. Innovative policy initiatives often attract committed and skillful executives to implementing institutions, particularly in the case of new agencies. But such people generally become burned out and disillusioned with bureaucratic routine after a few years, to be replaced by officials much more interested in personal security and organizational maintenance than in taking risks to attain policy goals.[24]

Condition 4: The program is actively supported by organized constituency groups and by a few key legislators (or the chief executive) throughout the implementation process, with the courts being neutral or supportive.

[23]For discussions of leadership and illustrations of its importance, see Heclo, *Government of Strangers*, ch. 5–6; Francis Rourke, *Bureaucracy, Politics, and Public Policy*, 2d ed. (Boston: Little, Brown and Co., 1976), pp. 94–101; Richard Bolan and Ronald Nuttall, *Urban Planning and Politics* (Lexington, Mass.: D.C. Heath, 1975); Eugene Bardach, *The Skill Factor in Politics* (Berkeley and Los Angeles: University of California Press, 1972); Andrew McFarland, *Power and Leadership in Pluralist Systems* (Stanford, Calif.: Stanford University Press, 1969), ch. 8; Phillip Selznick, *Leadership in Administration* (New York: Harper and Row, 1957); and Victor Vroom and Philip Yetton, *Leadership and Decision-Making* (Pittsburgh: University of Pittsburgh Press, 1973).

[24]Marver Bernstein, *Regulating Business by Independent Commission* (Princeton, N.J.: Princeton University Press, 1955), ch. 3; Downs, *Inside Bureaucracy*, ch. 2, 8, and 9. For some ambivalent evidence, see Kenneth Meir and John Plumlee, "Regulatory Administration and Organizational Rigidity," *Western Political Quarterly* 31 (March 1978): 80–95.

It is absolutely crucial to maintain active political support for the achievement of statutory objectives over the long course of implementation. If the first three conditions have been met, this essentially requires that sufficient support be maintained among legislative and executive sovereigns to provide the implementing agencies with the requisite financial resources annually, as well as assuring that the basic statute is not seriously undermined but instead modified to overcome implementation difficulties.

This seemingly rather simple requirement is, however, exceedingly difficult to accomplish, for a variety of reasons. First, the rather episodic issue-attention span of the general public and the mass media tends to undermine diffuse political support for any particular program among both the public and legislators.[25] Second, there is a general tendency for organized constituency support for a wide variety of programs—including environmental and consumer protection, as well as efforts to aid the poor—to decline over time, while opposition from target groups to the costs imposed on them remains constant or actually increases. This shift in the balance of constituency support for such programs gradually becomes reflected in a shift in support among members of the legislature as a whole and the committees in the relevant subsystem(s).[26] Third, most legislators lack the staff resources and/or the incentives to monitor program implementation actively.[27] The exception is constituent casework, which tends to be heavily skewed towards complaints. Without active political support from a few key legislators, implementing officials supportive of the program find it difficult to overcome the constant drumbeat of constituent complaints, as well as the delay and resistance inherent in implementing any program requiring substantial behavioral change (except in those instances where target groups support such change).

Despite these difficulties, the necessary infusion of political support can be maintained if two factors are present. The first is the presence of a "fixer" (or fixers)—that is, an important legislator or executive official who controls resources important to other actors and who has the desire and the staff resources to closely monitor the implementation process, to intervene with agency officials on an almost continuous basis, and to protect the budget and the legal authority of the implementing agencies.[28]

[25]Anthony Downs, "Up and Down with Ecology—the Issue-Attention Cycle," *Public Interest* (Summer 1972): 38–50.

[26]See James Q. Wilson, "The Politics of Regulation," in *Social Responsibility and the Business Predicament,* ed. Jame McKie (Washington, D.C.: Brookings, 1974), pp. 135–68; Paul Sabatier, "Social Movements and Regulatory Agencies," *Policy Sciences* 6 (Fall 1975): 301–42; and Barry Weingast, "A Positive Model of Public Policy Formulation: The Case of Regulatory Agency Behavior," working paper no. 25 (St. Louis: Center for the Study of American Business, 1978).

[27]See Hargrove, *Missing Link,* pp. 112–17; Morris Oguls, *Congress Oversees The Bureaucracy* (Pittsburgh: University of Pittsburgh Press, 1976); Malcolm Jewell and Samuel Patterson, *The Legislative Process in the U.S.,* 3d ed. (New York: Random House, 1977), ch. 18; and John Johannes, "Congressional Caseworkers: Attitudes, Orientations, and Operations" (Paper presented at the 1978 Annual Meeting of the Midwest Political Science Association, Chicago, Ill., April 1978).

[28]Bardach, *Implementation Game,* pp. 268–283. For example, Bardach describes a case in which this function was ably performed with respect to an important 1967 mental health law in California by a legislator who was the ranking Republican on the California Assembly Ways and Means Committee, who was widely acknowledged as the legislature's expert in this area, and who, moreover, viewed this legislation as the crowning achievement of his career. One might also cite the efforts of Senator Edmund Muskie with respect to federal pollution control legislation (see Bernard Asbel, *The Senate Nobody Knows* [Garden City, N.Y.: Doubleday, 1978]).

Except in very unusual circumstances, however, any particular "fixer" is unlikely to occupy a crucial position and/or to maintain an interest throughout the long process of implementation. This brings us to the second, and ultimately the most important requirement, namely, the presence of an organized supportive constituency (interest) group that has the resources to monitor closely program implementation, to intervene actively in agency proceedings, to appeal adverse agency decisions to the courts and to the legislature, and to convince key legislators that the program merits their active support.[29] For the paramount advantage of any organization over an individual is continuity. If the supportive constituency is present, "fixers" can generally be found and/or nurtured.

Programs involving intergovernmental relations, however, pose additional difficulties to the maintenance of political support. On the one hand, programs of intergovernmental "subordinates" (such as localities vis-à-vis states and the federal government) are often subject to revision and/or emasculation by superordinate units of government.[30] Unless a program's representatives occupy important positions at the superordinate level, there is little that can be done to maintain its legal (and sometimes financial) integrity. Conversely, superordinate

levels are usually confronted with substantial local variation in political support for program objectives and, consequently, in the compliance of local implementing officials with program directives. While such variation can, in principal, be overcome if the superordinate statute provides very substantial incentives for compliance and sufficient financial resources to enable superordinate officials essentially to replace local implementors, in practice the system is seldom structured to that degree, and thus superordinate officials are forced to bargain with recalcitrant local implementors.[31] The result is greater sensitivity to local demands and generally a suboptimal achievement of statutory objectives.

The discussion thus far has focused on the need for political support among the legislative and executive sovereigns of implementing agencies. But one must not neglect the courts. In most cases, the contemporary deference of most federal and state courts to agency decision making means that they play a rather minor role in the implementation process except on procedural issues and to assure

---

[29]See Sabatier, "Social Movements and Regulatory Agencies," pp. 317–27; Walter Rosenbaum, "The Paradoxes of Public Participation," *Administration and Society* 8 (November 1976): 355–83; and B. Guy Peters, "Insiders and Outsiders: The Politics of Pressure Group Influence on Bureaucracy," *Administration and Society* 9 (August 1977): 191–218.

[30]Probably the most extreme case is federal preemption of nuclear safety issues in power plant siting. For examples of the sometimes deleterious effects of new federal pollution control statutes on state programs, see Jones, *Clean Air,* ch. 8; and Harvey Lieber, *Federalism and Clean Waters* (Lexington, Mass.: D.C. Heath, 1974), ch. 7.

[31]For examples of the effects of variation in local support on the implementation of federal programs, see Murphy, "Title I of ESEA," pp. 35–63; Rodgers and Bullock, *Coercion to Compliance,* ch. 2–4; Paul Berman and Milbrey McLaughlin, "Implementation of Educational Innovation," *Educational Forum* 40 (March 1976); 345–70; and Rufus Browning, Dale Rogers Marshall, and David Tabb, "Implementation and Political Change: Sources of Local Variations in Federal Social Programs," in *Effective Policy Implementation,* ed. Mazmanian and Sabatier. See also Berman, "Macro- and Micro-Implementation," pp. 168–79; Elmore, "Organizational Models of Social Program Implementation," pp. 199–216; Jeffrey Pfeffer and Gerald Salancik, *The External Control of Organizations* (New York: Harper and Row, 1978); and Helen Ingram, "Policy Implementation through Bargaining. The Case of Federal Grants-in-Aid," *Public Policy* 25 (Fall 1977): 499–526.

conformity with explicit statutory directives.[32] But courts strongly opposed to a given statute have the authority to emasculate implementation through delay in enforcement proceedings, through repeatedly unfavorable statutory interpretations, and, in extreme cases, by declaring the statute unconstitutional.[33] On the other hand, there have been some instances where courts have substantially strengthened programs through favorable rulings.[34] Given the enormous potential role of the courts, we argue that successful implementation of statutory objectives requires that they be either neutral or supportive.

Condition 5: The relative priority of statutory objectives is not significantly undermined over time by the emergence of conflicting public policies or by changes in relevant socioeconomic conditions that undermine the statute's "technical" theory or political support.

Change is omnipresent in most contemporary societies, in part because most countries are immersed in an international system over which they have only modest control, in part because policy issues tend to be highly interrelated. Pollution control, for example, is linked to energy, to inflation and national monetary policy, to transportation, to

public lands, and to numerous other issues. As a result of this continuous change, any particular policy decision is susceptible to an erosion of political support as other issues become relatively more important over time. Obvious examples would be the effect of the Vietnam War and inflation on many Great Society programs and the effect of the energy crisis and inflation on pollution control programs.[35] Change can also be so extensive as essentially to undermine the technical assumptions upon which a policy is based, as when the migration of poor people from the South and Puerto Rico to northern industrial cities brought into serious question the ability of state and local governments to provide matching funds for welfare programs.

It is in responding to such changes that support for a particular program from key legislators, organized constituency groups, and implementing officials becomes crucial. If they are sensitive to the effects that changes in seemingly tangential policies and in technical assumptions can have on "their" program, they can take steps to see that these repercussions are addressed in any new legislation.[36]

This concludes our discussion of the conditions of effective policy implementation. To recapitulate: A statute or other basic policy decision will achieve its objectives if (1) it incorporates a valid "technical" theory linking target group behavior to those objectives; (2) it contains unambiguous policy directives and

---

[32]See Louis Jaffe, *Judicial Control of Administrative Action* (Boston: Little, Brown and Co., 1965); and Edward White, "Allocating Power Between Agencies and Courts," *Duke Law Journal* 1974 (April 1974): 195–244.

[33]The locus and scope of judicial review can, however, be regulated by statute. For example, judicial review of the decisions of the Illinois Pollution Control Board is limited to the appellate courts and to rather narrowly defined procedural issues. See Elizabeth Haskell and Victoria Price, *State Environmental Management* (New York: Praeger, 1973), pp. 17–20.

[34]One of the best examples is the effect of *U.S.* v. *Georgia* (1969) in accelerating southern school desegregation (see Rodgers and Bullock, *Coercion to Compliance*, ch. 2–3).

[35]See J. Clarence Davies and Barbara Davies, *The Politics of Pollution,* 2d ed. (Indianapolis: Pegasus, 1975), pp. 52–60; and Henry Aaron, *Politics and the Professors: The Great Society in Perspective* (Washington, D.C.: Brookings, 1977).

[36]An excellent example was the effort of Senator Muskie in resisting the efforts of the auto companies and utilities to use the energy crisis to emasculate the 1970 Clean Air Amendments.

structures the implementation process so as to maximize the probability of target group compliance; (3) the leaders of implementing agencies are supportive of those objectives and skillful in utilizing available resources; (4) the program is supported by active constituency groups and a few key legislators throughout the implementation process, with the courts being neutral or supportive; and (5) the program is not undermined by changing socioeconomic conditions. If all of these conditions are met, then any statute—no matter how ambitious—will be effectively implemented. In most cases, each of the conditions will have to be met if effective implementation is to take place; the exception would involve policies that seek only modest changes in target group behavior and/or in which target groups are amenable to mandated changes.[37]

Throughout this discussion, however, we have been somewhat vague about the actual process of policy feedback and evaluation. Moreover, while the set of conditions should (at the very least) serve as a useful checklist to policy formulators and to scholars, it provides little guidance about what can be done when one or all of the conditions cannot in practice be met. If this paper is to serve as a useful guide to implementation analysis and assessment, it must at least briefly address these two topics.

POLICY FEEDBACK AND EVALUATION

Thus far our attention has been focused on the extent to which implementing agencies and target groups act in a manner consistent with statutory objectives and ultimately on the extent to which those objectives are actually attained. In this respect we have mirrored the focus on formal goals of much of the literature on implementation assessment and program evaluation.[38]

But if one is interested in the evolution of policy and particularly with the political feedback process, a much wider range of impacts (or outcomes) needs to be considered. Of particular importance are unintended impacts that affect political support for the program's objectives. For example, any assessment of the implementation of school desegregation policy should be concerned not only with the amount of desegregation achieved but also with the effect of desegregation on "white flight" and ultimately on the amount of political and financial support for the public schools. Moreover, there is some evidence that political feedback is based primarily upon perceived, rather than actual, impacts and that policy elites evaluate a program not in terms of the extent to which it achieves its legal mandate but rather in terms of its perceived conformity with their policy preferences.[39]

---

[37]In the case of special education reform in Massachusetts, for example, the ultimate target groups (teachers and other local school officials) were apparently generally supportive of the mandated changes in their behavior. This essentially eliminated the need for a very hierarchically integrated decision process, and the program was rather successfully implemented despite a decided lack of skill on the part of state implementing officials. Nevertheless, uncertainty concerning the adequacy of financial resources and the relative priority of special education in the total educational program created significant obstacles to effective implementation. See Weatherly and Lipsky, "Implementing Special Education Reform," pp. 171–97.

[38]See, for example, Rutman, *Evaluation Research Methods,* pp. 28–29; and David Nachmias, *Public Policy Evaluation* (New York: St. Martin's, 1979), pp. 13–15. For a somewhat more inclusive view of impact analysis, see Frank Levy, Arnold Meltsner, and Aaron Wildavsky, *Urban Outcomes* (Berkeley and Los Angeles: University of California Press, 1974).

[39]While the literature on policy evaluation deals primarily with the correspondence between actual impacts and policy objectives, from the standpoint of political feedback it is perceived, rather than actual, impacts that are crucial. See Daniel Mazmanian and Paul

The actual process of policy evaluation and feedback occurs continuously on an informal basis as the implementing agencies interact with concerned constituency groups, legislative (and executive) sovereigns, and the courts. At periodic intervals, however, the process normally becomes more formal and politically salient as attempts are made to revise substantially the basic statute. For example, major efforts to amend federal air pollution control law seem to occur every three to four years. Some of these revisions can be attributed to continued resistance from affected target groups, while others can be traced to significant changes in relevant social and economic conditions. Whatever the source of proposed changes, it is important that supporters of the original objectives provide for independent evaluation studies to accurately assess the actual impacts of the program. Such systematic evaluation serves both to correct imperfections in program design and performance and to counteract the tendency for complaints to dominate the informal feedback process.

IMPLEMENTATION UNDER SUBOPTIMAL CONDITIONS

A frequently voiced criticism against both legislators and scholars is that they have been far more concerned with the passage of legislation than with its effective implementation. Over the past decade, however, a burgeoning interest in policy implementation and evaluation has occurred in the academic community. This has matched a corresponding shift of emphasis among legislators from the passage of major new policy initiatives to more effective implementation and oversight of existing programs. One of the principal purposes of this paper is to provide both communities an understanding of the conditions under which statutes (and other basic policy decisions) that seek to change the status quo can be effectively implemented— that is, can achieve their policy objectives.

Our discussion has shown that legislators and other policy formulators can go a long way toward assuring effective policy implementation if they see that a statute incorporates a sound technical theory, provides precise and clearly ranked objectives, and structures the implementation process in a wide number of ways so as to maximize the probability of target group compliance. In addition, they can take positive steps to appoint skillful and supportive implementing officials, to provide adequate appropriations and to monitor carefully the behavior of implementing agencies throughout the long implementation process, and to be aware of the effects of changing socioeconomic conditions and of new legislation (even in supposedly unrelated areas) on the original statute.

In practice, of course, even those legislators and other policy formulators concerned with effective implementation operate under substantial constraints that make it extremely difficult for them to perform all these tasks. Valid technical theories may not be available. Imperfect information, goal conflict, and multiple vetoes in legislative bodies make it very difficult to pass legislation that incorporates unambiguous objectives and coherently structures the implementation process.[40] Implementation

Sabatier, "The Role of Attitudes and Perceptions in Policy Evaluation by Attentive Elites: The California Coastal Commissions," in *Public Policy Analysis,* Sage Yearbook in Politics and Public Policy, vol. 8, ed. Helen Ingram and Dean Mann (Beverly Hills, Calif.: Sage, 1979).

[40]See Rein and Rabinovitz, *Implementation,* pp. 11–14; Carl Auerbach, "Pluralism and the Administrative Process," *Annals of the American Academy of Political and Social Science* 400 (March 1972); 1–13; and

must often be assigned to agencies that are not supportive of the policy objectives. Supportive interest groups and legislators with the resources to serve as "fixers" may not be available or may go on to other things over the long course of implementation.

Nevertheless, even under such suboptimal conditions, several steps can be taken at least to increase the probability of effective implementation.

1. If a valid "technical" theory linking target group behavior to policy objectives is not available or is clearly problematic, then the authors of the statute should make a conscious effort to incorporate in it a learning process through experimental projects, extensive research and development, evaluation studies, and an open decision process involving as many different inputs as possible.

2. If the legislature insists on passing legislation with only the most ambiguous policy directives, then supporters of different points of view can initiate litigation in the hopes of finding a court that will invalidate the law as an unconstitutional delegation of (legislative) authority. While not very promising, this strategy has been employed successfully at least once in a California case, with subsequent legislation providing much clearer guidance to the agency.[41]

3. If implementation cannot be assigned to strongly supportive agencies, then it is absolutely crucial to provide for intervention by outsiders through citizen suit provisions, periodic reporting to sovereigns, evaluation studies by prestigious and relatively independent outsiders, and perhaps special legislative oversight committees.

4. If there are no active supportive interest groups with the necessary resources to monitor implementation carefully, then identification and mobilization of such a group must be a major priority of supportive legislators and implementing officials—as any program is doomed in the long run without one. While it is occasionally possible to create new organizations from scratch, a more feasible strategy is to convince an existing organization with the requisite resources to expand its program to make program monitoring a major responsibility.[42]

5. If a "fixer" is not readily available, then program supporters must make a major effort to find or develop one. This may involve convincing a competent new legislator to specialize in this area or convincing an existing legislator that constituents strongly support the program and thus require it being given higher priority. If legislators in the relevant committees having jurisdiction over the implementing agencies are apathetic (or, worse, hostile) toward the new program, then efforts should be made to reorganize committee jurisdictions or

Nelson Rosenbaum, "Statutory Stringency and Policy Implementation: The Case of Wetlands Regulation," in *Effective Policy Implementation,* ed. Mazmanian and Sabatier.

[41]In 1971 a California appellate court held the Forest Practices Act of 1945 unconstitutional on the grounds that it improperly delegated its lawmaking authority without adequate standards (*Bayside Timber* v. *San Mateo County,* App., 97 Cal. Rptr. 431), which led to major amendments to the legislation, including considerable clarification of

the policy directives. This is of course a perfect example of what Lowi would term an application of the "Schechter Rule" (Lowi, *End of Liberalism,* ch. 10).

[42]For an example, see Sabatier, "Social Movements and Regulatory Agencies," pp. 310–17.

perhaps to create a special oversight committee with a program supporter as chairperson. Whatever the means, however, finding a "fixer" is of paramount importance for effective implementation.

In short, even if the conditions for effective implementation are not met at the time of the basic policy decision, policy formulators and other program supporters can still take a number of steps to approximate the ideal over time.

29. Stacking the Deck: Bureaucratic Missions and Policy Design

Jonathan Bendor, Serge Taylor, and Roland Van Gaalen

The air force is dominated by bomber pilots. The corps of engineers is dominated by civil engineers. The navy is dominated by carrier admirals. These agencies tend to develop a sense of mission, an orientation toward a particular means as well as particular ends (Halperin 1974). Indeed, devotion to the means can overwhelm an agency's attachment to the ends: "To say there is not a deeply ingrained prejudice in favor of aircraft among flyers . . . would be a stupid statement for me to make. Of course there is" (General Thomas White, air force chief of staff, quoted in Futrell 1980, 253). This phenomenon, often called goal displacement (Merton 1957), has numerous causes: homogeneous professional training of an agency's leadership (Kanter 1979; Kaufman 1960; McGregor 1974), genuine conviction that the national interest is well served by carrying out the mission, and career motivation (promotions are easier to obtain if we continue to do what we know how to do). Political superiors may, however, construe an agency's job in

broader terms. The corps of engineers is supposed to protect citizens against flood disasters; building dams is only one method for doing that. From the perspective of the secretary of defense, the navy is supposed to strengthen national defense. Deploying aircraft carriers is only a means to that end, and if technological changes in, for example, surface-to-surface missiles render carriers obsolete, then the secretary may want to change the navy's force structure.

The ability of politicians to alter the repertoire of agencies is, however, constrained by their lack of technical expertise. The relative merits of strategic bombers versus ICBMs are better known to specialists in the department of defense than to politicians. Indeed, policy alternatives are often generated by experts in the first place (Polsby 1984). Politicians dominate agenda formation in the sense of determining the *problems* that have priority but specialists dominate the generation of *solutions* (Kingdon 1984; Light 1983). Frequently—by no means always—the specialists are bureaucrats.[1]

This informational asymmetry gives bureaus an opportunity; their mission orientation provides a motive. When asked to generate policy proposals for re-

SOURCE: "Stacking the Deck: Bureaucratic Mission and Policy Design" by Jonathan Bendor et al., *American Political Science Review,* Vol. 81, No. 3, September 1987. Reprinted by permission of the American Political Science Association and the authors.

view by their political superiors, bureaucrats are tempted to bias the search for alternatives so that their superiors wind up selecting the kind of program the agency wants to pursue: "Thus alleged 'options' are often advocacy in more sophisticated guise, one real choice and two or three straw men" (Destler 1974, 135).[2] Such manipulation is the stuff of Washington folklore. In general, biased advocacy is the norm: "The sensitivity of military groups to new program needs depends largely upon service doctrine and service interests. The Air Force was active in pushing strategic deterrence and the Army in innovating European defense since each program was closely related to existing service doctrine. All the services were hesitant in pushing continental defense and limited war, however, which were alien to existing service doctrine" (Huntington 1961, 288; see also Bergerson 1980, 64–65; Coulam 1977, 93–96). Such descriptions point up the influence of career bureaucrats, an emphasis often found in public administration and organization theory (Allison 1971, chap. 3; Pfefer 1981, 119–21; Simon, Smithburg, and Thompson 1950, 533–34).

An equally well established research tradition has emphasized how politicians try to reassert their control over the bureaucracy. (On the White House's efforts to direct the bureaucracy, see, among others, Aberbach and Rockman 1976, Arnold 1976, Hess 1976, Lynn 1981, March and Olsen 1983, Moe 1985, Nathan 1975, Salamon 1981, and Seidman 1970.) One type of control rests on the ability of political executives to review and possibly reject all of a subordinate's options. This is, after all, a superior's formal prerogative. Recognizing this, a bureaucrat may be deterred from proposing an idea that furthers the agency's objectives rather than the superior's. Of course, the threat of a veto must be credible. If a subordinate

believes that the superior would be better off accepting the subordinate's preferred alternative than suffering the delay following a rejection of all proposals, the subordinate will consider the threat of rejection a hollow one and rig the agenda anyway.

A political executive can strengthen his or her hand by having more than one subordinate generate options, concurrently or sequentially. Stimulating competition among subordinates was central to Franklin Roosevelt's administrative strategy (Schlesinger 1958, 534–35), and with good reason: threatening to turn down a subordinate is more credible if there are other options waiting in the wings. (For experimental evidence see Sutton, Shaked, and Binmore 1986.) Though simultaneous competition may be rare—an executive must incur the cost of diverting the attention of subordinates from other problems—the sequential strategy may be fairly common.

A second type of control is to reward the bureaucrat for devising options that are useful to the superior. If the politician can evaluate the political worth of an alternative, then even if he or she cannot observe how an agency generates the proposals the politician may be able to induce the agency to keep his or her interests in mind. Investigating such incentive schemes has been an active area of research in the economics of organization (Arrow 1985). The analysis, known as principal-agent theory, has a simple logic. A superior (the principal) knows that the subordinate (agent) enjoys an informational advantage. For example, the agent may possess technical expertise or the principal may be unable to monitor the agent's actions perfectly. The principal believes the agent may exploit these advantages for the agent's own purposes. Anticipating this, the principal precommits him- or herself to a reward scheme *before* the agent acts.

The payoffs to the agent are contingent on outcomes the principal can observe. A key task in this research program is to examine the conditions under which a superior can induce a subordinate to choose precisely as the superior would have, had the latter chosen directly.

The ideas underlying principal-agent models have diffused into political science (Moe 1984), perhaps encouraging some scholars to believe that the older concern with bureaucratic influence has been unwarranted. Though politicians may be "mere dilettantes" on technical issues, they are professionals on strategic affairs, and, as we have learned from Neustadt (1960) and others, inducing a subordinate to do as one would wish is a matter of strategy. Hence descriptions of bureaucrats rigging the choice sets of politicians and political appointees may be seriously incomplete, for they focus only on the last steps of the decision process, neglecting how search may be conditioned by incentives created by superiors.

These issues are central to our understanding of policy making. If bureaucrats bias the search for options, we should investigate their policy goals and how they try to attain them. Alternatively, if politicians anticipate these problems and control them, students of the policy process may be able to ignore the bureaucracy, at least insofar as policy generation is concerned. As indicated, scholars disagree which view is more correct. It seems likely that—under the right conditions—each has merit; the problem is to specify just what those conditions are. To help us figure this out, we develop several models of political control, investigating the effects of both a review process and of incentives. In the first section, we study how a mission-oriented bureaucrat designs alternatives when he knows that in the final review his superior will reject unsatisfactory proposals and consider competing proposals. In the second section, we develop a principal-agent model to analyze how a superior could, in addition to reviewing proposals, use the carrot of bigger budgets to induce the bureaucrat to carry out the search the superior would prefer. (To avoid confusion, we assume the superior is female, the subordinate, male, in all three models.) We initially simplify the analysis by assuming in the first section that the bureaucrat has only programmatic preferences and in the second section that he cares only about budgets. In the third section we consider a more general model in which the bureaucrat is interested in both missions and budgets; as in the second section, the superior uses both types of control strategies. The models' main features are summarized in Table 29.1.

To keep the focus on substantive issues, we present the model informally in the text. The Appendix presents the mathematical version.

THE BASIC FRAMEWORK

The three sections share a common structure. A political superior in the executive branch, such as the president, a department secretary, or other high appointee, instructs a subordinate, such as

Table 29.1   The Models' Main Features

Parameters	Model 1	Model 2	Model 3
Bureaucrat's goals	mission only	budget only	missions and budgets
Superior's method of control	final review	final review and budgetary incentives	final review and budgetary incentives

a bureau chief, to prepare several proposals addressing a problem that concerns the superior. The superior knows that there are two qualitatively different kinds of programs she wants to evaluate: type x (e.g., missiles) and type y (e.g., planes). Indifferent to the programs' technological and administrative characteristics, she cares only about the political benefits they would produce. Not knowing which one would better serve her goals, she instructs the bureau to draft two proposals, one of each type. The bureau has a fixed amount of effort to devote to this task. Effort may be a complex function of person-hours allocated to each design, weighted by the ability of the staff. Let e_x denote the effort the bureau allocates to designing the type x program and e_y the effort it spends designing the type-y program. This allocation of search effort cannot be observed by the boss.

We assume a simple search technology. Let $X(e_x)$ represent the political benefits that accrue to the boss for a given search allocation, e_x; similarly for $Y(e_y)$.[3] To fit the uncertain quality of planning, we assume that X and Y are random variables. Exactly what the *realized* benefits are, for any given search allocation, depends on a host of idiosyncratic factors that cannot be predicted with certainty. Consequently, the bureaucrat knows the a priori distribution of benefits but will only discover the worth of a specific proposal after he has finished planning.

We assume that thinking improves the quality of solutions: $X(e_x') \geq X(e_x)$

Figure 29.1
More Design Time Produces
Stochastically Better Proposals

$$e_{Y_1} < e_{Y_2} < e_{Y_3}$$

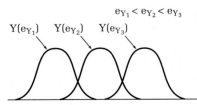

$Y(e_{Y_1})$ $Y(e_{Y_2})$ $Y(e_{Y_3})$

when $e_x' > e_x$, and similarly for Y. Graphically, this means that more design time shifts the distribution of possible proposals to the right (Figure 29.1). To follow standard terminology, $X(e_x')$ is *stochastically larger* than $X(e_x)$. To avoid pedantic repetition, we shall usually just say that one distribution is better than another.[4]

Once the bureau chief has prepared two proposals, he presents them to the superior. We assume that she knows the political benefits she will reap by implementing either proposal. If only one option is satisfactory, she chooses that one; if both are acceptable she picks the better of the two, denoted $\max(X, Y)$. In either case the decision process ends. If she finds neither acceptable, she turns them both down and invites other specialists—other agencies, her own staffers, outside think tanks, and individual policy entrepreneurs—to propose new alternatives.[5]

Let Z denote the amount of political benefits that would be generated by outside alternatives. Because these outside proposals are not the special province of the agency, we assume that their distribution is known by both the superior and the subordinate. In this second and final stage, the boss chooses the best of the three proposals, denoted $\max(X, Y, Z)$.

Thus in the basic model each decision maker must make a choice. Consider the superior's problem first. She must decide whether to accept the better of the bureau's two proposals in the first period or to wait, expecting that other policy specialists will generate something better. Her acceptance level a is a conditional rule of the form, "if $\max(X, Y)$ is above a, accept it; otherwise, defer the selection until the second period."[6] The level of the optimal acceptance or stopping rule a^* depends on the executive's utility function. We assume her utility is proportional to a proposal's political payoffs. In addition, she prefers sooner to later, discounting the value of future proposals by a parameter δ_s between zero and one.

To see how she would compute a^*, consider a particular value of max(X, Y) called m. If m is high, other proposals are unlikely to beat it. And if the executive is impatient (a low δ_s), the cost of waiting is great. In such circumstances, she would take m in the first round. If m is poor, the odds are good the outside competition will offer something better. And if she is patient, she does not incur significant delay costs. In such circumstances she would reject m and make her final decision later. In general she will reject m if and only if it is less than the discounted value of what she could get in the second round, $\delta_s E[\max(m, Z)]$ (see Figure 29.2). Thus, she sets a^* so that she is indifferent between taking $m = a^*$ now and taking the expected value of max(m, Z) later.

Consequently, the superior's optimal acceptance rule depends only on her knowledge of Z and on her utility function, but not at all on her beliefs about the distributions of X and Y or even on her knowledge of the realized value of the proposals. In game-theoretic terms, the superior has a best response to the bureau's choice that is not contingent on that choice: it is a dominant strategy for her to pick a^* in the above manner.[7] Thus, there is a fundamental difference between this control strategy of review and the control strategy of incentives introduced later. In the former, the superior will make her best move at every point in the process, rejecting a first period option only if she expects to improve upon it by waiting. In contrast, the incentive strategy presumes, in common with most principal-agent models, that the superior can *precommit* to a schedule of rewards before the subordinate makes his move. The second strategy requires precommitment: if the subordinate believed that his superior was not obligated to keep her promise once she inspected the agency's proposals, the incentives would lose their force.

The subordinate's problem is to pick a search strategy, e_y^*, that maximizes his expected utility, given his goals and the prevailing incentives. In the pure mission-oriented model we shall assume that he values the type-y program (planes) over type x (missiles), though either is preferred to letting an outsider win, so $u_y > u_x > u_z$.[8] For simplicity and with no loss of generality, we set u_z equal to zero. To ensure the two decision makers have conflicting interests we assume that X is better for the superior: if the bureaucrat devotes equal effort to each, then $p(X > b) \geq p(Y > b)$ for every benefit level b.

The bureaucrat prefers having a proposal accepted in the first period to having the same proposal accepted later. Thus $u_{y2} = \delta_b u_{y1}$, where the numerical subscripts denote the period and where δ_b, the bureaucrat's discount factor, is between zero and one. Similarly $u_{x2} = \delta_b u_{x1}$.

The tensions facing a mission-oriented bureaucrat are now evident. The agency would like to manipulate the superior's agenda so that she will accept a type-y proposal in the first round. However, the bureaucrat knows that x is a better kind of program for the boss, so to increase the odds of beating out the competition he may be forced to spend time designing xs.

Figure 29.2
The Expected Value of the "Good Tail" of Z

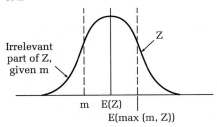

Irrelevant part of Z, given m

m $E(Z)$

$E(\max(m, Z))$

In the pure budgetary model the bureaucrat's expected utility depends only on the appropriation he will receive for the accepted program. His search strategy is therefore driven by the budget policy, which the superior designs in advance. The budget policies are described below. In the complex model, the bureaucrat still prefers planes to missiles to losing to an outsider and is also interested in funding. His optimal search strategy therefore must trade off these two goals.

Most principal-agent models focus on either of two kinds of informational asymmetry: the unobserved actions of subordinates (moral hazard) or their unobserved personal characteristics (adverse selection). Our work emphasizes moral hazard. Thus, in all three models, we allow the superior to know the bureaucrat's preferences; similarly, he knows her acceptance level.

MODEL 1: THE MISSION-ORIENTED BUREAUCRAT

In this section we investigate how a purely mission-oriented bureaucrat exploits his expertise in order to win approval of his pet program. First we examine absolute levels of stacking the deck, for example, when search will be extremely rigged. Next we use comparative statics to examine changes in search.

Clearly the bureau chief can control the process if his superior's acceptance level is low. There are two main reasons why the superior would be so undemanding. In each case the consequence is a rigged agenda.

PROPERTY 1.1. *If the outside competition is sufficiently poor, or the executive sufficiently impatient, the bureau stacks the deck completely by spending all its time designing the y alternative.*

Both conditions make intuitive sense. For the boss, the benefit of further search is the possibility of discovering a superior proposal; the cost, the cost of delay.[9] If the benefit is too low, or the cost too great, she will stop the process in the first period by accepting the bureau's better alternative. And if the bureau chief is sure he can satisfy his superior in the first round, he prefers to do so with a proposal consistent with his mission orientation.[10]

Now we move to the opposite extreme: a mission-oriented bureau that does exactly what its superior wants— more precisely, what the superior *would* want were she completely informed about the quality of the two types of programs. Let us call the search that a completely informed superior would carry out *unbiased* search. (In principal-agent models, the generic term for the choice of a fully informed superior is the "first-best" solution.)

PROPERTY 1.2. *A combination of strong outside competition and a patient superior can induce a mission-oriented bureaucrat to carry out unbiased search.*

In this situation the outside proposals are so promising that the agency has a chance of getting a proposal accepted only if it spends all its time on the superior type of program, x. Spending time on y is futile. In such circumstances the executive's first-best search would be to ignore y completely, which is just what the agency is driven to do.[11]

What counts here are the *relative* levels of the outside options, the acceptance threshold, and Y. If the bureaucrat knows that no matter how much time he spends working out the bugs of his mission program it still would be politically dreadful for his superior, then his only chance of getting a proposal accepted is to concentrate on x, even if the outside alternatives are mediocre.

Thus, a mission-oriented bureau tightly constrained by outside forces may do just what a fully informed boss would want. In these circumstances the control strategy of review works as well as could be desired. But Property 1.2 described sufficient conditions for unbiased search, not necessary ones. Can internal controls substitute for external ones? If the bureaucrat is neutral, that is, indifferent as between x and y, and has the same time preference as his superior, then he is trying to maximize the (time-weighted) probability of receiving her approval. Surely this orientation must make him do what she wants? Not necessarily.

PROPERTY 1.3. *Mission neutrality and identical time preferences do not guarantee unbiased search.*

Neutrality is insufficient: whereas the superior likes high values of max(X, Y), the bureau chief is indifferent between a proposal that just squeaks by and one that far exceeds the acceptance level.

Property 1.2 implied that search is not always biased toward the bureau's pet program. One might think that at least search will never be skewed toward the other type. This too is wrong.

PROPERTY 1.4. *Despite the bureaucrat's preference for the y program, a purely mission-oriented bureau may spend more time designing the x alternative than a fully informed superior would want.*

Consider this example. The superior is patient and will nearly always defer the final program choice until the second period. This worries the bureau chief who is impatient and craves a first-round decision. In the slim hopes of discovering an outstanding proposal that will induce his superior to look no further, he throws all his organizational resources into investigating the more promising type, x. The patient superior, however, considers a second-round decision nearly as good as a first-round selection. Therefore, unbiased search would approximately maximize the average value of the best of the three proposals. If there were diminishing returns to search, it would be suboptimal to devote all effort to x. The bureau, however, does precisely that.

Now we investigate how agenda manipulation shifts in response to changes in the model's parameters, first examining changes in the bureaucrat's preferences and subsequently investigating changes in the strength of the outside competition. To simplify the presentation we explain the results with the aid of figures; derivations are in Section 12 of the Appendix.

Changes in the Bureaucrat's Preferences

Over time, the composition of a bureau's dominant coalition can change (Kanter 1979, 102–8), in turn altering its leader's preferences for different programs. How will a purely mission-oriented chief shift his search pattern as his programmatic preferences change?

Consider an equilibrium before the parametric change. The benefit of paying more attention to y is an increased chance that it will be accepted multiplied by the utility of y. The cost of doing this is a reduced chance that x will be accepted multiplied by its utility. These expected marginal gains and losses were equal at the old optimal e_y^*. If the bureau comes to value y more, the marginal benefits of devoting more effort to y rise while the marginal costs are unchanged. Hence the bureau increases its focus on y. Symmetrically, if the bureau values x more, the marginal costs of e_y^* increase while the marginal benefits remain unchanged, so the agency attends less to y.

This result is intuitive. The bureau chief's liking for y over x represents conflict of interest between the superior and subordinate. As this bias falls, conflict diminishes, and search should be less skewed toward the type of program that is inferior from the boss' point of view.[12]

What happens if losing to the outsider becomes less unpleasant, that is, u_z rises? Because this means that the bureaucrat cares less intensely whether the executive chooses x or z, the implicit costs of devoting effort to its mission have fallen. Hence search is skewed more toward his preferred program.

The Effect of Improved Competition

We know from Properties 1.1 and 1.2 that the quality of outside proposals influences the bureau's strategy. In policy formation in the United States, the trend seems to be toward improved competition. Many observers have noted a growth of think tanks and policy entrepreneurs in Washington. This growth probably affects policy: the Reagan administration is reputed to listen to ideas from institutions like the Heritage Foundation.

How will a purely mission-oriented bureau respond if the quality of these competing proposals becomes stochastically better? Most beliefs about the restraining role of competition (e.g., a monopolist's ability to extract consumer surplus for itself) imply that the subordinate would stack the deck less as its

competition improves. Further, in this model, improved competition raises the executive's acceptance level, making her more demanding. Since the bureaucrat is less likely to beat his rivals and will be evaluated more stringently, won't he spend more time on the type of program that he knows is superior for the boss?

Not necessarily, as the following pair of examples shows. In the first example the bureaucrat makes the expected move of paying less attention to y; in the second he pays more attention. In both cases we simplify matters by assuming that the bureau has no chance of beating the outside competition in the second round, which allows us to focus only on the first period. (Alternatively one could assume that the bureaucrat discounts the future completely.) Improved competition still matters, however, because it raises the acceptance level in the first period.

The first example is shown in Figure 29.3. In the old status quo, the boss's acceptance criterion is moderately demanding. As revealed by the superiority of distribution Y, which occurs only when $e_y > e_x$, the bureau spends more time preparing y than x. The bureau does devote some time to x, possibly due to diminishing marginal returns to search.

The second picture in Figure 29.3 depicts the new status quo, in which greatly improved competition has induced the executive to jack up her acceptance threshold by a lot. Now the agency has

Figure 29.3
Bureaucrat Switches to x

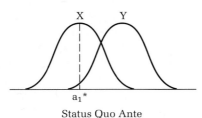

| X | Y | | Y (when $e_Y = 1.0$) | X (when $e_X = 1.0$) |

$a_1{}^*$ $a_2{}^*$

Status Quo Ante   New Situation

no choice: to have any chance of getting a proposal accepted it must spend all its time on x, the superior type. As expected, the bureaucrat becomes more docile in response to improved competition and tougher standards.

However, the next example of Figure 29.4 shows that just the opposite can happen. The status quo ante is the same as the previous example's. Then competition improves and the acceptance level increases, though less dramatically than before. Once again, to have any chance of designing an acceptable alternative, the agency must specialize. But unlike the previous example, y has a chance of being satisfactory, though of course the bureau is more likely to generate an acceptable proposal if it specializes in x. Which path the bureau chief chooses depends on how much he prefers y over x versus the relative chances of getting either one approved. If $u_y \times p(Y \geq a^*) > u_x \times p(X \geq a^*)$, given full specialization in each case, the bureau will focus more on y in response to improved competition.

This example is not bizarre; it is just a circumstance in which the bureaucrat's decision variable has increasing marginal utility and decreasing total utility. Clearly, if the bureau's rivals improve their proposals, the bureau chief's expected utility falls. The world has become a tougher place for the agency: it is less likely to win in either round. But because the administrator can do nothing about this, he focuses on the *relative* values of alternatives. And despite the fall of e_y's absolute value, its relative value can increase—as it did in the second example.[13]

How does the superior fare in the new environment? There are two answers here. The partial equilibrium answer, based on a fixed search strategy, is that she is unambiguously better off. If the second round is needed, she will get $\max(X, Y, Z)$, which can only get better if Z improves. Therefore, in the first period, she can afford to forego comparatively mediocre options that she would previously have approved. Hence, if the bureau does not adjust its search, improved competition must make the superior better off.

The complete equilibrium answer, however, is that the boss is *not* invariably better off. An example is presented in Figure 29.5. For simplicity, Z is a constant, z. The superior is patient, with an acceptance level just below z. For simplicity, we assume that both X and Y have only three values: for a given allocation of effort, the bureau could generate a poor, a mediocre, or a good proposal of each type of program.

In the old equilibrium (Figure 29.5a) the bureau spends more time thinking about y, resulting in a small chance of a spectacularly good plan, y_3. After z improves (Figure 29.5b) the bureaucrat realizes he can no longer afford to devote so much effort to y. Figure 29.5c shows the new equilibrium, after the bureau has adjusted its search by spending more time on x, thereby driving x_3 past the new z. The sharp decline of y_3 indicates that there are increasing returns to search from the superior's point of view. Because it is easy to ensure that the fall of y_3 more than offsets the increases of z and x_2, in this case improved competition ultimately hurts *both* the superior and the subordinate.

Of course it is possible that improved competition in the generation of policy alternatives typically en-

Figure 29.4
Bureaucrat Switches to y

Y (when $e_Y = 1.0$)   X (when $e_X = 1.0$)

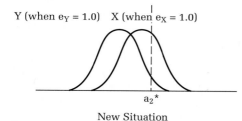

$a_2{}^*$

New Situation

(A) Old equilibrium

(B) New situation, old e_Y^* (superior is better off)

(C) New equilibrium (superior is worse off)

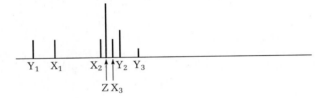

a* is not drawn (a* = Z − e)

Figure 29.5
Partial Equilibrium versus
Full Equilibrium Analysis

hances the well being of political superiors. If this is so, we suspect that it is because they take steps to ensure that their subordinates' interests are linked with their own. We examine such control strategies next.

MODEL 2: THE BUDGET-ORIENTED BUREAUCRAT

We now turn to the other end of the continuum to analyze the behavior of a bureau chief interested only in increasing his agency's appropriations. The basic structure remains the same: the bureaucrat generates proposals; the political executive makes the final choice.

Now, however, each actor enjoys a larger repertoire of choices. We shall examine in turn three new decision variables of the bureau chief. In addition to allocating effort, he can now (1) make his proposals more or less innovative, (2) reorganize his agency's planning to decrease or increase the correlation between his two proposals, and (3) draw on ideas floating in the "policy primeval soup" (in Kingdon's phrase) to alter correlation between his and outsiders' plans. (When examining Variables 1 and 3, we will suppress the distinction between the agency's two types of proposals, focusing directly on the derived distribution of max(X, Y).) The superior can design and precommit to incentive schemes. We consider three policies. The first is the simplest: if she accepts one of the agency's options, the bureau will receive a budget to administer that program. The funding grows in proportion to the program's political benefits. To maintain tractability we assume that the bureau chief is risk-neutral in the budget.

This incentive scheme is simple enough to be empirically plausible: all the superior needs to know is that the bureau chief prefers more funds to less. Moreover, because precommitting to an appropriation is a public matter, it is easier than precommitting to an acceptance level.

What behavior will this incentive scheme induce? Because here the bureau chief is interested only in funding and because he knows that his reward will increase in the quality of his better alternative, if the superior selects it, one might think that he will conduct unbiased search. However, consider the following properties.

PROPERTY 2.1. *The winner-take-all incentive policy does not guarantee that a budget-oriented bureaucrat will carry out unbiased search.*

Problems arise because this winner-take-all scheme makes the bureaucrat ignore the value of outside alternatives to his superior. Consequently he places a lower value on innovative searches that may lose to outsiders, even if such strategies—when they succeed—generate excellent proposals. Thus this incentive policy creates the following conflict:

PROPERTY 2.2. *The political executive always prefers riskier search to more cautious search, if the associated distributions have the same mean. Under the winner-take-all scheme, however, the bureaucrat does not always prefer riskier search.*

Note that these preferences do not derive from attitudes toward risk: both actors are risk-neutral. It is the logic of the relationship that drives them to have different views toward innovation. The superior knows that if the agency's proposals are poor, she can defer her decision in the hope that an outside alternative will be superior. Thus, she is protected from downside risk. And, of course, she likes the benign uncertainty of outstanding alternatives. Therefore she always wants the agency to try more innovative policy design (Kohn and Shavell 1974). The bureaucrat, however, is not always protected from downside risk. Indeed, risky search may increase the chance of losing to outside competitors (Figure 29.6). In general, if prospects look very good for the agency, the bureaucrat will prefer more cautious search; if matters are desperate—little chance of winning in either round—he will prefer bolder

Figure 29.6
Cautious versus Innovative Search

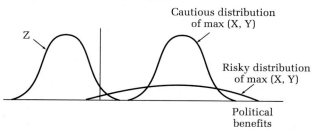

Cautious distribution
of max (X, Y)

Z

Risky distribution
of max (X, Y)

Political
benefits

search. Thus the logic of the situation can induce bureaucratic caution without assuming that administrators are personally averse to risk.

Implementation Budget Scheme

An intelligent superior might realize that the winner-take-all scheme is undesirable because it drives a wedge between her interests and her subordinate's. Alternatively it may be infeasible if the only rivals to the agency are staffers or think-tank analysts who lack the organizational resources for implementation. For either reason, we now consider a second incentive strategy: the executive decides in advance that the agency will administer whichever option she deems best, as well as the associated budget.[14] Thus, even if she picks an outside proposal the agency will implement it.

This scheme does diminish some of the conflicts created by the winner-take-all system: because the bureaucrat is interested only in budgets and will be funded to implement outsiders' proposals, he will not in his own search shy away from innovative ideas just because they run some risk of losing to an outside alternative. Nevertheless, it is not a panacea.

PROPERTY 2.3. *The implementation budget scheme does not ensure that a budget-oriented bureaucrat will carry out unbiased search.*

The remaining problem is conflicting time preferences. It is often asserted that career bureaucrats are more patient than political executives (e.g., Heclo 1977, 143). The latter typically have short stays in Washington and both sides know it. Therefore, in our model, the patient bureaucrat might prefer a second-period choice of a wonderful outside alternative—which the bureau, blessed with a correspondingly large budget, would implement—to a first-period choice of its own programs (recall that the bureaucrat has no mission preferences here).

PROPERTY 2.4. *The superior always prefers a first-period search yielding a stochastically better distribution of alternatives to one yielding an inferior distribution. The bureaucrat has the same preferences—if he is less patient than his superior. If he is more patient, he will under certain conditions prefer search that generates inferior distributions.*

The superior's preference comes as no surprise. Because the bureaucrat's reward depends on the quality of the accepted alternative, one might think that he too would always prefer superior search. So he does, if he is more anxious than his superior to reach an early resolution. But if he is more patient he may sabotage the first period, hoping to receive much more funding later. The implementation budget scheme makes the bureaucrat internalize the value of outside alternatives; indeed, now he may overvalue them (see Appendix, sec. 10).

Thus far the superior's control methods have been predicated on a genuine diversity among policy specialists: the outside proposals have been assumed independent of the agency's, and (given a search allocation) the agency's proposals have been independent of each other. Because in the real world policy ideas diffuse, experts might think in similar ways. The superior may want genuine pluralism maintained; would the bureaucrat also like this? To examine their possibly conflicting preferences for diversity, we consider two kinds of cognitive interdependence: the first concerns the relation between the agency's proposals; the second, the relation between the agency's plans and everyone else's. We take up each in turn. When considering the first type we continue to assume that the outside alternatives are independent of the bureau's.

An agency can organize its planning in several different ways. One office could be charged with the task, or each program could be the responsibility of separate offices. If there are separate units, they could communicate with varying intensity. The more "tightly coupled" the offices, the more correlated (positively interdependent) the alternatives are likely to be. (For a precise definition of *positively interdependent distributions,* see sec. 11 of the Appendix.) Hence, the organization of proposal generation can be a strategic choice: given a fixed allocation of effort, the agency can decide to organize its planning in either a tightly or a loosely coupled way. These choices matter. To focus only on the effects of interdependence, we assume that the *un*conditional distributions of the two plans are unaffected by how tightly coupled they are.

PROPERTY 2.5. *The superior would always prefer the agency to organize its search to reduce positive interdependence between its alternatives. A less patient bureaucrat has the same preferences. However, a more patient subordinate will under certain conditions prefer more correlated search.*

The intuition behind the superior's preference is straightforward. Tightly coupled planning is more likely to produce two good proposals; it is also more likely to generate two bad ones. Because the superior needs only one good option, the disadvantage of two poor alternatives outweighs the advantage of two good ones. Thus she prefers pluralistic policy design. Indeed, a more pluralistic process yields a superior distribution of $\max(X, Y)$ (Bendor 1985, 47; Bhattacharya and Mookherjee 1986), so even a risk-averse superior prefers loosely coupled search.

This superiority of low correlation implies that Property 2.4. obtains. Thus the bureaucrat, whose budgetary reward is contingent on the outcome, will also generally prefer loosely coupled search, unless he wants to sabotage the first round in order to wait for an outside option.

The second dimension of interdependence concerns the relation between the agency's search and the outsiders'. Typically, policy arenas form communities of common attention. Ideas for new programs diffuse in these networks (Heclo 1978; Kingdon 1984; Polsby 1984). When an agency designs policy proposals, it can draw in varying degrees on this fund of public knowledge. Thus, qualitatively different search strategies produce plans correlated in varying degrees with proposals from outside the agency. Would the superior prefer high or low correlation over time?

One might think that an extension of Property 2.5 would apply immediately: search that is loosely coupled over time is always better than more tightly coupled search. Not so, however: when time is introduced the problem becomes more complex.

PROPERTY 2.6. (a) *In sequential search the superior does* not *always prefer loosely coupled design strategies and* (b) *if the superior's stopping problem is classical in that her optimal strategy in the first period is to reject poor alternatives and to accept good ones, then she prefers less correlated search. However, even in this setting there can be conflict: the bureaucrat will under certain conditions prefer more interdependent search.*

The superior might prefer high correlation in the sequential setting—Result (a)—when good options are likely to be followed by much better ones. Consider the following simple example. In the first round, $\max(X, Y)$ will be either poor (m_1) or good (m_2). The two outside alternatives, z_1 and z_2, are strongly correlated with m_1 and m_2 respectively. Assuming that policy specialists learn from each other, the second-round proposals generally improve upon the earlier ones: z_1 is a bit better than m_1, and z_2 is much superior to m_2. Because z_1 is but a small improvement over m_1, the superior will accept m_1 if she discounts the future moderately. However, she will reject m_2 in the hopes of doing much better later. Given this pattern of accepting poor first-period proposals and rejecting good ones, if the agency could figure out a way to plan so that its alternatives were even more positively correlated with the later ones, the superior would prefer that the agency do so. (For example, if the alternatives were perfectly correlated, rejecting m_2 would be riskless since it would always be followed by the wonderful z_2.)

This example requires the counterintuitive acceptance strategy of accepting poor options and rejecting good ones. Yet, though it is counterintuitive, such a strategy can be an optimal stopping rule because, in a search context, alternatives have information value as well as intrinsic value. Poor alternatives are accepted not because they are intrinsically useful but because their appearance augurs ill. Conversely, good alternatives are rejected because they predict an even brighter future.

When the stopping rule is more conventional, loosely coupled search is again desirable—Result (b). Because the superior will initially spurn inferior options, she does not want the second set of proposals closely related to the first set. And because she accepts good alternatives in the first round, the value of high correlation—fine early options precede fine later ones—is irrelevant (see sec. 11 of the Appendix).

The bureaucrat's tastes, however, do not always run to less correlated search even in the classical setting. If, for example, he is sufficiently impatient, he will prefer any first-round proposal to any second-round one. Therefore he would want his superior to have an extremely low acceptance level. But more loosely coupled search can induce the superior to raise her standard, making the bureaucrat worse off.[15]

Because the above problems stem from conflicting time preferences, a sophisticated political superior would take these into account while designing incentives. One cure is simple. If her subordinate is more patient, she should scale down the budgetary payoff in the second period; if less patient, she should increase it. (Equivalently, she could increase the first-period payoff for a patient bureaucrat and decrease it for an impatient one.) Typically, one would expect a political executive to know that her subordinate is more patient; how much so would be uncertain. To simplify matters, we make the less plausible assumption that she knows δ_b precisely. Then finally we arrive at a scheme that induces unbiased search.

PROPERTY 2.7. *If the superior uses an implementation budget scheme and rescales the second-period budget by δ_s/δ_b, a budget-oriented bureaucrat will conduct unbiased search.*

Under this scheme, the bureaucrat's valuation of a second-period budget is proportional to δ_s/δ_b multiplied by his own discount of δ_b, so it is proportional to the superior's discount of δ_s. Therefore, the bureaucrat's induced utility function is now qualitatively the same as the superior's in both periods, eliminating all the conflicts over search strategies described in Properties 2.2 and 2.4–2.6. We should remember that the superior has induced this without knowing anything about the technical details of the search process, what the returns to policy analysis and design are, and so forth. Thus, bureaucrats' greater technical expertise may be countered by incentive systems that tie the career officials' goals to the fulfillment of politicians' objectives.

But the conditions guaranteeing unbiased search are restrictive. Most importantly, we have assumed in this section that the bureau chief is interested only in appropriations; he cares not a jot about the type of program he implements.

MODEL 3: BUDGETS AND MISSIONS

The most important case empirically is one in which bureaucrats are interested in both budgets and missions. We now assume that utility = k_1(program) + k_2(budget), where k_1 and k_2 are positive constants symbolizing relative intensity for programs and budgets respectively. (The earlier models are special cases in which either k_1 or k_2 is zero.) The problem is otherwise the same.[16]

Can the superior control this more complex subordinate? She can since she knows his programmatic preferences.

PROPERTY 3.1. *The following implementation budget scheme ensures that the bureaucrat will carry out unbiased search: (a) if the superior accepts a proposal in the first period, she appropriates a budget that increases linearly in the value of the accepted alternative; if she chooses x, she gives the agency an additional fixed amount of c_1, which gives the bureaucrat a utility of $k_1/k_2(u_y - u_x)$; (b) if the superior makes her decision in the second period, she again gives the agency a budget composed of a linear term plus a constant; the linear part is rescaled by δ_s/δ_b. If she chooses x, she adds a constant, c_2, which equals $\delta_b c_1$. If she accepts z, she adds a constant of c_3, which gives the bureaucrat a utility of $\delta_b k_1/k_2(u_y - u_z)$.*

These incentives neutralize the bureau chief's mission orientation. Because he is indifferent between, say, implementing y in the first period and implementing x plus getting the extra funding of c_1, only the variable part of the budget matters. And because that increases in the realized political benefits to the superior, the decision makers' interests are bound together.[17]

Thus, despite her ignorance of how alternatives are generated, the political superior can get exactly what she wants—if she knows exactly what the bureaucrat wants. Note that the incentive scheme is only moderately complicated; the hard part is obtaining accurate information about the bureaucrat's preferences. (The limitations of assuming perfect information are examined in the concluding section.)

However, although the political executive can induce unbiased search, because she does not know the search functions, it is unlikely that the above incentive scheme is *efficient*: other schemes might make both decision makers better off, once one factors budget costs into the superior's utility function. For example, suppose c_1—the cost of inducing the bureaucrat to treat x and y evenhandedly—is large and its expected benefit—the improvement in the average value of max(X, Y)—is small, say δ. For simplicity, assume that without the incentive of c_1, the bureaucrat will spend all his time on y and that his superior will choose y in the first period with certainty; with the compensation of c_1 he will devote all his attention to x, guaranteeing that it will be selected. In this circumstance, the incentive scheme of Property 3.1 is Pareto inefficient. The superior would be better off foregoing the ε improvement of unbiased search, saving the large sum of c_1; the subordinate is nearly indifferent as to having y approved versus the combination of having x approved and receiving the lump-sum appropriation of c_1 plus the tiny budget increase proportional to ε. Therefore if she gave him a small fraction of c_1 unconditionally, they would both be better off than under the incentive scheme that induces unbiased search.

Of course, in our model, the superior does not know the requisite facts about search, and though the administrator does have this information and therefore could point out when the incentive scheme is inefficient, the former cannot trust the latter not to exploit his greater expertise. Thus inefficient arrangements can arise here from a combination of asymmetric information and the subordinate's inability to commit to the mutually beneficial course of action of revealing his information.

Let us assume, therefore, that the scheme of Property 3.1 is in place. We can now readdress the comparative-static issues of the first model. Consider personnel matters. Just as politicians vary in their commitment to policies versus their drive to win elections, so do career bureaucrats vary in their dedication to programs versus their appreciation of bigger budgets. This variation would matter to political executives if they were concerned about the cost of implementing programs.

PROPERTY 3.2. *Assume that for a fixed level of benefits, the superior preferred smaller to larger budgets. Then, given the above budget policy,* (a) *the superior always prefers a less biased bureaucrat to a more biased one; and* (b) *the superior always prefers a bureaucrat more oriented toward budgets than one less oriented.*

The cost of neutralizing a mission orientation is less, the smaller the difference between u_y and u_x; hence, Result (a). Similarly, the more appropriations matter compared to programs (smaller ratios of k_1/k_2), the more cheaply neutrality is bought; hence Result (b).[18]

Thus, given this incentive structure, personnel policy has an important monotonicity property: the more the bureau chief approaches the pure, budget-oriented subordinate, the better off his superior is. This may parallel the electoral control of politicians. It is sometimes argued that politicians oriented toward winning would tend to drive out rivals oriented toward policy, particularly in competitive districts (Mayhew 1974, 13–15; Wittman 1983, 148–50). Similarly, one might expect budget-oriented bureaucrats to outlast more programmatically driven colleagues because the selection environment favors the former.

Now consider shifts in the policy arena. Recall that in the pure-mission model, the superior's prospects could decline if the outside proposals improved, a perverse consequence of the agency's response to tougher competition. This cannot happen when the appropriate incentives are in place.

PROPERTY 3.3. *Assuming the described budget policy, the superior's expected utility* always *rises if the outside alternatives become stochastically better.*

Indeed, almost all the parametric changes that had indeterminate effects on the superior's welfare in the pure-mission model now have, given the budget policy of Property 3.1, determinate and intuitive effects.[19] Pursuing its own interests, the mission-oriented agency's response to improved competition could wipe out the gains to the executive. However, once the agency's interests have been bound to those of the politician, it will not alter its search in a way that harms its superior. Accordingly, as a mental shortcut, one can simply consider how parametric changes affect the superior. Thus the right incentives make the bureaucracy irrelevant in an important sense: one need not study it if one is interested in how political leaders—

their careers, electoral prospects, and so forth—are affected by exogenous changes in policy arenas.[20] Further, because political benefits accruing to political executives are usually related to benefits accruing to various constituencies, if one is interested in macro issues—relations between voters, interest groups, and politicians and how these shift as policy ideas change—then, again, one can ignore the bureaucracy.[21]

CONCLUSIONS

These models have strikingly different implications concerning the political control of bureaucracy. In Model 1—the pure mission-oriented case—a superior using only the (credible) threat of rejecting a bureaucrat's proposals is sometimes unable to prevent her agenda from being completely rigged, and only under the most fortuitous circumstances will the subordinate carry out unbiased search. In Models 2 and 3, adding the appropriate budgetary incentive schemes induces the bureaucrat to plan just as a completely informed political executive would. Perhaps more importantly, when these incentives are in place, changes in the larger environment (such as the quality of options in the "policy primeval soup") affect the superior in the expected way, whereas in Model 1 such changes can, via the agency's mediating influence, have perverse effects. Thus Model 1 directs our attention to bureaucracy's role in policy formation; Model 3 implies we can ignore it.

Ignoring the inner workings of bureaucracies would economize on the information-processing resources of the discipline. Most descriptions of agencies' roles in policy generation and implementation are richly detailed. Theory is hard pressed to absorb such complexity; it is easier to assume that policy proposals need not be designed and that the beliefs and preferences of career bureaucrats can be set aside.

Of course, starting with simple theories is a sensible intellectual strategy. And Model 3 suggests that when the appropriate incentives are in place, a unitary-actor interpretation of the executive branch may be a reasonable approximation of "its" behavior. But a close examination of this principal-agent model suggests that caution is in order.

First, though the final reward structure ensures unbiased search, the bureaucrat's programmatic preferences still matter, for they affect the cost of the incentive scheme. Therefore, the classic issue of the compatibility of politicians' and bureaucrats' interests remains alive.

Second, the incentive scheme reflects a partial optimization. A complete optimization would require that the superior balance the benefits of improved search against the cost of inducing the improvement. Executives would find this more global calculation much more difficult, for it requires knowing or having beliefs about the probabilistic returns to search, and then trading off expected marginal gains of inducing bureaucrats to move toward unbiased search versus the marginal costs. Control strategies and outcomes would then be shaped by what politicians believed was feasible, by how they weighted the advice of specialists inside and outside government, and in general by the politics of belief formation. Once again, experts' policy preferences may matter.

Third, inducing unbiased search, even without maximizing net benefits, requires knowing the subordinate's goals exactly. This is implausible. Though agencies' mission orientations are part of Washington folklore, a political appointee will not know precisely how much a bureau chief prefers one program to another. Therefore an incentive scheme will never neutralize an agency's search exactly; there will be undercompensations and overcompensations.

To be sure, conclusions built on assumptions of perfect information may be robust, that is, introducing a "small" amount of uncertainty may lead only to "small" changes in results. For example, it has been shown recently that the control of politicians by voters in the classical spatial model is robust in this sense (Calvert 1985b); perhaps this will also hold true for the control of bureaucrats by politicians. Most importantly, one would like to know about two kinds of robustness. First, do small misperceptions of the subordinate's goals produce small errors in the incentive scheme, in turn diminishing the superior's expected benefits by just a bit?[22] Second, if the incentive scheme is "nearly" optimal, do the comparative-static results of Model 3—for instance that the superior prefers bureaucrats more oriented to budgets to those with more programmatic concerns (Property 3.2)—still hold up? Both questions are for future research to settle; clearly affirmative answers would give us more confidence in principal-agent models.

Fourth, the incentive scheme becomes more complex as the principal and agent differ on more dimensions. The scheme for the purely budget-oriented bureaucrat was simpler and required less information than the one designed for the administrator who cared about programs as well. In the real world, politicians and agency officials will differ by still more dimensions (Aberbach, Putnam, and Rockman 1981). Of course, politicians could deploy rough-and-ready reward schemes—indeed, we think these more common than refined ones. But as we saw with the first policy, the simple scheme of Property 2.1, rough-and-ready rewards are not likely to ensure the best results. In this domain it seems that simple control strategies are suboptimal, possibly significantly so.[23]

The basic idea of principal-agent models is that superiors, anticipating that subordinates might exploit informational asymmetries for their own purposes, establish controls with this in mind. This is a valuable corrective to an overemphasis on bureaucratic influence. But we are struck by how demanding the prerequisites for full control are. Indeed, we suspect that the modern tools of principal-agent analysis and search theory will demonstrate that rational superiors would not strive for complete control: even if feasible, it would be too expensive. Because of these limits, the older literature on bureaucratic influence still has much to teach us.

APPENDIX

This presentation of the model does not parallel the text's sequence. Note too that only mathematical properties not obviously established in the text are derived here.

1. The bureaucrat's fixed search budget (normalized to unity) is spent on generating proposals of two types, x and y: $e_x + e_y = 1$. The political benefits of these proposals to the superior are independent random variables X and Y, whose probability distributions are stochastically increasing in e_x and e_y, respectively. We assume that for equal effort levels e_x and e_y, X is stochastically larger than Y.

Whereas X and Y are available in both periods, the type-z proposal is generated by outside competition in the second period. Its political benefits are given by the random variable Z, which may or may not be independent of X and Y.

2. The superior can influence the bureaucrat's activities by providing him with a budget and manipulating this as an incentive scheme that may depend on which program (type x, y, or z) will be realized, the corresponding level of political benefits $(X, Y, \text{ or } Z)$, and the period (1 or 2) when the final choice is made by the superior. This budget function is known to the bureaucrat.

One would expect the budget function to be designed to counterbalance the bureaucrat's mission bias and to reflect the superior's utility function (see Properties 2.7 and 3.1). In that case, the bureaucrat would have an incentive to act more in accord with the superior's wishes. Under a *winner-take-all* incentive policy, the bureau receives no budget if an outside proposal of type z is accepted, whereas under an *implementation budget* scheme, the bureau receives an appropriation no matter which proposal is accepted.

3.   The bureaucrat is assumed to be an expected-utility maximizer. The only variables under his control are e_x and e_y, both nonnegative and summing to one. His utility function is of the form u(program, budget, period), where (1) program = x, y, or z (depending on which proposal is accepted by the superior), and

$$u(y, \cdot, \cdot) \geqslant u(x, \cdot, \cdot) \geqslant u(z, \cdot, \cdot)$$

i.e., the bureaucrat prefers y to x, and x to z, other things equal; (2) $u_2 > 0$, i.e., the bureaucrat prefers higher budgets, other things equal; and (3) period = 1 or 2 (depending on when the final choice is made by the superior), and $u(\cdot, \cdot, 1) > u(\cdot, \cdot, 2)$, i.e., the bureaucrat prefers period 1 to period 2, other things equal.

4.   In addition to determining the budget scheme, it is the superior's prerogative to decide which program will be realized, and when. The superior is also an expected-utility maximizer, and her utility function is of the form v(benefits, period) where (1) $v_1 > 0$, i.e., the superior prefers higher levels of political benefits (X, Y, or Z), other things equal; and (2) period = 1 or 2, and $v(\cdot, 1) > v(\cdot, 2)$, i.e., the superior prefers period 1 to period 2, other things equal. For convenience we have assumed that the budget is not an argument of her utility function.

5.   We impose the following important restrictions: (1) the superior rejects a first-period proposal only if she expects to improve on it by waiting; thus, she lacks the power to manipulate the bureaucrat by threatening decisions that would be to her own disadvantage to carry out; and (2) the bureaucrat in turn maximizes his expected utility without trying to influence the superior's acceptance rule or incentive scheme by using his control over e_x and e_y as a weapon.

6.   It is worth noting that the assumptions made so far do *not* guarantee that the superior's optimal strategy is "classical," i.e., to accept the better of X and Y in the first period if $\max(X, Y)$ is sufficiently large and otherwise postpone the decision to the second period and accept the best of X, Y, and Z. This *will* be the case, however, if we assume that (1) Z is independent of X and Y; and (2) v(benefits, 2) = δ_s v(benefits, 1) $\geqslant 0$ for some implicit discount rate $\delta_s \, \varepsilon \, [0, 1]$. Under those assumptions, the superior will accept the better realized value of X and Y, say m, in the first period if and only if

$$v(m, 1) \geqslant E\{v\{\max(m, Z), 2\}\}$$
$$= \delta, \, E\{v\{\max(m, Z), 1\}\}$$

which is equivalent to $m \geqslant a$ for some constant a, the *acceptance* level. If $m < a$, then it would be better for the superior to wait until the second period. Assumption (1) will be relaxed in section 11.

7.   Let S_x denote the event that the type-x proposal is accepted in either the first or the second period, S_{x1} the event that the type-x proposal is accepted in the first period, and similarly for S_{x2}, S_y, S_{y1}, S_{y2}, and $S_z = S_{z2}$. Then

$$S_{x1} = \{X \geqslant Y, X \geqslant a\}$$
$$S_{x2} = \{X \geqslant Y, X < a, X \geqslant Z\}$$
$$S_x = S_{x1} \cup S_{x2}$$
$$S_{y1} = \{Y > X, Y \geqslant a\}$$
$$S_{y2} = \{Y > X, Y < a, Y \geqslant Z\}$$
$$S_y = S_{y1} \cup S_{y2}$$
$$S_z = S_{z2} = \{\max(X, Y) < \min(a, Z)\}$$

To analyze how the probabilities of these events depend on e_x and e_y, the following observation is helpful: because e_x cannot take on two different values at the same period, the assumption that $X(e_x = e_x^+)$ is stochastically larger than $X(e_x = e_x')$ whenever $e_x^+ > e_x'$ is equivalent to the seemingly stronger assumption that $X(e_x = e_x^+) \geqslant X(e_x = e_x')$, and similarly for Y with respect to e_y.

It follows that if $e_x' + e_y' = e_x^+ + e_y^+ = 1$, $e_x^+ > e_x'$, and $e_y^+ < e_y'$, then

$$S_x(e_x = e_x', e_y = e_y') \subseteq S_x(e_x = e_x^+, e_y = e_y^+)$$
$$S_y(e_x = e_x', e_y = e_y') \supseteq S_y(e_x = e_x^+, e_y = e_y^+)$$
$$S_{x1}(e_x = e_x', e_y = e_y') \subseteq S_{x1}(e_x = e_x^+, e_y = e_y^+)$$
$$S_{y1}(e_x = e_x', e_y = e_y') \supseteq S_{y1}(e_x = e_x^+, e_y = e_y^+)$$

Therefore, if $e_x + e_y = 1$,

$$\frac{dP(S_x)}{de_y} \text{ and } \frac{dP(S_{x1})}{de_y}$$

are both negative, and since

$$\frac{dP(S_x)}{de_y} = \frac{dP(S_{x1})}{de_y} + \frac{dP(S_{x2})}{de_y}$$

so $\dfrac{dP(S_{x2})}{de_y} < \dfrac{dP(S_{x1})}{de_y}$

Similarly,

$$\frac{dP(S_y)}{de_y} \text{ and } \frac{dP(S_{y1})}{de_y}$$

are both positive, and

$$\frac{dP(S_{y2})}{de_y} > - \frac{dP(S_{y1})}{de_y}$$

8. If the budget function is such that max{budget : project = z} $\leqslant$ min{budget : project = x or y}, or any other condition guaranteeing that the bureaucrat always prefers his own proposals x and y to the outside competition of type z, and budget(period = 1) $\geqslant$ budget (period = 2),

other things equal, or any other condition guaranteeing that the bureaucrat's time preference cannot be reversed by the budget, then (1) *a higher acceptance level a makes the bureaucrat worse off.* This follows from the fact that if $a^+ > a'$, then $S_{x1}(a = a^+) \subseteq S_{x1}(a = a')$, $S_x(a = a^+) \subseteq S_x(a = a')$, $S_{y1}(a = a^+) \subseteq S_{y1}(a = a')$, $S_y(a = a^+) \subseteq S_y(a = a')$, and $S_z(a = a^+) \supseteq S_z(a = a')$; and (2) *a stochastically larger Z makes the bureaucrat worse off.* This follows by a very similar argument. Note that if Z becomes stochastically larger, the acceptance level a will increase as well.

9. A completely mission-oriented bureaucrat's utility function does not depend on the budget. Therefore, the above conclusions 8.1 and 8.2 apply.

Under a winner-take-all incentive policy, budget = 0 whenever project = z, so the first condition of section 8 is automatically met. Therefore, if the other condition is also satisfied, those two conclusions apply to this case as well.

10. It is obvious that the superior always prefers a stochastically larger distribution of max(X, Y). If the bureaucrat is purely budget oriented (i.e., his utility does not depend on the program type), the budget is proportional to the political benefits, and his utility function is such that it implicitly defines an optimal acceptance level a^+ from his perspective (analogous to the superior's acceptance level a; see section 6), then the bureaucrat also prefers a stochastically larger distribution of max(X, Y), provided that $a^+ \leqslant a$, i.e., he is less patient than the superior. To see this, note that in this situation both the budget and the period in which the final choice is made can only change to the bureaucrat's advantage. If, however, $a^+ > a$, it is conceivable (though not necessary) that the superior is more likely to accept proposals in the first period that do not meet the bureaucrat's own standard.

11. Given any two random variables U and V, a *correlation-decreasing transformation (cdt)* changes their joint distribution so that $p(U > s, V > t)$ is decreased for all s, t, without affecting the marginal distributions of U and V (Epstein and Tanney 1980).

1. Relaxing the assumption that X and Y are independent (given e_x and e_y), we will analyze the effect of a *cdt*. Given e_x and e_y , a *cdt* on the joint distribution of X and Y leads to a stochastically larger distribution of $M = \max(X, Y)$, which is in the superior's interest. If the bureaucrat is purely budget oriented (i.e., his utility is independent of the *program* type), and less patient than the superior, this helps him as well. If the bureaucrat has some mission bias, the effect of such a *cdt* on his welfare is indeterminate, since the probability that Y exceeds X can either increase or decrease.

2. Relaxing the assumption that $M = \max(X, Y)$ and Z are independent, consider a *cdt* on their joint distribution. As illustrated in the text (Property 2.6.a), this is not always in the superior's interest. Moreover, even if the superior's optimal decision rule is classical (that is, M is accepted in the first period if and only if $M \geqslant a$), then a *cdt* on M and Z is not necessarily good for the superior under a complete-equilibrium analysis. To see this, note that since she cannot precommit to a suboptimal acceptance level (i.e., a must be a best response), she will in general change her cutoff if the joint distribution of M and Z changes. In turn the new a may cause the bureaucrat to alter his search so much to the superior's disadvantage that the net effect on her welfare is negative. However, under the partial-equilibrium analysis of Property 2.6.b, the superior prefers a *cdt* since it has the effect of stochastically increasing $\max(M, Z) = \max(X, Y, Z)$ on the set $\{M < a\}$.

12. Suppose the bureaucrat's utility function is of the simple form.

$$u(program, budget, 1) = \begin{cases} 1 + budget \\ \text{if } program = y \\ c + budget \\ \text{if } program = x \\ budget \\ \text{if } program = z \end{cases}$$

$$u(program, budget, 2) = \delta_b$$
$$u(program, budget, 1)$$

where c and δ_b are both in the interval $[0, 1]$. Assume that the expected utility $E(u)$ is a concave function of e_y with an interior maximum satisfying $dE(U)/de_y = 0$ where $e_x + e_y \equiv 1$. By the results in section 7,

$$\frac{d^2 E(u)}{dc \, de_y} = \frac{dP(S_{x1})}{de_y} + \delta_b \frac{dP(S_{x2})}{de_y}$$

is negative. Therefore, as the relative utility of c of type x is increased, the bureaucrat's optimal e_y decreases, so e_x increases. This determinate result holds only for this special utility function. Even here, however, the remaining comparative statics on e_x and e_y are indeterminate. For example, analyzing the bureaucrat's response to a changed acceptance level a we have

$$\frac{d^2 Eu}{da \, de_y} = \left[\frac{d^2 P(S_{x1})}{da \, de_y} + \delta_b \frac{d^2 P(S_{x2})}{da \, de_y} \right] c$$

$$+ \frac{d^2 P(S_{y1})}{da \, de_y} + \delta_b \frac{d^2 P(S_{y2})}{da \, de_y}$$

since $u_y = 1$ and $u_z = 0$. Note that many of the *components* of the above equation cannot be signed. For example,

$$\frac{d^2 P(S_{x1})}{da\, de_y} = \frac{d}{da}\left(\frac{dP(S_{x1})}{de_y}\right)$$

$$= \frac{d}{da}\left[P(X > Y \mid X \geqslant a)\,\frac{dP(X \geqslant a)}{de_y}\right.$$

$$\left. + \frac{dP(X > Y \mid X \geqslant a)}{de_y}\,P(X \geqslant a)\right]$$

$$= P(X > Y \mid X \geqslant a)\,\frac{d^2 P(X \geqslant a)}{da\, de_y}$$

$$+ \frac{dP(X > Y \mid X \geqslant a)}{da}\,\frac{dP(X \geqslant a)}{de_y}$$

$$+ \frac{d^2 P(X > Y \mid X \geqslant a)}{da\, de_y}\,P(X \geqslant a)$$

$$+ \frac{dP(X > Y \mid X \geqslant a)}{de_y}\,\frac{dP(X \geqslant a)}{da}$$

Without further assumptions, the sign of this component cannot be determined, so neither can the overall expression for $d^2 Eu/da\, de_y$. Since changes in either Z or δ_s affect a, they are likewise indeterminate. Finally, grinding through similar comparative-static equations for δ_b and Y reveal that they cannot be signed either.

13. *For any given acceptance rule,* the superior prefers stochastically larger distributions of X, Y, and Z (obtained by adding nonnegative random variables Δ_x, Δ_y, and Δ_z, respectively). If the superior's utility function is linear or convex (risk-neutral or risk-seeking) in the benefits, she also prefers riskier distributions (obtained by adding random-noise terms ε_x, ε_y, and ε_z, respectively, satisfying $E(\varepsilon_i \mid X, Y, Z) = 0$ for $i = x, y, z$) (Rothschild and Stiglitz 1971). However, paralleling the effect of reduced correlation in section 11.2 above, the effect of riskier Z on the superior's welfare is indeterminate once one allows a and e_y to vary.

NOTES

1. Consider, for example, Polsby's finding that "The civilian control of atomic energy . . . started with a scientific laboratory threatened with extinction. As the laboratory searched for ways to remain useful, it began also to seek to innovate and to invent new policies. It is not uncommon to hear of such a sequence of events" (1984, 164).

2. A recent CBO study (Congressional Budget Office 1986) on infrastructure management observed that "federal programs do not constantly encourage broad searches for ways to improve the productivity of infrastructure. Most . . . are managed not to support and promote broad policy goals but instead to provide capital for predetermined types of projects" (p. 15). For more on domestic policy formation see Salamon 1981, 190.

3. These political benefits need not correspond to those of a conventional cost-benefit analysis: the politician's goals need not be normatively appropriate. Indeed, many bureaucrats probably believe that without technical guidance, politicians would often make inappropriate decisions based on narrow electoral criteria. Such officials may think that by manipulating the menu of alternatives they are offering a form of guidance.

4. This condition implies that average political benefits also increase with search.

5. One may wish to consider the jurisdictional structure as an object of long-run strategic interest (Hammond 1986). It is fixed for the short run modeled here. In any case, recall that giving one agency a temporary monopoly is not necessarily suboptimal for the superior, given the opportunity costs of a simulta-

neous generation of alternatives. Moreover, we will see that the model yields simultaneous *review* of alternatives as a special case.

6. Rejecting poor proposals and accepting good ones, the "classical" stopping rule (Kohn and Shavell 1974), is optimal if Z is independent of X and Y and the future is discounted. We generally assume independence; correlated search is covered in Properties 2.5 and 2.6.

7. Of course, her decision depends on what the realized value of $\max(X, Y)$ is. It is the conditional decision *rule* that can be formulated without observing the bureau's proposals.

8. This preference ordering approximates the air force's attitudes toward intermediate range ballistic missiles (IRBMs) in the 1950s. Initially unenthusiastic toward missiles and strongly oriented toward bombers, the dominant coalition in the air force became much more interested in IRBMs when it became evident it could lose out to the army's Jupiter missile (Armacost 1969, 55–56).

9. Suppose, for example, the superior was a political appointee, an assistant secretary who wanted to make her mark in a hurry. (For data on the length of tenure of political appointees in the Kennedy, Johnson, and Nixon administrations, see Heclo 1977, 105. For tenure data on senior career bureaucrats, see McGregor 1974, 24.)

10. Because the boss takes into account both benefits and costs, the two conditions are intertwined. For example, the more impatient she is, the better the outside competition can be and still be "sufficiently" poor so that the agenda is completely rigged.

11. Of course if the outside competition is sufficiently strong and the superi-

or sufficiently patient, the bureaucrat's search will be irrelevant to the boss because she will never accept his proposals.

12. These results imply another sufficient condition for complete agenda manipulation: if u_x is "sufficiently" small and the chance of getting y approved is not too small, the agenda will be totally rigged.

13. Similarly, it is easy to show that changes in the quality of the agency's alternatives, in the bureaucrat's discount parameter, or in the superior's acceptance level all have indeterminate effects on search (Appendix, sec. 12).

14. The winner-take-all scheme would not necessarily be undesirable if the supply of outside alternatives depended on the prospect of receiving a budget for the program, as was partly the case for the army's interest in missiles (Kanter 1979, 112). In this model, however, Z is exogenously fixed.

15. Let $m_1 = 1$, $m_2 = 2$, and $z_1 = 2$, and $z_2 = 4$; their unconditional probabilities equal $1/2$. The bureaucrat's discount is .2; the superior's, .4. If M and Z are perfectly positively correlated the superior will accept either m_1 or m_2; if they are independent she will reject m_1. She prefers the latter situation; the bureaucrat, the former.

16. Though the purely budget-oriented administrator was a special case, almost all of Model 2's results carry over to the more realistic setting of an administrator interested in both missions and funding. (One must assume, of course, that the two types of agents face the same budgetary policy.) The only results that do not generalize are the parts of Properties 2.4 and 2.5 describing the responses of an impatient bureaucrat.

17. This scheme is not the only way to induce unbiased search. Assuming that the costs of implementing the program would still be covered, the superior could, in the first period, subtract a fixed amount of c_1 if she chose y. When combined with appropriate second-period adjustments, *any* weighted average of penalty for y of αc_1 and bonus for x of $(1 - \alpha)c_1$ would have the desired effect of neutralizing the bureaucrat's mission orientation. There are infinitely many such combinations. A choice between bonuses and penalties would probably matter to the superior. If she is operating under an overall budget constraint, a bonus for choosing x would require transfering funds from another bureau to this agency; a penalty for choosing y would reduce the program size of this agency. However, the comparative-static results of Properties 3.2 and 3.3 are unaffected by this choice between carrots and sticks.

18. In a model of advice giving, Calvert has discovered the intriguing result that superiors may prefer more biased subordinates (1985a). However, because he has modeled asymmetric information quite differently from the approach taken here, his finding and ours are not comparable.

19. The one exception is a change in the bureaucrat's discount factor: inspecting the second-period terms in the budget policy of Property 3.1 reveals that a change in δ_b can make the superior either better or worse off.

20. Personnel shifts are another matter: as we have seen, these affect a superior's welfare because it costs less to obtain unbiased search from less biased bureaucrats.

21. Note that most of the comparative statics on the bureau's allocation of search effort are still indeterminate: for instance, improved Z could make it focus more on x or y. Therefore, those interested in the details of policy formation might still find the agency's behavior interesting. In either case, however, the new search would be unbiased.

22. Two other assumptions of perfect information should also be subjected to sensitivity analysis: that the bureaucrat knows the superior's acceptance level, and that both know the distribution of second-round possibilities. It is worth noting that if the superior has an unbiased but noisy perception of Z, her acceptance level is higher than it would be if she knows Z (Kohn and Shavell 1974, 115). The reason parallels her preference for more objectively innovative search: because she can always fall back on the agency's better alternative, her increased perception of very bad possibilities is irrelevant, but her belief in very good possibilities raises her aspirations. (In this case, interestingly, the political superior need not have optimistic biases in order to have unrealistically high policy aspirations.) Yet, although pure uncertainty imparts a bias to behavior, as perceptions become less noisy the acceptance level converges to the full-information a^*; thus here small amounts of uncertainty do indeed have only small effects on actions.

23. For an analysis of the control problems created by the multiplicity of political principals and the ensuing multiple-winning coalitions, see Hill 1985 and Hammond, Hill, and Miller 1986. For a more wide-ranging analysis of the problems politicians have in controlling bureaucratic agents, see Moe 1984.

REFERENCES

ABERBACH, JOEL, ROBERT PUTNAM, AND BERT ROCKMAN. 1981. *Bureaucrats and Politicians in Western Democracies.* Cambridge: Harvard University Press.

ABERBACH, JOEL, AND BERT ROCKMAN. 1976. Clashing Beliefs within the Executive Branch: The Nixon Administration Bureaucracy. *American Political Science Review* 70:456–68.

ALLISON, GRAHAM. 1971. *The Essence of Decision: Explaining the Cuban Missile Crisis.* Boston: Little, Brown.

ARMACOST, MICHAEL. 1969. *The Politics of Weapons Innovation.* New York: Columbia University Press.

ARNOLD, PERI. 1976. Executive Reorganization Theory. Paper presented at the annual meeting of the American Political Science Association, Chicago, IL.

ARROW, KENNETH. 1985. The Economics of Agency. In *Principals and Agents,* eds. John Pratt and Richard Zeckhauser. Cambridge: Harvard University Press.

BENDOR, JONATHAN. 1985. *Parallel Systems: Redundancy in Government.* Berkeley: University of California Press.

BERGERSON, FREDERICK. 1980. *The Army Gets an Air Force: Tactics of Insurgent Bureaucratic Politics.* Baltimore: Johns Hopkins University Press.

BHATTACHARYA, SUDIPTO, AND DILIP MOOKHERJEE. 1986. Portfolio Choice in Research and Development. *Rand Journal* 17:594–605.

CALVERT, RANDALL. 1985a. The Value of Biased Information: A Rational Choice Model of Political Advice. *Journal of Politics* 47:530–55.

CALVERT, RANDALL. 1985b. Robustness of the Multidimensional Voting Model. *American Journal of Political Science* 29:69–95.

Congressional Budget Office. 1986. *Federal Policies for Infrastructure Management.* Washington: GPO.

COULAM, ROBERT. 1977. *Illusions of Choice: The F-111 and the Problem of Weapons Acquisition Reform.* Princeton: Princeton University Press.

DESTLER, I. M. 1974. *Presidents, Bureaucrats, and Foreign Policy.* Princeton: Princeton University Press.

EPSTEIN, LARRY, AND STEPHEN TANNY. 1980. Increasing Generalized Correlation. *Canadian Journal of Economics* 13:16–34.

FUTRELL, ROBERT. 1980. *Ideas, Concepts, Doctrine: A History of Basic Thinking in the United States Air Force, 1907–1964.* New York: Arno.

HALPERIN, MORTON. 1974. *Bureaucratic Politics and Foreign Policy.* Washington: Brookings.

HAMMOND, THOMAS. 1986. Agenda Control, Organizational Structure, and Bureaucratic Politics. *American Journal of Political Science* 30:379–420.

HAMMOND, THOMAS, JEFFREY HILL, AND GARY MILLER. 1986. Presidential Appointment of Bureau Chiefs and the "Congressional Control of Administration" Hypothesis. Paper presented at the annual meeting of the American Political Science Association, Washington, DC.

HECLO, HUGH. 1977. *A Government of Strangers.* Washington: Brookings.

HECLO, HUGH. 1978. Issue Networks and the Executive Establishment. In *The New American Political System,* ed. Anthony King. Washington: American Enterprise Institute.

HESS, STEPHEN. 1976. *Organizing the Presidency.* Washington: Brookings.

HILL, JEFFREY. 1985. Why So Much Stability? The Role of Agency Determined Stability. *Public Choice* 46:275–87.

HUNTINGTON, SAMUEL. 1961. *The Common Defense.* New York: Columbia University Press.

KANTER, ARNOLD. 1979. *Defense Politics: A Budgetary Perspective.* Chicago: University of Chicago Press.

KAUFMAN, HERBERT. 1960. *The Forest Ranger: A Study in Administrative Behavior.* Baltimore: Johns Hopkins University Press.

KINGDON, JOHN. 1984. *Agendas, Alternatives, and Public Policies.* Boston: Little, Brown.

KOHN, MEIR, AND STEVEN SHAVELL. 1974. The Theory of Search. *Journal of Economic Theory* 9: 93–123.

LIGHT, PAUL. 1983. *The President's Agenda: Domestic Policy Choice from Kennedy to Carter.* Baltimore: Johns Hopkins University Press.

LYNN, LAURENCE. 1981. *Managing the Public's Business.* New York: Basic Books.

MCGREGOR, EUGENE. 1974. Politics and the Career Mobility of Bureaucrats. *American Political Science Review* 68:18–26.

MARCH, JAMES, AND JOHAN OLSEN. 1983. What Administrative Reorganization Tells Us about Governing. *American Political Science Review* 77:281–96.

MAYHEW, DAVID. 1974. *Congress: The Electoral Connection.* New Haven: Yale University Press.

MERTON, ROBERT. 1957. *Social Theory and Social Structure.* Glencoe, IL: Free Press.

MOE, TERRY. 1984. The New Economics of Organization. *American Journal of Political Science* 28:739–77.

MOE, TERRY. 1985. The Politicized Presidency. In *The New Direction in American Politics,* eds. John Chubb and Paul Peterson. Washington: Brookings.

NATHAN, RICHARD. 1975. *The Plot that Failed: Nixon and the Administrative Presidency.* New York: Wiley.

NEUSTADT, RICHARD. 1960. *Presidential Power.* New York: Wiley.

PFEFFER, JEFFREY. 1981. *Power in Organizations.* Marshfield, MA: Pitman.

POLSBY, NELSON. 1984. *Political Innovation in America.* New Haven: Yale University Press.

ROTHSCHILD, MICHAEL, AND JOSEPH STIGLITZ. 1971. Increasing Risk II: Its Economic Consequences. *Journal of Economic Theory* 3:66–84.

SALAMON, LESTER. 1981. The Presidency and Domestic Policy Formulation. In *The Illusion of Presidential Government,* eds. Hugh Heclo and Lester Salamon. Boulder: Westview.

SCHLESINGER, ARTHUR. 1958. *The Coming of the New Deal.* Boston: Houghton Mifflin.

SEIDMAN, HAROLD. 1970. *Politics, Position, and Power.* Oxford: Oxford University Press.

SIMON, HERBERT, DONALD SMITHBURG, AND VICTOR THOMPSON. 1950. *Public Administration.* New York: Knopf.

SUTTON, JOHN, AVNER SHAKED, AND KENNETH BINMORE. 1986. An Outside Option Experiment. London School of Economics. Typescript.

WITTMAN, DONALD. 1983. Candidate Motivation: A Synthesis of Alternative Theories. *American Political Science Review* 77:142–57.

Public Administration
and the Public

The nature of the relationship between public administrators and those they serve is a source of long-standing debate in public administration. It is rooted in complex and enduring issues of philosophy and governance: the qualities of a citizen and the relation of the governed to their government. The philosophers Hobbes and Rousseau, for example, had dramatically different views of the nature of the individual members of a society and their ability to form a compact or union. Hobbes believed man to be essentially brutish and unable to act in a common interest. Rousseau was more sanguine, arguing that man was fundamentally good and able to pursue interests broader than his own. More than a little of Hobbes' view carried into the debate over the roles of government and the citizen in the new American state. James Madison's argument that "if men were angels, no government would be necessary . . ."[1] reflected a view of the citizenry as self interested and given to faction. Thomas Jefferson, whose view that the best government was that closest to the people, shared neither Madison's view of citizens nor the proper role of government. While Madison's conception of the nature of the citizen led him to conclude that a good government was one that moderated narrow preference to create a broader good, Jefferson argued that direct citizen participation in a decentralized system was more legitimate. Many scholars have observed that the Constitution incorporated both perspectives; the debate continues into contemporary government. Hart's excellent discussion summarizes the major issues.

For public administration, the problem is exacerbated by two other, equally compelling, issues. First, the Constitution does not make clear how the administrative function fits into the overall scheme of things. Although most parts of the federal bureaucracy fall under the executive branch, they are subject to congressional and—increasingly—judicial oversight. The direction and oversight provided by each of these three branches of government may be legitimate, but they are not necessarily compatible, nor do they necessarily provide a coherent view of the public good. Thus, public

---

[1] James Madison, "Federalist #51" in *The Federalist Papers* (New York: Bantam Books, 1982) p. 238.

bureaucracies often must choose the "best" alternative, both in terms of program goals and citizens' interests. Many elected officials and many citizens do not consider this level of bureaucratic discretion legitimate, however, and the demand for improved control over public bureaucracy ensues.

Second, and closely related to this last point, is the issue of the insularity of large bureaucratic organizations, whether they be public or private. As organizations increase in size and become more bureaucratic in their behavior, they tend to exclude many external influences. To be more stable and more efficient, they adopt standardized rules and regulations; inevitably, they fit individual citizens and their demands into the niches the standards create. Victor Thompson's classic admonition that public administrators act "without sympathy or enthusiasm"[2] contrasts sharply with demands for greater bureaucratic responsiveness to the needs and circumstances of individual citizens.

What, then, is a public administrator to do in relation to citizen participation and the public good? Historically, there have been a number of efforts to accommodate and incorporate citizen views and perspectives into administrative activity. Perhaps the oldest is the "Blue Ribbon" commission or advisory panel. In this model, leading citizens and experts from the business and academic communities provide elected and top administrative officials with advice on policy and program issues. A second widely used technique is that of the public hearing, in which citizens are asked to provide their views on proposed actions or policies. Public hearings and discussions are an important part of many current environmental programs, for example.

In the 1960s, a more radical model of citizen participation, involving both decentralization and more direct citizen decision making, was introduced. Lyndon Johnson's "Great Society" included many programs intended to alleviate the problems of poverty and discrimination in America. Central to the "War on Poverty" were Community Action Programs (CAPs) and neighborhood multipurpose centers. Administrative arrangements and authority for the Community Action Programs differed sharply from those of previous efforts; the intergovernmental funding structure was essentially bypassed and the CAP agencies were accountable to the federal government and to their elected boards. The elected boards are most interesting in terms of citizen participation. Initially, they were to have one-third of their total membership elected from the target communities served by the programs. Later, that requirement was changed so that a majority of the CAP board was to come from the target areas. The boards had policy and budget authority; they were an example of direct citizen participation in administrative structures.

The neighborhood multipurpose centers also represented a new model in citizen participation and service delivery. The decentralized sites, the specific tailoring of programs and staff for each neighborhood, the opportu-

---

[2]Victor Thompson, *Without Sympathy or Enthusiasm* (University: University of Alabama Press, 1975).

nity to have several services delivered in one place, and the simple proximity of those delivering the services to those being served all departed from the traditional model of centralized, standardized program design and delivery. Although Community Action Programs and other similar efforts still exist, most have changed in significant ways, all of which have moved them away from the model of direct citizen participation and authority. The model they provided, however, continues to be important for both citizens and administrators.

For public administrators, the need to understand the citizens being served—and to be understood by them—has become increasingly acute. As government becomes more complex and as the problems it attempts to solve become more intractable, traditional bureaucratic insularity and remoteness become a serious part of the problems societies face. Recent efforts such as Total Quality Management and concerns with "Reinventing Government" place the citizen at the center of bureaucratic concerns. "Customer service" and quality emphasize the need for citizens to be consulted and integrated into major bureaucratic processes, not after the decisions have been made, but while they are being considered. As David Mathews argues in the summary which follows, the realization that citizens are the "yarn" from which the fabric of government can be woven is fundamental to both good government and those in the public service.

Carole Pateman observed that " . . . the more individuals participate, the better able they become to do so."[3] For public administrators, elected officials, and citizens alike, the need to create and support consistent patterns of citizen participation in the design, implementation, and evaluation of public programs is a major challenge. It is also a necessary first step in rebuilding confidence in government and its institutions.

[3]Carole Pateman, *Participation and Democratic Theory* (Cambridge: The University Press, 1970) p. 12.

30.   The Public in Practice and Theory

David Mathews

The first part of this essay consists of reflections on the practice of public administration at the federal level. It is, admittedly, personal and subjective. I

SOURCE: "The Public in Practice and Theory" by David Mathews as appeared in *Public Administration Review,* March 1984. Adapted from a lecture for the Maxwell School of Citizenship and Public Affairs, Syracuse University, June 30, 1983. Reprinted by permission.

deal with government as it operates in relation to the public (the citizenry). The second section is philosophic and obtusely abstract. It may seem full of semantic antics and frantic pedantics. In that section I deal with "public" not as a practice, but as an idea.

The objective of both is to get at the root causes of some of our current difficulties. What happens to governing when the public is not available as a matter of practice? That is the first question. What happens to governing (and all common endeavors) when the public is not available as an idea? That is the second question.

In all, this essay reports on "wrestling" with the idea of "public." "Wrestling with" is an inelegant but accurate description of the paper's tenor. That is to say, the report is not complete. It does not end with a flourish. There is no grand conclusion. It simply stops. It is progress to date. Most of all, this paper is an invitation. It is for those who are wrestling with similar problems. It suggests that we talk more to each other about what we are doing and what we have learned.

THE PUBLIC AS SEEN FROM GOVERNMENT

I did not enter the federal government with any strong ideological bent or preconceptions about what I would find. My values were basically democratic. I do admit to having come from a populist political tradition, but I do not think the populist tradition is hereditary—there is no such thing as a populist gene. I am sure I had my biases; I did say some intemperate things about the inherent unmanageability of the Department of Health, Education, and Welfare. But beyond that, I was open to learn from what I saw.

The way government operated in relation to the people and to democratic precepts was disquieting. It was not that bureaucrats were "bad" people whose values differ from ours. It was not that the government was in the hands of bunglers. The problem went deeper. It had to do with what happened to the public in public administration. The public was, for the most part, unavailable.

For some officials and bureaucrats, the public was unavailable because it was an abstraction. The abstraction was

to be honored in principle, to be recognized rhetorically, but in practice, the real public was not essential in the operation of government. The view was that ours was a representative democracy; therefore it was not necessary to deal with the public directly in ways other than through elections.

For those who believed that the public was essential in the governing and not restricted to voting, there were other obstacles that made the public still unavailable. In the view of these officials, the public was "unreachable," that is, there seemed no efficient way to get at the whole of the public. All you could do was to get in touch with part of the public—then only at great expense. And letting in part of the public—some special interest within the public—was thought worse than doing nothing at all.

Others found the public unavailable because it was not understandable. "Why talk to the public?" "You can hear anything you want." The bureaucrats making those statements did not mean to be derogatory, only candid. The public appeared as a conglomeration of factions with no common language and no common purposes—beyond those in the broadest of platitudes. The public spoke in a myriad of languages about a myriad of objectives, confused and conflicting. The public was unintelligible.

Others found the public unavailable because they were convinced that the public was uninformed. The general public simply did not, in fact could not, know enough to comprehend the issues government had to address. The detailed, often technical, knowledge that was necessary for government's decisions was considered more than you could reasonably expect even an educated public to master. In the Jefferson Lectures two years ago, Gerald Holton made this problem clear, even for the most ardent advocates of popular sovereignty, when he noted that nearly half of all policy decisions are now scientific and technical in nature.[1] That is a very important observation for those who are mindful that this is still a democracy in which everyone is to participate. Scientific and technical matters, by their very nature, are the province of a few, while a democratic government is the province of the many. The dilemma is obvious and acute.

It also has to be said that new governmental processes (i.e., those instituted in the late 19th century) often work against the public, regardless of the point of view of the bureaucrat—and in spite of laws requiring public participation. Henry Steele Commager[2] has well described the blurring of the distinctions between the executive, legislative, and judicial functions that led to the new practices.

Regulatory or rule-making activities are good examples. Regulations are ostensibly only administrative actions. In fact they are also legislative and judicial.

The problem is that regulation as legislation does not conform to our standards for democratic legislative processes. Its agents are not elected, and its debates occur largely in administrative offices. The devices for involving the public are crude. A notice, which nobody reads, appears in the *Federal Register*. Individuals may comment on the proposed regulation by writing letters, but these letters are received by the agency, reduced to ciphers, and entered in the appropriate column. And where are these figures reported? In the *Federal Register*.

And as for adjudication, regulations certainly have the force of law. You may be found guilty of not conforming to a particular regulation and sentenced accordingly. The difficulty is that "innocent unless proven guilty" is not the canon for regulation as it is for adjudication. It is superseded by an administrative canon where the burden of proof is on you, not the agency. The net result of these practices is not only to raise serious questions about democratic values, but also to impede public access to government.

THE QUESTION OF PUBLIC COMPETENCE AND CIVIC LITERACY

I do not take any of these reservations about public participation lightly. But when I left government service, I was drawn to the issue of the public's competence and to the imperatives of civic literacy. In the last five years, I have found the company of others concerned about the public's knowing and participating in our kind of bureaucratic, professional, technical, scientific democracy. That concern led to the establishment of the National Consortium for Public Policy Education as an informal council for the discussion of public policy education. Out of those discussions came a new organization, the Domestic Policy Association (DPA).[3] (I must apologize for the name, because it inaccurately implies a disinterest in foreign policy. The name's only virtue was to suggest that the DPA was an organization somewhat like the more recognizable Foreign Policy Association.)

No one believes that the country needs more forums or conferences. The purpose of the Domestic Policy Association is not to promote more meetings or to dispense more information on given issues; it is rather to increase the ability of people to see the whole of things and their interrelationships. The objective is to help the country find common ground by devising the kinds of forums where individual interests can come together into shared interests.

For those reasons, the model of public learning that the Domestic Policy Association is using is different. One of the partners in the association and one of America's best public philosophers, Daniel Yankelovich, insists that the present model of public learning is terribly flawed.[4] We proceed, he says, on the assumption that if 22 minutes of news will not do it, then maybe 44 will. Our approach to public learning is to dispense facts. The problem, he contends, is that facts do not automatically turn themselves into meaning. Yankelovich argues that instant reaction to events or even facts is not half so valid as the thoughtful process of reflection and conversation ("digestion," he would say) that has to go on to turn a multitude of unrelated bits of information into public wisdom. The Domestic Policy Association, therefore, is about perfecting new models of public learning—aiding "digestion," if you will.

The method that the association is using for its national issues forums is very simple. There are millions of "stations" (institutions) that "produce" (convene) public conferences. I would guess that the number of people who attend public issues forums at this university number in the tens of thousands. There are other public and private universities, community colleges, and libraries and museums, and a variety of community organizations that are all convening institutions for public forums. There is not, however, any network that links the programs of these producing stations or convening institutions together.

Happily, there is no regimentation on what is to be discussed in the country. But if there were a limited number of problems discussed in common by a representative number of all of these hundreds of convening institutions, two things would happen that are not happening now. First, we could accelerate the development of new methods or models of public learning. Second, we could build stronger ties between the public forums and the policy community. It is difficult for a policy maker to read the public if policy conferences occur in an entirely random fashion. It is next to impossible for the policy com-

munity to do anything about this gap if no one is building networks of public forums on common topics.

The Domestic Policy Association is proceeding, in this its pilot year, with three common topics that will be discussed in some 45 different communities across the country. A new kind of guide to interpreting issue discussions has been prepared by the Public Agenda Foundation. And the policy community will assemble at the end of those conferences to listen. They will meet the DPA participants at the Ford Library at the University of Michigan for a capstone conference to be presided over by former Presidents Ford and Carter.

The Domestic Policy Association has now been at work for over a year getting ready for this program. A number of educational institutions, community organizations, foundations, and governmental bodies have been willing to collaborate to create the DPA.

Our problem, quite frankly, has been with the concepts we use. Those interested in public policy education and civic literacy, in citizenship education, in citizenship participation, have often met with reactions that range somewhere between a polite yawn and genuine puzzlemet. It is difficult to develop programs in public policy education when the term "public" is one of nonmeaning. So I have been revisiting the uses (or disuses) of "public" as an idea.

WRESTLING WITH THE "PUBLIC" AS AN IDEA

Public policy education can be no more important than the public is. Education for public ends can be no more instructive than public as an idea allows. And the policy options available to use can be no richer than our understanding of the nature and function of "public." Those are the reasons I would trouble you with the following disquisition on what "public" means—or can mean.

The public may be unavailable in ideas in a fashion roughly analogous to the way it is unavailable in governmental practice. The obstacles to its availability are:

- "Public" is too ambiguous a term to be useful. A best, it suggests the masses, the vulgar, the ordinary.
- "Public" is not consonant with our cherished individualism; it seems anti-private and has the pinkish tint of collectivism.
- "Public," as in "the public good," is a hopelessly romantic concept of uniformity and consensus that is incompatible with our pluralistic pragmatism.
- "Public" is a synonym for "politics" or "government" and hence not available as an independent idea.

"Public," as one would judge from the way we use it, is a term of very ambiguous meanings. "Public" means a restroom that is rather dirty. "Public" means transportation used by those too poor to own a car. "Public" is also a school. But is "public," as in transportation, the same "public" as in school? No, most would say, not because of a clear notion of what "public" means, but because of a habit of hearing it used to describe life at its lowest common denominator. "Public" has become the most public of terms—open to almost any definition.

Understanding the public poses difficult conceptual problems. The first is to understand public in relation to private or individual, on the one hand, and common or collective, on the other. Is thinking about public a danger to our individuality? Is it just one step away from an insidious collectivism? Second, it is imperative to look at "public" in comparison with "political" or "governmental." Can we use the one term interchangeably for the other two? What is the public's relationship to all of the in-

struments of the polity, the state itself, the processes and institutions of politics, and the government?

In *The Company of Strangers,* Parker J. Palmer argues that "public" is not legitimately a synonym for either political processes or the government itself. "Public" is, he argues, pregovernmental, even prepolitical.[5]

In my own work, I found it useful to begin with the classical roots of "public."[6] There are two. The word "public" is rooted in *pubes,* the term for maturity, implying the ability to understand the consequences of individual actions on others, the ability to see beyond ourselves. The other origin of the word "public" is in the Greek word for "common" which itself derives from the expression for "caring with." It is a useful reminder that there is an indispensable emotional connotation to public; it is what we recall in the phrase "public spirit."

Public life is well-defined as life lived in recognition of the consequences of, and potential in, our relations with others, both direct and indirect, over extended time. But the public is not simply a thing; it is a capacity. Perhaps it is even useful to think of public as if it were a verb so that we could talk about the ability "to public."

With that clue in hand—"public" as capacity, "public" as maturity—we can proceed to answer the second question: are "public" and "private" antithetical? I think not. The public is not the antithesis of private; it is more its corollary. Richard Sennett's sense of public and private as alternate, but not contradictory, modes of expression is useful.[7] The Greeks had two words for private. One word described an individual who was able to understand only his or her own perspective. The Greek word for that kind of private person has become our word "idiot." The other term for private, though, is not at all negative, quite the contrary. The second word derives from the Greek *oikos* for family or household. There is nothing wrong in attending to one's own household, nor does it preclude attending to public matters. To think of "public" and "private" as antagonistic is to fail to understand the necessary interrelationship between the two. Pericles, you may recall, said that the Greeks properly had both private (household) and public duties.[8] "Public" and "private" are more corollaries than antitheses.

But what about "public" and "common"? At first, I was not inclined to report that "public" had a Greek root in the word *koinon*, "common." Concentrating on the Latin, I could have made my case much stronger. But "common" and "mature" states have similarities. Both are predicated on an appreciation for, or a recognition of, the importance of relationships. Recall that *koinon* derives from *kom-ois*, meaning to "care with." What an important leap of mind and spirit it was when people could see in looking at others, not just those in their family or kinship group, a bond, a relationship. That recognition is the basis for the idea of common as it is at the root of public.

The idea of "common," though admittedly on the same continuum as "collective," is a very different idea indeed. Parker points out in his book that when a government imposes collectivism on a state, it not only destroys private life, it destroys public life as well. "Common" has no meaning for the collective mentality. It is simply not necessary because the task of distinguishing between what is private and individual, between what is one's own and what is somebody else's, is not necessary.

The notion that the public is "public good," a single, uniform definition that we all agree to, is subject to the same kind of criticism as is the idea that "public" and "collective" are synonymous. Appreciating the range of consequences and potential in relationships,

in a heterogeneous society of individuals all with their idiosyncrasies, will not result in monolithic definitions of what is good.[9] At the other extreme, the pluralism of our society does not impose on us an insipid relativism nor the conclusion that the public good is simply the mean of self-interests.

Finally, there is the problem of the relationship between public and political and governmental. Is the public the same as the polity? Going back to an earlier reference to public, as in public schools, many would say that a public school is a school supported by government funds. In fact, a United States senator said to me not long ago, "The public schools are not really the 'public's' schools; they are the government's schools." The most consistent use of "public" today is as a synonym for government or political. What is a "public" official? Most would say that a public official is one who spends his or her life in politics or in an elected office in government. But is that easy substitution of terms justified?

There is probably no better place to start than with Dewey's excellent *The Public and Its Problems*.[10] Dewey understood the public well; he understood it as the capacity to understand relationships. But it is common in the literature now to see "the organized public," the government, or state substituted for the "public." We talk of a "private" and a "public" sector, but we usually mean the for-profit business sector in the first instance and the governmental sector in the second. The real public sector is awkwardly classed as the not-for-profit private sector. Actually, the public is a complete idea in itself, apart from the idea of the organized public. The root words for "public" are not the same as the root words for the "polity," the state, the government. The public consists of those people who act together with an understanding of their relationship to each other. The "polity," coming from the Greek *polis,* is the public organized to carry on the functions of the "city" (an association to pursue the good life not just city government).[11] The concept of government is a very distant cousin of public. "Government" comes from the Greek *kybernan* (to steer). It consists of institutions established by the public for the control or direction of certain, usually very limited, activities.

Perhaps it would be better if we understood the public's relation to the polity, or the state, much in the same way we understand hydrogen's relationship to water. Hydrogen is most certainly a part of water, but at the time, hydrogen is most certainly not water. So, the public is vital to the creation of government but still not the government. There is a public life apart from governmental life. The public is the base atom from which we construct the molecule of government. It is the yarn from which we weave the cloth of politics.

IF THE PUBLIC WERE AVAILABLE . . .

It follows that if the quality of the public, or the public life, is not good, or not as good as it could be, then the quality of the things that depend upon it are in jeopardy.

It is often remarked that we live in a time when governments cannot govern and leaders cannot lead. Our common endeavors fall asunder because of an absence of common purpose and will. You can see it in our schools, our churches, our criminal justice system. Our political processes may be failing us because they are immobilized by a myriad of special interests. Factions seem to have the upper hand. *The Deadlock of Democracy* is the way James MacGregor Burns characterized our situation.[12] Committees, such as the ones for a Responsible Federal Budget, the proposed Third Hoover Commission, and the like, attest to a widespread conviction that

the political system is not able to address the really tough policy issues and that broad-based, public coalitions have to be formed either to force action or redesign the system. The sense is that we have to get back in control somehow.

There can be no vital political life, no viable institutions of government, no sense of mastery over our shared fate, no effective common endeavors of any kind without there being a foundation of public awareness and spirit. What we may be groping for in commissions and in domestic policy associations may be the reconstitution of a public. Certainly if there were a public sphere, we would have more choices in solving our problems. Now we are limited to two options in making corrections. We can increase the responsibilities of the private (i.e., business) sector or we can improve the performance of government. But if the public sphere were once again real and available, we might not only have a third set of options, but we might also have options that would get us closer to the problems behind the problems.

If the idea of the public were available to us, the question of who is attending to giving us the healthiest, the richest, and the best public life possible would become important. Perhaps it is not exactly accurate to say that the public has to be created. But if the public is in some way like maturity, then it is correct to say that the quality of the public is, by definition, unassured, just as the degree of maturity is unassured. The question who and what creates public has everything to do with all that depends on public life—all political processes, all governmental institutions, all agencies of our common endeavor.

Absent public awareness and spirit, absent the ability to translate individual concerns into larger common concerns, absent the people's ability to understand not just the particulars, but the relationships of the whole, there is no capacity "to public." And with relations of the sort that we have in a country as diverse as ours, with issues as intertwined as they are, with trade-offs and hard choices as inevitable as they are, the task of "publicking"—of understanding both consequences and potential in relationships, over time—is no small task.

Educating for public life, educating the civic self takes on new meaning when the public is recognized for what it really is.[13] Civic literacy, the capacity of people to think about the whole of things, of consequences and potential, becomes education of the most crucial kind. Public policy education becomes imperative in light of what the public can and must do; indeed what it can alone do.

We have had civics and civic education, the disciplines of political science and public administration, but we need to go further to re-examine the relations of the civic enterprise to the whole of education—even to the liberal arts— where we could begin by recalling that the liberal arts were "invented" to make our kind of civic order possible.[14] We have attended somewhat to the education of the civic self, but we also need to think about the way the community is educated, about the way it, like an individual, comes to know itself.[15] We need to think about the quality of the places where the public is formed, about the quality of the forums and conferences and conversations where we come to know each other—about whether those forums reinforce our penchant for special issues and special interests or whether they promote our finding common interests. We have public information from all kinds of news media, but we need to go further to ask what models of public learning we are using and whether those models protect us from informed meaninglessness.

Most basic of all, we need to talk to each other more about what the public has meant, does mean, can mean. *Darkness at Noon,* Arthur J. Koestler's book about the Moscow trials, is not a scholarly work, but one of the characters speaks to the consequences of not caring what the public (the people) really means:

> A mathematician once said that algebra was the science for lazy people— one does not work out X, but operates with it as if one knew it. In our case, X stands for the anonymous masses, the people. Politics mean operating with this X without worrying about its actual nature. Making history is to recognize X for what it stands for in the equation.[16]

There are those in other generations who have written about what the public is and is not—Lippman, Dewey, Arendt. The topic is a rich one for us, too. My suggestion is that our public philosophy begin with "public" itself.[17]

NOTES

1. Gerald Holton, "Where Is Science Taking Us?" Jefferson Lecture, National Endowment for the Humanities, May 11–13, 1981.

2. Henry Steele Commager, *The American Mind: An Interpretation of American Thought and Character Since the 1880's* (New Haven, Conn.: Yale University Press, 1950), p. 339.

3. For further information, contact the Domestic Policy Association, 5335 Far Hills Avenue, Suite 300, Dayton, Ohio 45429.

4. Daniel Yankelovich, "The Public Agenda Foundation," unpublished speech to a national public affairs group, Washington, D.C., January 1980.

5. Parker J. Palmer, *The Company of Strangers* (New York: Crossroad, 1981).

6. For this and other words cited from the Greek and Latin, see Carl Darling

Buck, *A Dictionary of Selected Synonyms in the Principal Indo-European Languages* (Chicago: University of Chicago Press, 1949).

7. Richard Sennett, *The Fall of Public Man* (New York: Knopf, 1977). Also see Hannah Arendt, *The Human Condition* (Chicago: The University of Chicago Press, 1958).

8. The funeral oration of Pericles, 432 B.C.

9. On a related topic, "the public interest," see: Glendon A. Schubert, *The Public Interest: A Critique of the Theory of a Political Concept* (Glencoe, Ill.: Free Press, 1960).

10. John Dewey, *The Public and Its Problems* (Chicago: Swallow Press, 1954).

11. "As Aristotle put it, the *polis* was an association for the pursuit of the good life; as such it was not much like what we know as a state, a government, an organization; it was first and foremost something that we would recognize as an involvement, a thoroughgoing involvement, in which the basic quality of life each experienced was felt to be continuously at stake. To be a citizen was to be involved with others in the shared effort to live well." Robert

McClintock, "The Dynamics of Decline: Why Education Can No Longer Be Liberal," *Phi Delta Kappan* 60 (1979), p. 636.

12. James MacGregor Burns, *The Deadlock of Democracy: Four-Party Politics in America* (Englewood Cliffs, N.J.: Prentice-Hall, 1963).

13. I am indebted to William F. May, *The Humanities and the Civic Self* (Bloomington: Indiana University Press, 1979), for the phrase "civic self."

14. Freeman Butts, *The Revival of Civic Learning: A Rationale for Citizenship Education in American Schools* (Bloomington, Ind.: Phi Delta Kappa, 1980).

15. Christopher C. Harmon, "Liberal Education Should Do More Than Just Liberate," *The Chronicle of Higher Education,* October 14, 1981, p. 24, discusses the community, saying, "The community, no less than the individual, must come to know itself."

16. Arthur J. Koestler, *Darkness at Noon* (New York: MacMillan, 1941), p. 84.

17. A selective, annotated bibliography on books dealing with what "public" means, prepared by the Kettering Foundation research interns, is available through the foundation.

31. Theories of Government Related to Decentralization and Citizen Participation

David K. Hart

The most urgent question facing the United States is whether our democratic institutions, as presently constituted, are

SOURCE: "Theories of Government Related to Decentralization and Citizen Participation" by David Hart, *Public Administration Review:* Special Issue (October 1972). Reprinted by permission of the American Society for Public Administration.

capable of resolving the accelerating problems menacing the immediate future (47)(48)(56). The extent and severity of this crisis in democratic institutions is the subject of considerable debate (18)(29)(89), but most democrats agree that reforms are necessary. The democratic reform alternatives are numerous, but they can be clustered into two major categories: (1) proposals for strengthening contemporary representative democracy, and (2) proposals for replacing representative democracy with participatory democracy. The general purpose of this essay is to discuss some of the arguments for and against maximal citizen participation as a reform alternative.

It is necessary to explain the manner in which the subject will be approached. Included within the first category above are those who recommend increased citizen participation as the most effective way of reforming representative democracy. They would increase participation in selected areas by feasible increments until some optimal level has been reached. Their recommendations would create some problems, but few that would be insoluble, since citizen participation would take place within the existing system and is intended to strengthen that system. This category allows for a number of structural mixes and differential participations. The majority of the essays in this issue fall into this first category. They describe and evaluate the condition of existing participatory programs and contain useful recommendations as to how the cause of citizen participation may be best advanced.

The second category, however, is revolutionary, its advocates calling for immediate and total citizen participation in all areas of society (5)(115). Because a totally participatory system would require a complete renovation of our present society, many dismiss the position as both unrealistic and unworkable. Perhaps they are correct. However, the number of scholars advocating total (or near total) participation is increasing and the position has figured prominently in the programs advocated by many politically active groups.

Of more importance here, however, is the fact that this radical position calls immediate attention to the most important question about increased citizen participation: *why should people participate?* The answer is not self-evident, and whether one believes in increased participation within the present system or in a totally participatory society, eventually that answer must be given.

In order to get at that question, this essay will concentrate upon the second category, because in that admittedly extreme position the basic normative questions about citizen participation are most sharply illustrated. Those defending that position will be termed the "advocates," and attention will be focused upon their arguments. At times those arguments will be pushed to extremes to illustrate the normative questions more graphically.

Implicit in the writings of the advocates is a vision of an ideal "democratic character" essential for the realization of a totally participatory society. While the ideal democratic man, possessing the ideal democratic character, is nowhere clearly described, elements of his character emerge from the writings of the advocates: he is capable of handling all of the requirements for full participation; he will invariably participate when given the opportunity; he receives his greatest satisfactions from participation; he and his fellow participants will arrive at a consensus in the resolution of policy matters; and, most important, he understands that his full human potential can only be realized through participation. In short, a totally participatory society is his optimal environment. Obviously, he is an abstraction—an ideal type serving approximately the same function as the "rational man" in classical economic theories. Both abstractions can be knocked over rather easily by the practical minded, but that is beside the point. Such constructs serve many useful purposes.

Aside from their utility in the construction of formal theories, their use in an essay such as this allows the most basic assumptions and problems in the respective areas to be stated simply, whether in the extremes of pure economic rationality or pure democratic participation. Thus, one can get to the heart of the normative arguments without getting entangled in the complexities inevitable to the description of real situations, as important as those obviously are.

Two caveats must be entered. First, as Davis noted: "The heart of classical [participatory] democracy is moral purpose" (31, p. 43). Therefore, it will be necessary to intrude within the jurisdictional boundaries of political philosophy. This essay makes no pretense at being a sophisticated argument in political philosophy. Rather, it presents an agenda of the general arguments for and against maximal citizen participation. Their full explication and analysis must be left to the political philosopher.

Second, this is a curriculum development essay, which means it is designed to present the problems that should receive attention in a curriculum on the subject, without necessarily trying to solve those problems. A survey of the relevant literature was made and authors and issues were selected because they present specific aspects of the debate about participatory democracy rather well. Some readers will disagree with those choices, but in so doing, the purposes of the essay will have been well met. The intention herein is not to convert but to encourage debate.

Thus, this essay will concentrate upon the arguments surrounding the vital question: why should people participate. It will be divided into three sections: (1) decentralization, (2) the arguments supporting participatory democracy, and (3) the arguments against participatory democracy.

DECENTRALIZATION

Participatory democracy is impossible without the extensive decentralization of public organizations. Therefore, any discussion about participatory democracy must deal with that extremely complex subject. While there are many reasons for decentralization, for the advocates the primary justification is that a decentralized environment is the optimal condition for citizen participation. In political science, discussions about decentralization are usually dealt with under the heading of "federalism" (62). However, contemporary conditions have greatly complicated previous assumptions about federalism and decentralization. As a result, there is considerable confusion about the subject, the scope of which has been lucidly discussed by Fesler (51).

To illustrate, one of the most disturbing characteristics of contemporary society is the increasing concentration of power in a decreasing number of organizations, both governmental and private. Ellul is correct in his assertion that the major impetus for centralization is the inevitable result of the conjunction of technology, modern organization, and the state (48)(50). In addition, the direction and control of that power is devolving upon an administrative elite—a cadre of specialists in control of modern technical organizations (134). As that augmented power is concentrated in fewer central organizations, the presentation of power becomes monolithic, and in almost all confrontations the ability of the individual to affect organizational decisions bearing on his life diminishes rapidly. Because of this escalating power differential, centralization is evaluated as a negative, dehumanizing trend, at least for those who value the political participation of individual citizens. Almost in reaction, decentralization has taken on an increasingly positive meaning. The advocates have correctly recognized that in this time, power lies with the administrative apparatus and its administrative elite— hence, administrative decentralization is coming to be identified as the main way to redress the imbalance.

The Confusion about Decentralization: Political Science, Administrative Theory, and Public Administration

A major reason for the confusion about decentralization is that at least three disciplines converge upon it: public administration, political science, and administrative theory. Although the influence might be diminishing, public administration is still rooted in political science and is the inheritor of the traditions and assumptions of American federalism (Heaphy, 149). On the other hand, public administrators must practice their profession in the field, often under difficult and unprecedented conditions, and those traditional views have not been altogether helpful in solving their pragmatically proximate problems. With increasing demands for and legislation requiring decentralization, public administration has turned to administrative theory, which has had considerable experience with decentralization. As a result, there has been a considerable borrowing of concepts and empirical evidence for decentralization.

In administrative theory, decentralization has a relatively clear meaning and rather specific organizational implications (58)(135). The concepts and evidence are usually drawn from studies of business firms and administrative units. The attempts to extrapolate them as justifications and guides for the decentralization of public organizations has not been altogether successful (Waldo, 149). Thus, one of the most urgent needs in this area is the serious attempt at a synthesis of the concepts of participation and decentralization into a new normative paradigm, from which operational concepts and theories applicable to the specific problems of public administration can be drawn.

1. A definition of decentralization. It is difficult to define the term because the criteria are so complex. At a minimum, it entails the delegation of authority within a larger organization. Scott and Mitchell offer the following:

> Decentralization involves the division of an organization into autonomous or semiautonomous decision units where performance responsibilities and control are vested in subordinate organizational units. *In human terms, true decentralization maximizes the amount of individual judgmental discretion exercised by an administrator* (135 p. 150, emphasis added).

In this essay the host organization is the nation and decentralization entails the delegation of authority to subnational entities. Of the numerous implications that can be drawn from the foregoing quotation, the following seem rather important.

Decentralization must take place within a previously centralized organizational environment. It is not just the opposite of centralization, which would be anarchy, but represents a third alternative (58). The reality of decentralization can be measured by the amount of authority delegated to the subnational units to initiate policy independently, and the willingness of the delegating authority to support the decentralized units in those independent decisions. For the advocates, the last phrase in the foregoing definition is the primary reason for decentralization—it enables more people to participate more effectively.

While the conventional response in political science calls for the decentralization of executive, legislative, and judicial structures, with the fantastic growth of public bureaucracies the discussion must now include the decentralization of the administrative functions of government as well. This is particularly necessary, since for the majority of people their most frequent and personal contacts with government are with those public agencies, as Kaufman noted:

Chief executives, legislatures, and the courts make more decisions of *sweeping* effect, but the agencies make a far greater number of decisions affecting individual citizens in *intimate* ways. In them lies the source of much present unrest; in them, therefore, the remedies are sought (69, p. 5).

The majority of essays in this issue concern the multifarious problems involved in decentralizing for participation in local units and they will not be restated. In addition, the reader is referred to the excellent work on decentralization by Fesler (51), Kaufman (69), and Waldo (149), among others.

2. What goals are to be obtained through decentralization? Administrative theory specifies a number of goals to be obtained through decentralization, such as reducing costs, improving services and outputs, and the more effective utilization of human resources. The advocates, of course, are primarily interested in the last category, and most of them willingly concede that decentralization will, at least in the initial phases, cause efficiency to decline and costs to rise. But for them those criteria are not really germane. They are mainly concerned with the enhancement of the democratic character of individual citizens through participation in decentralized organizational environments. In short, if they had to make a choice, they would rather have inefficient decentralized government than efficient centralized government (59).

Decentralization can take a number of general forms, two of which will be noted here. First, decentralization is advocated to allow for increased participation by organizational members *within* the decentralized subunits. Decisions about policy initiation will then involve more members of the subunit, with corresponding benefits in character development. In this area, participative management is seen as a particularly useful tool (Meade, 149).

Second, decentralization is advocated in order to provide better services to relevant client publics. The imperative here comes from the dwindling public confidence in the ability of officials and administrators to represent adequately constituency interests in obtaining desired system benefits (69). Many believe that the most effective way to protect and advance client interests is to decentralize public organizations to allow for more equitable access for affected publics to policy-making processes—in other words, to lessen the power differential referred to above. Since, in the ideal, the decentralized units would be smaller and in closer geographic proximity with their clientele, citizen groups would be able to participate directly with them in the making of policy decisions. It is further assumed that this will make public agencies more responsive to the citizens (152).

Participation thus can take place through more effective client interaction with the decisional centers within the organizations. More appealing to the advocates, however, would be the inclusion of clients, or client representatives, as members of the intraorganizational policy-making groups. Either way, the primary purpose of decentralization is to enhance the range of participation for individual citizens. These new demands represent a client-based neopartisanship that cuts directly at previously valued professional administrative expertise and nonpartisanship. It is predicated upon the belief that citizens need advocates within public agencies, rather than neutral administrators (107).

Decentralization as Reaction to Centralization: Ideology or Democratic Commitment?

While most scholarly responses to the threats of centralization have been directed toward practical remedies to enhance the status of the individual (as the essays in this volume demonstrate), they have been paralleled by an unfortunate ideological trend. As centralized organizations, public and private, bulk larger and larger, decentralization has been enshrined as an ideology, throwing disparate groups into uncomfortable alliances, as Waldo has described with perception and wit (149, p. 259). While the commitment to an ideology of decentralization among groups contending for political power is a most important subject, what is of more concern here is that some scholars and practitioners have accepted that ideology in the same uncritical manner.

To expand, the ideology is most often expressed in some variant of the equation that "decentralization" equals "democracy." Once organizations are decentralized, all of the positive benefits associated with democracy will supposedly come to pass. Fesler takes this problem quite seriously and is worth quoting at length:

> Decentralization is a means to the achievement of a number of end-values. However, by close association with certain of those values, decentralization appears to have been transformed into a value in its own right, and so into an article of faith for "right-thinking people," and into an end-value for which political scientists need merely specify how it may be maximized. This transformation has been accompanied by a romantic idealization of decentralization which, along with the hardening of doctrine, seems dysfunctional for political science—just as would be an assertive and sentimental advocacy of centralization as the means to, or embodiment of, the nation's organic unity, economic efficiency, or historic destiny. We are all witnesses to how tragic can be the consequences of centralization as the means for maximizing values chosen by one or a few powerful men. But it does not follow

that the opposite value, decentralization, is an absolute good. If, as appears true, decentralization has hardened into a dogma that furnishes the conscious or unconscious premise of much political analysis and prescription, an effort to explore its articles of faith and even its mysteries may be timely (51, pp. 538–539).

The presumption is that if policy initiation for all public organizations is delegated to local levels, where people know one another, then the ensuing decisions will not only be arrived at democratically, but all citizens will benefit from both the participatory processes and the eventual policy output. However, it is obvious that democratic processes do not necessarily result from, nor are democratic ideals necessarily maximized by, decentralization. In fact, the opposite has often occurred and independent local political structures have worked against democratic ideals. Kristol tersely summed it up: "I wish only to stress a significant and frequently misconceived point: decentralization is one thing, democracy is another" (75, p. 22). It is therefore extremely important to emphasize the obvious: the commitment to democracy must precede the commitment to decentralization, if the latter is to be instrumental in promoting the former. To promote decentralization without that prior commitment can lead to unforeseen and sometimes antidemocratic results.

To conclude, it must be noted that the advocates do not limit their demands for decentralization to public organizations. In fact, they want all structures in society to be decentralized, whether private or public, to allow for similar participation. This will be covered in a later section, however. The final note is simply that, for the advocates, the primary justification for decentralization is that it provides a more adequate arena for the participation of the individual citizen.

ARGUMENTS SUPPORTING PARTICIPATORY DEMOCRACY

When one compares the arguments supporting contemporary representative democracy with the arguments supporting contemporary participatory democracy, it is evident that the advocates have not fully developed their normative premises, although Bachrach (5) has made a promising beginning. There is little doubt about the intensity of the advocates' commitment to their beliefs, but such intensity is not a sufficient reason why an entire society should renovate itself in order to provide for maximal citizen participation. Because they do call for such widespread change, it is quite important that advocates clearly articulate the arguments justifying their claims in order to convince on the basis of reason rather than ideology. Before summarizing some of their positive arguments it will be useful to examine the scope of the changes they propose.

The Scope of the Changes

The advocates of participatory democracy want nothing less than full citizen participation in policy making in *all* organizations. They are not content to be limited to electoral access to political leaders at periodic elections, and this is one of their major disagreements with the proponents of representative democracy. To use Pateman's terms (115, pp. 67–71), they insist upon the "full" participation of individual citizens, rather than "partial" participation or—the great evil—"pseudo"-participation.

For this reason, they attack many of the traditional justifications of contemporary representative democracy, which they believe only provide for partial citizen participation at best, and at worst compel pseudo-participation. To illustrate, most of the advocates condemn the assumptions about the utility of political competition which, of course, are central to contemporary representative democracy and the inevitable political parties (240). To them, competition for votes encourages the manipulation of citizens and comprises a form of pseudo-participation.

Therefore, the advocates urge immediate pervasive changes in all political, economic, and social systems to allow for maximal citizen participation. The reason for this is not impatience, but the significance they place upon the development of democratic character: the specific personality characteristics essential for the successful performance of the duties entailed by democratic citizenship. They believe the only adequate way for all citizens to develop that character is through participation, so citizen participation is the *sine qua non* for the evolution of democratic character and for the reformation of society.

The importance of this educative aspect of participation must be emphasized, for it is the basic justification advanced by the advocates. One suspects that one reason they have not been overly energetic in articulating the arguments supporting their position is that they believe in the accelerated political education of the citizen which results from participation and which produces a heightened appreciation for participation. Thus, one cannot fully understand the justificatory arguments for participation until one has been educated by participation, at which time the need for justification will have disappeared.

This means the more one participates the better, and that *all* institutions within a society must contribute to the democratic education of the citizen. Specifically, the requirements of nongovernmental organizations (such as the job, the school, etc.) work against the development of the democratic character. Most citizens, for instance, spend most of their time with, and direct most of their mental efforts to, the demands of their jobs. In our society, most of those jobs are hierarchically organized and decisions are made in superior-subordinate relationships (134). Such authoritarian conditions have a detrimental effect upon both citizen abilities and desires to participate in the processes of government.

Therefore, the advocates almost invariably call for much more than participatory *government*—they want a participatory *society*. In other words, all organizations must be governed by member participation. To illustrate, Pateman argues that all organizations (economic, educational, etc.) are "political" systems. Thus:

> Society can be seen as being composed of various political systems, the structure of authority of which has an important effect on the psychological qualities and attitudes of the individuals who interact within them; thus for the operation of a democratic polity at national level, the necessary qualities in individuals can only be developed through the democratization of authority structures in all political systems (115, p. 35)(5, p. 7).

The advocates believe their system is good and ought to be instituted, but they seem to have taken a justificatory shortcut. If *all* organizations are defined as political systems, and if *all* political systems should be democratic, then they are justified in claiming the traditional arguments in support of political democracy for their demands that *all* organizations be made democratic. However, there are powerful reasons why such as inclusive definition of the political is not acceptable, best stated by Sheldon Wolin in *Politics and Vision* in a chapter entitled "The Age of Organization and the Sublimation of Politics" (155): The advocates have not come to grips with the important questions he raises, and they must do so if their claims are to move beyond an "ideology."

Second, the advocates clearly realize that most of the decisions in which the mass of the citizens will be involved in a fully participatory decentralized society will be trivial, especially in comparison with decisions on national policy. Schattschneider, in arguing that the public must be protected against wasting its somewhat limited political energies in trivia, wrote: "The power of the people in a democracy depends on the *importance* of the decisions made by the electorate, not on the *number* of decisions they make" (132, p. 140).

To the contrary, the advocates argue it is precisely the number of decisions that is important, since participation in decisional *processes* is the means by which democratic character is developed. But returning to the point made by Schattschneider, it seems that one reason the advocates "politicized" all organizations is to counter such charges. If *all* organizations are political systems, then all decisions made within those organizations, no matter how trivial, become by definition "political" decisions, and thus are given a somewhat spurious significance (50).

Bootlegging the justifications developed specifically for democratic political systems over to a justification for democratizing organizations within a participatory society is a shaky transaction. The cause of participatory democracy will be much better served if the advocates will develop specific justifications for the society they propose.

The Need for Justification

The simplest approach for one committed to participatory democracy if to make an *a priori* commitment that maximal citizen participation is "good." One can then ignore the most troublesome problems of justification and concentrate upon the prescriptions for implementing a participatory system, or descriptions of the state of participation in the real world. However, such a course seriously weakens the case for participatory democracy. The advocates must make their normative premises quite clear.

The purpose of such intellectual efforts is not just to achieve academic tidiness. Aside from the obvious academic obligations involved, there are practical reasons, as Tussman observed: "Concern for the normative is not a speculative luxury, it is a practical necessity" (144, p. 16). There are at least five reasons why the justifications for participatory democracy must be clearly presented.

First, many detractors of citizen participation argue that the advocates simply desire to fragment existing power structures and reconstitute them, with themselves at the center. Thus, the cause of citizen participation is weakened because it is seen by some as instrumental to increasing the political power of the advocates.

Second, the arguments against a fully participatory system raised by the proponents of contemporary democracy are quite formidable and must be answered. For instance, in referring to the recent activist attentions given to participatory democracy, Dahl wrote:

> The most recent visitation of the vision was during the 1960's when it revealed itself to some elements of the New Left who, not realizing how much they were merely restating a very ancient tradition, insisted that people who are affected by decisions have the right to participate directly in making those decisions. Their demand for "participatory democracy" was simply a renewed assertion of Rousseau's primary democracy. By the end of the decade the ideology of participatory democracy appeared to be waning; quite likely it was only a youthful fashion of the sixties, which the youth of the seventies will disdain as the foolish idea of their elders (29, p. 81).

One can argue that the "youthful fashion" has attracted many reputable scholars and practitioners in public administration and has been seriously treated in administrative theory for many years. Nevertheless, the theorists of contemporary representative democracy have made some devastating attacks upon participatory democracy and they must be answered. At a minimum, the negative arguments which have persuaded some to conclude that participatory democracy is at best a fad, and at worst a danger (129) must be answered.

Third, the modifications of political, economic, and social systems proposed by the advocates are so vast that the values justifying the desired ends must be rigorously investigated and debated. This is required not so much because institutions must be changed, but because those changes will require *every* citizen to participate extensively. Given the general political apathy of most citizens (71)(78)(106), this represents a revolutionary request by itself. But the ensuing changes in human behavior are apt to be profound and we must be convinced that the end results are what we really want.

Fourth, assuming that the normative position is acceptable, if the required institutional changes are to be brought about it will be necessary to convince those in positions of power of the value of the new participatory forms. Most of them will, perforce, have their power, perquisites, and professional expertise either diminished or rendered unnecessary by the new participatory structures. As one author put it, in a more limited context, extensive participation implies a "negation of the expertise built up by the specialist" (69, p. 9). Those in the threatened positions will not be easily persuaded to adopt the new ways of doing things.

Fifth, and most important, the citizens themselves must be convinced. A participatory society will only work if they feel a personal and voluntary obligation to participate, for great labors will be required of them. Without that sense of obligation the only solutions would be compulsory or manipulated participation, both of which destroy the *raison d'être* for participation in the first place. *Everything* rests with the citizens and they will not be persuaded easily. For one thing, they have had so little experience with such participation that they cannot fully appreciate its potentials, as Pranger observed:

> A paradox arises here, however: only through creative political experiences can a society discover the best political action in the politics of participation. Yet citizens, more used to the politics of power, are mostly unfit to engage themselves in such new experiences with any expertise; disabled by their political culture, they prove uninterested and ignorant (123, p. 92).

While the evidence comes from limited, subnational situations, it has been demonstrated that even when given the opportunity most people are diffident, disinterested, or even hostile to the demands (or opportunities) of participation, as even Pateman grudgingly concedes (115, pp. 67–84)(25). Thus, powerful arguments must be presented if citizens are to be convinced (and not manipulated) to participate.

The arguments in favor of participatory democracy are numerous, but they can be grouped into four categories: the advantages for (1) citizen consent, (2) the political system, (3) political integration, and (4) the individual. Such groupings inevitably blur the subtleties of an argument, but they provide a convenient and efficient way of emphasizing the most effective arguments put forward by the advocates.

Participation and Citizen Consent

If democracy is to mean anything, those who submit to its rule must do so through voluntary consent. In order for that consent to mean anything, the citizen must be able to choose from among meaningful alternatives. Tussman states the problem as follows: "We cannot, of course, have it both ways: we cannot assert on the one hand that government is based on consent, and on the other hand that membership, and the subordination it entails, is involuntary" (144, pp. 37–38). Unfortunately, he dismisses the plight of the average citizen in one brief paragraph. He agrees that the alternatives for the citizen are difficult but that they are not insuperable, concluding: "Difficult as the alternative to citizenship may be, there is *sufficient* alternative to preserve the voluntary character of the consent which creates membership" (144, p. 38, emphasis added). That is hardly a realistic assessment.

The question of voluntary consent is, in my opinion, one of the major strengths of the participatory theorists. They recognize that whatever "voluntarism" might have existed in citizenship has now disappeared entirely. Tussman reasons that although it might be quite difficult for a dissenting citizen to go elsewhere, it can be done, and the recent exodus of war protesters would seem to lend credibility to his claim. However, there are at least two problems that make real escape impossible.

First, there is no free land left, in the sense of being able to avoid a political system of one kind or another. Unless one desires to hide away as a hermit, one can only exchange one hierarchical political system for another. Thus, an individual has only the possibilities of citizenship under differing kinds of political control. His only meaningful alternative is to change the political system within which he lives, if none of the other extant political systems measure up to his standard of what a political system should be.

Second, citizens are further entrapped within their own political system, at least in the developed countries. The life of the citizen is, for the most part, completely dominated by organizations (whether governmental, economic, or whatever) and such organizations are encompassing ever more aspects of life. Again, even on a subnational, nonpolitical level, most citizens are trapped. There is no escape from organizations, hence there is no real voluntarism. We seemingly cannot free ourselves from hierarchical organizations.

The advocates of maximal citizen participation have looked more realistically at that condition of human existence. They recognize that citizen consent, as the consent to be governed, is a thing of the past, if indeed it ever existed at all. In recognizing that the citizen is now effectively trapped, they propose a different form of voluntarism. Since men cannot escape either political systems or organizations, if freedom is to mean anything they must have control over their futures by having access to all the major decisional centers that affect their lives. Thus, the advocates confront the tangled problem of citizen consent in modern society. They follow Rousseau in their belief that freedom comes from obedience to the rules one has laid down for one's self and it is a most compelling argument.

The Advantages of Participation for the Political System

The advocates believe that contemporary representative democracy has undergone revisions in both theory and practice which have made meaningless any possible contributions by individual citizens (31)(150). While their bill of particulars is extensive, the main complaint is the reduction of the contribution of the individual citizen, for the most part, down to the act of voting. As Walker put it: "The concept of an active, informed, democratic citizenry, the most distinctive feature of the traditional theory, is the principal object of attack" (150, p. 285).

The advocates blame this devaluation upon many factors, but they single out a rather diverse group of influential scholars of contemporary representative democracy as being responsible for changing the theories of democracy to incorporate that devaluation. Their indictments may be too sweeping (56), but, nonetheless, they are very critical of Joseph Schumpeter, in particular; with Robert A. Dahl, Giovanni Sartori, and most "behavioralists" in political science not too far behind (44). The advocates emphasize their belief that the main purpose of democracy is the realization of the potentials of citizenship for each individual. As a result, the reduced role of the individual citizen is an intolerable state of affairs. There seem to be two major reasons for this devaluation: (1) a pervasive disillusionment with the individual citizen; and (2) the invasion of complex organizations into nearly every area of human life.

1. Disillusionment with the individual citizen. For various reasons, the generally rational images of man upon which early versions of democratic theory were based have been badly shaken (98). The main reason has been the numerous negative findings about the levels of political commitment and sophistication of ordinary people that have emerged from so many recent studies of political behavior. Study after study has demonstrated that the common man is not the rational, self-motivating, and thoughtful democrat of the Jeffersonian dream. Rather, the picture that emerges is of a lethargic, irrational, and prejudiced individual who neither understands nor is particularly committed to democratic principles (125). As a result, there has come a disillusionment with the individual citizen.

The literature in this area is vast and it cannot be summarized here (6)(106). Perhaps the most thoughtful summations were written by the late V. O. Key in *Public Opinion and American Democracy* (71). To return to the main point, of all the possible negative conclusions, the most galling to the advocates is the devaluation of the individual citizen, with a concomitant upgrading of governmental systems. The point can be well illustrated by the following quotation that represents the flavor of the later attacks:

> *Individual voters* today seem unable to satisfy the requirements for a democratic system of government outlined by political theorists. But the *system of democracy* does meet certain requirements for a going political organization. The individual members may not meet all the standards, but the whole nevertheless survives and grows. This suggests that where the classic theory is defective is in its concentration on the *individual citizen*. What are undervalued are certain collective properties that reside in the electorate as a whole and in the political and social system in which it functions (14, p. 312).

While the reference is to voting behavior, it is indicative of the transfer of significance from the citizen to the political system in contemporary theories of democracy. The present situation represents the success of the numerous demands that democratic theory be revised to reflect reality (Hartz, 22)(100): the imperative is to modify theories of democracy to conform to empirical findings, rather than to modify political systems to achieve the ideal.

This argument is well stated in an essay by Lane Davis (31). Among other things, he contends that such behavioral findings have become the criteria for evaluating the possible contributions the individual might make to the political system, rather than as simple descriptions of changeable conditions. This has had a most negative effect upon democratic theory. Most contemporary theories state that the major system benefits for the citizens in a democratic polity are the substantive policies that emanate from that government. For instance, according to Schumpeter the processes of democratic policy making are only instrumental to the policy output and have little value beyond that (133). In fact, some contemporary theorists go so far as to insist that the processes of democratic policy making must be protected from the masses. As Bachrach summarized, "The relationship of elites to masses is, in a vital way, reversed from classical theory: masses, not elites, become the potential threat to the system, and elites, not masses, become its defender" (5, pp. 8–9).

In other words, individual citizens cannot realistically be trusted to govern themselves and need benevolent, but firm, guidance from an informed and politically active minority. The participation of individual citizens is reduced to the inferior role of periodically selecting their political stewards. Perhaps Davis overstates the case, but he does put it well:

> In contemporary democracy, the active role of the citizen as a defining feature of democratic government is limited to the periodic choice of governors. Responsible government refers primarily to the accountability of a creative and active governing elite to those who have been the objects of its policies. The citizen has only a minimal involvement as a creative actor in what he judges. He must necessarily judge governors, their records and their promises, largely as a passive object of the actions of others. To the extent that this notion of responsibility is accepted and the citizens are considered primarily as objects rather than as creative actors, they must be considered as essentially irresponsible. They are to judge a world they

never made, and thus become a genteel counterpart of the mobs which sporadically unseated aristocratic governments in eighteenth- and nineteenth-century Europe (61, p. 45).

For the advocates, the low reputation of the democratic capabilities of the ordinary citizen is not viewed as irrevocable. They argue that both social structures and education have worked against the realization of the full potential of each man. If all structures, public and private, would be altered to allow for maximal citizen participation in all policy processes, the resultant educative benefits would make their ideal a reality.

2. The invasion of complex organizations. At the same time the reputation of the individual citizen has been on the decline, the spectacular increases in the pervasiveness, size, and success of complex organizations have made them the center of scholarly and popular attention (48)(58)(135). This has had two negative effects upon citizenship: because human energies have been so absorbed by the demands of organizational membership, there has come a devaluation of the specifically political. Secondly, there has grown an increased appreciation for the necessity for an administrative elite. For the advocates, the shift in emphasis from the individual citizen to the individual organization man, the organization, and its administrative elite is not acceptable. This development has come about because of a certain logic in the development of complex organizations.

To begin, the most salient facts about complex organizations are their necessary dependence upon hierarchical structure and positional power relationships for obtaining organizational objectives. Even though there are increasing numbers of scholars who disagree with these imperatives (81), bureaucratic organizations are prevalent (134). Two major criticisms can be levied against

this dependence. First, since citizens are entrapped within and profoundly affected by complex organizations throughout their lives, they are socialized to accept as normal the habitual organizational relationships of hierarchy and power. Such conditioning has an extremely adverse effect upon their abilities to assume the responsibilities of democratic citizenship.

Second, organizations that rely upon hierarchy and power must necessarily rely upon an administrative elite. One need only mention the name of Michels to bring to mind the litany about the inevitability of elites in organizations (16)(99). Given the prevailing ethic of competition, administrative elites, as well as the organizations of which they are a part, will inevitably compete for advantage. Unless there is a final authority which can moderate that competition, or even halt it, society will dissolve into chaos. That final authority, of course, rests with the political system, which is itself a congeries of organizations and, thus, dominated by its own elites.

Obviously, such a situation is unacceptable to the advocates of participatory democracy. They are not persuaded that the continued stability of a democratic regime depends upon the quality of the activist elites, as Key argued:

> The argument amounts essentially to the position that the masses do not corrupt themselves; if they are corrupt, they have been corrupted. If this hypothesis has a substantial strain of validity, the critical element for the health of a democratic order consists in the beliefs, standards, and competence of those who constitute the influentials, the opinion-leaders, the political activists in the order. That group, as has been made plain, refuses to define itself with great clarity in the American system; yet analysis after analysis points to its existence. If a

democracy tends toward indecision, decay, and disaster, the responsibility rests here, not in the mass of the people (71, p. 568).

If one accepts this position, it means that the fate of a democratic society rests on the moral sensibilities of a comparatively few elites.

The advocates believe that the abilities and consciences of a political (or an administrative) elite is too frail a reed upon which to rest the survival of the entire society. Among many other arguments there is evidence that quite often those political elites are not even aware of the opinions of their constituencies (91)(137). They would spread the responsibility out to the mass of the people through maximal citizen participation in all organizations. This would effectively undercut the power base of the elites, thus relieving society from an excessive dependence upon the few. It is an argument with substantial merit.

3. The revival of citizenship. The institution through which the reformation of society must be accomplished is a revivified democratic citizenship (10)(123). To be a citizen means that one assumes an official position within a democratic political system, with corresponding rights and obligations, which is quite different from the notion of citizenship as near passive membership. This distinction is central to the advocates' position and has been admirably expressed by Pranger (123), who is not, however, entirely within their camp.

If participatory democracy is to achieve its full potential, then the importance of its most significant office—that of citizen—must be recognized, supported, and expanded. However, the reputation of citizenship has been generally emasculated in contemporary representative democracies. Good citizenship has come to mean perfunctionary

and sporadic voting for political elites—one of the tragedies of the contemporary scene.

The advocates argue, correctly I believe, that one of the major responsibilities of a democratic government is to increase the quality of its citizens as citizens. Although Tussman is not as an advocate, he has stated the issue with force:

Democratic political life turns upon the office of the citizen and upon the demands of that office. The citizen is, in his political capacity, a public agent with all that that implies. . . . He must, in this capacity, be concerned with the public interest, not with his private goods. His communication must be colleagial, not manipulative. He must deliberate, not bargain. This is the program. And it is simply the application of tribunal manners to the electoral tribunal. *Nothing is more certain than that the abandonment of this conception spells the doom of meaningful democracy* (144, p. 108, emphasis added).

The advocates believe contemporary democracy has failed in this task and that a completely participatory society is the only way to proceed. They would probably state the proposition as follows: as the quality of the individual citizen is devalued, the quality of public policy will decline. Thus, while maximal citizen participation will not improve the quality of public policy immediately, one does learn by doing, and over time the quality of citizen participation will increase, which will then lead to qualitatively better policy decisions.

4. The revival of legitimacy. Finally, one of the most practical justifications concerns the perennial problem of system legitimacy. One of the major problems facing any government is to create and maintain a sense of the legitimacy of the extant regime among the citizenry. Many argue that our system seems to be disintegrating as the essential sense of legitimacy weakens (59)(89). To correct that condition, the advocates reason that if all citizens participate in policy decisions, the resultant policy (and the regime from which it issues) will be more legitimate in the minds of the citizens. For that reason, the advocates believe most of the current problems of compliance to governmental policy will disappear in a participatory system, for when citizens participate in making the policy decisions, it will produce accord among them.

The Advantages of Participation for Political Integration

The main reason the advocates call for a totally participatory society is due to their concern with the effects of organizational structures upon the human personality, with resultant predispositions toward, and reward for, conflict behavior. While they are primarily concerned with individuals, they believe, nevertheless, that such behaviors are destructive to society because they hinder the development of politically integrated societies. They believe a healthy society must be founded upon citizen consensus, not upon citizen conflict.

Thus, some of their strongest denunciations are directed toward claims of the social utility of conflict, of which competition is the legitimized variant. There is scant need to review the almost hallowed position "competition" holds in the American tradition. Most of our political institutions rely upon competitive struggles to recruit the major policy makers. Not only is competition the primary method of recruitment, it is also seen as a process which produces qualitatively better people. In addition, complex organizations, which have a powerful socializing influence upon their members, utilize competition to recruit primary decision makers. Because the recruitment, maintenance, and reward structures of complex organizations (political and otherwise) are predicated upon competition, competition is not only inevitable, it becomes a way of life. Such behavior destroys any chance of a society built upon consensus.

The problem cannot be resolved until the conflict-producing, competitive organizations are reformed. In other words, the accepted mode of competitive behavior within complex organizations must be altered. In the opinion of the advocates, the most effective way to do this is through maximal citizen participation in all policy decisions. The reasons for this are clear: since competitive organizations produce competitive people, it stands to reason that participative organizations will produce participative people. Therefore, the first step in creating a society built upon consensus is to compel all complex organizations to become fully participative. The advocates want an organic society wherein each individual is made to feel—and in fact is—indispensable to the whole.

Another facet of this argument is worth mentioning. Implicit is the assumption that through full citizen participation a universal sense of commonality will be discovered, which will: (1) cause all men to view one another as brothers, and (2) be the source of all laws and organizations. This will, of course, eliminate conflict, for when citizens disagree they can look inward to that common core and will know what they ought to do. In this matter the advocates come close to Rousseau's idea of the General Will—without which none of the Rousseauean prescriptions will work. Unfortunately, the advocates never really grapple with the problem of a substitute for the essential General Will (95).

The Advantages of Participation for the Individual

The major argument offered in defense of the massive revisions required to achieve a fully participatory society is the great benefits that accrue to the individual. The assumption is that participation produces better citizens, because through participation they realize their full potential. One of the most important aspects of that assumption is that there exists powerful symbiotic relationships between organizational structure and the developing human personality. Put simply, good processes produce good people. Thus the advocates are adamant about restructuring *all* institutions, rather than just reforming political institutions or improving the quality of education, or some other solution. For them, the structural framework with its demands for specific attitudes and behaviors is the key to the creation of a new society.

Obviously, the advocates have immense confidence in the positive educative value of participation. Pateman is worth quoting at length on this subject:

> The theory of participatory democracy is built round the central assertion that individuals and their institutions cannot be considered in isolation from one another. The existence of representative institutions at national level is not sufficient for democracy; for maximum participation by all the people at that level socialization, or "social training," for democracy must take place in other spheres in order that the necessary individual attitudes and psychological qualities can be developed. This development takes place through the process of participation itself. The major function of participation in the theory of participatory democracy is therefore an educative one, educative in the very widest sense, including both the psychological aspect and the gaining of practice in democratic skills and procedures. Thus there is no special problem about the stability of a participatory system; it is self-sustaining through the educative impact of the participatory process. Participation develops and fosters the very qualities necessary for it; the more individuals participate the better able they become to do so (115, pp. 42–43).

There are two parts of the quotation that should be emphasized. Reference is made to education in democratic processes, which is important, but not as important as the psychological development of the participants (68, p. 184). Participation builds the essential democratic character. Note, however, the assumption that all will be positively motivated by participation, which will make them want to participate more. In this way there is a constant improvement of the citizen and thus no problem with nonparticipation. So much of the advocates' argument hinges on this assumption that it must be subjected to the most rigorous analysis.

One of the most important commitments made by the advocates is their optimism about the efficacy of processes for the psychological development of the ideal democratic character. However, there are some important distinctions about the ways those processes will operate. While there is some overlap, the following three categories are fairly inclusive:

1. Process as release. Some advocate a participatory society by arguing that men must engage in the work of the polity if they are to realize the full potential of their humanness. They are little interested in what empirical research says man is and much more interested in what he ought to become. While they do not reject empirical findings, their belief in what man ought to be is prior to any empirical studies. Bachrach phrased it well:

> The emphasis in classical democratic theory upon citizen participation in all aspects of public affairs is based upon the premise that such involvement is an essential means to the full development of individual capacities. The self-developmental approach of the democrat has a common strain with the educational philosophies of such diverse men as Jesus, Freud, and Dewey. For each in his own way argued that man could know truth, and thus be freer than before, only through discovering it by himself (5, p. 4).

This is a compelling argument and it makes some large assumptions about innate human nature. It requires a vision of man for whom citizen participation is the primary means of releasing a basic human potential. Based upon the released human potential, education for really effective citizenship can begin.

2. Process as construction. Some advocates dismiss the idea that man has anything innate to be released, and concentrate upon the constructive potentials of education through participation. Specifically, they see man as innately malleable and believe he will become whatever he is made to be. Usually the commitment is not made specific, but it is implicit in their writings. It emerges in the assumption that structures and processes can mold men quite easily. In other words, if the appropriate participatory structures are established, individuals will become effective citizens.

The point may be clarified by contrasting "construction" with "releasing." There it is assumed that participation "releases" something innate in man—a potential always existing, but warped by hierarchical, power-oriented institutions. In the "construction" argument, the idea is that man is nothing and can

be made into anything, without destroying anything innate. The key lies in the educative structures and in a fully participative society; all participation is educative and contributes to the creation of democratic character.

3. Process as therapy. Both of the aforementioned approaches fall back upon the notion of participation as therapeutic. It is believed that most citizens are spiritually or psychologically sick and that only through participation will or can they be made well. In other words, process is justified as therapy— process as the healing of the sick. The illnesses of man are usually identified with one of the varying types of alienation (1)(15)(52) and participation is offered as the corrective. For instance, the healthy citizen will demonstrate strong feelings of political efficacy (209, p. 46), and further participation will build upon this base, to create a truly democratic character.

THE ARGUMENTS AGAINST PARTICIPATION

The advocates usually take notice of the arguments made against participatory democracy, but—with a few exceptions—they tend to dismiss them as either invalidated by the claimants' desire to maintain the status quo or as trivial, since they will become nonrelevant in a participatory society. However, the negative arguments must be answered on their own merits. The following five categories are offered as an aggregation of the most telling arguments against participatory democracy.

Contra-participation: The "Public Interest" and Citizen Opinion

The determination of the "public interest" is the most important question to be resolved by any democratic political system, since it provides the value criteria from which policy decisions should be made and against which they should be measured. The issues in that debate are extremely complex and cannot be repeated here (54)(57). However, the advocates are vulnerable in the matter of the public interest.

For instance, if a fully participatory society is achieved, there is the real possibility that the citizens will adopt policies that are antisocial or contrary to the public interest (even though the public interest may not be clearly defined). For example, suppose the decision was made to open all national parks to commercial development, or to vent all sewage into the waterways. In fact, the opposition to mandatory busing to achieve racial balance in the schools has mobilized busing opponents to participate quite vigorously. What is to prevent the political system from enforcing those policies if they are adopted by the citizen participants?

The response from the advocates is usually that it won't happen, since participation will produce a clear vision of the public interest. Unfortunately, there is little evidence to warrant much confidence in that proposition. Those who defend representative democracy have a much safer position: the checks and balances have been built into the system which—they contend—will deter either masses or elites from rushing into such foolish positions (26). The question, what will check mass opinion contrary to the public interest in a participatory society, without resorting to elite veto structures? must be answered by the advocates.

Contra-participation: The Logic of Organization

The advocates have not responded well to the charges that they have overlooked what the logic of organization will do to the participatory society. The imperative forces operating within organizations must be considered. Stated in their most familiar form, the negative features of the logic of organization lead to the "iron law of oligarchy" and the "tyranny of expertise" (99). The validity of these arguments in the present is usually acknowledged, but the tendency is to dismiss them as simple structural flaws, which will disappear in a fully participatory society. Perhaps. But the notion of an administrative elite has received considerable support from scholars and those contentions must be considered (134).

It will illustrate the point to dwell upon a rather paradoxical aspect of this issue, dealing with education and expertise. The need for expertise in an advanced society, consisting of interdependent complex organizations, cannot be denied. Therefore, policy makers are dependent to an increasing degree upon those who supply them with the requisite expert information. If a participatory society is to exist, its citizens must be educated beyond anything yet achieved by any known society. There are at least two important types of knowledge they need. The first is knowledge of democratic decisional processes, which can be gained by participation. The second is the technical knowledge necessary for making decisions and administering complex organizations.

In the first instance, citizens can learn by doing, as the advocates suggest. In the second instance, however, citizens cannot learn by doing, since necessary knowledge can only be obtained through specialized education. One, for instance, does not learn about nuclear physics by participating in policy decisions about breeder reactors. Without technical information, citizen participants cannot make intelligent evaluations of various programs. The requirement for such technical information inevitably forces policy makers to turn to experts. And, since experts are not of one opinion, choices must be made among competing claims. Thus, the policy makers must place more reliance upon one set of experts than upon another—which lays the groundwork for a cadre of technical elite (82).

Then there is the technical expertise needed to administer the necessary complex organizations. If the citizen attempts to gain such expertise only through participation, he will have time for nothing else. It is not sufficient to argue that complex organizations will be decentralized, and hence easier to administer. Even if that is accomplished, the decentralized units must be coordinated, so the problems inherent in such complexity return.

Therefore, if participatory democracy is to work, it must solve the most difficult problems involved in supplying the essential information. First, it will be necessary to guarantee that each citizen participant receives complete and accurate information. Since that is nowhere practiced in contemporary society, it will call for a massive change of heart among those who control the information flow. The logistical problems would be immense. Second, it will be necessary to guarantee that citizen participants have the time, education, and wit to understand the technical information they receive. Finally, the issue is further complicated by the even more important requirement for absolute truth in all communications. At a minimum, this means there can be no attempts to deceive and no public business can be conducted in secret (123, p. 53). "Integrity of communication" (144, p. 108) is of the utmost importance in a participatory society, because there are no effective checks upon the unanimous will of the citizens. If they act in unison on bad or untruthful information, they will not be stopped (4).

Contra-participation: The Problem of the Nonparticipant

The many questions concerning nonparticipation in a participatory system have not been adequately dealt with by the advocates. Nonparticipation is discussed, but is too often dismissed by assuming that once the structural barriers to full participation are removed, all citizens will want to participate (123, p. 27). However, even the evidence so often cited does not completely warrant their optimism (3). Also, there are different reasons for nonparticipation, each of which creates rather different problems. The following are illustrative:

1. Nonparticipation and sloth. In every society are the slothful who will not want to exert the effort to participate. What should be the response of a participatory society to such individuals? Can they be ignored, or do they represent a threat to the system? While some citizens are strenuously engaged in participating, others may wish to loaf. Should they be "carried" by the participators or should they be required to participate? Will others be tempted to follow their lead if they are allowed to go their way? This is not a minor issue, for the status of the slothful nonparticipant (who has no *valid* reason not to participate) in a participatory society tells us a great deal about the status of freedom and liberty in that society.

2. Nonparticipation and the desire for privacy. Participation must take place in public. There are some people who simply do not like public associations and wish to maintain their privacy. Should their personal desires not to participate be respected?

3. Nonparticipation and dissent. There will inevitably be some citizens who disagree with participatory democracy and will protest. What form will such dissent be allowed to take? What will be the status of the dissenter in a participatory society?

4. Nonparticipation: the contemplative and the creative. How should a participatory society deal with the creative individual, who, more often than not, must work in a solitary and nonpublic environment? Must he leave his seclusion and his work in order to participate? Which of his actions—his work or his participation—is of greatest benefit to society? A similar set of questions may be asked about the man who prefers the contemplative, rather than the participatory life (33).

Contra-participation: Policy Making in Crisis

Another assumption implicit in the writings of the advocates is that time will be forgiving—that there will be ample time for the citizen participants to meet, decide, learn, and meet again. But time is increasingly unforgiving and we have entered into an era of accelerating crises, so much of the policy making of the future will undoubtedly take place in crisis situations. What will that do to the quality of the policy decisions made? To illustrate, war is perhaps the greatest human crisis and war requires elites, because of the necessity for immediate, nondeliberative and secretive decisions. Will the other crises bring on the same requirements?

Contra-participation: Social Unanimity and Incipient Totalitarianism

In order for a fully participatory society to work, more citizen consensus will be required than presently exists. The advocates envisage a new society wherein all citizens are bound together in a community. Yet what happens if such a society comes about? The unanimity of the elites in a democracy is condemned by the advocates, yet they seem undeterred by the unanimity of the masses. Such unanimity raises the spectre of an incipient totalitarianism, but the advocates either ignore the problem or dismiss it. Pateman, for instance, is rather sarcastic

about totalitarianism, as if it were only a red herring raised by establishment elites to deter the implementation of participatory democracy. But the question of what happens to a society that is unanimous must be answered.

CONCLUSION

In conclusion, we must ask again the primary question why should people participate? What justifies the immense labors that will be required of all people if a participatory democracy is to work? In other words, why should they support the institution of a participatory system? An attempt has been made to outline a few of the arguments for and against participatory democracy. But the problems connected with the subject are exceedingly difficult as Waldo wrote:

> Participation is unquestionably "right" in my view. But the issues involved are of all but mind-paralyzing complexity, inconsistency and confusion abound, and we need to get above the level of the *ad hoc* partisan argument. Above all, we need to recognize that participation takes place in a context of a country or a society and must be related to that context (149, p. 264).

A few final observations remain to be made.

Practical research. Obviously, not enough is known about the complex and interrelated subjects of decentralization and citizen participation. Decentralized, participatory programs have been brought into being and are operating with varying degrees of success. One result has been to highlight the major intellectual efforts that still must be made. To illustrate, one need only read the excellent article on participation by Verba to realize the endless variables that must be considered (147). In addition, a great deal of attention has been attracted by the work of administrative theorists in the area of participative management (Meade, 149). The names of McGregor, Likert, and Argyris are seen more and more often in the literature of public administration. Some aspects of the so-called "new public administration" attempt to integrate that scholarship into a synthesis applicable to the problems of public administration (97). If some version of participatory democracy is to be achieved on a limited or total scale, it must be possible to design, with some confidence, the optimal mixes for differential decentralization and participations. But, before that can be done, we must be able to specify what we mean by "optimal." In other words, what end-values are we trying to optimize? This leads to the next observation.

Metaphysical crises.   We still seem unable to state clearly why people should participate, and this intellectual failure is more serious than any failures in practice. While he arrived at conclusions almost opposite those of the advocates, Schattschneider's indictment of the intellectual is quite applicable:

It is an outrage to attribute the failure of Ameican democracy to the ignorance and stupidity of the masses. The most disastrous shortcomings of the system have been those of the intellectuals whose concepts of democracy have been amazingly rigid and uninventive. The failure of the intellectuals is dangerous because it creates confusion in high places. Unless the intellectuals can produce a better theory of politics than they have, it is possible that we shall abolish democracy before we have found out what it is! (132, pp. 135–136)

The vision of what a contemporary participatory system could be is only now beginning to be spelled out. The books by Bachrach, Tussman, and Pranger, and the essays in the volumes by Waldo and Marini all give evidence of serious thought about this problem. But more is needed.

We need a new theory of democracy that will be adequate to the demands of the lethal probabilities of the future. Such a theory must incorporate the findings of the behavioralists, but it must not abandon the ideal of the democratic dream that guided classical democratic theory. Earlier it was stated that the questions raised in this essay would have to be explicated and analyzed by political philosophers. Let me carry that a step further. It is now time for a generation of "public administration philosophers" who will address themselves to the resolution of the extremely difficult normative questions that plague nearly every book and article written about this subject. The absence of such metaphysical speculation is the most serious problem facing those who believe in participatory democracy—regardless of the scale of implementation they advocate.

Curriculum.   Because this is a curriculum development essay, it is appropriate that the concluding comment should refer to what this means to curriculum. Kuhn has described most lucidly the great influence of the textbooks in the sciences (76)(156). They not only define the paradigm of "normal science" that students will practice, they also define the "reality" of the world. Such is the case with public administration and political science. The subject of political socialization is extremely complex, but there is reason to believe that schools, books, and civics curricula make significant contributions to defining the "realities" of democratic participation for our students (46)(61)(63)(80). To an extent, they establish the standards of a "normal" democratic politics that seems increasingly unequal to the challenges of the future. In most of those texts, the theory of democracy is based upon the ideas of the theorists of contemporary representative democracy. Thus, their vision of democracy comes to be accepted not just as a description, or a possibility, but as the fact and the evaluative standard.

Is it too much to suggest that a new vision of democratic participation, articulated by the scholars, tested in the field, and embodied in the textbooks, may bring the dream of democracy a little closer to reality for future generations? The task will be immensely difficult, but there is reason for optimism. As Miller and Rein wrote in another context: "But it seems to us our society is enmeshed in the right kind of struggle" (107, p. 24).

REFERENCES

The following list of books and articles was pared down from an original bibliography of over 500 items. Obviously, many difficult choices had to be made. Many articles were sacrificed because of excellent bibliographies contained in many of the books. An example is the massive amount of work done on the subject of political socialization. It is reflected in only a few references, but they contain useful bibliographies. The same is true for other subject areas.

1. Joel Aberbach, "Alienation and Political Behavior," *American Political Science Review,* Vol. LXII (March 1969), pp. 86–99.
2. Robert R. Alford and Harry M. Scoble, "Sources of Local Political Involvement," *American Political Science Review,* Vol. LXII (December 1968), pp. 1192–1206.
3. Gabriel A. Almond and Sidney Verba, *The Civic Culture* (Boston: Little, Brown, 1965).
4. Hannah Arendt, "Truth and Politics," in David Spitz (ed.), *Political Theory and Social Change* (New York: Atherton, 1967), pp. 3–37.
5. Peter Bachrach, *The Theory of Democratic Elitism; A Critique* (Boston: Little, Brown, 1967).
6. James David Barber, *Citizen Politics: An Introduction to Political Behavior* (Chicago: Markham, 1969).
7. Brian M. Barry, *Sociologists, Economics and Democracy* (London: Collier-Macmillan, 1970).
8. Weldon V. Barton, "Towards a Policy Science of Democracy," *Journal of Politics,* Vol. XXXI (February 1969), pp. 32–51.
9. Darryl Baskin, *American Pluralist Democracy: A Critique* (New York: Van Nostrand Reinhold Co., 1971).
10. Christian Bay, "Law or Justice? An Emerging Conception of Citizenship," in Robert T. Golembiewski, Charles S. Bullock, III, and Harrell R. Rodgers, Jr. (eds.), *The New Politics: Polarization or Utopia?* (New York: McGraw-Hill, 1970), pp. 32–48.
11. Daniel Bell, "Notes on the Post-Industrial Society—Part One," *Public Interest* (Winter 1967), pp. 24–35; "Notes on the Post-Industrial Society—Part Two," *Public Interest* (Spring 1967), pp. 102–118.
12. Wendell Bell, Richard J. Hill, and Charles R. Wright, *Public Leadership* (San Francisco: Chandler, 1961).
13. C. George Benello and Dimitrios Roussopoulos (eds.), *The Case for Participatory Democracy: Some Prospects for a Radical Society* (New York: Grossman, 1971).
14. Bernard R. Berelson, Paul F. Lazarsfeld, and William N. McPhee, *Voting* (Chicago: University of Chicago Press, 1954).

15. Robert Blauner, *Freedom and Alienation* (Chicago: University of Chicago Press, 1964).

16. T. B. Bottomore, *Elites and Society* (Baltimore: Penguin Books, 1964).

17. David Braybrooke, *Three Tests for Democracy: Personal Rights, Human Welfare, and Collective Preference* (New York: Random House, 1968).

18. Zbigniew Brzezinski, *Between Two Ages: America's Role in the Technetronic Era* (New York: Viking, 1970).

19. James M. Buchanan and Gordon Tullock, *The Calculus of Consent: Logical Foundations of Constitutional Democracy* (Ann Arbor: University of Michigan Press, 1962).

20. Walter Dean Burnham, "The Changing of the American Political Universe," *American Political Science Review*, Vol. LIX (March 1965), pp. 7–28.

21. Claude Burtenshaw, "The Political Theory of Pluralist Democracy," *Western Political Quarterly*, Vol. XXI (December 1968), pp. 577–587.

22. William N. Chambers and Robert H. Salisbury (eds.) *Democracy in Mid-Twentieth Century* (St. Louis: Washington University Press, 1960).

23. Charles Cnudde and Deanne Neubauer (eds.), *Empirical Democratic Theory* (Chicago: Markham, 1969).

24. Roger W. Cobb and Charles D. Elder, "The Politics of Agenda-Building: An Alternative Perspective for Modern Democratic Theory," *Journal of Politics*, Vol. XXXIII (November 1971), pp. 892–915.

25. Michel Crozier, *The Bureaucratic Phenomenon* (Chicago: University of Chicago Press, 1964).

26. Robert A. Dahl, *A Preface to Democratic Theory* (Chicago: University of Chicago Press, 1956).

27. ——, "Further Reflections on the 'Elitist Theory of Democracy'," *American Political Science Review*, Vol. LX (June 1966), pp. 296–305.

28. ——, "The City in the Future of Democracy," *American Political Science Review*, Vol. LXI (December 1967), pp. 953–970.

29. ——, *After the Revolution?* (New Haven: Yale University Press, 1970).

30. ——, *Polyarchy: Participation and Opposition* (New Haven: Yale University Press, 1971).

31. Lane Davis, "The Cost of Realism: Contemporary Restatements of Democracy," *Western Political Quarterly*, Vol. XVII (March 1964), pp. 37–46.

32. Richard E. Dawson and Kenneth Prewitt, *Political Socialization* (Boston: Little, Brown, 1969).

33. Sebastian de Grazia, "Politics and the Contemplative Life," *American Political Science Review*, Vol. LIV (June 1960), pp. 447–456.

34. Bertrand de Jouvenel, "Politics and Prevision," *American Political Science Review*, Vol. LIX (March 1965), pp. 29–38.

35. Robert Denhardt, "Organizational Citizenship and Personal Freedom," *Public Administration Review*, Vol. XXVIII (January/February 1968), pp. 47–54.

36. ——, "The Organization as a Political System," *Western Political Quarterly*, Vol. XXIV (December 1971), pp. 675–686.

37. Jack Dennis, "Major Problems of Political Socialization Research," *Midwest Journal of Political Science*, Vol. XII (February 1968), pp. 85–114.

38. D. J. Devine, *The Attentive Public:*

Polyarchical Democracy (Chicago: Rand McNally, 1970).

39. John P. Diggins, "Ideology and Pragmatism: Philosophy or Passion?" *American Political Science Review,* Vol. LXIV (September 1970), pp. 899–906.

40. Giuseppe Di Palma, "Disaffection and Participation in Western Democracies," *Journal of Politics,* Vol. XXXI (November 1969), pp. 984–1010.

41. ———, and Herbert McClosky, "Personality and Conformity: The Learning of Political Attitudes," *American Political Science Review,* Vol. LXIV (December 1970), pp. 1054–1073.

42. Anthony Downs, *An Economic Theory of Democracy* (New York: Harper & Row, 1957).

43. Peter Drucker, "The Sickness of Government," *Public Interest* (Winter 1969), pp. 3–23.

44. Graeme Duncan and Steven Lukes, "New Democracy," *Political Studies,* Vol. II (June 1963), pp. 156–177.

45. David Easton, "The New Revolution in Political Science," *American Political Science Review,* Vol. LXIII (December 1969), pp. 1051–1061.

46. ———, and Jack Dennis, *Children in the Political System: Origins of Political Legitimacy* (New York: McGraw-Hill, 1969).

47. Paul R. Ehrlich and Anne H. Ehrlich, *Population, Resources, Environment* (San Francisco: W. H. Freeman, 1970).

48. Jacques Ellul, *The Technological Society,* J. Wilkinson (trans.) (New York: Knopf, 1954, 1964).

49. ———, *Propaganda,* K. Kellen (trans.) (New York: Knopf, 1962, 1965).

50. ———, *The Political Illusion,* K. Kellen (trans.) (New York: Knopf, 1965, 1967).

51. James W. Fesler, "Approaches to the Understanding of Decentralization," *Journal of Politics,* Vol. XXVII (August 1965), pp. 536–566.

52. Ada W. Finifter, "Dimensions of Political Alienation," *American Political Science Review,* Vol. LXIV (June 1970), pp. 389–410.

53. Richard Flacks, "On Participatory Democracy," *Dissent,* Vol. XIII (November-December 1966), pp. 701–708.

54. Richard E. Flathman, *The Public Interest* (New York: Wiley, 1966).

55. Robert Y. Fluno, "The Floundering Leviathan: Pluralism in an Age of Ungovernability," *Western Political Quarterly,* Vol. XXIV (September 1971), pp. 560–566.

56. Jay W. Forrester, *World Dynamics* (Cambridge, Mass.: Wright-Allen, 1971).

57. Carl J. Friedrich (ed.), *The Public Interest* (Nomos V; Chicago: Atherton, 1962).

58. Robert T. Golembiewski, *Man, Management, and Morality* (New York: McGraw-Hill, 1965).

59. Paul Goodman, *People or Personnel and Like a Conquered Province* (New York: Vintage Books, 1968).

60. Fred I. Greenstein, "Lasswell's Concept of Democratic Character," *Journal of Politics,* Vol. XXX (August 1968), pp. 696–709.

61. ———, *Personality and Politics* (Chicago: Markham, 1969).

62. Morton Grodzins, "Centralization and Decentralization in the American Federal System," in Robert A. Goldwin (ed.), *A Nation of States* (Chicago: Rand McNally, 1963), pp. 1–23.

63. Robert D. Hess and Judith V. Torney, *The Development of Political Attitudes in Children* (Garden City, N.Y.: Anchor Books, 1968).

64. R. Jean Hills, "The Representative

Function: Neglected Dimension of Leadership Behavior," *Administrative Science Quarterly,* Vol. VIII (June 1963), pp. 83–101.

65. Henry S. Kariel, *The Decline of American Pluralism* (Stanford: Stanford University Press, 1961).

66. ——, "Expanding the Political Present," *American Political Science Review,* Vol. LXIII (September 1969), pp. 768–776.

67. ——, "Creating Political Reality," *American Political Science Review,* Vol. LXIV (December 1970), pp. 1088–1098.

68. Arnold S. Kaufman, "Human Nature and Participatory Democracy," and "Participatory Democracy Ten Years Later," in William E. Connolly (ed.), *The Bias of Pluralism* (New York: Atherton, 1969), pp. 178–212.

69. Herbert Kaufman, "Administrative Decentralization and Political Power," *Public Administration Review,* Vol. XXIX (January/February 1969), pp. 3–14.

70. Willmoore Kendall and George Carey, "The 'Intensity' Problem and Democratic Theory, *American Political Science Review,* Vol. LXII (March 1968), pp. 5–24.

71. V. O. Key, Jr., *Public Opinion and American Democracy* (New York: Knopf, 1961).

72. ——, with Milton C. Cummings, Jr., *The Responsible Electorate: Rationality in Presidential Voting—1936–1960* (Cambridge: The Belknap Press of Harvard University Press, 1966).

73. Otto Kirchheimer, "Private Man and Society," *Political Science Quarterly,* Vol. LXXXI (March 1966), pp. 1–24.

74. Manfred Kochen and Karl W. Deutsch, "Toward a Rational Theory of Decentralization: Some Implications of a Mathematical Approach," *American Political Science Review,* Vol. LXIII (September 1969), pp. 734–749.

75. Irving Kristol, "Decentralization for What?" *Public Interest* (Spring 1968), pp. 17–25.

76. Thomas S. Kuhn, *The Structure of Scientific Revolutions,* 2nd edition (Chicago: University of Chicago Press, 1970).

77. Robert E. Lane, "The Politics of Consensus in an Age of Affluence," *American Political Science Review,* Vol. LIX (December 1965), pp. 874–895.

78. ——, and David O. Sears, *Public Opinion* (Englewood Cliffs, N.J.: Prentice-Hall, 1964).

79. Kenneth P. Langton, *Political Socialization* (New York: Oxford University Press, 1969).

80. ——, and M. Kent Jennings, "Political Socialization and the High School Civics Curriculum in the U.S., *American Political Science Review,* Vol. LXII (September 1968), pp. 852–867.

81. Harold J. Leavitt, "Applied Organizational Change in Industry: Structural, Technological, and Humanistic Approaches," in James G. March (ed.), *Handbook of Organizations* (Chicago: Rand McNally, 1965), pp. 1144–1170.

82. Avery Leiserson, "Scientists and Public Policy," *American Political Science Review,* Vol. LIX (June 1965), pp. 408–416.

83. Frank Levy and Edwin M. Truman, "Toward a Rational Theory of Decentralization: Another View," *American Political Science Review,* Vol. LXV (March 1971), pp. 172–179.

84. Charles E. Lindblom, *The Intelligence of Democracy: Decision Making Through Mutual Adjustment* (New York: Free Press, 1965).

85. Seymour Martin Lipset, *Political Man* (Garden City, N.Y.: Doubleday, 1960).

86. ———, *The First New Nation* (New York: Basic Books, 1963).

87. Lewis Lipsitz, "Work Life and Political Attitudes: A Study of Manual Workers," *American Political Science Review,* Vol. LVIII (December 1964), pp. 951–962.

88. Michael Lipsky, "Protest as a Political Resource," *American Political Science Review,* Vol. LXII (December 1968), pp. 1144–1158.

89. Theodore Lowi, *End of Liberalism* (New York: Norton, 1969).

90. Herbert McClosky, "Consensus and Ideology in American Politics," *American Political Science Review,* Vol. LVIII (June 1964), pp. 361–382.

91. ———, Paul J. Hoffman, and Rosemary O'Hara, "Issue Conflict and Consensus Among Party Leaders and Followers," *American Political Science Review,* Vol. LIV (June 1960), pp. 406–427.

92. C. B. MacPherson, *The Real World of Democracy* (Oxford: Clarendon Press, 1966).

93. Duncan MacRae, Jr., "Scientific Communication, Ethical Argument, and Public Policy," *American Political Science Review,* Vol. LXV (March 1971), pp. 38–50.

94. Harvey C. Mansfield, Jr., "Whether Party Government is Inevitable," *Political Science Quarterly,* Vol. LXXX (December 1965), pp. 517–542.

95. Frank Marini, "Popular Sovereignty But Representative Government: The Other Rousseau," *Midwest Journal of Political Science,* Vol. XI (November 1967), pp. 451–470.

96. ———, "John Locke and the Revision of Classical Democratic Theory," *Western Political Quarterly,* Vol. XXII (March 1969), pp. 5–18.

97. ——— (ed.), *Toward a New Public Administration* (Scranton, Pa.: Chandler, 1971).

98. Max Mark, "What Image of Man for Political Science?" *Western Political Quarterly,* Vol. XV (December 1962), pp. 593–604.

99. John D. May, "Democracy, Organization, Michels," *American Political Science Review,* Vol. LIX (June 1965), pp. 417–429.

100. Henry B. Mayo, *An Introduction to Democratic Theory* (New York: Oxford University Press, 1960).

101. ———, "How Can We Justify Democracy?" *American Political Science Review,* Vol. LVI (September 1962), pp. 555–566.

102. Peter Medding, "'Elitist' Democracy: An Unsuccessful Critique of a Misunderstood Theory," *Journal of Politics,* Vol. XXXI (August 1969), pp. 641–654.

103. Kenneth A. Megill, *The New Democratic Theory* (New York: Free Press, 1970).

104. Richard M. Merelman, "On the Neo-Elitist Critique of Community Power, *American Political Science Review,* Vol. LXII (June 1968), pp. 451–460.

105. ———, "The Development of Political Ideology: A Framework for the Analysis of Political Socialization," *American Political Science Review,* Vol. LXIII (September 1969), pp. 750–767.

106. Lester W. Milbrath, *Political Participation: How and Why do People Get Involved in Politics?* (Chicago: Rand McNally, 1965).

107. S. M. Miller and Martin Rein, "Participation, Poverty, and Administration," *Public Administration Review,* Vol. XXIX (January/February 1969), pp. 15–24.

108. Edward N. Muller, "The Representation of Citizens by Political Authorities: Consequences for Regime Support," *American Political Science Review,* Vol. LXIV (December 1970), pp. 1149–1166.

109. J. P. Nehl, "Consensus or Elite

Domination: The Case of Business," *Political Studies* (Fall 1965), pp. 22–44.

110. Deane E. Neubauer, "Some Conditions on Democracy," *American Political Science Review*, Vol. LXI (December 1967), pp. 1002–1009.

111. Norman H. Nie, G. Bingham Powell, Jr., and Kenneth Prewitt, "Social Structure and Political Participation: Developmental Relationships," *American Political Science Review*, Vol. LXIII (June 1969), pp. 361–378; "Social Structure and Political Participation: Developmental Relationships," Vol. LXIII (September 1969), pp. 808–832.

112. Robert A. Nisbet, "The Twilight of Authority," *Public Interest* (Spring 1969), pp. 3–9.

113. Michael Parenti, "Power and Pluralism: A View From the Bottom," *Journal of Politics*, Vol. XXXII (August 1970), pp. 501–530.

114. Geraint Parry, *Political Elites* (London: George Allen and Unwin, Ltd., 1969).

115. Carole Pateman, *Participation and Democratic Theory* (London: Cambridge University Press, 1970).

116. J. Roland Pennock and John W. Chapman (eds.), *Equality* (Nomos IX, New York: Atherton Press, 1967).

117. ———, *Representation* (Nomos X; New York: Atherton Press, 1968).

118. ———, *Political and Legal Obligation* (Nomos XII; New York: Atherton Press, 1970).

119. ———, *Privacy* (Nomos XIII; Chicago: Aldine-Atherton, 1971).

120. Dorothy Pickles, *Democracy* (Baltimore: Penguin, 1970).

121. John Plamenatz, "Electoral Studies and Democratic Theory," *Political Studies*, Vol. VI (February 1958), pp. 1–9.

122. Paul F. Power, "On Civil Disobedience in Recent American Democratic Thought," *American Political Science Review*, Vol. LXIV (March 1970), pp. 35–47.

123. Robert J. Pranger, *The Eclipse of Citizenship: Power and Participation in Contemporary Politics* (New York: Holt, Rinehart & Winston, 1968).

124. ———, "The Status of Democratic Values and Procedures in a Changing Urban America," *Western Political Quarterly*, Vol. XXI (September 1968), pp. 496–507.

125. James W. Prothro and Charles M. Grigg, "Fundamental Principles of Democracy: Bases of Agreement and Disagreement," *Journal of Politics*, Vol. XXII (May 1960), pp. 276–294.

126. Douglas W. Rae, "Political Democracy as a Property of Political Institutions," *American Political Science Review*, Vol. LXV (March 1971), pp. 111–119.

127. Emmette S. Redford, *Democracy in the Administrative State* (New York: Oxford University Press, 1969).

128. David Ricci, *Community Power and Democratic Theory* (New York: Random House, 1971).

129. Giovanni Sartori, *Democratic Theory* (New York: Praeger, 1965).

130. ———, "Politics, Ideology, and Belief Systems," *American Political Science Review*, Vol. I. (June 1969), pp. 398–411.

131. John H. Schaar, "Some Ways of Thinking About Quality," *Journal of Politics*, Vol. XXVI (November 1964), pp. 867–895.

132. E. E. Schattschneider, *The Semisovereign People* (New York: Holt, Rinehart and Winston, 1960).

133. Joseph Schumpeter, *Capitalism, Socialism and Democracy*, 3rd edition (New York: Harper and Row, 1950, 1962).

134. William G. Scott, "Organization Government: The Prospects for a

Truly Participative System," *Public Administration Review,* Vol. XXIX (January/February 1969), pp. 43–52.

135. ———, and Terence C. Mitchell, *Organization Theory: A Structural and Behavioral Analysis,* revised ed. (Homewood, Ill.: Irwin-Dorsey, 1972).

136. Donald D. Searing, "Models and Images of Man and Society in Leadership Theory," *Journal of Politics,* Vol. XXXI (February 1969), pp. 3–31.

137. Roberta S. Sigel and H. Paul Friesema, "Urban Community Leaders' Knowledge of Public Opinion," *Western Political Quarterly,* Vol. XVIII (December 1965), pp. 881–895.

138. V. Subramaniam, "Representative Bureaucracy: A Reassessment," *American Political Science Review,* Vol. LXI (December 1967), pp. 1010–1019.

139. Dennis F. Thompson, *The Democratic Citizen: Social Science and Democratic Theory in the 20th Century* (London: Cambridge University Press, 1970).

140. Thomas Landon Thorson, *The Logic of Democracy* (New York: Holt, Rinehart and Winston, 1962).

141. ———, *Biopolitics* (New York: Holt, Rinehart and Winston, 1970).

142. Glenn Tinder, "Is Liberalism Out-of-Date?" *Journal of Politics,* Vol. XXIV (May 1962), pp. 258–276.

143. David Truman, "The American System in Crisis," *Political Science Quarterly,* Vol. LXXIII (December 1959), pp. 481–497.

144. Joseph Tussman, *Obligation and the Body Politic* (New York: Oxford University Press, 1960).

145. Sidney Verba, *Small Groups and Political Behavior* (Princeton: Princeton University Press, 1961).

146. ———, "Organizational Member-ship and Democratic Consensus," *Journal of Politics,* Vol. XXVII (August 1965), pp. 467–497.

147. ———, "Democratic Participation," *The Annals of the American Academy of Political and Social Science,* Vol. II (September 1967), pp. 53–78.

148. Donald Von Eschen, Jerome Kirk, and Maurice Pinard, "The Conditions of Direct Action in a Democratic Society," *Western Political Quarterly,* Vol. XXII (June 1969), pp. 309–326.

149. Dwight Waldo (ed.), *Public Administration in a Time of Turbulence* (Scranton, Pa.: Chandler, 1971).

150. Jack L. Walker, "A Critique of the Elitist Theory of Democracy," *American Political Science Review,* Vol. LX (June 1966), pp. 285–295.

151. Michael A. Weinstein, "A Critique of Contemporary Democratic Theories," *Western Political Quarterly,* Vol. XXIV (March 1971), pp. 41–44.

152. Orion F. White, Jr., "The Dialectical Organization: An Alternative to Bureaucracy," *Public Administration Review,* Vol. XXIX (January/February 1969), pp. 32–42.

153. Fred H. Willhoite, Jr., "Political Order and Consensus: A Continuing Problem," *Western Political Quarterly,* Vol. XVI (June 1963), pp. 294–304.

154. James Q. Wilson, "The Bureaucracy Problem," *Public Interest* (Winter 1967).

155. Sheldon S. Wolin, *Politics and Vision* (Boston: Little, Brown, 1960).

156. ———, "Paradigms and Political Theories," in P. King and B. C. Parekh (eds.), *Politics and Experience* (Cambridge: Cambridge University Press, 1968), pp. 125–152.

SECTION 10

Accountability and Ethics

Accountability and ethics are topics of constant concern in public administration. Public administrators play a very significant role in the development and implementation of public policies and the expenditure of vast resources. They sometimes wield vast regulatory and enforcement powers. They generate, maintain, and control a great amount of information. In democratic theory, public administrators must be subordinate to the legislature and political executive. But such subordination is not automatic. There is a wide variety of reasons why public administrators' actions may deviate from the expectations of the legislature and/or the law: self-interest, competing visions of the public interest, complexity of enforcement, responsiveness to various groups, professional values, and so forth. Although there are solutions to some specific problems of accountability, there is no overall formula for guaranteeing that public administrators will not act independently in ways that deviate from their political bosses' expectations and instructions.

Ethics are related to accountability. They are often conceptualized as a form of inner check on behavior. For instance, ethical behavior would generally preclude violating the law, even in minor ways, for the sake of one's self-interest, family, or friends. But ethics and legal compliance are not synonymous. Ethics may demand more, including on occasion that a truly bad law be circumvented. (For example, today would we judge unethical a public administrator of a century and a half ago who violated the Fugitive Slave Act on principle?)

Accountability and ethics are complex. Our terms are imprecise, and we must apply them in myriad shifting situations. The selections in this section map out the main issues. Their purpose is to clarify thinking about accountability and ethics more than to provide answers or prescribe applications.

In recent years, public administrators have often been urged to act as "public entrepreneurs," that is, to find new sources of revenues and to span the traditional boundaries between public and private organizations in implementing programs. In "Reconciling Public Entrepreneurship and Democracy," Carl J. Bellone and George Frederick Goerl consider the problems that public entrepreneurship may present for accountability and citizen participation. They call for a "civic-regarding entrepreneurship" as a means of assuring that democracy is strengthened.

Certainly, as a general principle, one would want public administrators to be civic regarding. But how can accountability to such a standard be attained? In "Accountability in the Public Sector: Lessons from the Challenger Tragedy," Barbara Romzek and Melvin Dubnick note that there are really four types of accountability systems: legal, political, bureaucratic, and professional. Would that they were harmonious! However, in the context of the Challenger disaster, Romzek and Dubnick show that the systems can undercut one another. The authors conclude that NASA's " . . . emphasis on political and bureaucratic accountability was a relevant response to changing institutional expectations in NASA's environment, but they were inappropriate for the technical tasks at hand." The question, therefore, is not how to have an accountability system, but rather how to have the right one or mix of them. As the case study shows, the stakes in making the correct choices may be very high indeed.

As he has often done throughout his remarkable career, Dwight Waldo provides conceptual clarity by asking the right questions. In "Public Administration and Ethics: A Prologue to a Preface," he reviews some of the grand ethical conflicts and provides "a map—of sorts" to ordering them. The conflicts are between public morality and private morality as well as between governmental law and "higher" law (such as religious obligation or, in the United States, natural law as vaguely incorporated into the constitutional scheme through the Ninth Amendment). The map is helpful, but "a need for navigation instruments" remains. In a concluding section on "observations and reflections," Waldo looks toward the future. He suggests how we must think about public administrative ethics if we are ever to achieve them.

32.   Reconciling Public Entrepreneurship and Democracy

Carl J. Bellone and George Frederick Goerl

The 1980s have been labeled the "age of the entrepreneur." Several commentators have given the Reagan administration credit for promoting the virtues of private enterprise, "leaner" govern-

SOURCE: "Reconciling Public Entrepreneurship and Democracy" by Carl J. Bellone and George Frederick Goerl, *Public Administration Review:* 52 (March/April 1992). Reprinted by permission of the American Society for Public Administration.

ments, and entrepreneurial budgets (those that lower tax burdens). The rise of the public-sector entrepreneur is found in the advent of tax limitation movements, declining federal grants to state and local governments, and the growing fiscal crises faced by governments at all levels of the federal system. Public administrators as entrepreneurs and agents of entrepreneurial states seek to find new sources of revenue, besides the more traditional taxes, to increase tax bases through economic development projects and to augment the number of private-sector entrepreneurs within their boundaries. Current attention paid to public-private partnerships as solutions to the fiscal and social problems of government symbolizes the importance currently attached to both private and public entrepreneurship.

However, the characteristic behavior of public entrepreneurs (as well as traditional public administrators), must be evaluated in terms of administrative responsibility if their actions are to be compatible with democratic values. Administrative responsibility can be viewed as simply following policies and directions of hierarchical superiors. Because this approach can lead to the Eichmann phenomenon, some authors have argued that administrative responsibility must include certain democratic values when administrators are carrying out administrative directives. Other authors have even described responsibility as requiring the administrator to become an active agent of democratic education and reform. John Burke urges administrators to correct any departures from democratic principles by politicians, to feel an obligation to democratic government as a whole, and to act effectively to achieve policy ends (Burke, 1986, pp. 42, 45, 50–54). Terry Cooper argues that public administrators, as "citizen-administrators," should be political educators for a citizenry that needs more information in order to play important political and citizenship roles (Cooper, 1984). In these two cases, theorists of administrative responsibility assume that the public administrator has a responsibility for furthering democratic values in the political process, in policy implementation, and for developing better opportunities for citizenship.

As entrepreneurs, public administrators, have taken on the added responsibility of finding new and add sources of revenue; but they have, at the same time, a vested political self-interest. The legitimacy of public entrepreneurs would seem to rest on their exercising administrative responsibility in the democratic manner described above so as to make public entrepreneurship compatible with democratic values and institutional roles. Four important characteristics of public entrepreneurs—autonomy, a personal vision of the future, secrecy, and risk-taking—need to be reconciled with the fundamental democratic values of accountability, citizen participation, open policymaking processes, and concern for the long-term public good (stewardship).

ENTREPRENEURIAL AUTONOMY VERSUS DEMOCRATIC ACCOUNTABILITY

First, a conflict exists between the autonomy/discretion desired by entrepreneurs and democratic accountability. With an increase in the complexity of revenue problems facing many governments, public administrators ask for greater discretion to carry out their entrepreneurial revenue searches (Lewis, 1980; Goerl and Bellone, 1983). Revenue crises have made public policy goals relatively less important in comparison to economic goals or revenue acquisition. In the name of revenue generation, programs and projects are set in motion that threaten to change drastically the character of a community and the authority relationships between professional public administrators and the citizenry. For example, user fees, redevelopment agencies, off-budget enterprises, investment revenues, tax-increment financing, and development fees can be seen as measures to avoid voter approval and, thereby, increase the autonomy of public officials and public administrators. Together with privatization, they contribute to the autonomy and discretion of public entrepreneurs while often making public accountability more difficult.

Because the public sector's bottom line is hard to measure, public accountability is most often attempted by measuring inputs or regulating administrative processes. Thus, through the budget process and administrative rules and regulation, legislative bodies have long sought to circumscribe the actions of public agencies in the belief that budgets and regulations ensure accountability (Gruber, 1987). A characteristic of public entrepreneurs, however, is their attempt to increase their influence over budget processes in order to be free from excessive rules and regulations. Public entrepreneurs ask for autonomy from line-item budget controls in order to be more effective and efficient. They want discretion to spend "their money" (public entrepreneurs are encouraged to see themselves as owners) for measures that they deem important and on items they, not others, choose. This means that, if public entrepreneurs are to be held accountable, measures of accountability must shift from an input or process focus to one based on an outcome analysis. Analysis of outcomes as a means to measure administrative accountability can be traced to the 1960s with program budgeting and evaluation.

A current example of outcome accountability for public entrepreneurs can be found in Fairfield, California, where the city council spends little time going over the city manager's budget or in holding budget hearings. Fairfield's budget is determined on a formula basis that includes cost of living, population growth, and available revenue indicies. Each department gets a predetermined percentage of the overall budget. Near the end of the year, however, each department head must come before the council and explain how the allocated money was spent to achieve the agreed-upon goals of the department. It should be noted, however, that because the

goals of departments can be hard to measure, the open-line of credit given department heads may not always result in effective public accountability.

PUBLIC ENTREPRENEURIAL VISION VERSUS CITIZEN PARTICIPATION

A second conflict for a public entrepreneur who desires democratic legitimacy is between entrepreneurial vision and democracy's need for citizen input. Terence Mitchell and William G. Scott have suggested that entrepreneurs may be no more prescient and knowledgeable than the rest of us (Mitchell and Scott, 1987, pp. 447–448). Democratic politics and administration both demand that citizens be able to contribute views on issues of importance to them. However, if entrepreneurs are to be innovators, it means that they need to come with visions or ideas that are, by definition, uncommon. The Reagan administration's Iran-Contra arms entrepreneurial scheme, implemented by Oliver North and others, and the vision of the former Mayor of Oakland, California, and others to reacquire the Oakland Raiders by guaranteeing ticket sales, are examples of private visions which, by most standards, were not compatible with the tenets of democratic participation and approval.

The Los Angeles Olympic Organizing Committee's decision to have the 1984 Olympics privately financed and the decision of the City of Santa Clara, California, to buy a $100 million amusement park in order to save it from closing, although not widely held visions, gained acceptance by the public and public officials through open discussion. In the latter case, the citizenry of Santa Clara got to vote on the proposal.

Only by testing entrepreneurial vision through a meaningful public participation process can public administrators and others ensure that public entrepreneurship is compatible with the values of democratic participation.

ENTREPRENEURIAL SECRECY VERSUS DEMOCRATIC OPENNESS

A third conflict is between the entrepreneur's need for secrecy and the democratic value of conducting the public's business in the open. Openness is defined as disclosure of information in policymaking stages that permits the public to be informed participants in the policymaking process. The Iran-Contra arms deal is a good example of an entrepreneurial activity requiring secrecy to be successful. Given the competitive nature of local governmental finance and land development, public-private entrepreneurial partnerships frequently require secrecy if they are to be successful. In the interest of the private developer, land-use decisions are often kept as secret as possible and, in the process, compromise the public's right to know.

Because many entrepreneurial deals are done in the face of competition from other cities, as in the case of auto malls in California and elsewhere, the pressure to help subsidize the private entrepreneur can yield large outputs of public money (Bellis, 1987). The wisdom of these, or, in the case of Oakland's fight to get "their" Raiders back, can produce major budgetary outlays, which may not prove to be very productive when open to public scrutiny and measured in term of the overall public interest.

ENTREPRENEURIAL RISK TAKING VERSUS DEMOCRATIC STEWARDSHIP

Fourth, entrepreneurial risk taking may conflict with the obligation to be a steward of the public good. Democratic stewardship is concerned with the prudent use of the public trust to achieve both long- and short-term goals compatible with a concept of the public interest. When directed by legislative or executive mandate, public administrators engage in risk-taking behavior (such as economic development projects) that are subject to changing business cycles. The administrator may face professional and ethical dilemmas if he or she believes that the risk taking demanded is unwise. When engaging in nonmandated risk taking, the responsibilities of the public administrator become even more a stewardship issue. High-risk investment schemes that have gone wrong and resulted in economic losses, failed arbitrage efforts in investing federal grant funds, and short-term borrowing to pay operating costs, as in the case of New York City's fiscal crises of the seventies, are all examples of entrepreneurial risk taking that ignored the prudent concern for the long-term public good (Shefter, 1985).

Entrepreneurial risk taking may be more congruent with democratic stewardship if it is preceded by public information, discussion, and formal acceptance by those who will have to bear the risks should they fail. Indianapolis found a professional football team to fill its stadium, but other cities have had a difficult time finding private developers to make their public entrepreneurial ventures profitable.

TOWARD A MORE "PUBLIC" PUBLIC ENTREPRENEURSHIP: THE CASE FOR A CIVIC-REGARDING ENTREPRENEURSHIP

The range of administrative and democratic responsibilities of public entrepreneurs helps describe the tension between such entrepreneurship and a democratic polity. Public administrators who seek to be entrepreneurial have added to their responsibilities by trying to generate new sources of revenue for financing public services and providing more services that pay for themselves. Given current fiscal crises, they have needed to be adept economic and political entrepreneurs. Although Mitchell and Scott (1987) raise questions as to how entrepreneurial public entrepreneurs or any entrepreneurs actually are, there is also the important question of how "public" are public entrepreneurs. The answer to this is to be found in the earlier discussion of administrative responsibility. Public entrepreneurs need to take their political authority seriously and follow the principles of democratic theory in policy design and implementation as Burke and Cooper stated. We propose that, following Cooper's line of reasoning, they also need to be concerned with a more active approach to administrative responsibility which includes helping to facilitate increased citizen education and involvement. We call this a civic-regarding entrepreneurship.

Certainly, not all public administrators are concerned with citizenship and public participation, although many observers argue that they should be (e.g., Frederickson, 1982). However, given the areas of conflict between public entrepreneurship and democracy listed above, it is important for a truly "public" entrepreneurship to be civic regarding.

To borrow from Benjamin Barber's distinction between thin and strong theories of democracy (strong theories being participatory), we maintain that only a thin theory of public entrepreneurship presently applies (Barber, 1985). The thin theory, in accord with liberal democratic theory, is of a public entrepreneurship that effectively and responsively generates public revenue in order to provide public services. To do this, public entrepreneurs must have the autonomy and discretion to demonstrate their economic and political talents in the public interest. The citizenry's role is one of evaluation and trust in the entrepreneur's success and responsiveness. However, the evaluation and trust asked of the citizenry is problematic because public service delivery quality is difficult to measure, and entrepreneurs can often fail. Consequently, a citizen's continued passivity may only be a sign of political alienation.

A strong theory of public entrepreneurship (a civic-regarding entrepreneurship), following Barber's distinction, should be participatory or one where the citizenry have greater opportunities to participate in the design and delivery of their public goods and services. As a result of the more-services-less-revenue paradox handed the public administrator by the voter, citizens can be held accountable, in part, for current deficiencies in public services and financial resources. These deficiencies have led to the growth of a public entrepreneurship characterized by increased efforts by administrators to be free of voter and taxpayer control. It is the citizen's distrust of "big" government and the services that it provides that has led administrative theorists to call for greater citizen participation and an improved citizenship as a way of helping to regain the trust of the voter or citizen. Greater cooperation between administrator and citizen is the desired goal.

A civic-regarding entrepreneurship emphasizing public participation offers a remedy for over-zealous pursuits of self-interests. It offers a program of action that could make public entrepreneurship and democracy more compatible. Through developing citizens' opportunities to participate, the quality of citizenship could be raised to a level where citizens themselves become more responsible agents of efforts to provide more public goods and services within the parameters of acceptable tax burdens.

At the highest level of political aspiration, a civic-regarding entrepreneurship can be seen to be attempts, to use George Frederickson's words, to "recover civism," which embraces among other things, political community, self-aware citizens, and more adaptable and responsive government (Frederickson, 1982). Expanding on Frederickson's call for our discipline to rediscover its own citizenship responsibilities, administrative theorists have stressed that public administrators should be held responsible for helping further "civic literacy" (Mathews, 1984, p. 124), civility (as in forbearance [Hart, 1984, p. 116]), and "civic capital." "Civic capital" can be defined as: "problem solving knowledge possessed by citizens, attitudes that guide civic action, and civic capacity for governance" (McGregor, 1984, p. 128). The goals of such efforts would be, to cite Charles Levine's (1984, p. 180) list, the raising of citizen trust in government, the citizen's sense of efficacy, and, hopefully, a shared conception of the common good.

A strong theory of public entrepreneurship requires a strong theory of citizenship. Better citizen participation, along with new sources of public revenue and better public policies and services, are high standards for public administrators to try to reach. These lofty aspirations, however, are abstract without clearer identification of the type of citizenship role one is talking about and specifications as to how opportunities for citizenship and a citizen's public education can be enhanced.

At a minimum, a civic-regarding entrepreneurship is no different from all other endeavors to increase citizen participation. However, as Dwight Waldo reminds us, not all citizen participation is of a public or collective character (Waldo, 1984); it can simply be expressions of self-interest, interest group liberalism, or special pleading. In addition, it can be more manipulative than facilitative and more symbolic than effective. It may also be more divisive than facili-

tative or benevolent. Lastly, it may require more concern for social-equity considerations than are found in liberal democracy (Bellah *et al.,* 1985; Frederickson and Hart, 1985).

There are different degrees or levels of political participation (Milbrath, 1965, pp. 5–38). In the case of administrative democracy, the same may be said. At a minimum, citizens can only take part in public service delivery systems if they receive public services. Not all do. Thus, considerable doubts exist as to fairness in such distributions of services. Equal access to high-quality public services should be a basic citizenship right that should not be jeopardized. However, fiscal limits threaten the provision of public goods and services. Thus, the entrepreneurial talents of public administrators are crucial to a civic-regarding entrepreneurship.

However, public administrators, as civic-regarding entrepreneurs, can go much further. They can increase the ability of citizens to complain about the quality of their public services and help to facilitate correcting efforts (Sharp, 1986). In similar fashion, New York City and other local governments that create uniform-service districts that enable a citizen to use a single site for reaching the appropriate service providers are also increasing the opportunities for greater involvement in ensuring service systems that are responsive (Mudd, 1984).

When it comes to providing the rationale for spending public funds, a civic-regarding entrepreneurship would entail creating citizen budget committees to help set priorities before any formal budget approval is made by the executive and legislative branches. Portland, Oregon; Dayton, Ohio; and, in some respects, New York City all try to get citizens more involved earlier in the budgetary process.

Because public entrepreneurship often is manifested in the form of economic development projects, any effort at a civic-oriented entrepreneurship needs to increase the ability of citizens to see, comprehend, criticize, amend, and jointly design the projects so that their neighborhood or community is not disrupted or victimized by the development efforts of others. Where neighborhoods are well defined, neighborhood associations, citizen advisory boards, etc., may be in order if citizens are to defend and enhance their own community (White, 1983; Marcuse, 1990). Although criticized for possibly raising the Not In My Back Yard problem, overall social equity concerns are better served by mutually agreeable zoning and development than when the citizenry and neighborhoods have no say.

Elevating citizen choice, as in the case of voucher systems, may still be the best way for enhancing citizen participation. Budget and land-use decisions are among the most important for all stakeholders. Being urged to become more responsible for one's public choices, with public sector staff providing needed information, may make citizen input far more informative for city staff and elected officials.

The use of citizen volunteers to help provide and produce public services has been suggested as another way of increasing opportunities for citizen participation. Volunteerism has increased in many fiscally troubled cities and counties out of self-defense. Neighborhood safety patrols and arson-prevention volunteers are cases in point. In upper-class suburbs, a highly educated citizenry often demands a high level of participation for themselves in the design and delivery of their public services. Such citizen volunteerism is a show of civic obligation and duty. It is a way of stretching scarce resources to enable citizens to provide more and better services than they would otherwise have received. It may also be a way of increasing the citizenship rights and especially the citizenship obligations of many people who would otherwise remain outside the service delivery systems of governments.

From an historical perspective, it has been entrepreneurial volunteers who have first provided most public services from the postal service, to the police, down to present-day neighborhood mediation services (Ellis and Noyes, 1978). Volunteers, when aided by government offices of volunteerism, have been crucial to a delivery of many services, especially new and more innovative social services that facilitate compassion, benevolence, and the equal distribution of public goods.

CONCLUSION

De Tocqueville and John Stuart Mill saw the jury as a key to a citizen's public education. Today, there are more vehicles for increasing the opportunities for a citizen's participation and civic education (Barber, 1985, pp. 261–311). Not all citizens may want to participate, and they should not be forced to do so under the tenets of liberal democratic theory (Meyers, 1990). However, as Morris Janowitz and Gerald Suttles have argued, there may not be enough opportunities for those who want to participate (Janowitz and Suttles, 1978). A civic-regarding entrepreneurship is about finding those opportunities. For those who find the opportunity to do so, a more deeply felt obligation to be better citizens may develop and perhaps a willingness to give more of themselves for the provision of needed public services. The willingness to pay is one important sign that civic-oriented entrepreneurship is present. A civic-regarding entrepreneurship is a reminder of our roles as both agents (participants) and members (with political obligations) to the polity (Tussman, 1960).

REFERENCES

BARBER, BENJAMIN, 1985. *Strong Democracy.* Berkeley: University of California Press.

BELLAH, ROBERT, *et al.,* 1985. *Habits of the Heart.* Berkeley: University of California Press.

BELLIS, DAVID, 1987. "Inner-City Competition Over Auto-Mall Development (or, How to Win Friends by Stealing Auto Dealers From Your Neighbors)." *Western Governmental Researcher,* vol. III (September), pp. 15–29.

BURKE, JOHN, 1986. *Bureaucratic Responsibility.* Baltimore: Johns Hopkins University Press.

COOPER, TERRY, 1984. "Public Administration in an Age of Scarcity: A Citizenship Role for Public Administration." In Jack Rabin and James S. Bowman, eds., *Politics and Administration.* New York: Marcel Dekker, pp. 306–309.

ELLIS, SUSAN J. AND KATHERINE NOYES, 1978. *By the People.* Philadelphia: Energize Press.

FREDERICKSON, H. GEORGE, 1982. "The Recovery of Civism in Public Administration." *Public Administration Review,* vol. 42 (November/December), pp. 501–508.

FREDERICKSON, H. GEORGE AND DAVID K. HART, 1985. "The Public Service and the Patriotism of Benevolence." *Public Administration Review,* vol. 45 (September/October), pp. 547–554.

GOERL, GEORGE F. AND CARL J. BELLONE, 1983. "The Democratic Polity's Search for the Knowledgeable Public Administrator: An Argumentative Essay." *International Journal of Public Administration,* vol. 5(3), pp. 217–266.

GRUBER, JUDITH, 1987. *Controlling Bureaucracies.* Berkeley: University of California Press.

HART, DAVID K., 1984. "The Virtuous Citizen, the Honorable Bureaucrat and 'Public' Administration." *Public Administration Revi[ew]* issue), pp. 111–12[0]

JANOWITZ, MORRIS A[N]... 1978. "The Social ... ship." In Rosemar[y] ... eskel Hansenfield, [eds.,] *ment of Social Se[rvice]...* ...ow York: Columbia University Press.

LEVINE, CHARLES, 1984. "Citizenship and Service Delivery: The Promise of Coproduction." *Public Administration Review,* vol. 44 (special issue), pp. 178–187.

LEWIS, EUGENE, 1980. *Public Entrepreneurship: Toward a Theory of Bureaucratic Power.* Bloomington, IN: Indiana University Press.

MARCUSE, PETER, 1990. "New York City's Community Boards: Neighborhood Policy as Results." In Naomi Carmon, ed., *Neighborhood Policy and Programmes.* New York: St. Martin's Press, pp. 145–163.

MATHEWS, DAVID, 1984. "The Public in Practice and Theory." *Public Administration Review,* vol. 44 (special issue), pp. 120–125.

McGREGOR, EUGENE B., 1984. "The Great Paradox of Democratic Citizenship and Public Personnel Administration." *Public Administration Review,* vol. 44 (special issue), pp. 126–132.

MEYERS, DIANA, 1990. "Democratic Theory and the Democratic Agent." In John Chapman and Alan Westheimer, eds., *Majorities and Minorities.* New York: New York University Press, pp. 126–150.

MILBRATH, LESTER, 1965. *Political Participation.* Chicago: Rand McNally.

MITCHELL, TERENCE AND WILLIAM G. SCOTT, 1987. "Leadership Failures, the Distrusting Public and Prospects of the Administrative State." *Public Administration Review,* vol. 47 (November/December), pp. 445–452.

MUDD, JOHN, 1984. *Neighborhood Services.* New Haven: Yale University Press.

iRP, ELAINE B., 1986. *Citizen Demand-Making in the Urban Context.* University, AL: University of Alabama Press.

SHEFTER, MARTIN, 1985. *Political Crises/Fiscal Crises.* New York: Basic Books.

TUSSMAN, JOSEPH, 1960. *Obligation and the Body Politic.* New York: Oxford University Press.

WALDO, DWIGHT, 1984. "Response." *Public Administration Review,* vol. 44 (special issue), pp. 107–109.

WHITE, LOUISE G., 1983. "A Hundred Flowers Blossoming, Citizen Advisory Boards and Local Administrators." *Journal of Urban Affairs,* vol. 5 (Summer), pp. 221–230.

33.   Accountability in the Public Sector: Lessons from the Challenger Tragedy

Barbara S. Romzek and Melvin J. Dubnick

On January 28, 1986, the space shuttle Challenger exploded in mid-flight and seven crew members lost their lives. The widely known details of that tragic event need not be retraced here. Opinion is growing, however, that the official explanations offered by the Presidential Commission on the Space Shuttle Challenger Accident (the Rogers Commission) fail to provide full answers to why the disaster occurred. We offer an alternative explanation which addresses institutional factors contributing to the shuttle accident.

I. SEEKING AN INSTITUTIONAL PERSPECTIVE

Two common threads ran through public discussions of the Challenger incident. First was the urge to pinpoint the technical problems contributing directly to the booster rocket explosion on the

shuttle. Second was the desire to uncover human and managerial errors that might have caused National Aeronautics and Space Administration (NASA) officials to overlook or ignore those technical flaws. By the time the Rogers Commission issued its findings on June 9, 1986, those technical and managerial issues dominated its conclusions.

On the first point, the verdict of the Commission was unequivocal:

> The consensus of the commission . . . is that the loss of the space shuttle Challenger was caused by a failure in the joint between the lower segments of the right solid rocket motor. The specific failure was the destruction of the seals that are intended to prevent hot gases from leaking through the joint during the propellant burn of the rocket motor. The evidence assembled . . . indicates that no other element of the space shuttle system contributed to this failure.[1]

The Commission was equally explicit about managerial problems at NASA being a "contributing cause" of the accident:

SOURCE: "Accountability in the Public Sector: Lessons from the Challenger Tragedy" by Melvin Dubnick and Barbara Romzek, *Public Administration Review:* 47 (May/June 1987). Reprinted by permission of the American Society for Public Administration.

The decision to launch the Challenger was flawed. Those who made the decision were unaware of the recent history of problems concerning the O rings [seals] and the joint and were unaware of the initial written recommendation of the contractor advising against the launch at temperatures below 53 degrees Fahrenheit and the continuing opposition of engineers at [Morton] Thiokol after the management had reversed its position. . . . If the decision-makers had known all the facts, it is highly unlikely that they would have decided to launch [the shuttle] on January 28, 1986.[2]

The Commission's report was notable for its conclusive tone regarding these specific findings. More interesting, however, is the untravelled investigative path which asks if the problems at NASA and in the space shuttle program were institutional as well as technical or managerial. The institutional perspective is familiar to students of organizational theory who, following the lead of Talcott Parsons and James D. Thompson, note three levels of organizational responsibility and control: technical, managerial, and institutional.[3]

At the *technical level,* organizations focus on the effective performance of specialized and detailed functions. At the *managerial level,* an organization provides for mediation among its technical components and between its technical functionaries and those "customers" and "suppliers" in the organization's "task environment." At the *institutional level,* the organization deals with the need for being part of the "wider social system which is the source of the 'meaning,' legitimation, or higher-level support which makes implementation of the organization's goals possible."[4]

Applying this framework to the study of specific program or project failures such as the Challenger, one can argue that critical problems can arise at any or all three levels. Thus, an investigation of such events would be incomplete without considering the possible implications of activity at each level. The fact that NASA and other public agencies must constantly contend with the institutional forces that surround them (i.e., the "wider social system" of which they are part) is worthy of attention because agency efforts to deal with those forces may contribute to shaping the outcomes of agency action.

Investigators might ignore the role of institutional factors for several reasons. Attention to such factors might raise questions that are too basic and too dangerous for the organization or its supporters. Thus, a commission composed of individuals committed to the enterprise under investigation[5] and to the political system in general[6] is unlikely to open up the Pandora's Box of institutional factors. In contrast, institutional factors might be overlooked because analysts lack a conceptual framework that facilitates such considerations. Assuming the latter explanation, we offer a framework useful for highlighting the institutional factors that might have contributed to the Challenger disaster.

II. AN "ACCOUNTABILITY" PERSPECTIVE

While often regarded as a unique public organization,[7] NASA has institutional characteristics similar in very important respects to other public sector agencies. As such, NASA has to deal with the diversity of legitimate and occasionally conflicting expectations emanating from the democratic political system of which it is a part (its institutional context). In the following pages we present a framework of public accountability as a means for examining NASA's management of its institutional pressures and its implications.

Managing Expectations

Accountability is a fundamental but un-
derdeveloped concept in American public administration. Scholars and practitioners freely use the term to refer to
answerability for one's actions or behavior. Administrators and agencies are accountable to the extent that they are required to answer for their actions.
Beyond this basic notion of answerability, there has been little refinement of the
term. Most of the discussion in the literature centers on the "best" strategy for
achieving   accountability,   with   the
Friedrich-Finer exchange of the 1940s
being the most cited example.[8]

From an alternative perspective, accountability plays a greater role in the
processes of public administration than
indicated by the idea of answerability.
In its simplest form, answerability implies that accountability involves limited, direct, and mostly formalistic responses   to   demands   generated   by
specific institutions or groups in the
public agency's task environment. More
broadly conceived, *public administration accountability involves the means
by which public agencies and their
workers manage the diverse expectations generated within and outside the
organization.*[9]

Viewed as a strategy for managing expectations, public administration accountability takes a variety of forms.

The focus here is on four alternative systems of public accountability, each
based on variations involving two critical factors: (1) whether the ability to define and control expectations is held by
some specified entity inside or outside
the agency; and (2) the degree of control
that entity is given over defining those
agency's expectations. The interplay of
these two dimensions generates the four
types of accountability systems illustrated in Figure 33.1

Regarding the first dimension, the
management of agency expectations
through accountability mechanisms
calls for the establishment of some authoritative source of control. Internal
sources of control rely on the authority
inherent in either formal hierarchical relationships or informal social relationships within the agency. External
sources of control reflect a similar distinction, for their authority can be derived from either formalized arrangements set forth in laws or legal contracts
or the informal exercise of power by interests located outside the agency.

A second ingredient in any accountability system is the degree of control
over agency choices and operations exercised by those sources of control. A
high degree of control reflects the controller's ability to determine both the
range and depth of actions which a public agency and its members can take. A
low degree of control, in contrast, pro-

Figure 33.1

Source of Agency Control

		Internal	External
Degree of Control Over Agency Actions	High	1. Bureaucratic	2. Legal
	Low	3. Professional	4. Political

vides for considerable discretion on the part of agency operatives.

Bureaucratic accountability systems (cell 1) are widely used mechanisms for managing public agency expectations.[10] Under this approach, the expectations of public administrators are managed through focusing attention on the priorities of those at the top of the bureaucratic hierarchy. At the same time, supervisory control is applied intensively to a wide range of agency activities. The functioning of a bureaucratic accountability system involves two simple ingredients: an organized and legitimate relationship between a superior and a subordinate in which the need to follow "orders" is unquestioned; and close supervision or a surrogate system of standard operating procedures or clearly stated rules and regulations.[11]

Legal accountability[12] (cell 2) is similar to the bureaucratic form in that it involves the frequent application of control to a wide range of public administration activities. In contrast to bureaucratic accountability, however, legal accountability is based on relationships between a controlling party outside the agency and members of the organization. That outside party is not just anyone; it is the individual or group in a position to impose legal sanctions or assert formal contractual obligations. Typically, these outsiders make the laws and other policy mandates which the public administrator is obligated to enforce or implement. In policy-making terms, the outsider is the "lawmaker" while the public administrator has the role of "executor."

The legal accountability relationship between controller and the controlled also differs from that found between supervisor and subordinate in bureaucratic accountability forms. In the bureaucratic system, the relationship is hierarchical and based on the ability of supervisors to reward or punish subordinates. In legal accountability, however, the relationship is between two relatively autonomous parties and involves a formal or implied fiduciary (principal/agent) agreement between the public agency and its legal overseer.[13] For example, Congress passes laws and monitors a federal agency's implementation of those laws; a federal district court orders a school board to desegregate its classrooms and oversees the implementation of that order; the local city commission contracts with a private firm to operate the city refuse dump. In each case the implementors are legally or contractually obliged to carry out their duties, and the enforcement of such obligations are very different from those found in situations where bureaucratic accountability systems are applied.[14]

Professional accountability[15] (cell 3) occurs with greater frequency as governments deal increasingly with technically difficult and complex problems. Under those circumstances, public officials must rely on skilled and expert employees to provide appropriate solutions. Those employees expect to be held fully accountable for their actions and insist that agency leaders trust them to do the best job possible. If they fail to meet job performance expectations, it is assumed they can be reprimanded or fired. Otherwise they expect to be given sufficient discretion to get the job done. Thus, professional accountability is characterized by placement of control over organizational activities in the hands of the employee with the expertise or special skills to get the job done. The key to the professional accountability system, therefore, is deference to expertise within the agency. While outside professional associations may indirectly influence the decision making of the in-house expert (through education and professional standards), the source of authority is essentially internal to the agency.

Typically the professional accountability organization will look like any other public agency with a manager in charge of a set of workers, but the relationships among them are much different. Under a bureaucratic accountability system, the key relationship would be that of close supervision. In contrast, under professional accountability the central relationship is similar to that found between a layperson and an expert, with the agency manager taking the role of the layperson and the workers making the important decisions that require their expertise.[16]

Political accountability (cell 4) is central to the democratic pressures imposed on American public administrators. If "deference" characterizes professional accountability, "responsiveness" characterizes political accountability systems (cell 4).[17] The key relationship under these systems resembles that between a representative (in this case, the public administrator) and his or her constituents (those to whom he or she is accountable). Under political accountability, the primary question becomes, "Whom does the public administrator represent?" The potential constituencies include the general public, elected officials, agency heads, agency clientele, other special interest groups, and future generations. Regardless of which definition of constituency is adopted, the administrator is expected to be responsive to their policy priorities and programmatic needs.

While political accountability systems might seem to promote favoritism and even corruption in the administration of government programs, they also serve as the basis for a more open and representative government. The urge for political accountability, for example, is reflected in open meetings laws, freedom of information acts, and "government in the sunshine" statutes passed by many state and local governments.

Table 33.1 summarizes the principal features of the four general types of accountability systems. Under the bureaucratic system, expectations are managed through a hierarchical arrangement based on supervisory relationships; the legal accountability system manages agency expectations through a contractual relationship; the professional system relies on deference to expertise; while the political accountability system promotes responsiveness to constituents as the central means of managing the multiple expectations.

Preferences for Accountability Systems

Given these alternative means for managing expectations, what determines the preference for one accountability approach over others in any particular situation? The appropriateness of a specific accountability system to an agency is

---

Table 33.1   Relationships Within Accountability Systems

Type of Accountability System	Analogous Relationship (Controller/Administrator)	Basis of Relationship
1. Bureaucratic	Superior/subordinate	Supervision
2. Legal	Lawmaker/law executor Principal/agent	Fiduciary
3. Professional	Layperson/expert	Deference to expertise
4. Political	Constituent/representative	Responsiveness to constituents

linked to three factors: the nature of the agency's tasks (technical level accountability); the management strategy adopted by those heading the agency (management level accountability); and the institutional context of agency operations (institutional level accountability).[18] Ideally, a public sector organization should establish accountability mechanisms which "fit" at all three levels simultaneously.

In the American political system, all four accountability types offer potentially legitimate means for managing *institutional level* expectations.[19] Under current institutional norms, no single type of accountability system is inherently more acceptable or legitimate than another. *In theory,* each of the four accountability systems can insure agency responsibility at the institutional level. Thus, in theory an agency might manage its expectations using the accountability system most appropriate in light of relevant institutional considerations. The same potential flexibility may not exist at the technical or managerial levels where the appropriateness of accountability mechanisms is more closely tied to specific tasks or the strategic orientations or idiosyncrasies of individual managers.

In reality, most U.S. public agencies tend to adopt two or more types of accountability systems at any time depending on the nature of existing environmental (institutional) conditions as well as their technical tasks and management orientations. We argue, however, that institutional pressures generated by the American political system are often the salient factor and frequently take precedence over technical and managerial considerations.[20] If this is the case, the challenge of managing expectations changes as institutional conditions change. If the environmental changes are drastic enough, they may trigger a different type of accountability system, one which attempts to reflect those new institutional conditions.

III. ACCOUNTABILITY UNDER DIFFERENT CHALLENGES: THE CASE OF NASA

NASA was an organizational initiative born in the midst of a national crisis and nurtured in the relatively protective shelter of an institutional consensus that lasted until at least 1970. That nurturing consensus focused attention on President Kennedy's mandate to land an American on the moon by the end of the 1960s. In addition, it fostered the belief that achieving that objective required complete deference to those experts who could get the job done. In short, it was a consensus which supported a professional accountability system.

Over time, the pressures to develop a politically responsive agency strategy became dominant. Even before the successful lunar landing of Apollo 11, changing institutional conditions were creating an organizational setting that encouraged more reliance on bureaucratic and political accountability mechanisms. This reliance on bureaucratic and political accountability systems produced circumstances which made the agency ill-equipped to contend with the problems that eventually led to the Challenger disaster. Furthermore, institutional reactions to the Challenger tragedy itself may be creating new pressures that are moving the agency toward a greater reliance on legal and bureaucratic accountability methods for managing expectations.

The Professionalization of the Space Program

NASA's earliest programs had three important characteristics: they involved clearly defined outcome objectives, highly technical methodologies for achieving those goals, and almost unqualified political (and therefore budgetary) support.[21] The task of overcoming the technical barriers to space exploration was central to the agency's mission, and NASA was able to invest its expenditures primarily in research and development projects associated with its missions.[22]

Those early conditions had a significant impact on the development and management of NASA. The agency's structure and recruiting practices reflected an institutional willingness to respect the technical nature of NASA's programmatic tasks. NASA's form of organization emphasized deference to expertise and minimized the number of political appointments at the top of the administrative structure (in this case, two political appointees with extensive professional expertise in public management).[23] NASA's initial staff consisted almost entirely of individuals with the relevant substantive knowledge, primarily aeronautical engineers.

These circumstances afforded NASA the opportunity to become among the most innovative organizations (public or private) in recent American history and a classic example of an agency operating under a professional accountability system. The locus of control over agency activities was internal; NASA's relationship to outside sources (including Congress, the President, and the general public) was that of expert to layperson. Internally, NASA developed a matrix structure in which managers and technicians were assigned to project teams based on the expertise they could offer to the particular task at hand. Technical experts in NASA were expected to make decisions based upon their expertise. Thus, within the agency the degree of control exercised over NASA technical personnel was relatively low. Much of this deference to NASA's technical experts was based on trust in their judgment as well as their expertise. The early managers at NASA "were highly technical people, who knew the spacecraft from the ground up, and they were all very conservative." If "an order to

launch came down from on high, they wouldn't do it without first giving everybody the bottom line."[24]

The professional accountability system was evident in the three centers under the Office of Manned Space Flight (OMSF): the Marshall Space Flight Center (Alabama), the Manned Spacecraft Center (Texas; later renamed the Johnson Space Center), and Kennedy Space Center (Florida). During the early 1960s, OMSF and its subunits acted with considerable autonomy. NASA's top management in Washington did occasionally pull in the organizational reins. In several cases (1961, 1963, and 1965), reorganizations were intended to redirect several key units toward new program goals as NASA moved from Project Mercury toward Project Apollo. Each of these changes led to a short-term centralization of control which was intentionally relaxed once programmatic arrangements were in place. In 1967, however, a major long-term effort was made to reduce the autonomy of the manned space flight centers in light of the agency's first major budget constraints and the launch pad fire that killed three astronauts.[25]

The Politicization and Bureaucratization of Accountability

Although many of the technical tasks facing NASA did not change significantly over the past 30 years, institutional pressures on the agency have undergone considerable change. In the late 1960s, NASA faced a leveling off of both its political and financial support. Beginning in the early 1970s there was more concern about the managerial challenges inherent in making NASA into an operational agency—a concern arising from pressures to make the shuttle system a fully operational program.[26] The result of these pressures was a reconfiguration of the accountability systems used by some of the agency's key units. Ironically, the very success of NASA's early programs generated those changes.

NASA's apparent victory in the "space race" coincided with an end to the nurturing consensus that permitted the agency to rely almost exclusively on professional accountability for managing expectations. With America's attention turned increasingly toward Vietnam and economic issues, the space program no longer took priority. A new consensus had to be constructed around some new programmatic mission, and in the late 1960s the idea of a space shuttle began to take form. According to its proponents, the shuttle would represent "a whole new way of space flight," one that would transform NASA from an agency committed to accomplishing specific and discrete program goals within given time constraints (e.g., Apollo) to an agency obligated to the continuous operation of a commercial-like enterprise.[27]

The effort to gain presidential endorsement for the space shuttle program made NASA more aware of and responsive to key actors in the political system. Building the necessary consensus was not easy in the highly volatile and competitive institutional context of the early 1970s. James Fletcher, NASA's Administrator from 1971 to 1977 (and the individual President Reagan brought back to head the agency after the Challenger disaster), needed to sell the space shuttle effort to Congress and the American public as well as the White House. Most of the opposition to the shuttle came from the Office of Management and Budget which was supported by negative assessments of the program by a presidential scientific advisory committee and the RAND Corporation.[28]

During this period NASA entered into political coalitions with groups that it had previously ignored or fought in the policy-making arena, as well as with its traditional supporters in government and among its contractors. The shuttle program, for example, was designed to attract the support of those who might take advantage of its capacity to launch satellites and conduct unique scientific and technological experiments in space. Aided by the military, the scientific community, and parts of the business community, NASA was able to get President Nixon's backing for the program in 1972 despite OMB's opposition. Political accountability was no longer secondary or peripheral to NASA.[29] It became a critical ingredient in guaranteeing its maintenance as a viable agency. In more recent years, that urge for public and political support was implicit in NASA's widely publicized efforts to include members of Congress and non-agency civilians on its shuttle flights. These programs represented NASA's efforts to cultivate or maintain general support for its activities.

Another important (and related) set of institutional constraints emerged in the form of major budget cutbacks and (in the late 1970s) greater pressures for privatization. From the height of its support in the late 1960s to the mid-1970s, NASA's budget was cut in half (in constant dollars). Recent estimates indicate that NASA went through a staff cut of 40 percent from the big-budget days of Apollo and that NASA's safety and quality control staff alone were cut by 71 percent between 1970 and 1986.[30] Operating with fewer resources, the agency had to economize; it became just like most other agencies in Washington. NASA experienced a new-found interest in efficiency and thus became more willing to use bureaucratic means for dealing with its financial problems.

NASA officials intended to accommodate these new institutional pressures by reducing the organizational costs that characterized NASA in the "old days" when external support and availability of resources were not major concerns. NASA has "had to pinch pennies to protect the shuttle, accepting lower-cost technologies and making what seem to have been extravagant claims for its economic potential."[31] Agency decentralization and field center specializations continued, and decentralization brought with it increasing reliance on bureaucratic accountability mechanisms. The shift allowed for economies due to a careful division of labor and compartmentalization of authority based on position. While professional accountability systems survived *within* some of the field centers, for the agency as a whole professional accountability patterns characteristic of the early NASA nearly disappeared. With decentralization in NASA came an isolation and competition among field centers.[32]

NASA's use of contractors was, to a certain extent, a manifestation of its efforts to manage changing institutional expectations. In addition to any technical and financial benefits they provided NASA, contractors had always proved very helpful politically in establishing support for the agency's programs and annual funding requests. During the 1970s the link between contract decision and political support became increasingly critical to NASA.[33]

Bureaucratically, contracting out established the ultimate superordinate/subordinate relationship between NASA's top managers and those carrying out the specific parts of the shuttle program. A contract establishes clear responsibilities and gives top management considerable leverage to apply pressures for better performance. It also allows top management to avoid the problems and costs associated with directly maintaining professional accountability mechanisms. Thus, contracting out not only enhanced the bureaucratization process at NASA; it also reduced reliance on deference to expertise characteristic of professional accountability systems.

Changing institutional conditions altered the locus of control over NASA's activities as well as the degree of control over agency activities. The result was a shift in the types of accountability systems relevant to NASA's operations. In place of the dominant professional accountability systems of the pre-Apollo 11 era, NASA created an elaborate mixture of accountability mechanisms that stressed the political and bureaucratic. It was under these conditions that decisions regarding the general schedule of space shuttle flights and specific launch times were being made when the Challenger lifted from its Kennedy Space Center pad on January 28, 1986.

The Case of the Challenger

Evidence gathered by the Rogers Commission Report and through the mass media illustrate the various forms of accountability in operation in NASA before the launch of the Challenger. The principal question is whether (and to what extent) the Challenger accident resulted from the efforts by NASA's leadership to manage changing institutional expectations through political and bureaucratic forms of accountability. Did NASA's emphasis on these accountability mechanisms eventually take precedence over the professional system of accountability that characterized NASA in the early 1960s? Were the problems that eventually led to the Challenger accident linked at all to the poor fit between agency tasks and agency accountability mechanisms? In our view, the answer to both questions is "yes."

Political pressures. The contention that NASA was feeling considerable political pressure to launch the Challenger on January 28 was widely rumored just after the Challenger accident, particularly stories about direct pressure emanating from the White House. The Rogers Commission emphatically denied the truth of those rumors.[34] Nonetheless, similar pressures existed and came from a variety of sources outside of NASA, including the White House.

On the official policy level, President Reagan announced in July 1982 that the first priority of the shuttle program was "to make the system fully operational." Given the costs involved in supporting the program, additional pressures emanated from an increasingly budget-conscious Congress.[35] Other pressures on NASA were due to widespread reporting of shuttle delays in the mass media. One top agency official argued that the press, in giving major coverage to numerous shuttle delays over the previous year, had "pressured" the agency to jeopardize flight safety. "I don't think it caused us to do anything foolish," he said. "But that's where the pressure is. It's not from anywhere else."[36]

These external pressures were easily translated into internal decisions that set an overly ambitious launch schedule.[37] In short, NASA set that schedule for the purposes of reducing the program's cost factors and appeasing various attentive publics, including the White House, Congress, the media, and the agency's military and private sector "customers" who were important actors in NASA's supportive political coalition.

These political pressures may not have been specifically addressed to the Challenger launch, but there is little doubt they were felt throughout the agency. The increasing emphasis on political accountability was bound to cause attitudinal as well as operational problems. "The pressure on NASA to achieve planned flight rates was so pervasive," concluded a congressional report, "that it undoubtedly adversely affected attitudes regarding safety."[38] An agency official noted that NASA's organization culture changed "when NASA felt itself under pressure to demonstrate that the shuttles were operational vehicles in a 'routine' transportation system."[39] Part of that "routinization" took the form of "streamlining" the reporting requirements for safety concerns. Less documentation and fewer reporting requirements replaced previous directives that all safety problems and responses were to be reported to higher levels in NASA's hierarchy. The "old requirements," it was argued, "were not productive for the operational phase of the Shuttle program."[40]

The same political accountability pressures had an impact on NASA's key shuttle program contractor, Morton Thiokol. The assent of Morton Thiokol management (and the silence of their engineers) to the Challenger launch recommendation was influenced in part by NASA's importance as a primary customer—a customer who was in the process of reviewing its contracts with the firm. The company's management did not want to jeopardize their relationships with NASA. As a result, rather than emphasizing deference to the experts who worked for them, Morton Thiokol deferred to the demands of NASA's top managers who, in turn, were under a self-imposed, politically derived launch schedule.

Bureaucratic pressures. Indications of preference for bureaucratic rather than professional forms of accountability in NASA are evident in the agency's shuttle program operations. By the early 1980s, NASA's managers were having difficulty coordinating their projects.[41] They came to rely increasingly on hierarchical reporting relationships, a clear manifestation of bureaucratic accountability. This had two effects. First, it increased the potential for "bureaupathological" behavior which the professional accountability system attempted to minimize.[42] Second, it reduced the cross-cutting communications channels which once characterized the less hierarchical and flexible matrix structure at NASA.

The failure of NASA's management system is a fundamental theme of the Rogers Commission. Supervisors were criticized for not passing on up the hierarchy their subordinates' recommendations. Managers were criticized for judgments that were contrary to those suggested by the available data. The Commission reported that its investigation revealed "failures in communication that resulted in a decision to launch [the Challenger] based on incomplete and sometimes misleading information, a conflict between engineering data and management judgments, and a NASA management structure that permitted internal flight safety problems to bypass key Shuttle managers."[43] But what the Rogers Commission perceived as a failure of the agency's management system was, in fact, an inherent characteristic of the bureaucratic accountability system adopted by NASA in order to meet the institutional expectations of the post-Apollo 11 era.

Under NASA's shuttle program, responsibility for specific aspects of the overall program was allocated to supervisors at lower levels in the reporting hierarchy, and the burden for giving the go ahead to launch decision makers shifted from the engineers and experts toward those supervisory personnel. As scheduling and other pressures increased, so did the reluctance of those supervisors to be the individual who threw a monkey wrench into the shuttle program machinery. Thus it is not surprising that lower-level managers tried to cope on their own instead of communicating their problems upward.[44]

The relevance of this problem to the Challenger disaster was illustrated time and time again in the testimony given before the Rogers Commission. NASA officials noted that individuals higher up in the agency had not been informed about the Rockwell engineers' reservations about ice on the launch pad nor the concerns of Morton Thiokol's personnel about weather conditions and the O-rings.[45] In another instance, when asked why he had not communicated

the Thiokol engineers' concerns about the O-ring seals to the Program Manager of the National Space Transportation System, the manager of the Solid Rocket Booster Project (based at the Marshall center) answered that he believed it was an issue that had been resolved at his level in the organization.[46] As one reporter observed, "no one at Marshall saw any reason to bother the managers at the top of NASA's chain of command—the normal procedure in the face of disturbing new evidence." This bureaupathological behavior reflects an attitude among employees at Marshall who feel they are competing with Johnson and the other centers. "Nothing [sic] was ever allowed to leave Marshall that would suggest that Marshall was not doing its job. . . ."[47]

The impact of the bureaucratic accountability system is also evident in testimony about discussions between NASA representatives and Thiokol engineers on the night before the Challenger launch. During an "off-line" caucus between Morton Thiokol management and their engineers (while NASA prelaunch review officials were "on hold"), a member of management asked one of his colleagues

to take off his engineering hat and put on his management hat. From that point on, management formulated the points to base their decision on. There was never one comment in favor . . . of launching by any engineer or other nonmanagement person in the room before or after the caucus. . . . [The engineers were] never asked nor polled, and it was clearly a management decision from that point. . . . This was a meeting where the determination was to launch, and it was up to [the Thiokol engineers] to prove beyond a shadow of a doubt [to Thiokol management and NASA] that it was not safe to do so. This is in total reverse to what the position usually is in a preflight conversation or a flight readiness review. It is usually exactly opposite that. (emphasis added)[48]

A final example of the bureaucratic accountability system's relevance to the failure of the Challenger focuses on an incident occurring in 1984. Problems with the O-rings were noticed and noted by Morton Thiokol engineers in February that year after the tenth Shuttle mission had been completed, and a report on the problem was ordered by the Office of the Associate Administrator for Space Flight before the launch of the eleventh flight in late March. A decision was made to launch the shuttle, but not before it was determined by the Associate Administrator, James Abrahamson, and NASA's Deputy Administrator, Hans Mark, that the O-ring problem had to be solved. A meeting to discuss the problem with relevant officials from the different NASA centers was called for May 30. It was a meeting that would have drawn attention to the technical factor that would later cause the shuttle tragedy; it was a meeting that never took place. By May 30, Abrahamson had left the agency to work on President Reagan's Strategic Defense Initiative, and Deputy Administrator Mark cancelled the meeting to visit Austin, Texas, where he was being considered for the position of University Chancellor. Abrahamson's successor, Jesse A. Moore, was never informed of the problem, and Mark's successor was not appointed for a full year. Thus, the O-ring problem was never communicated to the relevant experts for action. In Mark's words, it was "a classic example of having something fall between the 'cracks.'"[49] In our terms, it was another instance of bureaucratic accountability applied in inappropriate circumstances.

IV. A POST-COMMISSION ERA: THE NEW INSTITUTIONAL PRESSURES

Given the technical and managerial focus of the Rogers Commission Report and other investigations of the Challenger accident, it is not surprising that calls for changes in the space program tend to favor two objectives: punishing those in NASA who were to blame for the tragedy and instituting reforms that would guarantee that a similar event would not occur in the future. In both form and content, these efforts represented increased institutional pressures for NASA, pressures likely to lead the agency to develop new legal accountability mechanisms as well as increase its reliance on bureaucratic accountability mechanisms.

The search for scapegoats and legal responsibility for the Challenger accident are unsavory but perhaps unavoidable by-products of the Rogers Commission's focus on technical and managerial problems. If a technical problem existed, why was it not discovered in time; and if it was discovered in time, why was it not taken seriously by those in charge?[50] These are the questions which have led to personnel actions within NASA (and Thiokol) ranging from reassignments and resignations to early retirements. Beyond these actions, the families of most Challenger crew members either filed lawsuits or accepted legal settlements from the government and its subcontractors.[51]

On less personal levels, suggestions for reforms in the space agency have proliferated. On the surface many of these seem to signal a return to professional accountability. Some recommendations call for improving the role and voice of certain classes of individuals within NASA with special or unique insight into the risks associated with space exploration. There is, for example, a proposal for placing ex-astronauts in management positions at NASA.[52] At first glance, this looks like an attempt to reinvigorate the role of experts and professionals in the agency, but bringing former astronauts into NASA does not guarantee improvement in technical expertise and actually looks more like a thinly veiled attempt to use highly visible symbols of the space program to enhance the agency's damaged credibility.

Another proposal that at first seems to involve a return to professional accountability calls for establishment of explicit guidelines and criteria for use in making launch decisions. Supposedly these criteria would represent the accumulated wisdom of many experts in the field, but they can just as easily be regarded as another step away from deference to professional engineering judgments and toward imposing accountability that carries with it threats of legal liability if such checklists are not properly followed.

Legal accountability mechanisms are also manifested in the emphases in many other proposed reforms on establishing independent or external oversight bodies capable of vetoing decisions by agency personnel regarding safety issues. For example, the Rogers Commission called for the creation of an independent Solid Rocket Motor design oversight committee to review the rocket design and make recommendations to the Administrator or NASA.[53] Similarly, the Commission called for creation of a separate Office of Safety, Reliability and Quality Assurance outside the normal lines of the agency hierarchy to report directly to the NASA Administrator.[54] In both instances, actors outside the normal lines of the agency hierarchy would oversee key decision-making points within NASA dealing with the design and launch of future manned space flights.[55] While these bodies are not intended to exercise direct control over the day-to-day operations of NASA's

space shuttle program, such bodies would have jurisdiction over a wide range of agency actions.

It is also evident that congressional oversight of NASA activities is likely to focus a great deal more on details of technical and managerial matters than in the past.[56] In the past, Congress' role regarding NASA was that of patron rather than overseer. For the most part, congressional concerns about NASA were limited to the general priorities of the agency and its potential as a source of pork-barrel projects. In the near future, at least, members of relevant congressional committees and their staffs will become more involved in the details of NASA's operations.[57]

Other suggested reforms (some already being implemented) attempt internal changes in NASA that would complement this movement toward changing accountability. For example, recommendations for reorganizing the shuttle management structure include redefining the program manager's responsibilities to enhance that official's decision-making role. In addition, units within NASA are being reorganized to improve intraorganizational communications. Operationally, suggested reforms include a call for refinement of decision criteria used in equipment maintenance, landing safety, and launch abort procedures. These changes reinforce or legitimize the influence of bureaucratic structures within NASA by formalizing organizational relationships and operational procedures. In form and function, they attempt to move the bureaucratic structures of NASA closer to a centralized system more easily held legally accountable for the agency's future actions.

It was inevitable that the Challenger disaster would generate strong institutional pressures for NASA, and those pressures are creating new demands and expectations for the agency. Ironically, the direction of those pressures has been toward enhanced bureaucratic structures and growing reliance on legal accountability mechanisms which stress NASA's formal responsibilities for the safety of its astronauts. Since President Reagan ordered NASA to terminate its commercial operations temporarily, a major source of political pressure and support has been removed. Thus, we might expect a decline of political accountability in the space agency's operations. Nevertheless, political factors have not disappeared. At present, NASA lacks a clear sense of direction and faces programmatic competition from the military and commercial sectors. At the end of 1986, Dr. Fletcher's view was reported as follows: "the policy-making process is not so straightforward because there are 'so many players.'"[58] In addition, there is little likelihood that Challenger-related reforms will reflect the need for NASA to reestablish the priority of professional accountability systems which held sway in the agency during pre-Apollo 11 heydays.

V. CONCLUSION

The primary contention of this paper is that the Rogers Commission was shortsighted in focusing exclusively on the failure of NASA's technological or management systems. The problem was not necessarily in the *failure* of those systems, but rather in the *inappropriateness* of the political and bureaucratic accountability mechanisms which characterized NASA's management approach in recent years. The agency's emphasis on political and bureaucratic accountability was a relevant response to changing institutional expectations in NASA's environment, but they were inappropriate for the technical tasks at hand. To the extent that these accountability mechanisms were ill-suited to the technical nature of NASA's agency task, they comprised a major factor in the Challenger tragedy.

In more prescriptive terms, if the professional accountability system had been given at least equal weight in the decision-making process, the decision to launch would probably not have been made on that cold January morning. Had NASA relied exclusively on a professional system of accountability in making the decision to launch the Challenger space shuttle, perhaps deference would have been given to the technical expertise of the engineers. Their recommendation against launch might never have been challenged by the Project Manager for the Solid Rocket Booster.[59] Instead, the Thiokol engineers' initial recommendation against launch was ignored by their hierarchical superiors. Decision makers relied upon supervisors to make the decision rather than deferring to professional experts.

Will the post-accident push for greater emphases on the legal and bureaucratic accountability systems improve NASA's ability to successfully pursue its mission? If this assessment of the role of institutional factors in the success and failure of NASA's programs is correct, then the proposals for reform increase the chances of other failures. This conclusion is consistent with the thesis that adding safety mechanisms to already complex systems in fact may increase the chances that something can go wrong.[60] As NASA gets drawn further away from what it can do best—namely, mobilizing the expert resources needed to solve the technical challenges of space exploration—its chances for organizational success are diluted. Ideally, NASA needs to return to what it does best, using the form of accountability that best suits its organizational mission, i.e., a professional accountability based on deference to expertise.[61] The reality of NASA's institutional context, however, makes achievement of this ideal highly improbable. NASA no longer enjoys a nurturing institutional context; instead it faces increased environmental pressures calling for the adoption of political, bureaucratic, and legal accountability mechanisms. Such is the dilemma facing NASA and the challenge confronting all American public administrators.

NOTES

1. *Report of the Presidential Commission on the Space Shuttle Challenger Accident* (Washington: June 6, 1986), p. 40; hereafter cited as *Rogers Commission Report.*

2. *Rogers Commission Report,* p. 82.

3. See James D. Thompson, *Organizations in Action: Social Science Bases of Administrative Theory* (New York: McGraw-Hill Book Co., 1967), pp. 10–11.

4. Thompson, *Organizations in Action,* p. 11.

5. Besides current astronaut Sally Ride and former astronaut Neil Armstrong, the commission membership included: Eugene Covert, an MIT professor and frequent consultant to NASA who received the agency's "Public Service Award" in 1980; Robert W. Rummel, an aerospace engineer and private consultant who was also a recipient of a NASA public service award; and Major General Donald J. Kutyna, director of the U.S. Air Force's Space Systems program and former manager of the Defense Department's space shuttle program.

6. For example, Commission Chair Rogers was Attorney General for President Eisenhower and Secretary of State for Richard Nixon. David C. Acheson, a well-known Washington lawyer, had previously served as a U.S. Attorney, counsel for the Atomic Energy Commission, and Senior Vice President of COMSAT. Other members of the Commission were: two physicists, Richard P. Feynman and Albert D. Wheelan (Executive Vice President, Hughes Aircraft); astronomer, Arthur B. C. Walker, Jr.; test pilot, Charles E. Yeager; aeronautical engineer, Joseph F. Sutter; and Robert B. Hotz, former editor of *Aviation Week and Space Technology Magazine.*

7. See Paul R. Schulman, *Large-Scale Policy Making* (New York: Elsevier North Holland, Inc., 1980), pp. 22–41; James E. Webb, *Space Age Management* (New York: McGraw-Hill Book Co., 1968); Leonard R. Sayles and Margaret K. Chandler, *Managing Large Systems* (New York: Harper and Row, 1971); and Peter F. Drucker, *Management: Tasks, Responsibilities, and Practices* (New York: Harper and Row, 1974), chapter 47.

8. See discussion in Herbert A. Simon, Donald W. Smithburg, and Victor A. Thompson, *Public Administration* (New York: Alfred A. Knopf, Inc., 1950), especially chapters 24 and 25. Also, Carl Joachim Friedrich, "Public Policy and the Nature of Administrative Responsibility," in C. J. Friedrich and Edward S. Mason, eds., *Public Policy, 1940* (Cambridge: Harvard University Press, 1940), pp. 3–24; and Herman Finer, "Administrative Responsibility and Democratic Government," *Public Administration Review,* vol. 1 (Summer 1941), pp. 335–350.

9. This view of accountability is developed more fully in Barbara Romzek and Mel Dubnick, "Accountability and the Management of Expectations: The Challenger Tragedy and the Costs of Democracy," presented at the annual meeting of the American Political Science Association, the Washington Hilton, August 28–31, 1986.

10. See Max Weber, *Economy and Society; An Outline of Interpretive Sociology,* edited by Guenther Roth and Claus Wittich (Berkeley: University of California Press, 1987), chapter XI.

11. See Alvin Gouldner, *Patterns of Industrial Bureaucracy* (New York: The Free Press, 1954), pp. 159–162.

12. Philosophically and ideologically, the basis of legal accountability is found in the "rule of law" concept; see Friedrich A. Hayek, *The Road to Serfdom* (Chicago: University of Chicago Press, 1944), chapter VI; also see Theodore J. Lowi's call for "juridical democracy" in *The End of Liberalism: The Second Republic of the United States,* 2d ed. (New York: W. W. Norton and Co., 1979), chapter 11.

13. For a comprehensive application of the theory of agency, see Barry M. Mitnick, *The Political Economy of Regulation: Creating, Designing, and Removing Regulatory Forms* (New York: Columbia University Press, 1980).

14. While bureaucratic accountability relies on methods available to members, such as close supervision and rules and regulations, legal accountability is limited to the tools available to outsiders, such as monitoring, investigating, auditing, and other forms of "oversight" and evaluation.

15. See Carl Joachim Friedrich, "Public Policy and the Nature of Administrative Responsibility."

16. For an example of a professional accountability system, see the story of the Manhattan Project offered in Peter Wyden, *Day One: Before Hiroshima and After* (New York: Warner Books, 1985), Book One.

17. See Emmette S. Redford, *Democracy in the Administrative State* (New York: Oxford University Press, 1969); also see works by Paul Appleby and Herman Finer.

18. See James Thompson, *Organizations in Action.*

19. See Robert C. Fried, *Performance in American Bureaucracy* (Boston: Little, Brown and Co., 1976).

20. It is possible (at least theoretically) for different accountability mechanisms to operate within one agency at different levels of the organization. For example, a professional accountability mechanism may be in operation at the technical level of an organization while a legal accountability mechanism may be used to manage external expectations at the institutional or boundary-spanning level. See Thompson, *Organizations in Action.* For an application of this notion in a related area, see Donald Klingner and John Nalbandian, "Values and Conflict in Public Personnel Administration," *Public Administration Quarterly* (forthcoming).

21. See Hans Mark and Arnold Levine, *The Management of Research Institutions: A Look at Government Laboratories* (Washington: National Aeronautics and Space Administration, 1984), pp. 117–118. On the political support for NASA in those early years, see Don K. Price, *The Scientific Estate* (Cambridge, MA: The Belknap Press, 1965), pp. 222–223. On the effects of its budgetary support through 1966, see Paul R. Schulman, *Large-Scale Policy Making* (New York: Elsevier North Holland, Inc., 1980), pp. 87–88.

22. Through the Apollo program, NASA spent over 80 percent of its funding on research and development (R&D) efforts. See Philip N. Whittaker, "Joint Decisions in Aerospace," in Matthew Tuite, Roger Chisolm, and Michael Radnor, eds., *Interorganizational Decision Making* (Chicago: Aldine Publishing Co., 1972), p. 272.

23. On the early history of NASA by an "insider," see John D. Young, "Organizing the Nation's Civilian Space Capabilities: Selected Reflections," in Theodore W. Taylor, ed., *Federal Public Policy: Personal Accounts of Ten Senior Civil Service Executives* (Mt. Airy, MD: Lomond Publications, Inc., 1984), pp. 45–80. Some

analysts have defined that "nurturing consensus" as little more than a "political vacuum" in which the agency got to define its own programmatic objectives. See John Logsdon, *The Decision to Go to the Moon,* cited in Lambright, *Governing Science and Technology* (New York: Oxford University Press, 1976), pp. 41–42.

24. Henry S. F. Cooper, Jr., "Letter from the Space Center," in *The New Yorker* (November 10, 1986), p. 93.

25. Mark and Levine, *The Management of Research Institutions,* pp. 60, 200–202.

26. Schulman, *Large-Scale Policy Making,* pp. 62–74. Also Cooper, "Letter from the Space Center," p. 99.

27. Schulman, *Large-Scale Policy Making,* pp. 74–76; also Mark and Levine, *The Management of Research Institutions,* pp. 117–118.

28. Lambright, *Governing Science and Technology,* p. 43. Also see Wayne Biddle, "NASA: What's Needed To Put It On Its Feet?" *Discover,* vol. 8 (January 1987), pp. 36,40.

29. It is incorrect to think that NASA was apolitical even during its early years. Tom Wolfe describes a heated argument between John Glenn and NASA Administrator James Webb when Glenn bitterly complained of the number of trips he had to take at the request of members of Congress or the White House. See Wolfe's, *The Right Stuff* (New York: Bantam Books, 1979), p. 331. See also Mark and Levine, *The Management of Research Institutions,* p. 82, for a discussion of the importance of generating "new business" for the agency. The politics surrounding the shuttle are reflected in investigations of the role Fletcher played in awarding contracts for the shuttle project in 1973; see William J. Broad, "NASA Chief Might Not Take Part in Decisions on Booster Contracts," *The*

New York Times (December 7, 1986), pp. 1, 14.

30. W. Henry Lambright, *Governing Science and Technology,* pp. 21–22; and U.S. Congress, House, Committee on Science and Technology, *Investigation of the Challenger Accident,* Report, 99th Congress, 2d Session (Washington: U.S. Government Printing Office, 1986), pp. 176–177.

31. John Noble Wilford, "NASA May Be a Victim of Defects in Its Own Bureaucracy," *The New York Times* (February 16, 1986), p. 18E.

32. See Cooper, "Letter from the Space Center," especially pp. 85–96.

33. See Mark and Levine, *The Management of Research Institutions,* pp. 122–123, on NASA contracting. NASA's use of "pork barrel" politics dates to the agency's earliest years; see Amitai Etzioni, *The Moon Doggle* (Garden City, NY: Doubleday and Co., 1964), and Price, *The Scientific Estate,* pp. 21–23. The continuation of political considerations in NASA's contracting practices during the 1970s is demonstrated by the circumstances surrounding the competition for the shuttle's booster rocket contract which was eventually awarded to Thiokol in 1973; see Broad, "NASA Chief May Not Take Part in Decisions on Booster Contracts."

34. *Rogers Commission Report,* p. 176.

35. *Rogers Commission Report,* pp. 176, 201. Also Cooper, "Letter from the Space Center," pp. 99–100, and U.S. Congress, House, *Investigation of the Challenger Accident,* pp. 119–120.

36. William J. Broad, "NASA Aide Assails Panel Investigating Explosion of Shuttle," *The New York Times* (March 16, 1986), p. 23.

37. U.S. Congress, House, *Investigation of the Challenger Accident,* p. 120.

38. U.S. Congress, House, *Investigation of the Challenger Accident,* p. 122. Richard P. Feynman, a member of the Rogers Commission, speculated

about agency attitudes regarding safety. He believed the agency might have downplayed the riskiness of the shuttle launching to "assure" Congress of the agency's "perfection and success in order to ensure the supply of funds." See David E. Sanger, "Looking Over NASA's Shoulder," *The New York Times* (September 28, 1986), p. 26E.

39. John Noble Wilford, "NASA Chief Vows to Fix Problems," *The New York Times* (June 10, 1986), p. 22.
40. *Rogers Commission Report,* pp. 153–154.
41. Laurie McGinley and Bryan Burrough, "Backbiting in NASA Worsens the Damage from Shuttle Disaster," *The Wall Street Journal* (April 2, 1986), p. 1.
42. See Victor A. Thompson, *Modern Organization,* 2d ed. (University: University of Alabama Press, 1977), chapter 8.
43. *Rogers Commission Report,* p. 82.
44. On the factors which make it difficult for employees to pass bad news to upper levels of the organization, see Chris Argyris and Donald A. Schon, *Organizational Learning: A Theory of Action Perspective* (Reading, MA: Addison-Wesley Publishing Co., 1978).
45. *Rogers Commission Report,* p. 82.
46. Testimony of Lawrence Mulloy, *Rogers Commission Report,* p. 98.
47. Cooper, "Letter from the Space Center," pp. 89, 96.
48. Testimony of Roger Boisjoly, *Rogers Commission Report,* p. 93. Also see testimony of R. K. Lund, *Rogers Commission Report,* p. 94.
49. David E. Sanger, "Top NASA Aides Knew of Shuttle Flaw in '84," *The New York Times* (December 21, 1986), pp. 1, 22.
50. See William J. Broad, "NASA Had Solution to Key Flaw in Rocket When Shuttle Exploded," *The New York Times* (September 22, 1986),

p. 1; and David E. Sanger, "NASA Pressing Shuttle Change Amid Concerns: Fear of Short-Circuiting Safety Search Raised," *The New York Times* (September 23, 1986), p. 1.
51. In July 1986, the family of shuttle pilot Michael Smith filed a "wrongful death" suit against NASA and some of its top managers. Later settlements with other families were announced. See William J. Broad, "4 Families Settle Shuttle Claims," *The New York Times* (December 30, 1986), p. 1.
52. *Rogers Commission Report,* pp. 199–201.
53. *Rogers Commission Report,* p. 198.
54. *Rogers Commission Report,* p. 199.
55. *Rogers Commission Report,* pp. 198–199.
56. Members of Congress criticized the Commission for not going deeply enough into the question of which individuals bore direct responsibility for the accident. See Philip M. Boffey, "Shuttle Panel is Faulted for Not Naming Names," *The New York Times* (June 11, 1986), p. 16.
57. Philip M. Boffey, "NASA Challenged on Modification That Rockets Met Requirements," *The New York Times* (June 12, 1986), p. 18.
58. John Noble Wilford, "Threat to Nation's Lead in Space is Seen in Lack of Guiding Policy," *The New York Times* (December 30, 1986), p. 18.
59. *Rogers Commission Report,* p. 96.
60. See Charles Perrow, *Normal Accidents: Living With High Risk Technologies* (New York: Basic Books, Inc., 1984).
61. Our suggestion that a professional system of accountability is the most appropriate to NASA should not be construed as an endorsement of professional accountability under all circumstances. Rather, our point is to indicate that the type of accountability system needs to suit the agency task.

34.   Public Administration and Ethics: A Prologue to a Preface

Dwight Waldo

"No process has been discovered by which promotion to a position of public responsibility will do away with a man's interest in his own welfare, his partialities, race, and prejudices."—James Harvey Robinson

"You are welcome to my house; you are welcome to my heart . . . my personal feelings have nothing to do with the present case. . . . As George Washington, I would do anything in my power for you. As President, I can do nothing."—George Washington, to a friend seeking an appointment

"There is not a moral vice which cannot be made into relative good by context. There is not a moral virtue which cannot in peculiar circumstances have patently evil results."—Stephen Bailey

"The big organization dehumanizes the individual by turning him into a functionary. In doing so it makes everything possible by creating a new kind of man, one who is morally unbounded in his role *as functionary. . . . His ethic is the ethic of the good soldier: take the order, do the job,* do it the best way you know how, *because that is your honor, your virtue, your pride-in-work."*—F. William Howton

"It seems to be inevitable that the struggle to maintain cooperation among men should destroy some men morally as battle destroys some physically."—Chester Barnard

"The raising of moral considerations in any discussion on organizations usually causes discomfort. . . . Nonetheless, if morality is about what is right and wrong, then behavior in organizations is largely determined by such considerations."—David Bradley and Roy Wilkie

"The first duty of a civil servant is to give his undivided allegiance to the State at all times and on all occasions when the State has a claim on his service."—Board of Inquiry, United Kingdom, 1928

The subtitle of this presentation and the several heterogeneous epigraphs are directed toward emphasizing the central theme of this presentation, namely, that moral or ethical* behavior in public administration is a complicated matter, indeed, *chaotic.* While some facets of the matter have been treated with insight and clarity, nothing in the way of a comprehensive and systematic treatise exists—or if so I am unaware of it.[1] This situation may not reflect just accident or lack of interest. What may be reflected is the fact that a systematic treatise is impossible, given the scope, complexity, and intractability of the material from which it would have to be constructed and given an inability to find acceptable or defensible foundations of ideas and beliefs on which it could be grounded.

In this discussion I hope to indicate some of the subjects that might be given attention in a systematic treatise. I appreciate that even this hope may represent pretentiousness.

PUBLIC MORALITY AND PRIVATE MORALITY

An appropriate beginning is to note a distinction between public and private morality and the possibility of a conflict between them.[2] This is a very elementary distinction, but much evidence indicates that it is little understood. As presented in the media, including the columns of the pundits, morality in public office is a simple matter of obeying the law, being honest, and telling the truth. *Not so.*

Public morality concerns decisions made and action taken directed toward the good of a collectivity which is seen

or conceptualized as "the public," that is, as an entity or group larger than immediate social groups such as family and clan. Conventionally, "the public" in the modern West is equated with "the nation," or "the country." Thus when decisions are made and actions taken vis-à-vis other nations or countries a public interest is presumed to be in view. Similarly, when the decision or action is directed inward toward the affairs of the nation-state, a public or general interest is presumed to come before private or group interests.

In either case a decision or action justified as moral because it is judged to be in the interest of the public may be immoral from the standpoint of all, or nearly all, interpretations of moral behavior for individuals. The most common example is killing. When done by an individual it is, commonly, the crime of homicide. When done in warfare or law enforcement on behalf of the public it is an act of duty and honor, perhaps of heroism—presuming the "correct" circumstances. All important governments have committed what would be "sins" if done by individuals, what would be "crimes" if done under their own laws by individuals acting privately.

Those in government who decide and act on behalf of the public will from time to time, of *necessity* as I see it, be lying, stealing, cheating, killing. What must be faced is that all decision and action in the public interest is inevitably morally complex, and that the price of any good characteristically entails some bad. Usually the bad is not as simple and stark as the terms just listed signify; but sometimes it *is,* and honesty and insight on our part can begin with so acknowledging.

Ironically, the concept of "the public" is regarded, and I believe properly, as a good and even precious thing. It is a heritage from Greek and Roman antiquity. Its projection, elaboration, nurture, and defense are generally represented as

---

*Strictly speaking, *moral* signifies right behavior in an immediate and customary sense; *ethical* signifies right behavior as examined and reflected upon. But no warranty is given that this distinction is always made in what follows.

the work of inspired thinkers, virtuous statesmen, and brave warriors. How can this be, when sins and crimes are committed in the name of the public? The answer is twofold. First, my favorite question: Compared to what? Assuming government is desirable, or at least inevitable, what legitimating concept is better? At least the idea of government in the name of a public advances that enterprise beyond purely personal and often tyrannical rule. Second, once in motion, so to speak, the concept of the public becomes invested with, a shelter for, and even a source of, goods that we identify with words such as citizenship, security, justice, and liberty.

THE STATE AND HIGHER LAW

To see the matter of public and private morality in perspective it is necessary to understand the complicated relationship of both moralities to the concept of *higher law.* The concept of higher law, simply put for our purposes, holds that there is a source and measure of rightness that is above and beyond both individual and government. In our own history it is represented prominently in the justification of the Revolution against the government of George III, and it inspired the Declaration of Independence.

The classical Greek philosophers, from whom much of our tradition of political thought derives, sought a moral unity. Are the good man and the good citizen the same? Both Plato and Aristotle answered the question affirmatively, though Plato more certainly than Aristotle. In the comparatively simple world of the city-state this answer could be made plausible, given the Greek conviction of superiority and the elitist nature of citizenship: the polity creates citizens in its admirable image and is thus the source of man's morality; there can be no legitimate appeal from what it holds to be right.

But as Sophocles' *Antigone* signifies, the idea of a higher law—in this case the laws of Zeus as against those of the king, Creon—existed even in Athens. During the Hellenistic period, after the decline of the city-state, the idea of a natural law above and beyond the mundane world was elaborated, especially by the Stoics. A sense of personhood apart from the polity, and of the essential equality of humans *as* humans was developing, and this was accompanied by a growing belief that right and wrong rested on foundations beyond the polity. As Sabine put it in his history of political theory; "Men were slowly making souls for themselves." With Christianity these ideas were of course broadened and deepened. The idea of God's law, or natural law—and characteristically the two became conflated—was to become a powerful force in relation to both private and public morality.

For more than a millennium after the fall of Rome, during a period in which government all but disappeared in the West, the relationship of the two powers, the sacred and the secular—for most purposes to be equated with Church and secular authority—was at the center of political philosophy and political controversy; but the theoretical and logical supremacy of the higher law was seldom questioned. With the emergence of the modern state a new era opened. The authority of a state, even a secular state, to determine right and wrong for its citizens was powerfully asserted by political theorists, notably Machiavelli and Hobbes. On the other hand, the long era of higher-law thinking had left an indelible imprint on thought and attitude. That there is something to which one's conscience gives access and which provides guidance on right and wrong remains a strong feeling even among those who regard themselves as completely secular.

The discussion of higher law has indicated that the initial duality of public morality and private morality was simplistic. There is an important, and insufficiently appreciated, distinction between the two, as I hope was demonstrated. But two important matters are now apparent. One is that higher law does not equate with or relate only to private morality as against public. Its sanction can be claimed by the polity if the polity represents the sacred as well as the secular, that is, if there is no separation of church and state—or perhaps even if there is.

The other matter is that the public-private distinction is but one example, albeit a crucial one for our purposes, of a class of relationships that can be designated *collectivity-person*. The biological person is of course distinguishable from any collectivity: nation, party, union, family, whatever. But whether the person can have or should have moral standing apart from the collectivities that have created him and given him meaning is a large part of what ethics is about; for all collectivities of any durability and significance will claim, explicitly or implicitly, to be the source of moral authority. While the state may well, and in some cases inevitably will, claim moral supremacy, the individual will have to weigh its claims against his or her interpretations of competing claims of other collectivities *and* the claims of higher law and "conscience."

Plainly, the ethical landscape is becoming very cluttered and complex. More to this shortly. But first a few words on *reason of state*. Reason of state is public morality at its extreme reach. Plainly put, it is conduct that violates all or nearly all standards of right conduct for individuals; this in the interests of the creating, preserving, or enhancing state power, and rationalized by "the ends justify the means" logic. A few years ago I had occasion to review the literature on this subject in Political Science in the United States. Significantly,

what I found was very little, and this mostly by émigré scholars. Unbelievably, there is no entry for this important subject in the seventeen-volume *International Encyclopedia of the Social Sciences,* even though it was planned and executed during the moral-ethical hurricane of the Vietnam War. A number of historical factors, beyond exploring here, have led us to gloss over and even deny the complexities and contradictions that exist when public and private morality conflict, as inevitably they sometimes will.

A MAP—OF SORTS

A few years ago, attempting to address the subject "Ethical Obligations and the Public Service," I made a rough sketch of the ethical obligations of the public administrator as seen from one point of view. Later, this sketch was somewhat elaborated and refined in collaboration with Patrick Hennigan in a yet unpublished essay. It will serve present purposes to indicate the nature of this endeavor.

The sketch, or "map," as we called it, is of ethical obligations of the public administrator with special reference to the United States. The perspective taken is that of the *sources* and *types* of ethical obligations to which the public administrator is expected to respond. We identify a dozen, but as we indicate, the list is capable of indefinite expansion and does not lend itself to logical ordering.

First. Obligation to the Constitution

This is a legal obligation of course, but it is also a source of ethical obligations, which may be symbolized and solemnized by an oath to uphold and defend the Constitution. The upholding of regime and of regime values is a normal source of public-service obligation, and the Constitution is the foundation of regime and of regime values for the

United States. But note: not an unambiguous foundation. A great deal of our history, including a civil war, can be written in terms of different interpretations of the Constitution.

Second. Obligation to Law

Laws made under the Constitution are a source not just of legal obligation but also of ethical obligations, as public-service codes of ethics normally underscore. Note again the ambiguities and puzzles. What if the law is unclear? What if laws conflict? What if a law seems unconstitutional, or violates a tenet of higher law? What is the ethical status of regulations made under the law?

Third. Obligation to Nation or Country

By most interpretations, a nation or country or people is separable from regime, and plainly this sense of identity with a nation, country, or people creates ethical obligations. Indeed, in many situations the obligation to country—Fatherland, Motherland, Homeland, however it may be put—overrides the obligation to regime. Lincoln, justifying his actions in 1864: "Was it possible to lose the nation, and yet preserve the constitution?"

Fourth. Obligation to Democracy

As indicated in previous discussions, this is separable from obligation to Constitution, granted that the relationship is complicated and arguable. Whatever the intent of the Framers—and I do not expect agreement on that, ever—democracy happened: it came to be accepted as an ideology or ethic and as a set of practices that somewhat overlie and somewhat intertwine with the Constitution. The emotional and intellectual acceptance of democracy creates obligations that are acknowledged and usually felt

by the public administrator. But again, note the ambiguities: Is the will of the people *always* and *only* expressed in law? If in other ways, how? And how legitimated? Is the *will* of the people, however expressed, to be put ahead of the *welfare* of the people as seen by a public official with information not available to the people?

Fifth. Obligation to Organizational-Bureaucratic Norms

These may be logically divided between those that are *generic* and those that are *specific*. The generic obligations are deeply rooted, perhaps in human nature, certainly in history and culture. They are associated with such terms as loyalty, duty, and order, as well as, perhaps, productivity, economy, efficiency. Specific obligations will depend upon circumstance: the function, the clientele, the technology.

Sixth. Obligation to Profession and Professionalism

The disagreements among sociologists as to what precisely *profession* entails may be disregarded here. All would agree that a profession, indeed a well-developed occupation, has an ethos that acts to shape the values and behavior of members. This ethos concerns actions pertaining to fellow professionals, clients, patients, employers, and perhaps humanity in general. We have become much more aware of the strength and effects of professional values and behavior in public administration since the publication of Frederick Mosher's *Democracy and the Public Service.*

Seventh. Obligation to Family and Friends

Obligation to family is bedrock in most if not all morality. But in countries shaped by the Western political tradition it is formally accepted that *in principle* obligation to country and/or regime as well as to the public is higher than that to family. While the newspaper on almost any day will indicate that the principle is often breached, we are very clear and insistent on the *principle,* and on the whole we believe that the principle prevails. But in countries in which the concept of public is recent and inchoate and in which family or other social group remains the center of loyalty and values, the principle is breached massively, so much so that the creation of an effective government may be impossible.

Friendship is less than family, but shares with it the immediate, personal bond; and friendship as well as family is honored in moral tradition. To indicate the ethical problems that may arise from this source one has only to set forth a name: Bert Lance.

Eighth. Obligation to Self

Yes, to self: this is a respectable part of our moral tradition, best epitomized in the Shakespearean "This above all, to thine own self be true." Selfishness and egocentrism are by general agreement bad. The argument for *self* is that self-regard is the basis for other-regard, that proper conduct toward others, doing one's duty, must be based on personal strength and integrity. But, granting the principle, how does one draw the line in practice between proper self-regard and a public interest?

Ninth. Obligation to Middle-Range Collectivities

In view here is a large and heterogeneous lot: party, class, race, union, church, interest group, and others. That these are capable of creating obligations felt as moral is quite clear, and that these obligations are carried into public administration is also quite clear. When,

and how, is it proper for such obligations to affect administrative behavior, to influence public decisions?

Tenth. Obligation to the Public Interest or General Welfare

This obligation is related to Constitution, to nation, to democracy. But it is analytically distinct. It is often explicitly embodied in law, but also has something of a separate existence. The concept is notoriously difficult to operationalize, and has been repeatedly subject to critical demolition. But presumably anyone in public administration must take it seriously, if only as a myth that must be honored in certain procedural and symbolic ways.

Eleventh. Obligation to Humanity or the World

It is an old idea, and perhaps despite all a growing idea, that an obligation is owed to humanity in general, to the world as a total entity, to the future as the symbol and summation of all that can be hoped. All "higher" religions tend in this direction, however vaguely and imperfectly. It is certainly an ingredient in various forms of one-world consciousness, and it figures prominently in the environmental ethic and in ecological politics.

Twelfth. Obligation to Religion, or to God

Immediately one must ask, are these two things or the same thing? The answer is not simple. But that obligations are seen as imposed by religion or God is not doubted even by atheists. One could quickly point to areas of public administration in which these felt obligations are at the center of "what's happening"—or possibly not happening.

A NEED FOR MAPS

Obviously, this listing of sources and types of ethical obligations involved in public administration is rough. The number, twelve, is plainly arbitrary. Perhaps some of the items were wrongly included, or should be combined. Perhaps some should be further divided and refined. Certainly other items might be included: *science,* for example, since science is interpreted not just to require a set of proper procedures but to be an ethos with accompanying ethical imperatives. As we know, *face-to-face groups* develop their own norms and powerfully influence behavior, but were not even mentioned. And what of *conscience?* Is it to be regarded as only a passive transmitter of signals or as in part at least an autonomous source of moral conduct?

You will have noticed that I did not attempt to order the twelve types of obligations, that is, list them in order of importance or ethical imperative. This was neither an oversight nor—I believe—a lack of intelligence on my part, but rather reflected the untidiness of the ethical universe. Perhaps the list included incommensurables. In any event, we lack the agreed beliefs which would enable us to construct an order of priority, one to twelve, with the higher obligation always superior to the lower.

How are we to proceed? How can we achieve enough clarity so that we can at least discuss our differences with minimum confusion, the least heat and the most light? My own view is that a desirable, perhaps necessary, preliminary activity is to construct more and better maps of the realm we propose to understand. Granted that this expectation may reflect only the habits of academia; professors are prone to extensive preparation for intellectual journeys never undertaken. But I do not see how we can move beyond a confused disagreement until there is more agreement on what we are talking about.

If I am essentially correct, then what would be useful would be a serious and sizable mapmaking program. We need various types of maps, analogous to maps that show physical features, climatic factors, demographic data, economic activity, and so forth. We need maps of differing scale, some indicating the main features of a large part of the organizational world, some detailing particular levels, functions, and activities. Despite common elements, presumably—no, certainly—the ethical problems of a legislator are significantly different from those of a military officer, those of a regulatory commissioner different from those of a police chief, those of a first-line supervisor from those of a department head.

Simply put: If we are going to talk about ethics in public life it would be useful to know what we are talking about.

A NEED FOR NAVIGATION INSTRUMENTS

The metaphor of maps may not have been the most apt, but I now use one that may be less felicitous, that of navigation instruments. But at least the second metaphor is complementary: given maps, how do we navigate? How do we find our way through what the maps show us? Let me indicate the nature of some navigation equipment that would be of use.

First, it would be useful to have an instrument to guide us through the historical dimensions of our ethical problems in public administration. Above all, it would be useful to have an explication of the implications and consequences of the disjunction, noted in earlier discussions, between the rise of political self-awareness and the rise of administrative self-awareness. Both as a part of that inquiry and independently, what do we know about the rise and growth of administrative morality, of notions of stewardship, duty and obligations, reciprocal or unilateral? With respect to estate management, which has been so large a part of administrative history, have rules of proper conduct been widely divergent, or has the nature of the function disposed toward uniformity? Since estate management has been centrally involved in royal governance, from Sumer to the Sun King—and beyond —what effect has this had on bureaucratic morality? Perhaps it is worth more than mere mention that *estate* and *state* are cognates, both derived from the Latin *stare:* "to be or stand"; the essential notion in both cases is of substance, firmness, an organizing center.

Second, it would be useful to have instruments provided by the social sciences or derived from a survey of them. Immediately, we face the fact indicated in the epigraph from Bradley and Wilkie at the head of this chapter: "The raising of moral considerations in any discussion on organizations usually causes discomfort." In addressing organizational behavior as in contemporary social science generally, ethics is not just a neglected interest, it is a rejected interest. I shall return to this point; but what I have in mind presently need not cause serious discomfort, though it no doubt would strike many as a peculiar interest and a waste of energy. What I have in view is not an addressing of ethical issues as such, but rather a survey to determine what the several social sciences have to say about ethical matters, either directly or indirectly. For example, are ethical issues present in disguise—morality pretending to be science? We can see that the *yes* answer has often been true in the past, and not a few claim it is true now. What would the most honest, nonideological view reveal? Aside from this question, do the paradigms and tools of the several social sciences offer any handles for ethical inquiry?

Political Science, presumably, would be most centrally involved. And that brings me, inevitably, back to the theme of disjunction: what are the consequences for both Political Science and Public Administration, more broadly, *politics* and *administration,* of the fact that politics reached self-awareness in classical Greece and administration not until the late nineteenth century—this despite the fact that, even (especially?) in small and simple polities, politics and administration were inevitably intermingled.

The other social sciences, even Anthropology, need also to be surveyed. "Even Anthropology?"—an argument could be made that its determined lack of normativeness plus its comparativeness make it particularly germane. Sociology—beginning with its ancestry in Montesqieu and others, and certainly decisively in Comte, Spencer, Durkheim, Weber, Parsons, and other major figures—is rich with relevant material; whether in spite of or because of its scientific stance is hard to say. And Economics? One should not, of course, be put off with its scientific aura and impressive technical apparatus. Adam Smith, in his own view and that of his contemporaries, was a moral philosopher; and Irving Kristol has recently reminded us that Smith's *An Inquiry into the Nature and Causes of the Wealth of Nations* was not intended as a defense of the *morality* of free enterprise. Economics, both in what it attends to and in what it refuses to attend to, in the behavior it licenses and in the behavior it forbids, is very central to any inquiry into ethical conduct in administration: As a random illustration, the recent realization that noxious waste chemicals simply have been dumped in tens of thousands of locations. What sins are committed in the name of externalities and exogenous variables?

Third, ethics as a self-aware enterprise, together with the philosophic matrices from which differing ethical theories are derived, needs to be searched and ordered for the purposes of ethical analysis and judgment in public administration. It may be thought peculiar, to say the least of it, that only well into this discussion ethical theory as such is brought to the fore. But as I view the matter it deserves no high priority. For ethics has little attended to proper behavior in large-scale organization. Its central interests have been elsewhere, tending to oscillate between the probing of traditional relationships such as those of family and friendships and rather abstract and bloodless general principles of conduct. While there is to be sure a great deal in the literature that is relevant, its relevance becomes clear only by extrapolation and application.

Fourth, religion also needs to be surveyed with the object of determining what instruments of navigation it can provide. For our purposes attention should be centered on the Judeo-Christian stream of religious thought and practice, but all major religions should be included. Among the many subjects on which I am not expert are theology and religious history. However, it takes only a little knowledge and understanding to appreciate three things. The first is that theology as such, like ethics to which it is linked in many ways, has attended very little to proper conduct in formal organizations, at least those not religious. Second, as with ethics, there is in theology a great deal that can be made relevant by extrapolation and application. In fact, the writings of Reinhold Niebuhr moved vigorously in this direction; and perhaps I do less than justice to others of whose work I may be unaware. Third, the history and effect of religious institutions and the second, third and X-order effects of religious thought and practice are of so great import for organizational life that one could devote a career to the matter without doing more than explore a few areas. The point is made simply by referring to

the work under the heading of Protestant Ethic.

THE PYRAMID PUZZLE

Not surprisingly, many of the most interesting and significant questions concerning administration and ethics concern the theory and practice of hierarchy. Some of these questions are generic, in the sense that they apply to business and nonprofit private organizations as well as to public administration. But some have a special relevance to public administration, as they concern governmental institutions and political ideology. It will be instructive to focus briefly on this pyramid puzzle in the public context.

Central, at least to my own interest, is the fact that hierarchy is represented both as a force for morality and a source of immorality. Both cases are familiar to us, though perhaps not in the context of ethics.

The affirmative case has it that hierarchy is a force that works both for the soft values of democracy and the hard values of effectiveness, efficiency, and economy; indeed, that the achievement of the soft and hard values is complementary, not two things but a single thing. This is a central theme of old-line Public Administration, and the reasoning and conclusions are familiar: Democracy is, realistically, achievable only if power is concentrated so that it can be held accountable, and this is possible only through hierarchy. Otherwise, responsibility bleeds into the social surround. The devices for focusing citizen attention so that it could be made effective—devices such as the short ballot and party reform—were part of the old-line package. Responsibility was viewed as owed upward, subordinate to superordinate, to the top of the pyramid, then bridged over by the electoral principle to the people. Authority was viewed as moving the other direction, upward from the people through their elected representative, then bridged over to the top of the pyramid and descending, echelon by echelon, to every officer and employee.

That this way of viewing things has considerable logic and force strikes me as self-evident. It is plausibly, though hardly unarguably, based on Constitution and history, and can be bolstered with much evidence. It can be, and has been, buttressed by arguments from foreign experience and from business practice. Able and honorable persons have supported the main tenets of the argument. Thus Paul Appleby in his *Morality and Administration in Democratic Government:*[3] The hierarchical principle forwards effective government, but above all it is necessary to democratic government, insuring through its operation the triumph of the general interest over special interests. Thus Marver Bernstein in "Ethics in Government: The Problems in Perspective,"[4] arguing that serious ethical irregularities as well as inefficiencies are all but assured through the absence of hierarchical control in the arrangements for some regulatory agencies, which create conflicts of interest or in effect make the regulatory agencies captives of the interests to be regulated. Thus Victor Thompson in his *Without Sympathy or Enthusiasm: The Problem of Administrative Compassion,*[5] where he argues that the prescriptions for participation equal an invitation for the unauthorized to steal the "tool" of administration from its "owners," the public.

The case against hierarchy in turn has considerable logic and force. It also has roots in Constitution and history, and can be bolstered with much evidence. In this case persons who are able and honorable have stressed the contradictions involved in using hierarchy as a means of promoting democracy, the limitations of hierarchy as a means of achieving effectiveness and efficiency, and its complicity in forwarding immorality. Thus

Vincent Ostrom in his *The Intellectual Crisis in American Public Administration,*[6] arguing the spuriousness of the case for centralization, and the greater democracy achievable by organizing public administration into smaller units more in accord with "consumer" will and control. Thus the advocates of a New Public Administration,[7] who take social equity as guiding principle and seek to achieve it "proactively," through client-oriented and client-involving devices. Thus F. William Howton—quoted in one of the epigraphs[8]—who speaks for many who believe that hierarchy with its accustomed corollaries creates deformed humans with deadened consciences. Thus Frederick Thayer in his *An End to Hierarchy! An End to Competition!*[9] who finds hierarchy implicated in immorality as well as promoting inefficiency, and necessarily to be abolished if there is to be a tolerable future—indeed, perhaps, a *future.*

My aim is not to weigh the arguments, much less render a verdict, but rather to emphasize the tangle of ethical problems in and related to the principle and practice of hierarchy; this by way of illustrating the central position of ethical concerns in our professional business—whether or not we care to attend to them as ethical questions. But before passing on, let me pose one question that many would regard as the paramount one: What difference does democracy make with respect to the morality of actions taken by government? Rousseau, if I understand him correctly, argued that while the people can be *mistaken,* they cannot be *wrong.* Two examples to ponder, the first from history, the second hypothetical. (1) If the bombing of Haiphong was "immoral," was the firebombing of Hamburg and Dresden—which was massively greater—also immoral? If not, why not? (2) If the Holocaust had been carried out under a democratic government rather than a dictatorship, would an Eichmann have been any more or less immoral? In reflecting on this, bear in mind Herman Finer's notable essay on "Administrative Responsibility in Government,"[10] in which he holds with regard to the public servant: "The first commandment is subservience."

OBSERVATIONS AND REFLECTIONS

The spirit and nature of this discussion was indicated by the Chapter subtitle, A Prologue to a Preface. At most I can hope to point to some of the matters that would be worthy of attention in a more serious and systematic inquiry. In conclusion, the following further observations and reflections. I shall proceed discontinuously, serially.

First

The twentieth century has hardly been distinguished either by its observance of agreed moral codes or by its concentration on ethical inquiry. On the contrary, it has been distinguished by a "decay" of traditional moral codes, a widespread feeling that morality is "relative" if not utterly meaningless, and a disposition to regard ethical inquiry as frivolous, irrelevant. These currents of thought and feeling have been associated with a "falling away" from religious belief and a concomitant rise of "belief" in science and its philosophical—or antiphilosophical—aura.

These developments have coincided with the Organizational Revolution: an unprecedented increase in the variety, number, size, and power of organizations, at the center of which is government, public administration. It has coincided also, and relatedly, with the arrival of administrative self-awareness, with a new type of "scientific" interest in administrative study and a resulting increase in administrative technology.

So we confront this historical situation: Just at the time the organizational world is thickening and thus the need for ethical guidance increasing, not only does old morality erode but no serious effort is made to create new codes of conduct appropriate to the new situation; and the scientific mentality that is largely responsible for the Organizational Revolution simultaneously makes it difficult to take ethical matters seriously.

Second

In no country does the level of conscious ethical conduct in government reach the level of complex reality, but the United States may have one problem to an unusual degree. It has often been observed that Americans tend to view morality very heavily if not exclusively in sexual and pecuniary terms: in the public area, Elizabeth Rays on payrolls and Tongsun Parks passing envelopes of currency behind closed doors.

As I see it, a concern for *public* morality must indeed include a concern with the ordinary garden varieties of sexual and pecuniary misconduct within or affecting public life; we would have to be ignorant of history and oblivious to contemporary political life to think otherwise. However, as even my few shallow probes indicate, the matter of ethically proper conduct reaches far, far beyond the popular images of sex and money. It presents problems of conduct for which traditional morality, growing in and shaped to simpler times, provides little guidance. Or worse, it provides misguidance.

Third

Some of the better writings bearing on our subject emphasize the prevalence, perhaps even the necessity, of "moral ambiguity" in organizational life. Thus Stephen Bailey in his "Ethics and the Public Service";[11] I refer back to the epigraph from this essay emphasizing the "contextuality" of good and evil. Thus Melville Dalton in his *Men Who Man-*

age,[12] who concluded that persons from a middle-class background are more likely to become successful managers than persons from a working-class background, not because of superior ability or technical skill but because of a socialization that better prepares them to cope with moral ambiguity.

If we cannot *clarify* the ethics of the organizational world, perhaps it will help if we can advance *understanding* of the complexity and confusion. If ambiguity cannot be eliminated, then a "tolerance for ambiguity" becomes an essential operating skill. A *moral* quality as well as an operating skill? I shall not try to answer that.

Fourth

The following seems to be true, almost axiomatically: Moral complexity increases as memberships in organizations increase; persons in formal organizations in addition to traditional/nonformal organizations face greater moral complexity than those only in the latter; those in formal *public* organizations face more moral complexity than those in nonpublic organizations; and moral complexity increases as responsibilities in an administrative hierarchy increase.

If this is a correct view, then high-placed administrators (managers, executives) in public organizations are at the very center of ethical complexity. In this connection I refer you to the probing of morality in relation to administration in Chester Barnard's *The Functions of the Executive*[13]—from which comes the epigraph at the head of this chapter. *The Functions* is of course widely and correctly viewed as a seminal work. But it is a commentary on the interests of the past generation that this discussion of morality has been generally ignored.

Barnard believed that "moral creativeness" was an essential executive function. As the quoted sentence indicates, he believed also that the burden assumed could lead to moral breakdown. In a simi-

lar vein Stephen Bailey, in the essay cited in observation Third above, uses the metaphor "above the timber line" to signify the severe moral climate in which the high executive must operate and the dangers to which he is exposed.

Fifth

We have recently seen, and we presently see, the growth of a gray area, an area in which any clear distinction between the categories of *public* and *private* disappears, disappears in a complex and subtle blending of new organizational modes and legal arrangements. In this gray area, hierarchy is diminished, but does not disappear; new lateral and diagonal relationships grow up and operate along with it, making it formally and operationally difficult to answer the question: Who's in charge here?

As I view it, our ethical problems are compounded in this growing gray world. Who will be responsible for what to whom? In what will duty consist and by what can honesty be judged? One view is that, with hierarchy relaxed and freedom increased, the way is open for the development of authentic *personal* morality. Harlan Cleveland seeks a solution in the hope and prescription that managers in the "horizontal"[14] world that is emerging will regard themselves as "public managers"—because in fact they will be. I confess that on most days I find it hard to share either of these two varieties of optimism.

Sixth

As the epigraph from David Bradley and Roy Wilkie indicates, "the raising of moral considerations" in the study of organizations has not been popular. Indeed, the chapter on Morality and Organizations in their *The Concept of Organization*[15] is, to my knowledge, without a parallel in the scores of general treatments of organizational behavior or theory.

A number of factors, some pertaining to American public affairs and without need of mention, and some pertaining to the general climate of our intellectual life that are beyond explicating here, suggest that there may be a change in the situation, that we will begin to address seriously the ethical dimensions of our organizational world—here I allow myself a bit of optimism. This may be best done—perhaps it can be done only—by working from the empirical base legitimated in recent social science. It might begin, for example, with mapmaking, along the lines suggested earlier. Later, just possibly, we may be able to address the ethical as such.

One point of view has it that ethical inquiry is dangerous. Samuel Butler put it this way: "The foundations of morality are like all other foundations: if you dig too much about them, the superstructure will come tumbling down." But in our case, the digging has been done; the superstructure is already down. But then, the old superstructure was not to our purpose anyway. Perhaps on a new foundation we can use some of the fallen materials to build a superstructure that is to our purpose?

NOTES

1. Certainly Robert T. Golembiewski's *Men, Management, and Morality: Towards a New Organizational Ethic* (New York: 1965) is an able and useful work, and I do not wish to demean it. But the picture in my mind is of a work even broader in scope, one taking into account developments of the past decade. Neither do I mean to slight the useful work of Wayne A. R. Leys, done when ethics was *really* unfashionable: *Ethics and Social Policy* (New York: 1946), and *Ethics for Policy Decisions: The Art of Asking Deliberative Questions* (New York: 1952).

2. The analysis set forth in this section is a brief version of that in my "Re-

flections on Public Morality" (*6 Administration and Society* [November 1974], pp. 267–282).

3. Paul Appleby, *Morality and Administration in Democratic Government* (Baton Rouge, La.: 1952).

4. Marver Bernstein, "Ethics in Government: The Problems in Perspective" (*61 National Civic Review* [July 1972], pp. 341–347).

5. Victor Thompson, *Without Sympathy or Enthusiasm: The Problem of Administrative Compassion* (University, Ala.: 1975).

6. Vincent Ostrom, *The Intellectual Crisis in American Public Administration* (University, Ala.: 1973).

7. See the symposium, H. George Frederickson, ed., "Social Equity and Public Administration" (*34 Public Administration Review* [January/February 1974], pp. 1–51).

8. F. William Howton, *Functionaries* (Chicago: 1969).

9. Frederick C. Thayer, *An End to Hierarchy! An End to Competition! Organizing the Politics and Economics of Survival* (New York: 1973).

10. Herman Finer, "Administrative Responsibility in Democratic Government" (*1 Public Administration Review* [Summer 1941], pp. 335–350).

11. Stephen Bailey, "Ethics and the Public Service" (*23 Public Administration Review* [December 1964], pp. 234–243).

12. Melville Dalton, *Men Who Manage* (New York: 1959).

13. Chester Barnard, *The Functions of the Executive* (Cambridge, Mass.: 1947). See especially Chapter 17, The Nature of Executive Responsibility.

14. Harlan Cleveland, *The Future Executive: A Guide for Tomorrow's Managers* (New York: 1972).

15. David Bradley and Roy Wilkie, *The Concept of Organization: An Introduction to Organizations* (Glasgow: 1974).